the ITQ student's workbook

NICKI TALBOT

D1464992

Hodder Arnold

A MEMBER OF THE HODDER HEADLINE GROUP

Orders: please contact Bookpoint Ltd, 130 Milton Park, Abingdon, Oxon OX14 4SB. Telephone: (44) 01235 827720. Fax: (44) 01235 400454. Lines are open from 9.00 – 5.00, Monday to Saturday, with a 24-hour message answering service. Visit our website at www.hoddereducation.co.uk

British Library Cataloguing in Publication Data
A catalogue record for this title is available from the British Library

ISBN-10: 0 340 88973 X
ISBN-13: 978 0 340 88973 2

Published 2005
Impression number   10 9 8 7 6 5 4 3 2
Year   2009 2008 2007

Typeset by Fakenham Photosetting Limited, Fakenham, Norfolk.
Printed in Singapore for Hodder Arnold, an imprint of Hodder Education, a member of the Hodder Headline Group, 338 Euston Road, London NW1 3BH.

Contents

Note

Microsoft product screen shots reprinted with permission from Microsoft Corporation. Microsoft, Front Page, Hotmail, Outlook, PowerPoint, MSN and Windows are either registered trademarks or trademarks of Microsoft Corporation in the United States and/or other countries. Adobe product screen shots reprinted with permission from Adobe System Inc. Adobe, Photoshop and Pagemaker are either registered trademarks or trademarks of Adobe Systems Incorporated in the United States and/or other countries.

Acknowledgements

I would like to thank the following people for their assistance in creating this book:

- Mark Simmons of Milton Keynes College, who provided me with a lot of information and advice in the early stages of the book development.
- Abi Woodman and Matthew Smith, my editors at Hodder Arnold; this was my first experience of writing this type of book and they have been incredibly supportive.
- Steve Talbot – my always-supportive husband – who spent many hours working with the screenshots that are used throughout the book.

Introduction

The ITQ Student Workbook is designed to assist you in undertaking the ITQ qualification. If you are embarking on this qualification, then you probably already use a range of software in your daily work. Once you have chosen the units you will undertake to fulfil the ITQ criteria, you can refer to the appropriate unit in this book to ensure that you have the knowledge and skills required to successfully complete the unit (and if you don't the book will teach you).

The ITQ units

Each unit takes you through the skills and techniques that are necessary for that unit and provides a range of suggested tasks that you can perform in your workplace to provide the evidence required for the unit.

Some of the units are application-based, for example, Unit 208 – Word-processing software, Unit 209 – Spreadsheet software, etc. In these units, the relevant areas of the software with which you will need to be familiar are explained in detail with individual tasks so that you can practise new techniques and skills. Other units are more general and theoretical, for example, Unit 215 – Evaluate the impact of IT. In these units, the relevant areas that need to be demonstrated are discussed, to give you a broader knowledge and understanding of the issues involved. However, you may need to do further research to provide evidence for these units. Units 216 to 220 are stand-alone units which are designed for people who do not use IT in their primary role but still need to have some knowledge. The skills and techniques that need to be covered in these units have already been covered in other units in the book. These units therefore simply contain tables pointing you to the relevant place in the book where you will find information about that skill.

Software used in the book

The following software programs have been used throughout the book:

- Windows® operating system
- Microsoft® Office (Word, Excel, PowerPoint®, Outlook®, Access, FrontPage®)
- Adobe Photoshop®

There are also references to other software utilities, such as WinZip® and Norton AntiVirus™.

Two versions of the Windows® operating system are referenced: 2000 and XP. Two versions of Microsoft® Office are referenced: 2000 and XP. Screenshots showing Windows® 2000 and Office XP are used throughout the book, unless the other version of the software is markedly different, in which case this screenshot is also included. For example, in Unit 208 – Word-processing, the screenshots show Word 2002 where Word 2000 and Word 2002 are similar. However, in cases where the versions of the software are very different – for example, mail merge – both versions are covered in more detail.

Things you should know

Using shortcut keys

When executing a command in the software, there is generally more than one way to do this, for example, you can usually use a menu, a toolbar button or a shortcut key. The shortcut keys are referenced wherever appropriate. To use a shortcut key – for example, Ctrl+O – you hold down the Ctrl key on the keyboard and then press O.

Taking screenshots

There will be times when, in order to provide evidence that you have used a particular feature, you may wish to take a 'screenshot' (a copy of the screen). While you can send a screen print directly to the printer, you will find it more efficient to copy screenshots to the clipboard and then paste them into, for example, a Word document.

To take a screenshot of the entire screen, showing everything on the screen, press the Print Screen button on your keyboard. (This key is usually located on the right side, top row of the QWERTY keyboard and may have the text **Prt Scr** on it.)

To take a screenshot of just the active window – for example, if you have a dialog box open on the screen and you just want a screenshot of the dialog box – press Alt+Prt Scr.

Both these techniques copy the image to the clipboard. You can then switch into Word and paste the image onto the page using the normal Paste command. Once you have pasted the graphic onto the page, you are free to resize it, move it and work with it using the Picture toolbar in Word.

Make selective use of IT

| Unit value = 25 | **Overview** |

This unit assesses your ability to determine the appropriate use of IT in a variety of settings, such as home, work and school.

Competent people can work out how to use IT for more complex tasks and purposes, taking account of their own skills and capabilities. They can explain decisions and actions taken using IT, find and evaluate information using appropriate methods, organise information and review their own use of IT and feedback from others.

 ## Required skills and techniques for level 2

Explaining (use of IT)	Explaining which software tools and techniques were chosen and how effectively they were used for particular tasks and uses.
Finding and evaluating	Choosing and using appropriate methods of searching for relevant information. Reviewing sources and information to help choose what is most relevant, and to decide when enough has been found.
Organising	Using a variety of IT software tools and techniques to structure information to suit more complex tasks and audience needs, such as using large print for partially sighted readers.
Reviewing	Evaluating own strengths and weaknesses in using IT. Taking account of feedback from other people about own use of IT.

 ## Requirements of this unit

You will undertake *four* pieces of work for this unit. This unit requires you to 'explain the use of IT', which you can do using one or more of the four tasks that you will undertake.

Most of the skills and knowledge that you need to produce evidence in this unit can be learnt from the other units in this book. However, the emphasis in this unit is on explaining why you have made the decision to use a particular piece of software and why that software is the right tool for the job.

 ## What will I achieve?

By accomplishing a Level 2 in this unit, you will also have achieved Level 1 in most cases and Level 3 in some cases. Below is a table to show what levels you will have achieved.

Required skill	Level 1	Level 2	Level 3
Handling files	●	●	●
Combining information	●	●	
Editing text		●	
Formatting text	●	●	
Laying out	●	●	
Checking text	●	●	●
Improving efficiency	●	●	

 ## About this chapter

Because most of the areas covered in this unit are discussed elsewhere in this book, these tables contain 'signposts' to point you to the parts of the book that will aid your knowledge and understanding in a particular area.

 ## Skill requirements

1 Explaining (use of IT)

Skill to evidence	Applicable Unit
Knowledge of different software tools	Unit 202 – Operate a computer

2 Finding and evaluating

Skill to evidence	Applicable Unit
Choosing and using appropriate methods of searching for relevant information	Unit 206 – The Internet and intranets
Reviewing sources and information to choose what is most relevant	Unit 206 – The Internet and intranets

3 Organising

Skill to evidence	Applicable Unit
Using IT software tools and techniques to structure information	Unit 208 – Word-processing software Unit 209 – Spreadsheet software Unit 210 – Database software Unit 211 – Website software Unit 212 – Artwork and imaging software Unit 213 – Presentation software

4 Reviewing

Skill to evidence	Applicable Unit
Evaluating own strengths and weaknesses in using IT	Unit 215 – Evaluate the impact of IT
Taking account of feedback from other people about own use of IT	Unit 215 – Evaluate the impact of IT

Glossary of IT terms

Below is a list of terms you may come across in your use of computers. A lot of the terms are used in this book.

Application	Software designed for a specific use. Applications include word-processors, spreadsheets and database programs.
Bandwidth	How much data can be sent through a network or modem connection. It is measured in bits per second or bps. The higher the bandwidth, the more information can be transferred at one time.
Bitmap	A graphic image made up of dots or bits.
Bluetooth	Technology that enables wireless communication between compatible devices. Used for short-range connections between desktop and laptop computers, PDAs, digital cameras, scanners, mobile phones and printers. Uses radio waves, so can communicate through walls. Limited to 30 feet.
Boot up	The series of steps that take place when you turn on your computer. The term is derived from the expression 'pulling oneself up by the bootstraps'. A cold boot is when you turn the computer on from an off position. A warm boot is when you reset a computer that is already on.
Broadband	High-speed data transmission in which a single cable can carry a large amount of data at once. The most common types of Internet broadband are cable modems (which use the same connection as cable TV) and ADSL modems (which use your existing phone line).
Bug	A programming error that can cause a computer or a program to perform erratically, produce inaccurate results, or crash.
CD-ROM	A CD that contains a large amount of information, but can only be read from, not written to.
Cookie	Data sent to your computer by a Web server that records your actions on a website. When you visit the site after being sent the cookie, the site will load certain pages according to the information stored in the cookie or the site will remember your user name and password.
CPU	Central Processing Unit or 'brain' of the computer which processes instructions and complex functions. Usually referred to simply as the processor.
Crash	If an application (such as Word or Excel) will not respond to any command, your computer has 'crashed'. Other terms used are 'hang' and 'freeze'. When an application crashes it is not usually the fault of the user.
Cyberspace	Used to describe the virtual world of computers. Data floating around on a computer system or network is often referred to as being 'in cyberspace'. Cyberspace is now also used to refer to the global network of computers that is the Internet.

Data packet	Information is transmitted around networks (and the Internet) in the form of small data packets. When you send an e-mail message, for example, the message is broken into many small packets. Each packet contains the address of its origin and destination and information that connects it to related data packets. The process of sending and receiving packets is known as 'packet switching'. Packets from many different locations are sent on the same lines and are sorted and routed by various computers along the way (rather like the Post Office). Billions of packets are transferred each day and most packets take less than a few seconsd to reach their destination.
Desktop	The area on your screen where you move windows and icons around.
Dialog box	A box that appears on your computer screen that enables you to have a 'dialog' with your computer. You can type in commands, choose from drop-down lists, click on buttons, etc.
Disk defragmenter	A system tool within Windows® which allows the user to defragment a disk. Over time the files that are stored on a computer's hard disk can become fragmented and are stored in different parts of the disk. Defragmenting a disk puts all the parts of a file in one location. This reduces the time it takes to open a file.
Domain name	The name that identifies a website, e.g. microsoft.com is the domain name of the Microsoft® website. Domain names can be 'bought' or registered. Most companies have registered the domain of their company name.
Download	The process in which data is sent to your computer. When you receive information from the Internet, you download it to your computer. The opposite of this process – sending information to another computer – is called uploading.
Drag	This is a mouse action where you position the mouse pointer over the object to be dragged, press and hold down the left mouse button and then move the mouse. The object follows the mouse movement until you release the left mouse button.
Driver	A device driver is a program that enables an application to use a device such as a printer. Hardware devices such as printers, scanners and mice usually have a floppy disk or CD in the box with them. Not only does the hardware need to be physically connected to a port at the back of the system unit, but the driver needs to be installed using the floppy disk/CD.
DVD	Digital Versatile Disc. A high-capacity optical disc that looks like a CD but can store much more information. (A CD can store 650–700 MB of data; a single-layer, single-sided DVD can store 4.7 GB of data). DVD drives can read both DVDs and conventional CDs.
E-commerce	Electronic-commerce, or business over the Internet. Amazon.com is an e-commerce site. Two main types of e-commerce are Business-to-Consumer (B2C) and Business-to-Business (B2B).
E-mail	Electronic mail that is sent from one computer to another. The computers may be linked by a network or by modems. You can send messages any time of the day or night and you can send the same message to lots of people at the same time. You can attach files to e-mail messages, enabling files to be transferred.
Ergonomics	When it refers to computers, the study of healthy working practices using computers.
Extension	The notation at the end of a file name which indicates the type of a file it is. The extension appears after a full stop. For example, .doc, .xls, .ppt or .tmp.
Firewall	Used to protect a server or computer from damage by unauthorised users. A firewall can be implemented in hardware or software.
Folder	A workplace on a disk. Your PC's memory can be divided into various folders to separate your different projects.

FTP	File Transfer Protocol. A method of transferring files via the Internet from one computer to another.
Gigabyte	Memory size and disk capacity are measured in bytes. A gigabyte is approximately one billion bytes (or 1000 megabytes).
GUI	Graphical User Interface, pronounced 'gooey'. An interface (usually mouse-driven) that uses pictures and icons as well as words. The Windows® operating system, with its user-friendly icons and pull-down menus, is a GUI.
Hard disk/drive	A fixed disk installed inside the computer for storage. It is long-term memory for storing applications and data. The data is stored on a stack of disks that are mounted inside a metal casing.
Hardware	The physical elements of a computer that you can see and touch.
HTML	HyperText Markup Language. The language that Web pages are written in. HTML documents are displayed in a Web browser.
HTTP	HyperText Transfer Protocol. The protocol used to transfer data over the World Wide Web. All Web site addresses begin with http://.
Icon	An icon on your computer screen represents an object or a program on your hard drive. Icons are one of the fundamental features of the graphical user interface (GUI).
Illegal operation	The message displayed when a program on your computer has an error. It usually indicates a fault with the program that was running or with the operating system itself.
Interface	The means by which communication is achieved between the computer and another party (usually the user).
Internet	International Network. A global network of computers and servers which can communicate with each other, allowing people to share information. All the computers connected to it communicate with each other using Transmission Control Protocol/Internet Protocol (TCP/IP). The most common Internet applications are e-mail, file transfer, electronic bulletin boards and the World Wide Web.
Internet Explorer	The name of the Microsoft® Web browser that enables you to 'surf' the Internet.
Intranet	An intranet is an internal/private network used within an organisation. It uses the same technology as the Internet and is viewed using a browser, but is only available to those on the internal network.
IP	Internet Protocol. The protocol for transmitting data on the Internet. IP has also become popular as the protocol for company LANs.
IP address	A code made up of sets of numbers separated by dots that identifies a particular computer on the Internet. Every computer on a network (including the Internet) has an IP address (rather like a postal address). IP addresses can be static (remain the same) or dynamic (change each time you connect to the Internet).
ISDN	Integrated Services Digital Network – a digital network capable of carrying a wide range of services, including data, voice and video.
ISP	Internet Service Provider. The company who enables you to get connected to the Internet, either by dialling-up or using a cable or ADSL modem.
JPEG	Joint Photographic Experts Group compressed graphic file format. It is supported by most graphics applications.

LAN	Local Area Network. A group of computers which are physically linked. Local indicates a network usually in one area, such as an office or college. Most businesses today use LANs, which make it easy for employees to share information. With the development of wireless technology, wireless LANs are now becoming popular.
Mainframe	A high-performance computer made for high-volume, processor-intensive computing. Typically used by large businesses. A mainframe can execute many programs simultaneously at high speed.
Megabyte	Memory size and disk capacity are measured in bytes. A megabyte is approximately one million bytes. (A byte = 8 bits = 1 character.)
Microchip/ Microprocessor	Also known as processor or CPU. A chip that performs all the tasks. It is installed on the motherboard inside the computer. The most popular microprocessor used in PCs today is the Intel Pentium chip.
Modem	Short for Modulator-Demodulator. A piece of computer hardware that allows a computer to communicate with other computers via a phone line by converting digital signals to and from analogue signals. A modem can be internal or external to the PC. Most desktop PCs bought today come with an internal modem already fitted. Dial-up modems are gradually being replaced by cable and ADSL modems.
Monitor	The part of the computer containing the visual display unit (VDU). Popularly known as the screen.
Motherboard	The main electronic circuit board where the parts of a computer are plugged in.
Multimedia	Multiple media – text, graphics, audio, video, etc. Software that involves animation, sound and text is called multimedia software.
Multitasking	Term given when a processor can perform more than one task at a time.
Netiquette	Etiquette on the Internet. Good netiquette means respecting other Internet users and not doing anything online that will annoy or frustrate people. Areas where good netiquette is important are e-mail, online chat and newsgroups.
Network	A way of connecting computers so that they can share data, files, software and hardware (such as printers). The Internet is a global network. Computers can be networked using cables or wirelessly.
Newbie	A new user of a computer, a software program or the Internet may be referred to as a 'newbie'.
Newsgroup	A discussion group that discusses a particular topic. Users post messages to a news server which then sends them to the other participating news servers. Other users can then access the newsgroup and read the postings. To participate in a newsgroup, you have to 'subscribe' to it.
Operating system	The main control program of a computer. The operating system schedules tasks, manages storage and handles communication with the peripherals. Software programs cannot run without an operating system.
Packet	A small amount of computer data sent over a network. Data you receive from the Internet is delivered in many small packets. Each packet contains the address of where it came from, the address of where it is going to and information that connects it to its related packets. This process is known as packet-switching. The packets can travel along many different routes and are then sorted at the destination computer. Billions of packets are transferred every day and they each take less than a few seconds to reach their destination.

PDF	Portable Document Format. A multi-platform file format developed by Adobe® Systems. A PDF file can capture text, images and the formatting of documents from a variety of applications. To view a PDF file, you need Adobe Acrobat® Reader.
Peripheral	The hardware connected to a computer: mouse, keyboard, monitor, printer, scanner, external disk and tape drives, microphone, speakers, joystick, etc.
Port	The name given to a socket at the back of the system unit used to plug in external devices such as a mouse, keyboard, scanner or printer. There are three kinds of port – parallel, serial and USB. A parallel port is usually used for connecting a printer. A mouse can be connected to a serial or parallel port. A USB port can be used for scanners, printers and external storage devices (flash drives).
Print spool	A temporary file produced by the computer to hold printing instructions until they are executed by the printer.
Printer driver	Program that operates as an interface between the computer and the printer. It translates the print job into code that the printer can understand.
Program	A set of coded instructions for the computer to perform a specific task. There are two types of program: system and application.
RAM	Random Access Memory. The memory that is used to store application files and data files. RAM can be changed.
Recycle bin	An area of memory where deleted files and folders are temporarily stored. The Recycle Bin is like a 'safety net'. If you delete something from a folder and then decide you do need it after all, it can be restored from the Recycle Bin.
ROM	Read Only Memory. The memory that a computer uses to carry out its self-test routines when it is booted up. You cannot change Read Only Memory.
Router	This is a hardware device that routes data from one network to another. Rather like a traffic policeman directs traffic on the road, a router directs traffic across networks.
Search engine	Google, Yahoo and AltaVista are examples of search engines. They create indexes of websites based on their titles, keywords and text on the page. They can locate relevant websites when users enter keywords.
Server	A server 'serves' computers that connect to it. Users can access programs, files and other information from the server.
Software	The coded commands that enable the computer to carry out specific tasks.
Spam	The electronic equivalent of junk mail. Unsolicited e-mails and irrelevant postings to newsgroups are considered to be spam. A violation of netiquette.
System software	Also known as the operating system, this software enables your computer to work.
System unit	The box that contains the workings of the computer.
TCP/IP	Transmission Control Protocol/Internet Protocol. The language that is used by computers to communicate with each other on the Internet.
Upload	The opposite of downloading. Sending a file from your computer to another computer.
URL	Uniform Resource Locator or Web address. The first part of a URL indicates what type of resource is being used, such as http or ftp. The second part of a URL contains the address of the computer being located and the path to the file.

USB	Universal Serial Bus. A USB port can be used to connect a mouse, keyboard, printer, scanner, digital camera and removable drives. USB ports are faster than serial and parallel ports.
VDU	Visual Display Unit. More commonly known as the monitor.
Virus	A program that is written to corrupt information on computers. Viruses can create, move and erase files, use up your computer memory and cause your computer not to work properly. Some viruses can duplicate themselves, attach themselves to programs and travel across networks. Opening an infected e-mail attachment is the most common way to get a virus. You can use an anti-virus program to protect your computer from viruses.
WAN	Wide Area Network. Similar to a Local Area Network (LAN) but bigger. WANs are not limited to a single location. Many wide area networks span long distances via telephone lines, fibre-optic cables or satellite links. They can also be made up of smaller LANs that are interconnected. The Internet could be described as the biggest WAN in the world.
Web browser	The software program you use to open websites. The two most popular are Internet Explorer and Netscape Communicator.
Web page	Documents written in HTML and translated by a Web browser. A website is made up of a number of Web pages.
Website	A collection of Web pages. For example, the Microsoft® website contains hundreds of pages.
Window	An on-screen frame that lets you view your documents, worksheets, databases, drawings, etc. A window environment enables you to run multiple applications, each in its own window.
Windows	The most popular operating system for personal computers. It is made by Microsoft®. There are several versions of the Windows® operating system, including Windows® XP and Windows® 2000. Earlier versions of Windows® include Windows® 3.1, 95, 98, ME and NT. Windows® uses a graphical user interface (GUI).
Windows Explorer	The program in Windows® that helps you view the contents of your hard drives and other drives. You use this program to manage your files and folders.
Wizard	A set of easy to follow dialog boxes that guide you through various processes within the Windows® environment.
WWW	World Wide Web. One of the most popular services provided by the Internet. The World Wide Web consists of pages that can be accessed using a Web browser. HTTP is the protocol used to transfer Web pages to your computer.
WYSIWYG	What You See Is What You Get. A term given to an environment where you can see your document on the screen exactly as it will look in its final state.
Zip	A 'zipped' file is a compressed file. Zipping a file compresses it so that it is smaller. This is useful if you wish to send the file as an e-mail attachment or download a file from the Internet. To be able to use a zipped file, you need to unzip it first. There are various programs available which can do this – a popular one is WinZip®.

Operate a computer

Unit value = 20

Overview

You are likely to be in a role which involves setting up and using a wide range of different types of hardware (e.g. laptop, PDA, external disk drive, digital camera, webcam or scanner), storage media (e.g. floppy disk, CD-ROM or DVD), local area network (LAN) or wide area network (WAN); and using software for complex tasks (e.g. keeping a project budget or editing a photo for a brochure).

The operating system outlined in this chapter is Microsoft Windows®. Microsoft Windows® is the most popular operating system used in offices and homes around the world. It is necessary to have an operating system on your computer in order that you can interact with it and run any applications that you may want to use, e.g. Microsoft Office. The Windows® operating system 'manages' the hardware and software that you are using and provides a user-friendly interface to enable you to use and customize your computer's working environment.

Competent people can use most types of hardware, software and storage media effectively, including setting up hardware safely, using popular storage media, using popular software tools and understanding health and safety issues and compatibility issues.

Required skills and techniques for Level 2

Setting up	Connecting up a computer with other hardware and storage media safely. Linking a computer to other hardware safely.
Accessing	Accessing files on a local area network (LAN) or a wide area network (WAN).
Using storage media	Using common storage media. Identifying the best way to transfer files to different types of storage media. Archiving data to make the most of the storage space available.
Using tools and techniques	Using common tools and techniques appropriately, such as page setup, shortcuts and print preview.

Requirements of this unit

You will need to carry out at least *two* comprehensive tasks to demonstrate your competence and general skills in the everyday use of IT. You need to be able to demonstrate that you can connect basic hardware together and use a computer safely and effectively.

This unit focuses on four basic skills:

■ **Setting up** the computer. You should be able to disconnect and connect a computer safely, recognising the common connectors. In your workplace, you may be asked to move a PC to another desk in the office. This would involve disconnecting it and then connecting it correctly and safely again at the new location. (You would not be expected to carry out any installations.)

- **Accessing** files on a network. You can use the local area network that you probably have in the office, or the Internet (which is a wide area network).
- **Using storage media**, including floppy disks, re-writable CDs and DVDs, zip drives, USB devices, flash memory and other computers. You must show that you are aware of the capacities of the different media, can connect or insert them correctly and transfer data to them.
- **Using tools and techniques**. This will be demonstrated by using software applications for other units in the qualification. You should demonstrate that you can use the basic tools in all these software applications, such as opening, saving, print preview and printing.

Tasks in this unit

The tasks that appear throughout this unit are designed to help you practise using the feature that has just been discussed. However, if you wish, you can provide these as extra pieces of evidence in addition to the two main pieces that are required by the unit.

The tasks at the end of the unit are suggested ways in which you could provide the main evidence for this unit.

What will I achieve?

By accomplishing a Level 2 in this unit, you will also have achieved Level 1 in most cases and Level 3 in some cases. Below is a table to show what levels you will have achieved.

Required skill	Level 1	Level 2	Level 3
Setting up	●	●	●
Accessing	●	●	
Storage media	N/A	●	●
Tools and techniques	●	●	
Installing	N/A	N/A	
Customising	N/A	N/A	

What is a computer?

Below is a dictionary definition of a computer:

A programmable electronic machine for storing, processing and retrieving information. A computer has four functions: input data, process data, produce output and store results.

Simply put, a personal computer is a machine that gathers and processes information and then presents it back to you. This would all seem very simple but, from a business perspective, the desktop PC has literally changed the world. Information can now be brought instantly to the desk, empowering people and transforming what they can achieve in a day. Productivity has increased and more business can be taken on and managed. Records, details, files and information can be processed, accessed, stored and retrieved easily. Personal computers have created an entirely new way of working and businesses have benefited on a massive scale.

Computer hardware

Computer hardware means the physical parts of the computer that you can see and touch, the metal and plastic that makes the computer. There is the main part of the computer (often referred to as the system unit), which contains several devices and then there are 'peripherals' – these are the other pieces of hardware that plug into the system unit.

Peripherals can be further divided into two groups: input hardware and output hardware. Input hardware is any device that is used to enter information into a PC, e.g. keyboards, mice, scanners, digital cameras, microphones. Output hardware is any device that is used to convey information from inside the PC to the outside world, e.g. monitors, speakers, printers, MP3 players.

Some devices are considered to be both input and output, e.g. hard drives, floppy drives, Zip drives and CD-RW drives. (Devices that send and receive data, such as network interface cards and modems, are also input/output devices.)

The system unit

The system unit (case or tower) is the box where all the internal components of the PC reside. The main components are:

- The motherboard
- A central processing unit (CPU)
- Memory cards
- Storage devices
- A power supply

The **motherboard** is an electronic circuit board that contains sockets and switches that enable all the devices of the PC to be connected to it.

The **central processing unit (CPU)** is the 'brain' of the computer. The CPU interprets and carries out instructions and controls the devices connected to the PC. (Think of it as the 'Managing Director' of the PC.) A CPU is a microprocessor or microchip – the latest set is Pentium. Intel is a large manufacturer of microprocessors. A CPU's speed is measured in Hertz. The latest CPUs run at speeds of many gigaHertz (GHz) – which means they can perform billions of calculations per second.

Memory cards are used by the computer to hold information required by the processor. There are two types of memory: Read Only (ROM) and Random Access (RAM).

When you switch on your PC you will notice that it can take a few minutes before it is ready to start work. During this time the PC is running various routines and self-tests to ensure that all its parts are working properly. These routines are stored in ROM. Because ROM is permanent, it is used for programs that the computer requires all the time, like the start-up program that tells the computer how to get itself going when switched on. ROM chips are plugged into sockets on the motherboard.

RAM temporarily stores data, software and the operating system while the PC is operating. Data in RAM can be changed or erased. RAM holds 'live' data – the software you are using and the data files you are creating. When your computer is switched off, everything that has been stored in RAM disappears. The memory is available again the next time you switch the computer on. The same memory chips are used over and over to store different data or programs. For example, if you switch from a word-processing application to a spreadsheet application, the instructions for the spreadsheet application replace the instructions for the word-processing application in your computer's RAM. If you wish to permanently store data, you must save it to a storage device before exiting from an application. If you wish to be able to run large, complex applications, or you want to be able to run numerous applications at the same time, then the amount of RAM you have is important. RAM is measured in megabytes.

The most common **storage devices** are hard drive, floppy drive, CD drive, DVD drive and flash drive.

The **hard drive** (or disk) is located inside the system unit. The hard disk stores both the instructions and data the computer needs to run. Modern hard drives store gigabytes of data. A hard drive is a permanent storage device. Anything stored on the hard drive remains there until deleted. The first hard drive in a computer is assigned the drive letter C: by default.

The **floppy drive** reads information from and writes it to 3.5" diskettes. A standard floppy disk holds 1.44 megabytes of data. A floppy disk is a removable storage device. It can be used to transfer files from one PC to another.

CD (compact disc) and **DVD** (digital video disc) **drives** come in a variety of formats. CDs and DVDs are removable storage devices. One CD can hold about 700 megabytes of data, which is the equivalent of about 500 floppy disks.

- A CD-ROM drive can read data on CD-ROMs. You can use a CD-ROM to transfer information from the CD to your computer (i.e. a software program), but cannot write back to the CD (hence it is Read Only Memory).
- A CD-R drive can read data from CD-ROM discs and write to CD-R discs. A CD-R disc can have data written onto it only once. Once written to, a CD-R becomes a CD-ROM.
- A CD-RW drive is the same as a CD-R drive but you can use it to save information onto the same CD many times. You can also remove the information on the CD and use it again. The CD-RW drive uses CD-RW discs.
- A DVD-R drive can view DVDs and can read data from CDs. DVD-R drives can only read data, they cannot write to a DVD or CD.
- A DVD-RW drive can read information from a DVD and also save to the same DVD many times.

Removable **flash drives** are becoming very popular. They are an extremely efficient way of moving data from one computer to another. They are pocket-sized and attach to any computer with a USB port. (For information on USB ports, please see page 18.) They have various storage capacities, but can hold large amounts of data, digital photographs or MP3 music files.

N.B. Anything inserted into the USB port of your computer is usually instantly recognised by the Windows® operating system and ready to use.

In order for your computer to work, a **power supply** is required. The main power cable plugs into the back of the system unit case. The connection for the power supply is usually near to a fan, which helps to keep the power supply cool so that it can work efficiently.

Peripherals

Anything that is plugged into the back of the system unit is known as a peripheral, for example, monitor, keyboard, mouse, printer, scanner, etc.

The **monitor** displays what you have typed and shows you the results of the tasks you have asked the computer to perform. Monitors come in a range of sizes. They connect to the system unit through a Video Graphics Adapter (VGA) connection. Flat panel monitors are now becoming very popular – because there is no tube, they are much flatter so take up far less room on a desk. They also provide a very clear, crisp image.

The **keyboard** is an essential input device that you need to give instructions to your computer. A keyboard can be connected to the PS/2 connector on the back

of the system unit or a USB port. Wireless keyboards are now available which communicate with your computer via radio signals. The receiver is usually plugged into the USB port on the computer (see page 18).

The **mouse** is an optional input device (but one that most of us couldn't manage without). You use the mouse to move the pointer on the screen. There are usually at least two buttons on a mouse and these are used to choose options by clicking. (Laptop computers have different variations on the mouse, e.g. a touchpad.) Optical mice are becoming more popular today (they have no moving parts underneath and use a laser to detect the movement).

A mouse can be connected to the PS/2 connector on the back of the system unit, or a USB port. Wireless mice are now available which communicate with your computer via radio signals. The receiver can plug into the PS/2 connector or the USB port. (For more information on connections, see pages 18–19.)

A **printer** enables you to produce a copy of something on your computer on paper. A printer is usually connected to the computer via the parallel connection. (However, you can also get printers that will connect via the USB port.) Broadly, printers fall into two categories:

Inkjet printers produce the image by spraying drops of ink onto the paper. Most inkjet printers can print in black and white and colour. Inkjet printers are inexpensive and are the most popular option for an affordable colour printer.

Laser printers use lasers to bond toner onto the page. They produce a high quality output and there is no wet ink to get smudged. Most laser printers only print in black and white. (You can get colour laser printers but they are very expensive). Laser printers can print at higher speeds than inkjet printers.

A **scanner** converts an image (photograph or drawing) into a digital format which can then be saved as a file on your computer. When you purchase a scanner (which is hardware), it will usually come with a piece of software that is used to capture and transfer the image. A scanner is usually connected to the computer through the USB port.

Other hardware

Laptop computers are becoming very popular as people look for ways to be productive on the move. A laptop computer is a powerful, mobile computer. They come with integrated screen, keyboard and mouse pad. Laptop computers are ideal for people whose job involves travelling. You can work anywhere – from home, in airports and hotels, abroad and even in meetings.

A laptop computer can do everything a desktop computer can do and, with a modem and Internet connection, laptop users can access the Internet and a company network from anywhere in the world.

A **Personal Digital Assistant (PDA)** is a hand-held device which is portable, lightweight and compact, but still powerful. You can store contact details, run your schedule, jot notes, track expenses, write e-mails and browse the Web. You can synchronize your PDA with your computer so that information on both is always kept up-to-date.

Both laptops and PDAs offer a range of options to help you manage your time, stay in touch easily and use the power of online technology whenever you're on the move.

A **digital camera** can take digital images that can be fed directly into your PC. Digital cameras don't use film: they store images on memory cards. The camera can then be connected to the computer, usually via the USB port, and the images copied from the memory card in the camera onto the computer drive. A digital image is like any other image file stored on your computer. It can be viewed, edited, printed, sent via e-mail or uploaded to a website.

Attaching the hardware

There are different connections that you can use to connect peripheral devices to the system unit of your computer:

- **Serial** – this port on the system unit can be used to connect modems, mouse devices and PDAs.
- **Parallel** – this port on the system unit can be used to connect printers.
- **PS/2** – this port on the system unit can be used to connect keyboard and mouse devices.
- **USB** – this port on the system unit can be used to connect mouse devices, keyboards, printers, digital cameras, music players, scanners, PDAs, CD/DVD drives and external hard drives.

There are traditionally two steps to attaching a piece of hardware to your computer. The first step is physically connecting the hardware (e.g. monitor, mouse, keyboard, etc.) to your computer by plugging it into the appropriate port on the back of the system unit. The second step is installing the driver, a small piece of software which enables the computer to recognise the hardware and work properly with it. (When you purchase hardware, there will usually be a floppy disk or CD in the box, which contains the driver. The exception to this is hardware that is connected to the USB port of the computer. Any device connected to the USB port is instantly recognised by the operating system and installed automatically.)

The latest versions of the Windows® operating system (Windows® 2000 and XP are used in this book) have a list of many drivers and can usually find an appropriate driver when you install a piece of hardware. It is therefore not necessary to use the driver that comes with the hardware. This ability to simply plug the hardware into your computer and have the Windows® operating system install it automatically is known as 'plug and play'.

 ## Connecting a computer

Connecting a computer up to all its peripherals is not rocket science. The connections on the back of the system unit are usually colour-coded to make it easy to see what fits where. Even if the connections are not colour-coded, there is usually only one 'hole' that a device will fit into.

Place the hardware where you need it to be on and around the desk. Run the cables to the back of the system unit. Plug the monitor, keyboard and mouse into the appropriate connectors on the back of the system unit. (Ensure there is enough 'give' on the cables to enable you to move the monitor, keyboard and mouse on the desk.)

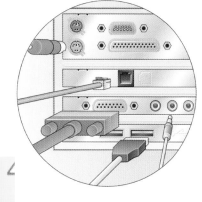

If necessary, connect the printer into the back of the system unit. You also need to connect any other peripherals, i.e. scanner, speakers, etc.

If there is a network or modem cable, connect this into the appropriate connector on the back of the system unit.

Finally, plug the power cable (there may also be a separate power cable for the monitor) into the system unit and into the power socket.

Once you have connected all the hardware to the system unit, you can switch the PC on. For every device that has a power cable, there will be an On/Off switch (system unit, monitor, printer, scanner, etc.).

TASK 1

1 **Have a look at your computer and identify the different components: system unit, monitor, keyboard, mouse, printer, scanner, etc. Identify the various storage devices you may have: floppy disk drive and CD/DVD drive.**

2 **Look at the back of your computer and note where the peripherals are plugged in: monitor, mouse, keyboard, printer and network connection. Also the power supply.**

3 **If you have an external USB device, plug it into the USB port and notice that your computer recognises that a device has been plugged into the USB port.**

What is software?

Software provides the instructions that computers follow to make the hardware work. A software program is a set of programming commands and statements that the computer follows to carry out tasks. Without software, hardware may look like a computer, but it won't act like one. Having a computer system without software is rather like having a music system without CDs. Software falls into two main categories: operating software (such as Windows®) and application software (such as Word and Excel).

Operating software

An operating system (such as Windows®) is the program that manages all of the other programs on the computer. It works behind the scenes managing the different requests that the application software may make, for example, loading up a file onto the screen (opening) or printing a file. Every PC, laptop and handheld device has to have an operating system. When you switch on a computer, after it has carried out the self-tests, it looks for the operating system and loads it.

General application software

Word-processing packages are used to produce written documents, such as letters and reports. Text can be formatted with different fonts, sizes and attributes, bullet points, numbering, etc. Text can be edited using cut, copy and paste or find and replace. In modern word-processing packages you can also create tables and mailshots. They also now contain a lot of tools that were previously only found in desktop publishing software.

Spreadsheet packages are used to store and manipulate figures. They are used for storing, working with and presenting financial information such as cashflow forecasts, budgets, balance sheets and accounts. Modern spreadsheet packages can carry out complex calculations and also produce graphs.

Presentation packages are used to create anything that will be presented to an audience (usually containing graphical elements). You can create the individual slides using text, drawings, graphics and charts. They also include tools, such as animation, that allow you to turn the individual slides into a professional presentation.

Database management packages are used wherever large amounts of information need to be stored and retrieved. Data can be entered, stored, sorted, searched and presented in reports.

Integrated packages, such as Microsoft® Office, contain more than one general software application. A package contains a number of separate applications but they can all work together very efficiently and easily.

Specific application software

Specific application software is designed to carry out a specific task, usually in a particular industry. A payroll application is an example of specialised application software. It is designed for payroll activities and could not be used for anything else. Below are some more examples:

Graphics applications are used to produce diagrams, drawings and pictures. Some can also work with photographic images. These applications are used in industries where high-quality graphic images need to be created. Examples of graphics applications include Paint, CorelDRAW®, Paint Shop™ Pro® and Photoshop®.

Computer-aided design (CAD) applications are used for designing, usually in the engineering and architectural industries. They enable the user to produce highly accurate, scale drawings and, using layers, the designer can show different information on each layer.

Application software can be bought 'off the shelf' or it can be written specifically for an industry or organisation. This type of software is often referred to as 'bespoke' software. (More information on this type of software is contained in Unit 214 – Specialist or bespoke software.)

Although there are many software applications available, they share common elements because they all operate using the Windows® operating system. You will soon realise that Word, Excel, PowerPoint®, Access and Outlook® all have the same 'look' and that basic features such as Open, Save, Print, Cut, Copy and Paste are carried out in the same way in all applications. This makes it easier for you to transfer your knowledge from one application to another.

In order to use different software applications efficiently, it is useful to learn the basic techniques that you can apply in any application. It is also useful to know the shortcuts that enable you to use the application more productively. Basic techniques, such as page setup, print preview, printing, saving, customizing toolbars and creating shortcuts are covered in this book in the appropriate unit for the specific piece of software.

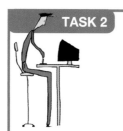

TASK 2

The next time you are using your computer, make a note of the different pieces of software you have installed. What is the operating system? What application software do you have?

 ## Getting started

Turning the PC on

You will need to switch on the system unit of the computer and any peripherals, e.g. monitor. (Any device that has its own power supply will have an On/Off switch.)

When you switch the computer on it goes through a process known as 'booting up'. It carries out a series of self-tests and then finds and loads the operating system. (The term 'booting up' apparently comes from the term 'pulling up your bootstraps' – a bootstrap is a small loop at the back of a leather boot that enables you to pull the entire boot on. The imagery suggests that your computer is preparing itself for work!)

Logging in

Because of the security features of most operating systems, you will normally have to 'log-in' to your account on the computer. Once your computer has 'booted up', the log-in screen will appear. Type in your user name and password and click on OK.

TASK 3

1 **Switch on the PC and all its peripherals. Note that it takes a little while for your computer to carry out its self-test and load up the operating system.**

2 **If prompted, log into the computer using the appropriate user name and password.**

 # Changing basic settings

Adjusting monitor brightness

You can adjust the brightness of the image on the monitor by using the controls on the front of the monitor itself. The buttons on the monitor will vary according to the manufacturer, but you will be able to change the contrast and brightness of the screen.

Adjusting settings using the control panel

You can adjust a number of settings on the computer using the operating system software. For more information on using the Control Panel in the Windows® operating system, see page 37.

TASK 4

Change the brightness and contrast using the controls on the monitor.

 # Accessing files on computer

If your computer is not connected to other computers it is called 'stand-alone'. In this situation, you can only access files that are stored on the hard drive of the computer or on floppy disks, CDs or flash drives. You can only use hardware that is directly connected to the computer.

Each storage device connected to a computer is assigned a letter:

A: is the drive letter assigned to the floppy disk drive.

C: is the drive letter assigned to the hard drive.

D: is the drive letter that is assigned to the CD/DVD drive (if it is the next letter available).

E: F:, etc. are available to be assigned to network drives.

N.B. The drive letter B: used to be assigned to 5¼" floppy disks. As these disks are rarely used today, this drive letter is no longer used.

The drive letters for the hard drive and floppy disk drive are always C: and A:. The drive letter assigned to the CD or DVD drive will depend which is the next letter available. In some caes, a hard drive may have been 'partitioned', i.e. split into sections. Each section is assigned a different letter, e.g. C:, D:, E: and F:. The CD or DVD drive is then assigned the next available letter, e.g. G:.

There are various ways you can view the drives, folders and files on your computer: **My Computer**, **Windows Explorer** and the **Open** or **Save** dialog box in an application.

My Computer

Double-click on the My Computer icon on the desktop.

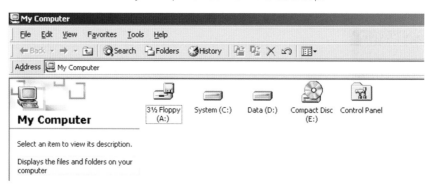

The My Computer window shows the drives that are available on the computer. (If it is a networked computer, it also shows the network drives that the user has access to.) To view the contents of a drive, double-click on the drive icon. The example above shows that the computer being viewed has a 3½ Floppy (A:), two hard drives (C:) and (D:) and a CD drive (E:).

When you double-click on the C: drive icon, the window shows the contents of the C: drive. A drive can contain folders (rather like cardboard folders in a filing drawer). Folders are indicated by the yellow folder icon and files are shown at the bottom of the list. The icon beside a file indicates the application that the file is associated with. To open a folder to view its contents, double-click on the folder. To open a file, double-click on the file. The appropriate application will be launched and the file opened.

Each folder can contain other folders and files. To go down through the structure of folders, double-click to open each folder. If you wish to go back to the previous folder, press the **Back** button on the toolbar.

As you navigate down through folders, a note of where you are going is shown in the Title Bar at the top of the screen (the Address Bar in Windows XP). The 'address' of the folder is called the path. The path starts with the drive letter you double-clicked and folders are separated by a backslash (\ ).

📁 C:\Documents and Settings\Nicki Talbot\My Documents\Letters

The path above shows that the user double-clicked on the C: drive icon, then opened the folder called Documents and Settings, then the folder called Nicki Talbot within Documents and Settings, then the folder called My Documents within Nicki Talbot and then the folder called Letters within My Documents.

TASK 5

1 **Use My Computer to explore the contents of your C: drive. Notice the different folders that are on the C: drive and open them to view their contents. Notice that within some folders there are other folders and within those folders there can be other folders, and so on.**

2 **Use the Back button to move back up out of a folder and notice the path on the Title Bar changing as you navigate into different folders.**

Windows Explorer

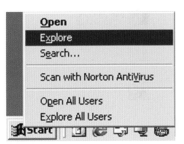

Another way to view the drives, folders and files on your computer is to use Windows Explorer.

Windows® XP: Choose **Start**, **All Programs**, **Accessories**, **Windows Explorer**.
Windows® 2000:Choose **Start**, **Programs**, **Accessories**, **Windows Explorer**.

Alternatively, you can right-click on the **Start** button and choose **Explore** from the shortcut menu.

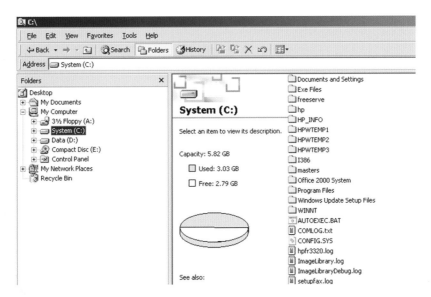

The drives are listed on the left side of the Explorer window. When you click on a drive in the list, the contents of the drive (folders and files) are shown in the right side of the window. In the example above, the C: drive is selected in the list on the left. The contents of the C: drive (folders and files) are shown on the right side of the screen.

If you wish to see the folder structure under a drive, click on the **+** to the left of the drive letter.

In the example on page 24, the **+** beside the C: drive icon has been clicked. The folder structure on the C: drive is now showing in the list on the left. (To collapse this part of the list again, click on the **−** button that is now showing beside the C: drive icon.)

To open a folder to view its contents, double-click on the folder (either on the left or right side of the screen). To open a file, double-click on the file. The appropriate application will be launched and the file opened.

Each folder can contain other folders and files. To progress down the structure

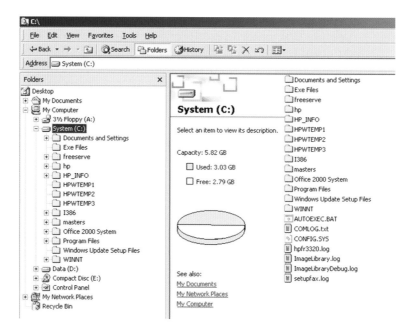

  of folders, double-click to open each folder. If you wish to go back to the previous folder, press the **Back** button on the toolbar.

As you navigate down through folders, a note of where you are going is shown in the Title Bar at the top of the screen. (In Windows® XP it is shown in the Address Bar.) The 'address' of the folder is called the path. The path starts with the drive letter you double-clicked and folders are separated by a backslash (\ ).

📁 C:\Documents and Settings\Nicki Talbot\My Documents\Letters

The path above shows that the user double-clicked on the C: drive icon, then opened the folder called Documents and Settings, then the folder called Nicki Talbot within Documents and Settings, then the folder called My Documents within Nicki Talbot and then the folder called Letters within My Documents.

TASK 6

1 **Use Windows Explorer to explore the contents of your C: drive.**

2 **Click on the + button beside the C: drive icon to see the folder structure on the C: drive. Notice the folders and open different folders to view their contents. Notice that within some folders there are other folders and within those folders there can be other folders, and so on.**

3 **Use the Back button to move back up out of a folder and notice the path on the Title Bar changing as you navigate into different folders.**

4 **Press the – button beside the C: drive icon to collapse the folder structure again.**

Viewing drives, folders and files within an application

You can view drives, folders and files from within the **Open** or **Save** dialog boxes in an application.

Within the application, choose **File, Open** (or click on the **Open** button) to open the Open dialog box.

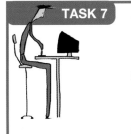

The example above shows the Open dialog box in Word. Click on the drop-down arrow at the end of the **Look in** box and choose **My Computer** from the list. You will now see the drives that are available from this computer.

Double-click on a drive letter to see the contents of that drive.

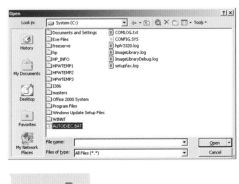

In this example, the C: drive letter was double-clicked in order to see the contents of the C: drive. The Folders and files that are on the C: drive are now listed. Double-click on a folder to move into it. Use the **Back** button to move back up to the previous level.

TASK 7

1 Open the Open dialog box in an application and choose the C: drive from the Look in list.

2 Double-click on folders to open them and navigate around the folder structure on the C: drive.

3 Use the Back button to come back up out of the folders.

Networks

In an office situation, it is desirable that computers are connected together. Connected computers can share resources, i.e. printers, scanners, etc., and also files. This is a much more efficient way of working. A network is a collection of computers and other devices that are connected by cables (or wireless connections) to enable them to communicate with each other. Network users can share and exchange information (files and programs), access business services (e-mail and other applications) and share resources (printers, scanners, etc.) easily and efficiently.

Networks lead to increased productivity – everything can happen faster and all users have access to the shared equipment. Networks can also reduce costs – e-mail communications significantly reduce telephone overheads. Finally, networking creates mobility. It allows the business resources to be accessed from anywhere on the network. Remote users can connect to the network and access files and resources that they need.

Local area network

The most common type of network for within an office is a local area network or LAN. This connects together a collection of computers and other devices. The network hardware physically connects the computers and devices. The network software allows each computer and device to be seen by the others on the network and enables communication between them.

There are two basic types of LAN: peer-to-peer and client/server.

A **peer-to-peer** network is fine for up to five computers. The network is controlled by a hub (a switch) which connects the computers and devices together. Each computer is the equal of, or 'peer' to the others. They are all able to share the files of each computer and the peripheral devices that are connected to each computer on the network.

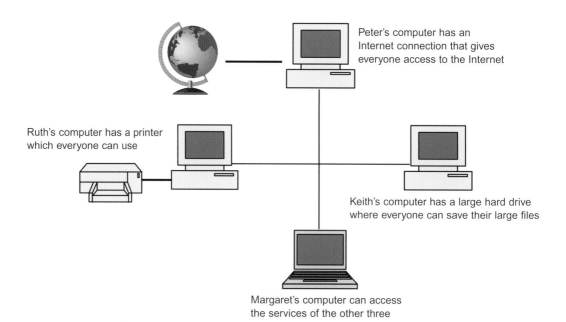

Peter's computer has an Internet connection that gives everyone access to the Internet

Ruth's computer has a printer which everyone can use

Keith's computer has a large hard drive where everyone can save their large files

Margaret's computer can access the services of the other three

There are some disadvantages with a peer-to-peer network. For example, if one of the computers on the network is not switched on or is not there (in the case of a laptop), then the files and resources of that computer cannot be used. Also, if everyone on the network is sending jobs to the printer, the computer that is attached to the printer is using a lot of processing power to manage the print jobs and it may become difficult for someone to work on that computer at the same time. If everyone is saving large files to one computer and that computer crashes, no one can access these files. Finally, a peer-to-peer network is not very 'scaleable', i.e. it cannot grow easily. Once there are more than five computers trying to share files or resources on another computer, the network will no longer be efficient.

A **client/server** network is best for more than five computers and if you want to be able to expand the network quickly and easily. In a client/server network there is one computer – called the server – where all the files are stored and all the peripheral devices are connected. Everything is done through the server and it manages the operations of the network, i.e. monitoring who is using files and queuing print jobs for the printer. A server is a network device that links computers, peripherals and business processes together efficiently.

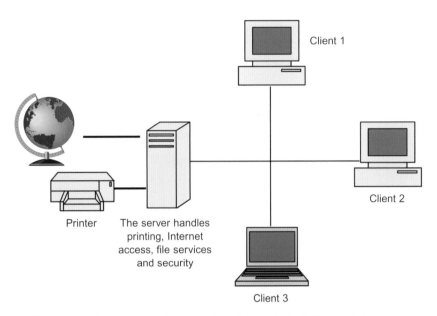

Client 1

Client 2

Client 3

Printer

The server handles printing, Internet access, file services and security

Because the server is a powerful computer, it is able to fulfil multiple requests quickly and efficiently and maintains the connections and control within the network. It sorts out communication 'bottlenecks' and allocates the processing power necessary to allow every user to optimise their productivity.

Wide area network

A wide area network (WAN) is a computer network over a larger geographical area. Typically, a WAN consists of two or more LANs. Computers connected to a wide area network are often connected through public networks, such as the telephone system. They can also be connected through leased lines or satellites. The largest WAN in existence is the Internet.

Working on a networked computer

If your computer is on a network, you will need to 'log-in' once the computer has started up. When you enter a user name and password, this information is checked with the server and, as long as the server recognises your credentials, it will let you into the network.

Once you have logged onto the network, you have access to any drives, files and resources that your user name has permission to access.

You can open files from network drives and save files to network drives. You can print to printers that are on the network and access other peripherals, such as scanners.

Folders ×
Desktop
My Documents
My Computer
Local Disk (C:)
Compact Disc (D:)
Apps on 'Vol456\London' (F:)
Data on 'Vol456\London' (H:)
Peter Smith on 'Vol456\Lon\Data\Users' (U:)
National on 'Vol456\London' (N:)
Public on 'Vol456\London' (P:)
Control Panel
Network
Recycle Bin
Internet Explorer
Application Explorer
My Briefcase

Accessing files on a network

If your computer is part of a network, then as well as the local drives on your own computer, you will be able to access drives on the network.

When you use My Computer or Windows Explorer, you will be able to see the network drives that you can access from your computer.

In the example to the left, the folder list shows that this computer has a hard drive (C:), a CD drive (D:) and also has access to network drives F:, H:, U:, N: and P:.

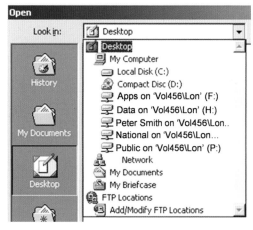

You will also be able to see all the drives to which you have access from within all applications.

The example on the left shows the Open dialog box in Word showing the drives that can be accessed.

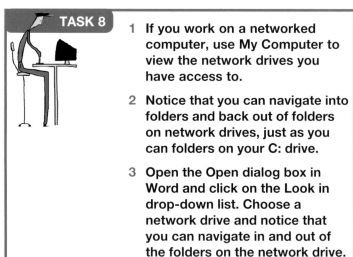

TASK 8

1 **If you work on a networked computer, use My Computer to view the network drives you have access to.**

2 **Notice that you can navigate into folders and back out of folders on network drives, just as you can folders on your C: drive.**

3 **Open the Open dialog box in Word and click on the Look in drop-down list. Choose a network drive and notice that you can navigate in and out of the folders on the network drive.**

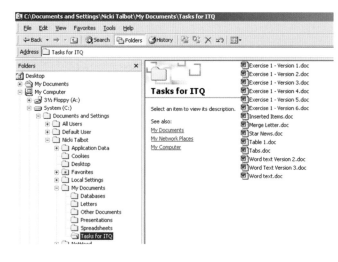

Opening files

You can open any file that you have access to, whether it is stored on a 'local' drive or on a network drive.

You can open any file that you see in My Computer or Windows Explorer by double-clicking on the file name. The appropriate application will be launched and the file opened.

In Windows Explorer you can navigate into a folder to view the files that are in that folder. In this example, the Tasks for ITQ folder is selected in the list on the left and the contents of this folder are shown in the right section of the screen. Each file has an association to an application. In the list above, all the files are Word documents (indicated by the Word icon to the left of the filename).

When a filename is double-clicked, the appropriate application will launch (in this case, Word) and the file will open. Alternatively, you can launch the application first and then open a file.

Launch the application you wish to use, i.e. Word, Excel, PowerPoint®, etc.

Choose **Open** from the **File** menu in the application.

Alternatively, click on the **Open** button on the Standard toolbar.

The **Open** dialog box opens as below:

Navigate to the drive and folder in which you wish to view the files. (The example above shows the contents of the Tasks for ITQ folder.) Select the file you wish to open and click on **Open**. (For more information on opening files in a specific application, refer to the unit for that application.)

Save

Saving files

When you open a file, the appropriate application is launched for that file. To save a file (if you have made changes to it), choose **Save** from the **File** menu.

Alternatively, click on the **Save** button on the Standard toolbar.

If you are saving a new file the **Save** dialog box opens **as** left:

Navigate to the drive and folder in which you wish to save the file. (The example above shows the Tasks for ITQ folder.) Give the file an appropriate filename (if you haven't previously saved it) and click on **Save**. (For more information on saving files in a specific application, refer to the unit for that application.)

 TASK 9

1 **Practise opening files from My Computer or Windows Explorer. Notice the icon to the left of the filename and the fact that the appropriate application is launched when you double-click on the file.**

2 **Launch one of your applications and practise opening files. Familiarise yourself with the Open dialog box and see how you can look into different drives and folders to see the files that are in those folders.**

3 **Notice that if you use Save in the application, the previous version of the file is overwritten. If you wish to access the Save dialog box, you must use Save As and then you can save the file with a different file name or in a different location.**

For more practice on opening and saving files, see the unit for the specific application.

Using storage devices

Files that you create can be stored on a variety of storage devices – the hard drive of your own computer, floppy disks, CDs or DVDs, flash memory or on network drives.

Saving to the hard drive

The hard drive (or disk) is located inside the system unit. Files saved to the hard drive of a stand-alone computer can only be accessed at that computer. Saving files to the hard drive is a quick and efficient process. The hard drive on your computer will, by default, have the letter C: assigned to it. If you save any file to a folder which starts with C:\, you are saving to the hard drive. To open the file again, you need to navigate to the same folder on the C: drive.

The example on the left shows the **My Documents** folder, which is on the **C:** drive of the machine. Files stored in this folder can only be accessed again at this computer.

Saving to a floppy disk

If you need to take information from one computer to another, you can use a floppy disk. The file can be saved to a floppy disk and then opened from the floppy disk on another computer. The largest capacity floppy disk is 1.44 MB. This is fine for text files, but is not large enough if you wish to transport multimedia files that may

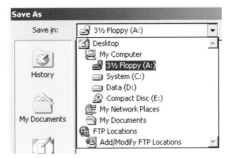

contain sound, photographs or video. Also, saving to a floppy disk is up to 10 times slower than saving to a hard drive.

To save to a floppy disk, insert the diskette in the floppy disk drive and choose 3½ Floppy (A:) from the **Save in** list in the Save As dialog box.

Give the file a name and click on **Save.** The file is saved to the **A:** drive (floppy disk). The floppy disk can now be removed from the machine and inserted into another machine. To open a file from the floppy disk, choose the **A:** drive from the **Look in** list in the **Open** dialog box. This will show you the contents of the A: drive. Click on the file that you wish to open and click on **Open**.

Saving to a CD or DVD

Another portable storage medium is CD or DVD. CDs can store from 650 MB to 850 MB of data (the equivalent of about 500 floppy disks). A DVD can have up to four layers, two on each side. It can store from 4.38 GB to 15.9 GB of data, depending on the number of layers.

CD and DVD drives come in a variety of formats: some can simply read files (CD-ROM), some can read and write files (CD-R) and some can read, write and re-write files (CD-RW).

CD and DVD drives are assigned the next available letter when they are installed. (For example, if your computer has a hard drive called C: and a floppy disk drive called A:, then a CD or DVD drive will be assigned the letter D:). To read information from a CD or DVD, insert it into the drive and navigate to the letter that has been assigned to it. (It will usually state that it is a CD/DVD as well as showing the drive letter.)

This example shows that the CD drive has been assigned the letter E:. The icon indicates that it is a CD drive.

You can view and open files on a CD if you have a CD-ROM drive. Navigate to the CD drive and open the files that are on that drive. However, to be able to save to a CD, you need to have a CD-R drive or a CD-RW drive.

To save data to a CD (sometimes called 'burning'), you need to use a special piece of software. Common CD writing software includes Nero and CD Creator. However, the Windows® XP operating system also contains a utility to write to CDs or DVDs.

Copying files to a CD in Windows® XP

Insert a blank CD into the CD recorder. Double-click on the My Computer icon on the desktop. Navigate to and select the files that you wish to copy to the CD.

Under **File and Folder Tasks**, click **Copy this file** or **Copy the selected items**. (If the files are in the My Pictures folder, click **Copy to CD** or **Copy all items to CD**.) In the **Copy Items** dialog box, click the CD recording drive and then click **Copy**.

Windows displays a temporary area where the files are held before they are copied to the CD. Check that the files that you wish to copy to the CD appear under **Files Ready to be Written to the CD**.
Under **CD Writing Tasks**, click **Write these files to CD**.
The CD Writing Wizard launches.
Type a name for the CD. Click on **Next.**
The files are written to the CD. A progress monitor appears while this is happening.

Once the writing process is complete, the final step of the Wizard appears. Click on **Finish.**
It is a good idea to use My Computer or Windows Explorer to check that the files are on the CD and will open.

Saving to an external hard drive (flash drive)

Most modern PCs have at least one Universal Serial Bus (USB) port. Many modern external devices, such as flash drives, scanners, printers and digital cameras, can connect to the computer via the USB port.

Removable flash drives are becoming very popular. They are very small yet can hold large amounts of data – from 32 MB to 1 GB. They are an extremely efficient way of moving data from one computer to another. These removable drives plug into the USB port of your computer. Both Windows 2000 and Windows XP will detect a device plugged into the USB port, so there is no need to 'install' the hardware. Simply plug it in.

When you plug in the flash drive, it is assigned the next available letter. You can copy files to the flash drive by choosing this drive as the destination for the copied file.

The example to the left shows that a flash drive has been plugged into the USB port of the computer and has been assigned the letter F:.

To read information from a flash drive or write to a flash drive, insert the device into the USB port and then navigate to the appropriate letter in the Save (or Save As) dialog box. (It will usually state that it is a 'removable drive' as well as showing the drive letter.)

Once you have copied files to this drive, you should remove the device properly. When you plug the device in, an icon will appear in the system tray on the Task Bar indicating that there is a device plugged into the computer.

Double-click on this icon and the Unplug or Eject Hardware dialog box will open.

Select the device that you wish to remove and click on **Stop**. Click on **OK** at the prompt. You will now receive the following message:

Click on **OK** and then **Close**. You can now safely remove the device from the USB port.

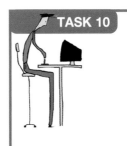

TASK 10

1 **Use My Computer or Windows Explorer to view the drives that are available on your computer. Note your 'local' drives, C: and A:. Also note if you have a CD drive and what letter it has been assigned.**

2 **Open a file within one of your applications and save it to a floppy disk. (Remember to use Save As.) Open that file again from the floppy disk.**

3 **If you have a CD-R or CD-RW, use the CD copying software to copy some files to a CD.**

4 **If you have an external drive, plug it into the USB port of your computer. View the drive in My Computer or Windows Explorer. Copy files to the external drive.**

 ## File management in My Computer and Windows Explorer

You can move, copy, rename and delete files in My Computer and Windows Explorer. You can also create new folders to store work in.

Selecting files in My Computer or Windows Explorer

To select a file in a folder, click on the file to highlight it.

To select multiple files that are adjacent to each other, click on the first file in the list, hold down the **Shift** key on the keyboard and click on the last file in the list. All the files in between are selected.

To select multiple files that are not adjacent to each other, click on the first file that you wish to select, hold down the **Ctrl** key on the keyboard and click on each subsequent file that you wish to select. All the files you click on are selected.

Creating a folder

Click on the drive or folder that you wish to create the new folder in. Choose **New, Folder** from the **File** menu.

A new folder will appear called **New Folder**. Type a name for the folder and press Return.

Moving or copying files

Select the file or files that you wish to move or copy. Choose **Copy To Folder** or **Move To Folder** from the **Edit** menu. (Copy leaves the file where it is but also puts a copy of it in the drive and folder you specify. Move moves the file to the drive and folder you specify.)

 Alternatively, click on the **Copy To Folder** or **Move To Folder** button on the Standard toolbar.

In Windows® 2000, the **Browse For Folder** dialog box will open; in Windows® XP, the **Copy Items** dialog box will open.

Navigate to the folder that you wish to move or copy the selected files into. Select the drive from the top of the list and then double-click on folder icons to open them. (If you wish to copy or move files to a floppy disk, insert the floppy disk into the A: drive prior to indicating the drive you wish to copy/move to. If you wish to copy or move files to an external hard drive, insert the device into the USB port of the computer prior to indicating the drive you wish to copy/move to.)

Once you have navigated to the appropriate folder, it will show in the **Folder** box in Windows® 2000. Click on **OK** in Windows® 2000 or **Copy** in Windows® XP. The

File management in My Computer and Windows Explorer

file or files will be copied or moved to the specified folder. If there are a number of files to be copied or moved, you may see a progress window appear on the screen with files 'flying across' from one folder to another.

You can use the Cut/Copy and Paste method if you prefer. This works in the same way as in an application: select the file or files that you wish to move or copy, choose **Cut** or **Copy** from the **Edit** menu, move to the destination folder and choose **Paste** from the **Edit** menu.

Deleting files

Select the file or files that you wish to delete. Choose **Delete** from the **File** menu.

Alternatively, click on the **Delete** button on the Standard toolbar.

If you are deleting a file from the hard drive of your computer, you will receive the following message:

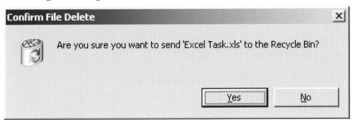

Click on **Yes** to complete the deletion. The file is sent to the Recycle Bin.

If you are deleting files from a removable storage device (e.g. floppy disk or CD) or from a network drive, you will receive the following message:

Click on **Yes** to complete the deletion. The file is not sent to the Recycle Bin.

The Recycle Bin

When you delete a file from the hard drive of your own computer, it is sent to the Recycle Bin. As its name suggests, files in the Recycle Bin can be 'recycled' or 'undeleted'.

You can access the Recycle Bin from My Computer or Windows Explorer. You may also have an icon on your desktop for it.

Click on the icon to open the Recycle Bin.

To restore a file from the Recycle Bin, select the file in the list and choose **Restore** from the **File** menu or click on the **Restore** button.

The files stored in the Recycle Bin still take up space on your hard drive, so it is a good idea to empty the Recycle Bin regularly. To empty the Recycle Bin choose **Empty Recycle Bin** from the **File** menu or click on the **Empty Recycle Bin** button.

Renaming files

Select the file that you wish to rename. Choose **Rename** from the **File** menu.

Alternatively, right-click on the file itself and choose **Rename** from the shortcut menu.

Type the new name for the file and press Return.

TASK 11

1 **Using My Computer or Windows Explorer, create a new folder on the C: drive of your computer.**

2 **Practise copying multiple files into the new folder you have created.**

3 **Rename some of the files you have copied into the new folder.**

4 **Delete the files you have copied into the new folder. Go into the Recycle Bin and restore the files you have just deleted.**

5 **Delete the folder you have created.**

File management in an application

You can carry out basic file management within an application. In the **Open** or **Save** dialog box you can create folders, move and copy files from one drive/folder to another, rename files and delete files.

To create a folder, navigate to the folder in which you wish to create the new folder and click on the **New Folder** button on the toolbar.

You can also use the shortcut key combination: Alt+%5.

Type a name for the new folder and click on **OK.**

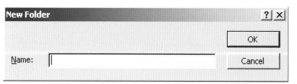

To move or copy a file, right-click on the file you wish to move or copy and choose **Cut** or **Copy** from the shortcut menu.

Navigate to the folder into which you wish to move or copy the file, right-click on a blank area of the folder window and choose **Paste** from the shortcut menu.

To rename or delete a file, right-click on the file you wish to **Rename** or **Delete** and choose the appropriate option from the shortcut menu.

Follow the on-screen prompts.

Printing

The Windows® operating system also manages your printers. You can install new printers and choose which printer to print to. Windows® also manages the print queue.

Choose **Start, Settings, Printers**. (Printers can also be accessed from the Control Panel in Windows® XP.)

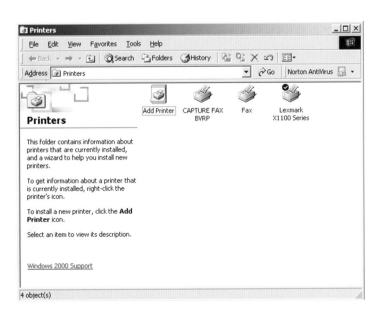

The Printers window shows you the Printers that you have access to from your computer. (Network printers are shown with a 'connector' underneath.)

One of the printers will have a tick against it – this indicates the 'default' printer (i.e. the one that you will print to when you press the Print button in an application).

To add a new printer, double-click on the **Add Printer** icon and follow the instructions in the Wizard.

To see the print queue for a printer (to see if there are any jobs in it), double-click on that printer icon.

To cancel the printing of a specific document, select the document in the print queue by clicking on it and choose **Cancel** from the **Document** menu.

To cancel the printing of all documents, choose **Cancel All Documents** from the **File** menu.

The Windows® operating system

When you switch on your computer it runs a series of self-tests. Once it has done this, it locates the operating system and launches it. Most computers today use the Windows® operating system. (There are various different versions in use – this book covers Windows® 2000 and Windows® XP, which are the two most up-to-date.)

Windows is a piece of software that manages all the functions of your computer. It is also a platform for the applications – they all need Windows® to work. Think of Windows® as the 'managing director' of the software. It works in the background while you are using an application to ensure that everything is working smoothly. It also controls the environment you work in, i.e. screen colours, keyboard, mouse, etc.

Most users don't spend much time at the Windows® desktop, they simply launch the applications they wish to use, e.g. Word, Excel, PowerPoint®, Outlook, but Windows® is always working in the background ensuring that your commands are given the processing power necessary to be carried out.

While Windows® is mostly used as a platform for getting into the applications you want to use, it does also have some useful accessories that you can use to personalise the environment.

The Windows® desktop

Once Windows® has launched and you have logged-in (if appropriate), you arrive at the Windows® desktop.

There are icons on the desktop which are like 'doorways' into different areas of Windows® or different applications. There may also be icons on the Quick Launch Bar which again allow quick access to applications.

The **Start** button at the bottom left of the screen opens the Windows® menu system. You can navigate to all the features of Windows® and all the applications you use by using the menus.

Windows® 2000

Windows® XP

Creating shortcuts

You can add shortcuts to the desktop for the applications or files that you use regularly, so that you don't have to go through the menu system to access them. There are various ways to create a shortcut on the desktop.

Choose **Start**, **Search**, **For Files or Folders** (**All Files and Folders**, in Windows® XP).

Type the name of the application or file that you wish to find in the **Search for files or folders named:** box (the **All or part of the file name:** box in Windows® XP) and click on **Search Now** or **Search**.

In this example the file called winword.exe is being searched for. A filename with an .exe extension indicates an 'executable' file – an application. Winword.exe is the file that launches the Word application.

The files matching your search criteria are returned in the **Search Results** window. Right-click on the file in the **Search Results** window and choose **Create Shortcut** from the shortcut menu.

The following message appears:

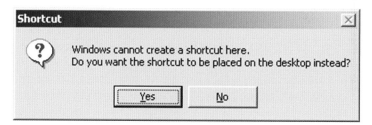

Click on **Yes.** A shortcut will be placed on the desktop. (You can tell a shortcut on the desktop as it has a small black arrow on top of the icon.)

It is important that you create a shortcut on the desktop, and do not move the actual file or application itself. If you place the 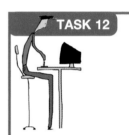 actual file or application on the desktop, it will greatly increase the time it takes for Windows to launch (because it has to build the desktop each time). Also, if you accidentally delete the icon from the desktop, you have deleted the file or application from your computer. By putting shortcuts on the desktop, you can delete the shortcut from the desktop without removing the actual file or application from the computer.

TASK 12

1 **If your system allows, search for an application and put a shortcut to it on your desktop.**

2 **Search for a file and put a shortcut to it on your desktop.**

The Control Panel

The Control Panel enables the user to customise the Windows® environment and all the devices that Windows® manages. To access the Control Panel, choose **Start**, **Settings**, **Control Panel**. (**Start**, **Control Panel** in Windows® XP.)

The Control Panel window contains icons to customise different areas of the Windows® environment.

Windows® 2000

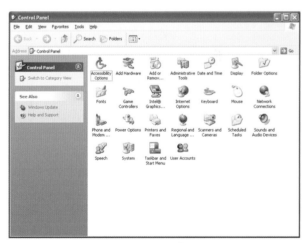

Windows® XP

To open the appropriate dialog box, double-click on the icon.

Date/Time

You can change the **Date/Time** setting on the computer. (You can also choose a different **Time Zone**.) This setting is sometimes disabled by the network administrator. (Changing the time can affect e-mail traffic from the server to your computer.) Make any changes you require and click on **OK.**

Display

You can change the **Background** colour on the desktop, the **Screen Saver** and the **Appearance** (colour schemes) of the screen using the controls in this setting. (Windows® XP also has a **Themes** tab.) Again, the Display Properties can be disabled in a networked environment. Make any changes you require and click on **OK.**

Keyboard

You can customise how your keyboard operates using the controls in this setting. On the **Speed** tab, you can control how long a delay there is before the keys repeat and also the repeat rate. You can also control the speed that the cursor blinks on the screen. The **Input Locales** tab enables you to specify the language of your keyboard. Make any changes you require and click on **OK.**

Mouse

You can customise how your mouse operates using the controls in this setting. (The tabs in this dialog box may vary according to the mouse driver you have installed). On the **Buttons** tab, you can control which buttons do what. (You can switch the buttons around if you are left-handed.) You can also control the double-click speed. On the **Pointers** tab, you may be able to choose from a range of different mouse pointer schemes. On the **Motion** tab, you can control how fast the mouse moves around the screen and its acceleration. Make any changes you require and click on **OK.**

Sounds and Multimedia

You can apply a sound to each event in Windows and you can also control the volume of the sound in this dialog box. (It is called Sounds and Audio Devices in Windows® XP.) Make any changes you require and click on **OK.**

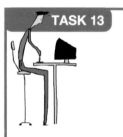

TASK 13

1 **Have a look at the icons in the Control Panel. Double-click on various icons and have a look at the options that are available.**

2 **Practise changing the settings for your mouse and keyboard.**

3 **If your system allows, explore the changes you can make using the Display icon.**

Windows® accessories

Although Windows® is mainly used as the manager of your software, it does have some accessories of its own that you might find useful. To see the accessories, choose **Start**, **Programs**, **Accessories**. (**Start**, **All Programs**, **Accessories** in Windows® XP).

The accessories include a calculator, a notepad, imaging software (which you can use with a scanner), a CD player (if you have a CD drive), some games and some system tools (these are discussed in Unit 204 – IT maintenance for users). Windows Explorer (see page 23) can also be accessed from this menu.

Why Windows®?

The main reason for the operating system being called 'Windows' is the fact that every program or utility you launch opens into its own window. These windows all share some common elements and once you have become familiar with them, you will begin to become more confident in navigating in, around and out of windows. Even if you have never used a software application before, you will immediately recognise how it looks and how to use some basic features.

Working with windows

Every window has a bar across the top – this is called the **Title Bar** and shows you where you are, e.g. Control Panel, Word, Excel, etc.

At the right end of the Title Bar are three **Window Control Buttons**.

Clicking on the button **Minimize** pushes the window to the bottom of the screen onto the Windows® taskbar. (It does not close the window and the window is available to use again by clicking on it on the taskbar.)

The example above shows the Control Panel minimized onto the Task Bar at the bottom of the screen.

The middle button is called **Maximize** or **Restore**. If a window opens in the middle of the screen, you can click on the **Maximize** button so that the window fills the entire screen. If a window is maximised, this button changes to the **Restore** button. Clicking on it again restores the window to the size and position it was in before it was maximised.

The last button is called **Close**. This closes the window.

Underneath the Title Bar is a **Menu Bar**. This contains words which, when clicked on, open a drop-down menu.

In the case of the Control Panel, the Menu Bar contains the words **File, Edit, View, Favourites, Tools** and **Help**. These menu words vary according to which application window you have opened.

Usually, underneath the Menu Bar there is a **Toolbar** (in Word, Excel, PowerPoint®, etc., there are two) containing buttons that carry out commands. They are offered as an alternative to choosing the feature from a menu.

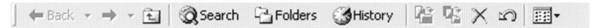

Finally, along the bottom of a window there is usually a **Status Bar**. This bar offers information about the currently selected item.

Once you have mastered the basics of navigating around windows, you can be confident that you can open a window with the knowledge that you can simply close it again if you don't want to do anything in that window.

As well as being able to **Minimize**, **Maximize** and **Close** windows, you can also move and resize windows.

To move a window, point to the Title Bar, click and hold the left mouse button and drag the window to a new location on the desktop.

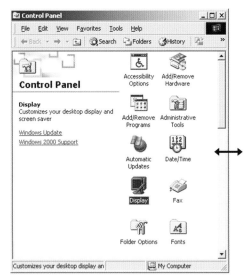

To resize a window, move the mouse over any border of the window. The mouse pointer changes to a double-headed black arrow. Click and hold the left mouse button and drag to resize the window.

TASK 14

1 **Practise opening different windows and minimising, maximising and closing them.**

2 **Practice resizing and moving windows.**

Dialog boxes

Dialog boxes are slightly different to windows. A dialog box opens when you need to have some 'dialogue' with your computer – when your computer needs some information from you or wants to confirm an operation. For example, if you choose **Print** from the **File** menu in Word, a dialog box opens so that you can choose options for printing your document.

A dialog box has a Title Bar across the top but it only contains one window control button – **Close**. There is usually also a **Help** button by the Close button. The contents of the dialog box vary depending which dialog box it is, but they all have an **OK** and **Cancel** or **Close** button. Clicking on **OK** carries out any changes you have made in the dialog box. Clicking on **Cancel** closes the dialog box without carrying out any changes (i.e. it removes the dialog box from the screen).

A dialog box can contain:

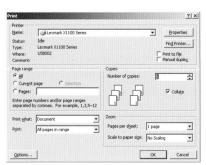

■ **Option buttons** – where you can choose only one of the options. In the figure left, the Page range area contains a set of option buttons.

■ **Check boxes** – where you can choose more than one box. The figure above contains three check boxes: Print to file, Manual duplex and Collate.

■ **List boxes** – which contain a list of options from which you can select. If the list is too long to see all of it, there will be scroll bars so that you can scroll up or down through the list.

■ **Drop-down list boxes** – which work in the same way as list boxes but, in order to view the list of options, you have to click on the drop-down arrow to open the list box. The figure above contains drop-down list boxes to choose the Name of the printer, for Print What and Print.

■ **Text boxes** – where you can type data. In the figure above, the Pages box in the Page Range area is a text box.

■ **Combo boxes** – where you can either type your selection in the box (like a text box), or pick from a list (like a list box). There are also drop-down combo boxes.

■ **Spin boxes** – where you can select a numerical value. To use a spin box, click on the up or down arrow to move the numerical value up or down. The figure above contains a spin box for Number of copies.

■ **Control buttons** – buttons such as OK, Print, Close and Cancel are control buttons that carry out commands. Some control buttons open another dialog box. In the figure on page 140, Properties, Find Printer, Options, OK and Cancel are all control buttons.

Archiving files and folders

You can change the properties of a file to mark it as ready for archiving. You can change the properties of a file from wherever the file is listed, i.e. **My Computer**, **Windows Explorer** or in the **Open** or **Save As** dialog box.

Right-click on the file and choose **Properties** from the shortcut menu.
Click on the **Advanced** button at the bottom of the **General** tab.

Tick the box **File is ready for archiving** and click on **OK**.

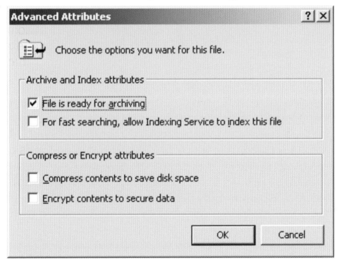

While you can use this facility to archive a file, it is good practice to carry out regular housekeeping with your folders and files. Delete folders and files that are no longer required and do not need to be kept.

Anything saved to a network drive will be backed up by the server, so you can delete it knowing that there is a copy on the server back-ups. (However, you will not be popular with your IT team if you make a habit of deleting files and then going to them to ask for them back!)

Anything saved to your C: drive is your responsibility. If you do save files to your C: drive (which is generally discouraged in a networked environment), back it up yourself (i.e. to floppy or CD) prior to deleting it from the hard drive.

TASK 15

1 **Select some files on your hard drive and mark them ready for archiving.**

2 **Remove this property from the files.**

Compatibility issues

In a world where we want to be able to communicate quickly and easily with anyone, anywhere, standards are growing in importance. Standards are usually set by companies working together to develop, establish, endorse and promote those standards. Sometimes these alliances are between companies selling complementary components that work together, for example, Microsoft® and Intel® have teamed up to ensure that the microchips that Intel produce and the operating systems that Microsoft® design work smoothly together. More often, however, companies that are direct competitors will agree on compatibility to build sufficient support for a new technology.

There are many standards in computer hardware: the 3½" floppy disk standard, the VGA video display standard for monitors, the standard for serial buses that transport data from one hardware component to another, the standard for microprocessors that drive the computer, Ethernet standards for computer networks and Internet protocols.

Standards in computer software include the Microsoft® Windows® operating system, the MPEG standard for compressing video data, the PostScript® page language for printing and Adobe Acrobat® for making documents 'portable'.

The setting of standards in the IT arena is very important to ensure the continued development, growth and exploitation of new technologies.

All hardware and software that is used in a computer must be compatible. If a piece of hardware is not compatible with another piece of hardware on your computer, there is what is referred to as a 'conflict'. When one piece of hardware is conflicting with another, it may result in neither of them working properly, if at all.

In an organisation, before hardware or software upgrades take place, the IT team will spend time checking the compatibility of the new systems and testing current software to ensure it will run properly on the new systems.

Microsoft® provides a website which makes it easy to check whether your hardware devices and your software are compatible with a Windows® operating system (2000 or XP). All Microsoft® software works efficiently together and is designed to work seamlessly with most modern hardware. However, problems can arise if you are using older software or software that has been designed specifically for your organisation. (This type of software would need to be tested prior to any upgrades to check that it will still work with the new software.) Also, although a lot of the software we use in offices today is designed by Microsoft®, there may be conflicts if you use software designed by a different software manufacturer, such as Lotus® or Macromedia®. (If you are using the Windows® operating system, then your application software is running using this operating system, which is made by Microsoft®.)

In order that your computer can communicate with other computers, inside or outside your organisation, there must be compatible standards. There must be standardised hardware and software formats and, in order to e-mail someone using the Internet, there must be standardised Internet protocols. For example, the International Telecommunications Union (ITU) has established universal standards for modems. All modems that are manufactured must adhere to these standards so that all modems are compatible, regardless of who manufactures them.

Health and safety issues

There are a number of health issues that are related to computer use. However, most of these issues can be avoided by the correct layout of the computer area and by following good practice when using a computer.

Back problems

Many computer users complain of backache, stiff neck and stiff shoulders. This often means they are not sitting in an appropriate position to use their computer or they have bad posture. Chairs must be the correct height for the desk and computer. A common scenario is where a computer sits on a side desk, at a right angle to the main desk. The user will tend to work with their hands to the side instead of sitting face on to the computer.

The risk of back, neck and shoulder problems can be minimised by having an appropriately designed chair that supports the lower back and is fully adjustable. A screen should be tilted and turned so that the user is not having to look to the side to view it. Document holders can reduce neck movement and the use of a footrest can ensure that the user is sitting in a correct position. Also, users must take regular breaks away from the computer.

Stress

For a lot of people, using a computer can be very frustrating. Repeated frustration can lead to stress. Frustration is usually down to a lack of training in the use of a piece of software, the software being too complex for a simple task, the computer being very slow to use, the computer environment being inappropriate (maybe too cluttered) or repeated hardware failure, i.e. printer getting jammed or computer crashing.

This frustration can be removed by providing users with adequate training and support, by choosing well-designed software that does the job quickly and efficiently and by having a hardware infrastructure in place that is capable of meeting the users' demands.

Eye strain

Looking at a screen for a long time can lead to eye strain, particularly if the screen is of a poor quality and flickers. The lighting in the room can also have an impact on the eyes. Users may complain of headaches and sore eyes.

In order to minimise this risk, screens should be checked regularly to ensure they are performing at optimum levels. The lighting in the room should be suitable for computer work. Computers should be sited to avoid glare and reflection and, where it is not possible to avoid this, screen filters should be fitted. Blinds could be fitted to windows to help reduce glare. The user's eyeline should be level with the top of the screen and the screen should be slightly tilted. Employers are obliged to pay for eye tests for users who spend long hours in front of a computer screen. Again, regular breaks should be taken away from the computer.

Repetitive Strain Injury (RSI)

It is accepted that prolonged use of a computer can cause RSI. RSI affects the fingers, wrists and shoulders – they swell and become stiff and painful. The risk of RSI can be reduced by ensuring keyboards are at the appropriate angle and using wrist supports while typing. Work should be varied so the user doesn't spend all day at the keyboard and the user needs to take regular breaks away from the computer.

Ozone irritation

Laser printers emit ozone which can be an irritant to some people. A few people experience problems with breathing, headaches and nausea. Ensure that laser printers are not sited right next to a desk and that there is good ventilation in the room.

Computers have been blamed for a whole range of health problems, from increased epilepsy to an increase in miscarriage in pregnant women. Much research has been done but no absolute conclusions can be drawn. Computer users need to use common sense when using a computer, just like any other piece of office machinery.

Ensure that computer leads are not trailing around the floor and that you will not fall over any computer hardware. Ensure that your desk is clutter-free and that you have a good position when working on the computer.

Health and Safety (Display Screen Equipment) Regulations 1992

Legislation makes it a legal requirement for employers to take various measures to protect the health of workers using computers. The legislation is quite wordy and complex, but below are some basic points from it.

Employers must:

- Provide adjustable chairs.
- Provide tiltable screens.
- Provide anti-glare screen filters.
- Ensure workstations are not cramped.
- Ensure room lighting is suitable.
- Plan work at a computer so that there are breaks.
- Provide information on health hazards and training for computer users.
- Pay for appropriate eye tests for computer users.
- Provide special glasses if they are needed.

(These regulations apply to computer users in offices, not students in schools and colleges.)

 ## Data transmission speeds

The time it takes to move data from one place to another varies depending on the devices being used.

Saving a file to a floppy disk can take up to 10 times longer than saving to a hard drive. Saving files to a network drive can also be a little slower than saving to the hard drive of your computer because your computer is having to communicate with the server.

Moving files to a CD is a slightly different process. The speed at which files will 'burn' to a CD depends on the speed of the CD drive you have. Speeds can also vary depending on the type of connection an external device is using to connect to your computer. For example, saving to a device connected via the parallel port on your computer is slower than saving to a device connected to the USB port on your computer.

The speed of sending data from one computer to another depends on the method by which you are communicating with the other computer. If you use the Internet to send and receive e-mails and to search the World Wide Web, it may help to understand the way in which the information travels.

The Internet is an 'international network' of linked computers. Data is sent from your computer in digital packets. These packets are routed from one computer to another until they reach the destination computer. (The packets don't necessarily travel along the same route – they may go different ways but they join together again at their destination.)

If you use a dial-up connection, you are using an analogue telephone line to send and receive data. Because the data from your computer is digital and the telephone line can only transmit an analogue signal, you need a modem (modulator/demodulator) which turns the digital signal into an analogue one so it can travel along the telephone line and turns the received signal back to a digital one when it reaches your computer. The transmission speed of data travelling along an analogue telephone line is relatively slow. The speed is measured in Kilobits (or Kbps) and for an analogue phone line it is 56 Kbps. How fast data can be transmitted is sometimes called the 'bandwidth'. (If you imagine a pipe that data travels up and down – an analogue telephone line is a very narrow pipe, so data cannot travel up and down it very quickly.)

There are many other ways that computers can communicate, but a popular technology at the moment is 'broadband'. Broadband can convert the analogue line into a digital line. As the term implies, the bandwidth is broader and therefore data can travel up and down this bigger pipe more quickly – anything from 500 Kbps to 2.5 Mbps, depending on the type of broadband being used.

Below is a table of some of the different ways to connect computers together and their speeds:

Technology being used	Downstream (Receive)	Upstream (Send)
56K modem (dial-up)	56 Kbps	56 Kbps
1-channel ISDN line	64 Kbps	64 Kbps
2-channel ISDN line	128 Kbps	128 Kbps
Bluetooth (wireless radio signal)	721 Kbps	721 Kbps
ADSL (broadband) slow	500 Kbps	400 Kbps
ADSL (broadband) fast	2.5 Mbps	640 Kbps
T1 leased line	1.554 Mbps	1.554 Mbps

Below is a table showing the time it would take to fill various storage media, using the different connections available:

Capacity	56K modem	ADSL (broadband) slow	ADSL (broadband) fast
1 MB hard drive	3 minutes	2.2 seconds	1.3 seconds
Floppy disk	4 minutes	3.1 seconds	1.8 seconds
600 MB CD	30 hours	21 minutes	13 minutes
1 GB hard drive	50 hours	36 minutes	21 minutes

Suggested tasks for evidence

All evidence for this unit must be produced in the workplace. The suggested tasks below provide guidance on the type of work that you can produce as evidence for this unit. You may come across one or more of these scenarios in your workplace. By following the guidelines below, you will have produced a piece of evidence for this unit.

To ensure that your work can be used as evidence towards your ITQ, take screenshots and print-outs wherever possible.

Suggested Task 1

Create a checklist that your colleagues could follow if they needed to connect up a computer and attach a printer.

Suggested Task 2

Whenever you use My Computer or Windows Explorer to carry out file management, take screenshots of the steps you carry out.

Whenever you access or save files to the network (i.e. in Word, Excel, etc), take screenshots of the steps you carry out.

Suggested Task 3

Create a short report in Word on the different types of storage media available and when they are appropriate to use. Make use of photographs or drawings and lay the report out in a two-column newsletter style.

Suggested Task 4

Create a short presentation in PowerPoint® on the different ways to transfer data from one machine to another. Discuss what can affect the speed of transfer.

Suggested Task 5

Create a health and safety checklist for the area around a computer desk. Carry out a simple risk assessment on your own work area and note the findings.

IT troubleshooting for users

Unit value = 15

Overview

You are likely to be in a role which involves using skills and experience to solve most types of errors (e.g. faulty cable connections, broken mouse, software that needs more memory to open or damage to software from viruses) and knowing about problems to do with compatibility.

The operating system outlined in this chapter is Microsoft® Windows®. Two versions are covered: Windows® 2000 and Windows® XP. The software applications outlined in this chapter are part of Microsoft® Office. Two versions are covered: Office 2000 and Office XP.

Competent people can solve errors on most types of hardware and software using their skills and experience. This includes restarting hardware and software, being aware of the types of errors that can occur with software and being aware of the compatibility issues that can arise (see Unit 202 – Operate a Computer).

Required skills and techniques for Level 2

Restarting	Restarting most hardware and software using tools supplied by the manufacturer.
Correcting errors	Choosing and using methods that have worked in the past to correct different types of errors. Checking that errors have been corrected.

Requirements of this unit

You will need to carry out at least *two* comprehensive tasks demonstrating skills, techniques and knowledge in everyday troubleshooting of your PC.

All IT systems experience errors sometimes. Generally the IT support team will deal with any hardware or software problems that may arise. However, there are things that users can do to solve simple errors themselves and useful information they can gather to assist the IT support team.

Of course, faults do not occur to order. The problems may arise while you are using software for the other units, so this unit will be completed as part of the overall completion of the required ITQ units. If problems do occur, make notes and take screenshots to show that you recognised the problem and the steps you undertook to rectify the fault.

Tasks in this unit

The tasks that appear throughout this Unit are designed to help you practise using the feature that has just been discussed. However, if you wish, you can provide these as extra pieces of evidence in addition to the two main pieces that are required by the unit.

The tasks at the end of the unit are suggested ways in which you could provide the main evidence for this unit.

What will I achieve?

By accomplishing a Level 2 in this unit, you will also have achieved Level 1 in all cases. Below is a table to show what levels you will have achieved.

Required Skill	Level 1	Level 2	Level 3
Restarting	●————————————●		
Correcting errors	●————————————●		

 # Introduction

While the design of computer hardware and software is becoming more sophisticated and the two elements are generally able to communicate well, there are inevitably times where the communication 'breaks down'. There are hundreds of hardware and software components that must all work together, so it is inevitable that, on occasion, there are glitches and performance problems do occur. This unit deals with recognising that a fault has occurred and knowing some basic steps to take to attempt to resolve the particular problem.

 # Troubleshooting a 'frozen' computer

You may be happily working away on your computer when the mouse and/or keyboard seem to stop working. The mouse won't move around the screen and the screen does not respond to keys on the keyboard. Your system has 'frozen' or 'hung' (the official term is 'has stopped responding'). This is rarely the fault of the hardware; the problem usually lies with the software application that you are using. There are some basic steps you can take to 'unfreeze' the system and then you will be able to continue working.

Wait . . .

Before taking any action, it is a good idea to wait a few minutes before jumping to the conclusion that the system has frozen. It could simply be that your PC is performing a resource-intensive task, so nothing else will respond for the moment. If this is the case, after a few minutes, the system should 'unfreeze' itself and you will be able to continue working normally. If, after a few minutes, the system is still not responding, then you will need to move onto the next option – exiting from the frozen program.

N.B. If you are forced to exit from a frozen program, you may lose data. It is good practice to save a file at regular intervals (say every 10 minutes) as you are working on it. Then, if you are forced to exit from a frozen program, you will not have lost too much data. Windows® XP and Office XP are very efficient at recovering files when your system stops responding.

Exiting from a program

There are two ways you can exit from a program in this situation.

Right-click on the program's button in the taskbar. A shortcut menu appears. Click on **Close** (see figure below). Either the application will close immediately, or you will have the opportunity to use the Task Manager to exit the application.

If your system does not respond to clicking the program button, use the Task Manager.

In Windows® 2000, you can use [Control]+[Alt]+[Delete] to open the Windows® Security dialog box. Click on **Task Manager**. Alternatively, the quick key combination to go straight into Task Manager is [Control]+[Shift]+[Esc].

In Windows® XP, [Control]+[Alt]+[Delete] takes you straight into the Task Manager.

The Windows Task Manager opens onto the **Applications** tab. This lists all the applications currently in use. The Status column indicates whether the application is working properly. This normally says 'Running' but if an application has frozen, it may say 'Stopped Responding'.

Click on the name of the program which has stopped responding and click on the **End Task** button at the bottom of the Task Manager window.

The End Program message box might appear to let you know that the program is not responding. To exit from the program, click on **End Now**.

The program will end and you can then restart the program to continue working.

In Office XP, when you restart the program, the **Document Recovery** message appears down the left side of the screen. This lists any files that have been 'recovered' during the End Task procedure.

Click on the file you wish to save. You can then **Close** the Document Recovery window.

Logging off

If you have tried to exit from the 'frozen' program using both of the methods above, but the program remains 'frozen' on the screen and your system is still not responding, you need to move onto the next option – logging off. Logging off will stop all programs currently running on your PC.

If your mouse will move, in Windows® 2000 you can use **Start**, **Shut Down** and then choose **Log off** from the drop-down list in the **Shut Down Windows** dialog box.

In Windows® XP, choose **Start**, **Log Off** and then click on **Log Off** in the **Log Off Windows** dialog box.

If you cannot use your mouse, in Windows® 2000 press [Control]+[Alt]+[Delete] and click on **Log Off** in the **Windows Security** dialog box. You will be asked if you are sure you want to log off. Click on **Yes.**

In Windows® XP press [Control]+[Alt]+[Delete] to open **Task Manager**. Press [Alt]+[U] to open the Shut Down menu and scroll down to the **Log Off** option in the menu. Press **Return**.

Once you have logged off, all the applications that were running will have been closed. You can log back on and continue working normally.

If you have tried to log off, but your system is still not responding, you need to move onto the next option – restarting your PC.

Restarting your PC

If your mouse will move, in Windows® 2000 click on **Start**, **Shut Down** and then choose **Restart** from the drop-down list in the **Shut Down Windows** dialog box.

In Windows® XP click on **Start**, **Turn Off Computer**. Click on **Restart** in the **Turn off computer** dialog box.

If you cannot use your mouse, in Windows 2000 press [Control]+[Alt]+[Delete], click on **Shut Down** in the **Windows Security** dialog box and choose **Restart** from the drop-down list in the **Shut Down Windows** dialog box.

In Windows® XP, press [Control]+[Alt]+[Delete] to open **Task Manager**. Press [Alt]+[U] to open the **Shut Down** menu and scroll down to the **Restart** option in the menu. Press **Return**.

Restarting your computer will take it through the shut down process and then start the machine again, as if you had just switched it on. This is the best way to restart your computer, as it goes through the appropriate shut down process before restarting.

The other option in the **Shut Down Windows** dialog box (Windows® 2000) or the **Turn off computer** dialog box (Windows® XP) is **Shut down/Turn Off**, which will take the computer through the shut down process, but it will not then restart.

Switching off the computer

If all else fails (which is very unusual), you may simply have to switch off the power to the system unit and then switch on again. This is known as 'cold-booting'. Only use this option as a last resort. Switching off the power to the computer without allowing it to go through the shut down process properly can cause problems in the future, especially if you do it regularly.

If you are forced to switch off the power to the PC, you may find you have to press and hold the power button for a few seconds before your computer switches off.

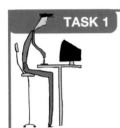

TASK 1

Familiarise yourself with Task Manager. Notice that it lists the applications that are currently running on the Applications tab. They should all show as 'Running'.

Basic troubleshooting

With experience, you can develop the skills needed to diagnose and resolve basic problems that may occur when using your PC. You may be able to resolve some problems yourself or, even if you do have to contact your IT support team, you will be able to tell them the steps you have already taken to try to resolve the problem.

Checklist for troubleshooting your PC

- **Stay calm and be patient!** Take your time and keep a clear head.
- **Read the screen**. When a problem occurs, a message will usually appear on the screen. Write down the message exactly as it appears, so you can tell your IT support team.
- **Check for the obvious**. The problem may simply be a loose connection or cable. Ensure all cables are securely attached to the PC and the device, e.g. printer, modem, speakers, etc. Make sure the device is turned on.
- **Quit all programs and restart the computer**. Quitting all programs and restarting will clear everything out of the computer's memory. This is a pretty good solution for most issues that may arise as you use your PC.
- **Focus on the software**. A lot of hardware problems are actually software-related. For example, a device might need an updated driver or some changes made to the settings in order to work properly.
- **Change one thing at a time**. If you are attempting to fix a problem, make one change at a time and test the PC to see if that change worked. If not, undo the change, make a different change and test the PC again. Continue doing this until you resolve the problem.
- **Ask the right questions**. When did the problem start? Is the problem always there or does it only happen when you enter certain commands? Asking the right questions will help you focus on exactly when the problem occurs, which might help find the solution.
- **Read the documentation**. A user guide is included with most hardware devices and software. Check this guide for a troubleshooting section showing common issues.
- **Make notes**. Take notes about the problem you encounter and what steps you take to resolve it. Include both successful and failed actions. This information will be useful if the same problem occurs again. Also, if you need to call on IT support, you will be able to tell them how you have already tried to resolve the problem.
- **Check the manufacturer's website**. Most manufacturers have a support area

on their website where you can view a Frequently Asked Questions (FAQ) list, search a database for help, or download software updates (known as patches).

■ **Never be afraid to ask for help**. If you cannot resolve the problem in a reasonable amount of time, call your IT support team.

What software version?

One of the basic things you should know is the version of the software that you are running. There are various versions of Microsoft® Windows® and Microsoft® Office on the market today. It will help your IT support team if they know which version you have.

To find out what version of the Windows® operating system you are running, click on the **Start** button. The version is shown up the left side of the Start menu.

To find out what version of a Microsoft® application you have, click on the **Help** menu in the application and choose 'About Microsoft . . . .' (usually the bottom entry in the menu).

An information box will open telling you the version that you have.

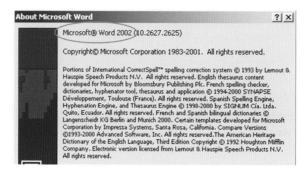

The PC won't start up

If your PC doesn't power on when you switch it on, there are a few things you can check before calling on IT support:

■ Press and hold the power button for a few seconds. Make sure you are pressing it in fully.
■ Make sure the mains outlet is working. Plug something else into the socket to check.
■ Disconnect and reconnect every cable attached to the PC. Try the power again.
■ Disconnect the mouse and keyboard and try the power again. (If the mouse or keyboard are damaged they may cause a short-circuit. Your PC will not start if this is the case.)

If the fan on the back of the system unit turns, it indicates that your PC's internal power supply is working. The motherboard of the computer could be damaged or the On/Off switch is not working. Call your IT support team.

If the fan on the back of the system unit does not start, this could indicate that your PC's internal power supply has failed. This could simply be a blown fuse. Call your IT support team.

If the power indicator lights up on the front of the system unit but nothing else happens, this could indicate that the hard drive or motherboard of the computer is damaged. Call your IT support team.

If the PC powers up, but doesn't boot, it could require a system restoration. Call your IT support team.

Troubleshooting using Help

The Microsoft Help system usually includes a troubleshooting section which will take you through a step-by-step process to troubleshoot an issue on your computer. The Windows® Troubleshooter can be accessed in the Help system.

Choose **Start**, **Help** (Windows® 2000) or **Start**, **Help and Support** (Window® XP). Click on the **Troubleshooting** link.

For example, to troubleshoot printing problems, click the **Troubleshooting** link in **Help** and click on the **Print** link in the list of Troubleshooters. This opens the **Print Troubleshooter**. Answer the appropriate questions to work through the troubleshooter.

Common Error Messages

Below is a table of error messages you might encounter, what they mean and what action you should take. You will see that most of the error messages are not the fault of the user, but the fault of the programmer of the software! Also, you can see that the best course of action for any error message is to exit from the application and, if necessary, restart the computer.

Error	What does it mean?	Action
Non-system disk or disk error	This message appears when you switch on the PC if you have a floppy disk in the drive.	Remove the floppy disk and press any key on the keyboard to continue.
General Protection Fault error	Each application runs in its own memory space. Each application must stay in its own memory space. If one application tries to store something in another application's memory space a General Protection Fault occurs.	Exit from the application that has caused the error and then re-open it. If the system has frozen, you may need to restart. You may lose some data.
Illegal Operation error	This error is not caused by an illegal operation by the user! Your application tried to perform an 'illegal operation'. This type of message is almost always the result of a programmer's error.	Exit from the application that has caused the error and then re-open it. If the system has frozen, you may need to restart. You may lose some data.
Unexpected Application error	The application is not being used in the way the programmer designed it to be used. This is the fault of the programmer for not anticipating every possible way that the user might use the application!	Exit from the application that has caused the error and then re-open it. If the system has frozen, you may need to restart. You may lose some data.
Fatal error	Processing is halted due to many different problems. The program or operating system cannot recover from this error.	Exit from the application that has caused the error and then re-open it. If the system has frozen, you may need to restart. You may lose some data.

Another error message you may encounter when you are copying a file to a floppy disk.

This means that the file you are trying to copy to the floppy disk is too large. You will need to copy the file to a larger capacity external storage medium (such as a CD or Flash drive). The following error occurs when you try to open the wrong file type in an application (for example, opening a Word document in PowerPoint®).

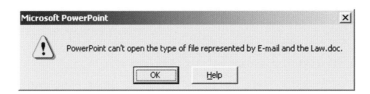

Microsoft PowerPoint ⚠ PowerPoint can't open the type of file represented by E-mail and the Law.doc.

OK   Help

Detect and Repair tools in the software

Most software applications now contain their own repair tools. In Microsoft® applications, the Detect and Repair tools can be found in the **Help** menu.

In Microsoft® Office, you can use this feature to detect and repair problems such as missing application files and the registry settings associated with installed Microsoft® Office applications. When this feature is used, all default settings are restored:

■ The Office Assistant character reverts to the default (Clippit).
■ The most recently used entries on the File menu are removed.
■ Menu and toolbar buttons and position revert to the default.
■ View settings within the application, such as the Calendar view in Outlook, revert to the default.

You will need to re-enter your user name and initials when you restart the Office applications.

This is a useful tool to use if you are considering reinstalling the program. You might find that running the Detect and Repair feature fixes whatever the problem was and there is no need to reinstall Microsoft® Office.

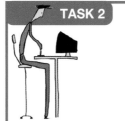

TASK 2

1 **Find out what versions of Microsoft® Windows® and Microsoft® Office® you have on your computer.**

2 **Familiarise yourself with the troubleshooting tools in Windows® and Office.**

3 **Locate the Detect and Repair tools in your Microsoft® Office applications.**

Getting help with an application

Most software contains a comprehensive range of help files.

Help in Microsoft® Windows 2000

In Microsoft® Windows 2000, the Help system can be accessed by choosing **Help** from the **Start** menu.

The Windows® 2000 help system has four tabs: **Contents, Index, Search** and **Favorites**.

The **Contents** tab lists the main help files by chapter. When you click on the chapter heading link, the contents of the chapter are listed. Each of these section headings is a link to a help file. In the example below, the **Introducing Windows 2000 Professional** link has been clicked which shows a list of sections under that heading. By clicking on the **What's new?** link, the help topic appears in the screen on the right.

The **Index** tab shows an alphabetical list of all the help topics. You can double-click on a topic in the list, or type a keyword to move to that topic in the list.

The **Search** tab enables you to search for help topics. Type in a keyword or keywords and click on List Topics. A list of topics that relate to your keyword are shown on the left side of the Help window. When you click on a topic in the list on the left, the help topic appears on the right side of the Help window. For example, if the keyword 'mouse' has been entered a list of help topics relating to the mouse will be returned.

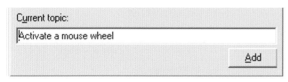

The **Favorites** tab enables you to put your 'favourite' help topics in a list. When you have used one of the other tabs to find the help topic you would like to store, click on the **Favorites** tab and click on **Add** at the bottom of the window.

Help in Microsoft® Windows® XP

In Microsoft® Windows® XP, the Help system can be accessed by choosing **Help and Support** from the **Start** menu.

The front screen contains links to different areas of help. You can also type a keyword into the Search box and click on the green arrow to search for help topics relating to that keyword.

The Microsoft® Office Assistant

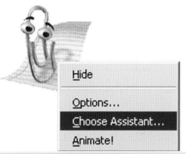

In Microsoft® Office 2000 and Microsoft® Office XP there is a 'character' called the **Office Assistant**. This character offers quick access to the large array of help files that are available in the applications.

To switch on the Office Assistant, choose **Show the Office Assistant** from the **Help** menu.

There is a range of Office Assistants you can choose from. To choose an Assistant, right-click on the Office Assistant that is currently on the screen and click on **Choose Assistant** in the shortcut menu.

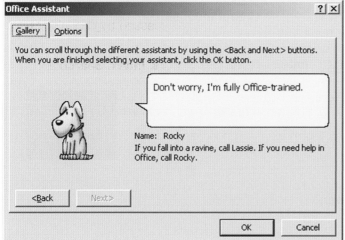

Click on **Back** and **Next** to view the available Office Assistants. They all have a name(!) and animations that they do. Click on **OK** to choose an Assistant.

The important thing is that you can click on the Office Assistant at any time and type your question to access the help files for that topic.

You can hide the Office Assistant by right-clicking on it and choosing **Hide** from the shortcut menu.

If you wish to switch the Office Assistant off, right-click on it and choose **Options** from the shortcut menu.

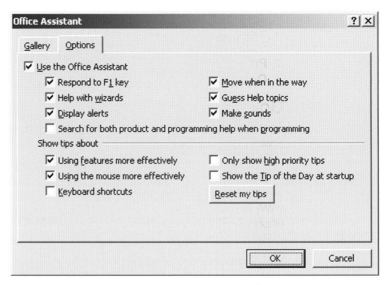

Deselect the **Use the Office Assistant** check box. Click on **OK.**

Using Microsoft® Office Help Files

If you wish to access help without using the Office Assistant, choose **Microsoft Help** from the **Help** menu.

Alternatively, you can press ⌐F1⌐

The Microsoft® Office Help screen has three tabs: **Contents, Answer Wizard** and **Index.**

The **Contents** tab lists the main help files by chapter. By clicking on the + beside a chapter heading, you can view the help topics under that chapter heading. In the figure on the left the **Creating a Document Quickly Using Wizards** chapter heading has been expanded to show the topics in that chapter. The **Create a document** topic has been selected and the content of that topic displays on the right side of the screen.

On the **Index** tab you can type a keyword or choose a keyword from the list. All the help topics relating to that keyword are then listed. By clicking on a help topic in the list, the content of that topic shows on the right side of the Help window.

The **Answer Wizard** allows you to type in a question and click on **Search.**

A list of help topics relating to your question is shown on the left side of the Help window. By clicking on a help topic in the list on the left, the content of that help topic will appear on the right side of the window. If you type 'changing font size' in the top box and click **search**.

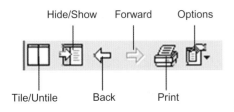

Hide/Show   Forward   Options

Tile/Untile   Back   Print

You can use the buttons on the toolbar to work with the help system:

- **Tile/Untile** – you can tile the Help window so that it sits beside your active window. Untiling the window makes it sit on top of the active window.
- **Hide/Show** – you can hide or show the left pane of the Help window. (The Help window takes up less room on the screen when hidden.)
- **Back** – go the previous help page.
- **Forward** – go to the next help page (once you have used Back).
- **Print** – print the help topic.
- **Options** – opens a menu of options for the help system.

Going online for help

As well as the help files that come with the application, you will be able to access a wide range of help topics on the manufacturer's website.

For example, Microsoft® has a huge website containing lots of information about the software you are using, tips and tricks for better PC use and a searchable 'knowledgebase' where you should be able to get answers to your questions. www.microsoft.com takes you to the home page. There are lots of links in the application's help system which will take you to the appropriate online help page.

By clicking on the Support link under Resources on the left side of the page, you can go to the Microsoft® Support home page or to the Knowledge Base.

The Support Home page has links to FAQs, Newsgroups, the Knowledge Base, software download and to Microsoft® Online Help.

To launch the Knowledge Base, click on the link **Search our Technical Database (Knowledge Base)**.

Complete the form: select the product from the drop-down list, type your keywords and choose the other options as required. Click on the green **Go** button. There are also hints and tips for effective searching on the Knowledge Base home page.

There is a large range of other websites which will assist you in troubleshooting your computer.

- www.computerhope.com is a very easy to follow site which contains information about common error messages and basic troubleshooting tips for software and hardware.
- www.everythingcomputers.com is another good site full of tips and tricks that includes lists of How Tos.

TASK 3

1 **Use the Windows® help system to find out about the options in the Control Panel. Print off the help topics.**

2 **Switch on and change the Office Assistant in your Microsoft® Office applications.**

3 **Use the Contents tab of the Microsoft® Word help files to locate the topic, 'Assign or remove a shortcut key'. Print the topic.**

4 **Use the Answer Wizard tab of the Microsoft® Word help files to locate information on creating a table. Print the topic.**

5 **Use the Microsoft® Knowledge Base to get information on managing templates in Word. Print one of the results.**

6 **Use www.google.co.uk to identify sites that offer help with your computer.**

Viruses

A virus is a piece of computer code (software) that is designed to cause, at the very least, inconvenience to a computer user and, at the very most, fatal damage to your computer. Once a computer is infected with a virus, that virus will 'propagate' itself and spread to anything else that is connected to that computer, i.e. another computer or even a portable storage device, such as a floppy disk drive or CD drive.

If you save a file from an infected computer onto a floppy disk, it is quite likely that the virus is on the floppy disk. If you introduce that floppy disk into another computer, the virus will spread to that computer. In a networked environment, viruses can spread extremely quickly around the network, because all the computers are connected to each other. Viruses have become more common in recent years, due to use of the Internet. Because the Internet is an international network of computers, it is an extremely fast way to spread a virus to computers around the world.

One of the most popular ways to send a virus to other computers is via an e-mail attachment. When the user at the receiving computer double-clicks on the attachment, the virus starts to propagate itself. Because that computer is probably on the Internet, the virus can then very quickly spread around the world and affect computers that are also connected to the Internet.

It is extremely important, whether running a PC in a stand-alone environment (i.e. not connected to other computers via a network) or in a networked environment, that you have up-to-date virus detection software installed. There are many different anti-virus software applications on the market – the most popular are Norton and McAfee®.

You can purchase anti-virus software in a box from a software retailer or you can purchase the software online and download it to your PC. Good quality anti-virus software, once installed, will automatically update itself whenever you go onto the Internet. This means that your anti-virus software is always up-to-date – new viruses are being written every day so the anti-virus software needs to be up-dated regularly.

In an office environment, the IT team will ensure that all machines are virus-protected and, if running a network, that the entire network is protected from viruses.

Dealing with viruses

If your anti-virus software finds a virus, either on one of the computer's drives, or in an incoming e-mail attachment, it will usually repair the file (i.e. remove the virus) or delete the file that contains the virus. If it cannot repair the file, it will 'quarantine' it (depending on the options that have been chosen in the software).

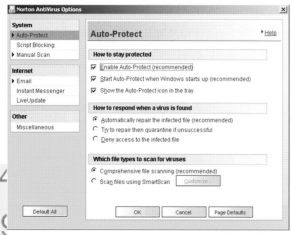

All anti-virus software deals with viruses in a similar way. The example left shows Norton AntiVirus™ 2003.

Under **Options**, you can choose how you want Norton AntiVirus™ to respond when a virus is found. It can **Automatically repair the infected file**, **Try to repair then quarantine if unsuccessful** or **Deny access to the infected file**.

You can schedule your anti-virus software to run a scan at regular intervals, or you can manually run a system scan.

If Norton AntiVirus™ finds a virus while it is performing a system scan and you have set it to automatically repair the infected file, the scan summary will list the files that were infected and specify whether they were repaired or deleted. The scan summary simply informs you what has been done. You do not need to do anything as Norton AntiVirus™ has already dealt with the virus.

If you wish to see details of the repair, click on **More Details**. When you have finished reviewing the repairs, click on **Finished.**

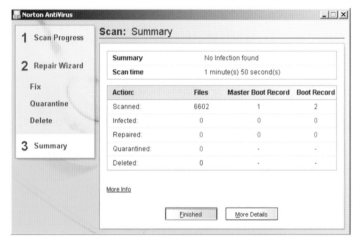

If Norton AntiVirus™ finds a virus while it is performing a system scan and the files could not be repaired, or you have set up the software so that it asks you what to do with a virus, the Repair Wizard opens. If Norton AntiVirus™ did not attempt a repair, the Repair Wizard opens in the Repair window. If Norton AntiVirus™ failed to repair the file, it 'quarantines' it and the Quarantine window opens.

In the Repair window, deselect any files that you do not want to fix (all the files will be ticked by default) and click on **Fix.**

In the Quarantine window, all the files that have been quarantined are listed. Click on **Quarantine**. Files that cannot be quarantined will be deleted. Click on **Delete** in the Delete window.

Auto-Protect, which is one of the features of Norton AntiVirus™, scans files for viruses when you move, copy or open them. If it detects a virus, you will receive an alert telling you that a virus was found and repaired or deleted. It will also tell you which virus was infecting the file. Click on **OK** to close the alert. If the file cannot be repaired you will receive two alerts – one telling you that the file was not repaired and another telling you that access to the file was denied. You can set Auto-Protect to quarantine any infected files that it cannot repair. If you do this, the alert will inform you of any files that have been quarantined.

If a virus has been found by Auto-Protect, run a full system scan on your computer to ensure that no other files are infected and follow the recommended steps in the Repair Wizard to protect your computer from the infected files.

Dealing with quarantined files

In the Norton AntiVirus™ main window, click on **Reports**.

Click on the **View Report** button for Quarantined items. The Quarantine window opens.

The toolbar at the top of the Quarantine window enables you to work with the quarantined files:

Add Item

Adds a file to quarantine. Use this to manually quarantine a file that you think may be infected. **You cannot add a file that is already in quarantine.**

Properties

Provides information about the selected file and the virus that is infecting it.

Repair Item

Attempts to repair the selected file. You can use this option if you have received new virus updates since the file was quarantined.

Restore Item

Returns the selected file to its original location without repairing it.

Delete Item

Deletes the selected file from the computer.

Submit Item

Sends the selected file to Symantec™. (You can use this option if you think the file is infected even if Norton AntiVirus™ did not detect it).

LiveUpdate

Runs LiveUpdate to check for virus updates. Use this if you haven't updated your virus definitions for a while.

As well as quarantined files, the Quarantine window also stores **Backup Items**. Norton AntiVirus™ makes a backup copy of a file before attempting a repair. After the repaired file is verified, the backup copy of the file can be deleted from the Quarantine window.

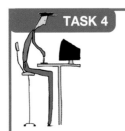
TASK 4

1 **If you have anti-virus software installed on your PC, familiarise yourself with the windows and options that it contains.**

2 **Talk to your IT support team about the anti-virus protection that they use to protect the network.**

Software updates

While software manufacturers strive to produce software that is 100% error-free, this is very rarely the case. If an error comes to light after the software has been released, the software manufacturer will release an update (sometimes known as a 'patch') to fix the bug. Once you have purchased and installed the software application on your computer, you can go to the appropriate site and download any updates or patches to keep your software up-to-date.

N.B. Do not download anything from the Internet unless you are sure that you have permission to do this. Always check with your IT support team before downloading a software update.

Because Microsoft® software is very widely used around the world, it is often a target for 'hackers' who try to find 'holes' in the software where they can get in and cause problems. Microsoft® are constantly issuing 'patches' for all supported versions of their software, so it is worth keeping an eye on the Updates page of the Microsoft® website.

On the home page of the Microsoft® website (www.microsoft.com) there are links to the Windows Update page and the Office Update page (under Resources on the left side of the page). You can also access the Windows® Update page by choosing Windows® Update in the Windows® XP Start menu, or in the Help and Support system.

These links take you to the appropriate page where you can find out if there are any updates to your software you should download.

Windows® Update scans your computer and tells you which updates you require. Some of the updates will be listed under 'Critical Updates' – they are critical to the operation of your computer and it is highly recommended that you download them as they will fix known issues and patch known security vulnerabilities.

Office Update enables you to choose from a range of updates that will ensure that your version of Office is running as efficiently and securely as possible. The Office Update site supports Office 2000, Office XP (2002) and Office 2003.

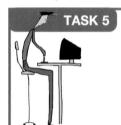

TASK 5

Locate the Microsoft® Windows® update site and the Microsoft® Office update site. Store the web addresses of these two sites in your Favorites folder.

 ## Suggested tasks for evidence

The evidence for this unit will need to be collected as and when problems and issues arise. The suggested tasks below provide guidance on the type of work that you can produce as evidence for this unit. You may come across one or more of these scenarios in your workplace. By following the guidelines below, you will have produced a piece of evidence for this unit.

To ensure that your work can be used as evidence towards your ITQ, take print-outs and screenshots where appropriate.

Suggested Task 1

Create a checklist that your colleagues could follow for basic troubleshooting they should carry out before calling IT support.

Suggested Task 2

Log all errors that occur and the steps taken to resolve the problem. Log steps that failed as well as the ones that were successful. Take screenshots to show different screens. Keep this log to refer to whenever errors occur. Create two categories: 'Errors I can fix' and 'Errors I can't fix'. This will be useful as a quick reference when an error occurs.

Suggested Task 3

Compile a list of useful sources of advice that you have found for hardware and software problems. This could include people, websites, books, help systems, etc.

IT maintenance for users

unit 204

Overview

You are likely to be in a role which involves carrying out maintenance regularly (e.g. organising files, backing up data, cleaning computers and printers, using the Defragmenter tool, etc.). You should also know what is involved in upgrading hardware and software and be aware of health and safety implications when using a computer.

A competent person can carry out appropriate routine and non-routine maintenance safely, including managing files, maintaining hardware and software and identifying health and safety risks.

 ## Required skills and techniques for Level 2

Managing files	Changing default settings for saving data.
Cleaning	Selecting suitable cleaning methods and materials. Cleaning hardware, such as keyboard, mouse roller ball and vents, to make it work efficiently. Cleaning hardware to keep it looking good.
Avoiding health and safety risks	Carrying out a risk assessment of own use of IT, including checking electrical loading of system.
Maintaining	Carrying out routine maintenance to printers, following manufacturer's instructions for users. Identifying any non-routine maintenance needed to hardware and carrying it out, by following manufacturer's guidelines.

 ## Requirements of this unit

You will need to carry out at least *two* comprehensive tasks demonstrating skills, techniques and knowledge in the routine and non-routine maintenance of your computer, managing files, cleaning the hardware and dealing with health and safety issues.

The term 'maintenance' means the actions that users can take in order to prevent or slow down the deterioration of functions on the computer. There are two parts to the maintenance of an IT system: cleaning, replenishing and safety of the hardware; and file management and performance of the software.

 ## Tasks in this unit

The tasks that appear throughout this unit are designed to help you practise using the feature that has just been discussed. However, if you wish, you can provide these as extra pieces of evidence in addition to the two main pieces that are required by the unit.

The tasks at the end of the unit are suggested ways in which you could provide the main evidence for this unit.

What will I achieve?

By accomplishing a Level 2 in this unit, you will also have achieved Level 1 in all cases and a Level 3 in some cases. Below is a table to show what levels you will have achieved.

Required skill	Level 1	Level 2	Level 3
Managing files	●	●	●
Cleaning	●	●	●
Avoiding health and safety risks	●	●	
Maintaining	●	●	
Enhancing performance	N/A	N/A	

 # Cleaning your computer

In order to keep your system looking good and to avoid a decrease in efficiency (due to a clogged fan, for example), you should regularly physically clean the external hardware elements of your computer. Ensure that the all computer components are switched off prior to cleaning.

Cleaning the system unit

The outside of the system unit should be cleaned periodically, to ensure that it is free from dust and dirt. You can use a damp cloth with a mild detergent to clean off any grubby marks. (Be careful that the cloth is not too wet – you do not want water getting into the system unit).

If there is a build-up of dust on the vent (fan) at the back of the system unit, this should be removed. It is important that the fan on your system unit continues to work efficiently, otherwise there is a risk that the system will overheat, which could create major problems.

Cleaning the monitor

What you clean the monitor with will depend on the type of monitor you have. You can purchase monitor cleaning wipes or spray which you use with a soft cloth – both of these work well on a traditional CRT monitor (the one that looks like a portable TV). However, be careful if you have a flat-screen monitor. The cleaning materials for these are different and you should never rub hard on a TFT panel.

Also check the back of the monitor for dust and grime. Wipe the other parts of the monitor with a damp cloth and remove any dust from vents.

Cleaning the keyboard

With continued use, the keyboard inevitably gets grubby from your fingers. It is a good idea to clean the keyboard when the computer is switched off, as you will have to lean on the keys to clean them. You can purchase specific keyboard cleaning products, but a damp (not wet!) cloth with a mild detergent works just as well. Damp cotton wool buds are useful for cleaning between the keys. You can also purchase a compressed air canister which has a long nozzle that you can place between the keys. The blast of air will remove dust and loose debris that has accumulated between the keys.

Cleaning the mouse

Just like the keyboard, the mouse can get grubby from continual contact with your hands. Again, you can clean the outside of the mouse with a damp cloth and mild detergent to remove any marks.

If you have a mouse with a roller ball, it is also a good idea to take the ball out and give the inside of the mouse and the ball a clean to remove dust that can build up over time. Dirt can often get itself wrapped around the internal mechanism of the mouse, which will impair its performance – remove any dirt from the inside of the mouse carefully.

It is a good idea to wipe your mouse mat regularly too, to remove any dust or debris which may affect the performance of the mouse.

Cleaning the printer

The external parts of a printer can be cleaned with a damp cloth and mild detergent. Depending on the printer you have, you may have to carry out routine cleaning to the inside components of the printer. Always check the manufacturer's guide to see if you should be carrying out routine cleaning.

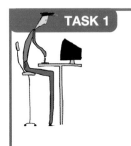

TASK 1

1 **Clean all the external hardware of your computer. Set up a schedule to do this on a regular basis.**

2 **Establish the type of monitor you have and obtain appropriate cleaning materials for it.**

3 **Check the vents at the back of the system unit to check they are clear of dust build-up.**

4 **Establish the type of mouse you have and, if necessary, take it apart to clean the internal mechanism.**

 ## General maintenance of hardware

Changing the printer cartridge

The printer cartridge will need replacing when it runs out. This is carried out differently depending on the printer, so it is not possible to outline here how to do it. However, if you need to do this yourself, you should always read the instructions for your printer (they will either be in a booklet or installed on your computer). This normally involves physically changing the cartridge and then carrying out a self-test print to ensure the new cartridge is performing to its optimum level.

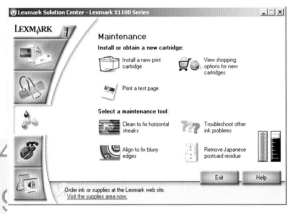

Carrying out routine printer maintenance

There are some basic maintenance steps you can take to ensure your printer continues to print at its best quality.

If your printouts have lines across them, or parts of the words are missing, you may need to clean the ink nozzles. Follow the instructions in the user guide booklet or in the software on your computer. If your printout appears jagged, you may need to run an alignment test. Again, follow the instructions in the user guide booklet or in the software on your computer.

For example, when you install a Lexmark printer, the Lexmark Solution Center is installed on your computer. You can use this piece of software to maintain the printer, i.e. install a new cartridge, print a test page, clean and align the printer heads and carry out other troubleshooting.

Most printers will have a similar feature that you can use to maintain the printer.

If your printer develops a fault, it is a good idea to refer to the software which will probably have a troubleshooting section. Also read the printed guide that you received with the printer. You should always do this first to establish if you can sort the problem out yourself before going to the expense of calling out an engineer.

It is a good idea to keep a maintenance log so that you know when you last cleaned the hardware and carried out routine tests and maintenance.

TASK 2

1 **Ensure that you know how to replenish the paper in the printer, should it run out.**

2 **The next time the printer ink or toner cartridge needs replacing, have a go at doing it yourself. Follow the steps in the manufacturer's guidelines and then carry out any self-tests that are required.**

 ## Managing files

Naming and storing files in your applications

When you save a file in an application, you will be prompted to give the file a name and choose where you wish to store it (the drive and folder).

It is a good idea to set up a logical 'filing system' right from the start and use a consistent naming system so you can easily remember what you have called files and where you have stored them. You can create folders on your computer, just like you have folders in a physical filing system. You can then keep all related files in the same folder. (You can access these folders from any application, so you can save Word documents, Excel spreadsheets, PowerPoint® presentations, etc., in the same folder).

Filing systems are personal to each individual user and it depends on the type of work you are creating as to what folders you might want to create.

You can create folders in the Save As dialog box in all Microsoft® Office applications. In this way, as you go to save a file, if there isn't an appropriate folder to put it in, you can create one.

The first time for any document that you choose **Save** from the **File** menu or click on the **Save** button on the Standard toolbar, the Save As dialog box opens.

Move to the folder that you wish to create the new folder in. To create a new folder, click on the **Create New Folder** button or press ⌐Alt⌐+⌐%5⌐.

Type a name for the folder.

To navigate to different drives and into different folders in your filing system, click on the **Look in:** drop-down list in the **Open** dialog box and the **Save in:** drop-down list in the **Save As** dialog box.

For more information on managing files in your applications, see Unit 202 – Operate a Computer.

Using Windows Explorer to manage files

Windows Explorer is a utility provided by the Windows operating system which enables you to see an overview of your drives, folders and files and manage them. For more information on how to use Windows Explorer to carry out file management, please see Unit 202 – Operate a Computer.

General housekeeping

It is obviously important that you do regular 'housekeeping' of your files to ensure that your filing system remains clutter-free and that your computer works efficiently.

You should regularly delete files that are no longer required. If you are on a network, your network drives will be backed up for you, so the file is still available to you on a back up, even if you delete it. If you work in a standalone environment, then it is up to you to back up prior to deleting files.

You can back up your files onto floppy disk, CD or Flash drive. If you work on a network, you can back up your files onto the server. The process of backing up files simply means copying them to another place – preferably in a different location to your own computer. In that way, should your computer be stolen, or the hard drive of your computer fail, you will still have a copy of all your files.

For more information about copying files to portable storage media, please see Unit 202 – Operate a Computer.

Deleting unnecessary files

When your computer does 'crash', temporary files are created. Over a period of time, if these files are not deleted, they can build up and clutter up your hard drive.

Choose **Start**, **Search**, **For Files or Folders** to open the Search window. (In Windows® XP, click on **Search** and then click on **Files or Folders**).

In the Search box, type *.tmp. (This will search for all files with a file extension of tmp. The * is a wildcard and means 'anything'.) Under **Look in** choose the hard drive (normally C:).

A list of temporary files will be returned. Select all the files in the list and press the **Delete** button on the toolbar (or press the **Delete** key on the keyboard).

N.B. To select multiple files, click on the first file in the list, hold down **Shift** and click on the last file in the list – all the files between will be selected.

Setting save options in Microsoft® Office

When you save a file in the Microsoft® Office applications (Word, Excel, PowerPoint®, etc.), you can set other save options for the file.

In the **Save As** dialog box, click on **Tools** and choose **Save Options** or **General Options** in Office 2002. In Office 2000, choose **General Options**.

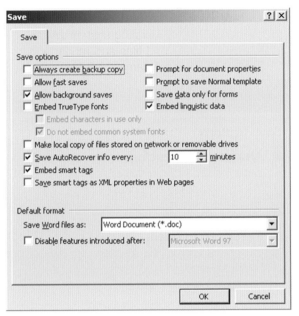

Word 2002/2000

The **Save Options** dialog box in Microsoft Word allows you to set a number of save options, including:

■ **Always create backup copy** – this means that whenever you save the file, the previous version of the file becomes a backup. (Backups are stored in the same folder as the original, with the filename extension .wbk.)

■ **Allow fast saves** – this speeds up interim saving as it only saves the changes made to a document. When you have finished creating the document, you must deselect this in order to carry out a complete save of your document.

■ **Allow background saves** – this saves the document in the background so that you can continue working in Word.

■ **Make local copy of files stored on network or removable drives (Word 2002 only)** – this creates a temporary file on the local hard drive. When you save, the changes are saved to the original file on the network or removable drive. However, if that file is not available, Word will prompt to save to the local copy, so no data is lost.

■ **Save AutoRecover info every * minutes** – Word creates an AutoRecover file and updates it every number of minutes specified. If your system should freeze or hang, Word will open the AutoRecover file when it is relaunched. Any unsaved data will be in the AutoRecover file. **However, it is important that you also save the file regularly.**

You can also choose the **Default Format** in which to save Word files. The default is Word Document (*.doc) but you can choose from a large list of different formats, including older versions of Word, Rich Text Format (RTF) or Web page.
    Make your choices and click on **OK.**

PowerPoint® 2002/2000

Save Options in PowerPoint® include:

■ **Allow fast saves** – this speeds up interim saving as it saves only the changes made to a presentation. When you have finished creating the presentation, you must deselect this in order to carry out a complete save of your file.

■ **Save AutoRecover info every * minutes** – PowerPoint® creates an AutoRecover file and updates it every number of minutes specified. If your system should freeze or hang, PowerPoint® will open the AutoRecover file when it is relaunched. Any unsaved data will be in the AutoRecover file. **However, it is important that you also save the file regularly.**

■ **Save PowerPoint® files as** – PowerPoint® files are saved as a PowerPoint Presentation by default. The file is saved as whatever version you are currently using – 2000 or XP. You can choose to have your files saved to an older version of PowerPoint® by default, or as Web pages.

Make your choices and click on **OK.**

Excel 2000/2002

Save Options in Excel include:

■ **Always create backup** – whenever you Save the workbook, the previous version of the file becomes a backup. (Backups are stored in the same folder as the original.)

■ **Password to open** – you can set a password so that the file can only be opened by those who know the password. (A password can be up to 15 characters long and is case sensitive.)

■ **Password to modify** – you can set a password so that the file can only be modified by those who know the password. Anyone can open the file to view it, but the user will be prompted for the password if they attempt to modify the file.

■ **Read-only recommended** – the file will open as Read Only. If the user makes changes to the file and tries to save it, they will be prompted to 'Save As' so that they create another file. The original file cannot be overwritten.

Make your choices and click on **OK.**

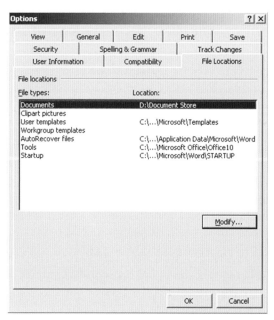

Setting the default file location in Microsoft® Office

You can specify a default file location in Word, Excel, PowerPoint® and Access. Whenever you access the **Open** or **Save As** dialog box, you are taken to the default file location. (If you navigated to a different drive or folder when you previously opened or saved during this session, you will be taken back to that drive and folder.)

You normally set the default file location to wherever you want to be taken when you **Open** or **Save** a file.

Word

Choose **Tools**, **Options** and click on the **File Locations** tab.

You can specify the default file locations for documents, clipart pictures, templates and AutoRecover files. Select the **File type** in the list that you wish to modify and click on **Modify**. Browse to the file location that you wish to set as the default. Click on **OK.**

Click on **OK** when you have finished making changes.

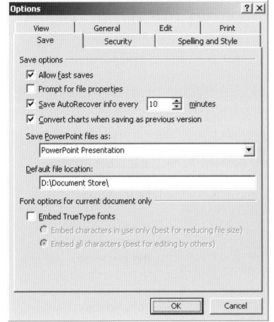

PowerPoint®

To set the default file location in PowerPoint®, choose **Tools**, **Options** and click on the **Save** tab.

Type the full path of where you want to navigate to in the **Default file location** box. Click on **OK** when you have finished making changes.

Excel

To set the default file location in Excel, choose **Tools**, **Options** and click on the **General** tab.

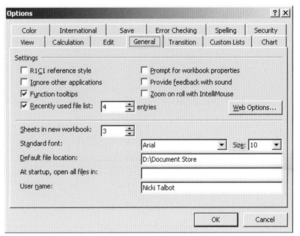

Type the full path of where you want to navigate to in the **Default file location** box. Click on **OK** when you have finished making changes.

Access

To set the default database folder in Access, choose **Tools**, **Options** and click on the **General** tab.

Type the full path of where you want to navigate to in the **Default database folder** box. Click on **OK** when you have finished making changes.

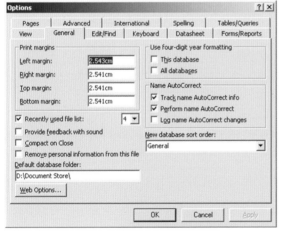

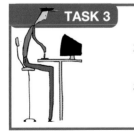

TASK 3

1 Delete all the *.tmp files from your hard drive.

2 The next time you save a file in Microsoft® Office, have a look at the Save options that are available.

3 Establish the default file location in Word, Excel and PowerPoint®. Change if you feel necessary.

General maintenance of computer systems

Windows® provides two utilities that help keep your hard drive well maintained and organised: disk cleanup and disk defragmenter. Both these utilities are easy to use, but you may find that, if you work in a networked environment, you do not have the permission to carry out these utilities. (You will need to speak to your IT support team.)

Disk Cleanup

This utility is a safe way to find and delete unnecessary files.

Choose **Start**, **Programs**, **Accessories**, **System Tools** and click on **Disk Cleanup**.

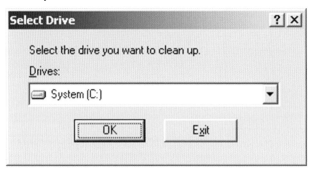

Select the drive you wish to clean up and click on **OK.**

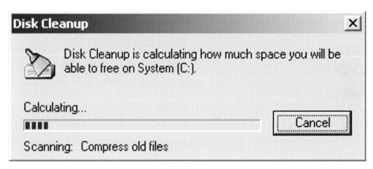

The Disk Cleanup status box opens to show you the progress of the Disk Cleanup utility. The first step is to calculate how much space can be created by cleaning the drive you have selected.

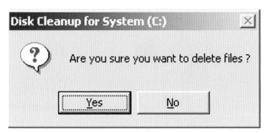

Disk Cleanup reports how much space can be freed up by deleting certain types of files. Tick the types of files that you wish to delete and click on **OK**.

Click on **Yes** at the prompt.

Disk Cleanup is carried out and closes automatically when finished.

Disk Defragmenter

Over a period of time the files that are saved on your hard drive can become 'fragmented'. Instead of being placed together in one space, the files are broken up and stored in different places on the hard drive, wherever there is space available.

Imagine a car park with an enthusiastic car park attendant who is determined to make use of every available piece of space. To start off, cars would be parked neatly altogether in one space, but then the car park attendant realises that there is no more space for whole cars, so starts taking the cars apart in order that he can fit a wheel in one little space and an engine in another space. (A ridiculous example, I know, but you get the idea.)

That's what happens to your files over a period of time. If there is not a big enough space on the hard drive to store the whole file, the file is split up and bits are stored in different places on the hard drive. This is known as fragmentation. Over a period of time, this will impair performance, as your hard drive has to work harder each time you request to open a file – it has to locate the various parts of the file in different places and put them back together. Disk Defragmenter tidies up the hard drive by reconstructing the fragmented files and storing them in one place again. It also reorganises files so that those that are used frequently are easy to access.

Choose Start, Programs, Accessories, System Tools and click on Disk Defragmenter.

The Disk Defragmenter window opens.

Select the drive in the list that you wish to defragment and click on **Defragment**. (**Analyze** enables you to check for fragmentation on a drive without actually defragmenting. It is a good idea to do this first so you can establish if you need to defragment the drive.)

The time that Defragmenter takes will depend on the size of the drive, the number of files on the drive and how much fragmentation there is. You can interrupt defragmentation by clicking on **Stop** or **Pause**. It is a good idea to carry out disk defragmentation when you do not need to use your PC for a while. The resources required to carry out this procedure will slow down your computer if you are trying to do other things at the same time.

As the drive is being defragmented, you will receive a display in the bottom part of the Disk Defragmenter window. The colour coding shows files that are fragmented, those that are not (Contiguous files), System files and Free space. The progress of the defragmentation appears in the status bar at the bottom of the Disk Defragmenter window.

When Defragmentation is complete, a message appears. Click on **Close**.

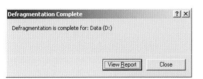

TASK 4

If you have permission, carry out Disk Cleanup and Disk Defragmenter on your hard drive.

Health and safety issues

For more information on health and safety issues, see Unit 202 – Operate a Computer.

It is important to choose a sensible position for your computer equipment. The workstation should be designed to enable you to reach all the necessary equipment without stretching and should be clear of obstruction. You should also consider:

- **Electrical safety** – there are obviously the restrictions of having to locate electrical equipment near sockets. However, it is essential that the equipment does not increase the risk of danger, either to the user or to the equipment itself.
  - Route long electrical cables and trailing flexes appropriately, secure and cover.
  - Check for frayed leads and damaged plugs regularly and, if found, replace.
  - Check the system is not overloaded. Ensure there are not too many extension leads being used.
  - Check that cables are not coiled – they can overheat and start a fire.
  - Check for wear and tear regularly – damage to flexes (cuts or cracks) and damage caused by spillages or dust.
- **Heat** – all ICT equipment gives off heat which will build up during the day. This is not ideal for the user or for the equipment. Ensure that ICT equipment is located in a well-ventilated, even air-conditioned, room. Turn off equipment when not in use to reduce the amount of heat being generated.
- **Light** – screens should be positioned to reduce reflection and glare from lights or windows. Blinds should be fitted to windows in the vicinity of screens. The screen should be cleaned regularly to give better visibility and reduce glare. All work surfaces should be non-reflective and clean.
- **Noise** – you might want to consider placing particularly noisy equipment away from users so they are not distracted.
- **Space** – there should be enough space around the workstation for the computer peripherals and also for papers, books and anything else required for the job. Also, there should be space for more than one user at a time to gain access.
- **Comfort and safety** – you should take frequent short breaks from the computer (10 minutes every hour) to allow the eyes to readjust. You should be comfortably positioned with easy access to all equipment. You should be able to adjust:
  - **screen** – the angle and height should be adjustable. The top of the screen should be roughly at eye level. You must be able to control brightness, screen colours and fonts. The screen should be sharply focused and should not flicker. If your screen does flicker, report it to your IT support team.
  - **keyboard** – the keyboard should be adjustable between flat or tilted. There should be room to move the keyboard on the desk to suit the individual user. There should be space in front of the keyboard for resting the wrists when not typing. Good keyboard technique is important – keep wrists straight, use a soft touch on the keys and do not overstretch the fingers.
  - **mouse** – position the mouse within easy reach so it can be used with the wrist straight. Sit upright and close to the desk so your mouse arm is not outstretched. Support your forearm on the desk and do not grip the mouse too tightly. Rest your fingers lightly on the buttons and do not press them hard. Flex your hands and fingers regularly to prevent cramp or aches.
  - **seating** – the height of the chair should be adjustable. Your lower arms should be roughly horizontal when working and your knees should fit

comfortably under the desk. Do not cross your legs but place both feet on the floor so that your thighs are roughly horizontal. Footrests should be available if necessary.

- **posture** – do not sit in the same position for long periods. Change your posture as often as you can. Take regular breaks away from the screen and do some stretches. A document holder may avoid awkward neck and eye movements.
- **peripherals** – these should be easy to reach without stretching (if on the desk) or clear of obstructions if anywhere else in the office.

It is a good idea to engender a health and safety culture within your workplace and to ensure that everyone recognises that they have a responsibility for health and safety in their workplace.

Upgrading

Hardware

Unfortunately, purchasing computer hardware is not just a one-off event for a business – it is a continuous, on-going process which needs a pretty hefty budget.

The technology involved in computers is moving at such a pace that a computer is out-of-date almost the minute it has been purchased. That is not to say you need to have the latest, all-singing, all-dancing PC. Most office-based tasks do not require the latest graphics card or huge amounts of memory. A PC in an office situation can continue working efficiently for anything up to 10 years.

Of course, it may be necessary to upgrade some of the parts of the computer. It is common to add more RAM (memory) to a computer to enhance its performance and perhaps to upgrade the graphics card. It is not uncommon to upgrade the central processing unit itself. It might be necessary to install a new CD or DVD writer.

Of course, you wouldn't be carrying out the upgrade itself, but there are some things you can do to ensure that disruption of your work is kept to a minimum.

- Prior to your computer being upgraded, back up your important files – just in case! Of course, if your files are stored on a network drive, then you don't need to worry about backing them up – backups will be kept by your IT team.
- Make a note of any shortcuts you have on your desktop and how to put them there. Also, any other Windows customisations you have carried out. You might find that Windows has been reinstalled after the upgrade, which means you will have lost all your personalised settings.
- Talk to the person carrying out the upgrade so that you understand what is going to happen and how it may impact on the performance of your PC. Ask them if there is anything else you need to do prior to the upgrade.

Software

Just like the hardware, the software can also become out-of-date. New versions of software are released regularly and it might be that a newer version contains features that would be useful to your organisation. Also, in order for your organisation to remain compatible with other organisations they deal with, they may regularly upgrade their software. Most software manufacturers will stop supporting a piece of software once it is a few years old and newer versions have been released.

Prior to any major software upgrade, your IT team needs to carry out extensive testing to ensure that the new software will work with existing software. It is obviously important that the software upgrade does not interrupt productivity and discovering that the installation of a piece of software means that another critical piece of software no longer works is a major problem!

Again, you would not be carrying out the software upgrade yourself, but there are a few steps you can take prior to the upgrade:

■ Back up your important files – just in case!! Of course, if your files are stored on a network drive, then you don't need to worry about backing them up – backups will be kept by your IT team.
■ Make a note of any customisations you have made to the existing version of the software. The upgrade may mean that you lose your personal settings and will have to set them up again.
■ Talk to the person carrying out the upgrade so that you understand what is going to happen and how it may impact on you. Your organisation should provide appropriate training if the upgrade is going to mean a major change to the way you work.

 ## Suggested tasks for evidence

The evidence for this unit will need to be collected on an ongoing basis as you use your PC. The suggested tasks below provide guidance on the type of work that you can produce as evidence for this unit. You may come across one or more of these scenarios in your workplace. By following the guidelines below, you will have produced a piece of evidence for this unit.

To ensure that your work can be used as evidence towards your ITQ, take printouts and screenshots where appropriate.

Suggested Task 1

Create a checklist of routine cleaning and maintenance of your computer and peripherals that you can carry out each month.

Suggested Task 2

Create a health and safety checklist for the area around a computer desk. Carry out a simple risk assessment on your own work area and note the findings.

Suggested Task 3

The next time you are carrying out file management (either in an application or using Windows Explorer), take screenshots to show the steps you are taking.

Suggested Task 4

Create a checklist of how to change the toner/ink cartridge in your printer.

Suggested Task 5

Create a short report discussing the pros and cons of upgrading hardware and software and any other issues that need to be considered.

Suggested Task 6

Run Disk Cleanup and Disk Defragmenter. Take screenshots to show the steps you are taking.

IT security for users

Unit value = 15

Overview

You are likely to be in a role which involves knowing how to avoid common security risks and control access to software and data and requires being aware of how to protect software and data when exchanging information by e-mail or when downloading information from the Internet.

Competent people are aware of what security risks there are and can select and use appropriate methods to keep security risks to a minimum, to protect software and data and to control access to data. They are aware of the laws and guidelines that affect the use of IT.

 ## Required skills and techniques for Level 2

Explaining (use of IT)	Explaining which software tools and techniques were chosen and how effectively they were used for particular tasks and uses.
Finding and evaluating	Choosing and using appropriate methods of searching for relevant information. Reviewing sources and information to help choose what is most relevant, and to decide when enough has been found.
Organising	Using a variety of IT software tools and techniques to structure information to suit more complex tasks and audience needs, such as using large print for partially sighted readers.
Reviewing	Evaluating own strengths and weaknesses in using IT. Taking account of feedback from other people about own use of IT.
Protecting	Setting password levels on software and data. Making backups of operating system data. Downloading software patches to fix security flaws. Taking appropriate action to keep risks to a minimum, when downloading software. Taking action to avoid risks from receiving and opening attachments from e-mails.

 ## Requirements of this unit

You will need to carry out at least *two* comprehensive tasks demonstrating skills, techniques and knowledge in using the standard protection systems that are available on your computer and showing that you understand the need to protect data using passwords and backups, know how to download patches to fix security flaws and are aware of the risks surrounding e-mail and the Internet.

 ## Tasks in this unit

The tasks that appear throughout this unit are designed to help you practise using the feature that has just been discussed. However, if you wish, you can provide these as extra pieces of evidence in addition to the two main pieces that are required by the unit.

The tasks at the end of this unit are suggested ways in which you could provide the main evidence for this unit.

 What will I achieve?

By accomplishing a Level 2 in this unit, you will also have achieved Level 1 in all cases and a Level 3 in some cases. Below is a table to show what levels you will have achieved.

Required skill	Level 1	Level 2	Level 3
Explaining (use of IT)	●	●	●
Finding and evaluating	●	●	●
Organising	●	●	●
Reviewing	●	●	●
Protecting	●	●	

 Controlling access to your computer and files

Passwords

If you operate a computer in a networked environment then you will have to 'log in' to the system. This process matches your log-on credentials (your user name and password) with the information stored by the server and you are then 'authenticated' and allowed into the network. For most users it seems to be a tedious process having to change your password every few weeks or months, but it is a necessary security measure to ensure that the wrong people cannot get into your computer and onto your network. Of course, there is no point changing your password regularly if it is easy to guess what it is (this is known as a weak password) and you should never tell anyone what your password is.

A weak password means that you use:

- No password at all.
- Your real name, your user name or your company name.
- The word 'password'.
- A password that you write down on a post-it note on your monitor.
- A password you haven't changed for more than two months.
- A password known by someone else.

A strong password:

- Is at least seven characters long.
- Does not contain your user name, real name or company name.
- Does not contain a complete dictionary word.
- Is significantly different from previous passwords (Password1, Password2, Password3 are not strong passwords).
- Contains a mix of upper and lower case letters, numbers and symbols (such as ! ~ # @ $ % &).
- Is changed regularly.

Of course, the most secure password in the world is no good if you cannot remember it! You need to decide on a policy that balances security with practicality. Enforcing a tough password policy on all users will just mean they write them down.

You can perhaps have different policies for different sets of users, e.g. you could insist that the HR/Personnel Department have stronger passwords. Users should be encouraged to think of their password in the same way as they would the key to the office – don't leave it lying around and don't give it to strangers.

It is also a good idea to set up the system so that it automatically locks after so many minutes of inactivity. When the user returns to their desk they have to unlock the computer by keying in the password. This stops opportunists wandering around the office and having a quick look at what's on a computer while the user is not there.

Document protection

As well as passwords to secure logging into the computer and network, you can also set passwords on the documents you create. Only those people who know the password will be able to work with the file.

You can set passwords on files when you save them. Alternatively, you can make a file "Read Only" which means it can be opened and 'read' but it cannot be changed and overwritten.

In Word 2002 and PowerPoint® 2002, click on **Tools**, **Security Options** in the **Save As** dialog box.

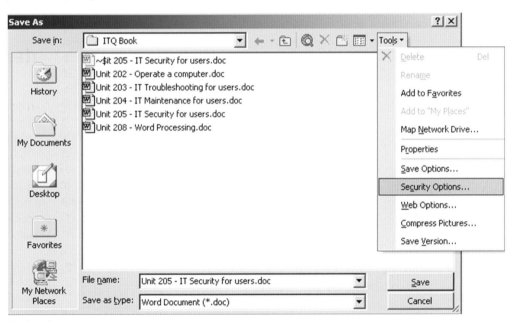

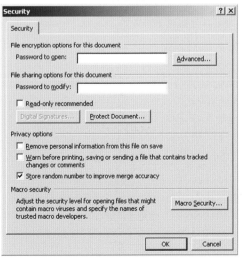

(In Word 2000 and PowerPoint® 2000 click on **Tools, General Options**.)

Choose the settings you require in the **Security** dialog box.

- **Password to open** – if a user tried to open this file, they would be prompted for the password. (The password can be up to 15 characters long.)
- **Password to modify** – anyone can open the document without the password, but the document will open as read only. Only those people who know the password can open the document for editing.
- **Read-only recommended** – the file opens as read only, which means if someone makes changes to it, they will have to use Save As to create a different document. The original version cannot be overwritten.

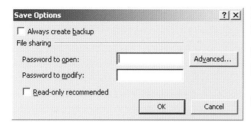

In Excel 2002 and 2000 click on **Tools, General Options** in the **Save As** dialog box.

Choose the settings you require in the **Save Options** dialog box.

As with Word, you can set **Password to open**, **Password to modify** or **Read-only recommended**.

TASK 1

1 **Consider your own password – is it a strong password? If it is not, consider changing it.**

2 **Explore the security options when saving documents in Microsoft® Office. (You will need to open a file and then choose Save As to open the Save As dialog box.) Open a file and apply different security options to it as you save it. Notice how these security settings affect the file when you next open it.**

 ## Backing up data

If you save all your work onto network drives, then you will not be responsible for ensuring those files are backed up. The network is backed up regularly, so should there be a system failure, you will not lose your files. However, if you save files onto the hard drive of your computer, or onto a portable storage medium (perhaps so you can take them home to work on them), until those files are back on the network, you are responsible for them, including backing them up.

There are two aspects to backing up data – the hardware that you use and the procedure for doing it – how often? There are two kinds of backup – complete and incremental. A complete backup is a complete copy of data onto another storage medium, e.g. a CD. An incremental backup only copies files that have changed to another storage medium. An incremental backup is obviously quicker to carry out, but it does mean you need all the incremental backups for a full restore.

Firstly, decide the medium on which you are going to back up – floppy disks are fine if you only have a small amount of data to copy. The capacity of the highest floppy disk is only 1.44 MB though, so if your files contain graphics or audio they are likely to be too large for a floppy disk. A CD is a popular option. You will need specific software to 'burn' to a CD. Windows® XP contains a CD burning utility (see Unit 202 – Operate a computer). Copying files to other storage media is also discussed in Unit 202 – Operate a computer.

 ## Security

The security measures discussed below should be deployed at a company level. It may well not be your responsibility to instigate a lot of them, but it is still important for each individual to be aware of security risks with computer equipment, in order that they can ensure they uphold the security policies that are in place.

Just as you would protect your home from potential intruders, so you should protect your computer equipment, both physically and when you are working with the data on the computer. You should be aware of the physical security of your equipment and also how you can protect your data from viruses, hackers and unauthorised users. It is extremely important to back your data up regularly – what would happen if you lost your critical business data? How long would it take to recover?

Physical security

As well as ensuring that the wrong people cannot access your computer data, it is important to think about the physical security of the computer hardware. Below are some points to think about – not all are in your control, but you can still consider how well they have been put into place:

- Obviously, there should be security measures in place to control who can come into your office building – entry points should be manned and visitors should be identified and logged in and out. Access to server rooms should be restricted and only authorised personnel should be allowed access. You should always query unescorted strangers in the building.
- When choosing a location for the server room, your IT team should consider its location and the risk from fire or flood.
- Windows and doors should be locked when not in use.
- Alarms should be tested regularly.
- There should be a 'clear desk' policy – all papers should be locked away when not being used.
- PCs and their major components should be security marked.
- The serial numbers of all hardware should be logged so they can be identified if stolen and recovered.
- Users should collect their documents from printers and photocopiers promptly.
- There should be policies in place for when equipment is taken off-site (particularly laptops).

Laptop security

Laptops, by their very nature, are easy to steal. About 67,000 laptops are stolen in the UK each year. As well as the hassle and expense of replacing the hardware, a laptop can contain hard-to-replace or confidential information which should not get into the wrong hands. Below are some specific pointers for laptop security:

- The laptop should be kept in a padded bag, to protect it against knocks or falls. Don't use a bag that looks obviously like a laptop bag though.
- The laptop should always be kept in sight. This is particularly important in crowded places like train stations and airports.
- Laptops should be kept in your hand luggage when travelling – don't leave them in hotel baggage-hold rooms.
- The laptop should be locked to something using a cable lock and (if possible) the hard drive should be removed when not in use.
- The laptop should be security marked. The serial number should be noted and it is a good idea to keep a note of all the software on it also.
- A laptop should never be left in sight in a locked car.
- A laptop should not be allowed to overheat, e.g. by leaving it in the boot of a car on a hot day.
- A backup of all the work on the laptop should be kept. If travelling, continuous backups should be made – one way is to e-mail documents back to your office or to your home. Sensitive files should not be carried around unless they are needed for that trip.
- A BIOS password to boot the laptop is a good idea. Your IT team could also disable booting from a floppy disk for extra security.

Virus protection

More information on viruses and using anti-virus software can be found in Unit 203 – IT troubleshooting for users.

Install anti-virus software

This should be installed on every computer on a network. Anti-virus software contains virus scanners that scan the contents of incoming e-mails (and files on the computer) for a 'virus signature'. (A signature is like a unique DNA sequence in the virus's code.) If it finds a virus, it will delete it. Hundreds of new viruses are written every month so anti-virus software must be updated regularly so that it can catch the latest viruses. Most good quality anti-virus software automatically downloads updates whenever the computer is online.

An additional line of defence is to install anti-virus software on the e-mail server itself. Every piece of e-mail coming into the server is then scanned.

Also be aware of hoaxes – there are just as many hoaxes as there are viruses! If you receive an e-mail saying you have been infected with a virus, always check the website of the manufacturer of your anti-virus software. This will tell you if that virus is a hoax and can be ignored. Chain e-mails are also a nuisance and should not be forwarded on.

Do not open suspect files

A golden rule is not to open any file attached to an e-mail from an unknown or suspicious source. Also take care when visiting websites or downloading from the Internet. If in doubt, don't!

Use the security features of your e-mail software

For example, Microsoft® Outlook 2003 has good security features built in and they are switched on by default. In other e-mail software, you will probably be able to block certain types of file attachments.

Block spam

Spam is unsolicited commercial e-mail. Around half of all e-mail being sent around the world is spam. Laws have recently been introduced to try to control the amount of spam being sent, but as with anything on the Internet, it is quite hard to police. (See page 84 for more information on spam.) Again, your e-mail software may have features that can block spam (or junk e-mail). If spam is a real nuisance to your company, you can purchase commercial spam-blocking software.

Types of virus

The term 'virus' is used to cover all sorts of computer programs that do things that you don't want them to do to your computer. There are different types of virus and some are listed below.

- **Worms** – this type of virus 'worms' its way into your computer (often as an e-mail attachment). Once it finds a home in your computer, it replicates itself either on your computer, or by going through your address book and sending an e-mail (also containing the virus) to everyone listed there.
- **Trojan horses** – this type of virus finds it way into your computer by 'hiding' in another apparently harmless program. They don't replicate like worms, but can still cause considerable damage.
- **Macro viruses** – this type of virus is hidden within a macro. When the macro is executed, the virus is released and can start to do damage. Microsoft® now includes a warning message in its Office applications which appears when you are opening a file that contains a macro. You can choose to disable the macros in the file.

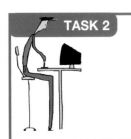

TASK 2

1 **Check the physical security of your own computer environment.**

2 **Establish what anti-virus software you have installed on the PC.**

Downloading from the Internet

Many organisations do not allow their users to download anything from the Internet. Downloading has to be done by the IT team, who can ensure that the information is from a trusted source and free from viruses, etc.

When downloading data or software from the Internet, know what you are downloading – some of the most harmful programs have harmless names, such as click.exe and setup.exe. Make sure you know the author of the program and only download from manufacturer's websites or well-known, reputable sites.

Be aware of copyright issues when downloading from the Internet. In general, software is protected by copyright and cannot be downloaded without charge. 'Freeware' is software where the copyright holder agrees to the software being used free of charge. 'Shareware' is software where the copyright holder agrees to the software being used for a specific period of time, in order to 'try it out'. The software stops working when the period expires and the user will be prompted to pay the licence fee if they wish to continue using the software. Clipart is readily available on the Internet and can usually be used free-of-charge – make sure, though. 'Public information' is not protected by copyright – this is free to use by all. The definition of public information can differ from country to country, but normally includes Acts of Parliament and official Government publications.

For information on *how* to download information from the Internet, see Unit 206 – The Internet and intranets.

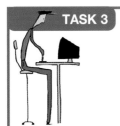

TASK 3

Establish if there are any policies in place in your organisation about downloading information from the Internet.

Keeping software up-to-date

A piece of software can take many hours of work and consist of millions of lines of code. A simple oversight can provide a 'backdoor' into an otherwise secure system. It is almost impossible to write 'bug-free' software. The more widespread a piece of software is, the more likely hackers are to target it. (This is why bugs come to light in Microsoft® software as this is the software that hackers are targeting constantly.)

It is therefore an ongoing process between hackers finding the weaknesses in the software and the developers writing code to close the 'holes'. This is why the software manufacturers release upgrades and 'patches' (pieces of code) to fix vulnerabilities in the software.

It is important that an organisation keeps their software up-to-date to ensure there are no unnecessary vulnerabilities. Patches can be downloaded from the manufacturer's website. To find out about patches for Microsoft® Windows, visit www.windowsupdate.com; to find out about patches for Microsoft® Office, visit www.officeupdate.com.

More information on patches can be found in Unit 203 – IT troubleshooting for users.

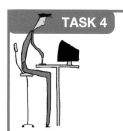

TASK 4

1 **Familiarise yourself with the two Microsoft® update websites.**

2 **Establish what other software you have installed on your computer and find out if they have websites for downloading updates to the software.**

 ## What's a firewall?

Another security measure that companies will take, if their users have Internet access, is to install a firewall. A firewall protects the network from unwanted communication. Firewalls can block all traffic between the Internet and your network that you haven't explicitly allowed. They can also hide the addresses of the computers behind the firewall, making the network 'invisible' to anyone outside. (Every piece of hardware on a network, or the Internet, has an IP address. Hackers will scan these IP addresses to see if any ports are open. If they find an open port, they can get into your network and start exploiting vulnerabilities in your software.)

There are two types of firewall: hardware and software. Hardware firewalls usually stand between the computers in your company and the Internet. Software firewalls can be installed on the machine that sits between the Internet and the company network. (You can also install software firewalls on individual PCs – for example, your home PC).

The Microsoft® Windows® XP operating system has a built-in firewall – Internet Connection Firewall. However, you can still use other makes of firewall. Two popular firewall products are Symantec™ (Norton) Firewall and ZoneAlarm.

To switch on Internet Connection Firewall, choose **Start**, **Control Panel**.

Double-click on Network Connections.

Right-click on the connection you use to get onto the Internet and choose **Properties** from the shortcut menu. The **Properties** dialog box opens as in the figure on the left.

Click on the **Advanced** tab. Check the **Protect my computer ...** box. Click on **OK.**

A firewall does not protect against:

■ Malicious traffic that doesn't come through the firewall, i.e. it gets into your network via another route, such as a wireless network.
■ Traffic that appears to be legitimate.
■ Viruses.
■ Users who use weak passwords.

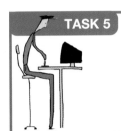

TASK 5

Establish if you have a firewall installed on your computer or on the network.

Laws and guidelines

Data Protection Act 1998

The Data Protection Act 1998 supersedes the previous act of 1984 and was brought into force in March 2000. However, a recent survey shows that there is a general lack of understanding among UK companies about the new Data Protection Act and the penalties that they may incur for non-compliance.

There are eight principles in the Data Protection Act:

1. **Personal data must be processed fairly and lawfully.** The subject must give permission for information to be kept about them. The only time that the subject's permission is not required is if the processing of the data is to protect them – for example, retrieving their medical records after a serious accident – or to comply with the administration of legal obligations.

2. **Personal data shall be obtained only for one or more specified and lawful purposes.** The 'data controller' must specify the purpose for which the personal data is to be obtained either to the subject or by notifying the Data Protection Commissioner.

3. **Personal data shall be adequate, relevant and not excessive in relation to the purpose for which it is processed.** Organisations are required to state the purpose for which data is processed and cannot process it for any other purposes without further notification. For example, a dating agency may collect and process data for the purpose of matching compatible people. They cannot then use that data to identify prospective customers for a different commercial activity, unless they notify the subjects or the Commissioner of their intention.

4. **Personal data shall be accurate and, where necessary, kept up-to-date.** The 'data controller' must take reasonable steps to ensure the accuracy of the data. Organisations must carry out checks at regular intervals. (This is usually done by sending the personal details held to the subject for them to verify the accuracy.)

5. **Personal data processed for any purpose shall not be kept longer than is necessary for that purpose.** For example, data may be collected from applicants for a job. The data can only be stored for the period of assessment, interview and selection. After that it should be destroyed.

6. **Personal data shall be processed in accordance with the rights of data subjects under the Act.** The subject is entitled to make a written request to the 'data controller' (usually accompanied by a fee) and be given details of their data within 40 days. The information they are given must include a description of their data, the purposes for which it is processed, people to whom it may be disclosed and the name of the organisation actually carrying out the processing of the data. The subject has the right to have inaccurate data amended or deleted. The subject also has the right to prevent processing that is likely to cause damage or distress (and to sue for compensation if damage or distress has been caused) and to prevent processing for direct marketing ('junk mail') purposes.

7 **Appropriate technical and organisational measures shall be taken against unauthorised or unlawful processing of personal data and against accidental loss or destruction of, or damage to, personal data**. The data must be kept private and secure. The 'data controller' must ensure that the data is backed up regularly, virus checked and restricted to named authorised persons, for example, by using passwords.

8 **Personal data shall not be transferred to a country or territory outside the European Economic Area, unless that country or territory ensures an adequate level of protection for the rights and freedoms of data subjects in relation to the processing of personal data**. (The European Economic Area is currently the member countries of the EU plus Iceland, Liechtenstein and Norway.) The only exemptions to this are if the data subject has given consent to the transfer or the transfer is necessary for reasons of public interest, is in the interests of the data subject or is for legal reasons.

Computer Misuse Act 1990

The Computer Misuse Act 1990 was passed to deal with the problem of hacking of computer systems. There are three offences under the Act:

■ **Unauthorised access to computer material**. This includes finding or guessing someone's password, then using it to get into a computer system and have a look at the data it contains. This is an offence even if no damage is done and no files are deleted or changed. The very act of accessing material without authorisation is illegal. This offence carries a penalty of imprisonment for up to six months and/or a fine.

■ **Unauthorised access with intent to commit or facilitate commission of further offences**. This builds on the previous offence. This offence, covers, for example, guessing or stealing an on-line banking password and using it to access a person's bank account and transfer the money to another account. This offence carries a penalty of up to five years' imprisonment and/or a fine.

■ **Unauthorised modification of computer material**. This could include deliberately deleting files, changing the computer setup or introducing a virus with the intent to impair the operation of the computer, or access to programs and data. This also includes using a computer to damage other computers, even though the computer used to do this is not modified in any way. This offence carries a penalty of up to five years' imprisonment and/or a fine.

Every employee should be made aware of this Act and their responsibility under it. Information about the Act should be distributed to all employees in an easy to understand form. Most people would agree that using a computer to commit fraud is clearly wrong. However, most would not realise that playing around with the computer settings can also be construed as computer misuse under the Act.

 ## Spam

What is spam?

There are thousands of companies who are taking advantage of the low cost of electronic communications to send mail to our Inbox. These unexpected, unsolicited, inappropriate and usually unwanted e-mails are referred to as 'spam' or 'junk mail'.

When is it spam?

According to the Mail Abuse Prevention System (MAPS) an electronic message is spam if the recipient's personal identity and context are irrelevant because the message is equally applicable to many other potential recipients, the recipient has not granted deliberate and explicit permission for it to be sent or the transmission and receipt of the message appears to benefit the sender more than the recipient. These conditions usually apply to bulk e-mails.

Where does the term 'spam' come from?

The term has its origins in the early days of the Internet in Multi-User Dungeons – (MUDs) online, real-time, interactive, text-based virtual environments. A user programmed his computer to type 'spam, spam, spam' over and over in a MUD until his connection was terminated by a system administrator. From these origins, the term spam began to be used to describe excessive multi-postings on Usenet groups (forums where users can publish articles about a specific topic; articles that are not about that topic are referred to as spam).

Why do people send spam?

Spam is the electronic equivalent of junk mail. Spam is generally sent to sell products and services. Physical junk mail (i.e. letters) costs an organisation a lot of money to send out so, if the posting is unsuccessful, they will probably stop. However, bulk e-mail costs very little, so these organisations are not really too concerned how successful it is in selling the product or service, as it doesn't cost them much anyway.

How can you tell where the spam has come from?

Usually you cannot tell where the spam has come from. Often the spammer will set up a one-time e-mail account from which to send the spam e-mailshot. Once the e-mailshot has been sent, the account is closed. Alternatively, the spammer will forge the headers on the e-mail to make it almost impossible to trace the origin of the spam.

How do spammers get e-mail addresses?

There are many ways. You may have dealt with a company who sells their mailing lists to third parties (although they must disclose this to you). Spammers also use 'robots' to scour the Internet and bring back any e-mail addresses they find. If you post to newsgroups, spammers can pick up your e-mail address.

If I unsubscribe, won't the spam stop?

This is usually a very clever trick by the spammers. They will send e-mails to thousands of addresses on a mailing list (many of which are probably invalid). They will invite you to unsubscribe by clicking on a link. However, by doing this, you are simply confirming to the spammer that your address is a valid one and they will then continue to use this and pass it onto others, so you will probably receive more spam!

Isn't spam illegal?

In December 2003, new regulations came into force in the UK to try to reduce the problem of spam. Under this EU Directive on Privacy and Electronic Communication (DPEC), anyone sending direct marketing messages by e-mail must comply with the rules or face a fine of up to £5000.

The regulations have two main areas:

- You cannot transmit unsolicited marketing material by e-mail to an individual subscriber (i.e. a consumer) unless the recipient has previously notified you that he or she consents to receiving such communications. Exceptions to this rule are:
- The recipient has actively invited the communication via a third party.
- The recipient has been made aware that he or she is likely to receive marketing messages and has not objected to receiving them. (There must be a clear and simple way for the recipient to object.)

- The sender has obtained the contact details of the recipient in the course of a sale or negotiations for the sale of a product or service and the marketing material being sent is about similar products and services.

You cannot transmit any marketing e-mail (solicited or unsolicited) to any subscriber (corporate or individual) where:

- The identity of the sender is disguised or concealed.
- A valid address (to which the recipient can send an opt-out request) has not been provided.

Where the consent of the recipient has been gained, this must be considered to be 'for the time being'. The recipient must be given the opportunity in every subsequent communication to 'opt out' (i.e. remove that consent). When an opt-out request is received, the contact details of that recipient should be suppressed.

Is spam a big problem?

Yes! There are many reasons why spam is a very big problem. Your Internet Service Provider must purchase bandwidth in order to be able to service all their customers efficiently. As their customer base grows, so their revenue increases and they can purchase new servers and more bandwidth in order to service their growing numbers of customers. Spam, however, increases the need for bandwidth and increases the load on e-mail servers with no added revenue to the ISP to compensate. The added cost ends up being passed onto the customer. Also, in the recent past, large e-mail servers have been shut down due to spam overload, depriving thousands of paying customers from receiving their e-mails. According to MessageLabs, the e-mail security company, spam now accounts for up to 55% of all e-mail. Their figures also show that during 2002/2003, the percentage of spam to legitimate e-mail has grown at a very fast rate – 2.3% in June 2002 to 55% in June 2003. The problem of spam has reached such proportions that it threatens the viability of e-mail and the Internet itself.

Another problem is the amount of physical resources it consumes. People spend about 15 minutes per day reading and deleting spam e-mails. In an organisation with many employees, this adds up to a lot of time and money.

How can I stop spam e-mail?

There are a number of things you can do to stop spam e-mail. Which one suits you will depend on the type of e-mail you normally receive and whether you have complete control over your e-mail account.

- Have two e-mail addresses. Only give out your 'proper' e-mail address to trusted sources, i.e. business colleagues, friends, etc. Set up a second web-based e-mail address (such as Yahoo or Hotmail) and use this when purchasing goods and services online, or filling in forms online. If you start to receive too much spam into this e-mail account, stop using it and set-up another one. (You will not have to inform anyone of the change as your 'trusted' sources don't use this e-mail address anyway).
- Use the filters in your e-mail software to examine the sender information and subject fields and to filter out e-mail containing specific keywords.
- Install server-based anti-spam software. If your organisation receives a large amount of legitimate e-mails from people with whom they have had no previous contact (for example, in a customer service department), it is obviously not practical to inform everyone of a new e-mail address. Server-based anti-spam software can apply rules for users and groups of users to filter out users who do not 'meet the rules'.

How does an e-mail spam filter work?

There are different kinds of filters. *User-defined filters* are included in most e-mail software today. With these filters you can forward e-mails to different folders or mailboxes according to headers or contents. You can also forward e-mail directly to the rubbish bin in your e-mail software. You will usually find that spam e-mails have some common characteristics, either in the sender's e-mail address or the subject line. By applying some rules to your incoming messages, you can eliminate a large number of spam e-mails. *Header filters* are more sophisticated. They look at the e-mail headers to see if they are forged. (Headers contain other information as well as recipient, sender and subject fields. They include information about the servers that were used in delivering the e-mail.) A forged header is usually a pretty good indication that the e-mail is spam. Not all spam has forged headers though, so this filter on its own is not sufficient. *Language filters* simply filter out any e-mail that is not in your native tongue. *Content filters* scan the text of an e-mail and use a form of 'logic' to decide whether the e-mail is spam. They can be very effective but may also filter out the odd newsletter or bulk e-mail that is legitimate. *Permission filters* block all e-mail that does not come from an authorised source. The first time you send an e-mail to a person who uses permission filters, you may receive an automated response inviting you to visit a web page and enter some information. Your e-mail address is then authorised and you will be able to send e-mails to this person.

Other privacy threats

The Internet is all about enabling people to communicate easily on a worldwide basis. However, it is also easy for intruders to connect to you without your invitation, or even your knowledge.

- **Hacker** – this term used to be used to describe an enthusiastic computer user. Someone who enjoyed learning about computer systems and programming languages and could be considered an 'expert' on such matters. However, the term hacker is now used to describe someone who breaks into computers and networks. A hacker is usually very clever with software programs. Some hackers do this just for the thrill, others are looking for information about companies and individuals.
- **Identity thief** – this is someone looking for your personal details, such as your birth certificate, in order to impersonate the actual owner of the information.
- **Personal profiler** – some websites sell the information they collect to third parties.
- **Stalker** – someone who visits chat rooms to try to meet women or children.
- **Con artist** – you will not have to be online for too long before you will start to receive electronic approaches from people offering you 'get-rich-quick' schemes and other dubious products.

Jargon buster

A lot of technical terms have been used in this chapter. Below is a list of these words and their meanings:

Term	Meaning
Back up	The process of copying files to a second medium (usually a disk or CD) as a precaution in case the first medium fails. One of the basic rules in using computers is to back up your files regularly.
BIOS	The **B**asic **I**nput/**O**utput **S**ystem is built into the computer when it is built. The BIOS contains all the code required to control the keyboard, screen, disk drives, etc. Because the BIOS is placed in a chip when the computer is manufactured, it cannot be damaged by a disk failure. It also enables the computer to boot.
E-mail header	The header is information that precedes the e-mail message. A header is part of the data packet and contains information about the file or the transmission. The header can only be accessed by the operating system or using a specialist software program.
Hacker	An individual who gains unauthorised access to computer systems for the purpose of stealing and corrupting data. Hackers, themselves, maintain that the proper term for such individuals is 'cracker'.
Log-in	Most computers on a network require a user name and password to get into the system. The user is 'authenticated' by the server and allowed to access the network and use resources on that network.
Patch	Also called a 'service patch'. A piece of code that is inserted into an executable program to fix a 'bug'. Patches are available to download from the Internet.
Robot	A program that runs automatically without human intervention. Usually a robot has some 'artificial intelligence' so that it can react to different situations. Two common types of robot are 'agents' and 'spiders'.

 ## Suggested tasks for evidence

The evidence for this unit will need to be collected on an ongoing basis as you use your PC. The suggested tasks below provide guidance on the type of work that you can produce as evidence for this unit. You may come across one or more of these scenarios in your workplace. By following the guidelines below, you will have produced a piece of evidence for this unit.

To ensure that your work can be used as evidence towards your ITQ, take print-outs and screenshots where appropriate.

Suggested Task 1

If you do not already have virus software installed on your PC (at home or at work), install it. Take screenshots to show the different stages.

Suggested Task 2

Run a virus scan on a floppy disk (or another drive on your system). Take screenshots to show the stages.

Suggested Task 3

Create a short report on what security patches are, how you can check whether you need any and how to download them.

Suggested Task 4

Create a backup of one of the folders on your system. Take screenshots to show the stages.

Suggested Task 5

Create a short report or presentation to discuss the security issues users must be aware of when using a computer and the Internet.

Internet and intranets

Unit value = 15

Overview

You are likely to be in a role which involves knowing about the benefits and drawbacks of different connection methods; understanding how to avoid Internet security risks; using and customising more advanced browser facilities; and searching for, finding and evaluating information.

A competent person can use a computer to access, retrieve and exchange information, including searching for information on the Internet and evaluating the information found, exchanging information via a Company intranet or the Internet and customising browser settings for optimum performance.

 ## Required skills and techniques for Level 2

Searching	Choosing a search engine that is appropriate for the information that is needed. Carrying out searches efficiently, such as by using meta search engines, wild cards, AND or NOT (Boolean notation).
Finding and evaluating	Choosing and using appropriate methods of searching for relevant information. Reviewing sources and information to help choose what is most relevant and to decide when enough has been found.
Exchanging information	Choosing and using appropriate methods of exchanging information, such as FTP or HTTP.
Customising browser software	Customising browser settings to improve the performance of software.

 ## Requirements of this unit

You will need to produce at least *two* comprehensive and different pieces of work, demonstrating skills, techniques and knowledge in using one of the most frequently used information exchange and gathering systems.

 ## Tasks in this unit

The tasks that appear throughout this unit are designed to help you practise using the feature that has just been discussed. However, if you wish, you can provide these as extra pieces of evidence in addition to the two main pieces that are required by the unit.

The tasks at the end of the unit are suggested ways in which you could provide the main evidence for this unit.

 ## What will I achieve?

By accomplishing a Level 2 in this unit, you will also have achieved Level 1 in all cases and a Level 3 in some cases. Below is a table to show what levels you will have achieved.

Required skill	Level 1	Level 2	Level 3
Searching	●————————————————●————————————————●		
Finding and evaluating	●————————————————●————————————————●		
Exchanging information	●————————————————●		
Customising browser software	N/A	●————————————————●	

Introduction

What is the Internet?

The term stands for International Network, which is exactly what the Internet is. It is a series of inter-connected networks which enable communication and the transfer of information between computers around the world. The Internet provides four main services:

- **E-mail** – the ability to communicate with anyone around the world using electronic mail.

- **World Wide Web** – a worldwide library of information delivered via web pages.

- **File Transfer** – the ability to transfer files from one computer to another using the File Transfer Protocol, FTP. Copying files from a remote host (server) to your computer is known as downloading. Copying files from your computer to a remote host (server) is known as uploading.

- **Telnet** – this enables you to establish a session with a remote computer from your own computer. Once the connection is made, you can log into that computer as if you were sitting in front of it. Telnet also allows two programs to work co-operatively by exchanging data over the Internet.

Where did it all begin?

The origins of the Internet go back to 1969. US military agencies set up a project to enable their research centres to keep in touch and exchange information more efficiently. This was known as ARPAnet (Advanced Research Projects Agency network). At the beginning it consisted of just four computers at universities in Utah, Los Angeles, Santa Barbara and Stanford. By 1972, ARPAnet consisted of 50 computers.

The UK joined in at the end of the 1970s when the first academic network, called Joint Academic Network (JANET) was established between five UK universities. At this stage, most of the computer networks in the US and Europe had few connections to other networks. In the 1980s networks began to interconnect and the term 'Internet' was first used.

The Internet's really spectacular growth began in the early 1990s. The introduction of the World Wide Web as one of the services that the Internet could deliver combined with improved telephone access made it easy to connect to the Internet and use it.

No one actually owns the Internet. Individuals, companies and other organisations own their part of the network and their own Web sites, but the Internet itself is a co-operative effort.

How does it work?

The Internet is an ever-expanding mass of networks, software and linking devices all with their own role to play – storing information, directing the flow of messages, giving users access to the network, or keeping the different parts of the network in touch.

Talking the same language

The reason that the computers and other hardware on the Internet can communicate with each other is because they all speak the same language – an agreed-upon set of rules, known as a protocol. The protocol used on the Internet is Transmission Control Protocol/Internet Protocol (TCP/IP). Transmission Control Protocol manages the way data is sent and received on each computer. Internet Protocol controls the way the data is routed across the networks that make up the Internet.

As well as the users' computers on the Internet, there are servers and routers which manage the connections and communication. When you work on the Internet, your computer connects to a **server**, which contains files, databases and other information you can access. Every network has at least one server – the Internet has hundreds.

Internet traffic

With all the 'traffic' on the Internet (messages and data travelling around from one computer to another), there has to be some direction and control. This job is handled by **routers**. Routers provide the links within and between the different networks. They find the best routes for data and messages to travel over the networks, rather like traffic policemen.

When you hit the Send button in your e-mail application, you are starting an electronic race to get your message delivered as quickly as possible. Your message is broken down into small chunks of data – known as packets. These packets contain the message and the unique address you are sending it to (rather like a postal address and post code). These packets are routed around the networks. Each packet may take a different route and arrive at a different time, so the message doesn't arrive in the same order that it was sent in. However, each part of the message has a unique identifier so that it can be reassembled in the correct order when it reaches its destination.

Your message travels across a number of relay points, controlled by routers. Their job is to find the most efficient physical path across the interconnected networks. Routers may switch the data packets from one path to another, to complete the trip in the most efficient way. Each router sends the packet along and hands it off to the next router. Each race – and there are millions of them going on simultaneously – is completed in a matter of seconds.

What is an intranet?

An intranet uses the same technology as the Internet and often looks the same. However, an intranet is a private network for use within an organisation. It is not accessible to the general public. Companies use intranets to manage projects, provide information to employees, distribute data, etc. Users of an intranet can exchange e-mail, send and receive files, browse web pages and connect to other computers within the intranet.

Connecting to an intranet

Because an intranet is usually hosted on a server that is internal to your organisation, you do not need to physically connect to the intranet. When you click on your intranet icon, you will normally be asked for a user name and password (rather like when logging onto the network), so that it can authenticate who you are before letting you in.

Getting connected

You need a combination of hardware and software to connect to the Internet. You will, of course, need a computer. For a basic dial-up connection you will also need a modem and a telephone line. You will then need an Internet Service Provider (ISP) who will provide you with the software and means to connect to the Internet.

Dial-up connection

A dial-up connection uses a telephone line to connect you to the ISP's servers, through which you can then connect to other servers and computers internationally.

Your computer uses a digital signal, but your telephone line (certainly if it is an ordinary telephone line) is analogue. A modulator/demodulator (**modem**) converts the digital signal from your computer into an analogue signal that can travel along the telephone line. Another modem at the destination computer will convert the analogue signal back into a digital signal that the computer can receive and understand.

Because a dial-up connection uses an ordinary telephone line, it can be slow. If you imagine that an ordinary telephone line is a narrow pipe, not much information can travel up and down it at the one time. If you need to transfer large files from one computer to another using the Internet, you will find that using a dial-up connection is painfully slow. Also, you have to dial-up and connect each time you want to use the Internet, which is not the most efficient way to work if you need regular access.

Broadband

For most businesses, a broadband Internet connection is a preferred option. There has been a lot of press coverage recently about broadband and whether you can get it at your business (or home) location. It is gradually becoming more and more available and will continue to grow in popularity in the years to come.

Broadband is an 'always on' connection, so there is no need to dial-up each time you want to connect to the Internet. Also, as its name suggests, it has a much broader bandwidth (a bigger pipe) so more information can travel up and down the pipe at faster speeds (up to 40 times faster than a dial-up connection).

The most common form of broadband is Asymmetric Digital Subscriber Line (ADSL). ADSL transforms the existing standard telephone line into a high-speed digital line capable of carrying the high-speed broadband service. To do this, you need a broadband modem and some phone adapters. Even though your Internet connection is always on, you can still make and receive telephone calls on the same line. Because of the way it works, it has an enormous capacity to carry traffic and, because it is digital, the quality of the data is very high.

Other forms of broadband include cable and satellite. Cable broadband is delivered through cables – like cable TV – so you need to be in a cabled area. Satellite broadband uses a satellite to send and receive information. Wireless broadband, as the name suggests, uses wireless technology (radio transmitters) to send and receive data (rather like a mobile phone). Alternatively, a leased line is a dedicated line reserved totally for one business. This is very fast and reliable, but also expensive.

Mobile phones

You can also connect to the Internet using a mobile phone. Bluetooth technology enables you to 'latch on' to the mobile phone network to access the Internet. A

WAP mobile phone enables you to access the Internet directly from the phone and 3G is the new generation of mobile phones, which offer a much wider range of Internet services.

Bluetooth

Bluetooth is a technology that enables communication between digital devices, such as computers, mobile phones, laptops and Personal Digital Assistants (PDAs). It is a short-range – usually around 10 metres – wireless connection.

It enables up to three pieces of hardware to be connected at one time. Information can then be exchanged between the devices. For example, you could connect a mobile phone to a PC using bluetooth and send information from the mobile phone to the PC. In the same way, you could use the mobile phone network to access the Internet.

WAP

WAP is a technology that enables e-mail and Web pages to be viewed on a mobile phone. The WAP browser on a mobile phone will display a text-only version of a Web page. New WAP mobile phones use a technology called General Packet Radio System (GPRS). This uses the mobile phone network to send and receive data at high speeds. GPRS provides a continuous connection to the Internet for the day, once it is logged in. You are only charged for the time it takes to download the information to the WAP phone.

Users of WAP phones can also send and receive e-mail from their phone. They must have an on-line e-mail account which is set up with the mobile phone service provider. The e-mail is created on the screen (rather like a text message) and then sent to the required e-mail address. To download your e-mails, you use WAP to connect to your e-mail account via the Internet.

3G phones

The first generation of mobile phones (known as 1G) developed during the 70s and 80s. These mobile phones enabled you to make voice calls. The phones used analogue transmission and could only be used in one country. The second generation of mobile phones (2G) began in the early 90s with the introduction of digital transmission. This allowed Short Message Service (SMS or 'texting') to be offered. Further advances in technology into the new millennium included WAP. (This is known as 2.5G.)

The third generation – **3G** – introduces broadband to the mobile phone and the possibilities are endless. Mobile phones now have the ability to send and receive all media quickly and efficiently and to deliver high-quality video conferencing. Web pages will become more accessible and can be received at much higher speeds than before. This generation of mobile phones also enables images, animations and clips as well as text to be sent to other phones using the same technology. Mobile phones now have built-in cameras, allowing images to be displayed on a mobile phone screen (rather like a digital camera). Images can be saved and sent to other mobile phones.

TASK 1

1 **Discuss with your IT department the type of connection that your company uses for Internet access. Compare this with the connection you use if you have a PC at home with which you connect to the Internet. Note the speed and efficiency of the connection.**

2 **Make a list of the benefits and drawbacks of a dial-up connection compared to a broadband connection.**

The World Wide Web

The World Wide Web is one of the most popular services provided by the Internet. It is a global collection of electronic documents or 'pages' that can be viewed on a computer using a Web browser (such as Internet Explorer).

The Web uses a protocol called HyperText Transfer Protocol (HTTP) to transfer specially formatted documents. The documents are created in a language called HyperText Markup Language (HTML). These documents support graphics, audio and video as well as links to other documents. When browsing, a user can jump from one document to another easily by clicking on a hyperlink.

Browsing the Web

In order to be able to view the content of a file created using HyperText Markup Language, you need a piece of software called a 'browser'. The latest versions of the Windows® operating system have an in-built browser, Internet Explorer. There is other browser software available, such as Netscape® Navigator or Opera. A browser reads the HTML code and converts it into the text and graphic images that you view on the computer screen. (The version of Internet Explorer covered in this book is 5.50.)

Browsing the Web, or 'surfing' as it is called, simply means typing in Web addresses and clicking on hyperlinks to jump from one page to another or from one site to another.

Web addresses

The correct term for a Web address is a Uniform Resource Locator (URL), although everyone uses the term Web address. A URL contains four parts:

- **http:** is the protocol that is being used (HyperText Transfer Protocol).
- **www.** Is a pointer to the host computer. It does not have to start www, but most Web addresses do.
- **Microsoft.com** is the name of the actual domain. (most organisations will purchase a domain that uses their company name, so it is easy to guess.)
- **/home/index.html** describes the folder path to the required page. You are usually taken to the Home page of the site to begin.

The part at the end of the domain name denotes the type of organisation: .com generally indicates that it is an American company, .co.uk indicates a UK company (although .ltd.uk is now also becoming popular for UK companies), .org or .org.uk usually indicates a non-profit making or charitable organisation, .gov.uk is used for UK Government departments and .net is used by ISPs and online companies.

Websites

The Web contains thousands of websites all containing a number of pages. On first sight, it can feel a bit like buying a magazine three miles thick with no contents page! However, each website belongs to an individual or an organisation and they can be broadly categorised as follows:

- **Institutional sites** – most Government departments and local authorities will have their own website. These are useful sources of information about a locality, local news, contact information, information about what a Government department does, etc.
- **ISP sites** – Internet Service Providers have their own sites containing information about pricing, support, downloadable software and other information for their customers or potential customers.
- **Sales or e-commerce sites** – online shops selling everything from books to groceries.

- **News sites** – all the major newspapers and magazines have websites. These sites are kept updated during the day, so they are able to deliver the latest, breaking news.
- **Company sites** – many companies now have their own website to inform about their products and services, to provide a service to their existing customers and to attract new customers.
- **Personal sites** – when you sign up with an ISP, you usually get some free Web space. Lots of people have decided to use their free space to create their own website, sharing information about themselves, their hobbies and even their pets with the rest of the world!

Internet Explorer

You may have the Internet Explorer **shortcut** on your desktop. If so, you can double-click on this shortcut to launch Internet Explorer.

Alternatively, click on **Start**, **Programs** and then choose **Internet Explorer** from the menu. (If you have Windows® XP, it is **Start**, **All Programs**, **Internet Explorer**.)

The browser window

The Internet Explorer screen shares the common elements of all Microsoft® applications.

There is a **Title Bar** across the top of the screen telling you which application you are in (Internet Explorer). Under the Title Bar is the **Menu Bar** which contains drop-down menus – File, Edit, View, Favorites, Tools, Help. Under the Menu Bar is the **Standard Toolbar** which contains buttons to access the main commands in Internet Explorer.

Under the Standard Toolbar is the **Address Bar**. To navigate to a Web address, type the address in this bar and click on Go at the end of the bar (or press Return on the keyboard).

The main part of the window is where you see the website to which you navigate.

The **Status Bar** runs along the bottom of the Internet Explorer window. When you navigate to a Web address, the progress of the transfer to that website is shown in the Status Bar.

Opening page http://www.microsoft.com/...

You can make use of the buttons on the Internet Explorer toolbar to navigate around the Web.

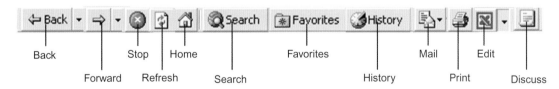

- **Back** – takes you back to the page that was displayed prior to the current one. (Click on the down arrow to display a list of the pages visited in this session. Click on a page in the list to jump to it.)
- **Forward** – takes you forward to the next page (once you have gone back). (Click on the down arrow to display a list of pages previously visited in this session. Click on a page in the list to jump to it.)
- **Stop** – stops the current page loading. Any elements that have already loaded will be displayed.

■ **Refresh** – refreshes or reloads the current page. Useful if the page has not loaded correctly or if it is a page that changes frequently, e.g. showing a live sports event.

■ **Home** – takes you to the page that first loads when you launch Internet Explorer. (This page can be changed using Internet Options.)

■ **Search** – opens the Search window down the left side of the screen.

■ **Favorites** – opens the Favorites window down the left side of the screen.

■ **History** – opens the History window down the left side of the screen.

■ **Mail** – launches the installed e-mail editor.

■ **Print** – prints the current page.

■ **Edit** – edits the current page in Excel, FrontPage®, PowerPoint® or Word.

■ **Discuss** – launches a discussion so that you can work collaboratively on a document. (This feature requires a Discussion server.)

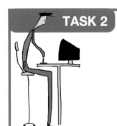

TASK 2

1 **Launch Internet Explorer and familiarise yourself with the browser window.**

2 **Click on the buttons on the toolbar to familiarise yourself with what they do.**

Surfing the Web

To start 'surfing', you simply type a Web address into the Address Bar at the top of the browser window.

Click on the **Go** button at the end of the address bar, or press **Return** on the keyboard.

As your browser locates the website and loads it onto the screen, the progress shows in the Status Bar at the bottom of the screen.

Once you have arrived at the website, you can click on the links to jump to different pages within that website. When the mouse pointer changes to a pointing finger icon, this indicates that you are on a link and can click to move to another part of the web page, another web page, or another website. Most links are apparent because they display as blue underlined text. However, pictures can also act as links.

You will notice that, as you click on links to move further into the website, the address on the address bar can become very long.

| Address | http://www.amazon.co.uk/exec/obidos/ASIN/034088973X/qid=1100783519/ref=sr_8_xs_ap_i1_xgl/026-3955396-4805264 |

The basic address, i.e. www.amazon.co.uk – takes you to the 'home' page of the site. The pages you move to when you click on the links also have their own Web address.

When you want to go to a different website, click in the address bar, type another Web address and click on Go (or press Return).

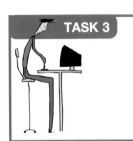

TASK 3

1   Type a Web address in the address bar of Internet Explorer to go to that website.

2   Practise clicking on links on the page and then using the Back button to return to the previous page.

Using Favorites

Favorites are rather like bookmarks for Web pages. If you find a Web page that is useful and informative, you can store the URL of this Web page in your Favorites list, which means you don't have to remember its Web address when you want to go back to it.

Once you are on the appropriate Web page, choose **Add to Favorites** from the **Favorites** menu.

You can also click on the **Favorites** button on the toolbar. The Favorites pane opens down the left side of the screen. Click on the **Add ...** button.

A third option is to right-click on the Web page and choose Add to Favorites from the shortcut menu.

The Add Favorite dialog box opens. A name for the Web page will be inserted in the **Name** box. You can change this name if you wish.

If you store a lot of Web addresses in your Favorites list, you might want to store them in different folders. To view the folders that are available, click on **Create in**. The dialog box expands. Click on the folder in which you wish to store this Favorite.

To create a new folder, click on **New Folder ...** , type a name for the folder and click on **OK.**

Navigating to a URL stored in Favorites

Click on the **Favorites** menu. The URLs that you have stored in Favorites, and any sub-folders that you have created, are listed.

To navigate to a URL stored in Favorites, click on the appropriate folder to show the URLs in that folder and then click on the URL you wish to go to.

Alternatively, you can press the **Favorites** button on the Standard toolbar. This will open the Favorites pane down the left side of the screen.

Click on a folder to open it and then click on the URL that you wish to go to.

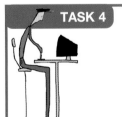

TASK 4

1   Store some Web addresses in Favorites.

2   Practise going back to the pages by using the link stored in Favorites.

Organising Favorites

If you store a lot of URLs in Favorites, you will need to manage this filing system in order that it remains an efficient way to navigate to a Web page quickly.

Choose **Organize Favorites** from the **Favorites** menu or click on **Organize ...** in the Favorites pane.

The Organize Favorites dialog box opens, as in the figure below.

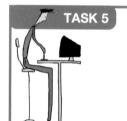

To create a folder at the top level, click on **Create Folder**.

To create a folder inside an existing folder, open the folder in which you wish to create the new folder and then choose **Create Folder**.

To rename a stored URL link, select the URL in the list and click on **Rename**. Type a new name for the URL link and press **Return**.

To move a stored URL link to a folder, select the URL in the list and click on **Move to Folder**. Select the folder to which you wish to move the URL link and click on **OK**.

To delete a URL link, select the URL in the list and click on **Delete**.

Click on **Close** when you have finished organising your Favorites.

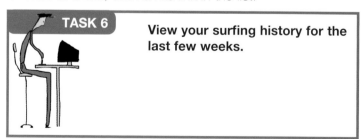

TASK 5

1 **Use Organize Favorites to create folders and place your links into folders.**

2 **Practise renaming, moving and deleting Favorites.**

Viewing History

As you navigate around the Web, Internet Explorer keeps track of the sites you have been visiting. To view a list of the sites you have visited, click on the **History** button on the Standard toolbar.

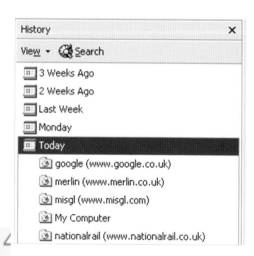

The History pane opens down the left side of the screen.

You can view History from **3 Weeks Ago**, **2 Weeks Ago**, **Last Week**, **Previous Day** or **Today**. When you click on the appropriate link, a list of the sites you have visited is shown. To return to a site, click on its link in the list.

TASK 6

View your surfing history for the last few weeks.

Saving a Web page as a file on your computer

When you store a Web page as a file on your computer, you can view the information on that Web page without having to connect to the Internet. If you decide you would like to store a Web page as a file on your computer, choose **Save As** from the **File** menu in Internet Explorer.

The Save Web Page dialog box opens.

Navigate to where you wish to save the Web page.

Type a name for the Web page (or accept the name that is already in the **File name** box) and click on **Save**.

The Web page is saved as an HTML file. You do not need to be connected to the Internet to view this Web page, as it is now stored on your computer. However, you do need to launch Internet Explorer before you can open the file and the file will not change if the Web page changes.

Choose **Open** from the **File** menu.

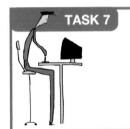

Type the name of the file you wish to open, or click on **Browse** ... to navigate to the Web page that you have saved on your computer. Select the file and click on **Open**.

TASK 7

1 **Save a Web page as a file on your computer.**

2 **Open the file to view its contents in your browser window.**

Sending a Web page or link in an e-mail

You can send an actual Web page, or a link to that Web page, in an e-mail message. Sending a link is more efficient as the e-mail message will be smaller and use less bandwidth.

Choose **Send** from the **File** menu and choose **Page by E-mail** or **Link by E-mail**.

This will launch a new message window of your e-mail application with the URL of the Web page or the link to the Web page already in the window. Complete the message and send in the normal way.

Page by E-mail

Link by E-mail

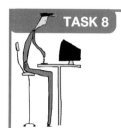

TASK 8

1 **Locate a Web page and send the page and/or the link in an e-mail to yourself.**

 ## Searching the Web

The Web is a global library of millions of websites each containing many pages. In order to make it easier to find what you are looking for in this global library, there are various search services you can use. These search services are called 'search engines'.

Search engines

Search engines contain databases of many web pages. There are two main types of search engine.

First there are those that create their listings by using computer programs called 'spiders'. These spiders find pages for inclusion in the database by following the links in pages they already have in the database. After the spider finds a page, it passes it to another program for indexing. This program identifies the text, links and content of the page and stores it in the search engine's database. The search engine then sifts through the millions of pages recorded in the index to find matches to a search and rank the matches in order of what is most relevant.

Secondly, there are human-powered directories. Anyone can submit the URL and a short description of a site to the directory. A person evaluates the submitted information and decides whether and where to include it in the directory.

How a search engine works

There are many search engines on the Web (Google, Yahoo, MSN Search, AltaVista, Lycos, to name a few). The rules they use to find and rank matches when you carry out a search mean that they can return slightly different results.

When you type in keywords to find sites containing those words, the search engine sifts through the millions of pages stored in its database and presents you with the ones that match your keywords. It even ranks the matches so the most relevant ones come first. However, in order to really get to what you are looking for, the search engine needs a little more information. If it was able to talk to you, it would ask you some questions to narrow down what you were looking for. Obviously, the search engine cannot talk to you, so in order to determine what is relevant when confronted with millions of web pages, it follows a set of rules known as an algorithm. Because each search engine's algorithm may vary slightly, they will each return slightly different results for the same keywords.

One of the main rules in an algorithm involves the location of and frequency with which your keywords appear on a page. The search engine will first of all check the HTML title of the page to see if it contains any of your keywords. Pages with the keywords in their title are assumed (rightly or wrongly) to be more relevant and ranked higher in the list of results. The search engine will then check to see if the keywords appear near the top of a Web page. Again, the assumption is that relevant pages will mention those words near the beginning. Finally, the search engine will analyse how often a keyword appears on the page in relation to other words. Those with a higher frequency are again assumed to be more relevant.

While all the major search engines follow the rule described above to some degree, they all do it slightly differently, which is why they can return different results.

Meta search engines

Meta search engines are slightly more sophisticated in that they send your search request to several different databases at the same time. A meta search engine does not own a database of Web pages; it simply sends your keywords to a number of databases owned by various search engine companies. They also try to be a little smarter by using technology that analyses and clusters the results to show themes.

However, meta searchers don't usually use the larger, more useful databases. They tend to return results from the smaller, free search engines.

Using Internet Explorer to search the Web

Internet Explorer uses a search engine called MSN Search to locate web pages.
Click on the **Search** button on the Standard toolbar of Internet Explorer.

This opens the Search pane down the left side of the screen.
You can **Find a Web page**, use **Previous searches** or **Find a map**.
Choose **Find a Web page** and type your keyword(s) in the box under **Find a Web page containing:**

Click on **Search**.
Links to pages containing your keyword(s) are listed in the Search pane.
Click on a link to move to that page.

TASK 9

Practise using the Search pane in Internet Explorer to locate websites containing keywords.

Using other search engines to search the Web

If you wish to use a different search engine, navigate to its site. Google™ is a popular search engine, www.google.co.uk

Type your keywords into the box on the Google™ home page and click on **Google Search**. (You can also choose to search **the web** or just **pages from the UK**.)

To find out how to use a particular search engine efficiently, use the Help files on the search engine site.

Most search engines follow these basic rules:

- They return only pages that contain all the words in your query, so you can narrow your search by including as many words as possible. You can type a phrase or a number of keywords with a **+** between the words. (You can also use **−** to indicate that the page should not contain the word. For example, London+hotels−hostels will return pages that contain the words 'London' and 'hotels', but not 'hostels'. If the page contains the word hostels as well as London and hotels, it will be excluded from the results. Use your keywords wisely. Try to be as specific as you can. Also remember that the order in which your keywords are typed will affect the search results.

- Most search engines ignore common words such as 'where' and 'how'. These words slow down the search without improving the results. If you want these words to be included in a search, either use the **+** sign or enclose the whole search query in quotes, for example, "How do I search the World Wide Web".

- Most search engines are not case sensitive. All letters will be treated as lower case, regardless of how you type them.

- Use quotation marks for proper names and phrases. If you enclose a set of words in quotation marks, the search engine searches for that phrase on the Web page. For example, a search for golf+clubs will return pages where the words golf and clubs appear, but not necessarily together. A search for "golf clubs" will return pages where these two words appear next to each other. This is more likely to yield the appropriate results.

- Some search engines use a system called 'word stemming'. This means that if you put in the word 'test', the search engine will also search for 'tests', 'tested', 'tester', 'testers', 'testing', etc.

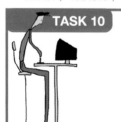

TASK 10

1 **Use Google™ (or a similar search engine) to practise finding sites containing your keywords.**

2 **Change the order in which you type the keywords to see how this yields different results.**

Using wild cards

If you are not sure how a word you are searching for is spelt, or you wish to widen the search, you can use wild card characters. There are three main wild card characters:

? replaces a single character in a search word. For example, b?ll will find ball, bell, bill, bull, etc. The missing letter will be in the same position as the ? and there must be a character in this position.

**$** replaces any single character or no character at all in a search word. For example, colo$r will find color and colour.

* replaces any number of characters or no characters at all in a search word. For example, a search for communi* would return the words communication, community, communities, communion, etc.

You cannot use a wild card character as the first character in a search. (Searches using wild card characters at the beginning of a search word or phrase would take much longer.)

Boolean operators

To include or exclude words in your search criteria, you can use Boolean operators. The three basic Boolean operators are **and, or** and **not**. Most search engines support Boolean operators, but make sure you know how the search engine handles them. (The **+** and **−** signs are substitutes for the **and** and **not** operators.)

■ **And** – the page must contain the word following the **and** operator.
■ **Or** – the page must contain one of the words on either side of the **or** operator.
■ **Not** – the page must not contain the word following the **not** operator.

You can combine these operators to create more complex search criteria. You can also 'nest' criteria within other criteria by using brackets. For example, to find pages that contain movies by George Clooney and Brad Pitt, you could type the following criteria: ('George Clooney' OR 'Brad Pitt') AND movies.

TASK 11

Practise using wild card characters and Boolean operators when searching for websites.

More advanced searching

Most search engines have the ability to do more advanced searching. There will usually be a link on their home page to the Advanced Search page. This example shows a screenshot of Google's advanced search form. You can see how you can really hone your search to the pages you require by inserting as many criteria as possible in the form.

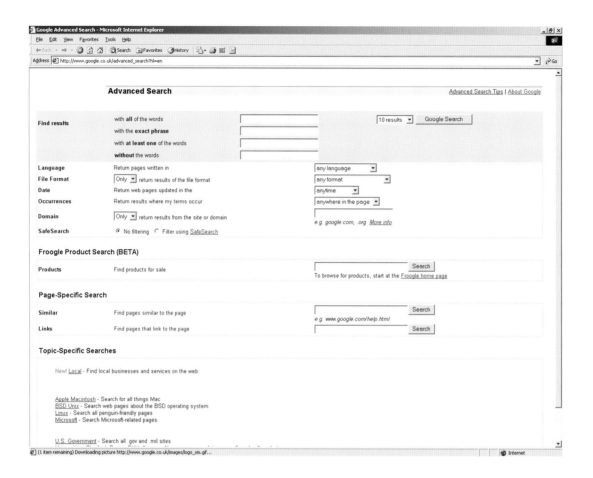

Saving searches

In Internet Explorer you can save searches so that you can undertake the same search again in the future, without having to enter the criteria again. If you use the Search pane in Internet Explorer, previous searches you have undertaken are saved automatically. Click on the **Search** button on the Standard toolbar to open the Search pane.

Click on **Previous searches**. Searches you have previously undertaken will be listed. Click on a link to return to that list of search results.

To clear the list of previous searches, click on the **Clear** button.

If you wish to save a page of search results, you can store that page in your Favorites list. (For more information on storing Favorites, see page 97.)

Evaluating search results

There are, of course, many different search engines on the Web. You will probably have a favourite which you use whenever you wish to do a search. However, it is a good idea to use more than one search engine when carrying out a search. As discussed in the previous section, they all return slightly different results. The top few results from each search engine used will yield the most relevant information.

When you carry out a search, even if you have used a number of keywords, thousands of Web pages will usually be returned. Because the search engine will have ranked the results in order of relevance, you will usually find that the top few entries in the list are the most useful. However, it is important to keep refining your search criteria (keywords) to narrow down the search to as a few relevant pages as possible. Remember to put the most important keywords first in your search criteria.

You must exercise your own judgement as to how relevant and how reliable the information on the pages may be. Web sites come and go all the time on the Web – some of the links returned may be to pages that have expired or been removed completely.

When you click on a link in the results list to go to that Web page, check when the web site was last updated. If it hasn't been updated for a long time, the information on it may be out-of-date.

Below is an example of the results list that Google™ returns.

The box at the top of the Google™ page shows the search criteria you have used to return this list. You can type in new search criteria and click on **Search** to carry out another search.

If you wish to carry out an Advanced Search, click on the link next to the Search button.

If you wish to set preferences for your searches, click on the Preferences link next to the Search button.

The pale blue bar supplies the statistics for the search. It tells you the number of results that have been returned for your search and the amount of time it took to complete your search. (In this case, 167,000 results have been found for London+Westminster+hotels and the search took 0.25 seconds.)

At the top of the results list there are usually some links shaded in pale blue. These are called 'OneBox' results and will usually contain the pages most relevant to your search criteria.

The first line of the result in the list is the title of the specific Web page that has been found. This title is a hyperlink so you can click on it to move to that Web page. The text below the hyperlink is an extract from the Web page itself. Your search keywords are highlighted in bold. At the bottom of each entry in the list is the URL of the returned result.

Exchanging information via the Internet

The Internet uses two protocols to exchange information: File Transfer Protocol (FTP) and HyperText Transfer Protocol (HTTP). For an introduction to FTP and HTTP, see Unit 207 – E-mail.

Using the command line to access an FTP server

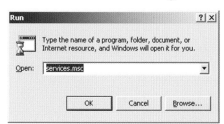

On any computer that is connected to the Internet, open the command line window by clicking on **Start** and **Run**. The Run window opens, as in the figure on the left.

Type the command **ftp:** *ftp address*. (You must know the address of the FTP server you wish to connect to. This is usually similar to a web address, but starts with 'ftp' rather than 'www'.)

You may then be asked to log into the FTP server. You can then use FTP commands to list the available files and upload or download files:

- **ls** – list the files in the current directory on the server.
- **cd** *name of directory* – change to the specified directory on the server.
- **lcd** *name of directory* – change to the specified directory on the local computer.
- **delete** *filename* – delete a file in the current directory on the server.
- **get** *filename* – copy a file from the remote server to your own computer.
- **mget** *filenames* – copy multiple files from the remote server to your own computer (you will be prompted for a Yes/No answer before transferring each file).
- **mget *** – copy all files from the current directory on the remote server to the current directory on your own computer.
- **put** *filename* – copy a file from your computer to the remote server.
- **quit** – exit the FTP environment.

Using a Web browser to view FTP files

You can only read files (not write them) on an FTP site using your Web browser, but it provides a very easy way to do this.

Launch your Web browser (e.g. Internet Explorer) and type ftp:// *ftp address* (just like typing a web address, but with ftp: at the beginning rather than http:). You may be prompted to log onto the FTP server.

The folders and files on the FTP server will be shown in a list with links. Click on the link for the directory to see the files in that directory. To open and view a file, click on its link in the list. To save a file to your own computer, right-click on the filename and choose **Save Target As** from the shortcut menu.

Using FTP software

It is quite likely that, should you need to move files using FTP, you will already have an FTP package installed on your computer.

There are many FTP programs available – many as freeware or shareware. Because there are so many available, it is difficult to choose just one for this book. However, opposite is an example of an FTP program called SmartFTP, to give you an idea of what the program looks like.

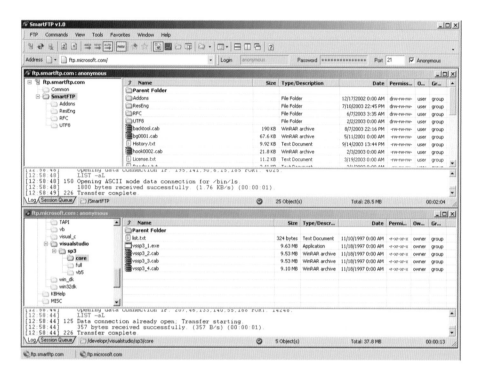

All FTP programs follow the same general principles and allow you to drag and drop files from your own computer (using My Computer or Windows Explorer) to the FTP server window. (The screenshot above shows the FTP server in the top section and the sender's own computer in the bottom section. Files can be transferred by simply dragging them from one window to the other.)

 # Internet Explorer maintenance

There are a number of tools in your Internet Explorer software that enable you to manage your browser and ensure that it continues to work efficiently and effectively.

Temporary Internet Files

As you navigate around the Web, files are created on your computer to store the Web pages you are visiting. This 'caching' of files means that Internet Explorer only has to load content that has changed since you last viewed a Web page instead of having to load all the content of the page each time. These files are not harmful, but will gradually build up on your computer. You should regularly delete them.

Choose **Internet Options** from the **Tools** menu.

The Internet Options dialog box opens. Click on the **General** tab.

Under **Temporary Internet files** click on **Delete Files …**

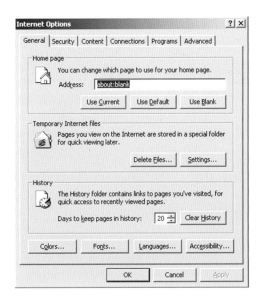

You can also specify settings for your Temporary Internet files. Click on the **Settings ...** button.

You can specify when Internet Explorer should check for new pages. This dialog box shows you where your temporary internet files are stored. You can also specify how much space should be taken up by temporary internet files.

Click on **OK** to save any changes.

Temporary internet files are stored in a folder on your C: drive. Instead of using Internet Options, you can use My Computer or Windows Explorer to delete these files. Navigate to the folder where the files are stored, select them and press Delete, just as you would with any other file.

Cookies

Cookies (apart from being something nice you can eat with your coffee!) are small text files that are placed onto your computer when you visit a website, to help your browser remember specific information. For example, the file might store a password and user ID for a specific website. If you visit a shopping site, you can leave the virtual store, return later and find that all the items are still in your shopping trolley – this is done by a cookie. Cookies can also store personal information, which can be used to identify or contact you. However, a website only stores the information that you provide. For example, a website cannot determine your e-mail address unless you provide it. The cookie is stored on your computer and sent back to the website that created it when you revisit that site.

There are different types of cookies: session cookies, persistent cookies and first- and third-party cookies.

■ A session cookie is stored in temporary memory and is deleted automatically when you close your browser.
■ A persistent cookie (also known as a permanent cookie or stored cookie) remains on your hard drive until it expires or is deleted. Persistent cookies are used to collect identifying information about the user.
■ A first-party cookie either originates from or is sent to the website you are currently viewing. These cookies are commonly used to store information such as your preferences when visiting that site.
■ A third-party cookie either originates from or is sent to a different website than the one you are currently viewing. For example, a site may contain advertising

from third-party websites and those third-party sites may use cookies. These cookies are commonly used to track your Web page use for advertising and marketing purposes. Third-party cookies can be persistent or temporary.

Whilst cookies are not harmful to your computer, they can build up over a period of time. If you decide to delete your cookies, be aware that, if you use sites where you have to log-in using a password, this password will no longer be stored once you have deleted the cookies. (Unfortunately, it is usually not possible to tell which cookies are password cookies and which cookies are other types of cookies.)

Cookies are stored in a folder on your hard drive called Cookies. (This is usually in your account folder, Documents and Settings\User Name). You can use My Computer or Windows Explorer to navigate to this folder.

Select the cookies that you wish to delete and click on **Delete** on the toolbar or press **Delete** on the keyboard.

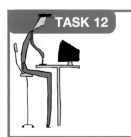

TASK 12

1 **Locate the temporary internet files on your computer and delete them.**

2 **Locate the cookies on your computer and delete them.**

 ## Customising Internet Explorer

As with all Microsoft applications, you can use Options to customise the application to suit the way you like to work.

Choose **Internet Options** from the **Tools** menu.

The Internet Options dialog box has several tabs: **General**, **Security**, **Content**, **Connections**, **Programs** and **Advanced**.

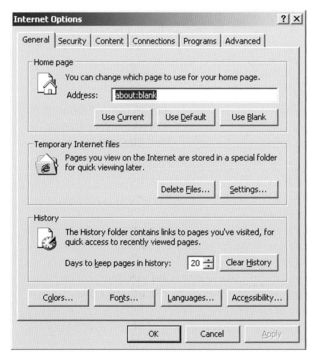

The **General** tab

■ In the **Home page** section you can set the default home page. This is the first page that will load each time you launch Internet Explorer (assuming you are online). It is a good idea to set a Web page that will load up quickly or no page at all.

If you wish to use the page that is currently on the screen, click on **Use Current**. If you wish to use Microsoft's default page (www.msn.co.uk), click on **Use Default**. If you wish Internet Explorer to show a blank screen to start with, click on **Use Blank**.

■ In the **Temporary Internet files** section you can delete and specify settings for temporary Internet files. (For more information on temporary Internet files, see page 107.)

■ In the **History** section you can specify the number of days' history to store and you can also clear the history that is stored about the Web pages you have visited. Your surfing history shows when you click on the History button on the Standard toolbar. (For more information on History, see page 98.)

You can also specify **Colors**, **Fonts**, **Languages** and **Accessibility** options for Internet Explorer.

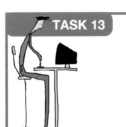

TASK 13

1 **Set up a page to be used as the default page when you launch Internet Explorer.**

2 **Specify settings for the storage of History.**

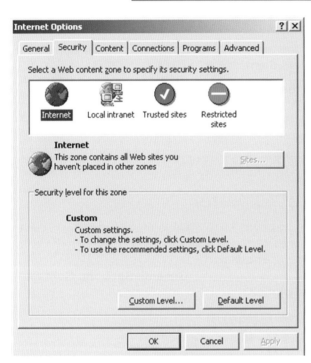

The **Security** tab

Internet Explorer divides the Internet into zones. You can assign a website to a zone that has an appropriate security level. Whenever you open or download content from a website, Internet Explorer checks the security settings for that website's zone.

There are four zones:

- **Internet** – this zone contains anything that is not assigned to another zone. The default security level for this zone is Medium.
- **Local intranet** – this zone contains internal sites (i.e. those that are on your company Intranet). The default security level for this zone is Medium.
- **Trusted sites** – this zone contains sites that you have assigned to the zone that you trust. You believe you can download content from these sites without worrying about potential damage to your computer. The default security level for this zone is Low.
- **Restricted sites** – this zone contains sites that you have assigned to the zone that you don't trust. The default security level for this zone is High.

To change the security level for a zone, click on the zone that you wish to change. If the zone is using default settings, drag the slider up or down to choose the appropriate security level. (To apply default settings, click on **Default Level**).

To set custom settings for the zone, click on **Custom Level**. Apply the security settings you require and click on **OK**.

The Content

The **Content Advisor** tab enables you to specify ratings to control what Internet content can be viewed on the computer. Once you have switched on Content Advisor, only rated content that meets or exceeds your criteria can be viewed.

With Content Advisor you can adjust the ratings settings in four areas: language, nudity, sex and violence. You can specify what types of content can be viewed with or without your permission, set up a list of websites that can never be viewed and those that can be viewed and you can set a password so that the Content Advisor settings cannot be changed without the password.

When you first switch on Content Advisor, it is set to the most conservative settings, i.e. those least likely to offend. You can adjust these settings to suit your own preferences.

Not all Internet content is rated. If you allow other people to view unrated sites on your computer, they may see what you consider to be inappropriate material.

Switching on Content Advisor and adjusting settings

Click on the **Enable ...** button. The Content Advisor dialog box opens. The Content Advisor has four tabs: **Ratings**, **Approved Sites**, **General** and **Advanced**.

To set ratings in the four areas, click on the **Ratings** tab. Select the area – Language, Nudity, Sex, Violence – in the list and then drag the slider across to the level you require.

To create a list of approved/not approved Web sites, click on the **Approved Sites** tab.

Type the URL of the site you wish to add to the list and specify whether this site should be allowed **Always** or **Never**. (You can remove sites from the list by clicking on the **Remove** button.)

To allow users to view sites with no rating, to set the password for Content Advisor or to view the Rating systems used, click on the **General** tab.

When you click on **OK** in the Content Advisor, you will be prompted to create a supervisor password. You will be prompted for this password every time you want to make a change to the Content Advisor settings.

Type the password in both boxes and click on **OK**.

The **Connections** tab

You can choose the type of connection your browser uses:

- **Never dial a connection** is used where you access the Internet via a company network or broadband.
- **Dial whenever a network connection is not present** is used on a computer that sometimes accesses the Internet via a company network and sometimes over a dial-up connection (e.g. when you use a company laptop from home).
- **Always dial my default connection** is used if you always dial-up to the Internet and you want the browser to make the connection.

The **Programs** tab

You can specify which program is launched automatically when you choose an Internet service (such as E-mail, Calendar, etc).

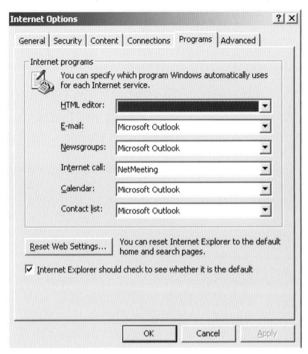

The **Advanced** tab

This contains a long list of options under various headings, including Accessibility, Browsing, Multimedia, Printing and Security. You can select and deselect options, depending on your preferences. (If you are not confident about this, it is best to leave the default settings in place).

Click on **OK** to apply any changes you have made in Internet Options.

Other issues

Netiquette

If you simply use the Internet to locate Web pages and read the information on Web pages, this does not involve anyone else. However, as soon as you start to use the Internet to communicate with other people, there are certain 'rules' that you should follow and standards you should adhere to.

For more information on netiquette, see Unit 207 – E-mail.

Security risks: More information on security can be found in Unit 205 – IT Security for Users.

Laws and guidelines: More information on laws and guidelines can be found in Unit 205 – IT Security for Users.

Downloading software patches: Information on patches can be found in Unit 203 – IT Troubleshooting for Users and Unit 205 – IT Security for Users.

 ## Suggested tasks for evidence

The evidence for this unit will need to be collected on an ongoing basis as you use your PC. The suggested tasks below provide guidance on the type of work that you can produce as evidence for this unit. You may come across one or more of these scenarios in your workplace. By following the guidelines below, you will have produced a piece of evidence for this unit.

To ensure that your work can be used as evidence towards your ITQ, take screenshots at every stage to show the steps you are taking. Appropriate print-outs should also be provided.

Suggested Task 1

Research your own Internet connection. What type does your organisation use? Do you have a connection at home? If you use a different connection at work and at home, compare these two connections for speed, performance, quality, etc. Write a short report on the advantages and disadvantages of each.

Suggested Task 2

Research a topic related to your job or organisation. Use three different search engines to find information on this subject.

Store the pages that contain the relevant information in your Favorites. Navigate to these pages again and print them.

Write a short report of your findings, extracting the appropriate information from the Web pages.

Suggested Task 3

If you use an FTP program, copy a file using the program. Take relevant screenshots to show the FTP program before the file is copied and after the file is copied.

Suggested Task 4

Write a checklist of maintenance that should be regularly carried out if you use Internet Explorer to surf the Internet (i.e. clearing out temporary internet files and cookies). Write a checklist of ways that you can customise Internet Explorer.

E-mail

Overview

You are likely to be in a role which involves using advanced e-mail facilities (e.g. for setting up groups of e-mail addresses, adding a signature, using RTF or HTML to alter the design and format of e-mails and compressing attachments).

The e-mail software outlined in this unit is Microsoft® Outlook. Microsoft® Outlook is part of the Microsoft® Office suite of applications. It offers a comprehensive e-mail facility to send, receive and manage e-mails. However, it offers a lot more than that and is used in many offices today to manage e-mail, calendars and scheduling, contacts, tasks and projects and to store and share information relating to the business.

Competent people can use the more advanced facilities of an e-mail application to send and receive messages, including formatting e-mails and using the tools available in the software. They should also be aware of the laws and guidelines affecting the use of e-mail.

 ## Required skills and techniques for Level 2

Sending and receiving	Using more advanced facilities, such as adding a signature or setting the priority of messages.
	Sending messages to groups of people set up in an address book.
	Sending and receiving instant messages with and without attachments.
	Compressing messages on sending and decompressing messages that have been received.
	Archiving e-mails where necessary, such as by using folders and subfolders.
Using address books and other facilities	Setting up groups for sending e-mails.
	Compressing and decompressing e-mail attachments.
Formatting e-mails	Changing design and format of e-mails, such as by using RTF, HTML and plain text.
Exchanging information	Choosing and using appropriate methods of exchanging information, such as FTP or HTTP.
	Using interactive sites.

 ## Requirements of this unit

You will need to produce at least *two* comprehensive and different pieces of work, demonstrating skills, techniques and knowledge outlined in the unit.

This unit asks you to demonstrate knowledge of and skill in using some of the more advanced features of an e-mail application so that you can communicate better and more securely both in the workplace and at home.

You need to be able to set up groups of contacts in your e-mail software, to compress files to send as attachments and to use features such as signatures, auto replies, etc. You should also show that you can create e-mails in different formats, i.e. HTML and Rich Text.

Tasks in this unit

The tasks that appear throughout this unit are designed to take you step-by-step through the feature being discussed. It is recommended that you use the tasks completed as evidence in addition to the two main pieces that are required by the unit.

The tasks at the end of the unit are suggested ways in which you could provide the main evidence for this unit.

 ## What will I achieve?

By accomplishing a Level 2 in this unit, you will also have achieved Level 1 in all cases. Below is a table to show what levels you will have achieved.

Required skill	Level 1	Level 2	Level 3
Sending and receiving	●	●	●
Using address books and other facilities	●	●	
Formatting e-mails	●	●	
Exchanging information	●	●	

 ## Introduction

E-mail has become the main way that people within organisations communicate with each other. It has meant that we can communicate with colleagues around the world on a 24 hours a day, 7 days a week basis. It is quick and easy to use and has impacted on the way that organisations do business – everything can happen more quickly. It is also becoming a popular method of communicating with friends and relatives from a home PC. There are many e-mail applications available – they fall into two distinct categories: client e-mail and Web e-mail.

Client e-mail software (such as Outlook) is installed on the computer. When the user goes 'online', e-mails are downloaded from the server into the client application. With this type of e-mail, the user can disconnect from the Internet and still use their e-mail application – they can read and deal with e-mails and compose replies. They only need to go 'online' when they wish to send the messages. With this type of e-mail application the user would usually have to access their e-mails from their 'client' computer, i.e. their desktop computer in the office or a laptop they carry around with them.

Web e-mail (such as Hotmail) is a free, easy to use e-mail service. However, to use the service, you must connect and go the Hotmail site. Therefore, the user has to be 'online' the whole time they are working with their e-mail. Because Hotmail is hosted on the Web, it can be accessed from any computer that has Internet access. This is useful for people who wish to travel around, but do not want to have to take their computer with them wherever they go.

Some Internet Service Providers provide access to e-mail in both ways: you can use client (POP) e-mail to download your messages when you are at home but you can use Web e-mail to access your e-mails from any computer with Internet access when you are travelling.

Microsoft
Outlook

Launching Outlook

Outlook can be launched by **double-clicking** on the **Outlook** shortcut on the desktop (if there is one).

Alternatively, click on **Start, Programs** and then choose **Microsoft Outlook** from the menu. (If you have Windows® XP, it is **Start, All Programs, Microsoft Outlook**.)

The Outlook screen

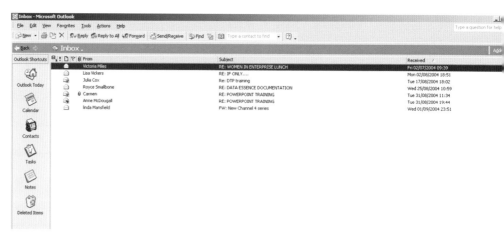

There are many different screens in Outlook and it depends how your software is set up as to which screen it will launch into. The screen above shows the Inbox folder. This is the place to be when you want to work with e-mail.

There are some elements of the screen which remain the same regardless of which area of Outlook you are working in.

The **Title Bar** across the top of the screen informs you that you are in Microsoft Outlook and which part of Outlook you are in (in this case, Inbox).

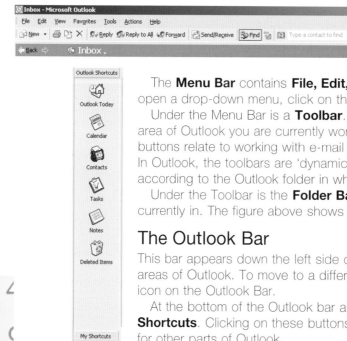

The **Menu Bar** contains **File, Edit, View, Favorites, Tools, Actions, Help**. To open a drop-down menu, click on the menu word on the Menu Bar.

Under the Menu Bar is a **Toolbar**. This contains buttons that are relevant to the area of Outlook you are currently working on. When you are in the Inbox, the buttons relate to working with e-mail – New, Print, Reply, Reply to All, Forward, etc. In Outlook, the toolbars are 'dynamic'. This means that the buttons change according to the Outlook folder in which you are working.

Under the Toolbar is the **Folder Banner**. This tells you which folder you are currently in. The figure above shows that the user is in the **Inbox.**

The Outlook Bar

This bar appears down the left side of the screen and contains links to the main areas of Outlook. To move to a different part of Outlook, click on the appropriate icon on the Outlook Bar.

At the bottom of the Outlook bar are two buttons, **My Shortcuts** and **Other Shortcuts**. Clicking on these buttons will change the Outlook Bar to show icons for other parts of Outlook.

The Folder List

The Folder List is another bar that you can switch on. Click on the **View** menu and choose **Folder List**.

The Folder List shows all the folders that you can access in Outlook. The advantage of the folder list is that it shows any sub-folders that you might have created under the main folders. For example, to manage your e-mail, you may have created sub-folders within your Inbox to store messages. (For more information on creating folders, see below). To expand a folder and view the sub-folders within it, click on the **+** beside the folder.

Some people work with both the Outlook Bar and the Folder List switched on, others just use one or the other. (Click on the appropriate entry in the **View** menu to switch the Outlook Bar or Folder List on or off.)

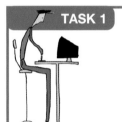 **TASK 1**

Familiarise yourself with the Outlook screen. Turn on the Folder List and turn off the Outlook Bar. Switch on the Preview Pane (also in the View menu).

 ## Outlook folders

Outlook provides a folder for each of the main areas: **Calendar, Contacts, Delete Items, Drafts, Inbox, Journal, Notes, Outbox, Sent Items, Tasks**.

■ The **Inbox** folder is where new e-mails arrive.
■ The **Outbox** folder is where e-mails that you have created and on which you have pressed the **Send** button wait to be sent if you are not connected. If you work on a network, you are probably connected to the Internet all the time. Messages will pass straight through the Outbox and go on their way to their destination.

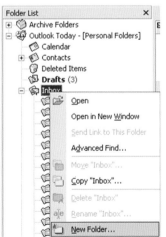

■ The **Sent Items** folder stores every message that you send.
■ The **Drafts** folder stores messages that you are creating but do not wish to send yet. If you press the **Save** button in the **New Message** window rather than **Send**, the message is put in the Drafts folder.
■ The **Deleted Items** folder stores all items that you have deleted from other folders.

You can create your own folders, either 'top-level' folders or sub-folders of one of the existing folders. For example, you may decide to create some sub-folders within your **Inbox** folder, so you can store messages relating to the same subject in one folder.

Click on the folder in which you wish to create the sub-folder (in this example, the Inbox folder).

Choose **New, Folder** from the **File** menu.

Alternatively, right-click on the existing folder (e.g. Inbox) and choose **New Folder** from the shortcut menu.

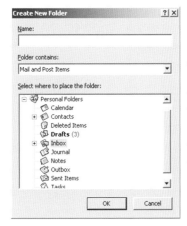

You can also press [Control]+[Shift]+[E]

The Create New Folder dialog box opens.

Type a **Name** for the new folder and click on **OK.** A new folder is created and added to your Folder List.

When you view your **Folder List**, any folder that has a **+** to the left of the folder name indicates that there are sub-folders within that folder. In the example below, the **Inbox** folder has a **+** to the left of it.

To view the sub-folders within the folder, click on the **+**. In the example below, the **Inbox** folder has been expanded to show there is a sub-folder – Calypso Project – inside it.

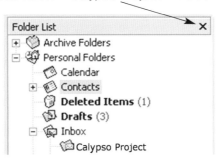

Working with received e-mail

You can use the Outlook Bar or the Folder List to move into your Inbox.

The Inbox lists the e-mail messages you have received. You can see who the message is from, the subject of the message and the date and time that it was received.

Unread messages display in bold and the icon to the left of the message is a closed envelope. Once a message has been read, it no longer displays in bold and the icon to the left of the message is an open envelope.

To read a message, double-click on it and it will open into its own window. Once you have read a message, you can use the buttons on the toolbar to deal with the message.

- **Reply** – reply to just the person who sent you the e-mail.
- **Reply to All** – reply to everyone who received the original e-mail (everyone in the **To** and **Cc** box).
- **Forward** – forward the message to someone else.
- **Print** – print the message.
- **Copy** – copy text in the message to the clipboard. (First select the text that you wish to copy.)
- **Flag** – flag the message as a reminder. (You can flag messages to remind yourself to deal with them.)
- **Move to Folder** – move the message into one of your folders in Outlook. (For more information on creating folders, see page 117.)
- **Delete** – send the message to the **Deleted Items** folder.
- **Previous Item** – view the previous message in the Inbox (without having to go back out to the Inbox).
- **Next Item** – view the next message in the Inbox (without having to go back out to the Inbox).

Some e-mail applications also have a **Reply with History** option. Using this option, the reply would include all the previous messages in this thread that had been sent and replied to.

You can also work with messages in the Inbox (without having to open them first).

The buttons on the toolbar in the Inbox allow you to print, move, delete, reply to and forward messages.

 **TASK 3**

1 **Open a message in your Inbox by double-clicking on it. Look at the buttons that are available on the toolbar once you have opened the message window.**

2 **Read a message in your Inbox by using the Preview Pane (on the View menu). Notice the buttons that are available for working with the message without having to open it into a separate window.**

Moving messages

Once you have read a message, you can move it into a different folder by clicking on the **Move to Folder** button on the Standard toolbar.

Choose from the list the folder into which you wish to move the message or click on **Move to Folder ...**
The Move Item to dialog box opens.

Select the folder that you wish to move the message into and click on **OK**. (To create a new folder, click on **New ...** Type a name for the new folder and click on **OK**.)

You can also move or copy a message by selecting it in the Inbox. Click on the message in the Inbox that you wish to move or copy and choose **Move to Folder** or **Copy to Folder** from the **Edit** menu.

The Move/Copy Items dialog box opens. Select the folder that you wish to move or copy the message into and click on **OK**.

Alternatively, to move messages from your Inbox into different folders you can simply drag the message to a different folder. Point to the message with the mouse, click and hold the left mouse button and drag the message to the folder in the Folder List into which you wish to move it. When you release the mouse button, the message is moved into the highlighted folder.

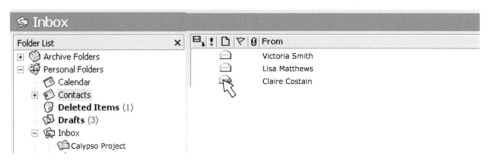

Deleting messages

Once you have read a message, you can delete it by clicking on the **Delete** button on the Standard toolbar.

Alternatively, press [Control] + [D]

The message is moved into the **Deleted Items** folder. The **Deleted Items** folder is like a 'bin' for anything you delete from any other folder in Outlook. Of course, this folder will gradually become full of items you have deleted from other folders, so you should delete the items from this folder regularly. When you delete items from the Deleted Items folder, they are permanently deleted.

Click on the **Deleted Items** icon on the **Outlook Bar** or click on the **Deleted Items** folder in the **Folder List**. Select the message(s) in the list that you wish to delete. To select adjacent messages, click on the first message that you wish to select, hold down **Shift** on the keyboard and click on the last message that you wish to select. All the messages in between are also selected. To select non-adjacent messages, click on the first message that you wish to select, hold down **Ctrl** on the keyboard and click on each message in turn that you wish to select.

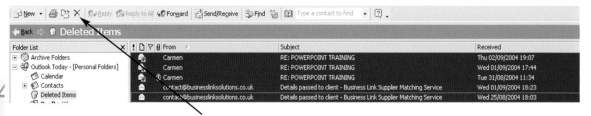

Click the **Delete** button on the Standard toolbar. The following message appears:

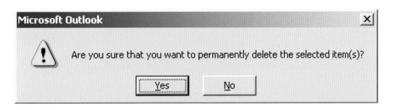

Click on **Yes** to permanently delete the selected messages from Outlook.

To move a message from another folder into the Deleted Items folder you can simply drag the message to this folder. Point to the message with the mouse, click and hold the left mouse button and drag the message to the Deleted Items folder. When you release the mouse button, the message is moved into this folder.

You can permanently delete messages from the Inbox, bypassing the Deleted Items folder. Select the message(s) that you wish to delete permanently and press [Shift] + [D].

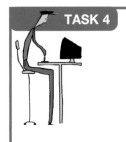

TASK 4

1 **Move some of the messages in your Inbox into the 'My ITQ' folder using the different methods described above. (If necessary, move them back to the Inbox.)**

2 **Copy a message from the Inbox into the 'My ITQ' folder.**

3 **Delete the message you have just moved into the 'My ITQ' folder.**

Finding messages

There are various ways you can quickly find messages in your different folders.

The columns in the each folder can be sorted by their column headings. For example, in the **Inbox**, you can sort the messages alphabetically by who they are **From** or the **Subject,** or in date order by the date and time **Received**. To sort a column, click on the appropriate column heading.

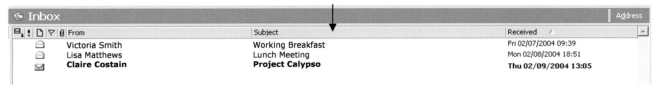

Alternatively, you can use the **Find** feature to find messages in a folder.

Click on the folder in which you wish to find a message, in the folder list.
Choose **Find** from the **Tools** menu.

Alternatively, press the **Find** button on the Standard toolbar.

You can also use [Control] + [E]

In Outlook 2002, the **Find** bar opens across the top of the folder.

| Look for: | ▾ Search In ▾ Inbox | Find Now Clear |

You can change the folder that you wish to search by clicking on the drop-down arrow by **Search In.** Choose which folders you wish to search in from the list.

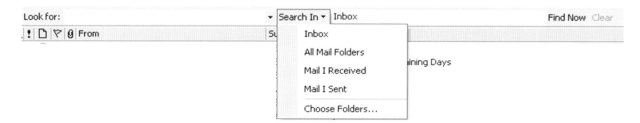

To clear the search screen and view all the messages again, click on **Clear** at the end of the Find bar.

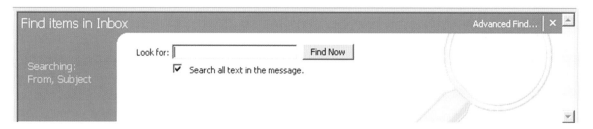

In Outlook 2000, the **Find** pane opens at the top of the folder.

Type the word you wish to find in the **Look for:** box and click on **Find Now**. (All the text in each message is searched, as well as the message header). The messages which contain your keyword are returned in a list.

To clear the search screen and view all the messages again, click on **Clear Search**.

TASK 5

1   **Practise sorting the columns in the Inbox by the different column headings – From, Subject, Received.**

2   **Use the Find feature to find messages in different folders.**

Sending mail messages

Creating a new mail message

To create a new mail message, choose **New**, **Mail Message** from the **File** menu.

Alternatively, you can press the **New Mail Message** button on the **Standard** toolbar.

You can also use ⌘Control + N

The new message window opens.

To address the message to someone, you can either type their e-mail address in the **To** box or click on the **To ...** button to open the Address Book.

To copy the message to someone, you can either type their e-mail address in the **Cc** box or click on the **Cc ...** button to open the Address Book (see below).

Click in the **Subject** box and type a subject for your message. (This will appear in the recipient's Inbox.)

Click in the message area and type your message.

Once you have read the message and are happy with it, click on the **Send** button at the left end of the toolbar to send the message.

You can also use ⎡Control⎤ + ⎡Return⎤

Using the Address Books

When you click on the **To ...** or **Cc ...** button in the new message window, the **Select Names** dialog box opens (see below).

If your organisation runs Outlook on an Exchange Server, then you will have access to the **Global Address List**. This list of addresses will have been set up by the e-mail 'administrator' (someone, probably in the IT Department, who sets up the software) and will contain a list of everyone in the organisation.

You will be able to see which address book you are looking at in the top right corner in the **Show Names from the:** box.

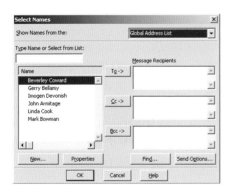

You can also store information about your own business and personal contacts in the **Contacts** folder of Outlook. (For more information on the Contacts folder, see page 124.)

If you have names and e-mail addresses stored in this folder, you can choose this as the Address Book to look in. Click on the down-arrow in the **Show Names from the:** box and choose **Contacts** from the list.

Type a name in the **Type Name** box or select a name in the list. Click on the **To** button to put the name into the **To** box on the right side of the Select Names dialog box.

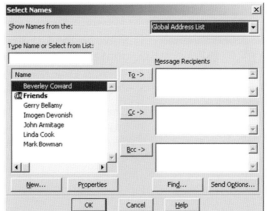

Continue typing names or picking them from the list and choosing **To** or **Cc** to put the name into the appropriate box.

When you have finished selecting names from the list, click on **OK**.

The names you have chosen will now appear in the **To** and **Cc** fields of the mail message.

| To... | Beverley Coward (bcoward@beds.co.uk); Imogen Devonish (devonish@btinternet.com) |
| Cc... | John Armitage (john.armitage@fiction.co.uk) |

TASK 6

1 Compose an e-mail to a colleague – start to type their name in the To box and see if Outlook offers you their name in a shortlist. Type a subject in the Subject box and type the body of the message. Send the message.

2 Click on the To button in a new message window to open the Select Names dialog box. Practise looking up names in the Global Address List. If you have any names stored in Contacts, show names from Contacts.

The Contacts folder

The Contacts folder in Outlook allows you to store information about the people you communicate with and come into contact with in your work.

Click on the **Contacts** icon on the Outlook Bar or click on the **Contacts** folder in the Folder List to move to this area of Outlook.

To create a new contact, choose **New**, **Contact** from the **File** menu.

| New ▾ | 🖨 | ☐ | ✗ | ▾ | 🗄 | ◌ |
| New Contact | | | Ctrl+N |

Alternatively, you can press the **New Contact** button on the **Standard** toolbar.

You can also use `Control` + `N`

The new contact window opens.

The **General** tab enables you to enter name, company, address and contact information. The white area at the bottom of the window is where you can type any other information that you might want to store about the contact.

The **Details** tab allows you to store other information about the contact, such as Department, Manager's name, nickname, etc.

Enter the information you wish to store in the appropriate boxes and then click on **Save and Close** on the toolbar.

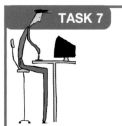

TASK 7

1 Move to the Contacts folder and create a new contact file for people that you communicate with outside your own organisation. Fill in information on the General tab and the Details tab.

2 Change the current view of the Contacts folder (on the View menu) to Address Cards, Detailed Address Cards, Phone List, etc.

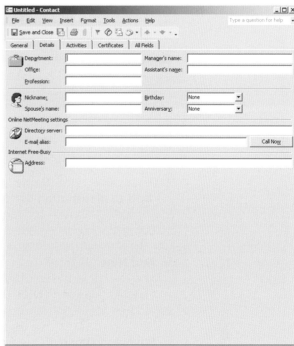

 ## Distribution lists

If you have a Global Address List, you may already have some distribution lists set up in the Address Book. A distribution list is a collection of e-mail addresses. It provides an easy way to send messages to a group of people. For example, the Marketing Team distribution list will contain the names (and e-mail addresses) of all members of the marketing team. A message sent to this distribution list will go to all the people in the list. A distribution list is identified by an icon displaying two heads.

You cannot amend the distribution lists set up in the **Global Address List** but you can create your own. These are stored in your **Contacts** folder. These distribution lists are only available to you, but you can share them by copying them and sending them to others.

Creating a distribution list

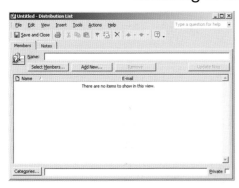

Click on the **Contacts** icon on the **Outlook Bar** or click on the **Contacts** folder in the **Folder List** to move to this area of Outlook.

Choose **New Distribution List** from the **Actions** menu.
  The Distribution List window opens.

Type a name for the Distribution List in the **Name** box. (For example, if the distribution list is to contain the e-mail addresses of the Marketing team, you might call it 'Marketing Team'.)
  To select members from your address books, click on **Select Members . . .**

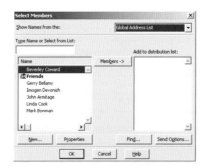

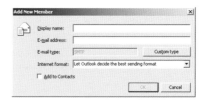

Select a name in the **Name** list and click on the **Members** button to put them in the **Add to distribution list** on the right side. Repeat for each person you want to add to the distribution list. (You can pick names from all your address books.) Click on **OK** once you have added all the names.

To type in names and e-mail addresses that are not in your address books, click on **Add New ...**

Type the name that you wish to be displayed for that person and type their e-mail address. Click on **OK**. Repeat these steps for each new person you wish to add to the distribution list.

When you have added all the names that you require in the Distribution List, click on **Save and Close** on the toolbar.

Sending messages to a distribution list

Move to the **Inbox** folder and click on the **New Message** button.

Click on the **To ...** button to open the **Select Names** dialog box. Click on the drop-down arrow by the **Show Names from the:** box. Choose **Contacts** from the list.

You will recognise a Distribution List by the 'heads' icon to the left of the Name in the list. (The example below shows a distribution list called Friends). Select the distribution list you wish to use and click on **To** (or **Cc** if you want to send a copy of the mail to the distribution list). Click on **OK.**

The name of the distribution list will appear in the **To** (or **Cc**) box of the new mail message window.

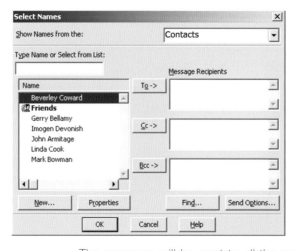

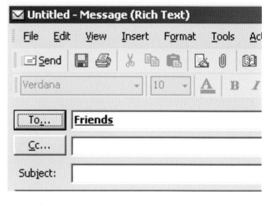

The message will be sent to all the members of this distribution list.

Managing distribution lists

If you need to add, delete or change the names in the distribution list or you just want to see who is in a distribution list, move to your **Contacts** folder. Locate the distribution list entry in the Contacts folder and double-click on it.

The distribution list opens and shows the people in the list. You can add names to the list by clicking on **Select Members ...** or **Add New ...** or you can remove names from the list by selecting them and clicking on **Remove.** If you wish to amend an entry, double-click on the entry.

Make the required changes and click on **OK**.

TASK 8

1 **Create a distribution list of a group of people (remember you can create distribution lists that contain names from both the Global Address List and your own Contacts). Give the distribution list an appropriate name.**

2 **Test the distribution list by sending an e-mail to it. Explain to the recipients that you are simply testing your distribution list and ask them to let you know if they received your e-mail.**

Attachments

An 'attachment' is a file that has been sent with an e-mail message. Not only can you read the message, but you can open the attachment and view the contents of the file.

Receiving an attachment

If you receive a message that contains an attachment, a paper clip icon will appear in the Inbox next to the message.

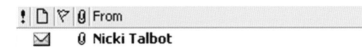

When you double-click on the message to read it, the attachment will either appear in the header area of the message or as an icon in the message area, depending what mail format is being used. (For information on different mail formats, please see page 138.)

Double-click on the icon to open the attachment and view it. The attachment is temporarily saved in an Outlook folder. If you decide to keep the attachment, you must save it to another folder on your system. For more information on saving attachments and then removing them from the message, please see page below.

Opening an attachment

When an attachment is received by your computer, it attempts to make a 'file association'. If it recognises the application that the attachment was created in (i.e. you also have this application on your computer), it will assign the appropriate icon to the attachment. For example, if a Word attachment is received and you have Word on your computer, it will recognise the attachment and make the file association to Word. The attachment will have the Word icon and when you double-click on the icon, Word will launch and the document will be opened.

You can only open attachments that were created in an application that you have on your computer. If you receive an attachment that was created in an application that your computer does not recognise, it is unable to make a file association. When you double-click on the attachment, the **Open With ...** dialog box will open. You must select the application in which you wish to open the attachment.

In the example (left), an attachment – flyer 25 June 04.pub – has been sent with a message. The attachment was created in an application called Microsoft Publisher which is not installed on the receiving computer. The receiving computer does not therefore recognise the file and the user is asked to choose which application should open the attachment.

It is quite likely, however, if your computer does not have the required application, that you will not be able to open the attachment to view it in a readable format.

Saving an attachment

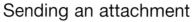
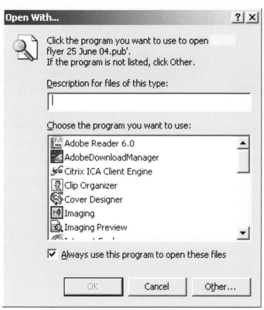

If you decide you wish to store the attachment on your own computer, you can save it. Right-click on the attachment and choose **Save As** from the shortcut menu.

The Save Attachment dialog box opens.

Navigate to the folder into which you wish to save the attachment, change the name of the attachment, if required, and click on **Save**.

Once you have saved the attachment to your own system, it is good practice to remove the attachment from the message. (If you do not, you are storing the message twice, taking up more room on your system).

To remove the attachment from the message, right-click on the attachment icon and choose **Remove** from the shortcut menu. (Alternatively, select the attachment icon and press Delete on the keyboard.)

Sending an attachment

Create the mail message as normal, completing the **To** and **Cc** boxes and the **Subject** box. Type the message in the message area.

Choose **File** from the **Insert** menu.

Alternatively, you can press the **Insert File** button on the **Standard** toolbar.

Insert File

The Insert File dialog box opens, as shown below.

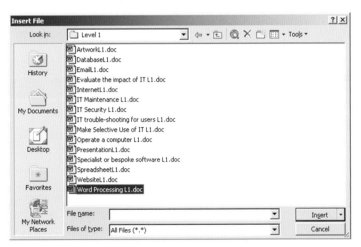

Navigate to the file that you wish to attach to the e-mail message. Select it and click on **Insert**.

The attachment will either appear in a separate line in the message header area or as an icon in the main part of the message, depending on what mail format you are using. (For information on different mail formats, please see page 139.)

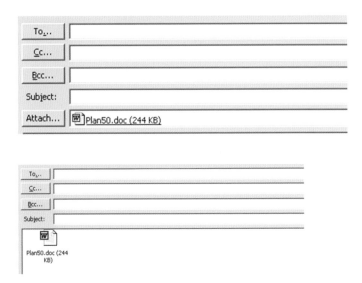

TASK 9

1 Create a new message and address it to yourself. Attach a Word file that you have stored on your computer. Send the message.

2 When you receive the message, open it and double-click on the attachment to view it. Save the attachment to your ITQ folder on your computer. Remove the attachment from the message. Delete the message.

Compressing attachments

In some organisations, a limit is set on the size of attachments you can send with an e-mail message. For example, anything over 1 MB is considered quite a large attachment.

In order to establish the size of a file, right-click on the file in **My Computer**, **Windows Explorer** or in the **Open** or **Save** dialog box in the application and choose **Properties** from the shortcut menu.

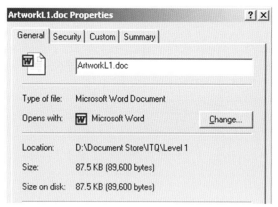

In order to send a large attachment with an e-mail (for example, an Access database file), you may need to compress the file before sending it. Compression software uses specific code and algorithms to reduce the size of the file.

A popular compression application is **WinZip®**. This is a small application that enables you to compress files before sending them over the Internet. Windows® XP includes a zipping utility. As long as the recipient of your message also has compression software installed on their computer, they can decompress the files in order to view them. (Files that are compressed using WinZip® are referred to as 'zipped' files.)

Compressing a file using WinZip®

Use **My Computer** or **Windows Explorer** to locate the file that you wish to compress.

Right-click on the file and choose **WinZip** from the shortcut menu. In this example a file called Plan50.doc has been selected.

Click on **Add to Zip file** in the sub-menu. The Add dialog box opens.

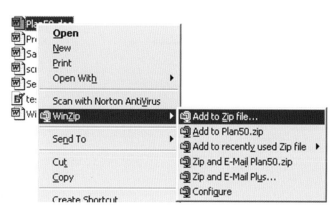

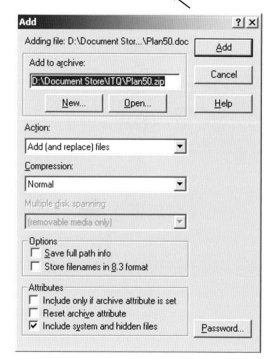

The **Add to archive** box shows the full pathname of the selected file and the name that will be given to the compressed version. (In this example, the pathname of the file is D:\Document Store\ITQ\ and the filename that will be created is Plan50.zip).

Click on **Add**.

A 'zipped' version of the file is created and stored in the same folder as the original, uncompressed, file.

To send the compressed file as an attachment, follow the instructions for attaching a file and insert the file with the .zip file extension.

Using the Windows® XP zip facility

Windows® XP has a utility which enables you to create compressed (or zipped) folders. Files that you move into a compressed folder are automatically compressed (zipped). Files zipped by using the Windows® XP zip facility can be opened by other compression software, such as WinZip®.

To create a compressed folder, navigate to the drive and folder in which you wish to create the compressed folder and select this folder. Choose **New** from the **File** menu and choose **Compressed (zipped) Folder**.

Type a name for the folder and press **Enter**. A compressed folder has a zipper on the folder icon.

To compress files, simply drag them into the compressed folder.

To extract files from a compressed folder (in order to decompress them), you can simply drag them out of the compressed folder to another location.

Alternatively, if you wish to extract all the files from a compressed folder, right-click on the compressed folder and choose **Extract All** . . . from the shortcut menu. The Extract Wizard is launched.

Specify the folder to which you wish to extract the files. (You can type the path to the folder or click on **Browse** . . . to navigate to the folder.) Click on **Next** and the files will be extracted.

Once you have put files into a compressed folder, you can attach that folder to an e-mail you are sending. The files can be decompressed using Windows® XP or another compression program, such as WinZip®.

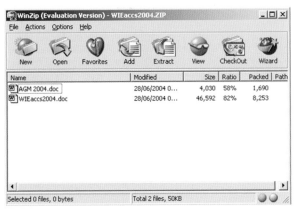

Decompressing attachments

If you receive a zipped file and you have compression software on your computer, when you double-click on the attachment, the software will be launched. This section discusses decompression using WinZip®.

The files that are contained within the zipped file will be listed. You can double-click on each file in turn to open and view it. If you wish to store the file on your own system, you need to **Extract** it from the zip. You can extract individual files or all the files. To extract an individual file, select the file in the list and click on the **Extract** button. (Notice that **Selected files** is chosen in the **Files** section of the Extract dialog box.)

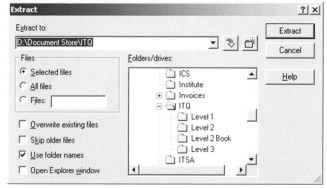

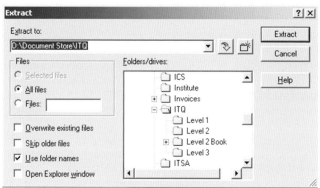

Choose the location (folder) that you wish to extract the file to and click on **Extract**. Repeat this process for each file that you wish to extract from the zip file.

Alternatively, to extract all the files, do not select an individual file but click on **Extract.** (Notice that **All files** is chosen in the **Files** section of the Extract dialog box.)

Choose the location (folder) that you wish to extract the files to and click on **Extract**.

If you do not have the application called WinZip®, you can purchase it on the Internet. (You can also download a free evaluation copy.) The web address for this application is www.winzip.co.uk.

There are other decompression applications available, such as SnapZip, SecureZip and 7-Zip. However, WinZip® is by far the most popular. They all work in a similar way – you compress files prior to sending and decompress them on arrival.

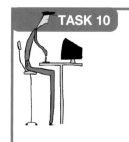

TASK 10

1 **Locate a large file on your computer and zip it using your compression software. Create a new message to yourself and attach this zipped file. Send the message.**

2 **When you receive the message, double-click the attachment and extract the zipped file to your ITQ folder on your computer.**

Using other mail tools

Setting the importance of a message

You can flag your message as being of high or low importance. In the New Mail Message window, click on the **Importance: High** or **Importance: Low** button on the Standard toolbar.

Importance: High   Importance: Low

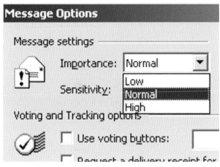

Alternatively, you can choose the message importance by clicking on the **Options** button on the Standard toolbar and choosing **Low, Normal** or **High** from the **Importance** drop-down list in the Message Options dialog box.

When the message arrives in the recipient's inbox, a red exclamation mark (high importance) or a blue arrow (low importance) will appear next to the message header, to let the recipient know that you have flagged the message.

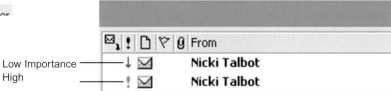

Low Importance
High

Setting other message options

In the Message Options dialog box, you can set other options for your message before you send it.

Sensitivity

If you are sending a message that is Personal, Private or Confidential, you can flag this by choosing the appropriate option from the **Sensitivity** drop-down list in the Message Options dialog box. When the message arrives in the recipient's Inbox, it will be flagged as Personal, Private or Confidential. However, this will only appear if the recipient has the Sensitivity column set up in their Inbox.

Voting buttons

If you are sending a message that simply requires a Yes or No answer, then you can use voting buttons. (These only work if you are running Outlook on an Exchange Server.)

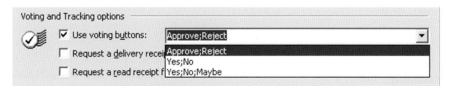

Tick the **Use voting buttons** box and choose the voting buttons you wish to use from the drop-down list (**Approve:Reject**, **Yes:No**, **Yes:No:Maybe**). When the recipients open the message to read it, they will be able to click on the appropriate button to respond to you.

Delivery receipt and read receipt

If you wish to receive a notification that your message has been delivered and/or read, you can tick these boxes in the Message Options dialog box. For the delivery receipt, a notification will be sent to you when the message has arrived in the recipient's Inbox. For the read receipt, a notification will be sent to you when the message has been read by the recipient. The notification arrives in your Inbox, like any other message. It will tell you that your message has been delivered and read and the date and time that this took place. (Rather like a registered post receipt.)

☐ Request a delivery receipt for this message

☐ Request a read receipt for this message

Spell checking messages

You can manually check the spelling of a message prior to sending it.

Choose **Spelling** from the **Tools** menu in the message area of the New Message window.

The Spelling dialog box opens.

The spelling check stops on the first word that is not in the dictionary. Choose from the following options:

- ■ **Ignore** – ignore this occurrence of the word and move on.
- ■ **Ignore All** – ignore all occurrences of this word during the check.
- ■ **Change** – change the word to the selected suggestion (first click on the word you require in the list of Suggestions).
- ■ **Change All** – change all occurrences of this word to the selected suggestion.
- ■ **Add** – add the word to the dictionary (future spell checks will not then stop on the word).

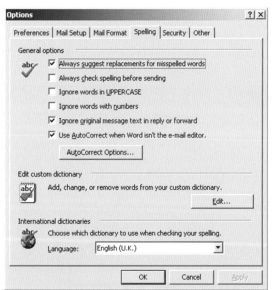

Continue clicking on the appropriate option to work through the misspelled words. You will be told when the spell check is complete.

Click on **OK.** You can now send the message.

Alternatively, you can switch on the spelling check so that it automatically runs whenever you press the **Send** button to send a message.

Choose **Options** from the **Tools** menu. Click on the **Spelling** tab.

Select the box **Always check spelling before sending**. Click on **OK**.

TASK 11

1 **Create a new message and address it to yourself. Look at the message options you have available on the toolbar and by clicking on the Options button. Set the message importance to High and use Voting Buttons. Request a read receipt for the message. Spell check the message and send it.**

2 **When you receive the message, notice the red exclamation mark next to the message in your Inbox. When you open the message to read it, you will be able to use the voting buttons. A read receipt will now be sent back to your Inbox letting you know that you have read the message!**

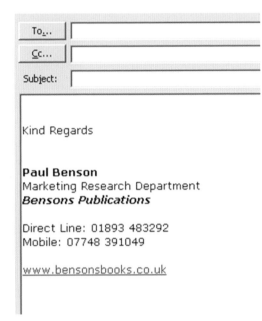

Kind Regards

Paul Benson
Marketing Research Department
Bensons Publications

Direct Line: 01893 483292
Mobile: 07748 391049

www.bensonsbooks.co.uk

Setting up a signature

You can set up a 'signature' that you can use at the end of e-mail messages you send. You can have more than one signature – for example, you might like to have a formal signature for writing to people you don't know well and an informal signature for when you write to colleagues and friends. On the left is an example of a signature at the end of a message.

To create a signature, choose **Options** from the **Tools** menu.

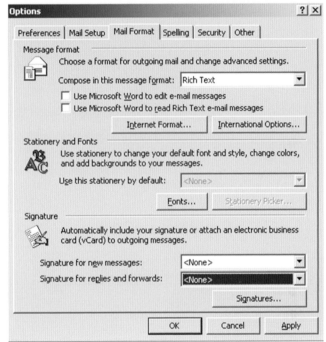

Click on the **Mail Format** tab at the top of the Options dialog box.

Click on the **Signatures ...** button at the bottom right of the dialog box to open the **Create Signature** dialog box. (In Outlook 2000, click on **Signature Picker ...**)

Click on the **New ...** button to create a new signature.

Type a name for the signature, e.g. Formal or Informal (you give the signature a name before creating it). Choose whether you want to start the signature from scratch (blank), or use an existing signature or file as the starting point.

Click on **Next**.

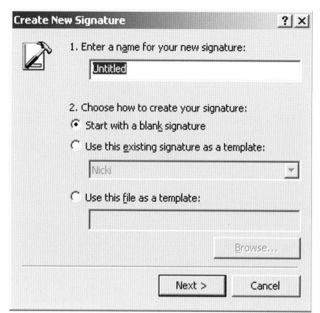

Type your signature in the box.

To change the font, style and size of the text, select it and click on the **Font** button to open the Font dialog box. To change the alignment of text or to apply bullets, select the text and click on the **Paragraph** button to open the Paragraph dialog box.

Creating a vCard

Alternatively, you can create a virtual business card (**vCard**). If you add a vCard to your signature at the end of a message, the recipient can easily open the vCard and save your information into their **Contacts** folder.

Set yourself up as a Contact in your **Contacts** folder (see page 124).

Follow the steps in the previous section to create a signature. In the vCard options section of the Create Signature dialog box, click on **New vCard from Contact**.

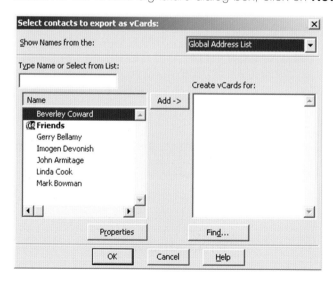

Select yourself in the **Name** list and click on **Add**. Click on **OK**.

Click on **Finish** when you have set up your signature and/or chosen your vCard.

Your new signature will now appear in the list of available signatures. When you click on the signature in the list, you will see a Preview of that signature at the bottom of the dialog box.

You can **Edit** and **Remove** existing signatures in the Create Signature dialog box. Click on **OK** to close the dialog box.

Using a signature

In the **Signature** section of the **Options** dialog box, there are two choices:

To have a signature automatically appear at the bottom of every new message you create, choose the signature you want to use from the **Signature for new messages** drop-down list in Outlook 2002 or from the **Use this Signature by default** drop-down list in Outlook 2000.

To have a signature automatically appear at the bottom of every message you reply to or forward, choose the signature you want to use from the **Signature for replies and forwards** drop-down list in Outlook 2002. In Outlook 2000 you have to use the same signature for new messages and replies, but you can choose not to have a signature when replying or forwarding by deselecting the check box.

If you do not wish to have a signature automatically appear at the end of messages, choose **None** from both drop-down lists. (You can manually insert a signature at the end of a message.)

Click on **OK**.

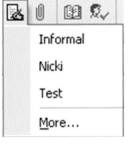

If you have chosen that a signature should automatically appear at the bottom of every new message you create, whenever you open a new mail message window, your signature will already be at the bottom of the window.

If you chose None from the list, you can insert a signature manually in a new mail message. At the position where you wish the signature to be placed, choose **Signature** from the **Insert** menu.

Alternatively, click on the **Insert Signature** button on the Standard toolbar.

Choose the Signature you wish to insert from the list.

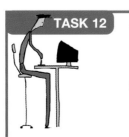

TASK 12

1 **Create two signatures for your own use – a formal signature and an informal signature. Use the informal signature for all new mail messages (default).**

2 **Open the new mail message window and see the informal signature at the bottom of the message window. Delete this signature and manually insert the formal signature.**

The Out of Office assistant

If you are going to be away from the office for a period of time, you can set up the Out of Office feature to automatically respond to messages you receive. (This feature only works if you are running Outlook on an Exchange Server).

Choose **Out of Office Assistant** from the **Tools** menu.
The Out of Office Assistant dialog box opens.

Type the text with which you wish to reply in the **AutoReply** box. Set up any other rules you may want to apply to messages received in your absence. Click on **OK**.

It is a good idea to send yourself a test message to check that the Out of Office message is returned to you.

When you are going to be away from the office, choose **Tools**, **Out of Office Assistant** and click 'I am currently Out of the Office' to activate the message.

When you return to the office, choose **Tools**, **Out of Office Assistant** and click 'I am currently In the Office' to disable the message.

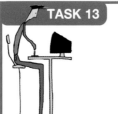

TASK 13

1 **Set up the Out of Office Assistant in Outlook. Switch the Out of Office Assistant on and send yourself a message to test that you receive the out of office message.**

2 **Switch the Out of Office Assistant off.**

 ## Formatting e-mails

There are three formats in which you can create messages when using Outlook: **Plain Text**, **Rich Text** and **HTML** (HyperText Markup Language).

Plain text format is a format that all e-mail programs understand. However, plain text format does not support the use of bold, italic, coloured fonts and other text formatting. It also doesn't support pictures displayed directly in the message body (although you can send pictures as attachments).

Outlook Rich Text Format (RTF) is a format that Microsoft® e-mail applications understand. RTF supports text formatting, including bullets, alignment and linking.

HTML format supports all text formatting, numbering, bullets, alignment, pictures, styles, stationery, signatures and Web pages. Most popular e-mail applications now support HTML. However, some do not and some e-mail applications remove HTML formatting. You should be aware that the recipient may not see all the formatting that you have put on the message. Also, the more formatting the message contains, the larger the message and the more bandwidth it takes up when sending and receiving.

Changing mail format

To change the format for a message you are creating or a message you have received, choose the format you require from the **Format** menu in the message window.

To change the format for all messages you send, choose **Options** from the **Tools** menu. Click on the **Mail Format** tab at the top of the dialog box.

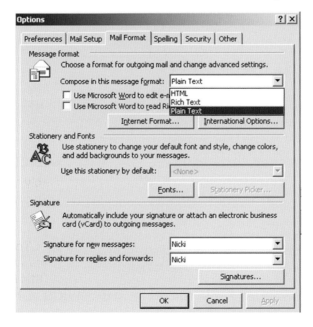

Choose the format you require from the **Compose in this message format** drop-down list. Click on **OK**.

Applying formatting to individual messages

If you are using Rich Text or HTML format, you can apply font and paragraph formatting to your message. Select the text that you wish to format by clicking and dragging over it with the mouse. To change the font, choose **Font** from the **Format** menu.

You can change the **Font**, **Font style** and **Size** of the text. You can also add **Effects** and change the **Color**. The sample box shows you how your changes will look. Click on **OK** to apply the changes to the selected text.

To format a paragraph, choose **Paragraph** from the Format menu.

You can change the **Alignment** of the text in the selected paragraph. You can also apply **Bullets** to selected text.

Click on **OK** to apply the changes to the selected text.

Alternatively, you can use the buttons on the **Formatting** toolbar to apply formatting to the text in the message body.

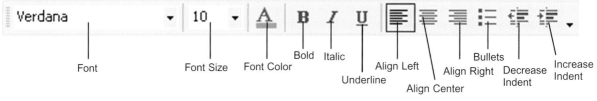

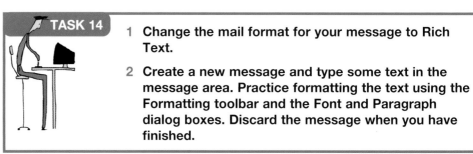

Font   Font Size   Font Color   Bold   Italic   Align Left   Align Right   Decrease   Increase
                                                                                                           Bullets   Indent
                                                        Underline   Align Right Decrease   Indent
                                                                            Align Center   Indent

TASK 14

1 **Change the mail format for your message to Rich Text.**

2 **Create a new message and type some text in the message area. Practice formatting the text using the Formatting toolbar and the Font and Paragraph dialog boxes. Discard the message when you have finished.**

Archiving messages

Everyone who uses Outlook in an organisation has a 'mailbox'. This mailbox is stored on a server with everyone else's mailbox. As you send and receive mail and store mail in different folders, the size of your mailbox grows and grows. If you then multiply this by the number of users of Outlook in the organisation, you can see that, very quickly, these mailboxes can take up a huge amount of space on the server.

In order to keep your mailbox on the server to a reasonable size (some companies specify the size you are allowed), you should archive your Outlook folders. Archiving creates another set of Outlook folders which, by default, are stored on your C: drive (although you can change this). In this way, the mailbox on the server is maintained at a workable level. You can still access your archive folders just as you access your live folders.

Archiving a folder

Select the folder that you wish to archive in the folder list.

Choose **Archive** from the **File** menu. The Archive dialog box opens.

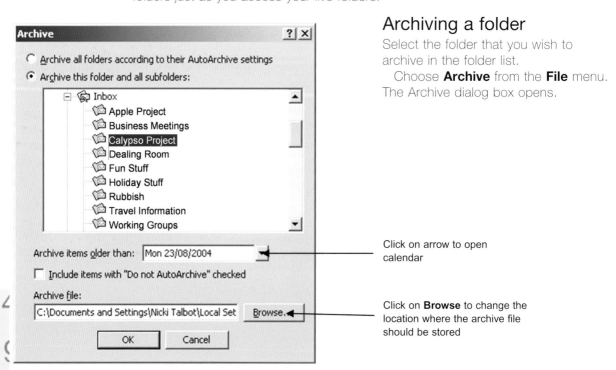

Click on arrow to open calendar

Click on **Browse** to change the location where the archive file should be stored

Choose **Archive this folder and all subfolders**. Select the date that you wish to **Archive items older than** from the drop-down calendar. Check the location of the archive file and amend if necessary.

Click on **OK**.

 Archiving

The archive process starts. A moving icon will appear in the status bar at the bottom right of the Outlook screen to show the progress of the archive.

The folder you have just archived is moved to the archive.pst file (in the location specified in the Archive dialog box). As you archive folders, the same structure is created in the archive file (for example, Inbox and its sub-folders, Deleted Items, Sent Items, etc.)

Viewing archived folders

Once you have archived a folder, an Archive Folders item appears at the top of the folder list. Click on the + beside Archive Folders to view the folder structure in the archive.

If you cannot see Archive Folders in the Folder List, choose **Open**, **Outlook Data File** from the **File** menu. (In Outlook 2000, choose **Open**, **Personal Folders File (*.pst)** from the **File** menu.)

Navigate to where the archive file has been created. Select the archive.pst file and click on **OK**.

Archive Folders will now appear in the Folder List.

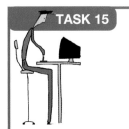

TASK 15

1 **Click on one of your folders in the Folder List and archive it. Choose an appropriate date in the Archive items older than box.**

2 **Once you have run the archive, open the archive folders list so that the folder you have just archived appears in the folder list.**

E-mail 'netiquette'

'Netiquette' is a set of rules for behaving appropriately online. Below are ten simple guidelines for ensuring you do not offend anyone when in 'cyberspace':

1 Don't forget that the person on the other end is human. It is easy when typing on a computer screen to forget that there is actually a live human being at the other end of your message. You are not able to use facial expressions, gestures and tone of voice to communicate what you really mean, so it is much easier for your meaning to be misinterpreted.

2 Be mindful of other people's time (and bandwidth). When you send an e-mail, you are taking up someone's time. Ensure that the time they spend reading

your mail is not wasted. It is easy to copy many people in on a message you are sending. Think carefully about who really needs to see the message. Everyone receives enough e-mail without receiving messages that we don't really need to get.

    Also, be aware that by sending a very large message (or attachment) you are taking up bandwidth and you may prevent others from working efficiently while the server is trying to deal with your large file. Before sending a large file to others via e-mail, think carefully about whether you really need to send it.

3 In a 'virtual' world you cannot be judged on how you look. However, you can be judged on the quality of your writing. Presentation and spelling do count, even in e-mail messages – they give the recipient an impression of you. Ensure that you know what you are talking about and pay attention to the content of your writing.

4 Don't start a 'flame' war. 'Flaming' is when you express a strong emotional opinion in order to get people to respond in an equally emotional way. By sending this kind of e-mail, you can unleash a barrage of angry, emotional e-mails which serve no constructive purpose and take up bandwidth.

5 Be forgiving when 'newbies' make mistakes. Everyone was new to cyberspace once and it is up to you to help people who perhaps don't know the netiquette.

6 DO NOT TYPE IN CAPITALS. This is the equivalent of shouting. It is also more difficult to read text that is typed in capitals.

7 Do not leave the Subject field blank when sending an e-mail. For efficiency, the Subject field should always contain a concise description of the content of the e-mail.

8 Avoid heavy formatting in e-mail messages. Many people still work with plain text messages and receiving a heavily formatted message means they have to convert it to plain text before being able to respond. Also, for someone on a dial-up connection, it will take a lot longer to download a message that contains lots of formatting and graphics. (Apart from anything else, it will take you longer to create the message in the first place!)

9 When sending a message to a group of people, it is courteous to put the e-mail addresses in the Bcc field. In this way, the recipients of the e-mail do not see who else you sent the e-mail to. By putting all the addresses in the To field, you allow everyone to see the e-mail addresses of everyone else – some people may not be happy about you doing this without their permission.

10 Do not use Return Receipt for every e-mail you send. This is annoying and intrusive to the recipient, especially if they are asked if they wish to confirm receipt on every e-mail you send to them! Use Return Receipt only when it is critical for you to know that the e-mail has been opened.

Exchanging information via the Internet

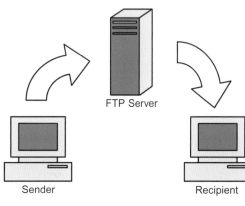

FTP Server

Sender

Recipient

The Internet uses two protocols to exchange information: File Transfer Protocol (FTP) and HyperText Transfer Protocol (HTTP).

    FTP is the simplest way to exchange files between computers on the Internet. FTP is usually used to transfer Web page files from their creator to the computer on which the website resides. It is also used to download programs and other files from the Internet to an individual's computer.

    FTP can be accessed using the Run command within Windows®, or you can use a specific FTP program. Your browser uses FTP whenever you request to download something from a Web page.

Information on transferring files using FTP can be found in Unit 206 – The Internet and intranets.

HTTP is a set of rules for transferring files (including text, graphics, images, sound, video and other multimedia files) on the Web.

Not only does HTTP transfer the original file but it will also transfer files that are referenced by the original file. (For example, if there are links to image files in the original file, these will also be transferred.)

Every time you type in a web address or click on a hyperlink on a Web page, your computer puts in an HTTP request to the host server of that website. The server receives the request and sends back the requested page.

Differences between FTP and HTTP

FTP is a protocol used to upload files from an individual computer (i.e. one on which a Web page has been designed) to a server on the Internet (a computer that hosts the file and enables others to view it) and to download files from a server on the Internet to an individual computer.

HTTP is a protocol used to transfer files from a server computer to a browser (e.g. Internet Explorer) on an individual's computer, in order that the user can view a Web page. Unlike FTP where entire files are written to a place on disk specified by the user, HTTP only transfers the contents of a Web page into a browser for viewing.

FTP is a two-way system as files can be uploaded and downloaded. HTTP is a one-way system as files are only transferred from the server to the computer's browser.

 # Using a Web-based e-mail system

There are a number of different Web-based e-mail services available (most of which are free). Two of the most popular are Hotmail® and Yahoo®. Web-based mail differs from client/server mail in that you do not have the e-mail application installed on your computer. Instead, you log into a website using a personal log-in and this gives you access to your Inbox. Web-based e-mail services offer basic e-mail features, such as sending and receiving e-mails, attaching files to e-mails and being able to organise your mail using folders.

Web-based e-mail accounts are useful if you wish to be able to retrieve your e-mails from any computer. As long as the computer has Internet access, you will be able to go to the website, sign in and use your Inbox in the normal way.

The disadvantage of a Web-based e-mail account is that you have to be online while you are reading and writing e-mails. With a client/server e-mail application installed on your own computer, you can receive e-mails and then disconnect (if appropriate) while reading and writing replies. You can then reconnect to send. You will also find that a dedicated e-mail application (such as Outlook) has a lot of features to assist you in dealing with e-mail. Web-based e-mail systems tend to be more basic and simply allow you to send and receive messages.

It is unlikely that you would need a Web-based e-mail system at work. You will probably have an e-mail application, such as Outlook, installed on your computer, which you will use. However, Web-based e-mail accounts are useful if you wish to send and receive personal e-mail.

Setting up a Web-based e-mail account

The guidelines below are for creating a Hotmail® account. However, the process is similar whichever Web-based e-mail system you choose to use.

Launch your Web browser and type **www.hotmail.com** in the address bar. This will take you to the Hotmail® home page. You can click on the **New Account Sign-Up** link to set up an e-mail account.

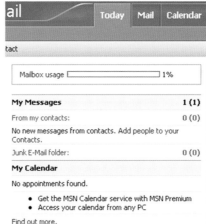

You will be asked to complete a form with some personal details. You also need to choose the name you require for your Hotmail® account and a password for logging in.

Using a Web-based e-mail account

Once you have set-up your e-mail account, you will be able to log-in whenever you want to check for received e-mails and to send e-mails.

Launch your Web browser and go to **www.hotmail.com**.

At the log-in screen, type your Hotmail® **e-mail address** and your **Password**. Click on **Sign In**.

Once you are signed in, you will be taken to the Today screen. This gives you an overview of the contents of your mailbox: if any messages are from your stored contacts and whether you have any messages in your Junk E-Mail folder.

It will also show you what is on your calendar (if you have signed up for this facility).

To move to your mailbox, click on the **Mail** tab at the top of the screen.

Down the left side of the mailbox screen is a list of your folders – **Inbox, Junk E-Mail, Sent Messages, Drafts** and **Trash Can**.

The toolbar across the top of the mailbox contains buttons for working with your mail messages.

- ■ **New** – create a new e-mail message. (By clicking on the down-arrow, you can choose to create new contacts, folders, etc.)
- ■ **Delete** – delete the selected messages. (Put a tick in the box to the left of the message header to select a message.)
- ■ **Block** – block messages from the selected senders. (Select the messages in the mailbox first.)
- ■ **Junk** – move the selected message into the Junk E-Mail folder.
- ■ **Find** – find messages stored in your folders.
- ■ **Put in Folder** – move the selected messages to the folder you choose from the drop-down list.
- ■ **Mark As Unread** – mark a message that has been read as unread again.

Managing folders

To work with your folders, click on the **Manage Folders** link on the left side of the Mailbox screen.

You will be shown a list of the folders and how much space they are taking up.

To create a new folder, click on the **New** button on the toolbar. You can also rename a folder by selecting it in the list and clicking on **Rename**. You can delete a folder by selecting it in the list and clicking on **Delete**.

Creating and managing contacts

Just like in Outlook, you can store the names and e-mail addresses of people you communicate with frequently. Click on the **Contacts** tab at the top of the Hotmail screen.

- ■ **New** – create a new contact.
- ■ **Edit** – edit an existing contact. (Select the contact in the list first.)
- ■ **Delete** – delete a contact. (Select the contact in the list first.)
- ■ **Put in Group** – put a selected contact into a group. You can send messages to groups of contacts (rather like distribution lists in Outlook).
- ■ **Send Mail** – send mail to a selected contact.
- ■ **Synchronize** – synchronise your Hotmail® contacts with contacts stored in other e-mail applications.
- ■ **Card View** – view your contacts as business cards
- ■ **Print View** – open a window that enables you to print your contacts.
- ■ **List View** – the default view for Contacts is in a list.

Composing a new message

Click on the **New** button in the mailbox.

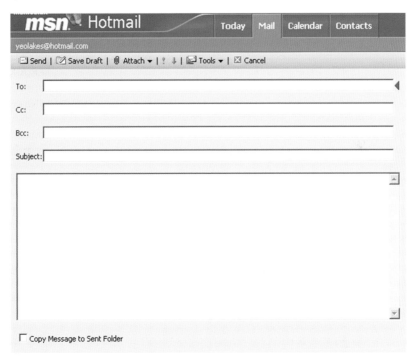

The New message window in Hotmail is similar to that in Outlook. There are **To, Cc** and **Bcc** boxes. (Bcc stands for 'Blind Carbon Copy'. The recipients in the **To** and **Cc** boxes are not aware you have sent the message to the recipients in the **Bcc** box.) Type the subject of the message in the **Subject** box and type the message in the main white area on the screen. If you wish to keep a copy of the message you are sending in the Sent Folder, you must check the box at the bottom of the message window: **Copy Message to Sent Folder**. (This differs from Outlook where messages you send are automatically stored in the Sent Items folder.)

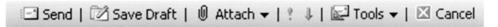

- **Send** – send the message you have just created.
- **Save Draft** – save the message you have just created in your Drafts folder. You can open the message from the Drafts folder later, to edit, send or delete.
- **Attach** – attach a file or Contact information to the message you are creating.
- **High Importance** – set the importance of the message to High.
- **Low Importance** – set the importance of the message to Low.
- **Tools** – use the Dictionary or Thesaurus.
- **Cancel** – close the window and discard the message.

Sending attachments

When you press the **Attach** button in the new message window, you will be prompted to **Browse** for the file you wish to attach. This is exactly the same as when you attach a file using Outlook.

 ## Using the ITQ electronic portfolio facility

An electronic portfolio facility is an Internet-based service which is being used by some ITQ centres to enable learners to upload their evidence and assessors to view that evidence. The learner can log into the electronic portfolio at any time to view it and to upload evidence. The assessor can log into the electronic portfolio at any time to view the evidence.

It also enables employers, who may be acting as 'witnesses' to create witness statements easily. They can also log into the portfolio and do this.

The electronic portfolio records all user activity and can store documents, scans, pictures, audio and video files. The assessor is able to monitor the progress and activities of the learner. The pieces of evidence can be viewed online by the assessor and the learner can be e-mailed straight away with feedback. The learner and assessor can see easily how much of the qualification has been achieved and what is needed for completion.

N.B. If you are using an electronic portfolio facility to provide your documentation to your ITQ provider, this can be used as evidence of exchanging information electronically. Take screenshots and print-outs to show your use of this facility.

 ## Risks associated with e-mail

Using the Internet to send and receive information brings with it some risks. By connecting to other computers (whatever method you use) you are exposing yourself to the risk of information being received by your computer that you do not want.

However, by being aware of the risks, you can take some simple steps to minimise them. In an office environment, your IT team will ensure that your PC is protected from risk and this is not an area that you would normally be responsible for. However, in the home environment, it is up to you to ensure that you have protected your PC from any potential risks.

Viruses

A virus is a computer program (a piece of code) that is loaded onto your computer without your knowledge. It usually causes some unexpected and undesirable event, such as lost or damaged files. Viruses can replicate themselves and spread to other computers. They can be transmitted by downloading programs from a website or by using an external device (such as a floppy disk) that is infected.

A popular method of transmitting viruses is by sending them as an attachment to an e-mail. If you receive an e-mail message from someone you do not recognise and you are prompted to open an attachment, do not do so until you have authenticated the sender and know that the attachment is genuine.

Viruses are a fact of life in a world where computers are connected together. If your computer is connected to other computers via a company network, or on the Internet, you should have an up-to-date virus protection program installed. Norton and McAfee® are large suppliers of anti-virus software. Of course, new viruses are being written all the time, so not only do you need to purchase an anti-virus software program, but you need to keep it up-to-date. When your install Norton or McAfee® anti-virus software, you register the product online and then you will receive automatic updates whenever you connect to the Internet.

For more information on virus protection, see Unit 205 – IT security for users.

Spam or chain e-mails

The Internet definition of spam is 'unsolicited junk e-mail sent to large numbers of people to promote products or services'.

Increasingly, some companies are using e-mail as a direct marketing tool. Legislation has recently been passed in the UK to control the amount of junk or spam mail that is received. However, as the Internet is international, it is extremely hard to police this kind of legislation, so you will still receive spam mail. There are steps you can take to reduce the amount of junk e-mail that you receive.

Organisations that sell lists of e-mail addresses use programs that scan Web pages and 'harvest' e-mail addresses. If you do need to use an e-mail address on a web page, alter it slightly. For example, if your e-mail address is pat@smithsons.co.uk, change it to patNOJUNKMAIL@smithsons.co.uk. Anyone who is going to use your e-mail from the website would know to remove the NOJUNKMAIL part, but a computer program would not.

Avoid giving out your main e-mail address. Only give this out to trusted business associates, friends, family, etc. If you want to enter your information onto websites, i.e. to receive brochures, information, etc., set up a second e-mail account (such as a Hotmail account). If you need to sign-up for information on the Internet, for your work, your IT department could set up a second e-mail account in your Outlook. You can set up a rule so that all messages addressed to that e-mail address are moved into a special folder.

Outlook has features that enable you to control the junk mail that you receive. It will search for commonly used phrases in e-mail messages and automatically move messages containing these phrases from your Inbox into a special junk e-mail folder, your Deleted Items folder, or any other folder you specify. (The list of terms that Outlook uses to filter suspected junk e-mail is in a file called filters.txt which is located in C:\Program Files\Microsoft Office\Office10\1033\filters.txt.)

You can also filter messages with a list of senders of junk e-mail. As you receive unwanted e-mail messages, you can create a list of the e-mail addresses of these senders and block mail from them.

Sometimes you will receive a mail that tells you to reply to the sender with REMOVE in the subject line, if you wish to be removed from their mailing list. In some cases, the sender uses this as a method of checking that the e-mail did get to a working e-mail address. By replying, you have confirmed that the e-mail did reach someone. It is a good idea not to reply to these messages.

Automatically move junk mail from your Inbox in Outlook

Choose **Organize** from the **Tools** menu.
Alternatively, click the **Organize** button on the Standard toolbar.

Organize

Click on **Junk E-Mail**.

Click on the drop-down list and choose to **Automatically move Junk messages to Junk E-Mail**. Click on **Turn on** to enable the feature.

Click on the drop-down list and choose to **Automatically move Adult Content messages to Junk E-Mail**. Click on **Turn on** to enable the feature.

A Junk E-Mail folder will now be created in your folder list and any messages that are deemed by Outlook to be junk or have adult content, will automatically be moved into this folder. For more information on the rules that Outlook uses to define junk and adult content, click on the link under the boxes in the Organize pane.

Add senders to your junk e-mail list

Point to a message in your **Inbox** and click with the right mouse button.
Choose **Junk-E-mail** from the shortcut menu and then click on **Add to Junk Senders list**.

Chain e-mail

Chain e-mail is the electronic version of chain letters. They are messages which advocate their own reproduction, e.g. 'Please forward this message to 10 other people'. For people who are vulnerable to psychological manipulation, chain letters can exude an aura of mystical power. Their preposterous claims play on the irrational wishes or fears of recipients. There is always a promise of rewards for complying: good luck, money or a clear conscience. On the flip side, threats of calamity are usually thrown in for good measure.

E-mail messages which can be forwarded to multiple recipients with the click of a mouse button have made it extremely easy to circulate 'chain'-type messages. These chain e-mails always ask you to forward them to a number of people.

In order to stop the propagation of these messages, you should not forward any chain messages you receive. Simply delete them.

Other issues

In a business environment, it is quite likely that each user of the e-mail system will have a limit to the amount they can keep stored in their e-mail account at any one time. Each e-mail message takes up space on a server and if everyone kept everything they received, the server would soon fill up. As well as doing housekeeping and archiving regularly to remove e-mails from the server (see page 140), in Outlook 2002 you can also control the size of e-mails that you will allow to be downloaded into your Inbox. You can specify that very large e-mails are not put into your Inbox.

Choose **Send/Receive Settings** from the **Tools** menu and click on **Define Send/Receive Groups**.

Alternatively, press ⌨Control+⌨Alt+⌨S

The Send/Receive Groups dialog box opens.

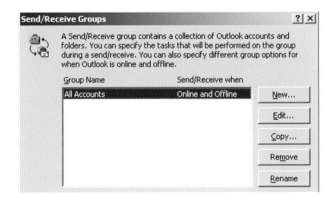

Click on **Edit ...**

Click on the Folder in the list that you wish to specify limits for.

Click on **Limit Message Size** and under **Message size limit**, check the **Don't download messages larger than** box and specify a size in the box. Whilst the size of messages that an e-mail server can deal with efficiently will vary from business to business, a general rule of thumb is that more than 1 MB (including attachments) is a large message. If you specify a message size limit and you are sent a message that exceeds this limit, Outlook bounces the message back to the sender explaining that it is too large. The sender would need to reduce the size of the message (for example, by removing attachments) or ask you to increase the size of messages that you will accept.

Click on **OK**.

 # Legal matters

For information on legal matters relating to general Internet use, please see Unit 205 – IT security for users and Unit 206 – The Internet and intranets.

The law and e-mail

UK law still applies when working on the Internet. However, because the Internet is international and you are simply a click away from another country, it is sometimes hard to police these laws – what is against the law in one country might be allowed in another. However, you should always abide by UK law when using the Internet.

The same basic rules which apply to business letters also apply to e-mails:

- You should have a standard footer (signature) stating your company name and other details. This should include your registered office address, a contact e-mail address, registered number and country of registration. This would normally be set up by your IT Department.
- You may want to include a standard disclaimer in all your e-mail messages. This might state that the e-mail is confidential and intended for the use of the

recipient only, that anyone receiving the e-mail in error should not use or disclose its contents and that the e-mail does not form part of a contract and is not legally binding. Again, this would normally be set up by your IT Department.

■ The content of an e-mail is covered by the same laws as the content of a letter. Do not send or forward e-mails that would be illegal, offensive or discriminatory if sent as ordinary documents.

Commercial e-mails are covered by a range of regulations:

■ You must clearly show the purpose of the e-mail and who it is coming from.
■ You must provide a valid address which recipients can use to opt out of receiving further e-mails from you.
■ You cannot send marketing e-mails to consumers without their prior consent – unless their e-mail address was collected in the course of a previous sale or sale negotiation.
■ Any promotional offers contained in your e-mails must be obvious, clear and easily accessible.

E-mails can present high risks:

■ Because e-mails seem less formal, employees may write things which they would not put in a letter.
■ E-mails are easy to distribute widely. A misguided e-mail sent round the office could be forwarded round the world in a matter of seconds.
■ E-mails (and Internet sites) are easily stored and used as evidence.
■ If an e-mail is being sent or forwarded to an international recipient, the sender should make themselves aware of the laws of that country.

Contracts and e-commerce

■ An e-mail can create a legally binding commitment.
■ The content of e-mails sent and received before a contract is concluded can form part of the contractual agreement.
■ Digital signatures can be used to authenticate messages, i.e. to verify that the message has indeed come from the sender's computer. A digital signature contains a certificate which includes a public key and a private key. The private key remains on the sender's computer and the public key is sent in the digitally signed message to the recipient. When the recipient receives the digitally signed message, they can save the certificate containing the public key to their contact list. Once this is done, when the sender sends an encrypted message (i.e. so it cannot be read by anyone else), the public key on the recipient's computer allows them to read (decrypt) the message.
■ You can obtain a digital ID from within Outlook by clicking on the **Get a digital ID** button.

Data protection

Collecting and handling personal data using e-mail falls under the Data Protection Act 1998. You must comply with the act:

■ You must not use an individual's personal data for direct marketing purposes if they request you not to do so.
■ Employers must ensure they comply with regulations on the monitoring of employees' e-mail use.

For more information on the Data Protection Act, please see Unit 205 – IT security for users.

Monitoring

A good monitoring system can help an organisation control inappropriate or illegal use of e-mail. If an organisation is going to monitor e-mails, they must inform employees that they intend to do this. It is a good idea to make this a part of the employment contract and e-mail and Internet use policies.

- You can install software which produces a log of all e-mails sent and received, together with addresses.
- Under the Regulation of Investigatory Powers Act, employers can inspect individual e-mails without an employee's consent for specific business purposes, including:
  - Recording transactions and other important business communications.
  - Making sure employees comply both with the law and with internal policies.
  - Preventing abuse of the telecoms system.
  - Checking e-mails when an employee is on leave.
- If employers wish to monitor e-mails for other purposes, they must get permission to do so (from both the sender and the receiver).

Responsibility

Employers are responsible for the actions of their employees on their e-mail system.

E-mail marketing

New legislation was introduced into the UK in December 2003 to govern the use of e-mail marketing. It is now an offence for UK companies to send marketing e-mail unless there is a pre-existing customer relationship. This legislation only applies to an individual's named e-mail address. It is still acceptable for a company to send a marketing e-mail to a business account, such as 'info@' or 'sales@'. If your company is involved in sending marketing material by e-mail, you should familiarise yourself with the new legislation. There is a useful document – New Laws for E-Mail Marketing – which can be downloaded from the Fact Sheets section of the website www.first-steps.info.

 # Suggested tasks for evidence

Below are more suggestions for the type of task you can create in the workplace which would serve as evidence for this unit.

Suggested Task 1

Your manager has asked you to log all e-mail activity for a day.

- Provide printouts of your Inbox and Sent Items folders, to show messages sent and received.
- Take screenshots to show the housekeeping you have been doing, e.g. moving messages into appropriate folders, archiving, etc.
- Show that you are using signatures and other options when sending messages.

Suggested Task 2

Your manager has asked you to send an HTML newsletter to a group of people.

- Create the newsletter using HTML format in Outlook.
- Create a distribution list with at least five names in.
- Attach a file that you have compressed to the newsletter.

Suggested Task 3

A colleague does not know how to create a signature or use the Out of Office feature in Outlook. Create a step-by-step checklist for using these features.

Suggested Task 4

Create a set of archived folders in Outlook. Use screenshots to show the folder structure prior to the archiving and the folder structure after archiving. Also create a short report on what archiving does and why it is important to archive regularly.

Suggested Task 5

Your manager is interested in purchasing compression software. Do some research on the Internet about different compression products available. Write a short report discussing the benefits and costs of each product.

Suggested Task 6

Your manager has asked you to write a checklist for responsible e-mail use, e.g, how to manage spam, chain e-mails, etc.

Suggested Task 7

Set up an Internet e-mail account. Use screenshots to show the setting up process. Create folders in the mailbox of this new account. Take screenshots to show the new folders.

Word-processing software

Overview

You are likely to be in a role which involves using a wide range of tools and techniques to produce professional looking documents (e.g. producing mail merged business letters and invoices, more complex reports and content for web pages).

The word-processing software outlined in this chapter is Microsoft® Word. Microsoft® Word is part of the Microsoft® Office suite of applications. It offers a set of comprehensive tools for producing letters, memos and reports. It also offers a large range of desktop publishing tools that enable the user to produce newsletters and other graphical material. It is used in offices to deal with and manage the large range of printed documents that need to be produced.

A competent person can use word-processing software effectively to produce professional looking documents that communicate clearly and accurately.

Required skills and techniques for Level 2

Handling files	Using appropriate techniques to handle, organise and save files.
Combining information	Linking information within the same type of software. Adding information from one type of software to information produced using different software.
Editing	Using a wide range of editing techniques appropriately: ■ size and sort ■ inserting special characters and symbols ■ mail merge.
Formatting text	Formatting documents using a wide range of tools and techniques: ■ tabs ■ columns – adding columns to a whole document or part of a page ■ styles – applying an existing style to a word, line or paragraph ■ pages – headers and footers, inserting page breaks ■ files – change format to RTF or HTML. Formatting in line with an organisational house style.
Laying out	Using appropriate tools and techniques for creating, editing and formatting tables: ■ insert tables ■ create, add and delete columns ■ modify column width and row height ■ add borders and shading. Selecting, changing and using appropriate templates.
Checking text	Using appropriate proofreading techniques. Checking line, paragraph and page breaks. Checking headings, subheadings and other formatting are used appropriately.
Improving efficiency	Setting up shortcuts.

Requirements of this unit

You will need to produce at least *two* comprehensive and different pieces of work, demonstrating skills, techniques and knowledge outlined in this chapter. The two pieces of work must demonstrate as many different Word features as possible. It is a good idea to use headers and footers in all documents provided as evidence and include the date in the header/footer. (Evidence must not be more than six months old.)

This unit asks you to demonstrate that you are capable of using a word processor to produce a professional looking document, which communicates some given information in the most appropriate way. If your organisation uses standard templates, you will be expected to select the most appropriate template to use.

In your workplace, you would normally be given some sort of handwritten notes or draft narrative, along with an idea of the document's purpose and a list of the recipients. If your organisation uses mail merge, then it would be appropriate to include that as part of one of the tasks.

 ## Tasks in this unit

The tasks that appear throughout the unit are designed to take you step-by-step through the feature being discussed. It is recommended that you use the tasks completed as evidence in addition to the two main pieces that are required by the unit.

The exercises at the end of the unit are suggested ways in which you can provide the main evidence for this unit.

 ## What will I achieve?

By accomplishing a Level 2 in this unit, you will also have achieved Level 1 in most cases and Level 3 in some cases. Below is a table to show what levels you will have achieved.

Required skill	Level 1	Level 2	Level 3
Handling files	●————	———●	●
Combining information	●————	———●	
Editing text		●	
Formatting text	●————	———●	
Laying out	●————	———●	
Checking text	●————	———●————	———●
Improving efficiency	N/A	●	

 ## Launching Word

Word can be launched by **double-clicking** on the **Word shortcut** on the desktop (if there is one).

Alternatively, click on **Start**, **Programs** and then choose **Microsoft Word** from the menu. (If you have Windows® XP, it is **Start, All Programs, Microsoft Word**.)

Creating a new document

When you first launch Word a new blank document appears on the screen. This document is based on the Normal template which is for a blank A4 piece of paper with margins set and using a default font. To begin working, simply start typing.

If you want to create a new document (based on the Normal template) at any time, click the **New Document** button on the Standard toolbar.

Alternatively, press [Control]+[N].

New

TASK 1

Type the following passage of text on the blank page:

You will find Word an extremely exciting package, allowing you to produce documents from simple letters to complex newsletters with columns, tables and graphics.

There are many desktop publishing features in Word which allow you to create drawings, organisation charts and graphs.

Creating standard text is easy using Styles and Autoformat and creating standard documents is made easy by using Templates.

Saving a document

If you wish to keep the document, so that you can use it again, you will need to save it. The first time you save a document, you will be prompted to give the document (file) a name and to choose which folder you wish to save it into.

Click on the **File** menu and choose **Save**.

Save

Alternatively, click on the **Save** button on the Standard toolbar.

You can also use [Control]+[S]

The **Save As** dialog box will open.

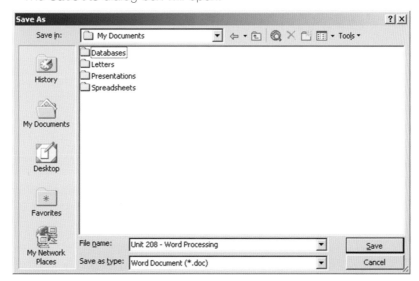

You have to do two things in this dialog box: decide where you want to store the document (in a folder) and what you want to call the document (file).

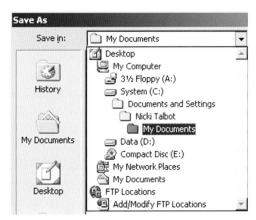

Choosing where to store the file

To change to a different 'filing drawer', click on the drop-down arrow at the end of the **Save in:** box to open a list of available locations where you can store your file. Choose the location from the list by clicking on it. In a lot of organisations, files are stored on a network drive rather than on your own computer, for security reasons. Click on the drop-down arrow in the **Save in:** box and choose the drive from the list.

What are folders?

Imagine a physical filing system where you might have labelled cardboard sleeves in the filing cabinet with papers relating to that topic in the sleeve. Folders on your computer are like the cardboard sleeves. Files are the papers that go inside the labelled sleeve. (For more information on how to create the filing system on your computer, see Unit 202 – Operate a computer.)

The Save As dialog box shown below has opened into the **My Documents** folder. Within this folder are folders labelled **Databases, Letters, Presentations** and **Spreadsheets**. If you want to store your file in any of these folders, double-click on the appropriate folder name to open that folder.

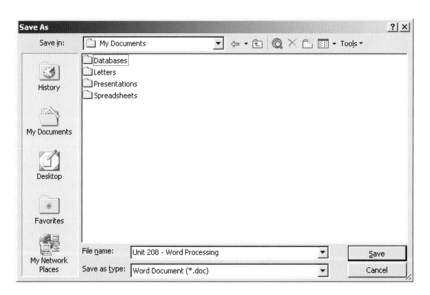

Navigating around folders

Once you have chosen the appropriate drive ('filing cabinet') from the Save in: list, the main area of the Save As dialog box will display the folders that are already in that filing cabinet.

To open a folder, double-click on the appropriate folder name.

Use the **Back** or **Up One Level** buttons to move up out of a folder.

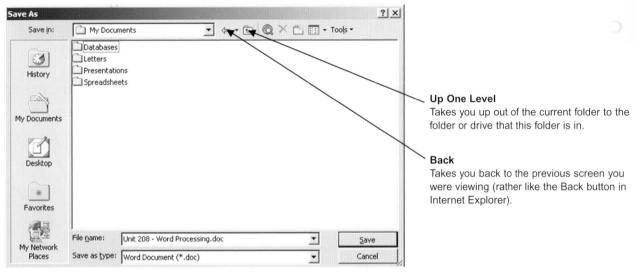

Up One Level
Takes you up out of the current folder to the folder or drive that this folder is in.

Back
Takes you back to the previous screen you were viewing (rather like the Back button in Internet Explorer).

Creating a new folder

If you wish to create a new folder to store your work in, navigate to the appropriate drive where you wish to create the folder (using the Save in: drop-down list).
    Click on the **Create a New Folder** button in the Save As dialog box.

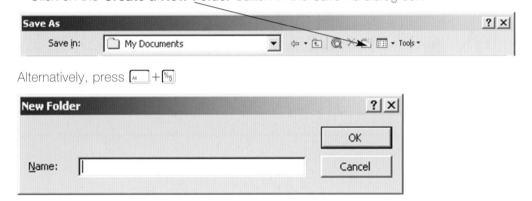

Alternatively, press [Alt]+[%5]

Type a name for the new folder and click on **OK**.

Naming a file

Once you have chosen the appropriate drive and folder, you need to give your document a name.
    Type a name for the document in the **File name** box and ensure that it will be saved as a Microsoft Word Document (**Save as type** should be set to Word Document (*.doc)).
    Your filename can be up to 250 characters long – use an obvious name for your file so that you remember what you called it in the future! You do not need to type the .doc filename extension as this will be added automatically. (The filename extension will not be visible in Windows Explorer if you have not set it to show file extensions.)

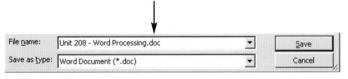

Once you have chosen the appropriate folder and given the file a name, click on the **Save** button at the bottom right of the dialog box.

Once you have saved the document, the name of the file will appear in the Title Bar across the top of the screen.

Unit 208 - Word Processing.doc - Microsoft Word

All Word documents have the file extension .doc. This helps you recognise which of your files are Word documents when you are viewing files in folders.

The Word icon also appears to the left of the file in the Open or Save dialog box.

If you have previously saved the document and then made some changes to it, choosing Save will overwrite the previous version of the document with the newly updated version. (It still has the same name and is stored in the folder that you initially put it in.)

TASK 2

1 **Open the Save As dialog box.**

2 **Navigate to the appropriate drive letter where you store your work.**

3 **Create a new folder called 'Tasks for ITQ'.**

4 **Name the file 'Word Text' and save it into the Tasks for ITQ folder.**

Closing the document

Once you have saved the file, if you wish to remove the document from the screen, you need to close it.

Choose **Close** from the **File** menu.

Alternatively, you can click on the **Close Window** button at the top right of the screen.

Close Window button

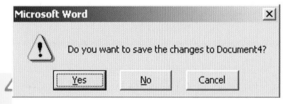

If you haven't previously saved the document or you have made more changes since you last saved the document, this message will appear on the screen.

Click on **Yes** to save any further changes you have made and close the file. If you do not wish to save any changes you have made, click on **No.** Clicking on **Cancel** will remove the dialog box from the screen without closing the file. If you wish to close the document, you will need to choose **File, Close** again.

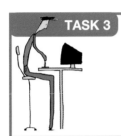

TASK 3

Close the file 'Word Text'.

 ## Opening an existing document

You may wish to open a document that you have already starting working on and previously saved.

Open

Choose **Open** from the **File** menu.
Alternatively, click on the **Open** button on the Standard toolbar.
You can also use Control + O
The Open dialog box will appear.
To change to a different drive, click on the drop-down arrow at the end of the **Look in:** box to open a list of locations. Choose the drive that you wish to view from the list.

Once you have chosen the appropriate drive from the Look in: list, the main area of the Open dialog box will display the folders that are already on that drive. To open a folder, double-click on the appropriate folder name.

Locate the document you wish to open, click on it and then click on the **Open** button at the bottom right of the dialog box. (Alternatively, you can double-click on the file.)

TASK 4

1 **Open the file called 'Word Text'.**

 ## Using Save As

If you have opened an existing document and made changes to it, but you do not wish to overwrite the original document, you can use **Save As**. You can then give the new version of the document a different name or store it in a different folder.

Choose **Save As** from the **File** menu and follow the same steps as for saving a document.

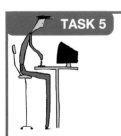

TASK 5

1 **Make the following changes to the text entered in Task 1:**

Change the word 'extremely' for the word 'very'.

Change the sentence which begins 'There are many ... ' to read 'There are a lot of ... '.

Add the words 'and efficient' after the word 'easy' in the third paragraph.

2 **Save the document in your Tasks for ITQ Folder with the file name 'Word text version 2'. (Use Save As.)**

Printing the document

If you wish to have what is known as a 'hard copy' of a document, you can print it onto paper.

Using Print Preview

Before you print the document onto paper, you can view the document as it will look when printed by using Print Preview.

Choose **Print Preview** from the **File** menu.

Print
Preview

Alternatively, click on the **Print Preview** button on the Standard toolbar.

The Print Preview screen opens and you can see your document displayed as it will look when printed.

The buttons across the top of the Preview screen allow you to work with the preview.

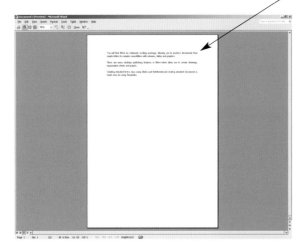

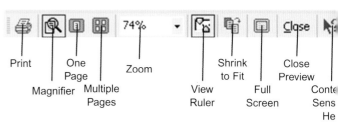

Print · Magnifier · One Page · Multiple Pages · Zoom · View Ruler · Shrink to Fit · Full Screen · Close Preview · Context-Sensitive Help

- **Print** – opens the Print dialog box.
- **Magnifier** – switches on the magnifying glass. You can click on the document to zoom in and click again to zoom out.
- **One Page** – previews the document one page at a time.
- **Multiple Pages** – enables you to choose how many pages you wish to preview.
- **Zoom** – enables you to choose the percentage you wish to zoom in or out. You can also choose Page Width, Text Width, Whole Page or Two Pages.
- **View Ruler** – switches on the ruler across the top of the Preview screen.
- **Shrink to Fit** – adjusts the document size so that the text ends at the bottom of a page. (So that you don't have some text spilling onto another page at the end of the document.)
- **Full Screen** – hides some elements of the screen (i.e. menu bar and toolbar) so that you can view more of the document.
- **Close Preview** – closes the Preview window and returns to the main document window.
- **Context-Sensitive Help** – enables you to get information about the screen. Click on this button and then click on the button or menu item that you require help with. A help box opens with a description of the button/menu item you have clicked on.

Printing

Print

Once you are happy with how your document looks in Print Preview, you can print the document.

If you wish to print one copy of the document based

on the current settings in the Print dialog box, you can click on the **Print** button on the Standard toolbar.

If you wish to open the Print dialog box, in order that you can make choices about the printing, choose **Print** from the **File** menu.

Alternatively, use [Control] + [P]

The Print dialog box opens.

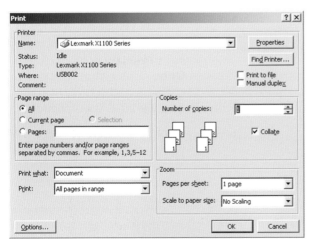

You can choose which printer you wish to print to by clicking on the **Name** drop-down list and choosing a printer from the list. (You may only be able to print to one printer, which will already be showing in the Name box.)

Choose a **Page range**:

- **All** – prints all the pages in the document.
- **Current page** – prints the page that the cursor is currently sitting in.
- **Pages:** – type a page range in the box. For example, to print pages 1, 3 and 5, type 1, 3, 5. To print pages 5-12, type 5-12.

Choose the **Number of copies** you wish to print.

Click on **OK** to print the document.

TASK 6

1. **Preview the document in the Print Preview window.**
2. **Print one copy of the document.**
3. **Save and close the document.**

Editing a Word document

Insert and overtype

When you start creating a document in Word, you are in 'Insert' mode. This means that if you move your cursor between two characters or words and you type, the existing text moves along to make room for the new text to be 'inserted'.

You can switch into 'Overtype' mode by clicking on the **Insert** key (to the right of the standard keyboard). The Insert key is a switch key: click it once to switch into Overtype mode and click it again to switch back to Insert mode.

You can see which mode you are in by looking at the Status Bar at the bottom of the Word screen. When you are in Insert mode, the word **OVR** is dimmed.

Page 22	Sec 1	22/108	At 17.5cm	Ln 17	Col 1	REC TRK EXT OVR

When you are in Overtype mode, the word **OVR** is shown in black.

Page 22	Sec 1	22/108	At 18.2cm	Ln 17	Col 1	REC TRK EXT OVR

Deleting text

There are two keys on the keyboard that you can use to delete text from the screen: the **Delete** key and the **Backspace** key.

If your cursor is sitting to the left of the word you wish to delete, use the **Delete** key. If your cursor is sitting to the right of the word you wish to delete, use the **Backspace** key. The **Delete** key deletes to the right of the cursor and the **Backspace** key deletes to the left of the cursor (as indicated by the arrow on the Backspace key).

Using undo

There is a very useful feature in Word which will undo any editing changes you have made. For example, if you have selected a paragraph of text and deleted it by mistake, you 'undo' the deletion. In fact, if you have made any changes to your document (i.e. applying formatting, inserting a table, etc.) and then you change your mind, you can undo the action.

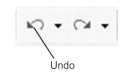

Undo

To use undo, click on the **Edit** menu and click on **Undo.** (The last action you performed will be showing.)

Alternatively, click the **Undo** button on the Standard toolbar.

You can also use ⌨Control⌨+⌨Z⌨

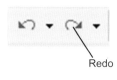

Redo

If you have undone something and then decide you did want it after all (!), you can use the **Redo** command.

Using Find and Replace

Find and Replace is a feature that enables you to find words or formatting in a document and replace them with other words or formatting.

If you wish to simply find a word or words in a document, choose **Find** from the **Edit** menu.

Alternatively, use ⌨Control⌨+⌨F⌨

The Find and Replace dialog box opens.

Type the word that you wish to find in the **Find what:** box. Click on **Find Next** to start the search.

Word stops on the first occurrence of the word. If this is not the occurrence of the word you wish to find, click on Find Next again to move to the next occurrence of that word. Continue clicking on Find Next until Word stops on the occurrence of the word you require. Click on **Cancel** to close the Find dialog box.

Search options

To choose more options for your Find, click on the **More** button in the Find and Replace dialog box.

The Search Options of the Find and Replace dialog box are revealed:

- **Search:** – choose whether you wish to search **All** the document, or just **Up** or **Down** from where your cursor currently is.
- **Match case** – tick this box if you only want to find words in the same case as the search word.

- **Find whole words only** – tick this box if you want to find whole words, i.e. if you type the word 'sort' in the Find box, the find would also find 'resort', unless you tick this box.
- **Use wildcards** – when searching for words, you can use wildcards. For example, b?ll will find ball, bull, bell and bill (the ? represents one character). The asterisk (*) can be used to represent any number of characters, e.g. con* would find any word that starts with the characters 'con' but then has anything after. If you are going to use wildcards in your search, you must tick this box to indicate that the ? or * are wildcards and not literal characters.
- **Sounds like (English)** – this will find words that sound like the search word. For example, if you type 'read' in the Find box and tick this box, it also finds 'red' and 'reed'.
- **Find all word forms (English)** – this will find all forms of a word. For example, if you type 'run' in the Find box and tick this box, it also finds 'ran' and 'running'.

Finding formatting

As well as finding words in your document, you can search for words with a specific formatting (e.g. bold) or just the formatting on its own. If you wish to find a word with specific formatting, type the word in the Find what: box.

Click on the **Format** button in the Search Options section of the Find and Replace dialog box.

Click on the appropriate formatting in the menu – Font, Paragraph, Tabs, Language, Frame, Style or Highlight – then choose the format you wish to find in the dialog box that opens.

The example below shows that the word 'occurrence' is being searched for, but only where it appears with Bold and Underline formatting.

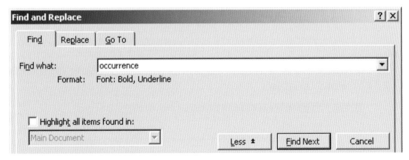

If you just wish to search for formatting in the document, don't type a word in the Find what: box but simply choose the formatting from the Format menu at the bottom of the dialog box.

Replacing words in the document

If you wish to find a word or words in your document and replace it with a different word or words, choose **Replace** from the **Edit** menu.

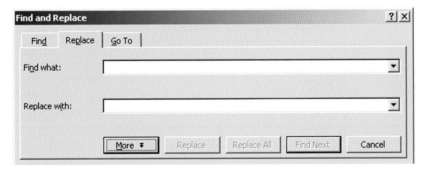

Type the words that you wish to find in the **Find what:** box. Type the words that you wish to replace them with in the **Replace with:** box.

Click on **Find Next** to start the search.

Word stops on the first occurrence of the word. If this is not the occurrence of the word you wish to replace, click on Find Next to move to the next occurrence of that word. If you do wish to replace this word, click on **Replace**. Continue clicking on Find Next or Replace to work through the document, replacing the word where necessary.

To replace all the words in the document without stopping, click **Replace All**.

When Word has finished searching through the document, this message appears.

Click on **OK** and then click on **Close** to close the Find and Replace dialog box.

You can use Search Options and search for formatting and replace with other formatting, just as for the Find feature.

TASK 7

1 **Open the file called 'Word text version 2'.**

2 **Use Find and Replace to find the word 'very' and replace it with the word 'extremely'.**

3 **Use Find and Replace to find the word 'allow' and replace it with the word 'enable'.**

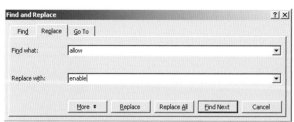

4 **Use Find and Replace to apply bold formatting to the words 'Styles' and 'AutoFormat'.**

5 **Save the document.**

6 4

7 9

) (

Moving and copying text in a document

If you wish to rearrange the text in a document (i.e. move it around), you can use a feature called Cut and Paste. If you wish to copy text in your document to another place, you can use a feature called Copy and Paste.

Using Cut or Copy and Paste is a four step process:

1 Select the text that you wish to move or copy. (To select, click to the left of the text you wish to select, hold down the mouse button and drag the mouse across the text. The text is highlighted.)

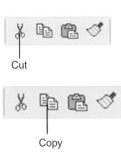

Cut

2 Choose **Cut** or **Copy** from the **Edit** menu.
Alternatively, click on the **Cut** or **Copy** button on the Standard toolbar.
You can also use [Control]+[X] or [Control]+[C]
The text is placed in a temporary storage area called the Clipboard. If you Cut the text it disappears from the screen.

3 Move the cursor to the place where you want to move the text to.

Copy

4 Choose **Paste** from the **Edit** menu.

Alternatively click on the **Paste** button on the Standard toolbar.

You can also use [Control]+[V]
The text appears on the screen at the cursor position.

Paste

What is the Office Clipboard?

The Office Clipboard is a temporary storage area. When you use the Cut or Copy command, the text is placed on the clipboard. You can use the Paste command to insert the text elsewhere, as many times as you need to.

The Office Clipboard works across all the Office applications: Word, Excel, PowerPoint®, Access and Outlook. You can also use the Office Clipboard to collect and paste multiple items (up to 12 in Office 2000 and 24 in Office XP). For example, you can copy a drawing object in Microsoft® Excel, switch to Microsoft® PowerPoint and copy a bulleted list, switch to Microsoft® Internet Explorer and copy a page of text, and then switch to Word and paste the collection of copied items.

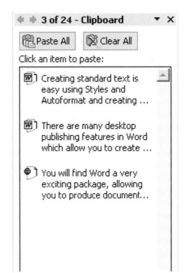

In Office XP, once you cut or copy more than one item to the clipboard, the Clipboard Task Pane appears down the right side of the screen. You can use this task pane to manage the items currently sitting on the clipboard.

In Office 2000 the Clipboard is a toolbar. Choose **Toolbars** from the **View** menu and then click on **Clipboard** to switch on the Office Clipboard. (It doesn't switch on automatically.)

Using drag and drop to move text

Another way to move text in a Word document is to use the drag and drop feature.

1 Select the text you wish to move. (To select, click in front of the text, hold down the mouse button and drag the mouse over the text. The text will be highlighted.)

2 Point to the selected text and click and drag with the mouse pointer. The selected text is 'picked up'.

3 Move the mouse pointer to where you want to move the text to and 'drop' the text.

You will find Word a very exciting package, allowing you to produce documents from simple letters to complex newsletters with columns, tables and graphics.

There are many desktop publishing features in Word which allow you to create drawings, organisation charts and graphs.

Creating standard text is easy using **Styles** and Autoformat and creating standard documents is made easy by using Templates.

You will find Word a very exciting package, allowing you to produce documents from simple letters to complex newsletters with columns, tables and graphics.

There are many desktop publishing features in Word which allow you to create drawings, organisation charts and graphs.

Creating standard text is easy using **Styles** and Autoformat and creating standard documents is made easy by using Templates.

Creating standard text is easy using **Styles** and Autoformat and creating standard documents is made easy by using Templates.

You will find Word an extremely exciting package, allowing you to produce documents from simple letters to complex newsletters with columns, tables and graphics.

There are many desktop publishing features in Word which allow you to create drawings, organisation charts and graphs.

TASK 8

1 **Use Cut and Paste to move the second paragraph of your document ('There are a lot of ... ') and make it the first paragraph.**

2 **Use drag and drop to move the third paragraph ('Creating standard text ... ') and make it the second paragraph. Save the document.**

There are a lot of desktop publishing features in Word which enable you to create drawings, organisation charts and graphs.

Creating standard text is easy and efficient using **Styles** and **Autoformat** and creating standard documents is made easy by using Templates.

You will find Word an extremely exciting package, allowing you to produce documents from simple letters to complex newsletters with columns, tables and graphics.

3 **Use Copy and Paste to copy all the text in the document into a new document. (Copy the text to the clipboard and then start a new document.) Save this new document in your 'Tasks for ITQ' folder with the file name 'Word text version 3'.**

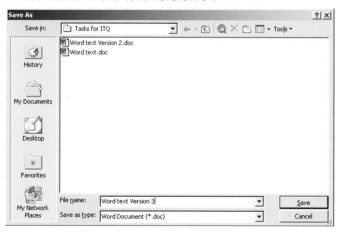

4 **Close all the files that are open.**

Formatting a Word document

There are many formatting options available in Word, to enable you to improve the appearance of text in the document and the layout of your document.

Font formatting

You can apply formatting to the text in your document using the Formatting toolbar or the Font dialog box.

The Formatting toolbar runs across the top of your screen (below the Standard toolbar). You can choose from drop-down lists or click on buttons to apply the more popular formatting options.

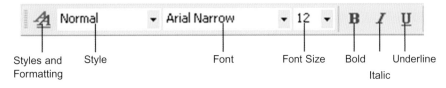

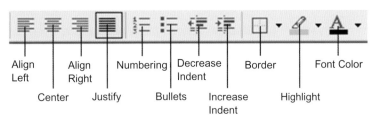

Before you can apply formatting to existing text, you need to select the text. Once you have selected the text, choose the option you require from a drop-down list or click on a button to 'switch it on'.

- **Styles and Formatting** – opens the Styles and Formatting task pane down the right side of the screen.
- **Style** – enables you to choose from a list of styles.
- **Font** – enables you to choose from a list of fonts.
- **Font Size** – enables you to choose from a list of font sizes.
- **Bold** – applies **bold** formatting to selected text (click on the button again to release it and remove the bold formatting).
- **Italic** – applies *italic* formatting to selected text (click on the button again to release it and remove the italic formatting).
- **Underline** – applies <u>underline</u> formatting to selected text (click on the button again to release it and remove the underline formatting).
- **Align Left** – aligns the selected text to the left margin.
- **Center** – centres the selected text between the left and right margins.
- **Align Right** – aligns the selected text to the right margin.
- **Justify** – justifies the selected text so that it lines up at the left and right margins.
- **Numbering** – applies numbering to the selected text.
- **Bullets** – applies bullets to the selected text.
- **Decrease Indent** – decreases the indent (moves the text back to the left once you have applied an indent).
- **Increase Indent** – moves the text to the right, away from the left margin.
- **Border** – applies a border to the selected text. Click on the drop-down arrow to open a palette of different borders that you can apply.
- **Highlight** – applies highlighting to the selected text. Click on the drop-down arrow to open a palette of different highlight colours that you can use.

■ **Font Color** – applies a font colour to the selected text. Click on the drop-down arrow to open a palette of different font colours that you can use.

For some of the more common formatting, you can select the text and use shortcut key combinations:

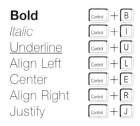

Bold   Control + B
Italic   Control + I
<u>Underline</u> Control + U
Align Left   Control + L
Center   Control + E
Align Right   Control + R
Justify   Control + J

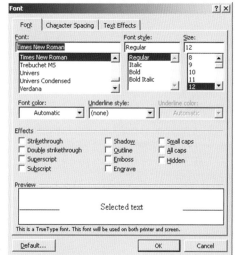

You can also use the Font dialog box to apply formatting to selected text.

Choose **Font** from the **Format** menu.

You can choose a **Font**, a **Font style** and a **Size** from the lists. You can choose a **Font color**, an **Underline style** and an **Underline color** from the drop-down lists. You can apply other **Effects** by ticking the appropriate boxes.

A preview of your selected text will appear in the **Preview** window at the bottom of the dialog box.

Once you have made your selections, click on **OK** to apply the changes.

TASK 9

1 **Open the file called 'Word Text'.**

2 **Select all the text in the document and change the font to Arial Narrow and the size to 11. Justify the text in the document. Change the font colour to blue.**

3 **Select the words 'columns, tables and graphics' and apply Bold. Select the word 'easy' in the third paragraph and apply Italic. Select the word 'Templates' and apply Underline.**

4 **Type a heading at the top of the document – Microsoft Word. Centre the heading and change the font to Arial 14. Bold and Underline the heading.**

5 **Save the document.**

Paragraph formatting

To format the paragraphs in your document, you use the Paragraph Dialog Box. If you wish to format just one paragraph, click in the paragraph that you wish to format. If you wish to format more than one paragraph, select the paragraphs that you wish to format.

Choose **Paragraph** from the **Format** menu.

The Paragraph dialog box opens, as in the figure on page 169.

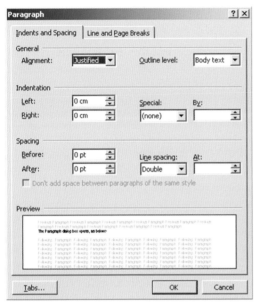

You can change the **Alignment** of text in a paragraph by choosing the alignment you require from the drop-down list.

You can use **Indentation** to indent the text in a paragraph. **Left** indents the text away from the left margin by the measurement you specify, **Right** indents the text away from the right margin by the measurement you specify. (You can choose First line or Hanging from the **Special** drop-down list.)

You can use **Spacing** to specify spacing before and/or after lines in the paragraph. You can choose Single, 1½ or Double line spacing from the **Line spacing** drop-down list.

A preview of your paragraphs will appear in the **Preview** window at the bottom of the dialog box.

Once you have made your selections, click on **OK** to apply the changes.

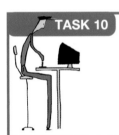

TASK 10

1 **Click in the second paragraph of the document. Indent this paragraph 2 cm from the left margin and 2 cm from the right margin.**

2 **Select all the paragraphs in the document and change to double line spacing.**

3 **Save the document.**

Document layout

The second tab of the Paragraph dialog box allows you to control the flow of text in your document.

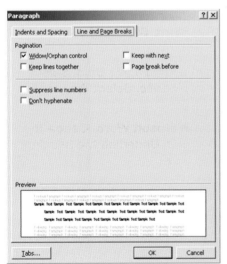

If you are working on a multi-page document, you can specify that lines and paragraphs should be kept together and where page breaks should fall. You can also control the occurrence of widows and orphans. (A widow is where just the last line of a paragraph goes onto the next page. An orphan is where the first line of a paragraph is on a page and the rest of the paragraph is on the next page.)

Page breaks

As you type on the Word page, when you reach the bottom margin of the page, a page break is automatically inserted and your cursor is taken to the top of the next page. In order to control how your paragraphs flow in a multi-page document, you can insert a manual page break.

Choose **Break** from the **Insert** menu.

Choose **Page break** and click on **OK**.

Alternatively, you can use `Control` + `Return`

Page Breaks are displayed in different ways, depending which 'view' you are using to view your document.

Document views

The views can be chosen from the **View** menu. There are four views you can choose from:

- **Normal** – this view shows all the text formatting, but simplifies the layout of the page. In Normal view, certain elements of the screen do not appear. Page breaks are shown by a horizontal dotted line going across the page.
- **Web Layout** – this view is useful if you are creating a page for an intranet or the Internet (or any other document that will be viewed on screen). You can see backgrounds that you have applied and the text is wrapped to fit the window. Graphics are shown as they would appear in a Web browser.
- **Print Layout** – this view allows you to see exactly how text, graphics and all other elements of your document will be positioned on the printed page. This view 'simulates' the actual pages of the document. Page breaks are shown by the end of one page and the start of another page.
- **Outline** – this view is useful for viewing the structure of the document. You can easily move, copy and reorganise the text in the document by simply dragging the headings to new locations. You can also 'collapse' the document, to just see the main headings, or 'expand' the document to see the body text between the headings.

Formatting marks

Another useful feature that enables you to see the page breaks you have inserted into a document is to show the formatting marks (returns, spaces, tabs and page breaks) in the document.

Click on the Show/Hide button on the Standard toolbar.

Show/Hide

Alternatively, press [Control]+[°8]

Formatting marks will now appear in your document.

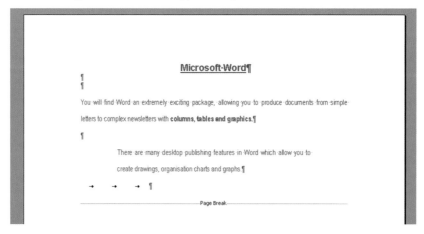

A dot appears to show a space between every word.
The ¶ symbol indicates where the return key has been pressed.
The → symbol indicates where the tab key has been pressed.
Page Breaks are shown.

It is easier to delete a page break or a return, etc., when you can actually see the marker for it.

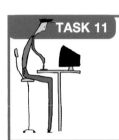

TASK 11

1 **Insert a page break in your document in front of the third paragraph ('Creating standard text ... '). The document will now appear on two pages.**

2 **Save and close the document.**

Page Setup

You can further control the layout of your document by using the commands in the Page Setup dialog box. Choose **Page Setup** from the **File** menu.

Page Setup in Word 2002

The Page Setup dialog box opens.

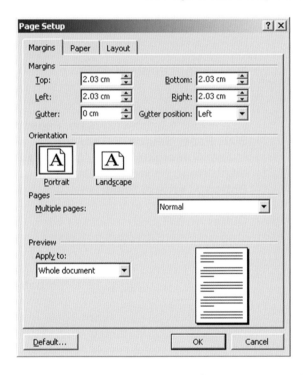

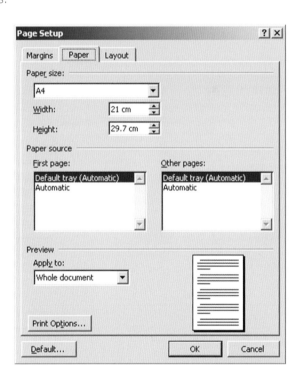

The Page Setup dialog box has three tabs across the top – **Margins, Paper** and **Layout.**

On the **Margins** tab you can change the margins of the document – **Top, Bottom, Left** and **Right**. You can also set a margin and position for the **Gutter**. (If you are producing a book-style document, the gutter margin alternates on each page, to leave extra space for binding. You can choose whether you wish the gutter to be Top or Left, depending on where you plan to bind the book.) You can change the page **Orientation** from Portrait to Landscape.

Once you have made changes, click on **OK** to apply the changes to your document and close the dialog box or click on the next tab if you wish to make more changes.

On the **Paper** tab you can change the **Paper size** that you wish to set the document up for. (The default is set to A4 because we mostly use this paper size when printing documents.) Under **Paper source**, you can choose which tray the paper should come from (if you use a multi-tray printer).

Once you have made changes, click on **OK** to apply the changes to your document and close the dialog box or click on the next tab if you wish to make more changes.

On the **Layout** you can choose where each new **Section** in the document should start (if you have broken the document into sections). For more information on Sections, see page 174.

You can choose to have different **Headers** and **Footers** appearing on odd and even pages, or a different first page header and/or footer. (For more information on headers and footers, see page 204). Under **From edge**, you can specify how far from the edge of the paper the header and footer should appear (how far from the top edge of the page – header and bottom edge of the page – footer).

You can change the **Vertical alignment** of the document. (For example, if you have created an invitation on an A4 page, you may wish to centre the text vertically as well as horizontally. To centre vertically, use this option in the Page Setup dialog box).

Once you have made changes, click on **OK** to apply the changes to your document and close the dialog box. (By default, any changes that you make in the Page Setup dialog box are applied to the whole document, unless you have selected text first, or the document is broken into sections – see page 174).

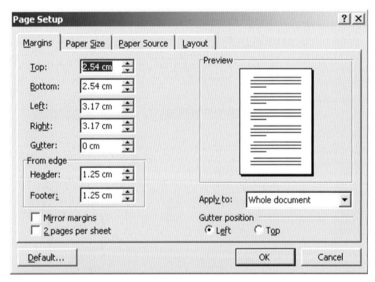

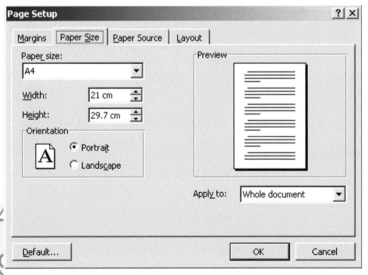

Page setup in Word 2000

The Page Setup dialog box opens.

The Page Setup dialog box has four tabs across the top – **Margins, Paper Size, Paper Source** and **Layout.**

On the **Margins** tab you can change the margins of the document – **Top, Bottom, Left** and **Right**. You can also set a margin and position for the **Gutter**. (If you are producing a book-style document, the gutter margin alternates on each page, to leave extra space for binding. You can choose whether you wish the gutter to be **Left** or **Top**, depending where you plan to bind the book.) Under **From edge**, you can specify how far from the top or bottom edge of the paper the header or footer should appear. Once you have made changes, click on **OK** to apply the changes to your document and close the dialog box or click on the next tab if you wish to make more changes.

On the **Paper Size** tab you can change the paper size that you wish to set the document up for. (The default is set to A4 because we mostly use this paper size when printing documents.) You can change the page **Orientation** from Portrait to Landscape.

Once you have made changes, click on **OK** to apply the changes to your document and close the dialog box or click on the next tab if you wish to make more changes.

On the **Paper Source** tab, you can choose which tray the paper should come from (if you use a multi-tray printer).

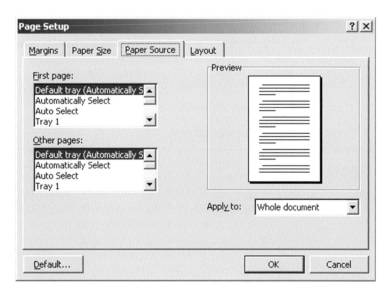

Once you have made changes, click on **OK** to apply the changes to your document and close the dialog box or click on the next tab if you wish to make more changes.

On the **Layout** tab you can choose where each new **Section** in the document should start (if you have broken the document into sections). For more information on sections, see page 174. You can choose to have different **Headers** and **Footers** appearing on odd and even pages, or a different first page header and/or footer. (For more information on headers and footers, see page 204.)

You can change the **Vertical alignment** of the document. For example, if you have created an invitation on an A4 page, you may wish to centre the text vertically as well as horizontally. To centre vertically, use this option in the Page Setup dialog box.

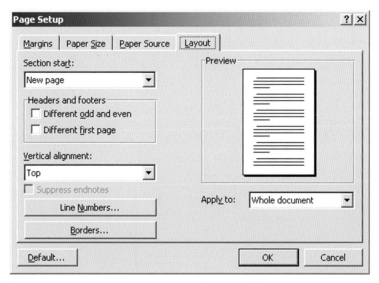

Once you have made changes, click on **OK** to apply the changes to your document and close the dialog box.

By default, any changes that you make in the Page Setup dialog box are applied to the whole document, unless you have selected text first, or the document is broken into sections.

TASK 12

1 **Open the document called 'Word text version 2'.**

2 **Change the margins for the document to 3 cm top and bottom and 2 cm left and right.**

3 **Change the page orientation to landscape.**

4 **Change the vertical alignment to centre.**

5 **Save and close the document.**

Sections

If you wish to have different page layouts or different headers and footers within one document, you need to break that document into 'sections'. There are two types of section break, continuous and next page. A continuous section break inserts a section break, but the text above and below the section break remains on the same page. (You would therefore have two sections on one page.) A more common type of section break is a next page section break. This forces text after the section break onto the next page.

To insert a section break, choose **Break** from the **Insert** menu.

Select the type of break you require under Section break types. (An Even page section break forces the text following the break onto the next even page in the document. An Odd page section break forces the text following the break onto the next odd page in the document.)

Section breaks are shown if you switch on formatting marks. (See page 170). The status bar at the bottom of the screen tells you which section of the document you are currently in.

Once you have divided your document into sections, you can apply features such as margins, page orientation, columns, headers and footers, etc., to individual sections in your document (rather than to the whole document). If you open the Page Setup dialog box in a document that is divided into sections, the Apply to: box shows **This section** rather than **Whole document**.

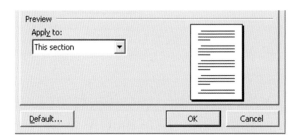

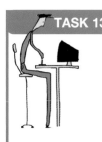

TASK 13

1. **Open the file called 'Word Text'.**

2. **Switch on formatting marks and delete the page break you inserted previously.**

3. **Insert a next page section break in front of paragraphs two and three. (Your document will now be on three pages and in three sections.)**

4. **Change the first section of the document to landscape orientation.**

5. **Change the margins in the second section of the document to 3 cm top and bottom and 4 cm left and right.**

6. **Save and close the file.**

Tabulation

If you want to display columns of data spaced across the page, you can use tabs.

Name	Class	Teacher
Stuart Smith	Gorillas	Mrs Hubbard
Sarah Peters	Giraffes	Mrs Kellerman
Betty Cooper	Monkeys	Mrs Thomson
Michael Howard	Crocodiles	Miss Thornton
Peter Richards	Lions	Mr Clarke

In every new document you start in Word, default tabs are set at approximately 1 cm across the page.

 The Tab key

You cannot see these default tabs on the ruler, but if you press the Tab key on the keyboard the cursor will move about 1 cm each time.

These tabs are useful if you wish to move the cursor across the page. (You should never use the space bar to create space across the page.)

However, if you wish to layout text across the page using tabs, you will find it easier to set your own tabs on the ruler. You will be able to see the tab markers on the ruler. Any tabs you set will override the default tabs.

If the ruler is not already switched on, choose **Ruler** from the **View** menu to switch it on.

There are four types of tab you can set:

L	left tab	text aligns on the left side
⊥	centre tab	text centres itself around the tab position
⅃	right tab	text aligns on the right side
⊥:	decimal tab	text aligns according to the decimal points in the numbers

At the left end of the ruler is the tab selection box.

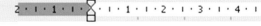

The box shows what looks like a small black **L**. This is a left tab marker. If you click on the tab selection box, the left tab marker changes to a centre tab marker. If you click again it changes to a right tab marker and so on. When you point to the tab selection box, a yellow tool tip appears to let you know what type of tab is being displayed.

Setting tabs using the ruler

Select the type of tab you require by clicking on the selection box.

In this example a left tab has been selected

Click on the ruler at the position where you want to set the tab. (You will need to click in the bottom half of the ruler, under the markers.) The tab marker will appear on the ruler.

Repeat this process for as many tabs as you want across the ruler.

Click to set the
tab on the ruler

A left tab is set
on the ruler

In your document, to type text at the first tab setting on the ruler, press the Tab key on the keyboard to move to that position.

Type the first piece of text. Press the Tab key again to move to the next tab setting on the ruler (do not press the space bar).

Once you have typed the text, you may decide to adjust the tab settings, in

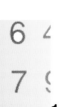

order to move the text on the page. Select the text that you wish to move by clicking and dragging with the mouse to highlight it. (Word selects whole lines, so you may need to select more text than you want to actually move.)

Name	Dept	Title	Ext. No.
Tom	Sales	Manager	2876
Peter	Accounts	Accountant	3849
Sarah	Marketing	Manager	3294

In this example, only the Ext. No. column needs to be moved to the right a little, but whole lines are selected.

To move the text, click and drag the appropriate tab marker on the ruler. (Be careful not to drag it off the ruler or it will disappear.) A guide line will appear down the page as you drag the tab marker, to help you see where to put the tab marker down.

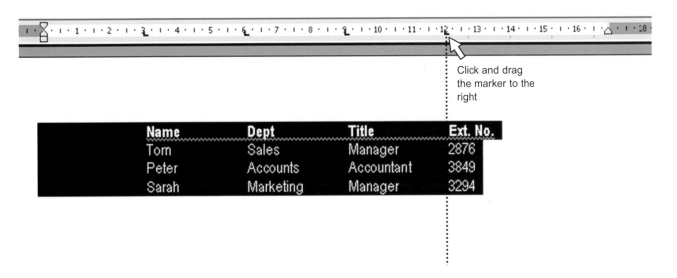

Click and drag the marker to the right

Name	Dept	Title	Ext. No.
Tom	Sales	Manager	2876
Peter	Accounts	Accountant	3849
Sarah	Marketing	Manager	3294

When you release the tab marker the text will realign to the new tab position.

Name	Dept	Title	Ext. No.
Tom	Sales	Manager	2876
Peter	Accounts	Accountant	3849
Sarah	Marketing	Manager	3294

To remove a tab from the ruler, point to the tab marker on the ruler and click and drag the marker off the ruler. The tab will disappear from the ruler.

Changing the tab

You may have set a left tab for some text and then decide you wish to change the tab to a centre tab.

Select the text for which you wish to change the type of tab. (Remember, Word selects whole lines, so you may need to select more text than you want to actually change.) Drag the tab you no longer require off the ruler.

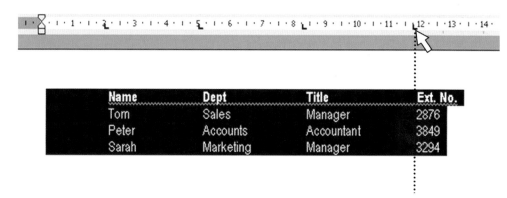

The text will move to the next tab on the ruler – DON'T PANIC! In this example, when the left tab marker was removed, the text found the next default tab. (You don't see these markers on the ruler.)

Name	Dept	Title	Ext. No.
Tom	Sales	Manager	2876
Peter	Accounts	Accountant	3849
Sarah	Marketing	Manager	3294

Select the tab you require by clicking on the tab selection box. Click on the ruler to set the new tab. The text will now align to the new tab. Adjust the position of the new tab marker by dragging it on the ruler.

In this example, a centre tab has been chosen from the tab selection box and then placed on the ruler. The text realigns to the new tab marker.

Name	Dept	Title	Ext. No.
Tom	Sales	Manager	2876
Peter	Accounts	Accountant	3849
Sarah	Marketing	Manager	3294

Setting tabs using the dialog box

You can also set tabs using the Tabs dialog box. Choose **Tabs** from the **Format** menu.

The Tabs dialog box opens.

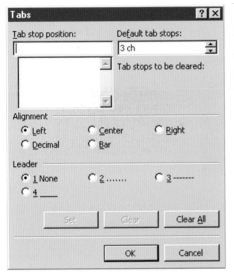

Type the tab position in the **Tab stop position** box, e.g. 3 cm. Select the **Alignment** of the tab: Left, Center, Right, Decimal or Bar. (A Bar tab inserts a vertical line at the tab position.) Select the type of **Leader** you require if you want dots running from the cursor position to the tab position. There are three different types of leader. An example of each is shown below.

Chapter 1 1

Chapter 2 ———————————————————————2

Chapter 3 _____3

Click on **Set** to set the tab. Repeat this process for each tab you require.

To remove a tab, select it in the list of tab stop positions and click on **Clear**. To remove all tabs, click on **Clear All**.

Click on **OK** to carry out the changes.

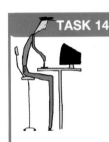

TASK 14

1 **Start a new Word document.**

2 **Set left tabs across the ruler at 2 cm, 6 cm and 10 cm.**

3 **Type the following text:**

DEPARTMENT	FLOOR	ROOM NO.
Personnel	2nd	215
Accounts	4th	422
Sales	7th	702
Marketing	6th	613

4 **Select the text you have just typed and move the second left tab to 7 cm and the third left tab to 11 cm.**

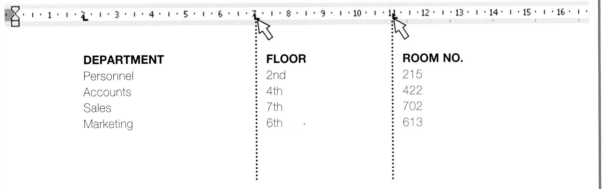

DEPARTMENT	FLOOR	ROOM NO.
Personnel	2nd	215
Accounts	4th	422
Sales	7th	702
Marketing	6th	613

5 **Select just the room numbers (not the heading, Room No.). Remember, Word will select whole lines.**

DEPARTMENT	FLOOR	ROOM NO.
Personnel	2nd	215
Accounts	4th	422
Sales	7th	702
Marketing	6th	613

TASK 14

6 **Remove the third left tab from the ruler.**

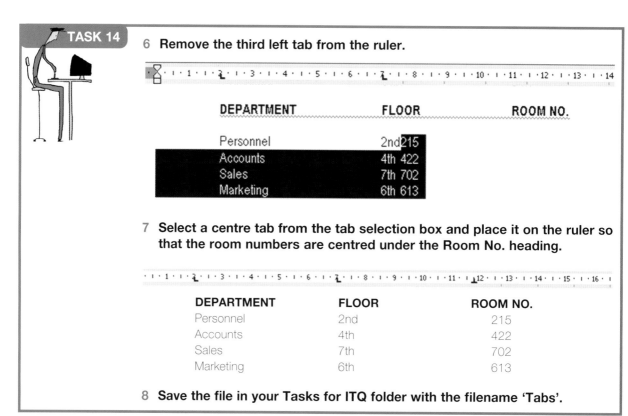

7 **Select a centre tab from the tab selection box and place it on the ruler so that the room numbers are centred under the Room No. heading.**

DEPARTMENT	FLOOR	ROOM NO.
Personnel	2nd	215
Accounts	4th	422
Sales	7th	702
Marketing	6th	613

8 **Save the file in your Tasks for ITQ folder with the filename 'Tabs'.**

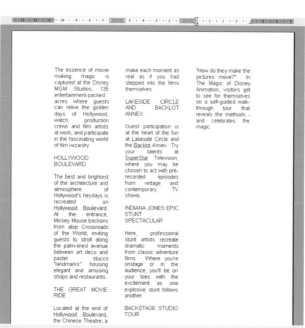

Columns

You can create newspaper style columns in a Word document. The text will flow to the bottom of one column and then wrap into the top of the next column. Below is an example of a document laid out using three columns.

You can switch on columns before you begin to type. The text will flow into the number of columns you have specified. Alternatively, you can select existing text and format it into columns.

To set up columns quickly, you can use the Columns button on the Standard Toolbar.

Columns

2 Columns

Click and hold the mouse button down and drag across to specify from one to four columns

To open the Columns dialog box, choose **Columns** from the **Format** menu. The Columns dialog box opens.

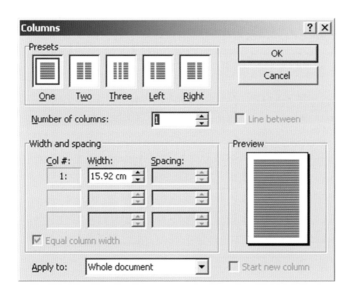

Click on the **Presets** (One, Two or Three), or choose the number you require in the **Number of columns** box. (You can also choose Left and Right to have one narrow and one wide column.)

By default, columns are set to **Equal column width**. As you choose the number of columns, the width of each column and the spacing between the columns is automatically calculated depending on your margin settings. If you wish to specify the width and spacing of columns yourself, you can insert this into the appropriate boxes.

Click on **OK** to set the page layout to columns. If you have the ruler switched on, you will be able to see the column layout.

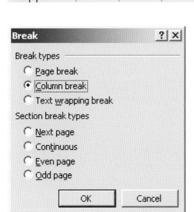

Starting a new column

Position the cursor where you wish to start a new column and choose **Break** from the **Insert** menu.

Choose **Column Break** and click on **OK**. Your cursor will move to the top of the next column.

Moving between columns

If you wish to move the cursor between columns, hold down the **Alt** key on the keyboard while pressing the up or down arrow. (**Alt+up arrow** takes you to the previous column, **Alt+down arrow** takes you to the next column).

Changing column width and spacing using the ruler

You can change the width of each column and the space between columns by using the ruler. First, you need to open the Columns dialog box (Format, Columns) and untick the **Equal column width** tick box.

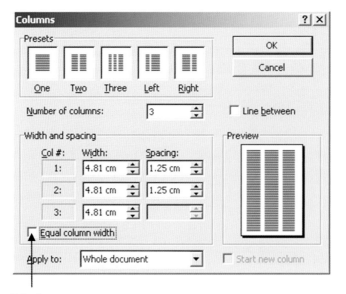

Take the
tick out of
this box

To change the width of a column, point to the grey area on the ruler between the columns. The mouse pointer becomes a double-headed black arrow. Drag left or right.

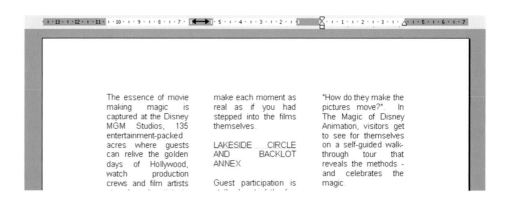

The essence of movie making magic is captured at the Disney MGM Studios, 135 entertainment-packed acres where guests can relive the golden days of Hollywood, watch production crews and film artists

make each moment as real as if you had stepped into the films themselves.

LAKESIDE CIRCLE AND BACKLOT ANNEX

Guest participation is

"How do they make the pictures move?". In The Magic of Disney Animation, visitors get to see for themselves on a self-guided walk-through tour that reveals the methods - and celebrates the magic.

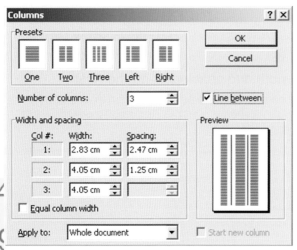

To change the space between two columns, point to the edge of the grey area on the ruler. The mouse pointer becomes a double-headed black arrow. Drag left or right.

Inserting a vertical line between columns

Choose **Columns** from the **Format** menu to open the Columns dialog box.

Tick the **Line between** box. Click on **OK**.

Applying columns to selected text

You may find it quicker to type your text in normal one column layout, then select the text and convert to columns after.

If you wish to apply column layout to just part of a

page, select the text that you wish to format in columns and choose **Columns** from the **Format** menu.

Notice that the **Apply to:** box at the bottom of the dialog box shows 'Selected text' rather than 'Whole document'. The column layout that you choose will be applied to just the selected text.

If you select text on part of a page and format it in column layout, Word inserts a section break above and below the column formatting (for more information on sections, see page 174).

TASK 15

1 **Start a new document and type the following text:**

STAR NEWS

Yes, for five lucky readers, Star News is offering book tokens to the value of £50.00. So all you bookworms among us, check your lucky numbers at the top of the newsletter and ring Star News' office for the winning combinations.

For those of you going on holidays this year, some books could be just what you need to help you relax and wind down.

Don't forget though, when you get back from your holidays to read your Star News newsletter for all your tasty bits of gossip!

2 **Select the main body of the text (excluding the heading) and put the text into three-column layout. Justify the text.**

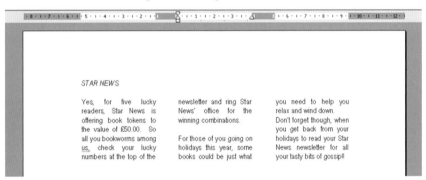

3 **Insert a column break at the start of each new paragraph.**

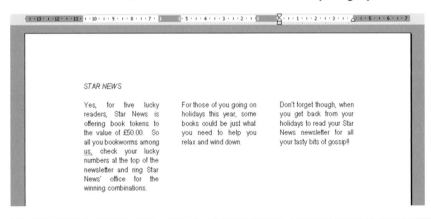

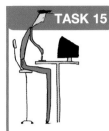

TASK 15

4 **Centre the heading across the columns and make it bold.**

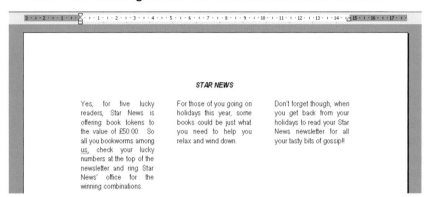

5 **Put a vertical line between the columns.**

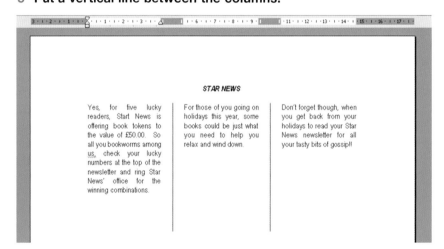

6 **Click on the heading Star News. Look at the status bar and notice that this is in Section 1. Now click in one of the columns. Look at the status bar and notice that this is in Section 2. (Because you only formatted part of the document into columns, Word has broken the document into two sections.)**

7 **Save the file into your Tasks for ITQ folder with the filename 'Star News'.**

 ## Inserting items into a Word document

Comments

You can create an on-screen comment in a Word document. Place the cursor at the position in the document where you wish to insert the comment.

Choose **Comment** from the **Insert** menu.

Comments in Word 2002

A red line runs from the cursor position to the right side of the page and a red comment box opens.

[Comment:]

Type your comment in the box.

To edit a comment, click in the comment box and amend the text.

If you send the document to someone and they are reading the document on-screen, they can move their mouse over the comment box to see the name of the person who made the comment.

To respond to a comment, click in the comment box for the comment you wish to respond to and choose **Comment** from the **Insert** menu. Another comment box appears, attached to the original comment box. Type your response in the second box.

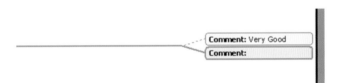

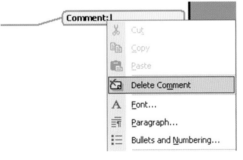

To delete a comment, right-click on the comment box and choose **Delete Comment** from the shortcut menu.

Comments in Word 2000

The text at the cursor position is highlighted in yellow and the Comment pane opens at the bottom of the screen. Type your comment in the Comment pane. Close the Comment pane.

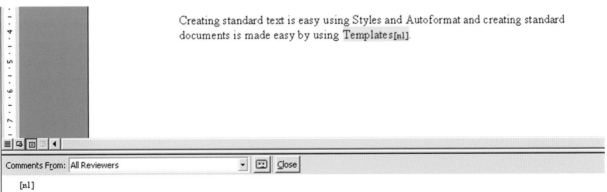

If you send the document to someone and they are reading the document on-screen, they can move their mouse over the highlighted text to see the comment and the name of the person who made the comment.

To edit or delete a comment, right-click on the highlighted text and choose **Edit Comment** or **Delete Comment** from the shortcut menu.

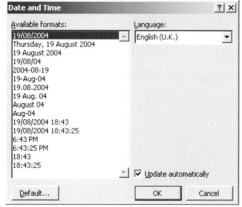

Insert date and time

You can insert the date and/or time into your document. You can also ask that the date and time update automatically, which means every time you open the document (or print the document in the case of the time), the current date and time show.

Place the cursor in your document where you wish to insert the date and time.

Choose **Date and Time** from the **Insert** menu. The Date and Time dialog box opens as below:

Choose the date and/or time format you require from the **Available formats** list. If you wish the date and time to update automatically, tick the **Update automatically** box. Click on **OK**.

Inserting files

You can insert an existing file into the file that is currently open. For example, if two people are working on different parts of the same report, you can use this command to insert the file containing the second part of the report into the file containing the first part of the report.

Open the file into which you wish to insert the second file. Move the cursor to where you wish to make the insertion.

Choose **File** from the **Insert** menu.

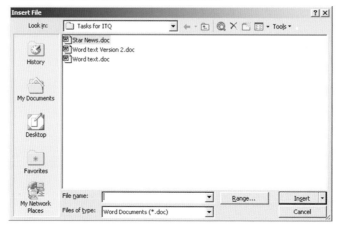

Navigate to the appropriate folder and select the file you wish to insert. Click on **Insert**.

Inserting symbols and special characters

As well as the characters that you can type using the keyboard, you can also insert symbols and special characters into your documents.

Place the cursor where you wish to insert the symbol or special character and choose **Symbol** from the **Insert** menu.

The Symbol dialog box opens.

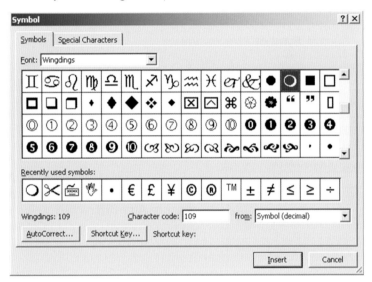

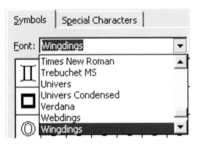

Choose the **Font** group from which you wish to view symbols by clicking on the drop-down arrow by the **Font** box.

Click on the symbol that you wish to use and click on **Insert**. The symbol is inserted at the cursor position.

You can insert more than one symbol while you have the dialog box open. (If the dialog box is sitting on top of your text and you cannot see the symbols you are inserting, move the dialog box by pointing to the blue title bar across the top and clicking and dragging with the mouse.)

Click on **Close** once you have finished.

To insert special characters, click on the **Special Characters** tab at the top of the Symbol dialog box.

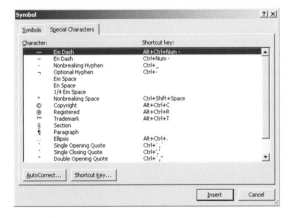

Click on the character that you wish to use and click on **Insert**. The special character is inserted at the cursor position.

Once you have inserted symbols and special characters into your document, you can work with them just as you would text you had typed using the keyboard. You can select the symbols and special characters and change the font size, font colour and add other font enhancements.

Assigning symbols and special characters to shortcut keys

If you use a particular symbol or special character a lot, you can assign that character to a shortcut key which makes it quicker to insert it into your document each time you need it.

Choose **Symbol** from the **Insert** menu. The Symbol dialog box opens.

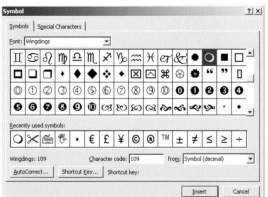

Click on the symbol or special character that you wish to assign to a shortcut key and click on **Shortcut Key . . .**

The Customize Keyboard dialog box opens.

Any current key assignments will be shown in the **Current keys** list. The cursor will be flashing in the **Press new shortcut key** box.

On your keyboard, press the shortcut key combination you wish to assign to this symbol. A shortcut key can comprise **Ctrl**+(letter or number) or **Alt**+(letter or number) or **Alt**+**Ctrl**+(letter or number).

Click on **Assign** and then **Close**.

When you wish to insert that symbol, press the shortcut key combination that you have assigned to it.

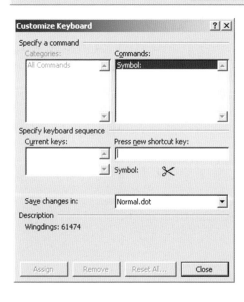

TASK 16

1 **Open the file called 'Word text version 3'.**

2 **Place the cursor by the word 'graphs' and type the comment 'Graphs are produced using Microsoft Graph'.**

3 **Move the cursor to the end of the last paragraph in the document and press Return four times. Insert the current date into the document using any format you wish from the list. Ensure the date will update automatically.**

4 **Press Return four times after the date and insert the file called 'Tabs' into this document.**

5 **Press Return two times and insert the following symbols into the document:** ✍➢☺💣.

6 **Enlarge these symbols to font size 20.**

7 **Save the document in your Tasks for ITQ folder with the filename 'Inserted Items'.**

Inserting AutoText

The AutoText feature enables you to store phrases and paragraphs of text that you use regularly and then recall these paragraphs onto the screen using shortcut keys.

There are a number of standard phrases already set up as AutoText. To insert a phrase stored in AutoText, choose **AutoText** from the **Insert** menu.

A sub-menu opens which contains categories of AutoText items. Click on a category to see the AutoText items stored in that category.

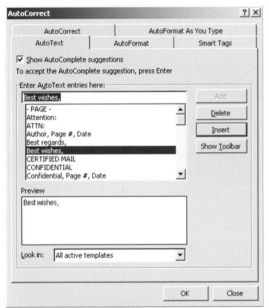

To use an AutoText item in the menu, click on it. The text is inserted in your document at the cursor position.

To open the AutoText dialog box, choose **AutoText** from the **Insert** menu and then click on **AutoText ...**

The AutoText dialog box opens.

All the AutoText items are listed. When you select an AutoText item in the list, a preview of what text is included in the AutoText item is shown at the bottom of the dialog box.

To insert an AutoText item, select it in the list and click on **Insert**.

Creating your own AutoText items

Type the text that you wish to store as an AutoText item. Select the text you have typed and open the AutoText dialog box (Insert menu).

The first few words of the text you have typed appear in the **Enter AutoText entries here** box. Delete this and type a short name to identify the text. (A good method is to use the first few letters of what you have typed). Click on **Add**. The AutoText dialog box closes.

You can use the dialog box to insert the text each time you want to use it (see above), or you can use a shortcut key combination. Type the name that you assigned to the AutoText item and then press **F3**.

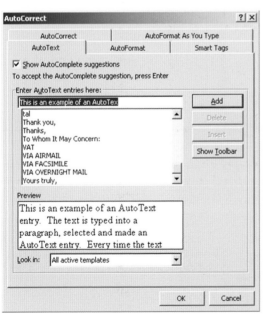

TASK 17

1 **Start a new Word document.**

2 **Type the following paragraph:**

   AutoText makes using standard phrases and paragraphs very easy. Simply type the text, select it and store it as an AutoText item. When you wish to use the text, type the short name you gave the AutoText item and press F3.

3 **Select the text and open the AutoText dialog box.**

4 **Type a short name for the AutoText item (for example, AutoT) and click on Add.**

5 **Practise recalling the text to the screen by using the short name followed by F3.**

6 **Repeat this process to create other AutoText items and practise recalling them to the screen.**

7 **Close the document without saving. (Your AutoText entries are already stored, even though you don't save the document).**

Inserting a text box

If you wish to place text in a box on the page and want to be able to move the box around easily, you can insert a text box.

Choose **Text Box** from the **Insert** menu.

The mouse pointer changes to a 'crosshair':

Click and drag with the mouse to draw the box. (Click and hold the mouse button down and then drag down and to the right.)

When you release the mouse button, the text box appears on the screen with the cursor flashing inside it.

Type the text that you wish to put into the text box. Click outside the text box once you have finished.

A text box can be moved to any place on the page and can be resized. You can also rotate text box.

Moving a text box

If you wish to move the text box on the page, point to the edge of the text box with the mouse pointer and click to select it.

Point to the dotted border around the edge of the text box. The mouse pointer now has a four-headed arrow attached to it.

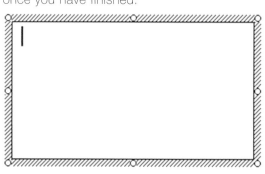

A text box can be moved to any place on the page and can be resized. You can also rotate a text box.

A text box can be moved to any place on the page and can be resized. You can also rotate a text box.

Click and drag the box to move it on the page. (As you move the box, it appears with a dashed border.)

When you release the mouse button, the text box moves to the new location.

Resizing a text box

If you wish to resize a text box, click on the edge of the text box to select it. Move the mouse over one of the white circle handles (white squares in Word 2000) around the edge of the box. The mouse pointer changes to a double-headed black arrow.

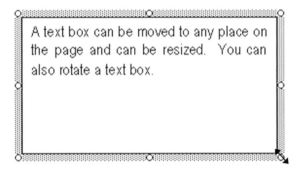

A text box can be moved to any place on the page and can be resized. You can also rotate a text box.

Click and drag this arrow inwards or outwards, depending on whether you wish to make the box smaller or larger.

(Resizing using the handles on the left or right of the text box will make the box narrower or wider. Resizing using the handles on the top or bottom of the text box will make the box shallower or deeper. Resizing using the handles in the corners of the text box will resize horizontally and vertically at the same time.)

Linking text boxes

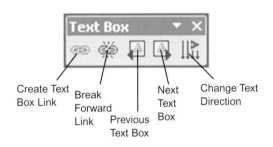

Create Text Box Link · Break Forward Link · Previous Text Box · Next Text Box · Change Text Direction

If you have inserted a number of text boxes onto the page, you can ensure that the text flows from one text box to the next by linking the text boxes.

Insert all the text boxes that you wish to have in your document.

Click on the first text box to select it and click on the **Create Text Box Link** button on the Text Box toolbar.

The mouse pointer changes to a pitcher icon. Move the mouse pointer over the box that you wish to link to this first text box – the mouse pointer now changes to a pouring pitcher icon. Click with the mouse to link the two text boxes. Repeat this process to link all the text boxes.

As you type text in a linked text box, when there is too much text for the first text box, it will flow automatically into the next text box and so on.

To break the link between text boxes, click on the text box for which you wish to break the link and click the **Break Forward Link** button on the Text Box toolbar.

Once you have linked text boxes, you can use the **Previous Text Box** and **Next Text Box** buttons to move between linked text boxes.

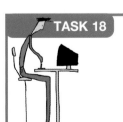

TASK 18

1 **Open the file called 'Star News'.**

2 **Create two text boxes at the bottom of the column layout. Link these two text boxes.**

3 **Now open the file called 'Word text version 2'.**

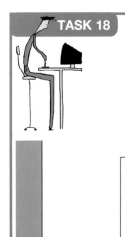

TASK 18

4 **Select the text in this document and copy it to the clipboard. Close this document.**

5 **Click inside the first text box and paste the text.**

6 **Resize the text boxes so that the text flows between the two.**

7 **Save and close the document.**

There are a lot of desktop publishing features in Word which enable you to create drawings, organisation charts and graphs.

Creating standard text is easy and efficient using **Styles** and **Autoformat** and creating standard documents is

made easy by using Templates.

You will find Word an extremely exciting package, allowing you to produce documents from simple letters to complex newsletters with columns, tables and graphics.

Inserting pictures into a document

You may wish to insert a picture or logo into a document. You can use the Microsoft Clip Art Gallery which will offer you a range of pictures that you can use in your documents or you can insert a picture, such as a company logo, that is already stored on your computer or network.

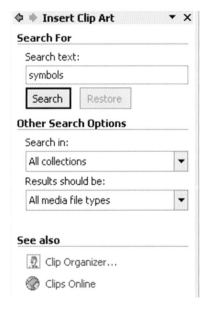

Inserting clip art in Word 2002

Open the file that you wish to insert the picture into. Choose **Picture** from the **Insert** menu and click on **Clip Art**.

The **Insert Clip Art** task pane appears down the right side of the screen. You can search for an appropriate clip art by typing keywords in the **Search text** box. Click on **Search** and clips that contain your keywords will be shown in the task pane.

In this example, the keyword 'symbols' has been typed into the **Search text** box. This returns the following list:

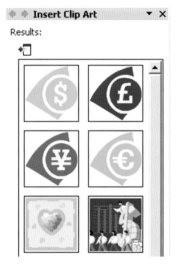

Click on a clip to insert it into your document.

Alternatively, you can click on the **Clip Organizer** link at the bottom of the task pane.

The Microsoft Clip Organizer dialog box opens.

To view the categories of clips that are available in each folder, click on the + icon beside the folder you wish to view. For example, to view the categories in the Office Collections folder, click on the + icon to the left of the folder name.

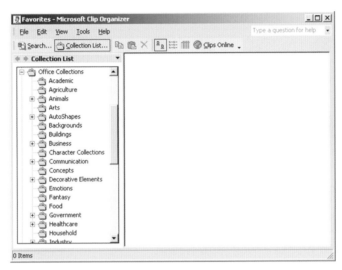

To view the clips in a category, click on the category name in the list on the left. The clips in that category will show on the right side of the screen. (If there is a + icon beside a category name, that indicates that there are more sub-categories under the main category. Click on the + icon to see the sub-categories. Click on the category to view the clips in it.)

To insert a clip from the Clip Organizer, point to the clip that you wish to insert and click on the drop-down arrow that appears.

Choose **Copy** from the shortcut menu

Click in your document and press the **Paste** button on the Standard toolbar (or choose **Paste** from the **Edit** menu; use [Control]+[V]; or right-click and choose **Paste** from the shortcut menu).

Inserting clip art in Word 2000

In Word 2000, choosing **Insert, Picture, Clip Art** will take you straight into the Clip Art Gallery.

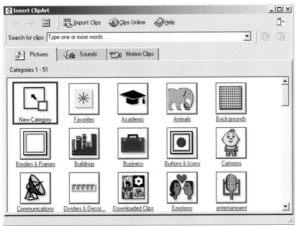

Double-click on a category to open it and view the clips in that category.

Click on the picture you require and choose **Insert Clip** (the top button) on the toolbar that appears next to the picture.

TASK 19

1 **Open the file called 'Star News'.**

2 **Move to the end of the document and insert a picture from the Clip Art Gallery.**

3 **Save the document.**

Inserting a stored picture

If you have been sent or have scanned a photograph or picture or you have taken a digital photograph, you will need to save the picture onto your computer first. There are many different picture file formats.

Image file formats

.bmp	A bitmap is made up of a series of small dots. When a bitmap is resized, it loses definition and the individual dots that make up the picture become visible. You can change the way colours look in a bitmap by adjusting the brightness and contrast and converting colour to black and white or greyscale. To change specific colours in a bitmap, photo editing software must be used.
.jpg	JPEG (Joint Photographics Expert Group) is an image file format that compresses the image by removing unnecessary image data (thus making the file size smaller). Many digital cameras automatically save images into this format. The JPEG format works well for high-colour photographs and is suitable for storing and using images electronically. However, because of the data loss generated as it compresses the file, a printed image from a JPEG file is not particularly high quality.
.gif	GIF (Graphics Interchange Format) is similar to JPEG in that it compresses the image to remove unnecessary data. However, because a GIF file is limited to 256 colours it is more effective for drawn images than for colour photographs.
.tif	TIFF (Tagged Image File Format) is the standard graphics format for high-quality graphics. It is widely used in applications such as Photoshop and scanners often save the scanned image as a TIFF file by default.

Image file formats

.wmf   Windows® Metafile is a graphics file format used to exchange information between Microsoft® Windows® applications. A WMF file contains a series of commands that the Windows® operating system converts into the graphic image you see on the screen. Using WMF files saves space when many bitmaps are being used by different components of the Windows® operating system.

.png   PNG (Portable Network Graphics) is a new graphic format similar to GIF. PNG is now a standard for the Web. PNG allows storage of images with a greater colour depth than GIF. A PNG file contains a number of 'chunks' which contain certain information about the image. These 'chunks' are either critical or ancillary. A program can safely ignore an ancillary chunk, thus reducing the size of the image file.

JPEG and GIF are the most commonly used image file formats on the Web. The most common picture format is JPEG as this format compresses the file to its smallest size, which is useful if you want to send the picture via e-mail.

Once you have saved the picture onto your computer, you can insert it into a Word document. Choose **Picture** from the **Insert** menu and then click on **From File**.

The Insert Picture dialog box opens.

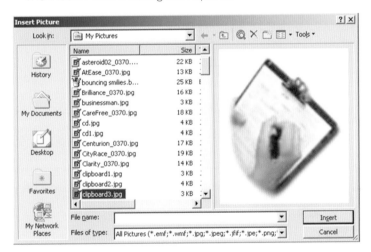

There are different ways you can view pictures in the Insert Picture dialog box. Click on the Views drop-down list to change the view.

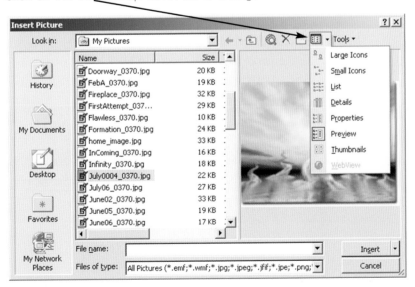

The dialog box is showing the picture using the Preview view. The Thumbnails view also enables you to see the pictures themselves. The other views will list the filenames rather than the pictures.

Open the drop-down list by the **Look in:** box and navigate to the drive and folder that your picture file is stored in. Double-click on a folder to open it, or use the **Back** or **Up One Level** buttons to move up out of a folder.

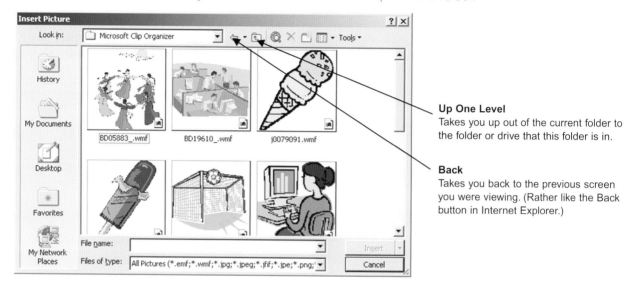

Up One Level
Takes you up out of the current folder to the folder or drive that this folder is in.

Back
Takes you back to the previous screen you were viewing. (Rather like the Back button in Internet Explorer.)

Locate the picture you wish to insert, click on it to select it and then click on the **Insert** button at the bottom right of the dialog box. (Alternatively, you can double-click on the file.) The picture will be inserted into the document.

TASK 20

Insert a picture already stored on your computer into the 'Star News' file.

How text works with pictures

Before you can start moving or resizing the picture that you have inserted, you need to choose how you want the text on your page to react to the picture. There are various text wrapping options. When you click on the picture you have just inserted, the Picture toolbar will appear. If it doesn't appear automatically, choose **Toolbars** from the **View** menu and click on the **Picture** toolbar to switch it on.

Text Wrapping

Click on the Text Wrapping button on the toolbar. A menu of options appears.

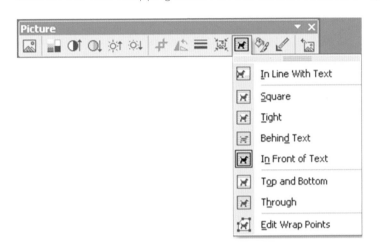

- **In Line With Text** – places the picture at the insertion point in the line of text.
- **Square** – wraps text around all sides of the box that contains the picture.
- **Tight** – wraps text around all sides using the contours of the picture itself.
- **Behind Text** – places the picture behind the text. The text does not wrap around the picture.
- **In Front of Text** – places the picture in front of the text. The text does not wrap around the picture.
- **Top and Bottom** – flows the text above and below the picture.
- **Through** – flows the text right through the picture object as if it was not there.

Positioning a picture on the page

To move a picture on the page, click on the picture with the mouse to select it. (The selection handles in Word 2002 are white circles, the selection handles in Word 2000 are white squares.) When the mouse pointer is on the picture, a four-headed arrow is attached to it.

Click and hold the left mouse button and drag the picture to its new location. As you drag the picture, a dashed border appears.

When you release the mouse button the picture is moved to the new location.

Resizing a picture on the page

To resize a picture, click on it to select it. Move the mouse over one of the selection handles (white circles or squares). The mouse pointer changes to a double-headed black arrow.

Click and drag this arrow inwards or outwards, depending whether you wish to make the picture smaller or larger. (Resizing using the handles on the left or right of the picture will make the picture narrower or wider. Resizing using the handles on the top or bottom of the picture will make the picture shallower or deeper. Resizing using the handles in the corners of the picture will resize horizontally and vertically at the same time.)

Rotating a picture in Word 2002

To rotate a picture, click on it to select it.

Move the mouse over the green circle at the top of the picture. The mouse pointer changes to a circular black arrow.

Click and drag this arrow to the right or left. The picture rotates in the direction you are dragging.

As you drag the handle, a dashed border appears. When you release the mouse button the picture is rotated.

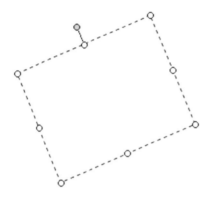

Rotating a picture in Word 2000

Click on the **Free Rotate** tool on the Drawing toolbar. The mouse pointer changes to a circular black arrow and the handles around the picture are now green circles. Move the mouse over one of the green circles.

Click and drag this arrow to the right or left. The picture rotates in the direction you are dragging.

As you drag the handle, a dashed border appears. When you release the mouse button the picture is rotated.

TASK 21

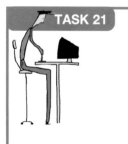

1 Click on the first picture you inserted into the document. Choose Tight as the text wrapping option. Repeat this process with the second picture.

2 Move the pictures so they are sitting in the column layout of the document.

3 Resize both pictures so they are much smaller. Notice how the text wraps around the pictures.

4 Choose different text wrapping options and watch how they effect how the text wraps around the picture.

5 Rotate the pictures using the rotate handle.

6 Save the document.

Formatting a picture

You can also specify settings for the picture in the Format Picture dialog box. Double-click on the picture to open this dialog box.

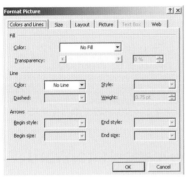

This dialog box has tabs across the top: **Colors and Lines**, **Size**, **Layout**, **Picture**, **Text Box** and **Web**.

The **Colors and Lines** tab enables you to put the picture in a box by choosing a **Line** colour and style for around the edge of the picture and a **Fill** colour inside the box.

The example below shows a picture with a blue dashed line around the edge and a red fill colour.

The **Size** tab enables you to specify a height and width for your picture (rather than simply resizing using the handles). You can also specify a rotation angle (rather than simply rotating using the handle).

If the **Lock aspect ratio** box is ticked, the height and width will change in relation to each other, i.e. when you specify the height measurement, the width measurement will change automatically so the picture still has the same dimensions.

You can also **Scale** the picture as a percentage of its original size (100%). (Ensure the **Relative to original picture size** box is ticked.)

The **Layout** tab enables you to choose text wrapping (like the button on the toolbar) and the horizontal alignment of the picture (where it should sit on the page).

The **Picture** tab enables you to **Crop** the picture. (By cropping a picture, you can slice off edges of the picture). Choose which side of the picture you wish to crop and by how much.

This example shows the picture having been cropped by 0.5 cm on the left and right sides.

You can also work with the **Image control** settings on the **Picture** tab. Click on the drop-down arrow by **Color** and choose Automatic, Grayscale, Black and White or Washout.

| Automatic | Grayscale | Black and White | Washout |

To adjust the **Brightness** and **Contrast** of the picture, either drag the slider to the left or right or choose a percentage in the box.

TASK 22

1 **Use the Format Picture dialog box to change the size of the pictures in your document.**

2 **Change one picture to Grayscale and the other picture to Washout.**

3 **Save and close the file.**

Inserting information from another application into Word

There are two ways you can bring information from another application, such as Excel, into Word.

You can insert the information as an 'embedded object' – the object is created in the source file and inserted into the destination file with no link. Once the information is embedded in the destination file, it becomes part of that file. If the object in the source file is updated, the embedded object is not updated. Changes can be made to the embedded object in the destination file. This is an efficient way to present in a Word document information from a different application.

Alternatively, you can insert the information as a 'linked object' – the object is created in the source file and inserted into the destination file with a link. If the object in the source file is updated, the linked object in the destination file is also updated. This is useful when you want to include some information in a Word document, but wish to maintain that information in a different application. For example, if you wish to present some data that is stored in an Excel worksheet in a report you are producing in Word, you can insert that data as an object in the Word document. If you want to be able to update the data in Excel and have that data automatically update in the Word document also, you can insert it as a linked object.

In Word an 'object' is something other than text (e.g. a drawing, clip art, a photograph, a text box). Objects can be moved and resized on the page. If you bring information in from another application, it is inserted into the Word document as an object.

Insert an existing file as an embedded object

Place the cursor where you wish to insert the file.
Choose **Object** from the **Insert** menu.

The Object dialog box opens.
Click on the **Create from File** tab.

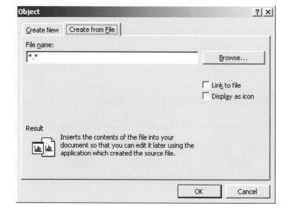

Click on **Browse ...** to locate the file you wish to insert.

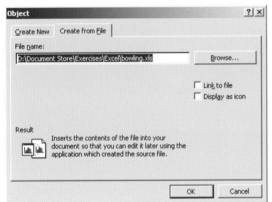

Choose the appropriate drive and open the folder for the file you wish to insert. Select the file and click on **Insert**.

The path of the file (location and file name) appears in the File name line of the Object dialog box. Click on **OK**. The file is inserted as an embedded object in the Word document. This object can be moved and resized (see page 196 for information on how to change the text wrapping options of the object).

If you wish to change the content of the object, double-click on the object and the source application is activated. For example if you inserted an Excel spreadsheet into a Word document. If the figures need to be altered, double-click on the object to activate an embedded version of Excel.

	A	B	C	D	E	F
1	**Name**	**Age**	**Bowling Average**			
2	Joan Simmonds	54	250			
3	Bill Smith	60	300			
4	Harry Ramsden	65	300			
5	Barbara Street	59	270			
6	Harriet Barlow	56	240			
7	Sid Thomas	53	340			

Sheet1 / Sheet2 / Sheet3 /

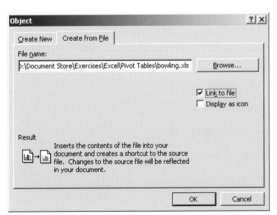

Insert an existing file as a linked object

If you wish to insert information into a Word document, but link that information to its original source, repeat the steps above for inserting an embedded object. In the Object dialog box, once you have located the file you wish to insert, tick the **Link to file** box and then click on **OK**.

The file is inserted as a linked object in the Word document. This object can be moved and resized. (See page 196 for information on how to change the text wrapping options of the object).

If you wish to change the content of the object, double-click on it and the source application is launched. Make any changes to the data on the Excel spreadsheet. (These changes will also be reflected in the linked object in Word). Save and close the file in Excel when you have finished updating it.

Insert information using copy and paste

Open the file that contains the information that you wish to paste into a Word document.

Select the data or object that you wish to copy. Choose **Copy** from the **Edit** menu, click on the **Copy** button or press [Control]+[C] to copy the selected information to the clipboard. (For information on using Copy and Paste and the Clipboard, see page 165).

Open the document in Word into which you wish to paste this information and move to the location where you wish to insert the information. Choose **Paste** from the **Edit** menu, click on the **Paste** button or press [Control]+[V] to paste the information onto the Word page. The information now becomes part of your Word document and can be amended and formatted just as if you had created it in Word.

Insert and link information using copy and paste

Open the file that contains the information that you wish to paste and link into a Word document.

Select the data or object that you wish to copy into Word. Choose **Copy** from the **Edit** menu, click on the **Copy** button or press [Control]+[C] to copy the selected information to the clipboard. (For information on using Copy and Paste and the Clipboard, see page 165).

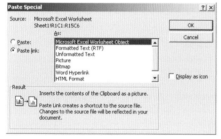

Open the document in Word into which you wish to paste and link this information and move to the location where you wish to insert the information.

Select **Paste Special** from the **Edit** menu. The Paste Special dialog box opens.

Choose **Paste link** and click on **OK**. The file is inserted as a linked object in the Word document.

TASK 23

1 **Launch Excel and type the following data onto the worksheet.**

Name	Age	Bowling Average
Joan Simmonds	54	250
Bill Smith	60	300
Harry Ramsden	65	300
Barbara Street	59	270
Harriet Barlow	56	240
Sid Thomas	53	340

2 **Save the file in the Tasks for ITQ folder with the filename 'Excel Data'.**

3 **Switch into Word and open the file called 'Star News'.**

4 **Insert the file 'Excel Data' into the Word document as a linked object.**

5 **Change the text wrapping option to Square and move the object so that it is centred under the two text boxes.**

TASK 23

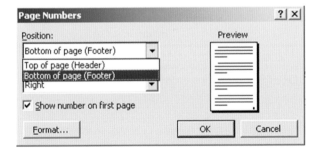

There are a lot of desktop publishing features in Word which enable you to create drawings, organisation charts and graphs.

Creating standard text is easy and efficient using **Styles** and **Autoformat** and creating standard documents is made easy by using Templates.

You will find Word an extremely exciting package, allowing you to produce documents from simple letters to complex newsletters with columns, tables and graphics.

Name	Age	Bowling Average
Joan Simmonds	54	250
Bill Smith	60	300
Harry Ramsden	65	300
Barbara Street	59	270
Harriet Barlow	56	240
Sid Thomas	53	340

6 **Double-click on the object and change the data as follows:**

Name	Age	Bowling Average
Joan Sampson	55	150
Bill Smithers	61	250
Harry Ramsbottom	66	260
Barbara Streeter	60	275
Harriet Barrett	57	230
Sid Thompson	54	300

7 **Save and close the Excel file and check that the data has updated in the Word document.**

8 **Save and close the Word file.**

Inserting page numbers

You can set up a page number to appear in the top or bottom margin area of every page in your document.

Choose **Page Numbers** from the **Insert** menu. The Page Numbers dialog box opens.

You can choose to have the page number appear at the Bottom of page (Footer) or the Top of page (Header). Click on the **Position** drop-down arrow and choose from the list.

You can choose to have the page number appear aligned at the left or right side of the page or in the centre of the page. Click on the **Alignment** drop-down arrow and choose from the list.

If you select Inside, the page numbers will appear on the 'inside' edges of a book-style document, i.e. on the right side of even pages and the left side of odd pages. If you select Outside, the page numbers will appear on the 'outside' edges of a book-style document, i.e. on the left side of even pages and the right side of odd pages.

Page Numbers   ? ×

Position:

Bottom of page (Footer) ▼

Top of page (Header)
Bottom of page (Footer)
Right ▼

☑ Show number on first page

Format...   OK   Cancel

Preview

Page Numbers   ? ×

Position:

Bottom of page (Footer) ▼

Alignment:

Right ▼

Left
Center
Right
Inside
Outside

OK   Cancel

Preview

The Preview area of the dialog box allows you to see where your page number will appear.

Once you have made your choice, click on **OK**. A page number will appear on every page in your document, at the location you have specified.

If you do not want the page number to appear on the first page of your document, for example, if it is a title page, remove the tick from the **Show number on first page** box. Click on **OK**.

The **Format** button in the Page Numbers dialog box enables you to choose from a range of different number formats for your page number.

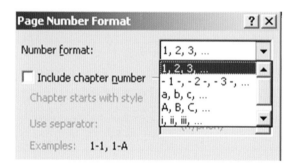

TASK 24

1 **Open the file called 'Word Text'.**

2 **Insert a page number at the bottom centre of every page in the document.**

3 **Change the page number to the top of the page and choose Inside as the alignment.**

4 **Save and close the file.**

Creating headers and footers

If you wish to have text appear in the top margin (header) or bottom margin (footer) of every page in your document, or you want to be able to add formatting to the page number, you must use the Header and Footer feature. On page 205 there is an example of a header and a footer.

HEADERS & FOOTERS

A header prints in the top margin on every (or every other) page of a document. A footer prints in the bottom margin.

If you are responsible for planning travel then you can tackle this either in an amateurish, just-do-what-is-needed way or with a professional, well-organised approach. The difference lies in the detail. Anyone can ring a travel agent but a good PA will check the fine print, make sure the trip doesn't coincide with local holidays and have information to hand on climate, local customs and medical precautions. The good PA will also be capable of coping with group bookings, liaising with those who are away and keeping the office well organised in their absence. Finally, by knowing the full range of services and alternatives available and who to contact for more information, a good PA will keep the costs of business travel within or below budget.

This is a footer   Page 2   ©Nicki Talbot 2004

To insert a header or footer into your document, choose **Header and Footer** from the **View** menu.

The cursor will move into the Header area of the page and the Header and Footer toolbar will appear.

The text in the main part of your document will be greyed out.

There are two tabs set on the ruler – a centred tab between the left and right margins and a right tab on the right margin. You can type text at the left side of the header area, press tab to move to the centred tab and type text in the centre and press tab again to move to the right tab and type text at the right side of the page.

The buttons on the Header and Footer toolbar enable you to insert fields which will show up-to-date information in the document, such as page number, current date, etc., and to work with headers and footers.

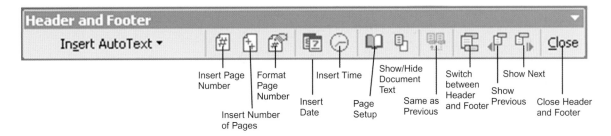

- **Insert AutoText** – opens a menu containing all the stored AutoText items. You can insert an AutoText item by clicking on it in the menu (see page 189 for more information on AutoText).
- **Insert Page Number** – inserts the current page number at the cursor position.
- **Insert Number of Pages** – inserts the total number of pages in the document at the cursor position. (You can use Insert Page Number and Insert Number of Pages together to create 'Page ? of ?').
- **Format Page Number** – enables you to change the number format and choose the number from which you want to start counting.
- **Insert Date** – inserts the current date at the cursor position. (This is governed by the Date/Time settings in the Windows Control Panel.) The date will update each time the document is opened or printed.
- **Insert Time** – inserts the current time at the cursor position. Again, the time will update each time the document is opened or printed.
- **Page Setup** – opens the Page Setup dialog box so that you can adjust the margins of your header and footer. You can also choose to have different headers and footers on odd and even pages, or a different first page header and/or footer.
- **Show/Hide Document Text** – shows or hides the main document text. (You will notice that the main document text shows in grey on the screen when you are in the header or footer area. If you prefer, you can hide the main document text completely while you are working on your headers and footers.)
- **Same as Previous** – you use this button to 'detach' a header or footer from the previous one, when your document is broken into sections. This enables you to have different headers and footers on different pages in a document.
- **Switch between Header and Footer** – this moves the cursor from the header area to the footer area and back.
- **Show Previous** – shows the previous header if you are in the header area and the previous footer if you are in the footer area.
- **Show Next** – shows the next header if you are in the header area and the next footer if you are in the footer area.
- **Close Header and Footer** – this closes the header and footer area and returns the cursor to the main document text.

Move to the footer area of the page (press the **Switch between Header and Footer** button).

As with the header area, tabs are already set on the ruler when you are in the Footer area. You can type at the left side of the page, press Tab to type in the centre of the page and/or press Tab to type at the right side of the page.

When you have finished typing headers and footers, click on the **Close** button on the Header and Footer toolbar. Your cursor will return to the main document text. The main document text now appears black and the headers and footers appear in grey so that you can distinguish which is the main part of the document and which is the header/footer text.

If you want to have different headers and footers appearing on different pages in a multi-page document, you need to break the document into sections (see page 174).

If you go into the header or footer area of a sectioned document, the section you are in is indicated.

Each header and footer in your document will be the same as the previous one. The **Same as Previous** button on the Header and Footer toolbar is always on unless you switch it off.

If you do not wish a header or footer to be the same as the previous one, release the **Same as Previous** button on the toolbar before you type the text for that header or footer.

TASK 25

1 **Open the file called 'Star News'.**

2 **Insert a footer into the document to read:**

   Newsletter Issue 4   Page 1   ©Star News Inc 2002

3 **Insert the page number as a field.**

4 **Format the footer using Arial, font size 9.**

5 **Save and close the file.**

6 **Open the file called 'Word Text'. (This document is already broken into three sections.)**

7 **Remove the page number from the pages and insert the following headers in Arial, font size 9:**

   Section 1 – Overview of Microsoft Word

   Section 2 – Desktop Publishing Features

   Section 3 – Styles and AutoFormat

8 **Save and close the file.**

 ## Creating tables

If you wish to lay out text across the page you can use tabs, or alternatively, a table.

DEPARTMENT	FLOOR	ROOM NO.
Personnel	2nd	215
Accounts	4th	422
Sales	7th	702
Marketing	6th	613

There are two ways you can create a table in Word: draw table or insert table.

Drawing a table

Choose **Draw Table** from the **Table** menu. The mouse pointer changes to a pencil icon. Click and drag the pencil icon to draw the table on the page. (You can only draw one line at a time.)

The Tables and Borders toolbar also appears.

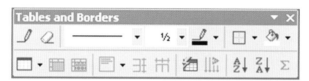

The first button on the toolbar is 'on' – this is the pencil. If you make a mistake, you can use the second button on the toolbar (**Eraser**) to rub a line out. Use this tool in the same way as the pencil – click and drag. Click on the pencil and eraser buttons alternately to draw and rub out the lines of your table.

TASK 26

1 **Start a new document in Word and practise drawing a table using the pencil icon and the eraser icon.**

2 **Close the document without saving it.**

Inserting a table

Choose **Insert** from the **Table** menu and then choose **Table** from the sub-menu.

The Insert Table dialog box opens.

Use the up and down arrows to choose the **Number of columns** and **Number of rows** you want in the table (or type in the number you require in the boxes).

Click on **OK**. A standard table will appear on the page, with the number of columns and rows you have specified. Type the text you require in each cell of the table and use the **Tab** key on the keyboard to move into the next cell.

If you wish to make a row deeper in order to type more text in the cell, press the **Return** key on the keyboard.

When you reach the last cell in the table, pressing the **Tab** key creates a new row in the table.

TASK 27

Start a new document and insert a table with 3 columns and 9 rows.

Selecting parts of a table

Before you can make changes to your table, you need to select the appropriate cell, column or row that you wish to change.

Point to the cell you wish to select (just inside the left cell border). The mouse pointer changes to a black arrow pointing to the cell. Click and the cell you are pointing at will be selected.

To select more than one cell, click and drag across the cells you wish to select.

Point to the row that you wish to select (just outside the table on the left). The mouse pointer becomes an arrow pointing towards the row. Click and the complete row will be selected.

To select more than one row, drag the mouse down.

Point to the column that you wish to select (just above the table). The mouse pointer changes to a black arrow pointing down towards the column. Click and the complete column will be selected.

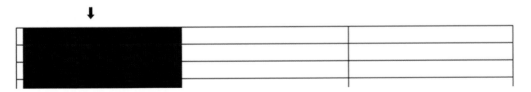

To select more than one column, drag the mouse across the columns.

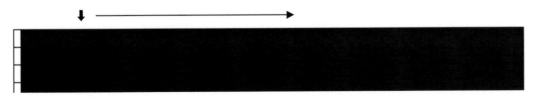

You can also use the Table menu to select different parts of the table. Choose **Select** from the **Table** menu and then choose which part of the table you wish to select from the sub-menu.

TASK 28

Practise selecting different parts of the table using the mouse and the menu.

Resizing rows and columns

The quickest way to resize rows and columns in a table is to use the resizing handles on the table itself. When you move the mouse over a column or row border, the mouse pointer changes to a double-headed black arrow.

To resize a column, click and drag the resizing handle left or right.

To resize a row, click and drag the resizing handle up or down.

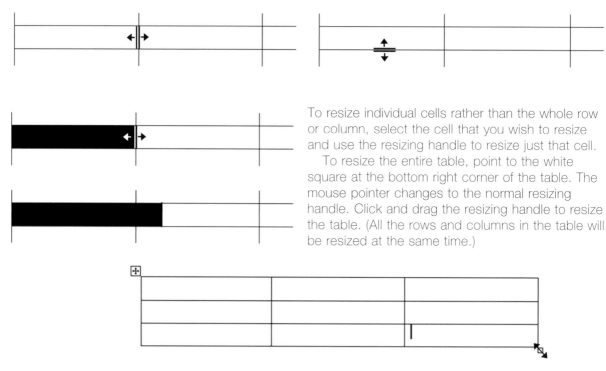

To resize individual cells rather than the whole row or column, select the cell that you wish to resize and use the resizing handle to resize just that cell.

To resize the entire table, point to the white square at the bottom right corner of the table. The mouse pointer changes to the normal resizing handle. Click and drag the resizing handle to resize the table. (All the rows and columns in the table will be resized at the same time.)

TASK 29

1 **Practise resizing the rows and columns in your table using the resizing handles.**

2 **Practise resizing the whole table using the resizing handle.**

Inserting and deleting rows and columns

Choose **Insert** from the **Table** menu and then select what you want to insert and where from the sub-menu.

You can insert columns to the left or right and above or below the one your cursor is placed in.

Select the row(s) or column(s) you wish to delete. Choose **Delete** from the **Table** menu and then select what you want to delete from the sub-menu.

Merging and splitting cells

Sometimes you may want to merge two or more adjacent cells to create a larger cell.

Select the cells that you wish to merge. Choose **Merge Cells** from the **Table** menu. In this example the cells in the first row of the table have been merged to allow for a centred heading above the data.

BUDGET 2004			
Quarter 1	Quarter 2	Quarter 3	Quarter 4

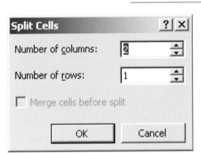

You may wish to split an existing cell to create a number of smaller cells.

Click in the cell you wish to split. Choose **Split Cells** from the **Table** menu.

Choose the **Number of columns** and/or **Number of rows** you wish to split the cell into. Click on **OK**.

In this example the first cell in the third row of the table has been split into three smaller cells.

BUDGET 2004			
Quarter 1	Quarter 2	Quarter 3	Quarter 4

You can also use the Merge Cells and Split Cells buttons on the Tables and Borders toolbar. (The buttons on this toolbar are discussed on page 220.)

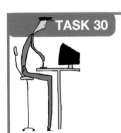

TASK 30

1 **Insert three rows and one column into the table.**

2 **Delete three rows and one column from the table.**

3 **Select the first row of the table and merge the cells in this row.**

4 **Click in the first cell of the third row of the table and split the cell into three columns.**

Splitting a table

You can split an existing table into two separate tables. (For example, you may wish to type some text in the middle of the table.)

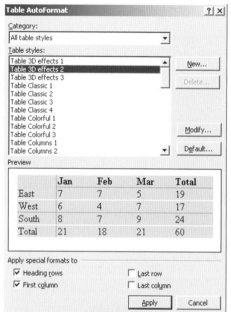

Click in the cell of the table where you wish the split to occur. Choose **Split Table** from the **Table** menu.

Two separate tables are created and the cursor is now sitting between the two tables.

The AutoFormat gallery

The AutoFormat gallery contains a number of pre-defined formats that you can apply to your table. These formats include borders, shading, fonts, font sizes, alignment, etc.

Choose **Table AutoFormat** from the **Table** menu. The Table AutoFormat dialog box opens.

Choose from the list of **Table styles** by clicking on a style. The Preview pane at the bottom of the dialog box shows you what the style you have selected looks like. To apply an AutoFormat to your table, click on **Apply**. You can modify the existing AutoFormat styles – click on the style you wish to modify and then click on **Modify ...** The Modify Style dialog box opens.

You can change the formatting of the selected AutoFormat. When you have finished making changes, click on **OK**. This amended AutoFormat will be available for you to use on any new tables you create.

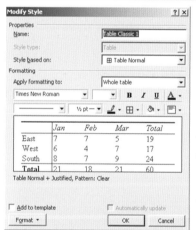

In Word 2002, you can create a new AutoFormat style based on an existing one – click on the style on which you wish to base the new style and then click on **New ...** The New Style dialog box opens as below.

Give the new AutoFormat a name and choose the formatting you wish to include in the AutoFormat. When you have finished choosing options, click on **OK**. This new AutoFormat will be available for you to use on any new tables you create.

If you wish a particular AutoFormat to be the default style for all tables you create – click on the style and then click on **Default ...**

Choose whether you wish to set this AutoFormat as the default for this document only or all new documents you create. Click on **OK**.

The AutoFormat gallery in Word 2000 is not quite as comprehensive as in Word 2002. You can choose from a range of table format styles and you can amend a style, but you cannot create new styles, delete styles or make a style the default style.

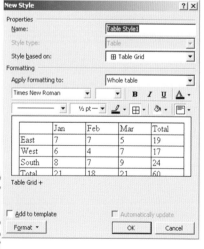

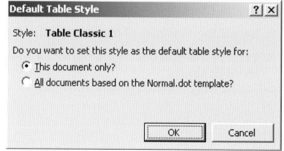

1 **Apply different AutoFormats to your table.**

2 **Amend an existing AutoFormat.**

3 **Create a new AutoFormat if you are working in Word 2002.**

4 **Close the document without saving.**

AutoFit columns

Word can adjust the size of columns automatically using the AutoFit options.

Select the column(s) you wish to adjust. Choose **AutoFit** from the **Table** menu and then choose which AutoFit option you want from the sub-menu.

- **AutoFit to Contents** – the column resizes to fit its contents.
- **AutoFit to Window** – useful when creating tables for a Web page – the table will resize when the window is sized.
- **Fixed Column Width** – you specify the size you want the column width to be.

If you wish to adjust the size of columns or rows so that they are the same size, select the columns or rows that you wish to adjust. Choose **AutoFit** from the **Table** menu and then select **Distribute Rows Evenly** or **Distribute Columns Evenly** from the sub-menu.

Repeating heading rows

If you are creating a large table which will print onto more than one page, you can set the first row(s) of your table (which normally contain the headings of the table) to automatically repeat at the top of each new page. This is a very useful feature as it makes it much easier to understand what the data in the table means, without having to refer back to the first page of the table every time.

Select the row(s) that you wish to repeat on each page and choose **Heading Rows Repeat** from the **Table** menu.

DEPARTMENT	FLOOR	ROOM NO.
Personnel	2nd	215
Accounts	4th	422
Sales	7th	702
Marketing	6th	613

(The best way to check this is to view your table in Print Preview. Your rows will be repeated at the top of the second and subsequent pages.)

TASK 32

1 **Start a new document and insert a table with 3 columns and 9 rows.**

2 **Type the following data into the table:**

Consultant	Consultancy hours to date	Rate per hour
Smith & Co	100	£40.00
Higgins Ltd	60	£30.00
Stone & Son	75	£7.00
Pete's Pizza Pad	40	£5.00
Abbey Investments	55	£25.00
Spire Fundholdings	30	£15.00
James James & Jones	200	£17.00
Tech-Compleat plc	85	£36.00

3 **AutoFit the columns to fit the contents.**

Consultant	Consultancy hours to date	Rate per hour
Smith & Co	100	£40.00
Higgins Ltd	60	£30.00
Stone & Son	75	£7.00
Pete's Pizza Pad	40	£5.00
Abbey Investments	55	£25.00
Spire Fundholdings	30	£15.00
James James & Jones	200	£17.00
Tech-Compleat plc	85	£36.00

4 **Select the second two columns and distribute them evenly.**

Consultant	Consultancy hours to date	Rate per hour
Smith & Co	100	£40.00
Higgins Ltd	60	£30.00
Stone & Son	75	£7.00
Pete's Pizza Pad	40	£5.00
Abbey Investments	55	£25.00
Spire Fundholdings	30	£15.00
James James & Jones	200	£17.00
Tech-Compleat plc	85	£36.00

5 **Set up the first row of the table to repeat on each printed page.**

6 **Save the document in your Tasks for ITQ folder with the filename 'Table 1'.**

Converting between text and a table

You can convert text you have already typed into a table and you can convert a table you have created back to normal text. If you wish to put existing text into a table, the text must be separated by tabs or commas to indicate where each new column should begin and each new row should begin on a new line.

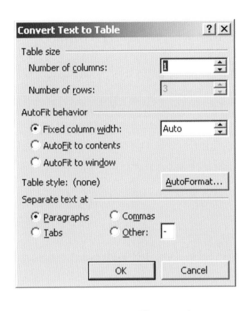

Select the text that you wish to put into a table. Choose **Convert** from the **Table** menu and choose **Text to Table ...** from the sub-menu.

The Convert Text to Table dialog box opens.

Choose how many columns and rows you want in your table under **Table size** and how the text should be separated under **Separate text at**. Click on **OK**.

Click in a table you wish to convert to text. Choose **Convert** from the **Table** menu and click on **Table to Text ...**

The Convert Table to Text dialog box opens.

Choose how you want the columns to be separated when the table is removed. Rows are always separated using paragraph marks. Click on **OK**.

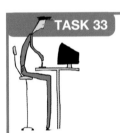

TASK 33

1 **Click in the table you have created in 'Table 1'.**

2 **Resize the columns to ensure that the headings appear on one line.**

3 **Convert the table to text, using tabs to separate the columns.**

Consultant	Consultancy hours to date	Rate per hour
Smith & Co	100	£40.00
Higgins Ltd	60	£30.00
Stone & Son	75	£7.00
Pete's Pizza Pad	40	£5.00
Abbey Investments	55	£25.00
Spire Fundholdings	30	£15.00
James James & Jones	200	£17.00
Tech-Compleat plc	85	£36.00

4 **Convert the text back into a table.**

Consultant	Consultancy hours to date	Rate per hour
Smith & Co	100	£40.00
Higgins Ltd	60	£30.00
Stone & Son	75	£7.00
Pete's Pizza Pad	40	£5.00
Abbey Investments	55	£25.00
Spire Fundholdings	30	£15.00
James James & Jones	200	£17.00
Tech-Compleat plc	85	£36.00

5 **Save the document.**

Sorting data in a table

You can sort data in a table. For example, if you have created a table containing name and address information and there are separate columns for first name and last name, you can sort the table by last name.

Click in the Table and choose **Sort ...** from the **Table** menu. The Sort dialog box opens.

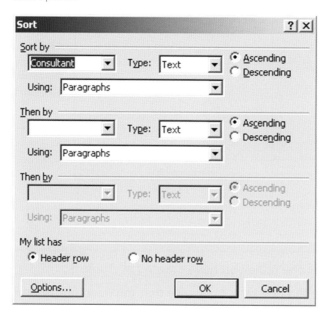

If your table has column headings, the dialog box will use these headings to identify which column to sort by.

Choose the column by which you want to sort from the **Sort by** drop-down list. Choose whether that column contains text, numbers or dates from the **Type** drop-down list. Click on **Ascending** to sort from A–Z or **Descending** to sort from Z–A.

You can have more than one level of sort. For example, you may want to sort your table by the last name column and then by the first name column. Choose the first column by which you want to sort and then choose the next column from the **Then by** drop-down list. Again, choose whether that column contains text, numbers or dates from the **Type** drop-down list and choose to sort Ascending or Descending. You can choose up to three levels of sort, i.e. you can sort by up to three different columns.

Click on **OK** when you have set up your sort options.

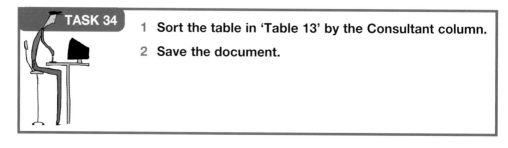

TASK 34

1 **Sort the table in 'Table 13' by the Consultant column.**

2 **Save the document.**

Hiding the gridlines

Sometimes you might use the Table feature in order to lay out text easily on a page. For example, when creating Minutes of meetings, it is useful to use the Table feature to lay out the text.

When you create a table, a thin black border grid appears on your table by default. You can remove the borders (see page 220), but you will still be able to see the gridlines. The figure below is an example of minutes laid out using a table. The borders have been removed, but the gridlines are still visible.

			ACTION
1.	Apologies There were no apologies.		
2.	Matters Arising Karen has now sorted out the water machine. She still needs to order more bottles from Spring Water.	Karen	

If you do not want the reader to see the structure of the table (i.e. the gridlines), choose **Hide Gridlines** from the **Table** menu. The example below shows the same Minutes table with the gridlines hidden.

ACTION

1.   Apologies

There were no apologies.

2.   Matters Arising

Karen has now sorted out the water machine. She still needs to   Karen
order more bottles from Spring Water.

Table Properties

The Table Properties dialog box contains four tabs across the top: **Table, Row, Column** and **Cell**. You can make more changes to your table, rows, columns or cells using this dialog box. Choose **Table Properties** from the **Table** menu. The Table Properties dialog box opens.

On the **Table** tab you can specify a width for your table. Tick the **Preferred width** box and specify the width in centimetres that you want your table to be.

You can choose the **Alignment** of your table on the page. When you insert a table, it will stretch from the left margin to the right margin. However, if you have resized columns, the table may no longer fill the page from margin to margin. You may then wish to align your table at the left margin, in the centre or at the right margin. You can also choose to indent the table away from the left margin. Choose a measurement in the **Indent from left:** box.

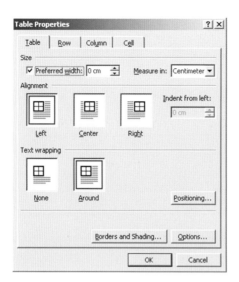

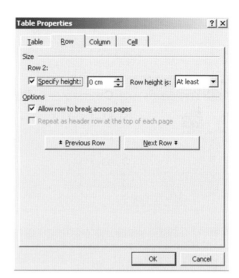

You can also choose how text on the page should wrap around a smaller table. You can create a small table on the page and have the text wrap around the outside of it.

You can also access the **Borders and Shading** dialog box (see page 220) from this tab of the Table Properties dialog box.

On the **Row** tab you can specify the height of selected rows. Tick the **Specify height** box and specify the height in centimetres that you want your rows to be.

You can specify whether a row should be allowed to go across a page break. If you are creating a long table, you can decide whether a row should be split across a page break, or whether the complete row should be taken onto the next page. Tick the **Allow row to break across pages** box.

You can also specify whether the selected row should be repeated at the top of each printed page. (This is the same as choosing **Heading Rows Repeat** from the **Table** menu.)

The **Previous Row** and **Next Row** buttons enable you to move to the previous or next row in the table without having to close the dialog box.

On the **Column** tab you can specify the width of selected columns. Tick the **Preferred width** box and specify the width in centimetres that you want your columns to be.

The **Previous Column** and **Next Column** buttons enable you to move to the previous or next column in the table without having to close the dialog box.

On the **Cell** tab you can specify the width of selected cells. Tick the **Preferred width** box and specify the width in centimetres that you want your cells to be.

You can also choose the **Vertical alignment** of the text in a cell. If you make a row deeper by resizing it, the text stays at the top of the row. Choose the preferred vertical alignment from this tab of the dialog box.

Click on **OK** to apply all your changes.

TASK 35

1   **Change the alignment of the table in 'Table 1' to Center.**

2   **Make the first row deeper, using the resizing handle. Change the vertical alignment of the headings in the first row to Center.**

Consultant	Consultancy hours to date	Rate per hour
Abbey Investments	55	£25.00
Higgins Ltd	60	£30.00
James James & Jones	200	£17.00
Pete's Pizza Pad	40	£5.00
Smith & Co	100	£40.00
Spire Fundholdings	30	£15.00
Stone & Son	75	£7.00
Tech-Compleat plc	85	£36.00

3   **Save the document.**

Adding borders and shading to a table

When you insert a table onto the Word page, it already has a thin black border grid. However, you may wish to change the borders and apply shading to cells. You can access the Borders and Shading dialog box by choosing **Table Properties** from the **Table** menu and then clicking on the **Borders and Shading** button on the **Tables** tab. Alternatively, you can choose **Borders and Shading** from the **Format** menu.

Apply borders

Select the cells in your table for which you wish to adjust the borders before opening the Borders and Shading dialog box. Click on the **Borders** tab at the top of the dialog box.

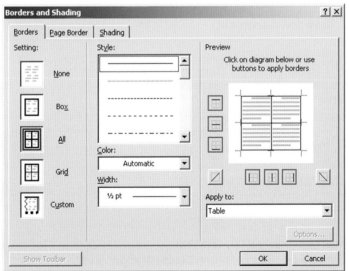

■ **Setting** – specifies the type of border you want: **Box** (borders around the edge), **All** (all borders), **Grid** (different outside and inside borders) or **Custom** (a different style for each border).

■ **Style** – solid, dotted, dashed, double, etc. style of line.

■ **Color**

■ **Width** – thickness of line.

■ **Preview** – shows you exactly what you will get when you click on OK. Click on the border buttons or the Preview area to apply the other formatting.

■ **Apply** – applies your choice to the whole table or just to the selected cells.

Click on **OK** when you have made the changes.

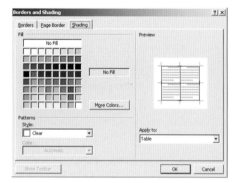

Apply shading

Select the cells in your table to which you wish to apply shading and open the Borders and Shading dialog box. Click on the **Shading** tab at the top of the dialog box.

Choose the colour that you wish to shade the selected cells from the **Fill** palette. (Click on **More Colours** to view more colours.)

Choose a shading style from the **Style** drop-down list. You can choose a % of shading or you can choose a pattern from this list. Once you have chosen a pattern, you can choose a pattern colour from the **Color** drop-down list.

Choose to **Apply** your choice to the whole table or to just the selected cells. Click on **OK**.

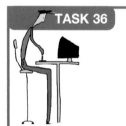

TASK 36

1 **Select the whole table in 'Table 1'.**

2 **Apply a solid 1½ pt Violet line to the borders around the edge of the table and a dashed ½ pt Bright Green line to the borders inside the table.**

3 **Apply Light Yellow shading to the top row of the table.**

4 **Save the document.**

Using the Tables and Borders toolbar

The Tables and Borders toolbar will appear automatically if you choose **Draw Table** from the **Table** menu. However, if you have used **Insert Table** to create your table and you wish to use the Tables and Borders toolbar, you can either choose **Toolbars** from the **View** menu and click on **Tables and Borders,** or click the **Tables and Borders** button on the Standard toolbar.

Tables and Borders

The Tables and Borders toolbar can be 'docked' at the top of the screen (like the Standard and Formatting toolbars) or can be displayed as a 'floating palette' on the screen. If it is docked, point to the left end of the toolbar and click and drag it to where you want it on the screen to make it a floating palette. As a floating palette, you can resize the toolbar to display it how you wish.

The top row of the toolbar contains buttons to work with the formatting of the table.

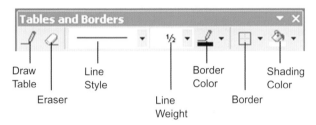

■ **Draw Table** – click on this button if you want to draw more rows or columns.
■ **Eraser** – click on this button to erase lines you have drawn using the pencil.

Before using the following buttons, select the appropriate part of your table first:

■ **Line Style** – click on the drop-down arrow to choose a line style from the list.
■ **Line Weight** – click on the drop-down arrow to choose a line weight from the list.
■ **Border Color** – click on the drop-down arrow to choose a border colour from the palette.
■ **Border** – click on the drop-down arrow to choose a border from the palette.
■ **Shading Color** – click on the drop-down arrow to choose a shading colour from the palette.

The bottom row of the toolbar contains buttons for features that can also be found in the Table menu.

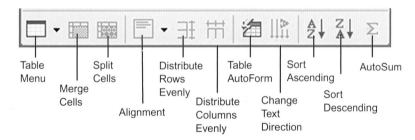

■ **Table Menu** – click on the drop-down arrow to open a menu of options for working with rows and columns.
■ **Merge Cells** – select more than one cell and click on this button to merge them into one cell.
■ **Split Cells** – click in a cell and click on this button to split the cell into more than one row and/or column.
■ **Alignment** – click on the drop-down arrow to choose the horizontal and vertical alignment of the text in the cell.
■ **Distribute Rows Evenly** – select more than one row and click on this button to make the rows the same height.
■ **Distribute Columns Evenly** – select more than one column and click on this button to make the columns the same width.
■ **Table AutoFormat** – click on this button to open the Table AutoFormat gallery.
■ **Change Text Direction** – click on this button to change the direction of the text in a cell. You can click on the button to cycle around the available options.
■ **Sort Ascending** – click on this button to sort a column in ascending order (A–Z).

- **Sort Descending** – click on this button to sort a column in descending order (Z–A).
- **AutoSum** – click on this button to add rows or columns of figures in a table.

TASK 37

1 **Select the table in 'Table 1'.**

2 **Practise making changes to the table using the Tables and Borders toolbar.**

3 **Save and close the document.**

 ## Mail Merge

If you wish to send the same letter to a group of people, rather than typing each letter individually, you can use the Mail Merge facility in Word to merge your standard letter with an address list (names and addresses and any other variable information). Each letter is personalised for the recipient. This is how companies produce mass-mailings. It is very quick and easy to use.

The Mail Merge Process

There are three stages to creating a mailing: create the layout of the letter, create the address list and carry out the merge process. It doesn't matter in what order the first two stages are carried out, but obviously the merge process has to be last.

The letter can be created during the mail merge process, or it can be a letter that has already been created.

The address list can be created during the mail merge process, or it can be a Word table, Excel spreadsheet or Access database that already contains the required information. You can also create mailing labels using the mail merge process.

The mail merge process does vary quite markedly between Word 2002 and Word 2000. Guidelines for mail merge in Word 2002 are shown first, followed by Word 2000 (page 231).

Mail Merge in Word 2002

Choose **Letters and Mailings** from the **Tools** menu and then choose **Mail Merge Wizard** from the sub-menu.

The Mail Merge task pane opens on the right side of the screen. Select the type of document you are working on. You can set up a mail merge to be sent via e-mail rather than traditional post.

Click on the link ➠ Next: Starting document.

Choose how you want to start the document. If you have not yet created the letter or if you have opened the letter you want to use and it is on the screen, choose **Use the current document**.

Mail Merge ▾ ✕

Select document type

What type of document are you working on?

- ◉ Letters
- ○ E-mail messages
- ○ Envelopes
- ○ Labels
- ○ Directory

Letters

Send letters to a group of people. You can personalize the letter that each person receives.

Click Next to continue.
Step 1 of 6

➪ Next: Starting document

Mail Merge ▾ ✕

Select starting document

How do you want to set up your letters?

- ◉ Use the current document
- ○ Start from a template
- ○ Start from existing document

Use the current document

Start from the document shown here and use the Mail Merge wizard to add recipient information.

Step 2 of 6

➪ Next: Select recipients

➪ Previous: Select document type

The other options are:

- **Start from a template** – if you want to create a new document based on a template.
- **Start from existing document** – if you want to use a letter you have already created, but haven't yet opened.

Click on the link ➟ Next: Select recipients. (Note that you can also go back to the previous step of the Wizard.)

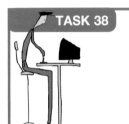

TASK 38

1   **Start a new document and choose Letters and Mailings, Mail Merge Wizard from the Tools menu.**

2   **Choose Letters in the Task Pane. Click on Next.**

3   **Choose Use the current document. Click on Next.**

Choose where the address list is coming from.

- If you have already created a list in a Word table, an Excel spreadsheet or an Access database, choose **Use an existing list**.
- If you want to mail Contacts you have stored in Outlook, choose **Select from Outlook contacts**.
- If you haven't yet created an address list, choose **Type a new list**.

The options in the second section of the task pane change according to what you select in the top section. If you choose **Use an existing list**, you will be invited to **Browse** to locate the file. If you choose **Select from Outlook contacts**, you will be requested to **Choose Contacts Folder**. Locate the Outlook Contacts folder that you are going to use. It is advisable to create a separate Contacts folder in Outlook first, containing the details of just the people you wish to mail.

In this example, the list has not yet been created, so **Type a new list** has been selected.

Click on the link **Create ...** to create your data list. The New Address List dialog box opens.

Creating a data list

The first stage of creating the data list is to decide which field names you require. Imagine your data list is a table containing data. The field names are the column headings of the table.

The New Address List dialog box offers standard fields that you can complete. To customise this list of field names, click on **Customize ...**

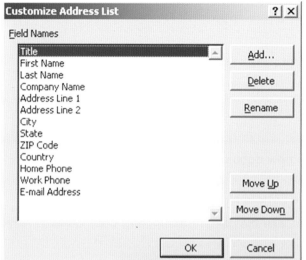

You can remove field names from the list, add new field names to the list and Rename field names. You can also rearrange the list using the **Move Up** and **Move Down** buttons. Click on the field you wish to move and press the appropriate button.

To remove a field name, click on the field name in the list and click on **Delete**.

To add a new field name to the list, click on **Add ...**

Type a name for the field and click on **OK**.

To rename a field name, select the field name in the list and click on **Rename**.

Type the new name for the field in the **To:** box and click on **OK**.

When you have finished customising the Address List, click on **OK**. You will be returned to the New Address List dialog box. The changes you have made to the field names will be reflected. You now need to enter the names, addresses and other information for the letter into this list.

The first blank record is showing. Type the first set of data into the list (this becomes a record) and then click on **New Entry** to move to the second blank record. Repeat this process for each set of data you need to enter.

If there is no data to go into a field, you can leave the field blank. For example, sometimes there is no Address2.

If you wish to delete a record from the list, locate the record using the View Entries section of the list and then click on **Delete Entry**. The **Find Entry** button enables you to find a record in your list by searching on a particular field. The **Filter and Sort** button enables you to sort the records in your list by any field and to filter the list according to specified criteria.

The View Entries section at the bottom of the dialog box enables you to view records in the list.

- **First** – takes you to the first record in the list.
- **Previous** – moves back through the records one at a time.
- **Record Number** – click in the box and type the record number that you wish to move to.
- **Next** – moves forward through the records one at a time.
- **Last** – takes you to the last record in the list.

When you have finished entering all the records of data, click on **Close**. You will now be prompted to save the Address List.

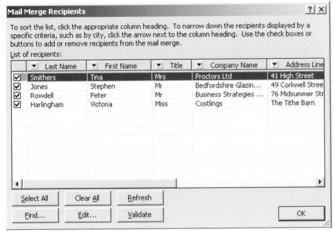

By default, you will be taken into the **My Data Sources** folder to store your address list. You can choose a different folder to store the address list in if you wish. Type a filename for the address list and click on **Save**.

Microsoft® Office Address Lists are given the file extension .mdb. However, you can open them in Word.

The Mail Merge Recipients dialog box now opens, showing a list of the data records you have entered.

You can sort this list by clicking on the appropriate column heading. For example, to sort by Last Name, click on the **Last Name** column heading.

You can filter the list by clicking on the down arrow in the column heading you wish to filter by. For example, if you wish to only merge to recipients living in Bedford, click on the down arrow to the left of the Town/City column heading and choose Bedford from the list. Only those records that have Bedford in the Town/City field will now be shown.

Once you have filtered the list, the column that you filtered by is indicated by a blue (rather than black) drop-down arrow. In order to view all the records again, click on the blue drop-down arrow and choose (All) from the list.

You can choose which recipients to add or remove from the mail merge, by clicking on the tick box to the left of their entry. If the box is ticked, that record is included in the mail merge. If the tick is removed, that record is not included in the mail merge.

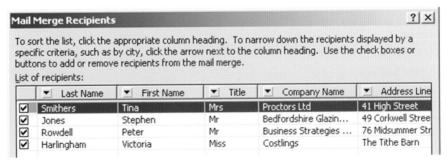

You can Select All records in the list by clicking on the **Select All** button, or you can deselect all records in the list by clicking on the **Clear All** button.

If you have a long list of recipients and you wish to find a specific record in the list, click on the **Find ...** button.

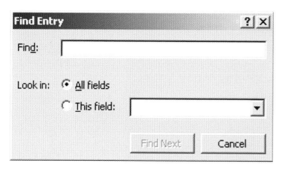

Type the word that you wish to find in the data list in the **Find:** box. Select **All fields** or **This field** and then pick a field from the drop-down list. Click on **Find Next**. The first record that matches your find criteria will be selected in the recipient list.

If you need to edit a record in the recipient list, select the record and click on **Edit ...** The Address List dialog box opens where you can edit the individual fields for this record.

If the information for your data list is being supplied by another file, i.e. a Word table, an Excel spreadsheet or an Access database, the **Refresh** button will update the recipient list to reflect any changes that have been made in the source file.

When this file is chosen as the data list, it is put into the Mail Merge Recipients list.

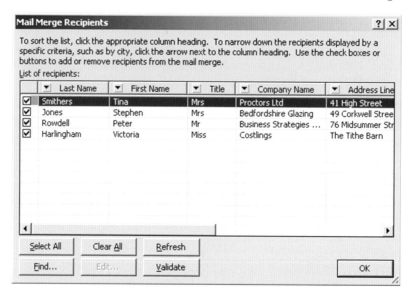

If a new record is added to the Excel spreadsheet, the Mail Merge Recipients list will not update until the **Refresh** button is pressed.

If you have address validation software installed on your computer, you can type in the Post Code and click on the **Validate** button. The correct address for the selected post code will be returned.

Click on **OK** when you have finished working with the list.

If you decide to use a different address list, click on **Select a different list** in the Task Pane.

If you wish to edit the existing list, i.e. to add or edit records, click on **Edit recipient list** in the Task Pane.

Click on the link ➡ Next: Write your letter.

Note that you can also go back to the previous step of the Wizard, should you wish to change anything.

TASK 39

1 Click on **Type a new list** and click on **Create**.

2 In the New Address List, click on **Customize** and ensure you have the following fields:

Title
FirstName
LastName
Address1
Address2
Town/City
County
PostCode
Amount

Remove any other fields from the list. Click on **OK**.

3 Enter the following four records of information into the Address List:

Title	Mrs	**Title**	Mr
First Name	Dorothy	**First Name**	Jonathan
Last Name	Smithers	**Last Name**	Thompson
Address1	26 Newtown Lane	**Address1**	The Blue Cottage
Address2	Chessil Village	**Address2**	Thorney Lane
Town/City	MILTON KEYNES	**Town/City**	MARLBOROUGH
County	Buckinghamshire	**County**	Wiltshire
PostCode	MK16 4AY	**PostCode**	MB17 4BY
Amount	100,000.00	**Amount**	50,000.00
Title	Mr	**Title**	Miss
First Name	Steve	**First Name**	Tina
Last Name	Barrett	**Last Name**	Dunsford
Address1	43 High Street	**Address1**	72 Green Lane
Address2		**Address2**	Bromham
Town/City	YEOVIL	**Town/City**	BEDFORD
County	Somerset	**County**	Bedfordshire
PostCode	BA21 4DZ	**PostCode**	MK42 7AP
Amount	250,000.00	**Amount**	750,000.00

4 Click on **Close**.

5 Save the address list in your Tasks for ITQ folder with the filename 'Address List 1'.

Using an existing data list

If the data list has already been created (it can be a Word table, an Excel spreadsheet or an Access database), choose **Use an existing list** in Step 3 of the Mail Merge Wizard.

Click on **Browse ...** The Select Data Source window opens.

Locate the file you wish to use as the data list. Select it and click on **Open**. Click on the link ⇒ Next: Write your letter.

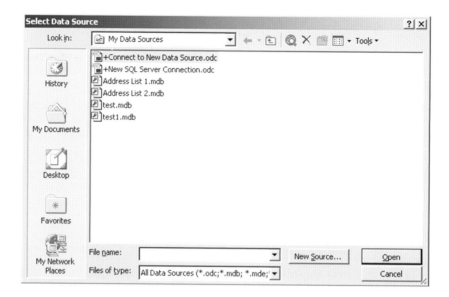

Creating the letter

You will now be returned to the current document. If you have not yet created the letter, you can do this now. Alternatively, you may have already opened the letter you are going to use prior to starting the Mail Merge Wizard.

Type the letter in the normal way. When you reach a place where you need to insert data from the data list, insert the appropriate field name in the letter. Position the cursor at the point where the field needs to be inserted and click on **More items ...** in the Task Pane.

The Insert Merge Field dialog box opens.

Select the field name in the list and click on **Insert**. When the merge is carried out, the field names indicate which data needs to be brought in from the data list. Click on **Close.**

You must remember to include appropriate spaces and returns between your field names. You must put the field names exactly where you want the data to be inserted from the data list when you merge the letter. For example, the name and address block should look like this:

«Title» «First_Name» «Last_Name»
«Address1»
«Address2»
«TownCity»
«County»
«Post_Code»

not like this:

«Title»«First_Name»«Last_Name»«Address1»«Address2»«TownCity»«County»«Post_C ode»

Continue creating your letter by typing text and inserting merge fields where appropriate. You will need to close the Insert Merge Field dialog box each time and click on **More items ...** when you want to open it again.

When you have finished creating your letter with the appropriate text and fields, click on the link ➡ Next: Preview your letters.

Note that you can also go back to the previous step of the Wizard.

TASK 40

Type the following letter using today's date. Insert the appropriate merge fields into the letter.

Ref: 19375

Today's date

«Title» «First_Name» «Last_Name»
«Address1»
«Address2»
«TownCity»
«County»
«Post_Code»

Dear «Title» «Last_Name»

NATIONAL LOTTERY

We have great pleasure in informing you that you have won the sum of £«Amount» in the National Lottery.

Please contact the undersigned to arrange for collection of your winnings.

Yours sincerely

Paul Shoesmith
Lottery Manager

Viewing the merged data

You will now be able to see your letter as it will look when the data from the address list has been merged into the letter.

The letter containing data from the first record in the data list is shown.

```
Ref    19375

22 August 2004

Mrs Dorothy Smithers
26 Newtown Lane
Chessil Village
MILTON KEYNES
Buckinghamshire
MK16 4AY


Dear Mrs Smithers

NATIONAL LOTTERY

We have great pleasure in informing you that you have won the sum of £100,000.00 in the
National Lottery.

Please contact the undersigned to arrange for collection of your winnings.

Yours sincerely



Paul Shoesmith
Lottery Manager
```

To preview the next letter, click on the forward button on the Mail Merge task pane (>>). To view the previous letter, click on the backward button on the Mail Merge task pane (<<).

To find a specific recipient's letter, click on **Find a recipient ...**

Type the word you wish to find in the **Find:** box and select **All fields** or **This field** and choose a field from the drop-down list. Click on **Find Next.**

Making corrections

Make changes

You can also change your recipient list:

Edit recipient list...

Exclude this recipient

When you have finished previewing your letters, click Next. Then you can print the merged letters or edit individual letters to add personal comments.

If you discover there are errors in the letter itself, click on **Previous: Write your letter** on the task pane to view your letter with the fields instead of the merged data. Make the necessary corrections to the letter.

If you discover there are errors in the data, click on **Edit recipient list . . .** on the task pane.

The Mail Merge Recipients dialog box opens. Select the record you wish to edit and click on **Edit ...**

Click on **Close** and **OK** once you have finished making the changes.

When you are happy with both the letter and the address data, click on the link ➡ Next: Complete the merge.

Editing individual letters

Merge to New Document

Merge records

⦿ All

◯ Current record

◯ From: [   ]   To: [   ]

OK   Cancel

Choosing **Edit individual letters ...** on the task pane, opens the Merge to New Document dialog box.

Choose whether you wish to merge **All** the records in the data list or just the **Current record** to a new document. You can also specify the record numbers to be merged in the **From** and **To** boxes. For example, if you only want to merge records 1–10 of the data list, type 1 in the From box and 10 in the To box.

When you click on **OK**, the selected records are merged into a new document. (For example, if there are 100 records in the address list, merging to a new document will create a

100-page document, one letter per page for each record in the address list.) You can make changes to specific records and use the normal Print command to print the letters you require.

Printing merged letters

Choosing **Print . . .** on the task pane, opens the Merge to Printer dialog box.

Choose whether you wish to merge **All** the records in the data list or just the **Current record** to the printer. You can also specify the record numbers to be merged in the **From** and **To** boxes. For example, if you only want to merge records 1–10 of the data list, type 1 in the From box and 10 in the To box.

When you click on **OK**, the **Print** dialog box will open in order that you can choose which printer to print to, etc.

TASK 41

1 **Click on Preview your letters on the task pane to view the letters as they will look when merged with the data list.**

2 **Check each of the letters using the forward and back buttons on the task pane.**

3 **If there are any errors in the letter, click on Previous: Write your letter and make the appropriate corrections. If there are any errors in the data list, click on Edit Recipient List and make the appropriate corrections to the records. Click on Close and OK to return to the letter.**

4 **Click on Next: Complete the merge on the task pane.**

5 **Choose Edit individual letters . . . in the task pane.**

6 **Choose All in the Merge to New Document dialog box and click on OK.**

7 **A new document window opens, containing the four merged letters. Save this document in your Tasks for ITQ folder with the filename 'Merged Letters'. Close the document.**

Completing the process

Once you have merged the letters to the printer or to a new document, you need to save and close the letter.

If you merged the letter to a new document, close it. The form letter is the active window. Save this letter.

TASK 42

Save and close both the letter and the data list.

Mail Merge in Word 2000

Choose **Mail Merge . . .** from the **Tools** menu.

The Mail Merge Helper dialog box opens.

The Mail Merge Helper offers a three-step process to performing a mail merge.

Step 1 concerns the main document (usually a letter), Step 2 concerns the names, addresses and other variable information that will go into the letter (known as the data source) and Step 3 puts the letter and data source together (Merge).

Click on **Create** and choose **Form Letters** from the menu.

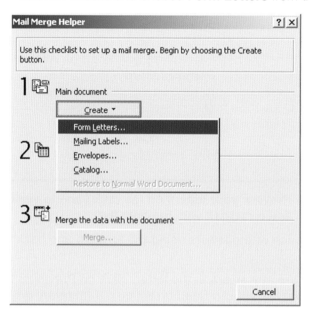

You will be asked how you wish to start the letter. If you haven't yet created the letter, or you have opened the letter you want to use and it is on the screen, click on **Active Window**.

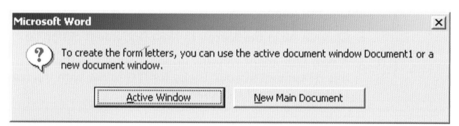

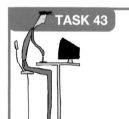

TASK 43

1 **Start a new document and choose Mail Merge from the Tools menu.**

2 **Click on Create and choose Form Letters from the menu.**

Click on **Get Data** in the Mail Merge Helper.

If you haven't yet set up the data source (names and addresses), choose **Create Data Source**.

If the data source has already been created (it can be a Word table, an Excel spreadsheet or an Access database), choose **Open Data Source**. You will then be prompted to browse to the relevant data file.

If you want to use your Outlook address book as the data source in the Mail Merge, choose **Use Address Book**.

Creating the data source

The first stage of creating the data source is to decide which field names you

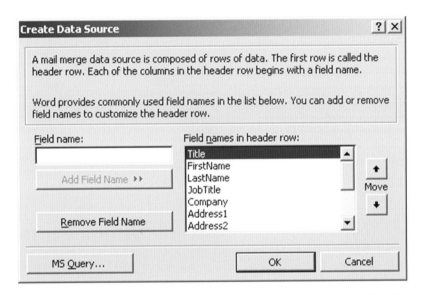

require. Imagine your data source is a table containing data. The field names are the column headings of the table.

You will be offered a list of standard field names. You can remove field names that you do not wish to use from the list and you can add new field names to the list.

To remove a field name that you do not wish to use, click on the field name in the list and click on **Remove Field Name**.

To add a new field name to the list, click in the **Field name** box and type a name for the field. (You cannot use spaces in a field name.) Click on **Add Field Name**.

You can also rearrange the order of the field names in the list. Click on the field name you wish to move and click the up or down arrow to the right of the list.

Click on **OK** when you have finished customising the list.

You will be prompted to save the data source. Choose the folder that you wish to store it in and give it an appropriate file name. Click on **Save**. N.B. Note that you are saving the data source before you have entered any records of information into it. Once you have entered the data, you must save the data source again.

Once you have saved the empty data source, you will be prompted to Edit it, i.e. to enter the records of data into it. Click on **Edit Data Source**. The Data Form

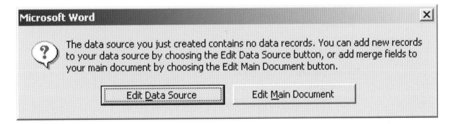

appears on the screen. You enter the names, addresses and other information for the letter into this form.

When the Data Form opens, the first blank record is showing. Type the first set of data into the form (this becomes a record) and then click on **Add New** to move to the second blank record. Repeat this process for each set of data you need to enter.

If you wish to delete a record from the data source, locate the record using the Record navigator buttons and then click on **Delete**. The **Restore** button will undo

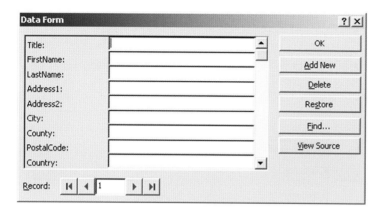

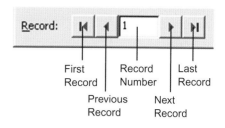

any changes you have made to the displayed record. The **Find** button enables you to find a record in your data source by searching on a particular field. The **View Source** button enables you to see the actual table of information that is being created as you enter records into the Data Form.

The Record Navigator buttons at the bottom of the dialog box enable you to move to different records in the data source.

- **First Record** – takes you to the first record in the data source.
- **Previous Record** – moves back through the records one at a time.
- **Record Number** – takes you to the record number that you type in the box.
- **Next Record** – moves forward through the records one at a time.
- **Last Record** – takes you to the last record in the data source.

If there is no data to go into a field, you can leave the field blank. For example, sometimes there is no Address2.

When you have finished entering all the records of data, click on **OK**.

You will be returned to the active window (your document).

TASK 44

1 **Click on Get Data and choose Create Data Source.**

2 **In the Create Data Source dialog box, ensure you have the following fields:**

   Title
   FirstName
   LastName
   Address1
   Address2
   Town/City
   County
   PostCode
   Amount
   Remove any other fields from the list.

3 **Save the data source into your Tasks for ITQ Folder with the filename 'Data Source 1'.**

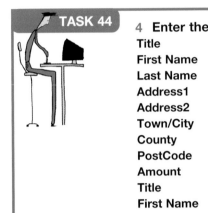

TASK 44

4 Enter the following four records of information into the data form:

Title	Mrs	**Title**	Mr
First Name	Dorothy	**First Name**	Jonathan
Last Name	Smithers	**Last Name**	Thompson
Address1	26 Newtown Lane	**Address1**	The Blue Cottage
Address2	Chessil Village	**Address2**	Thorney Lane
Town/City	MILTON KEYNES	**Town/City**	MARLBOROUGH
County	Buckinghamshire	**County**	Wiltshire
PostCode	MK16 4AY	**PostCode**	MB17 4BY
Amount	100,000.00	**Amount**	50,000.00
Title	Mr	**Title**	Miss
First Name	Steve	**First Name**	Tina
Last Name	Barrett	**Last Name**	Dunsford
Address1	43 High Street	**Address1**	72 Green Lane
Address2		**Address2**	Bromham
Town/City	YEOVIL	**Town/City**	BEDFORD
County	Somerset	**County**	Bedfordshire
PostCode	BA21 4DZ	**PostCode**	MK42 7AP
Amount	250,000.00	**Amount**	750,000.00

5 Click on OK.

Using an existing data source

If the data source has already been created (it can be a Word table, an Excel spreadsheet or an Access database), choose **Open Data Source** from the Mail Merge helper.

You will then be prompted to browse to the relevant data file.

Select the file you want to use as the data source and click on **Open.**

Creating the letter

Once you have created or opened the data source, you can now set up the letter. If you have not yet created the letter, start to type the letter in the normal way. If you had previously opened the letter that you wish to use, it will appear in the active window.

The Mail Merge toolbar appears across the top of the document.

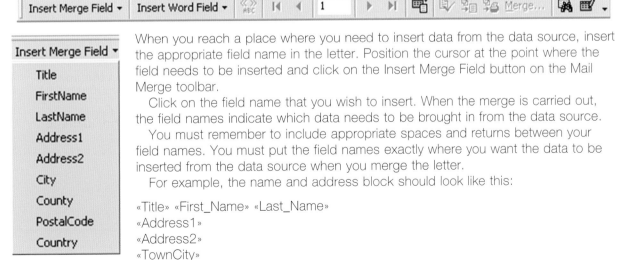

When you reach a place where you need to insert data from the data source, insert the appropriate field name in the letter. Position the cursor at the point where the field needs to be inserted and click on the Insert Merge Field button on the Mail Merge toolbar.

Click on the field name that you wish to insert. When the merge is carried out, the field names indicate which data needs to be brought in from the data source.

You must remember to include appropriate spaces and returns between your field names. You must put the field names exactly where you want the data to be inserted from the data source when you merge the letter.

For example, the name and address block should look like this:

«Title» «First_Name» «Last_Name»
«Address1»
«Address2»
«TownCity»

«County»
«Post_Code»

not like this:

«Title»«First_Name»«Last_Name»«Address1»«Address2»«TownCity»«County»«Post_C ode»

Continue creating your letter by typing text and inserting merge fields where appropriate.

NET/189475

22 August 2004

«Title» «First_Name» «Last_Name»
«Address1»
«Address2»
«TownCity»
«County»
«Post_Code»

Dear «Title» «Last_Name»

We have much pleasure in informing you that you have been specially selected to receive a free gift of a «Gift_Name».

Please contact the undersigned in order that we can rush your free gift to you without delay.

Yours sincerely

Peter Oxbridge
Free Gifts Manager

TASK 45

1 **Type the following letter using today's date. Insert the appropriate merge fields into the letter.**

Ref: 19375

Today's date

«Title» «First_Name» «Last_Name»
«Address1»
«Address2»
«TownCity»
«County»
«Post_Code»

Dear «Title» «Last_Name»

NATIONAL LOTTERY

We have great pleasure in informing you that you have won the sum of £«Amount» in the National Lottery.

Please contact the undersigned to arrange for collection of your winnings.

Yours sincerely

Paul Shoesmith
Lottery Manager

Viewing the merged data

Once you have finished creating your letter, you are ready to carry out the merge process. However, before you do it is advisable to view the letter with the merged data in order to check that everything is correct.

Click on the View Merged Data button on the Mail Merge toolbar.

You will now be able to see your letter as it will look when the data from the data source has been merged into the letter. The data you are being shown is from the first record in the data source. To view other letters, use the Record Navigator on the Mail Merge toolbar to move forwards or backwards through the records.

Making corrections

If you discover there are errors in the letter itself, click on the **View Merged Data** button again to view your letter with the fields instead of the merged data. Make the necessary corrections to the letter.

If you discover there are errors in the data, click on the **Edit Data Source** button on the Mail Merge toolbar.

The Data Form will open. Navigate to the record you need to correct and make the necessary amendments. Click on **OK** once you have finished making the changes.

If you are happy with the letter and the data source, you are ready to carry out the Merge process.

Merging to a new document

You can merge the data source and letter and create a new document that contains all the merged letters. (For example, if there are 100 records in the data source, merging to a new document will create a 100-page document, one letter per page for each record in the data source.)

Click on **Merge to New Document** on the Mail Merge toolbar.

You can make changes to specific records and use the normal Print command to print the letters you require.

Merging to the printer

You can merge the letters directly to the printer. Click on **Merge to Printer** on the Mail Merge toolbar. The normal Print dialog box will open in order that you can make printing choices.

Using the Merge dialog box

Clicking on the **Merge ...** button on the Mail Merge toolbar will open the Merge dialog box.

Under **Merge to** you can choose **New document** or **Printer** from the drop-down list. You can also choose to merge to **Electronic mail** if you wish to send your mailing via e-mail.

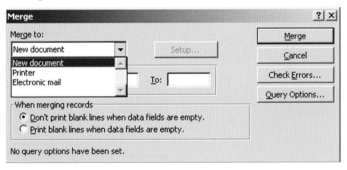

Under **Records to be merged,** you can choose whether you wish to merge **All** the records in the data source, or you can specify the record numbers to be merged in the **From** and **To** boxes. For example, if you only want to merge records 1–10 of the data source, type 1 in the From box and 10 in the To box.

In the **When merging records** area, you can choose **Don't print blank lines when data fields are empty** or **Print blank lines when data fields are empty**. The former (not printing blank lines) is the more common option. This is useful if, for example, some of your addresses do not contain data in the Address2 field.

Once you have chosen your options, click on **Merge**.

TASK 46

1 **Click on the View Merged Data button on the Mail Merge toolbar to view the letters as they will look when merged with the data source.**

2 **Check each of the letters using the Record Navigator.**

3 **If there are any errors in the letter, switch off View Merged Data and make the appropriate corrections. If there are any errors in the data source, click on the Edit Data Source button and make the appropriate corrections to the records. Click on OK to return to the letter.**

4 **Click on the Merge button on the Mail Merge toolbar.**

5 **Choose New document from the drop-down list under Merge to.**

6 **Ensure the Don't print blank lines when data fields are empty option is selected.**

7 **Click on Merge.**

8 **A new document window opens containing the four merged letters. Save this document in your Tasks for ITQ folder with the filename 'Merged Letters'. Close the document.**

Completing the process

Once you have merged the letters to the printer or to a new document, you need to save and close the data source and the letter.

If you merged the letter to a new document, the form letter will be the active window. Save this letter. When you close it, the following message appears on the screen:

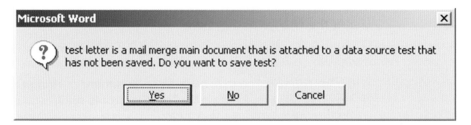

This message explains that the letter you are about to close is attached to a data source that has not been saved. The data source was originally saved when it was empty and now it contains records of data. Click on Yes to save the data source in order that you can use it again in the future.

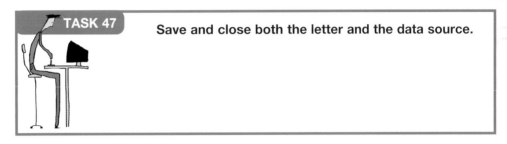

TASK 47

Save and close both the letter and the data source.

 ## Styles and templates

Word has a range of existing styles that you can apply to words, lines or paragraphs. You can also create your own styles that you can apply to text in your document.

In this example, the heading 'Word Styles' has been formatted using the built-in heading style, Heading 1.

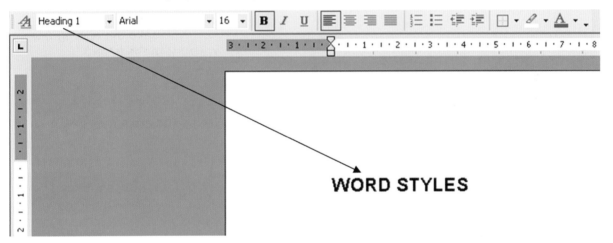

A style is a set of formatting characteristics that you can apply to text, tables and lists in your document to quickly change their appearance. When you apply a style, you apply a whole group of formats in one simple step. A style can include font and paragraph formatting, tabs, borders, shading, bullets and numbering.

For example, instead of carrying out three separate steps to format a title as:

- Arial
- 16 pt
- Centred

you can simply apply a style which contains all this formatting.

Your organisation may have styles that it uses. These styles will already be in your style list and you should have some guidelines as to when and in which documents certain styles should be used.

There are four types of style you can apply in Word 2002:

- A character style affects selected text within a paragraph, such as the font and size of text and bold and italic formats.
- A paragraph style controls the appearance of a paragraph, such as text alignment, tabs, line spacing and borders, and can also include character formatting.
- A table style provides a consistent look to borders, shading, alignment and fonts in tables.
- A list style applies alignment, numbering or bullet characters and fonts to lists.

Word 2000 has character, paragraph and list styles but no table styles.

Applying an existing style to text in a document

The quick way to apply a style is to use the Style list on the Formatting toolbar.

Click on the Style List drop-down arrow on the Formatting toolbar to open a list of styles that you can apply in your document.

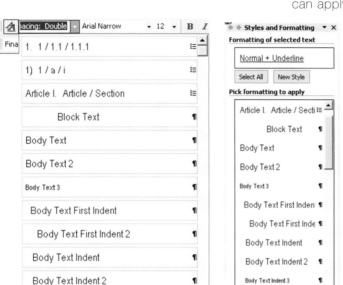

Alternatively, you can access the list of styles by using the command in the **Format** menu.

In Word 2002, choose **Styles and Formatting** from the **Format** menu to open the Styles and Formatting task pane.

To see all the styles that are available, choose **All Styles** from the **Show** list at the bottom of the task pane.

In Word 2000, choose **Style** from the **Format** menu to open the Style dialog box.

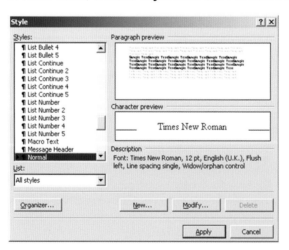

To view all the styles that are available, choose **All styles** from the **List** drop-down.

Applying a character style

Select the text to which you wish to apply the style to.

In Word 2002, click on the **Style List** on the Formatting toolbar and choose a style from the list or choose **Styles and Formatting** from the **Format** menu and click on a style in the task pane.

In Word 2000, click on the **Style List** on the Formatting toolbar and choose a style from the list or choose **Styles** from the **Format** menu to open the Style dialog box. Click on a style in the **Styles** list and click on **Apply**.

In this example, the Heading 1 style has been applied to the text in the paragraph heading.

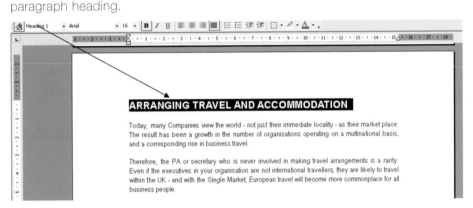

ARRANGING TRAVEL AND ACCOMMODATION

Today, many Companies view the world - not just their immediate locality - as their market place. The result has been a growth in the number of organisations operating on a multinational basis, and a corresponding rise in business travel.

Therefore, the PA or secretary who is never involved in making travel arrangements is a rarity. Even if the executives in your organisation are not international travellers, they are likely to travel within the UK - and with the Single Market, European travel will become more commonplace for all business people.

The Heading 1 style includes the following formatting:

- Font: Arial
- Font size: 16 pt
- Font enhancements: Bold
- Alignment: Left
- Space above paragraph: 12 pt
- Space below paragraph: 3 pt

There is a range of built-in heading styles, from Heading 1 to Heading 9.

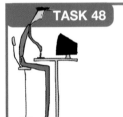

TASK 48

1 **Open the file called 'Word text version 3'.**

2 **Insert the heading 'What can Word do?' at the top of the document.**

3 **Apply the Heading 1 style to this heading.**

Applying a paragraph style

If you wish to apply the style to just one paragraph, you can just click in the paragraph. If you wish to apply the style to more than one paragraph, you need to select the paragraphs.

In Word 2002, click on the **Style List** on the Formatting toolbar and choose a style from the list or choose **Styles and Formatting** from the **Format** menu and click on a style in the task pane.

In Word 2000, click on the **Style List** on the Formatting toolbar and choose a style from the list or choose **Styles** from the **Format** menu to open the Style dialog box. Click on a style in the **Styles** list and click on **Apply**.

In this example, the Body Text First Indent style has been applied to the paragraphs.

The Body Text First Indent style includes the following formatting:

- Font: Arial
- Font size: 12 pt
- Font enhancements: None
- Alignment: Left
- Space above paragraph: 0 pt
- Space below paragraph: 6 pt
- Indent: 0.37 first line indent

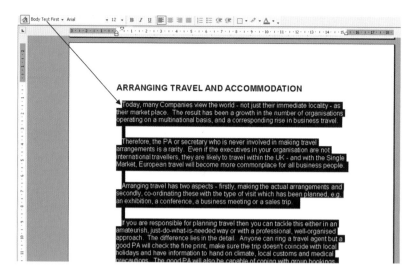

There is a range of built-in body text styles, ranging from Body Text to Body Text 3 and Body Text Indent to Body Text Indent 3.

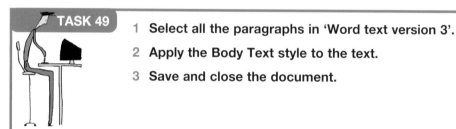

TASK 49

1 Select all the paragraphs in 'Word text version 3'.

2 Apply the Body Text style to the text.

3 Save and close the document.

Applying a table style

Click in the table to which you wish to apply the style.

In Word 2002, click on the **Style List** on the Formatting toolbar and choose a style from the list or choose **Styles and Formatting** from the **Format** menu and click on a style in the task pane.

In Word 2000, click on the **Style List** on the Formatting toolbar and choose a style from the list or choose **Styles** from the **Format** menu to open the Style dialog box. Click on a style in the **Styles** list and click on **Apply**.

In this example, the Table 3D effects 2 style has been applied to the table.

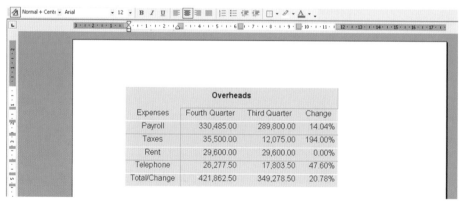

Overheads			
Expenses	Fourth Quarter	Third Quarter	Change
Payroll	330,485.00	289,800.00	14.04%
Taxes	35,500.00	12,075.00	194.00%
Rent	29,600.00	29,600.00	0.00%
Telephone	26,277.50	17,803.50	47.60%
Total/Change	421,862.50	349,278.50	20.78%

Table styles do not appear in the Style list. Instead, the style box shows the style that is being used for the text in the table.

The Table 3D effects 2 style includes the following formatting:

- Borders: Thin black and thin white horizontal (alternating); one thin black vertical
- Shading: 25% grey
- Alignment: Centred and right

There is a range of built-in table formats, ranging from Table 3D effects 1 to Table Web 3.

TASK 50

1 **Open the file called 'Table 1'.**

2 **Apply the Table Colorful 1 style to the table.**

3 **Save and close the document.**

Applying a list style

Select the list to which you wish to apply the style.

In Word 2002, click on the **Style List** on the Formatting toolbar and choose a style from the list or choose **Styles and Formatting** from the **Format** menu and click on a style in the task pane.

In Word 2000, click on the **Style List** on the Formatting toolbar and choose a style from the list or choose **Styles** from the **Format** menu to open the Style dialog box. Click on a style in the **Styles** list and click on **Apply**.

In this example, the List Bullet style has been applied to the list.

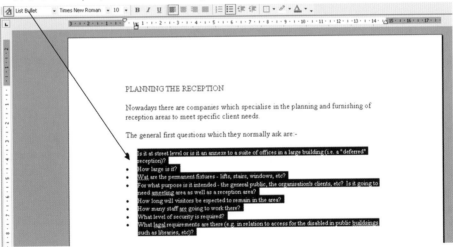

The List Bullet style includes the following formatting:

- Alignment: Justified
- Indent: 0.63 cm hanging indent
- Tabs: 0.63 left
- Bullet: List Bullet

There is a range of built-in list formats, ranging from List to List Number 5.

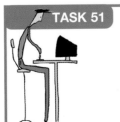

TASK 51

1 **Open the file called 'Word text version 2'.**

2 **Select all the text in the document and apply the List Number 2 style.**

3 **Save and close the document.**

What are templates?

A template is like a 'blueprint' for a document. It determines the basic structure of the document. It contains settings such as margins, tabs, columns, line spacing, fonts, etc. It also includes any text that will always appear in any document created using that template. For example, a Fax template will usually include text such as From, To, Fax Number, Number of Pages, etc.

Templates are used to create uniform standards in everyone's documents. For example, if everyone in an organisation uses a letter template, then everyone's letters will have the same background, layout and fonts, thus creating a 'corporate image'.

Templates also make it easier for the person creating the document, who doesn't have to worry about layout and fonts, etc., as these are already set up. They can just concentrate on adding the content of the document.

The Normal template

The Normal template is a 'global' template on which all the other templates are based. Settings in a global template are available in all documents. When you press the **New** button on the Standard toolbar, you create a new document based on the Normal template. This template is a blank A4 page with margins set and using a default font.

Creating a new document based on a template

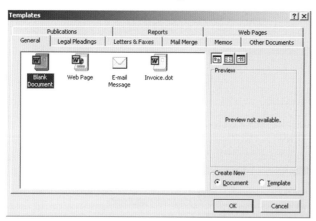

There is a standard range of other templates you can use when creating documents. In addition, your organisation may have created a set of templates that you are to use when creating certain types of document, for example, letters, faxes, reports, etc.

To access other templates, choose **New** from the **File** menu.

In Word 2002, the New Document Task Pane will appear down the right side of the screen.

Click on **General Templates** under **New from template** to open the Templates dialog box.

In Word 2000, the Templates dialog box opens when you choose **New** from the **File** menu.

The templates are divided into categories which appear on different tabs at the top of the dialog box: **General, Legal Pleadings, Letters & Faxes, Mail Merge, Memos, Web Pages, etc**. Click on a category tab to see the templates that are stored in that category.

If you wish to use a template, click on it to select it and then click on **OK**.

Left is an example of one of the built-in Word templates: Contemporary Letter.

Most of the built-in Word templates have been created so the user can

simply click on the placeholder text and replace it with their own text, making it very easy to complete.

Organisational templates

Your organisation may have a range of templates that you are to use when creating letters, faxes, reports, etc. Templates stored in the Templates folder will appear on the **General** tab of the Templates dialog box. Alternatively, your organisation may have created their own folder for in-house templates, which will appear as a separate tab in the Templates dialog box.

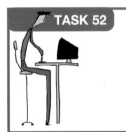

TASK 52

1 Create a letter based on the Professional letter template.

2 Replace the placeholder text.

3 Save the letter in your Tasks for ITQ folder with the file name 'Template 1'.

TASK 53

1 Create a web page based on the Personal Web Page template.

2 Replace the placeholder text to get an idea of how easy it would be to create a Web page using the template.

Proofing tools

Spelling and Grammar checker

Spelling and Grammar

The Spelling and Grammar checker is useful for checking the accuracy of your document. To launch it, click on the **Tools** menu and choose **Spelling and Grammar**.

Alternatively, click on the **Spelling and Grammar** button on the Standard toolbar.

You can also use **F7**

The Spelling and Grammar checker is launched and stops on the first word that is not in its dictionary.

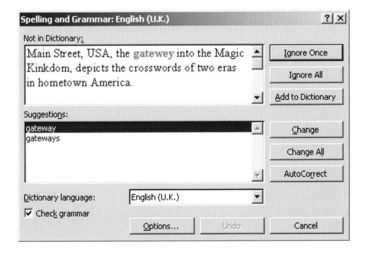

The word that is not recognised is shown in red and a list of **Suggestions** is offered in the bottom section of the dialog box. Click on the appropriate button to deal with the current word and move on.

■ **Ignore Once** – ignores the word this time but stops on it again if it comes across the same word in this spell check.
■ **Ignore All** – ignores all occurrences of the word during this spell check.
■ **Add to Dictionary** – adds the word to the dictionary so that the spell checker does not stop on it again (useful for words that you use regularly).
■ **Change** – changes this occurrence of the word to the word you have selected in the Suggestions list. The spell checker will stop again if it comes across the word again during this spell check.
■ **Change All** – changes all occurrences of the word to the word you have selected in the Suggestions list.
■ **AutoCorrect** – adds the selected word to the AutoCorrect list, which means if you type it incorrectly in the future, it will be automatically corrected by Word.

Each time you click on a button, the spelling and grammar check continues to the next word. Possible spelling errors are shown in red and possible grammatical errors are shown in green.

Grammatical errors usually include things such as sentence structure, incorrect words used in a particular context and fragmenting.

Once the Spelling and Grammar check is complete, the following message appears:

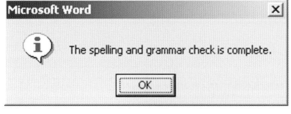

Click on **OK**.

One of the drawbacks of the spelling checker is that it will not stop on words that are spelt correctly but used in the wrong context, e.g. where and wear. Even if you run the spelling and grammar checker, you still need to proofread your document.

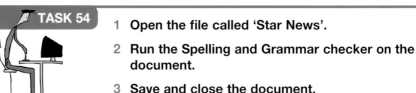

TASK 54

1 **Open the file called 'Star News'.**

2 **Run the Spelling and Grammar checker on the document.**

3 **Save and close the document.**

Proofreading and checking for inconsistencies

No one likes to read text on-screen, but it is a very useful skill to acquire. It only takes minutes to go through your document to ensure that there are no glaring typos and that you have used formatting, styles and layout consistently.

Below are some pointers for successful and efficient proofreading:

■ Use the spelling and grammar checker to get started. Remember, though that these tools cannot be used instead of proofreading – they will not pick up everything.
■ Read the document backwards, sentence by sentence. Reading the document backwards makes it easier to spot unclear sentences and redundant text.
■ Read the document backwards, word by word. You will notice typos and spelling mistakes easier this way.
■ Point at each word as you read it aloud.

- Circle verbs – this helps you to locate where the passive voice has been used, 'strong' verbs and shift in tense.
- Circle prepositions – you can identify unnecessary 'wordiness'.
- Create an 'editing checklist' for yourself of mistakes you commonly make. Keep this list updated and use it each time you proofread a piece of work.
- Read through the document several times, looking for different problems each time, i.e. verb tense, passive voice, to/two/too, etc.
- Create a 'draft' document – use double spacing and a large font – to make it easier to proofread and check.
- Use the find and replace function to check for unnecessary commas, extra spaces after full-stops, typos, etc.

Checking for layout

It is useful to use Print Preview to check the layout of your document. Click on the **File** menu and choose **Print Preview** (or press the **Print Preview** button on the Standard toolbar). For more information on Print Preview, see page 160.

Checking for consistency

Another part of your document you should check are headings and sub-headings. You need to ensure that these have been used consistently throughout the document. If you have used Styles in the document, you can use the **Find** feature to check that each heading has the appropriate style. (For more information on using Find, see page 162).

Document statistics

If you want to know how many pages, words, paragraphs, etc., there are in your document, click on the **Tools** menu and choose **Word Count**.

Word will provide you with various statistics about the current document. Click on **Close** when you have finished.

Saving a Word document as a different file type

When you save documents in Word, they are automatically saved with a .doc filename extension. This means that the documents can be identified by Word and opened.

However, there may be times when a document you have produced in Word needs to be opened using an application other than Word, for example, if a colleague doesn't have Word on their computer but uses another word-processing application, such as WordPro.

Rich text format

Rich text format (.rtf) is a standard encoding that most other computer programs can understand. If you save a file in rich text format it can be opened by most applications.

Choose Save As from the File menu.

In the Save As dialog box, click on the drop-down arrow by **Save as type** and choose **Rich Text format (*.rtf)** from the list. Click on **Save**.

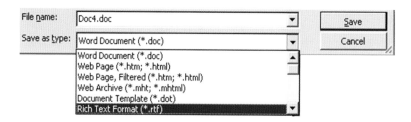

 **TASK 55**

1 **Open the file called 'Word Text'.**

2 **Save the file into your Tasks for ITQ folder in Rich Text Format.**

Web page format

If you have created a Word document that is going to be uploaded to an intranet or the Internet, you might have been instructed to save that file in HTML format. HTML stands for HyperText Markup Language and is the language used in files on the Internet. Word provides a very simple way to save a document in HTML.

Choose **Save as Web Page** from the **File** menu.

The Save As dialog box opens. The **Save as type** box has already changed to Web Page (*.htm; *.html).

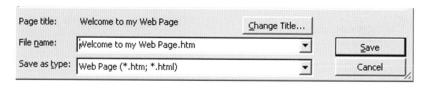

As well as giving the document a file name, a page title has been given to the document, for when it is displayed on the Internet. You can change the title by clicking on **Change Title ...**

Click on **Save** when you have made the appropriate changes.

 ## Improving efficiency

There are various ways in Word that you can improve your efficiency. This book contains details of shortcut keys where these can be used instead of opening a menu and scrolling down it to select the required option, or clicking on a button.

Word menus help you to see where you can use a button or a shortcut key. A button on the left of a menu command indicates that there is a button on the toolbar that will carry out the same command. A shortcut key on the right of a menu command indicates that a shortcut key can be used to carry out the same command.

If you prefer to use your keyboard to carry out commands, you can assign commands to the keyboard. See later in this section for details on how to do this.

If you prefer to use toolbar buttons to carry out commands, you can assign commands to buttons. You can add new buttons to the existing toolbars and remove buttons that you don't use.

Creating keyboard shortcuts

If you prefer to use the keyboard, you can assign commands to keyboard

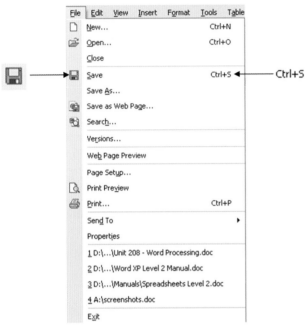

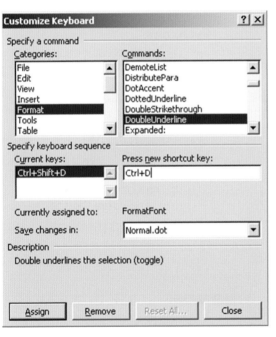

shortcuts. There are quite a lot of keyboard shortcuts already assigned. Below are some of the more popular ones:

- Ctrl+B   Bold
- Ctrl+I   Italic
- Ctrl+U   Underline
- Ctrl+S   Save
- Ctrl+P   Print
- Ctrl+X   Cut
- Ctrl+C   Copy
- Ctrl+V   Paste

To create your own shortcut keys, click on **Tools** and choose **Customize ...** The Customize dialog box opens.

Click on the **Keyboard ...** button at the bottom of the dialog box. The Customize Keyboard dialog box opens.

Choose a Category from the **Categories** list on the left. The commands in that category are listed in the **Commands** list on the right.

For example, in the figure on the left, **Format** has been chosen in the Categories list. All the formatting commands appear in the Commands list on the right. **Double Underline** has been chosen in the Commands list.

Click on the command that you wish to assign to a shortcut key from the Command list. If this command already has a shortcut key assigned to it, this will appear in the **Current keys:** box. You may decide that you do not need to assign a new shortcut key and you will use the shortcut key already assigned to the command. If this is the case, click on **Close** to close the Customize Keyboard dialog box.

To assign a new shortcut key to this command, type the shortcut key combination in the **Press new shortcut key:** box. Commands can be assigned using the shortcut key combinations:

- **Ctrl**+letter or number
- **Alt**+letter or number
- **Alt**+**Ctrl**+letter or number

For example, if you assigned a command to the shortcut key Control+H, you would need to hold down **Ctrl** while pressing **H**. If you assigned a command to Alt+Control+H, you would need to hold down **Alt** and **Ctrl** on the keyboard at the same time as pressing **H**.

Click on **Assign**. If you wish to assign another command to a shortcut key, repeat the process above. Click on **Close** when you have finished assigning commands to shortcut keys.

Be careful when assigning shortcut keys to commands, that you do not use a shortcut key combination that is commonly used for something else. For example, most people use Control+B for **Bold**, so if you assign this shortcut key combination to a different command, you could get some unexpected results!

TASK 56

Check to see if the following commands already have a shortcut key assigned to them. If not, assign them to shortcut keys on the keyboard:
- **File Close**
- **File Page Setup**
- **File Print Preview**
- **Edit Paste Special**
- **Insert Section Break**
- **Double Underline**
- **Table Properties**

Toolbars

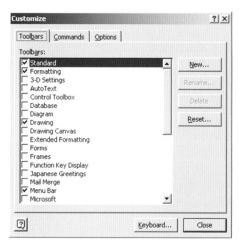

When you launch Word, the **Standard** and **Formatting** toolbars appear across the top of the screen. There is a range of other toolbars that are useful when using a specific feature (for example, Mail Merge). These toolbars can be customised – you can take buttons off them and add new buttons to them, to suit the way you like to work.

To see a list of all the toolbars that are available, click on **Toolbars** in the **View** menu or choose **Tools**, **Customize** and click on the **Toolbars** tab.

Click on **Tools** and choose **Customize ...** The Customize dialog box opens.

Click on the **Commands** tab at the top of the dialog box.

Choose a Category from the **Categories** list on the left. The commands in that category are listed in the **Commands** list on the right. In this example, **File** has been chosen in the Categories list. All the file commands appear in the Commands list on the right.

Click on the command that you wish to have a button for. Point to the button icon and click and drag the button onto the toolbar that you wish to put it on. Release the mouse button.

In this example, the Close button has been selected in the Commands list.

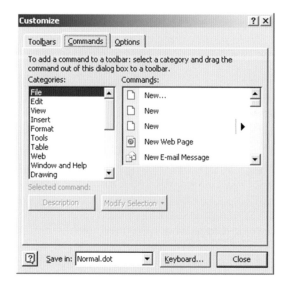

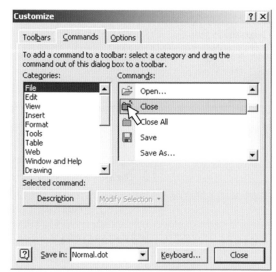

The **Close** icon is then dragged onto the Standard toolbar and dropped where it is required.

A black bar appears to help you see where the button will be placed on the toolbar.

When the mouse button is released, the **Close** button appears on the toolbar.

The grey area at the right end of the toolbar is not part of the toolbar. If you try and drop a button onto this area, the button will not appear.

To remove a button from a toolbar, click on **Tools** and choose **Customize** . . .

Once the Customize dialog box is open, point to the button that you wish to remove from the toolbar and click and drag it down and off the toolbar. When you release the mouse, the button disappears. It is still in the Commands list so that you can put it onto the toolbar again in the future, if you wish.

You do not need to save the file that is currently open on the screen to save toolbar changes. As soon as you assign a shortcut key or put a button on the toolbar, it is saved.

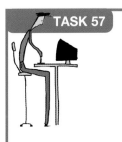

TASK 57

1 **Add the following buttons to your Standard toolbar:**
- **Close**
- **Page Setup**
- **Office Clipboard**

2 **Add the following buttons to your Formatting toolbar:**
- **Double Underline**
- **1½ spacing**
- **Double spacing**

3 **Remove these buttons from the toolbar.**

 ## Producing evidence for this unit

All evidence for this unit must be produced in the workplace. By completing the exercises below, you will have produced two pieces of work that cover all the criteria at Level 2. Following the exercises there is a list of other tasks that you can complete to provide evidence for this unit.

To ensure that your work can be used as evidence towards your ITQ, create appropriate files and take print-outs and screenshots at every stage to show the changes you are making to a document. The finished document should also be provided.

Exercise 1

1 Start a new document and type the following text in single line spacing:

TIME MANAGEMENT
How You Relate To Time
If you think words such as valley-like, white, hollow, available, unclaimed, ready, blank or empty best apply to time, you view time as something to be filled. You are probably not under very great time pressures.
If you think words such as spent, tiring, mountainous, jammed, relentless, restless, tense or bumpy best apply to time, you view time as an enemy. This is dangerous. You may be overstressed by environment and responsibilities.

Your Environment
Environment refers to the major people, places and things that affect the way people shape their time. Some of these environmental factors may seem beyond your control. What can you do about a spouse who never writes phone messages down? Suppose a computer would simplify your life, yet your company cannot afford one? What do you do if your boss is the most disorganised human being on earth?

Where do the hours go?
How many hours do you spend a week watching TV? During what hour do you receive the most phone calls at work? How much reading do you do weekly?
If you are an average Briton, each week you watch TV for 25 hours, read for just under 3 hours and receive the most phone calls between 10.00 am and 11.00 am.

LINING UP YOUR DUCKS: PRIORITISE!
The Index Card/Post-It System
If you prefer a more user-friendly system for putting your tasks in order, try this variation of the ABC system. Write each of your duties on a separate index card. Lay the cards out on a flat surface, then place them in order of importance or needed action.

The Inventory System
Another variation of the ABC approach, the inventory system, is primarily results orientated. Rather than having A,B,C values drive a person's activity, the inventory approach assumes that a person learns most by reviewing how he or she handled the day then applying what was learned to the next day's behaviour.

The Payoff System
The payoff approach fits well into a long tradition of viewing time as a sort of currency. 'Time is money' declared Benjamin Franklin, over 200 years ago, when the leisurely pace of rural America still dominated life. Now, with the flood of information, duties and events that overwhelm people every day, time has become a far more valuable commodity.

PROCRASTINATION – THE THIEF OF TIME
What's Behind Procrastination
At the root of procrastination, argue psychologists, almost always lurks some hidden fear or conflict. A person may be obliged to achieve certain results, but a

multitude of opposing emotions serve to short-circuit action. Although the procrastinator may act as if the threat, fear or conflict is gone, it is still there, where it generates stress and, ultimately, corrodes success.

Internal Forces
Four of the causes of procrastination are primarily inner rooted. They come from the psychological makeup of the procrastinator. To defeat procrastination you need to put considerable energy into behaviour change. Sounds impossible? It's not. A number of proven and clear strategies can enable you to effect genuine and lasting change.

External Forces
Even if you don't tend to procrastinate, your environment can impose procrastination on you. Unpleasant or overwhelming tasks – and unclear goals or task flow – are enough to make anyone want to postpone the inevitable.

2   Save the file in your Tasks for ITQ folder with the filename 'Exercise 1 – Version 1'.
3   Change the margins of your document to 2.54 cm Top, Bottom, Left and Right.
4   Rearrange the paragraphs under LINING UP YOUR DUCKS: PRIORITISE! so they are in the following order:
- The Payoff System
- The Inventory System
- The Index Card/Post-It System

5   Find the word 'tiring' and replace it with the word 'exhausting'. Find the word 'major' and replace it with the word 'main'. Find the word 'Briton' and replace it with the word 'Brit'.
6   Save the file in your Tasks for ITQ folder with the filename 'Exercise 1 – Version 2'.
7   Change the three main headings (in capitals) to Arial 14 pt, Bold, Italic and Blue. Centre them.
8   Change the sub-headings (there are nine) to Arial 12 pt, Italic, Underline and Red.
9   Fully justify the text and change the line spacing to 1.5.
10 Indent the first two paragraphs 1.5 cm from each margin.
11 Insert a page break before each main heading. (You will now have three pages.)
12 Save the file in your Tasks for ITQ folder with the filename 'Exercise 1 -Version 3'.
13 Convert the text in the section headed PROCRASTINATION – THE THIEF OF TIME into two column layout. Insert a column break to force the paragraph headed 'External Forces' into the second column.
14 Type the heading The ABC System after the main heading LINING UP YOUR DUCKS: PRIORITISE! Format this heading like the other sub-headings and then type the following text:

The ABC system is the 'grandfather' of prioritising strategies. In a nutshell, it says that all tasks should be given an A,B,C value.
Insert a table as below:

A TASKS	Those that must be done and soon
B TASKS	Those that should be done soon
C TASKS	Those that can be put off without creating dire consequences
D TASKS	Those that, theoretically, do not even need to be done

Change the row height and vertically centre the text in the rows. Add coloured borders to the table.

15 Save the file in your Tasks for ITQ folder with the filename 'Exercise 1 – Version 4'.

16 Apply the built-in Heading 1 style to your main headings (there are three of them).

17 Apply the built-in Heading 2 style to your sub-headings (there are ten of them).

18 Create a header which reads 'Time Management'. Create the header in Arial 9pt and centre it.

19 Create a footer which inserts the current page number in the centre and type ©(Your Name) at the right side. Create the footer in Arial 9pt.

20 Save the file in your Tasks for ITQ folder with the filename 'Exercise 1 – Version 5'.

21 Put page 2 into a separate section. Change the page orientation of this section to landscape.

22 Insert a picture at the bottom of page 2. Move the picture to the centre of the page under the text.

23 Insert a text box at the bottom of the last page and type the following text inside it:

GOOD TIME MANAGEMENT IS ACHIEVABLE
BUT MUST ACT NOW . . . !

Format the font as Arial 14pt Bold and centre the text in the box.

24 Run the spelling and grammar checker on the document.

25 Preview the document to check the layout and print one copy of the completed document. Save the document in your Tasks for ITQ folder with the filename 'Exercise 1 – Version 6'.

Your completed document should look like the document shown on pages 255–7.

TIME MANAGEMENT

TIME MANAGEMENT

How You Relate To Time

If you think words such as valley-like, white, hollow, available, unclaimed, ready, blank or empty best apply to time, you view time as something to be filled. You are probably not under very great time pressures.

If you think words such as spent, exhausting, mountainous, jammed, relentless, restless, tense or bumpy best apply to time, you view time as an enemy. This is dangerous. You may be overstressed by environment and responsibilities.

Your Environment

Environment refers to the main people, places and things that affect the way people shape their time. Some of these environmental factors may seem beyond your control. What can you do about a spouse who never writes phone messages down? Suppose a computer would simplify your life, yet your company cannot afford one? What do you do if your boss is the most disorganised human being on earth?

Where do the hours go?

How many hours do you spend a week watching TV? During what hour do you receive the most phone calls at work? How much reading do you do weekly?

If you are an average Brit, each week you watch TV for 25 hours, read for just under 3 hours and receive the most phone calls between 10.00 am and 11.00 am.

© (Your name)

TIME MANAGEMENT

LINING UP YOUR DUCKS: PRIORITISE!

The ABC System

The ABC System is the 'grandfather' of prioritising strategies. In a nutshell, it says that all tasks should be given an A, B, or C value.

A TASKS	Those that must be done and soon
B TASKS	Those that should be done soon
C TASKS	Those that can be put off without creating dire consequences
D TASKS	Those that, theoretically, do not even need to be done

The Payoff System

The payoff approach fits well into a long tradition of viewing time as a sort of currency. 'Time is money' declared Benjamin Franklin, over 200 years ago, when the leisurely pace of rural America still dominated life. Now, with the flood of information, duties and events that overwhelm people every day, time has become a far more valuable commodity.

The Inventory System

Another variation of the ABC approach, the inventory system, is primarily results orientated. Rather than having A,B,C values drive a person's activity, the inventory approach assumes that a person learns most by reviewing how he or she handled the day then applying what was learned to the next day's behaviour.

The Index Card/Post-It System

If you prefer a more user-friendly system for putting your tasks in order, try this variation of the ABC system. Write each of your duties on a separate index card. Lay the cards out on a flat surface, then place them in order of importance or needed action.

© (Your name)

2

TIME MANAGEMENT

PROCRASTINATION – THE THIEF OF TIME

What's Behind Procrastination

At the root of procrastination, argue psychologists, almost always lurks some hidden fear or conflict. A person may be obliged to achieve certain results, but a multitude of opposing emotions serve to short-circuit action. Although the procrastinator may act as if the threat, fear or conflict is gone, it is still there, where it generates stress and, ultimately, corrodes success.

Internal Forces

Four of the causes of procrastination are primarily inner rooted. They come from the psychological makeup of the procrastinator. To defeat procrastination you need to put

considerable energy into behaviour change. Sounds impossible? It's not. A number of proven and clear strategies can enable you to effect genuine and lasting change.

External Forces

Even if you don't tend to procrastinate, your environment can impose procrastination on you. Unpleasant or overwhelming tasks – and unclear goals or task flow – are enough to make anyone want to postpone the inevitable.

GOOD TIME MANAGEMENT IS ACHIEVABLE

BUT YOU MUST ACT NOW ...!

3   © (Your name)

Exercise 2

1 Start a new document and type the following paragraph of text:

Our current brochure contains examples of the types of rug we can produce, but of course, the design is entirely up to you. We can create designs from your sketches or photographs. Alternatively, we are happy to discuss your ideas with you.

Save the file in your Tasks for ITQ folder with the filename 'Text 1'.

2 Use Mail Merge to create a mail merge letter as below:
Ref: 1839/CJD

Date (Insert date field)

(Name of Recipient)
(Address of Recipient)

(Dear Name of Recipient)

RUBY'S RUGS

Thank you for the interest you have shown in our company. Ruby's Rugs has been producing woollen rugs for over 20 years at our workshop in the beautiful Buckinghamshire countryside. All our rugs are hand-finished to the highest standards and designed to your own specification.

Please find enclosed the brochure that you requested.

Yours sincerely

Ruby Hodder
Chief Rug Maker

3 The letter needs to contain the following fields of information:
   ■ Title
   ■ First Name
   ■ Last Name
   ■ Address Line 1
   ■ Address Line 2
   ■ Town/City
   ■ County
   ■ Post Code

4 Insert the file 'Text 1' at the end of the letter before 'Yours sincerely'.
5 Spell check the letter.
6 Merge the letters with a new or existing address list.
7 Print the merged letters.
8 Save the letter in Rich Text Format (RTF) in your Tasks for ITQ folder with the filename 'Ruby's Rugs Letter'.
9 Save the data source (address list) in your Tasks for ITQ folder with the filename 'Address List'.

Further suggested tasks for evidence

Below are more suggestions for the type of task you can create in the workplace which would serve as evidence for this unit.

Suggested Task 1

Your manager has asked you to create a newsletter about your organisation and what it does. Consider the following and then produce the newsletter:

- How should the newsletter be laid out? One, two or three columns?
- Should the newsletter have pictures? Where should they go? What size should they be?
- Should the newsletter also include a table?
- Should there be headers and/or footers?
- Who is the newsletter for? (Perhaps produce two different layouts suitable for different readers.)

Suggested Task 2

Send a letter accompanying the newsletter to ten people. Use the Mail Merge feature to personalise each letter. (Take screenshots to show that you are using mail merge.)

Suggested Task 3

Log each step that you took in Task 1 and note whether you accomplished the step easily or whether you experienced any problems. Is there anything that you would do differently another time?

Suggested Task 4

Customise your toolbar to suit your own use. Assign shortcut keys to the keyboard for your own use. Take screenshots of the dialog boxes to show the process.

Spreadsheet software

Unit value = 20

Overview

You are likely to be in a role which involves using more complex formulas and functions (e.g. mathematical, statistical and financial) and tools (e.g. monthly expenditure and sales figures, cash flow forecasts and graphs of results).

The spreadsheet software outlined in this unit is Microsoft® Excel. Microsoft® Excel is part of the Microsoft® Office suite of applications. It offers a comprehensive set of tools for working with and manipulating figures. It is used in offices for budgets, cashflow projections, cost and profit analysis and anything involving calculating with figures. It is also used extensively to store lists of information and has many database features to work with these lists, including sorting and filtering.

A competent person can use spreadsheet software to produce more complex spreadsheets, including combining different types of information, entering and editing data, formatting data, using functions and formulas and using tools to analyse and interpret spreadsheet data.

 ## Required skills and techniques for Level 2

Handling files	Using appropriate techniques to handle, organise and save files.
Combining information	Linking information within the same type of software. Adding information from one type of software to information produced using different software.
Entering and editing spreadsheet data	Inserting data into multiple cells at once. Using a wide range of editing techniques appropriately in more complex spreadsheets.
Formatting spreadsheets	Formatting more complex spreadsheets using a range of appropriate tools and techniques: ■ cells – colour, shading and borders ■ charts – change chart type, move and resize charts ■ pages – headers and footers, adjust page setup for printing.
Checking spreadsheets	Checking that page breaks fall in appropriate places and that the formatting is appropriate. Checking the accuracy of results and sorting out errors in formulas.
Functions and formulas	Using appropriate functions and formulas such as mathematical, statistical, financial and relational in more complex spreadsheets.
Analysing and interpreting	Using appropriate tools and techniques such as filters for analysing more complex data.
Presenting spreadsheets	Using appropriate methods, such as the range of graphs and charts provided by the software to present more complex data.
Improving efficiency	Setting up shortcuts.

Requirements of this unit

You will need to produce at least *two* comprehensive and different pieces of work, demonstrating skills, techniques and knowledge outlined in the unit.

This unit asks you to demonstrate valid uses of spreadsheet software, for example, to sort, analyse and display data. You need to demonstrate your knowledge of the use of spreadsheets to communicate information to a wide range of audiences.

In your workplace, you may be asked to present data in an appropriate format for the audience, produce more complex spreadsheets for a wide variety of uses and analyse and interpret data stored on a spreadsheet.

Tasks in this unit

The tasks that appear throughout the unit are designed to take you step-by-step through the feature being discussed. It is recommended that you use the tasks completed as evidence in addition to the two main pieces that are required by the unit.

The tasks at the end of the unit are suggested ways in which you could provide the main evidence for this unit.

What will I achieve?

By accomplishing a Level 2 in this unit, you will also have achieved Level 1 in most cases. Below is a table to show what levels you will have achieved.

Required skill	Level 1	Level 2	Level 3
Handling files	●————————●		
Combining information	●————————●		
Entering and editing spreadsheet data		●	
Formatting spreadsheets	●————————●		
Checking spreadsheets	●————————●		
Functions and formulas	●————————●		
Analysing and interpreting	●————————●		
Presenting	●————————●		
Improving Efficiency	N/A	●	

Launching Excel

Excel can be launched by **double-clicking** on the Excel **shortcut** on the desktop (if there is one).

Alternatively, click on **Start**, **Programs** and then choose **Microsoft Excel** from the menu. (If you have Windows XP, it is **Start, All Programs, Microsoft Excel**.)

Creating a new spreadsheet

New

When you first launch Excel, a new workbook is automatically created. This workbook contains three blank sheets. To begin working, simply start entering data into the cells.

If you want to create a new workbook at any time, click the **New** button on the Standard toolbar

Alternatively, press [Control]+[N]

TASK 1

Launch Excel and type your first name into cell A1 on the blank worksheet.

 ## Saving a spreadsheet

Save

If you wish to keep the workbook on the computer, so that you can use it again, you will need to save it. The first time you save a workbook, you will be prompted to give the file a name and to choose which folder you wish to save it into.

Click on the **File** menu and choose **Save**.

Alternatively, click on the **Save** button on the Standard toolbar.

You can also use [Control]+[S]

The Save As dialog box will open.

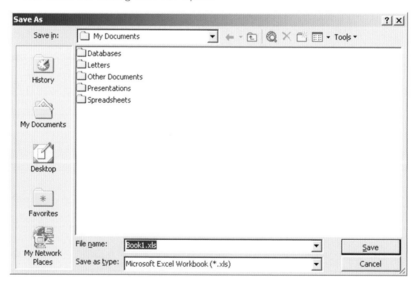

You have to do two things in this dialog box: decide where you want to store the workbook (in a folder) and what you want to call the workbook (or file).

If your files are stored on a network drive, rather than your own computer, click on the drop-down arrow in the **Save in:** box and choose the drive that you wish to go to from the list.

Once you have moved to that drive, the main area of the Save dialog box will display the folders that are on that drive (folders are indicated by the yellow icon). Double-click on a folder to move into it. Use the **Back** or **Up One Level** buttons to move up out of a folder. ⇦ ⬆

Navigate to the drive and folder that you wish to store your workbook in.

Type a name for the workbook in the File name box and ensure that it will be saved as a Microsoft Excel Workbook (under **Save as type** – it should be set to Microsoft Excel Workbook (*.xls)).

Your filename can be up to 250 characters long – use an obvious name for your file so that you remember what you called it in the future! You do not need to type the .xls filename extension as this will be added automatically. (The filename extension will not be visible in Windows Explorer if you have not set it to show file extensions.)

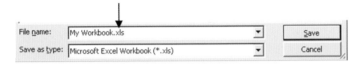

Once you have chosen the appropriate folder and given the file a name, click on the **Save** button at the bottom right of the dialog box.

Once you have saved the workbook, the name of the file will appear in the Title Bar across the top of the screen.

Microsoft Excel - My Workbook.xls

All Excel workbooks have the file extension .xls. This helps you recognise which of your files are Excel workbooks when you are viewing files in folders.

The Excel icon also appears to the left of the file in the Open or Save dialog box.

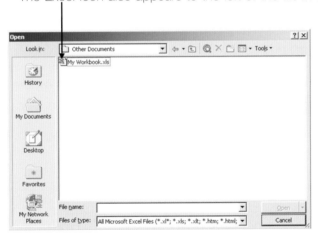

If you have previously saved the workbook and then made some changes to it, choosing Save will overwrite the previous version of the workbook with the newly updated version. (It still has the same name and is stored in the folder that you initially put it in.)

 **TASK 2**   **Save the workbook in your Tasks for ITQ folder with the filename 'Budget'.**

Closing the workbook

Once you have saved the file, if you wish to remove the workbook from the screen, you need to close it.

Choose **Close** from the **File** menu.

Alternatively, you can click on the Close Window button at the top right of the screen.

Close Window button

If you haven't previously saved the workbook or you have made more changes since you last saved the workbook, the following message will appear on the screen.

Click on **Yes** to save any further changes you have made and close the file. If you do not wish to save any changes you have made, click on **No**. Clicking on **Cancel** will remove the dialog box from the screen without closing the file. If you wish to close the workbook, you will need to choose **File**, **Close** again.

TASK 3   **Close the workbook that is on the screen.**

Opening an existing spreadsheet

You may wish to open a workbook that you have already starting working on and previously saved.

Open

Choose **Open** from the **File** menu.

Alternatively, click on the **Open** button on the Standard toolbar.

You can also use Control + O

The Open dialog box will open.

To change to a different drive, click on the drop-down arrow at the end of the **Look in:** box to open a list of locations. Choose the drive that you wish to use from the list.

Once you have chosen the appropriate drive from the **Look in:**

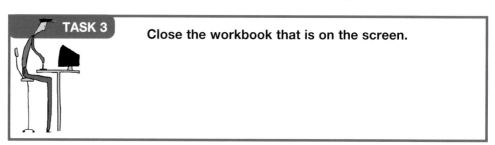

list, the main area of the Open dialog box will display the folders that are already on that drive.

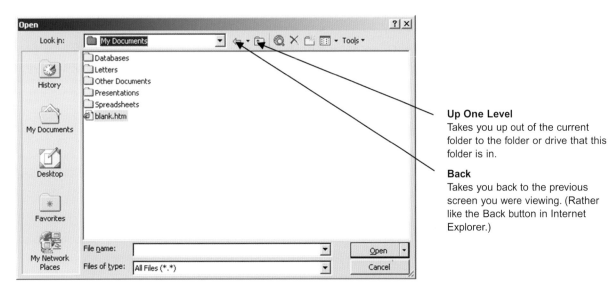

To open a folder, double-click on the appropriate folder name. Use the **Back** or **Up One Level** buttons to move up out of a folder.

Locate the workbook you wish to open, click on it and then click on the **Open** button at the bottom right of the dialog box. (Alternatively, you can double-click on the file.)

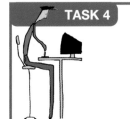

TASK 4

1 **Navigate to the Tasks for ITQ folder and open the workbook named 'Budget' again.**

2 **Type your last name into cell A2 on the worksheet.**

Using Save As

If you have opened an existing workbook and made changes to it, but you do not wish to overwrite the original file, you can use **Save As**. You can then give the new version of the workbook a different name or store it in a different folder.

Choose **Save As** from the **File** menu and follow the same steps as for saving a workbook.

TASK 5

Save the workbook in your Tasks for ITQ folder with the filename 'Budget Version 2'.

Renaming a workbook

If you change your mind about what you would like the workbook to be called after you have saved and closed it, you can rename it.

Choose **File, Open** or click on the **Open** button on the Standard toolbar to open the Open dialog box. Navigate to the file you wish to rename. Point to the file with the mouse and right-click to open the shortcut menu. Click on **Rename**.

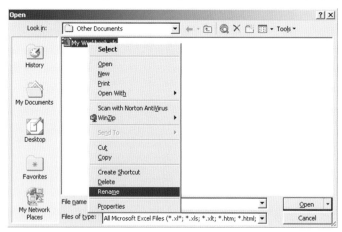

Type the new name for the file and press **Return** on the keyboard.

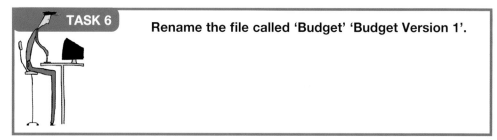

TASK 6

Rename the file called 'Budget' 'Budget Version 1'.

The Excel screen

The **Title Bar** across the top of the screen informs you that you are in Microsoft Excel and gives the name of the current workbook you are working in. (Workbooks are numbered by Excel until you save them and give them a filename.)

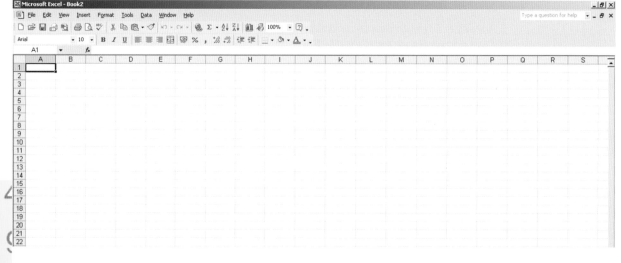

The **Menu Bar** contains menus – **File, Edit, View, Insert, Format, Tools, Data, Window, Help**. To open a drop-down menu, click on the menu word on the Menu Bar.

Under the Menu Bar are **Toolbars**. These contain buttons which you can use for the more popular features, instead of using the menus.

Under the Toolbars is the **Formula Bar**. This bar shows when a formula (a calculation) has been used in a cell on the worksheet.

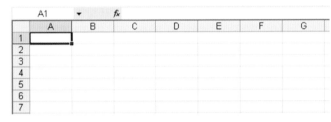

The main part of the screen is taken up by the worksheet. A worksheet consists of rows, columns and cells. Each cell on the worksheet has a 'cell reference' – the column letter and row number. For example, the first cell on the worksheet has the cell reference **A1.**

Selecting parts of the worksheet

To select one cell on the worksheet, click on that cell. The 'active' cell has a heavier black border around it.

To select more than one cell on the worksheet, click on the first cell you wish to select, hold down the mouse button and drag to select the other cells you wish to select. (More than one cell on the worksheet is called a 'range'.)

If you wish to select a row or column on the worksheet, click on the row number or column letter of the row or column you wish to select. The complete row or column is selected.

TASK 7

1 Open the workbook called 'Budget Version 2'.

2 Familiarise yourself with the Excel screen and practise selecting cells, rows and columns on the worksheet.

3 Close the workbook when you are finished. (You do not need to save any changes.)

 ## Entering and editing data

Entering data into a cell

To enter data into a cell, click on the cell and start typing. The data that you have typed will appear in the cell and also on the Formula Bar at the top of the worksheet.

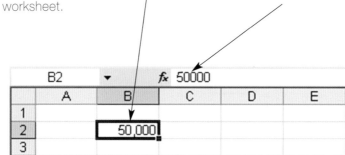

Entering data into multiple cells

If you wish to enter the same data into multiple cells at the same time, select the cells that you wish to contain the data, type the data into the first cell and press Control + Return .

Editing data in a cell

To overwrite the existing contents of a cell, click on the cell and start typing. The new data immediately overwrites what was in the cell before.

To edit the existing contents of a cell, double-click on the cell. The cursor now appears inside the cell. You can use Backspace and Delete and type new data to amend the contents of the cell. Press **Return** on the keyboard when you have finished editing the cell.

Deleting data in a cell

If you wish to delete the contents of a cell, click on the cell and press **Delete** on the keyboard.

TASK 8

1 **Open the workbook called 'Budget Version 1'.**

2 **Delete your name from cell A1 and input the following data:**

ITEMS	AMOUNT	JAN	FEB	MAR	APR
Furniture & Fittings	1800	32	1011	12	192
Bedding & Linen	1500	74	0	0	0
Electricity	13900	672	999	1118	1127
Cleaning	4600	378	742	416	409
Gas	13600	1023	1245	1000	1010

3 **Click on cell B1 and change the title in this cell to BUDGET. Your worksheet should look like this:**

4 **Click on the Save button to save the changes you have made.**

Microsoft Excel - Budget Version 1.xls

File Edit View Insert Format Tools Data Window Help

Arial ▾ 10 ▾ B I U ≡ ≡ ≡ 国 % ,

A27 ▾ *fx*

	A	B	C	D	E	F
1	ITEMS	BUDGET	JAN	FEB	MAR	APR
2	Furniture &	1800	32	1011	12	192
3	Bedding &	1500	74	0	0	0
4	Electricity	13900	672	999	1118	1127
5	Cleaning	4600	378	742	416	409
6	Gas	13600	1023	1245	1000	1010
7						

Using Undo

The Undo feature enables you to undo any editing or formatting changes you have made to the worksheet. You can undo changes up until you save the workbook. Once you save the workbook, the undo list is reset.

To undo a change you have made, choose **Undo** from the **Edit** menu.

Alternatively, press the Undo button on the Standard toolbar.

You can also use ⌨Control + Z

Working with rows and columns

When you start a new workbook, each worksheet in that workbook has 256 columns by 65,536 rows. After you have typed data onto the worksheet, you can insert rows and columns where they are required.

Inserting a row

Rows are inserted above the row that is currently active (i.e. the row that the cursor is sitting in). Click in the row below where you wish to insert the new row.

Choose **Rows** from the **Insert** menu.

A new row is inserted above the row the cursor is in.

A4 ▾ *fx*

	A	B	C	D	E	F	G	H	
1	ITEMS	BUDGET	JAN	FEB	MAR	APR	SPENT	BALANCE	
2	Bedding & Linen	1500	74	0	0	0	74	1426	
3	Cleaning	4600	378	742	416	409	1945	2655	
4									
5	Electricity	13900	672	999	1118	1127	3916	9984	
6	Furniture & Fittings	1800	32	1011	12	192	1247	553	
7	Gas	13600	1023	1245	1000	1010	4278	9322	

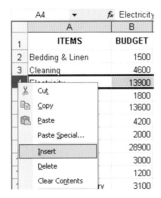

You can also use the shortcut menu to insert a new row. Point to the row number below where you wish to insert the new row. Right-click and choose **Insert** from the shortcut menu.

Inserting a column

Columns are inserted to the left of the column that is currently active (i.e. the column that the cursor is sitting in). Click in the column to the right of where you wish to insert the new column.

Choose **Columns** from the **Insert** menu.

A new column is inserted to the left of the column the cursor is in.

	A	B	C	D	E	F
1	ITEMS	BUDGET		JAN	FEB	MAR
2	Bedding & Linen	1500		74	0	0
3	Cleaning	4600		378	742	416
4	Electricity	13900		672	999	1118
5	Furniture & Fittings	1800		32	1011	12
6	Gas	13600		1023	1245	1000

You can also use the shortcut menu to insert a new column. Point to the column letter to the right of where you wish to insert the new column. Right-click and choose **Insert** from the shortcut menu.

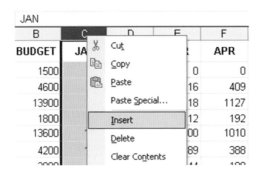

Deleting a row

If you do not require a row in your worksheet, select the row that you wish to delete by clicking on the row number at the left of the worksheet.

	A	B	C	D	E	F	G	H	I
1	ITEMS	BUDGET	JAN	FEB	MAR	APR	SPENT	BALANCE	
2	Bedding & Linen	1500	74	0	0	0	74	1426	
3	Cleaning	4600	378	742	416	409	1945	2655	
4	Electricity	13900	672	999	1118	1127	3916	9984	
5	Furniture & Fittings	1800	32	1011	12	192	1247	553	
6	Gas	13600	1023	1245	1000	1010	4278	9322	
7	Kitchen & Catering	4200	1515	332	289	388	2524	1676	

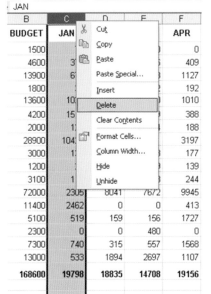

A5	▼	fx Furniture & Fittings	
	A	B	C	D
	ITEMS	BUDGET	JAN	FEB
1				
2	Bedding & Linen	1500	74	0
3	Cleaning	4600	378	742
4	Electricity	13900	672	999
5		1800	32	1011
6	Cut	13600	1023	1245
7	Copy	4200	1515	332
8	Paste	2000	127	0
9	Paste Special...	28900	10421	5908
10		3000	131	268
11	Insert	1200	29	101
12	Delete	3100	110	29
13	Clear Contents	72000	2305	8041

Choose **Delete** from the **Edit** menu.

Alternatively, you can use the shortcut menu to delete a row. Point to the row number that you wish to delete. Right-click and choose **Delete** from the shortcut menu.

Deleting a column

If you do not require a column in your worksheet, select the column that you wish to delete by clicking on the column letter at the top of the worksheet.

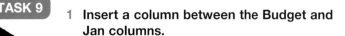

C1	▼	fx JAN		
	A	B	C	D	E
1	ITEMS	BUDGET	JAN	FEB	MAR
2	Bedding & Linen	1500	74	0	0
3	Cleaning	4600	378	742	416
4	Electricity	13900	672	999	1118
5	Furniture & Fittings	1800	32	1011	12
6	Gas	13600	1023	1245	1000
7	Kitchen & Catering	4200	1515	332	289
8	Laundry	2000	127	0	344
9	Maintenance	28900	10421	5908	2111
10	Medical Supplies	3000	131	268	298
11	Postage	1200	29	101	119
12	Printing & Stationery	3100	110	29	693
13	Provisions	72000	2305	8041	7672
14	Rates/Council Tax	11400	2462	0	0
15	Sundries	5100	519	159	156
16	Telephone	2300	0	0	480
17	Trips/Entertainment	7300	740	315	557
18	Vehicles	13000	533	1894	2697
19	TOTALS	168600	19798	18835	14708
20					
21					

Choose **Delete** from the **Edit** menu.

Alternatively, you can use the shortcut menu to delete a column. Point to the column letter that you wish to delete. Right-click and choose Delete from the shortcut menu.

JAN

B	C	D	E	F
BUDGET	JAN			APR
1500		Cut		0
4600	3	Copy		409
13900	6	Paste		1127
1800		Paste Special...		192
13600	10	Insert		1010
4200	15	Delete		388
2000	1	Clear Contents		188
28900	104	Format Cells...		3197
3000	1	Column Width...		177
1200		Hide		139
3100	1	Unhide		244
72000	2305	8041	7672	9945
11400	2462	0	0	413
5100	519	159	156	1727
2300	0	0	480	0
7300	740	315	557	1568
13000	533	1894	2697	1107
168600	19798	18835	14708	19156

TASK 9

1. **Insert a column between the Budget and Jan columns.**

2. **Insert a row above row 1 on the worksheet and type the heading AMOUNT SPENT SO FAR in the new cell A1.**

3. **Delete the column you have just inserted. Your worksheet should look like this:**

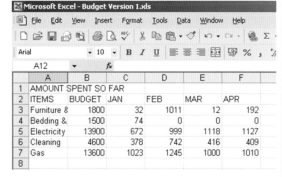

4. **Save the changes you have made to the workbook.**

Working with data

Moving data on the worksheet using cut and paste

Select the cells that contain the data you wish to move.

A4	▼	*fx* Electricity

	A	B	C
1	ITEMS	BUDGET	
2	Bedding & Linen	1500	
3	Cleaning	4600	
4	Electricity	13900	
5	Furniture & Fittings	1800	
6	Gas	13600	
7	Kitchen & Catering	4200	
8	Laundry	2000	
9	Maintenance	28900	
10	Medical Supplies	3000	
11	Postage	1200	

Cut

Choose **Cut** from the **Edit** menu.
Alternatively, click on the **Cut** button on the Standard toolbar.

You can also use Control + X

3	Cleaning	4600
4	Electricity	13900
5	Furniture & Fittings	1800
6	Gas	13600
7	Kitchen & Catering	4200
8	Laundry	2000

A moving border appears around the selected cells.
Click on the cell where you wish to move the data to.
Choose Paste from the Edit menu.
Alternatively, click on the **Paste** button on the Standard toolbar.

You can also use Control + V
The data is moved to the new location.

Paste

A13	▼	*fx*

	A	B	C
1	ITEMS	BUDGET	
2	Bedding & Linen	1500	
3	Cleaning	4600	
4	Electricity	13900	
5	Furniture & Fittings	1800	
6	Gas	13600	
7	Kitchen & Catering	4200	
8	Laundry	2000	
9	Maintenance	28900	
10	Medical Supplies	3000	
11	Postage	1200	
12	Printing & Stationery	3100	
13			
14			

Moving data on the worksheet using drag and drop

Select the cells that contain the data you wish to move. Point to the border of the selected cells. The mouse pointer has a four-headed arrow attached to it.

A4		ƒx Electricity	
	A	B	C
1	ITEMS	BUDGET	
2	Bedding & Linen	1500	
3	Cleaning	4600	
4	Electricity	13900	
5	Furniture & Fittings	1800	
6	Gas	13600	
7	Kitchen & Catering	4200	
8	Laundry	2000	
9	Maintenance	28900	
10	Medical Supplies	3000	
11	Postage	1200	

A4		ƒx Electricity	
	A	B	C
1	ITEMS	BUDGET	
2	Bedding & Linen	1500	
3	Cleaning	4600	
4	Electricity	13900	
5	Furniture & Fittings	1800	
6	Gas	13600	
7	Kitchen & Catering	4200	
8	Laundry	2000	
9	Maintenance	28900	
10	Medical Supplies	3000	
11	Postage	1200	
12	Printing & Stationery	3100	
13			
14			
15			
16			
17	Provisions	72000	

Copy

Hold the left mouse button down and drag the selected cells to the new location on the worksheet. (A dashed border appears as you drag the selected cells.)

When you release the mouse button, the selected cells are relocated.

Copying data using copy and paste

If you wish to copy data to another location on the worksheet, or to another worksheet, you can use the copy command.

Follow the steps for moving data, but use the **Copy** command rather than the **Cut** command.

Choose **Copy** from the **Edit** menu.

Alternatively, click on the **Copy** button on the Standard toolbar.

You can also use [Control]+[C]

Copying data on the worksheet using drag and drop

If you wish to copy data to another location on the worksheet using drag and drop, follow the steps for moving data using drag and drop. However, hold down the [Control] key as you drag the data.

TASK 10

1 **Using cut and paste, move the Furniture & Fittings heading and data to Row 8.**

2 **Using cut and paste, move the Bedding & Linen heading and data to Row 3.**

3 **Using drag and drop, move the Cleaning heading and data to Row 4.**

4 **Using drag and drop, move the Furniture & Fittings heading and data to Row 6.**

5 **Using copy and paste, copy the last three items (Electricity, Furniture & Fittings and Gas) onto Sheet 2.**

6 **Save the changes to the workbook.**

Resizing rows and columns on the worksheet

When you start a new workbook, all the rows and columns on the worksheet are of a standard size. However, you may decide to resize the rows and columns in order to improve the layout of the worksheet on the printed page.

Resizing rows using the mouse

Point to the number of the row you wish to resize. Move the mouse to the bottom border of the row number tile. The mouse pointer changes to a double-headed black arrow (the resizing handle).

	A	B	C	D	E	F	G	H
	ITEMS	BUDGET	JAN	FEB	MAR	APR	SPENT	BALANCE
2	Bedding & Linen	1500	74	0	0	0	74	1426
3	Cleaning	4600	378	742	416	409	1945	2655

J10 fx

Click and drag the resizing handle down to make the row deeper or up to make the row narrower.

	A	B	C	D	E	F	G	H
	ITEMS	BUDGET	JAN	FEB	MAR	APR	SPENT	BALANCE
2	Bedding & Linen	1500	74	0	0	0	74	1426
3	Cleaning	4600	378	742	416	409	1945	2655

J10 fx

Resizing columns using the mouse

Point to the column letter of the column you wish to resize. Move the mouse to the right border of the column letter tile. The mouse pointer changes to a double-headed black arrow (the resizing handle).

Click and drag the resizing handle to the right to make the column wider or to the left to make the column narrower.

J10 fx

	A	B	C
1	ITEMS	BUDGET	JAN
2	Bedding & Lir	1500	74
3	Cleaning	4600	378
4	Electricity	13900	672
5	Furniture & Fi	1800	32
6	Gas	13600	1023
7	Kitchen & Ca	4200	1515
8	Laundry	2000	127
9	Maintenance	28900	10421
10	Medical Supp	3000	131
11	Postage	1200	29
12	Printing & Sta	3100	110
13	Provisions	72000	2305
14	Rates/Counci	11400	2462
15	Sundries	5100	519

J10 fx

	A	B	C
1	ITEMS	BUDGET	JAN
2	Bedding & Linen	1500	74
3	Cleaning	4600	378
4	Electricity	13900	672
5	Furniture & Fittings	1800	32
6	Gas	13600	1023
7	Kitchen & Catering	4200	1515
8	Laundry	2000	127
9	Maintenance	28900	10421
10	Medical Supplies	3000	131
11	Postage	1200	29
12	Printing & Stationery	3100	110
13	Provisions	72000	2305
14	Rates/Council Tax	11400	2462
15	Sundries	5100	519

Resizing rows using the dialog box

Select the row or rows that you wish to resize. Choose **Row, Height** from the **Format** menu.

The Row Height dialog box opens.

Specify the height that you require the selected rows to be. (Row heights are measured in point sizes, i.e. what size font will fit into the row.) Click on **OK**.

Resizing columns using the dialog box

Select the column or columns that you wish to resize. Choose **Column, Width** from the **Format** menu.

The Column Width dialog box opens.

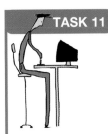

Specify the width that you require the selected columns to be. (Column widths are measured in characters, i.e. how many characters will fit into the column.) Click on **OK**.

TASK 11

1 Use the resizing handle to make row 1 deeper.

2 Use the resizing handle to resize column A to accommodate the text in it.

3 Use the dialog box to change the height of rows 2–7 to 20.

4 Use the dialog box to change the width of columns C–F to 6. Your worksheet should look like this:

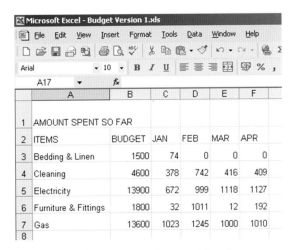

5 Save the changes to the workbook.

Formatting the worksheet

Using the Formatting toolbar

The Formatting toolbar sits across the top of the Excel screen.

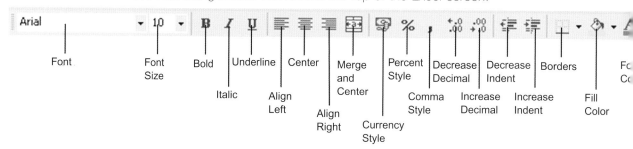

Before using the buttons on the Formatting toolbar, select the cell or cells that you wish to format.

- **Font** – click on the drop-down arrow to open a list of available fonts. Click on a font in the list to apply it to the selected cells.
- **Font Size** – click on the drop-down arrow to open a list of font sizes. Click on a font size in the list to apply it to the selected cells.
- **Bold** – click on the button to apply bold to the selected cells.
- **Italic** – click on the button to apply italic to the selected cells.
- **Underline** – click on the button to apply underline to the selected cells.
- **Align Left** – click on the button to align the data in the selected cells to the left.
- **Center** – click on the button to align the data in the selected cells in the centre.
- **Align Right** – click on the button to align the data in the selected cells to the right.
- **Merge and Center** – click on the button to merge the selected cells into one cell and centre the data in the merged cell.
- **Currency Style** – click on the button to apply currency formatting to the data in the selected cells. (This puts a £ sign in front of the figure, a comma as a thousands separator and two decimal places, if you have set your options to British.)
- **Percent Style** – click on the button to apply percentage formatting to the data in the selected cells. (This multiplies the number by 100 and adds the percent sign.)
- **Comma Style** – click on the button to apply comma formatting to the data in the selected cells. (This adds a comma as a thousands separator and two decimal places.)

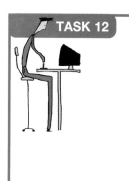 **TASK 12**

1 **Using the Formatting toolbar, change the font size of the heading in cell A1 to 12 point. Also make it Bold and Italic.**

2 **Select the headings in row 2 and apply Bold and Center.**

3 **Select the item names in cells A3 to A7 and make them Italic.**

4 **Select the cells A1 to F1 and merge and centre the heading in cell A1. Your worksheet should look like this:**

5 **Save the changes you have made.**

Microsoft Excel - Budget Version 1.xls

File Edit View Insert Format Tools Data Window Help

	A	B	C	D	E	F
1	AMOUNT SPENT SO FAR					
2	ITEMS	BUDGET	JAN	FEB	MAR	APR
3	Bedding & Linen	1500	74	0	0	0
4	Cleaning	4600	378	742	416	409
5	Electricity	13900	672	999	1118	1127
6	Furniture & Fittings	1800	32	1011	12	192
7	Gas	13600	1023	1245	1000	1010
8						

- **Decrease Decimal** – click on the button to reduce the number of decimal places being displayed in the selected cells by one place.
- **Increase Decimal** – click on the button to increase the number of decimal places being displayed in the selected cells by one place.
- **Increase Indent/Decrease Indent** – click on the buttons to indent the data in the selected cells away from the left side of the cell or to decrease the indent.
- **Borders** – click on the drop-down arrow to open the Border palette. Click on the border that you wish to apply to the selected cells.
- **Fill Color** – click on the drop-down arrow to open the Fill Color palette. Click on the fill colour that you wish to apply to the selected cells.
- **Font Color** – click on the drop-down arrow to open the Font Color palette. Click on the colour that you wish to apply to the data in the selected cells.

Using the Format Cells dialog box

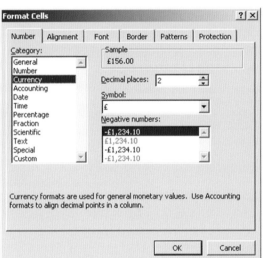

Before using the Format Cells dialog box, select the cell or cells that you wish to format.

Choose **Cells** from the **Format** menu.
The Format Cells dialog box opens.

This dialog box has five tabs relating to formatting: **Number, Alignment, Font, Border** and **Patterns.**

On the **Number** tab, you can select a number format from the **Category** list and specify settings for that number format. For example, by clicking on Currency in the list, you can choose the currency symbol you wish to use (if any), the number of decimal places to be displayed and how you want negative numbers to be displayed.

On the **Alignment** tab you can set the **Horizontal** and **Vertical** alignment of data in cells. You can switch on **Wrap text** (text will wrap within a cell), **Shrink to fit** which will shrink the contents to fit the cell and **Merge cells** which will merge selected cells into one cell. You can also choose the **Text direction** of text in a cell and choose the **Orientation** of data in a cell by dragging the red diamond round on the dial.

On the **Font** tab you can change the **Font**, **Font style** and **Size** of data in cells and apply other font enhancements such as **Underline** and **Color**. You can switch on other **Effects**.

On the **Border** tab you can choose the **Color** and **Line Style** and apply **Borders** to the selected cells.

On the **Patterns** tab you can choose **Cell shading** and/or **Patterns** to apply to the selected cells.

Click on **OK** when you made your choices on the various tabs.

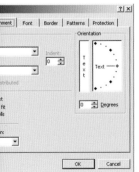
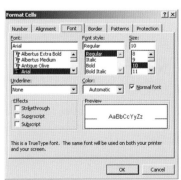
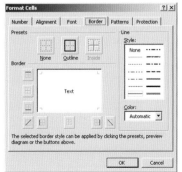
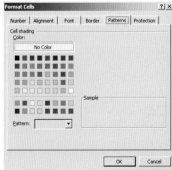

TASK 13

1 Click in cell G2 and type the heading **AMOUNT SPENT**. Click in cell H2 and type the heading **BALANCE REMAINING**.

2 Format these headings to match the other headings. Use the Format Cells dialog box to wrap both of these headings within their cells. (You may need to adjust the row height and column widths).

3 Select the headings in cell A2–H2 and centre them vertically in their cells.

4 Select the main heading – Amount Spent So Far – and merge and centre it again, across columns A–H. Also, centre it vertically in the cell.

5 Select the data on the worksheet (cells B3–F7) and apply currency formatting (two decimal places and the £ sign). (You might need to adjust the width of the columns.)

Your worksheet should now look like this:

6 Save the changes you have made.

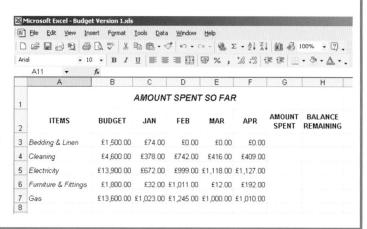

ITEMS	BUDGET	JAN	FEB	MAR	APR	AMOUNT SPENT	BALANCE REMAINING
Bedding & Linen	£1,500.00	£74.00	£0.00	£0.00	£0.00		
Cleaning	£4,600.00	£378.00	£742.00	£416.00	£409.00		
Electricity	£13,900.00	£672.00	£999.00	£1,118.00	£1,127.00		
Furniture & Fittings	£1,800.00	£32.00	£1,011.00	£12.00	£192.00		
Gas	£13,600.00	£1,023.00	£1,245.00	£1,000.00	£1,010.00		

Applying borders

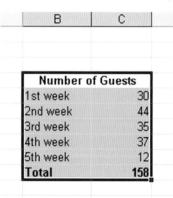

The lines that appear on the worksheet are called gridlines. These lines do not print unless you specify that you want them to print. However, the best method of creating lines that will print is to apply **borders**. There are two ways to apply borders: using the Borders palette on the Formatting toolbar or by using the **Borders** tab of the Format Cells dialog box.

Select the cells on the worksheet to which you wish to apply borders.

To use the Borders palette, click on the down arrow beside the Border button on the Formatting toolbar.

Click on the type of border that you wish to apply to the selected cells. (In Excel 2002 you can also choose **Draw Borders** and use the mouse as a pencil to draw borders where you want them.)

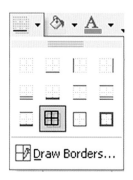

Alternatively, once you have selected the cells to which you wish to apply borders, choose **Cells** from the **Format** menu and click on the **Borders** tab of the Format Cells dialog box.

Select the **Color** and **Line Style** that you require and click on the appropriate border button to apply the borders you want. Click on **OK**.

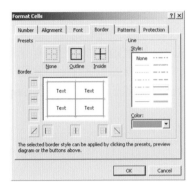

	B	C	D
	Number of Guests		
	1st week	30	
	2nd week	44	
	3rd week	35	
	4th week	37	
	5th week	12	
	Total	**158**	

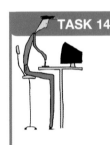

TASK 14

1 Select cells A2 to H7 and apply a thin blue border to all cells in that range.

2 Select cells A2–H2 and apply a heavier black border along the bottom of the cells.

3 Select cells A7–H7 and apply a heavier black border along the bottom of the cells.

Your worksheet should now look like this:

4 Save the changes you have made.

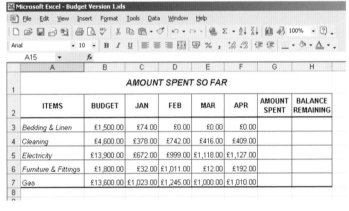

Applying shading

You can also colour the cells on the worksheet using **shading**. There are two ways to apply shading: using the Fill Color palette on the Formatting toolbar or by using the **Patterns** tab of the Format Cells dialog box.

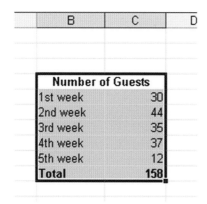

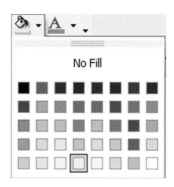

Select the cells on the worksheet to which you wish to apply shading.

To use the Fill Color palette, click on the down arrow beside the Fill Color button on the Formatting toolbar.

Click on the cell shading colour you wish to apply.

Alternatively, once you have selected the cells to which you wish to apply shading, choose **Cells** from the **Format** menu and click on the **Patterns** tab of the Format Cells dialog box.

Select the cell shading you require. Alternatively, click on the **Patterns** down arrow to open a palette of patterns and colours that you can apply to the selected cells. Click on **OK**.

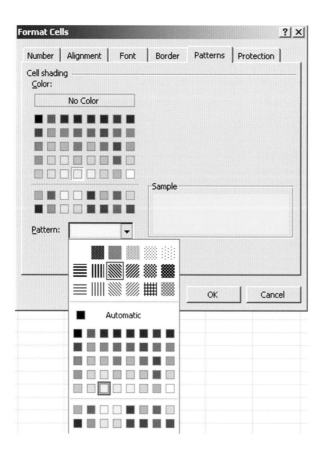

TASK 15

1 **Select the cells A2-H2 and apply a pale shading. Your worksheet should now look like this:**

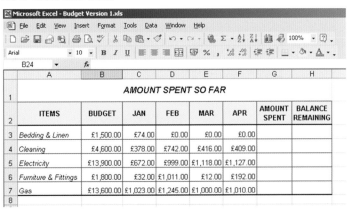

2 **Save the changes you have made and close the workbook.**

Removing formatting from cells

If you wish to remove formatting from cells, you can follow the same process as when you applied the formatting and individually switch off each formatting. However, it is quicker to use the **Clear** command.

Select the cells that contain the formatting you wish to remove and choose **Clear** from the **Edit** menu.

Click on **Formats** in the sub-menu. The formatting is removed from the cells, but the contents remain.

If you wish to simply delete the contents of a cell, click on the **Delete** button on the keyboard. However, any formatting in the cell is not removed and any new data entered into that cell will still have the formatting applied to the cell.

If you wish to remove the formatting from the cell as well as the contents, choose **All** from the **Clear** sub-menu.

Page setup and printing

Before the worksheet is printed, you should use the Page Setup dialog box to layout the worksheet for the printed page (usually A4 paper). Everything you do in the Page Setup dialog box affects how the worksheet will look when printed, not how it looks on-screen.

Using Page Setup

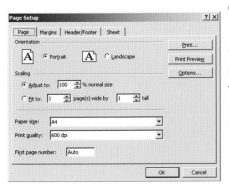

Choose **Page Setup** from the **File** menu.
The Page Setup dialog box opens.

Changing page orientation and scaling

By default, your worksheet will print onto portrait orientation. If you wish to change the page orientation to landscape, choose **File**, **Page Setup**, click on the **Page** tab and click the **Landscape** button.

If you wish to enlarge or reduce the size of your worksheet (e.g. to squeeze it onto one page), you can scale it. Choose **File**, **Page Setup**, click on the **Page** tab and use the spin button to scale the worksheet to smaller than 100% or larger than 100%.

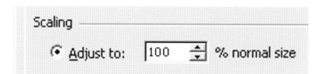

(It is helpful to make use of **Print Preview** when scaling, so you can see the results of your actions.)

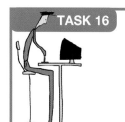

TASK 16

1 **Open the workbook called 'Budget Version 1' and use Page Setup to change the page orientation to Landscape.**

2 **Enlarge the worksheet to 120% normal size.**

3 **Save the changes you have made.**

Changing margins and alignment

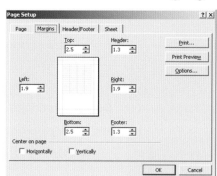

If you wish to change the margins, choose **File**, **Page Setup**, click on the **Margins** tab and use the spin buttons to adjust the margins. (The smaller the margin, the larger the work area and vice versa.) You can adjust the **Top, Left, Bottom** and **Right** margins on the printed page. You can also adjust the **Header** and **Footer** margin to control where headers and footers appear on the printed page.

To centre your worksheet on the page, choose **File**, **Page Setup**, click on the **Margins** tab and check the boxes to **Center on page Horizontally** (between the left and right margins) and/or **Vertically** (between the top and bottom margins).

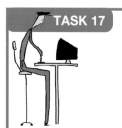

TASK 17

1 **Change the top margin of the page to 3.5 cm and centre the worksheet on the A4 Landscape page Horizontally.**

2 **Save the changes you have made.**

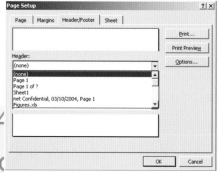

Creating headers and footers

A header is information that appears in the top margin area of every printed page and a footer is information that appears in the bottom margin area of every printed page. You can choose from a range of preset headers and footers, or you can create your own.
Choose **File**, **Page Setup** and click on the **Header/Footer** tab.

To choose a preset header or footer, click on the drop-down arrow for **Header** or **Footer** and choose from the list. The information is taken from user names, file names and sheet names.

Alternatively, you can create your own header and/or footer. Click on **Custom Header** or **Custom Footer**.

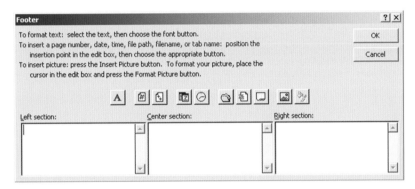

There are three sections in the Header or Footer dialog box: **Left section**, **Center section** and **Right section**. You can type in any of the sections, or use the buttons to insert fields.

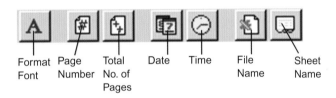

| Format Font | Page Number | Total No. of Pages | Date | Time | File Name | Sheet Name |

- **Format Font** – select any text you have typed and click on this button to format it. You can change the font, font style, font size and underline and add other text effects.
- **Page Number** – inserts the current page number. It will appear as a code – &[Page] – in the Header/Footer dialog box.
- **Total Number of Pages** – inserts the total number of printed pages. It will appear as a code – &[Pages] – in the Header/Footer dialog box.
- **Date** – inserts the current date. This will update each time the file is opened. The date will appear as a code – &[Date] – in the Header/Footer dialog box.
- **Time** – inserts the current time. This will update each time the file is opened or printed. The time will appear as a code – &[Time] – in the Header/Footer dialog box.
- **File Name** – inserts the name of the current file. The file name will appear as a code – &[File] – in the Header/Footer dialog box.
- **Sheet Name** – inserts the name of the current sheet. The sheet name will appear as a code – &[Sheet] – in the Header/Footer dialog box.

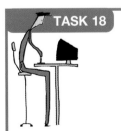

TASK 18

1 Create a header showing the file name in the centre of the page. The header should be in Arial 9 pt.

2 Create a footer showing the date at the left side of the page and the page number at the right side of the page. The footer should be in Arial 9 pt.

3 Save the changes you have made.

Other Page Setup options

The **Sheet** tab of the Page Setup dialog box offers you more options for setting up the printed page.

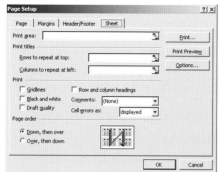

You can set a **Print area** if you only want to print a portion of the worksheet. Click in the **Print area** box to put the cursor in the box. Click on the red arrow button at the end of the Print area box to collapse the Page Setup dialog box. Click and drag on the worksheet to indicate the area you want to print. Click on the red arrow button to expand the Page Setup dialog box again.

You can choose to have rows and/or columns repeating on each printed page. For example, if you have headings at the top of a worksheet, you can indicate that this heading row should print again at the top of each printed page. Click in the **Rows to repeat at top** box or the **Columns to repeat at left** box, depending whether it is a row or column you wish to repeat. (You can have both rows and columns repeating on each printed page and more than one row or column.) Click on the red arrow button at the end of the box to collapse the Page Setup dialog box. Click and drag on the worksheet to indicate the rows or columns you wish to repeat. Click on the red arrow button to expand the Page Setup dialog box again.

You can choose to print gridlines (instead of using borders). Tick the **Gridlines** box. Gridlines print as a thin black line. **Be careful – asking for gridlines to print may give you more gridlines than you want**. You will get more control by applying borders where you want them, rather than printing gridlines.

If you have a colour worksheet and you print to a colour printer, but you only want a black and white print-out, tick the **Black and white** box.

If you don't want to see any formatting, borders or shading – just a print-out of the raw data – tick the **Draft quality** box.

If you wish to be able to see the row numbers and column letters on the printed page, tick the **Row and column headings** box.

You can insert Comments on the worksheet by choosing **Comment** from the **Insert** menu. Comments appear on the screen in a yellow box. If you wish to print the Comments you have inserted on screen, choose the appropriate option from the **Comments** drop-down list in the **Page Setup** dialog box.

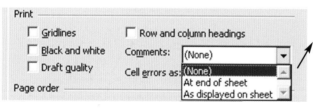

Finally, if you have a large amount of data, which will print on a number of printed pages, you can specify the order that it should print – **Down, then over** or **Over, then down**.

Print Preview

Before you print your worksheet, you may wish to view it as it will look when printed.

Choose **Print Preview** from the **File** menu.

Alternatively, press the Print Preview button on the Standard Toolbar.

Print
Preview

The Print Preview screen will open. Your worksheet displays on A4 paper and a set of buttons appears across the top of the screen.

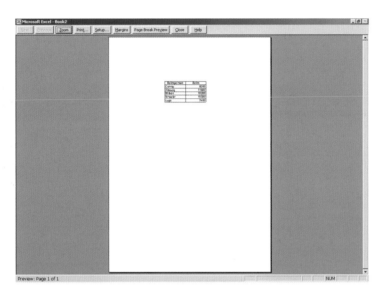

- **Next** – shows the next page if the worksheet goes over more than one printed page.
- **Previous** – shows the previous page if the worksheet goes onto more than one printed page.
- **Zoom** – zooms in on or out on the print preview. (You can also click on the sheet itself.)
- **Print** – opens the Print dialog box.
- **Setup** – opens the Page Setup dialog box. (This can also be accessed from the File menu.)
- **Margins** – switches on margin markers. You can move the margins by dragging the margin markers with the mouse.
- **Page Break Preview** – shows the worksheet divided into A4 pages. You can move the page breaks on the worksheet by dragging them.
- **Close** – closes the Print Preview window and returns to the worksheet.
- **Help** – accesses the online help files.

TASK 19

Preview the worksheet. It should look like this:

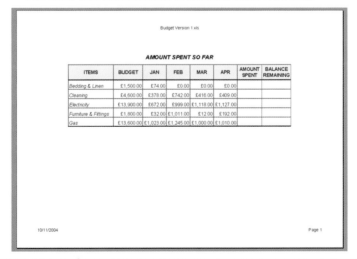

Page Break Preview

If you have created a large spreadsheet that will print onto more than one page of A4 paper, you can check where the page breaks will occur by using Page Break Preview.

Choose **Page Break Preview** from the **View** menu.

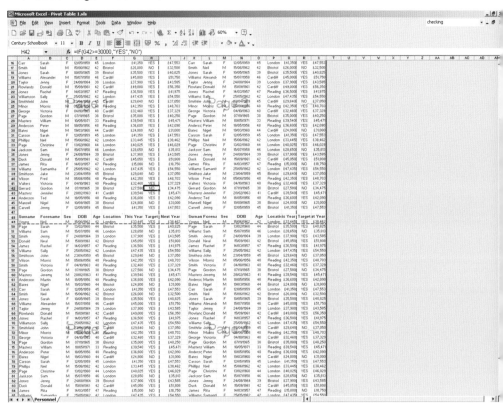

You can adjust where the page breaks will be by dragging the blue page break lines in this view.

	A	B	C	D	E	F	G	H	I	J
1	Surname	Forename	Sex	DOB	Age	Location	This Year	Target	Next Year	Surname
2	Young	Neil	M	15/06/1962	42	London	£33,445	YES	£38,462	Young
3	Page	Sarah	F	13/02/1960	44	Bristol	£35,500	YES	£40,825	Page
4	Williams	Sam	M	15/07/1958	46	London	£28,650	NO	£35,813	Williams
5	Smith	Jenny	F	24/08/1964	40	London	£37,900	YES	£43,585	Smith
6	Donald	Neal	M	15/09/1961	43	Bristol	£45,050	YES	£51,808	Donald
7	James	Rachel	F	14/03/1957	47	Reading	£36,500	YES	£41,975	James
8	Williams	Sally	F	25/05/1962	42	London	£47,435	YES	£54,550	Williams
9	Smithson	John	M	23/04/1959	45	Bristol	£29,640	NO	£37,050	Smithson
10	Wilson	Morris	M	05/06/1956	48	Reading	£42,350	YES	£48,703	Wilson
11	Smith	Victoria	F	04/10/1963	41	Reading	£32,460	YES	£37,329	Smith
12	Page	Gordon	M	07/11/1965	38	Bristol	£27,580	NO	£34,475	Page
13	Masters	Jeremy	M	28/02/1963	41	Reading	£39,540	YES	£45,471	Masters
14	Anderson	Martin	M	18/05/1956	48	Reading	£36,600	YES	£42,090	Anderson
15	Bates	Nigel	M	19/03/1960	44	Bristol	£24,800	NO	£31,000	Bates
16	Carr	Sarah	F	12/05/1959	45	London	£41,350	YES	£47,553	Carr
17	Smith	Neil	M	15/06/1962	42	Bristol	£26,000	NO	£32,500	Smith
18	Jones	Sarah	F	10/05/1965	39	Bristol	£35,500	YES	£40,825	Jones
19	Williams	Alexander	M	15/07/1958	46	Cardiff	£45,000	YES	£51,750	Williams
20	Taylor	Jenny	F	24/08/1964	40	London	£37,900	YES	£43,585	Taylor
21	Rowlands	Donald	M	15/09/1961	43	Cardiff	£49,000	YES	£56,350	Rowlands
22	Jones	Rachel	F	14/03/1957	47	Reading	£36,500	YES	£41,975	Jones
23	Williamson	Sally	F	25/05/1962	42	London	£47,435	YES	£54,550	Williamson
24	Smithfield	John	M	23/04/1959	45	Cardiff	£29,640	NO	£37,050	Smithfield
25	Minor	Morris	M	05/06/1956	48	Reading	£42,350	YES	£48,703	Minor
26	George	Victoria	F	04/10/1963	41	Cardiff	£32,460	YES	£37,329	George
27	Page	Gordon	M	07/11/1965	38	Bristol	£35,000	YES	£40,250	Page
28	Masters	William	M	10/05/1971	33	Reading	£39,540	YES	£45,471	Masters
29	Anderson	Peter	M	18/05/1956	48	Reading	£36,600	YES	£42,090	Anderson

Printing

Print

If you wish to print one copy of the current worksheet you can press the Print button on the Standard toolbar.

The worksheet will be sent directly to print.

However, if you wish to open the Print dialog box, in order to make some choices before printing, choose **Print** from the **File** menu.

You can also use Control + P

The Print dialog box opens, as below.

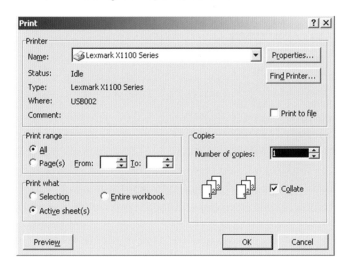

You can choose the printer to which you wish to print from the **Name** drop-down list.

You can choose to print **All** pages, or just a page range.

You can choose the **Number of copies** you require and whether you wish to print all the data on the **Active sheet**, just a **Selection** or the **Entire workbook**.

Click on **OK** to print.

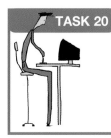

TASK 20

1 **Print two copies of the worksheet.**

2 **Save and close the workbook.**

Functions and formulas

Cell references

Every cell on an Excel worksheet has a 'cell reference'. This is made up of the column letter and the row number that the cell appears in.

	A	B	C	D
1		Wages (£)	Trade Union Deduction (1%)	Total after Trade Union deduction
2	F Bloggs	40.00		
3	B Briggs	207.00		
4	V Grange	218.50		
5	H Higgins	195.50		
6	J Jones	195.50		
7	J Morgan	400.00		
8	S Simple	250.00		
9	J Smith	300.00		
10				

The screenshot above shows that cell **B2** is the active cell. The cell itself has a heavier black border around it and the column letter and row number are highlighted.

When you write formulas (calculations) on the worksheet, you use the cell references to refer to the cells in the calculation.

Adding a row or a column

If you wish to add up a row or column of values on the worksheet, you can use the AutoSum button on the Standard toolbar.

AutoSum

Click in the cell at the end of the row or at the bottom of the column where you want the result to appear and press the AutoSum button.

SUMIF	▾ ✗ ✓ ƒx =SUM(B2:B9)			
	A	B	C	D
1		Wages (£)	Trade Union Deduction (1%)	Total after Trade Union deduction
2	F Bloggs	40.00		
3	B Briggs	207.00		
4	V Grange	218.50		
5	H Higgins	195.50		
6	J Jones	195.50		
7	J Morgan	400.00		
8	S Simple	250.00		
9	J Smith	300.00		
10	Total	=SUM(B2:B9)		
11		SUM(**number1**, [number2], ...)		
12				

A moving border indicates the range of cells that will be added. If this is the right range, press **Enter** on the keyboard. If this is not the right range, click and drag with the mouse to indicate the correct range and then press **Enter**. The result of the calculation appears in the active cell (i.e. the one the cursor is currently sitting in).

B10	▼	f_x =SUM(B2:B9)	
	A	B	C	D
1		Wages (£)	Trade Union Deduction (1%)	Total after Trade Union deduction
2	F Bloggs	40.00		
3	B Briggs	207.00		
4	V Grange	218.50		
5	H Higgins	195.50		
6	J Jones	195.50		
7	J Morgan	400.00		
8	S Simple	250.00		
9	J Smith	300.00		
10	Total	1806.50		
11				
12				

As an alternative, you can select the range that you wish to add up. (It is a good idea to also include the empty cell where you want the result to appear.)

B2	▼	f_x 40	
	A	B	C	D
1		Wages (£)	Trade Union Deduction (1%)	Total after Trade Union deduction
2	F Bloggs	40.00		
3	B Briggs	207.00		
4	V Grange	218.50		
5	H Higgins	195.50		
6	J Jones	195.50		
7	J Morgan	400.00		
8	S Simple	250.00		
9	J Smith	300.00		
10	Total			
11				
12				

Press the AutoSum button. The result is inserted into the empty cell that you selected.

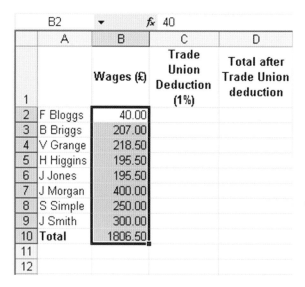

You can also use [Alt]+[+=] to activate AutoSum.

TASK 21

1 **Open the workbook called 'Budget Version 1'.**

2 **Type the text 'Totals' in cell A8 Make the text Bold and Italic and adjust the row height to 20).**

3 **Use AutoSum to add up the Budget column and the Jan, Feb, Mar and Apr columns.**

4 **Use AutoSum to calculate the Amount Spent So Far for each item. (Be careful that you don't include the Budget figure in these calculations.)**

5 **Use AutoSum to add up the Amount Spent column. Your worksheet should look like this:**

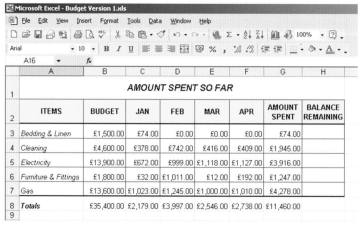

6 **Save the changes you have made.**

Formulas

If you need to do calculations with the data on the worksheet, you can write a calculation yourself (this is called a formula). Alternatively, you can use a built-in function.

A formula is made up of cell references (A1, D7, etc.) and mathematical operators. The four common mathematical operators are:

- ▪ Add   +
- ▪ Subtract   −
- ▪ Multiply   *
- ▪ Divide   /

If you use a desktop computer, as well as being able to access these symbols on the keys on the main part of the keyboard, these symbols also appear on the number keypad to the right of the main area of the keyboard. (To use the symbols on the number keypad, ensure that NUM LOCK is switched on.)

A formula starts with an = sign. This lets Excel know that you are not typing text or data into the cell, but are going to create a formula. For example, in the figure below, the value in cell B3 (Hourly Rate) is multiplied by the value in cell C3 (Hours Worked); the formula looks like this:

=B3*C3

SUMIF	▼ X ✓ *fx* =B3*C3		
	A	B	C	D
1				
2	Name	Hourly Rate	Hours Worked	Pay Due
3	Elaine Harrison	£7.50	50	=B3*C3
4	Jonathon Black	£10.00	35	
5				

Cell references are used in formulas rather than actual values so that, should the values in the cells change, the formula will automatically recalculate the resulting value.

Formulas are laid out in the same way that you would write a calculation on paper, except that the values are replaced with their cell references. Brackets, or parentheses, work in the same way too, to change the order of the mathematical calculation.

Creating a formula

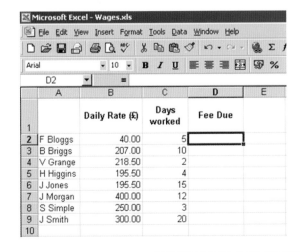

To calculate the Fee Due for F Bloggs (Daily Rate multiplied by Days worked), click in cell D2 (the cell where the result will appear). Type = to start the formula.

Click on the first cell that you need to include in the formula, **B2**. Excel inserts this cell reference into your formula. Type the mathematical operator ***** and then click on the second cell that you need to include in the formula, **C2**. The formula will look like this: =**B2*C2**

Press Enter when you have finished writing the formula.

The result of the calculation appears in the active cell, but the calculation itself appears in the formula bar.

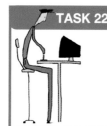

D2		*fx* =B2*C2		← Actual Formula used

	A	B	C	D
1		Wages (£)	Days Worked	Fee Due
2	F Bloggs	40.00	5	200.00 ← Result of calculation
3	B Briggs	207.00	10	
4	V Grange	218.50	2	
5	H Higgins	195.50	4	
6	J Jones	195.50	15	
7	J Morgan	400.00	12	
8	S Simple	250.00	3	
9	J Smith	300.00	20	
10				

TASK 22

1 **Write a formula to calculate the Balance Remaining for Bedding & Linen (Budget – Amount Spent).**

2 **Save the changes you have made.**

Copying a formula

Once you have written a formula, you do not need to write it again and again for each row or column it needs to refer to. There are various ways to copy the formula.

Click on the cell that contains the formula you have just written. Choose **Copy** from the **Edit** menu.

Alternatively, click on the Copy button on the Standard toolbar.

You can also use ⌨+C

Copy

D15		*fx* =B2*C2		

	A	B	C	D
1		Wages (£)	Days Worked	Fee Due
2	F Bloggs	40.00	5	200.00
3	B Briggs	207.00	10	
4	V Grange	218.50	2	
5	H Higgins	195.50	4	
6	J Jones	195.50	15	
7	J Morgan	400.00	12	
8	S Simple	250.00	3	
9	J Smith	300.00	20	
10				

Select the cells into which you wish to copy the formula.

D3		f_x =B2*C2		
	A	B	C	D
1		Wages (£)	Days Worked	Fee Due
2	F Bloggs	40.00	5	200.00
3	B Briggs	207.00	10	
4	V Grange	218.50	2	
5	H Higgins	195.50	4	
6	J Jones	195.50	15	
7	J Morgan	400.00	12	
8	S Simple	250.00	3	
9	J Smith	300.00	20	
10				

Choose **Paste** from the **Edit** menu.
Alternatively, click on the Paste button on the Standard toolbar.
You can also use [Control]+[V]

Paste

D3		f_x =B3*C3		
	A	B	C	D
1		Wages (£)	Days Worked	Fee Due
2	F Bloggs	40.00	5	200.00
3	B Briggs	207.00	10	2070.00
4	V Grange	218.50	2	437.00
5	H Higgins	195.50	4	782.00
6	J Jones	195.50	15	2932.50
7	J Morgan	400.00	12	4800.00
8	S Simple	250.00	3	750.00
9	J Smith	300.00	20	6000.00
10				

The formula is pasted into the selected cells. The row and column references change according to where the formula is copied to.

You can also use the fill handle to copy a formula. Click on the cell that contains the formula you wish to copy. Move to the bottom right corner of the cell over the small black square – the fill handle will appear.

Drag the fill handle over the cells into which you wish to copy the formula.

D2		= =B2*C2			
	A	B	C	D	E
1		Daily Rate (£)	Days worked	Fee Due	
2	F Bloggs	40.00	5	200.00	
3	B Briggs	207.00	10		
4	V Grange	218.50	2		
5	H Higgins	195.50	4		
6	J Jones	195.50	15		
7	J Morgan	400.00	12		
8	S Simple	250.00	3		
9	J Smith	300.00	20		
10					

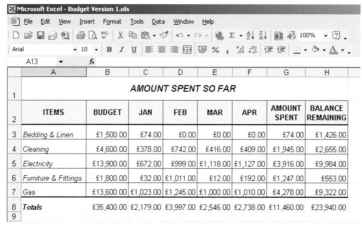

D2	▼	fx =B2*C2		
	A	B	C	D
1		Wages (£)	Days Worked	Fee Due
2	F Bloggs	40.00	5	200.00
3	B Briggs	207.00	10	
4	V Grange	218.50	2	
5	H Higgins	195.50	4	
6	J Jones	195.50	15	
7	J Morgan	400.00	12	
8	S Simple	250.00	3	
9	J Smith	300.00	20	
10				

TASK 23

1 **Copy the formula you have just created to calculate Balance Remaining for Bedding & Linen into the other rows in that column (to calculate the Balance Remaining for each item).**

2 **Use AutoSum to add up the Balance Remaining column. Your worksheet should now look like this:**

Microsoft Excel - Budget Version 1.xls

File Edit View Insert Format Tools Data Window Help

A13

	A	B	C	D	E	F	G	H
1		AMOUNT SPENT SO FAR						
2	ITEMS	BUDGET	JAN	FEB	MAR	APR	AMOUNT SPENT	BALANCE REMAINING
3	Bedding & Linen	£1,500.00	£74.00	£0.00	£0.00	£0.00	£74.00	£1,426.00
4	Cleaning	£4,600.00	£378.00	£742.00	£416.00	£409.00	£1,945.00	£2,655.00
5	Electricity	£13,900.00	£672.00	£999.00	£1,118.00	£1,127.00	£3,916.00	£9,984.00
6	Furniture & Fittings	£1,800.00	£32.00	£1,011.00	£12.00	£192.00	£1,247.00	£553.00
7	Gas	£13,600.00	£1,023.00	£1,245.00	£1,000.00	£1,010.00	£4,278.00	£9,322.00
8	Totals	£35,400.00	£2,179.00	£3,997.00	£2,546.00	£2,738.00	£11,460.00	£23,940.00
9								

3 **Save the changes you have made and close the workbook.**

Relative cell referencing

Excel uses 'relative cell referencing' when it copies a formula to other cells. This means that if you take a formula written in row 2 on the spreadsheet – for example, B2-C2 – and copy it down to row 3 on the spreadsheet, the formula becomes B3-C3. The row number changes relative to the cell to which the formula is copied. (It works in the same way if you copy a formula across columns.)

The above example shows the formula B2-C2 having been copied down through rows. The cell reference of the formula changes to reflect the row it has been copied to.

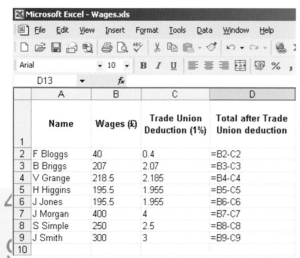

Microsoft Excel - Wages.xls

File Edit View Insert Format Tools Data Window Help

Arial 10 B I U

D13

	A	B	C	D
1	Name	Wages (£)	Trade Union Deduction (1%)	Total after Trade Union deduction
2	F Bloggs	40	0.4	=B2-C2
3	B Briggs	207	2.07	=B3-C3
4	V Grange	218.5	2.185	=B4-C4
5	H Higgins	195.5	1.955	=B5-C5
6	J Jones	195.5	1.955	=B6-C6
7	J Morgan	400	4	=B7-C7
8	S Simple	250	2.5	=B8-C8
9	J Smith	300	3	=B9-C9
10				

Absolute cell referencing

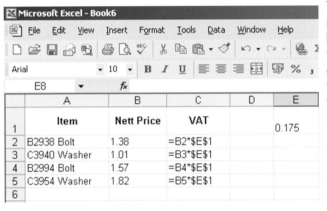

	A	B	C	D	E
1	Item	Nett Price	VAT		0.175
2	B2938 Bolt	1.38	=B2*$E$1		
3	C3940 Washer	1.01	=B3*$E$1		
4	B2994 Bolt	1.57	=B4*$E$1		
5	C3954 Washer	1.82	=B5*$E$1		
6					

There are times when you want to be able to place a value in a cell on the worksheet and have Excel refer to it all the time when writing formulas (for example, when doing VAT calculations). In order that you can still copy the formula down through rows or across columns, you need to make this cell reference fixed – known as an 'absolute cell' reference.

To make a cell reference absolute, you place a dollar ($) sign in front of each part of the cell reference, for example, **$B$3**. By placing a dollar sign in front of the column letter and the row number, you are saying 'absolute column B, absolute row 3'.

The worksheet above shows that the cell reference E1 has been made absolute. When the formula is copied from cell C2 to C3, C4 and C5, the cell reference E1 remains the same. In this case, the information in cell E1 is needed for all the formulas.

Rather than typing the dollar signs, you can use [F4]. As you build the formula, after you click on the cell that you wish to make absolute, press F4. This will put the dollar signs around the cell reference.

TASK 24

1 **Start a new workbook and type the following data onto the worksheet:**

ITEM	NETT PRICE	VAT	TOTAL PRICE
White Wine	£2.29		
Sugar	£0.55		
Baked Beans	£0.27		
Chocolates	£1.56		
Washing Powder	£2.33		

2 **Type 17.5% in cell H1 on the worksheet.**

3 **Calculate the VAT for White Wine, using the information in cell H1.**

4 **Make the H1 cell reference absolute and then copy the formula to the other items.**

5 **Calculate the Total Price for each item. Your worksheet should look like this:**

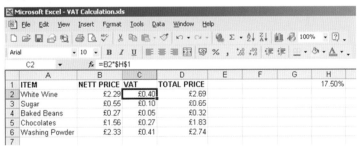

6 **Save the workbook in your Tasks for ITQ folder with the filename 'VAT Calculation'.**

7 **Close the workbook.**

Using built-in functions to perform calculations

Excel has many built-in functions to assist you in carrying out calculations on your data. The sum function adds data and is the most commonly used function. It has been assigned to a button (AutoSum) to make it very easy to use.

Using functions is slightly different in Excel 2000 and Excel 2002. Guidelines for functions in Excel 2000 are shown first, followed by Excel 2002.

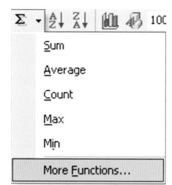

Excel 2002

The AutoSum button in Excel 2002 has a drop-down arrow beside it. Clicking on this drop-down arrow opens a menu of other commonly used functions – Sum, Average, Count, Max and Min.

To access the complete list of available functions, click on **More Functions ...** at the bottom of this menu.

Alternatively, you can choose **Function** from the **Insert** menu.

The Insert Function dialog box opens.

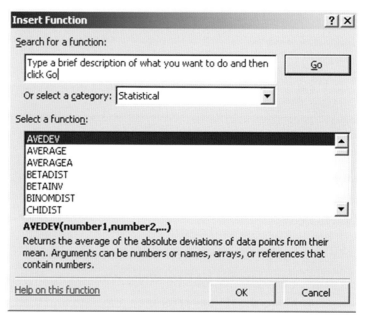

Click in the **Search for a function** box and type a brief description of what you want to do. Click on **Go** to search for a function. Alternatively, choose a function category from the **select a category** drop-down list.

To see a complete list of all the functions, choose **All** from the category list.

The functions in the chosen category are listed at the bottom of the Insert Function dialog box. When you click on a function in the list, a description of that function appears at the bottom of the dialog box.

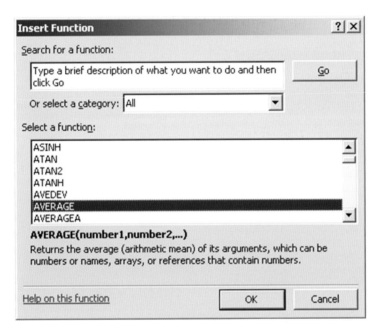

Once you have found the function you want to use, select it in the list and click on **OK** to open the function palette.

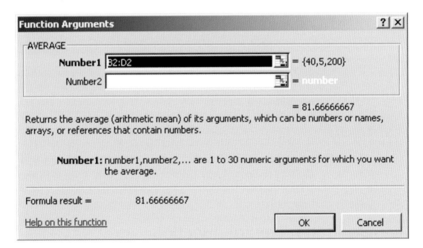

The Function Arguments will vary according to which function you have chosen. You will usually need to indicate individual cells or a range of cells. Click on **OK** when you have finished entering the data for the function arguments.

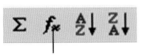

Paste
Function

Excel 2000

Choose **Function** from the **Insert** menu.
Alternatively, click on the Paste Function button on the Standard toolbar.
The Paste Function dialog box opens, as below:

The functions are divided into categories. To see a complete list of all the functions, choose **All** from the **Function category** list on the left. When you click on a Function in the list on the right, a description of that function appears at the bottom of the dialog box.

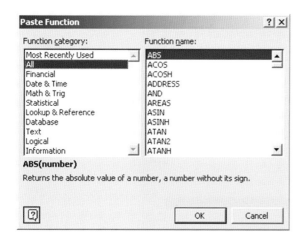

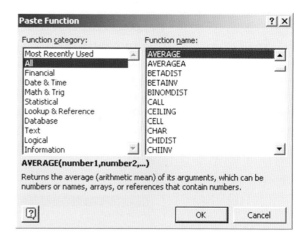

Once you have found the function you want to use, select it in the list and click on **OK** to open the Function palette.

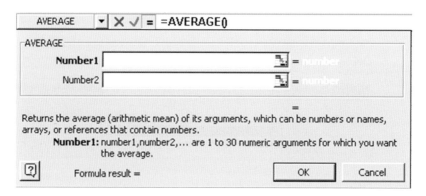

The Function palette will vary according to which function you have chosen. You will usually need to indicate individual cells or a range of cells. Click on **OK** when you have finished entering the data into the Function palette.

For more information on setting up specific functions, please refer to the pages later in this section.

Using the Average function

You can use the Average function to calculate the average of selected values on the worksheet.

Excel 2002

Click in the cell where you want the result to appear and choose **Average** from the drop-down list by the AutoSum button.

A moving border indicates the range that will be averaged and the formula that Excel will write on your behalf appears in the active cell and on the formula bar.

If this is the right range, press **Enter** on the keyboard. If this is not the right range, click and drag with the mouse to indicate the correct range and then press **Enter**.

	A	B	C	D	
1		Wages (£)	Days Worked	Fee Due	
2	F Bloggs	40.00	5	200.00	
3	B Briggs	207.00	10	2070.00	
4	V Grange	218.50	2	437.00	
5	H Higgins	195.50	4	782.00	
6	J Jones	195.50	15	2932.50	
7	J Morgan	400.00	12	4800.00	
8	S Simple	250.00	3	750.00	
9	J Smith	300.00	20	6000.00	
10	Average Fee	=AVERAGE(B2:B9)			
11		AVERAGE(**number1**, [number2], ...)			
12					

AVERAGE ▾ ✕ ✓ *fx* =AVERAGE(B2:B9)

Alternatively, you can choose **More Functions** at the bottom of the drop-down list and pick **Average** from the list of functions. Click on **OK** to select this function and then indicate the range in the Function Arguments dialog box.

Excel 2000

Click in the cell where you want the result to appear and choose **Function** from the **Insert** menu. Alternatively, click on the Paste Function button on the Standard toolbar.

The Paste Function dialog box opens showing the **Most Recently Used Category**. The Average function is usually in this category. If you cannot see it, choose the **Statistical** category from the list on the left side. The Average function will be in the list on the right side.

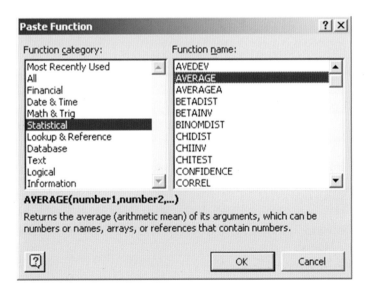

Click on it and click on **OK**. The Function palette opens.

AVERAGE	▼	✕ ✓	=	=AVERAGE()

AVERAGE

Number1		▥	= number
Number2		▥	= number

=

Returns the average (arithmetic mean) of its arguments, which can be numbers or names, arrays, or references that contain numbers.

Number1: number1,number2,... are 1 to 30 numeric arguments for which you want the average.

?	Formula result =		OK	Cancel

Number1 is the first range of values on the worksheet for which you wish to calculate the average. Excel will already have selected a range on the worksheet. If this is the correct range, click on **OK**.

If this is not the correct range, you need to select the correct range on the worksheet. If the Function palette is in the way, you can move it by clicking and dragging it on the worksheet.

Alternatively, you can collapse the Function palette by clicking on the red arrow button, so that you can see the worksheet.

Number1		▥
Number2		▥

Click on the red arrow button again when you want to expand the dialog box.

Click and drag with the mouse on the worksheet to select the correct range. Click on **OK** in the Function palette.

AVERAGE	▼	✕ ✓	=	=AVERAGE(B2:B9)

B2:B9

		Wages (£)	Days Worked	Fee Due
1				
2	F Bloggs	40.00	5	200.00
3	B Briggs	207.00	10	2070.00
4	V Grange	218.50	2	437.00
5	H Higgins	195.50	4	782.00
6	J Jones	195.50	15	2932.50
7	J Morgan	400.00	12	4800.00
8	S Simple	250.00	3	750.00
9	J Smith	300.00	20	6000.00
10	Average Fee	AGE(B2:B9)		
11				

If you wish to average across more than one range of values in the workbook, click in the **Number2** box and repeat the above process. You can average up to 30 ranges in a workbook. (The ranges can be on different sheets in the workbook.)

TASK 25

1 **Start a new workbook and enter the following data onto the worksheet:**

NAME	WAGES (£)
F Bloggs	470.00
B Briggs	207.00
V Grange	218.50
H Higgins	195.50
J Jones	195.50
J Morgan	400.00
S Simple	250.00
J Smith	300.00

2 **Type the text 'Average Wage' in cell A10. Make the text Bold.**

3 **Calculate the average wage paid. Put the result in cell B10. Your worksheet should look like this:**

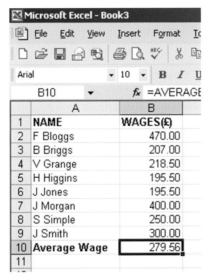

4 **Save the workbook into your Tasks for ITQ folder with the filename 'Wages'.**

Using the Max and Min functions

If you wish to know the maximum or minimum value in a range of values, you can use the **Max** or **Min** function.

Excel 2002

Click in the cell where you want the result to appear and choose **Min** or **Max** from the drop-down list by the AutoSum button.

A moving border indicates the range that will be used and the formula that Excel will write on your behalf appears in the active cell and on the formula bar.

AVERAGE	▾ ✗ ✓ ƒx =MAX(B2:B9)		
	A	B	C	D
1		Wages (£)	Days Worked	Fee Due
2	F Bloggs	40.00	5	200.00
3	B Briggs	207.00	10	2070.00
4	V Grange	218.50	2	437.00
5	H Higgins	195.50	4	782.00
6	J Jones	195.50	15	2932.50
7	J Morgan	400.00	12	4800.00
8	S Simple	250.00	3	750.00
9	J Smith	300.00	20	6000.00
10	**Average Fee**	225.81	8.88	2246.44
11	**Maximum Fee**	=MAX(B2:B9)		
12		MAX(**number1**, [number2], ...)		
13				

If this is the right range, press **Enter** on the keyboard. If this is not the right range, click and drag with the mouse to indicate the correct range and then press **Enter**.

Alternatively, you can choose **More Functions** at the bottom of the drop-down list and pick **Min** or **Max** from the list of functions. Click on **OK** to select the function and then indicate the range in the Function Arguments dialog box.

Excel 2000

Click in the cell where you want the result to appear and choose **Function** from the **Insert** menu. Alternatively, click on the Paste Function button on the Standard toolbar.

The Paste Function dialog box opens showing the **Most Recently Used Category**. The Min and Max functions can usually be found in this category. If you cannot see them, choose the **Statistical** category from the list on the left side.

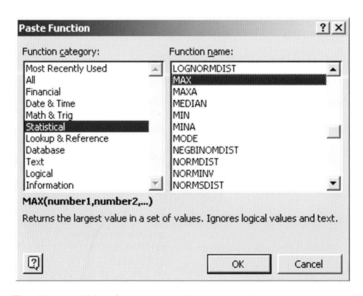

The Min and Max functions will be in the list on the right side. Click on the one you wish to use and click on **OK**.

The Function palette opens.

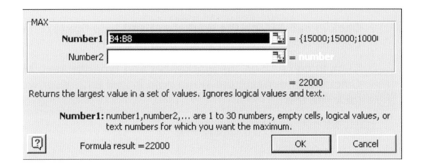

Number1 is the first range of values on the worksheet for which you wish to determine the maximum. Excel will already have selected a range on the worksheet. If this is the correct range, click on **OK**.

If this is not the correct range, you need to select the correct range on the worksheet. If the Function palette is in the way, you can move it by clicking and dragging it on the worksheet.

Alternatively, you can collapse the Function palette by clicking on the red arrow button, so that you can see the worksheet.

Click on the red arrow button again when you want to expand the dialog box.

Click and drag with the mouse on the worksheet to select the correct range. Click on **OK** in the Function Palette.

MAX	▼ X ✓ = =MAX(B2:B9)		
B2:B9|			
		Wages (£)	Days Worked	Fee Due
1				
2	F Bloggs	40.00	5	200.00
3	B Briggs	207.00	10	2070.00
4	V Grange	218.50	2	437.00
5	H Higgins	195.50	4	782.00
6	J Jones	195.50	15	2932.50
7	J Morgan	400.00	12	4800.00
8	S Simple	250.00	3	750.00
9	J Smith	300.00	20	6000.00
10	Average Fee	225.81	8.88	2246.44
11	Maximum Fee	=MAX(B2:B9)		
12				

If you wish to find the maximum of more than one range of values in the workbook, click in the **Number2** box and repeat the above process. You can average up to 30 ranges in a workbook. (The ranges can be on different sheets in the workbook.)

TASK 26

1　Click in cell **A11** on the worksheet and type the text 'Minimum Wage'. Calculate the minimum wage paid in cell **B11**.

2　Click in cell **A12** on the worksheet and type the text 'Maximum Wage'. Calculate the maximum wage paid in cell **B12**. Your worksheet should look like this:

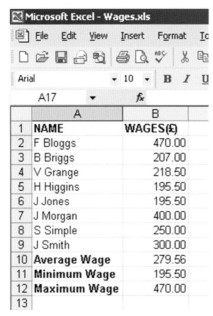

3　Save the changes you have made.

Using the Count function

If you wish to count the number of values in a range, you can use the Count function.

Excel 2002

Click in the cell where you want the result to appear and choose **Count** from the drop-down list by the AutoSum button.

A moving border indicates the range that will be used and the formula that Excel will write on your behalf appears in the active cell and on the formula bar.

If this is the right range, press **Enter** on the keyboard. If this is not the right range, click and drag with the mouse to indicate the correct range and then press **Enter**.

Alternatively, you can choose **More Functions** at the bottom of the drop-down list and pick **Count** from the list of functions. Click on **OK** to select the function and then indicate the range in the Function Arguments dialog box.

AVERAGE	▼ ✕ ✓ *fx* =COUNT(B2:B9)		
	A	B	C	D

	A	Wages (£)	Days Worked	Fee Due
1				
2	F Bloggs	40.00	5	200.00
3	B Briggs	207.00	10	2070.00
4	V Grange	218.50	2	437.00
5	H Higgins	195.50	4	782.00
6	J Jones	195.50	15	2932.50
7	J Morgan	400.00	12	4800.00
8	S Simple	250.00	3	750.00
9	J Smith	300.00	20	6000.00
10	**Average Fee**	225.81	8.88	2246.44
11	**Maximum Fee**	400.00	20.00	6000.00
12	**No. of Wages paid**	=COUNT(B2:B9)		
13		COUNT(**value1**, [value2], ...)		
14				

Excel 2000

Click in the cell where you want the result to appear and choose **Function** from the **Insert** menu. Alternatively, click on the Paste Function button on the Standard toolbar.

The Paste Function dialog box opens showing the **Most Recently Used Category**. The Count function can usually be found in this category. If you cannot see it, choose the **Statistical** category from the list on the left side.

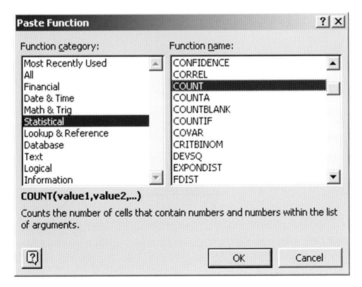

The Count function will be in the list on the right side. Click on it and click on **OK**.

The Function palette opens.

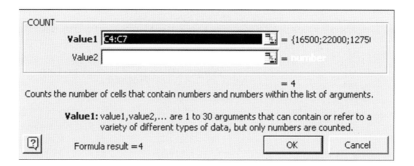

Value1 is the first range on the worksheet that you wish to count. Excel will already have selected a range on the worksheet. If this is the correct range, click on **OK**.

If this is not the correct range, you need to select the correct range on the worksheet. If the Function palette is in the way, you can move it by clicking and dragging it on the worksheet.

Alternatively, you can collapse the Function palette by clicking on the red arrow button, so that you can see the worksheet.

Click on the red arrow button again when you want to expand the dialog box.

Click and drag with the mouse on the worksheet to select the correct range. Click on **OK** in the Function Palette.

	COUNT ▾ ✕ ✓ = =COUNT(B2:B9)			
B2:B9				
		Wages (£)	**Days Worked**	**Fee Due**
1				
2	F Bloggs	40.00	5	200.00
3	B Briggs	207.00	10	2070.00
4	V Grange	218.50	2	437.00
5	H Higgins	195.50	4	782.00
6	J Jones	195.50	15	2932.50
7	J Morgan	400.00	12	4800.00
8	S Simple	250.00	3	750.00
9	J Smith	300.00	20	6000.00
10	**Average Fee**	225.81	8.88	2246.44
11	**Maximum Fee**	400.00	20.00	6000.00
12	**No. of Wages paid**	=COUNT(B2:B9)		
13				

If you wish to count more than one range of values in the workbook, click in the **Value2** box and repeat the above process. You can count values in up to 30 ranges in a workbook. (The ranges can be on different sheets in the workbook.)

Other Count functions

The count function only counts values in a range. However, there are a range of other count functions which can be useful when counting items in a list.

- **CountA** – counts the number of cells that are not empty. This is useful if you want to count items in a range that are words rather than figures.
- **CountBlank** – counts the number of empty cells in a range. This is useful if you need to know whether any cells are blank in a range.
- **CountIF** – counts the number of items in a range that meet a given condition. For example, to just count the name Parker in a list of names.

TASK 27

1 **Click in cell A13 on the worksheet and type the text 'No. of Wages paid'. Calculate the number of wages paid in cell B13. Your worksheet should look like this:**

	A	B
		fx =COUNT(B2:E
1	NAME	WAGES(£)
2	F Bloggs	470.00
3	B Briggs	207.00
4	V Grange	218.50
5	H Higgins	195.50
6	J Jones	195.50
7	J Morgan	400.00
8	S Simple	250.00
9	J Smith	300.00
10	**Average Wage**	279.56
11	**Minimum Wage**	195.50
12	**Maximum Wage**	470.00
13	**No. of Wages paid**	8
14		

Microsoft Excel - Wages.xls

File Edit View Insert Format Tools

Arial   10   **B** *I* U

B13

2 **Save the changes you have made and close the workbook.**

Using the Round function

The Round function will round a number or calculation on the worksheet to a specified number of digits.

	A	B	C	D	E	F	G
1				Supermarket Price Comparison			
2							
3	Item	Safeway	Tesco	Asda	Co-op	Average	Rounded Average
4	White Wine	1.29	1.72	1.89	1.45	1.5875	
5	Sugar	0.55	0.62	0.61	0.59	0.5925	
6	Baked Beans	0.27	0.25	0.26	0.24	0.255	
7	Lemonade	0.89	0.99	1.02	0.97	0.9675	
8	Tomato Soup	0.25	0.27	0.31	0.32	0.2875	
9	Salad Cream	0.76	0.88	0.74	0.76	0.785	
10							

G4   fx

In the example above, the average price needs to be rounded to two decimal places.

Click in the cell where you want the result to appear and choose **Function** from the **Insert** menu. Alternatively, choose **More Functions** from the drop-down list by the AutoSum button (Excel 2002) or click on the Paste Function button on the Standard toolbar (Excel 2000).

The Insert Function dialog box opens.

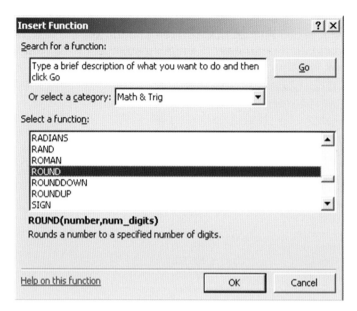

Select the Round function from the list (in the **Math & Trig** category) and click on **OK**.

The Function Arguments dialog box opens.

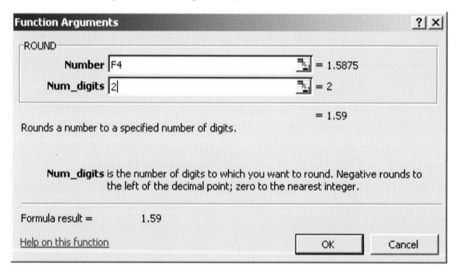

The **Number** is the cell reference of the number you wish to round (in the example, this is **F4**). The **Num_digits** is the number of digits you wish to round to (in this example, 2).

If the Function Arguments box is in the way, you can move it by pointing to its Title Bar and clicking and dragging it on the worksheet. Alternatively, you can collapse the Function Arguments box by clicking on the red arrow button, so that you can see the worksheet.

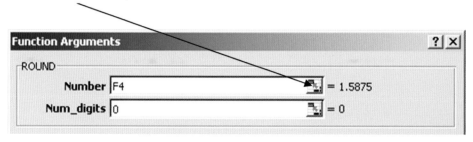

Function Arguments [?] [X]

Click on the red arrow button again when you want to expand the dialog box.
Click on the cell on the worksheet that contains the figure that you wish to
round. Click in the **Num_digits** box and type the number of digits you wish to
round to. Click on **OK**.

G4	▼		_fx_ =ROUND(F4,2)	◄────── Formula			
	A	B	C	D	E	F	G
1				Supermarket Price Comparison			
2							
3	Item	Safeway	Tesco	Asda	Co-op	Average	Rounded Average
4	White Wine	1.29	1.72	1.89	1.45	1.5875	1.59 ◄── Result
5	Sugar	0.55	0.62	0.61	0.59	0.5925	
6	Baked Beans	0.27	0.25	0.26	0.24	0.255	
7	Lemonade	0.89	0.99	1.02	0.97	0.9675	
8	Tomato Soup	0.25	0.27	0.31	0.32	0.2875	
9	Salad Cream	0.76	0.88	0.74	0.76	0.785	
10							

The result is entered in the active cell and the formula itself appears on the Formula
Bar.

TASK 28

1 **Open the workbook called 'VAT Calculation'. Click onto Sheet 2 and type
the following data:**

ITEM	SAFEWAY	TESCO	ASDA	CO-OP	AVERAGE ROUNDED AVERAGE
White Wine	1.29	1.72	1.89	1.45	
Sugar	0.55	0.62	0.61	0.59	
Baked Beans	0.27	0.25	0.26	0.24	
Lemonade	0.89	0.99	1.02	0.97	
Tomato Soup	0.25	0.27	0.31	0.32	
Salad Cream	0.76	0.88	0.74	0.76	

2 **Calculate the Average price for White Wine in cell F2 and copy the
formula to the other items.**

3 **Calculate the Rounded Average (using the Round function) for White
Wine. Copy the formula to the other items. Your worksheet should look
like this:**

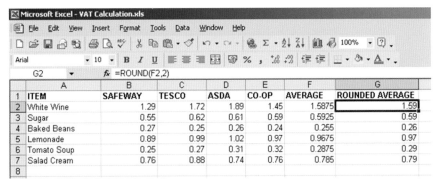

4 **Save and close the workbook.**

The PMT and FV Functions

The **PMT** and **FV** functions are just two of the functions in the **Financial** category. Periodic Monthly Term (PMT) enables you to calculate loan repayments based on constant repayments and a constant interest rate. Future Value (FV) enables you to calculate the future value of an investment based on constant payments and a constant interest rate.

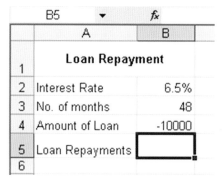

These functions need more than one piece of information (argument). The **PMT** function needs to know the amount of the loan, the interest rate and the number of monthly payments. The **FV** function needs to know the interest rate, the number of monthly payments and the amount paid in each month.

Below is an example of when the **PMT** function would be used. The **FV** function works in a similar way.

Click in the cell where you want the result to appear and choose **Function** from the **Insert** menu. Alternatively, click on the Paste Function button on the Standard toolbar (Excel 2000) or choose **More Functions** from the drop-down list by the AutoSum button (Excel 2002).

Select the **PMT** or **FV** function from the list (in the **Financial** category) and click on **OK**.

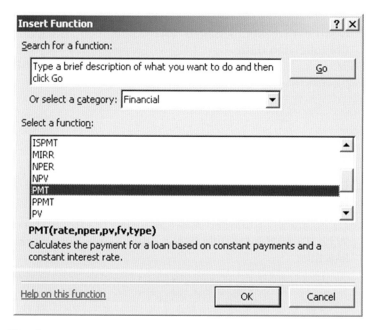

The Function Arguments dialog box opens.

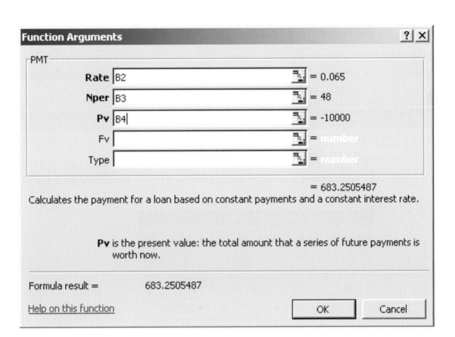

The **Rate** is the interest rate for the loan (in this example, the interest rate appears in cell **B2**). The **Nper** is the number of months over which the loan is to be repaid (in this example, the number of months appears in cell **B3**). The **Pv** is the present value of the loan, i.e. how much is being borrowed (in this example, the amount being borrowed appears in cell **B4**). The **Pv** is shown on the spreadsheet as a negative figure as this is how much is owed. By showing the Pv as a negative figure, the loan repayments will show as a positive figure.

Click on the cell on the worksheet that contains the interest rate. The cell reference is inserted into the **Rate** box in the function palette. Click in the **Nper** box and click on the cell on the worksheet that contains the number of months the loan will be taken over. The cell reference is inserted into the **Nper** box in the function palette. Click in the **Pv** box and click on the cell on the worksheet that contains the amount of the loan. (The loan amount should be entered as a negative value on the worksheet). The cell reference is inserted into the **Pv** box in the function palette.

Click on **OK** when you have finished entering the appropriate cell references.

The result is entered in the active cell and the formula itself appears on the Formula Bar.

If the Function Arguments box is in the way, you can move it by pointing to its Title Bar and clicking and dragging it on the worksheet. Alternatively, you can collapse the Function Arguments box by clicking on the red arrow button, so that you can see the worksheet.

Click on the red arrow button again when you want to expand the dialog box.

TASK 29

1 **Start a new workbook and type the following data on the worksheet:**
   LOAN INFORMATION

Interest Rate	6%
No. of Months	48
Amount of Loan	-10000

   Loan Repayments

2 **Calculate the loan repayment in cell B5. Your worksheet should look like this:**

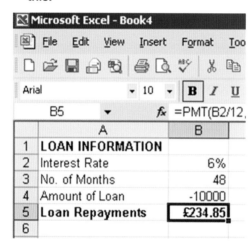

3 **Save the workbook in your Tasks for ITQ folder with the filename 'Loan Information'. Close the workbook.**

The IF function

IF functions are used where you want to be able to analyse data in a cell and ask Excel to perform an action dependent upon the data. For example, if different bonuses are awarded depending on sales figures, you can ask Excel to perform a test to see whether the sales figures are greater than a specified figure and then calculate the bonus based on this.

An IF function has three parts: a logical test to test the condition, an action that you want Excel to do if the test is true and one that you want Excel to do if the test is false.

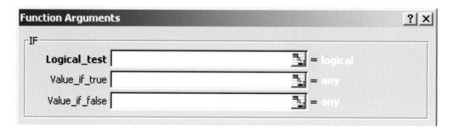

The IF function is a 'logical' function and uses logical operators:

■ Equal to   =
■ Greater than   >
■ Less than   <

■ Greater than or equal to>=
■ Less than or equal to   <=
■ Not equal to   ≠

In the example below, the school secretary wishes to establish whether each child is required to take a test (a test is required if they are aged 9 or over).

	A	B	C
	Name of Child	**Age**	**Test Required**
1			
2	Benjamin Taylor	8	
3	Stuart Timmins	12	
4	Penelope Bailey	7	
5	Sarah Barnings	10	
6	Jonathan Eggleton	11	
7	Bridget Smith	9	
8	Thomas Mannings	8	
9	Timothy Stott	10	
10	Brenda McAlison	11	
11	Emma Lawson	12	
12	James Browning	9	
13	Jennifer Moss	7	
14	Trudy Sullivan	10	
15	Simon Cuthbert	12	
16	Sally Pratt	8	
17	William Grant	9	
18	Stephen Little	11	
19	Louise Napps	12	
20	Lesley Ark	7	
21	Kieran Kensey	8	
22			

Click in the cell where you want the result to appear and choose **Function** from the **Insert** menu. Alternatively, click on the Paste Function button on the Standard toolbar (Excel 2000) or choose **More Functions** from the drop-down list by the AutoSum button (Excel 2002).

The Insert Function dialog box opens.

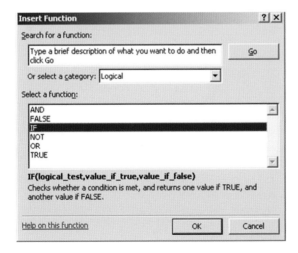

Select the **IF** function from the list (in the **Logical** category) and click on **OK**. The Function Arguments dialog box opens.

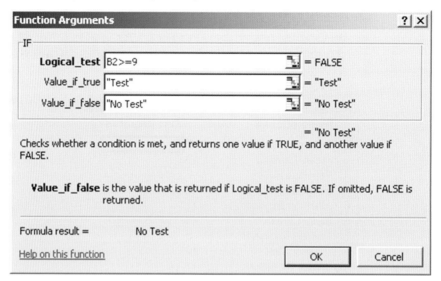

Logical_test is the test that you wish to perform. In this example, the logical test is **B2>=9** (to establish whether the number in cell B2 is greater than or equal to 9). Click in the **Value_if_true** box and type what result you want to be returned if the test is true (i.e. B2 is greater than or equal to 9) – in the example, the word 'Test' is returned. Click in the **Value_if_false** box and type what result you want to be returned if the test is false (i.e. B2 is less than 9) – in the example, the words 'No Test' are returned.

Click on **OK** once you have completed the three parts of the IF function.

	A	B	C	D
			=IF(B2>=9,"Test","No Test")	← Formula
1	Name of Child	Age	Test Required	
2	Benjamin Taylor	8	No Test ←	Result
3	Stuart Timmins	12		
4	Penelope Bailey	7		
5	Sarah Barnings	10		
6	Jonathan Eggleton	11		
7	Bridget Smith	9		
8	Thomas Mannings	8		
9	Timothy Stott	10		
10	Brenda McAlison	11		

The result is entered in the active cell and the formula itself appears on the Formula Bar.

For **Value if true** and **Value if false**, you can ask Excel to simply return an answer – 'Yes', 'No', 'True', 'False', 'Test', 'No Test', etc. Alternatively, you can ask Excel to do a calculation. For example, if cell B2 is greater than 20 you can ask that Excel should multiply cell B2 by 20 – **B2*20**. If cell B2 is not greater than 20 you can ask that Excel should divide cell B2 by 20 – **B2/20**.

If you need to see the worksheet behind the Function palette, drag the Function palette on the worksheet. Alternatively, you can collapse the Function palette by clicking on the red arrow button.

Click on the red arrow button again when you want to expand the dialog box.

Click on **OK** in the Function palette.

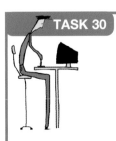

TASK 30

1 Open the workbook called 'VAT Calculation'.

2 Move to Sheet 2 and type the heading 'CHEAPEST?' in cell H1.

3 Write an IF statement to compare the prices of Tesco and Asda. The IF should return which is the cheaper price. Copy the IF statement to the other items. Your worksheet should look like this:

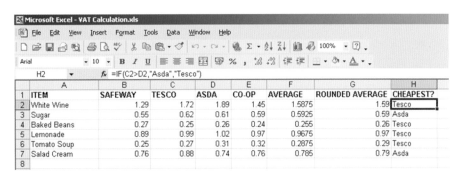

Microsoft Excel - VAT Calculation.xls

File Edit View Insert Format Tools Data Window Help

H2   fx =IF(C2>D2,"Asda","Tesco")

	A	B	C	D	E	F	G	H
1	ITEM	SAFEWAY	TESCO	ASDA	CO-OP	AVERAGE	ROUNDED AVERAGE	CHEAPEST?
2	White Wine	1.29	1.72	1.89	1.45	1.5875	1.59	Tesco
3	Sugar	0.55	0.62	0.61	0.59	0.5925	0.59	Asda
4	Baked Beans	0.27	0.25	0.26	0.24	0.255	0.26	Tesco
5	Lemonade	0.89	0.99	1.02	0.97	0.9675	0.97	Tesco
6	Tomato Soup	0.25	0.27	0.31	0.32	0.2875	0.29	Tesco
7	Salad Cream	0.76	0.88	0.74	0.76	0.785	0.79	Asda
8								

4 Save and close the workbook.

5 Open the workbook called 'Wages'. Type a heading 'BONUS' in cell C1.

6 Write an IF statement to calculate the Bonus. If wages are more than £250.00 the bonus is 10% of wages. If wages are less than £250.00 the bonus is 7.5% of wages. Copy the IF statement down for all employees. Your worksheet should look like this:

7 Save and close the workbook.

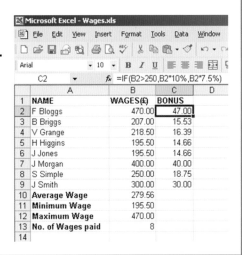

Microsoft Excel - Wages.xls

File Edit View Insert Format Tools Data Window

Arial   10   B I U

C2   fx =IF(B2>250,B2*10%,B2*7.5%)

	A	B	C	D
1	NAME	WAGES(£)	BONUS	
2	F Bloggs	470.00	47.00	
3	B Briggs	207.00	15.53	
4	V Grange	218.50	16.39	
5	H Higgins	195.50	14.66	
6	J Jones	195.50	14.66	
7	J Morgan	400.00	40.00	
8	S Simple	250.00	18.75	
9	J Smith	300.00	30.00	
10	Average Wage	279.56		
11	Minimum Wage	195.50		
12	Maximum Wage	470.00		
13	No. of Wages paid	8		
14				

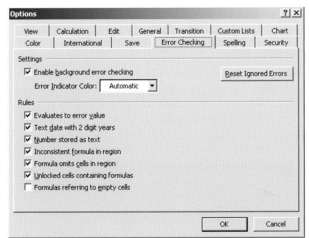

Checking for errors in formulas

If a formula cannot properly calculate, Excel will display an error value. Page 316 has a list of the error values, their possible causes and solutions.

Correcting problems in formulas

In Excel 2002 you can use rules to check for problems in formulas (rather like a grammar checker). These rules will find common mistakes in your formulas.

To switch these rules on or off, choose **Options** from the **Tools** menu.

Click on the **Error Checking** tab of the Options dialog box.

Error Value	Causes	Solutions
#####	■ The column is not wide enough. ■ A negative date or time is used.	■ Increase the width of the column. ■ Apply a different number format.
#VALUE!	■ The wrong 'argument' or 'operator' has been used.	■ Do not enter text when the formula requires a number or logical value. ■ Do not select a range when the formula requires a single value.
#DIV/0!	■ The number is divided by zero.	■ Ensure the divisor is not 0. ■ Ensure the cell reference used is not a blank cell.
#NAME?	■ Excel does not recognise text in a formula.	■ Use a named range that does exist. ■ Verify the spelling of the named range. ■ Do not use a label in a formula when labels are not allowed. ■ Ensure the name of the function is spelt correctly. ■ Do not use text without putting it in quotation marks. ■ Use a colon(:) in a range reference. ■ Refer to another sheet by enclosing its name in quotation marks.
#N/A	■ A value is not available to a function or formula.	■ Ensure no data is missing. ■ Ensure that a LOOKUP can find a matching value.
#REF	■ A cell reference is not valid.	■ Ensure that the cell referred to by the formula has not been deleted. ■ Do not use a link to a program that is not running.
#NUM!	■ Invalid numeric values in a formula or function.	■ Do not use a text argument in a function that is numeric. ■ Ensure the result is a number which is not too large or too small to be represented in Excel.
#NULL!	■ The specified intersection of two areas that do not intersect.	■ Ensure you are using the correct range operator. ■ Ensure ranges do intersect.

Tick the **Enable background error checking** box and then tick the rules you require. Click on **OK**.

If a cell contains a formula that breaks one of the rules, a triangle appears in the top left corner of the cell. When you click on a cell that contains a triangle, an information smart tag appears.

Click on the smart tag to open a menu of options for the problem in the cell. Choose the appropriate solution. Alternatively, you can check for errors on the worksheet one at a time. Choose **Error Checking** from the **Tools** menu.

The first error on the worksheet will be reported in the Error Checking dialog box.

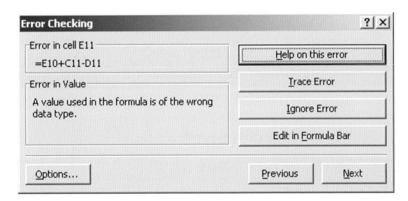

Click on the appropriate button on the right side of the dialog box. (These buttons will change according to the error.) Click on **Next** to move to the next error on the worksheet. (You can also use **Previous** to move back to the previous error.) A message will appear once you have checked all the errors on the worksheet. Click on **OK**.

Checking for accuracy in formulas

While Excel provides a range of tools to help you check for errors in formulas. It is a good idea to simply check the accuracy of formulas by adding up the figures elsewhere (even on a calculator). By doing a quick double-check, you will be able to establish if the results on the worksheet are accurate. If the result on the calculator differs to the result on the worksheet, this indicates that the wrong cells have been referenced in a formula. You would need to check back through each formula to ensure it is referencing the right cells.

Charts

If you wish to show your data graphically in Excel, you can create a chart from the worksheet data. You can have a chart on the worksheet itself or on a separate sheet in the workbook. The chart that is created from the worksheet data is automatically linked, so that if the data on the worksheet changes, the chart updates to reflect the new data.

Select the data that you wish to show on the chart (include any column or row headings). If you want to select data that is in separate places on the worksheet, hold down **Ctrl** as you click and drag to select the separate areas.

Once you have selected all the headings and data that you wish to show on the chart, choose **Chart** from the **Insert** menu.

ITEMS	BUDGET	JAN	FEB	MAR	APR	SPENT	BALANCE
Bedding & Linen	1500	74	0	0	0	74	1426
Cleaning	4600	378	742	416	409	1945	2655
Electricity	13900	672	999	1118	1127	3916	9984
Furniture & Fittings	1800	32	1011	12	192	1247	553
Gas	13600	1023	1245	1000	1010	4278	9322
Kitchen & Catering	4200	1515	332	289	388	2524	1676
Laundry	2000	127	0	344	188	659	1341
Maintenance	28900	10421	5908	2111	3197	21637	7263
Medical Supplies	3000	131	268	298	177	874	2126
Postage	1200	29	101	119	139	388	812
Printing & Stationery	3100	110	29	693	244	1076	2024
Provisions	72000	2305	8041	7672	9945	27963	44037
Rates/Council Tax	11400	2462	0	0	413	2875	8525
Sundries	5100	519	159	156	1727	2561	2539
Telephone	2300	0	0	480	0	480	1820
Trips/Entertainment	7300	740	315	557	1568	3180	4120
Vehicles	13000	533	1894	2697	1107	6231	6769
TOTALS	168600	19798	18835	14708	19156	72497	96103

317

Alternatively, you can click on the Chart Wizard button on the Standard toolbar.
   The Chart Wizard is launched. This takes you through a four-step process to create the chart.

Chart Wizard

Selecting the chart type

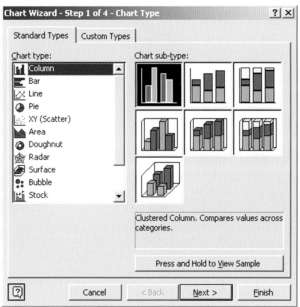

You can choose from a range of **Standard Types** including Column, Bar, Line, Pie and Scatter. Select a Chart type from the list on the left and you can choose from a range of sub-types for that chart type (including 2-D and 3-D). There are more chart types available on the **Custom Types** tab.
   The data you wish to display will often dictate the type of chart that is best. If you really aren't sure, allow the Chart Wizard to choose for you. If you wish to see how your data will look using a particular chart type, click and hold on **Press and Hold to View Sample** to see an example.
   Click on **Next** once you have made your choice. (You can click on **Back** at any time if you change your mind.)

Selecting the data

Step 2 of the Chart Wizard provides you with visual feedback of what your data will look like when plotted onto the type of chart you have chosen.

The **Data range** box shows you the ranges you have selected on the worksheet. (If you wish to check or amend these ranges, click on the red arrow button at the end of the Data range box to collapse the Chart Wizard.

Data range: `='Budget 1'!$A$1:$B$18,'Budget 1'!$G$1:$G$18`

You will now be able to see the selected ranges on the worksheet. Select different ranges if necessary.

Click on the red arrow button again to expand the Chart Wizard dialog box.

By choosing **Series in** Rows or Columns, you can choose how you want the headings and data to be displayed on the chart. When you make choices in the Wizard, the preview at the top of the box changes so you can see how your choice affects the chart.

The **Series** tab shows which ranges on the worksheet are providing the labels and data for the different elements of the chart.

Click on **Next** when you have made your choices. (You can click on **Back** at any time if you change your mind.)

Selecting chart options

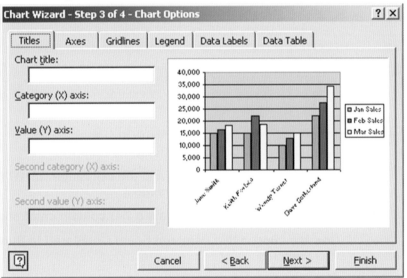

The Chart Options step of the Wizard varies according to what type of chart you have chosen.

- The **Titles** tab allows you to type a title for the chart and labels for each of the axes.
- The **Axes** tab enables you to choose what you want the axes to display. You can also switch axes on and off.
- The **Gridlines** tab enables you to switch gridlines on or off. You can have horizontal gridlines (coming from the value axis) and/or vertical gridlines (coming from the category axis). You can also choose to have major and/or minor gridlines.
- The **Legend** tab enables you to switch the legend (key) on or off. You can also choose where you want the legend to appear on the chart.
- The **Data Labels** tab enables you to switch data labels on and also choose what you want the data labels to display. Data labels will appear at the top of each column of a column chart, at the right end of each bar in a bar chart, etc.
- The **Data Table** tab enables you to switch on a data table, which will appear under the chart. The data table will show the actual data that is plotted onto the chart.

Click on **Next** to move to the final step of the wizard.

Selecting the chart location

The final step of the wizard enables you to choose the location of the chart. You can put it on a new sheet in the workbook. You are given the opportunity to name the new sheet. If you don't type a name for the sheet, it will be called Chart1.

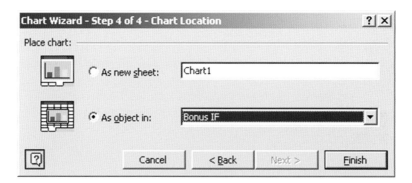

Alternatively, you can have the chart as an embedded object on the worksheet. Choose which worksheet you want it on from the drop-down list. The chart will be displayed as an object on the worksheet. You can move and resize the object.

Click on **Finish** to complete the Chart Wizard. Your chart will now be created and inserted in the location you have specified.

If you quickly want to create a default column chart on a separate sheet in the workbook, select the headings and data and press ⎘

TASK 31

1 **Open the workbook called 'Budget Version 1'.**

2 **Select the cell range A2–B7 and the cell range G2–G7 (remember to use Ctrl to select non-adjacent ranges).**

3 **Use the Chart Wizard to create a 2-D column chart showing this data.**

4 **Give the chart a title, 'Amount Spent Compared to Budget'. Label the X axis 'Items'.**

5 **Place the Legend at the bottom of the chart.**

6 **Place the chart on a new sheet.**

7 **Save the changes you have made.**

The Chart menu

When you have created a chart on a separate sheet or you click on a chart on the worksheet, a **Chart** menu appears in the menu bar.

The first four options in the **Chart** menu – Chart Type, Source Data, Chart Options and Location – take you back into the appropriate step of the Chart Wizard.

Adding data to a chart

The chart is automatically linked to the data that is plotted onto it. If the data changes on the worksheet, the chart will update to reflect the change.

In this example, the Budget figure for Cleaning is 4600, as reflected on the chart.

The Budget figure for Cleaning has changed to 8600 and the new figure is reflected on the chart.

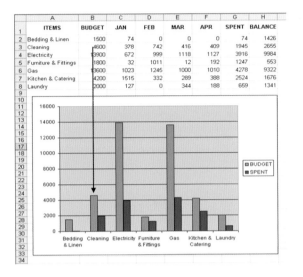

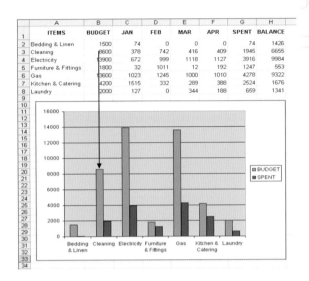

However, you can also add another complete set of data to a chart. Choose **Add Data** from the **Chart** menu.

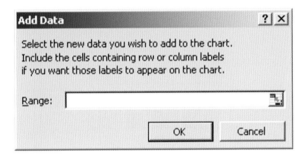

Click onto the worksheet that contains the data and select the range that you now wish to plot onto the chart. (Include row and column headings as well as the data.)

	A	B	C	D	E	F	G	H	I
1	ITEMS	BUDGET	JAN	FEB	MAR	APR	SPENT	BALANCE	
2	Bedding & Linen	1500	74	0	0	0	74	1426	
3	Cleaning	8600	378	742	416	409	1945	6655	
4	Electricity	13900	672	999	1118	1127	3916	9984	
5	Furniture & Fittings	1800	32	1011	12	192	1247	553	
6	Gas	13600	1023	1245	1000	1010	4278	9322	
7	Kitchen & Catering	4200	1515	332	289	388	2524	1676	
8	Laundry	2000	127	0	344	188	659	1341	
9									

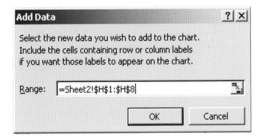

Click on **OK**. The new set of data is added to the chart.

TASK 32

1 **Add the data range H2–H7 to your chart.**

2 **Save the changes you have made.**

Adding data labels

Select the data point or data series that you want to add data labels to and choose **Chart Options** from the **Chart** menu.

Click on the **Data Labels** tab and specify what kind of data labels you want: **Series name**, **Category name** or **Value**. Series name labels the data series with the row heading, Category name labels the data series with the column heading and Value labels the data series with the actual figure on the spreadsheet.

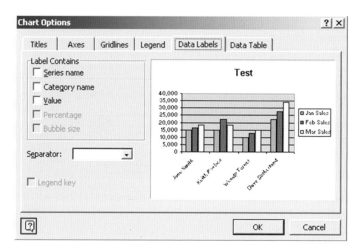

Click on **OK**.

Adding a chart title and axis titles

Choose **Chart Options** from the **Chart** menu and click on the **Titles** tab.

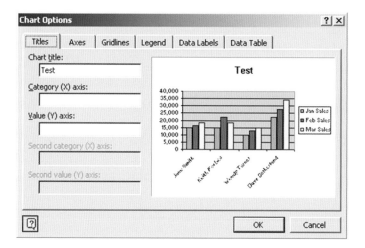

Click in the appropriate box: Chart title, Category axis or Value axis. Type the titles you require. Click on **OK**.

Adding a legend

The 'legend' is the key to the chart. It shows the colour being used for each heading.

Choose **Chart Options** from the **Chart** menu and click on the **Legend** tab.

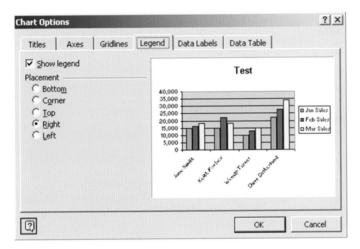

Tick the **Show Legend** box and choose where you want the legend to appear in the Chart Area – Bottom, Corner, Top, Right or Left. Click on **OK**.

Adding gridlines

Choose **Chart Options** from the **Chart** menu and click on the **Gridlines** tab.

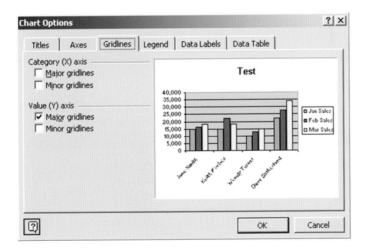

Specify which gridlines you want: major and/or minor and whether you want vertical (category) or horizontal (value) gridlines. To see what the gridlines look like, click in the box and the gridlines will appear in the preview. Click on **OK**.

Adding a trendline

You can add a trendline to a 2-D chart. Choose **Add Trendline** from the **Chart** menu.

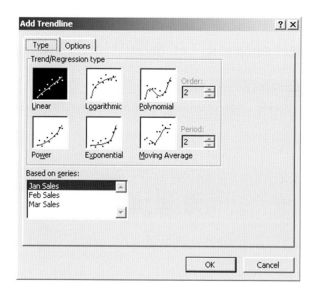

Choose the type of trendline you require and click on **OK**.

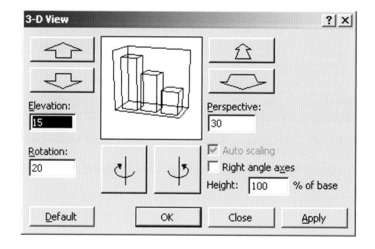

TASK 33

Add a linear trendline to the chart.

Changing the 3-D view

You can alter the view of a 3-D chart. Choose **3-D View** from the **Chart** menu.

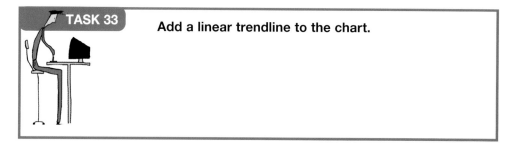

You can change the **Elevation, Rotation** and **Perspective** of the 3-D view. Click on the arrow buttons or type the amount you require in the boxes.

To switch back to the default view, click on **Default**.

Click on **OK** to apply the changes to your chart.

TASK 34

1 **Delete the trendline from the chart and change the chart type to a 3-D column chart.**

2 **Change the 3-D view to Default.**

3 **Save the changes you have made.**

Moving and sizing an embedded chart

To move a chart on the worksheet, click just inside the chart area to select it. Black squares appear around the chart area.

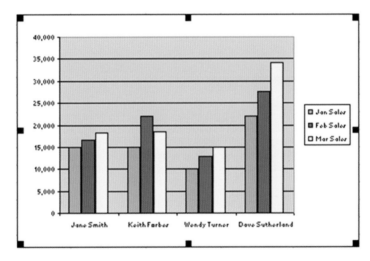

Click and hold the mouse button. The mouse pointer changes to a four-headed arrow. Drag the chart object to the new location on the worksheet.

To change the size of the chart, click just inside the chart area to select it. Black squares will appear around the edge of the chart area. Move the mouse over one of the black squares and it will change to a double-headed arrow. Click and drag this resizing handle to resize the chart.

If you wish to resize the chart but keep its original dimensions, click and drag a corner resizing handle.

Deleting an embedded chart

To delete an embedded chart, click on the chart to select it and press the Delete key on your keyboard.

Editing a chart

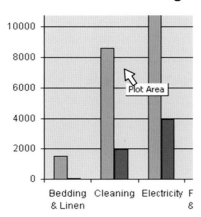

When you create a chart in Excel, the colours, fonts, etc., used in the chart are defaults. You can change any part of the chart – the Y-axis and Y-axis title, the X-axis and X-axis title, the data labels, the chart title, the data markers, the legend, the category names, the tick marks, the plot area, the chart area and the gridlines. Even the colours of the bars, columns or pie slices can be changed. As you move the mouse around the chart, ScreenTips appear to indicate what part of the chart you are pointing at.

Double-click on the part of the chart you wish to change. You will be taken into the appropriate dialog box to make your changes.

Formatting the chart title

Double-click on the chart title. The Format Chart Title dialog box will open.

This dialog box has three tabs: **Patterns, Font** and **Alignment**. You can put a box around the chart title and fill the inside of the box. The **Font** tab enables you to format the font of the chart title. The **Alignment** tab enables you to change the alignment of the chart title and rotate the title. Make any changes you require and click on **OK**.

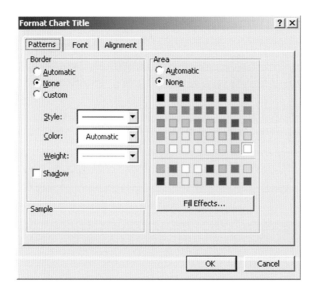

Formatting the value axis

To change the scale of the value axis, point to it and double-click. The Format Axis dialog box will open.

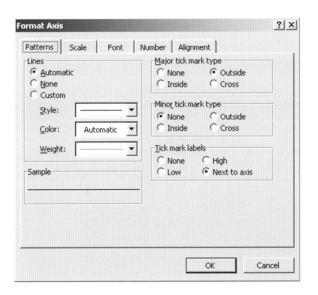

This dialog box has five tabs: **Patterns, Scale, Font, Number** and **Alignment**. On the **Patterns** tab you can format the axis line and also choose whether you want tick marks to appear on the axis. The **Scale** tab enables you to change the scale of the value axis. You can choose the Minimum and Maximum number on the axis and also choose the units that the axis should be divided into. The **Font** tab enables you to format the font of the data on the axis. The **Number** tab enables you to choose how you want the values on the axis to be displayed. The **Alignment** tab enables you to rotate the text on the axis and choose the text direction. Make any changes you require and click on **OK**.

Formatting the gridlines

Point to one of them and double-click. If you don't have any gridlines on the chart, use Chart Options in the Chart menu to add them. The Format Gridlines dialog box will open.

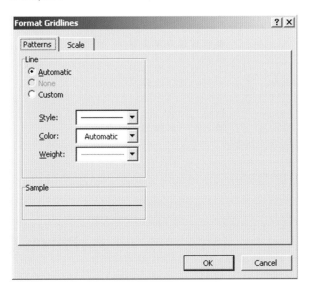

This dialog box has two tabs: **Patterns** and **Scale**. You can change how the gridlines look on the **Patterns** tab. The **Scale** tab is the same as the Scale tab in the Format Axis dialog box. Make any changes you require and click on **OK**.

Formatting the legend

Point to the legend (key) and double-click. The Format Legend dialog box will open.

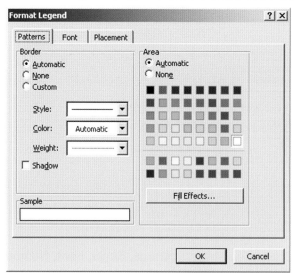

This dialog box has three tabs: **Patterns, Font** and **Placement**. The **Patterns** tab enables you to format the line and fill colour of the legend box. The **Font** tab enables you to format the font of the legend. The **Placement** tab enables you to choose where you want the legend to appear on the chart. Make any changes you require and click on **OK**.

Changing the chart background

To change the chart background, point to the Chart Area and double-click. The Format Chart Area dialog box will open.

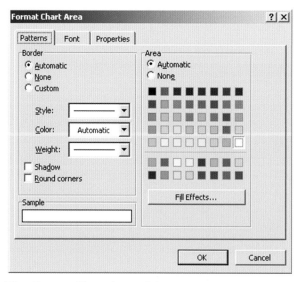

The Format Chart Area dialog box has three tabs: **Patterns, Font** and **Properties**. The **Patterns** tab enables you to format the line and fill colour of the chart box. The **Font** tab enables you to format the font used in the whole chart. The **Properties** tab enables you to control how the chart object will act on the worksheet. Make any changes you require and click on **OK**.

Working with colours

Remember, your chart will look very colourful on a colour monitor, but if you are going to print to a black and white printer, you need to assign contrasting colours so that it will be easy to understand the legend even in black and white. Purple and dark pink might look lovely together on screen, but will appear very similar when printed in black and white.

TASK 35

1　**Change the chart title to Arial 14 pt, Bold and Italic.**

2　**Change the scale of the Y-axis to have major units of 1000.**

3　**Change the gridlines to dashed lines.**

4　**Move the Legend to the top of the chart.**

5　**Remove the fill colour from the chart area.**

6　**Change the colours of the columns to Dark Blue, Red and Yellow respectively.**

7　**Save the changes you have made.**

Printing charts

If your chart is on a separate sheet in the workbook, then you can print just that sheet. The chart will print as A4 landscape and will fill the page.

If your chart is embedded in a worksheet, you have two choices for how you print it. To print the chart on its own, select the chart by clicking on it prior to printing. The chart will print as A4 landscape and will fill the sheet of paper. To print the worksheet data with the chart, click on any cell on the worksheet. By default, worksheets print A4 portrait. (However this can be changed in the Page Setup dialog box). Assuming it fits, you will see the worksheet data and the chart on the same page. (It is a good idea to use print preview to see how it looks prior to printing).

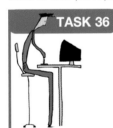

TASK 36

1　**Print the chart.**

2　**Save and close the workbook.**

 # Linking worksheets

Rather than putting all the data onto one sheet in the workbook, you may wish to split the data onto separate sheets (for example, one sheet for each month in a year). You can still calculate data across the sheets by linking. There are two ways to link data: by writing a formula that refers to another sheet or sheets (this is called **3-D referencing**) or by using **Paste Link**. (For information on how to write formulas and use functions, please refer to page 291.)

Referring to another sheet in a formula

You can write formulas that refer to cells on other sheets in a workbook. Click in the cell where you want the result to appear and begin to write the formula. When you need to refer to a cell that is on another worksheet, click on the sheet tab first, then click on the cell. Continue writing the formula, referring to other sheets and cells where appropriate.

For example, to subtract a figure in cell B2 on the current sheet from a figure in cell B2 on a different sheet, start the formula, =**B2**.

IF	▾ ✗ ✓ *fx* =B2			
	A	B	C	D
1	Item	Total Price	Profit	
2	C2943 Card Folder	£4.90	=B2	
3	B2940 Paper 80 gsm	£2.97		
4	C3945 Coloured Card - 100 sheet pack	£7.49		
5				

Type the mathematical operator: −.

Then click onto the other sheet (in this case, it is called 'Purchase Cost'), and click on cell B2. The sheet name and cell reference are inserted into the formula. It now looks like this:

=B2−'Purchase Cost'!B2

IF	▾ ✗ ✓ *fx* =B2-'Purchase Cost'!B2			
	A	B	C	D
1	Item	Total Cost		
2	C2943 Card Folder	£3.27		
3	B2940 Paper 80 gsm	£1.50		
4	C3945 Coloured Card - 100 sheet pack	£5.49		
5				

The sheet name is shown in quotation marks (this indicates that it is the name of the sheet). The sheet name and the cell reference are separated by a **!**.

Press **Return** on the keyboard or click on the green tick on the Formula Bar.

✗ ✓ *fx* =B2-'Purchase Cost'!B2

The result of the formula is entered into the active cell on the current sheet.

C2	▾ *fx* =B2-'Purchase Cost'!B2			
	A	B	C	D
1	Item	Total Price	Profit	
2	C2943 Card Folder	£4.90	£1.63	
3	B2940 Paper 80 gsm	£2.97		
4	C3945 Coloured Card - 100 sheet pack	£7.49		
5				

TASK 37

1 **Open the workbook called 'Wages'.**

2 **Move to Sheet 2. Copy and paste the names from Sheet 1.**

3 **Type a heading in cell B1, WAGES + BONUS.**

4 **Calculate the Wages + Bonus for F Bloggs. Copy the formula to the other employees.**

   Your worksheet should look like this:

5 **Save and close the workbook.**

Microsoft Excel - Wages.xls

File Edit View Insert Format Tools Data

Arial   ▾ 10 ▾ B I U

B2   *fx* =Sheet1!B2+Sheet1!C2

	A	B	C
1	NAME	WAGES + BONUS	
2	F Bloggs	517.00	
3	B Briggs	222.53	
4	V Grange	234.89	
5	H Higgins	210.16	
6	J Jones	210.16	
7	J Morgan	440.00	
8	S Simple	268.75	
9	J Smith	330.00	
10			

6

7

3-D referencing

If you refer to a range of other sheets when you are creating a formula, this is known as 3-D referencing. A 3-D reference is a range that spans two or more sheets in a workbook.

=SUM(May:July!B2:B6)

This formula shows that cells B2 through to B6 on the sheets called May through to July are being summed.

To create this formula, click in the cell on the worksheet where you wish the result to appear (in this example, B2).

Because you are 'summing', you can click on the AutoSum button to start the formula.

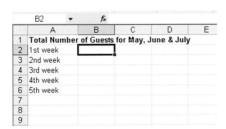

Click on the May tab, hold down the Shift key and click on the July tab. All the sheets from May to July are selected. (You have now selected a sheet range.) Release the Shift key.

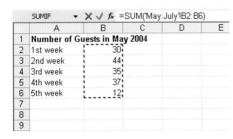

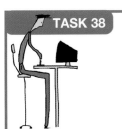

Now select the range of cells B2 to B6 on the current sheet. Press Enter on the keyboard to complete the formula and return you to the cell where you started.

TASK 38

1 **Start a new workbook and rename the three sheets January, February and March.**

2 **Insert a new sheet into the workbook and call this sheet 'Totals'.**

3 **Type the following data on the January sheet:**

NAME	WAGES
Tony	£2390.00
Ken	£1983.00
Susan	£1549.00
Kathy	£2395.00

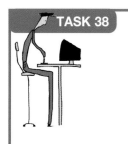

TASK 38

4 Copy and paste this information onto the February, March and Totals sheets.

5 Change the wages amounts on the February and March sheets. Delete the figures from the Totals sheet.

6 On the Totals sheet, calculate the total wages paid for January, February and March for Tony. Use a 3-D reference. The formula should look like this:
=SUM(January:March!B2)

7 Copy this formula for the others.

8 Save the workbook in your Tasks for ITQ folder with the filename Total Wages. Close the workbook.

Using Paste Link

Select the cells in the workbook that you wish to copy to a new location.

	A	B	C	D	E
1	Employee Name	Jan Sales	Feb Sales	Mar Sales	Total Qtr 1 Sales
2	Jane Smith	15,000	16,500	18,250	49,750
3	Keith Forbes	15,000	22,000	18,500	55,500
4	Wendy Turner	10,000	12,750	15,000	37,750
5	Dave Sutherland	22,000	27,500	34,250	83,750
6					

Copy

Choose **Copy** from the **Edit** menu.
Alternatively, press the Copy button on the Standard toolbar.

You can also use Control + C.
Move to the new location and choose **Paste Special** from the **Edit** menu.
The Paste Special dialog box will open.

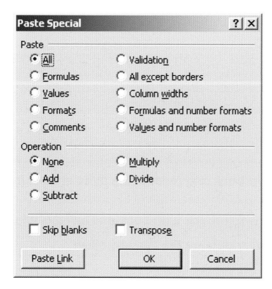

Click on the **Paste Link** button in the bottom left corner of the dialog box.

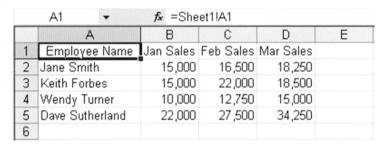

	A	B	C	D	E
1	Employee Name	Jan Sales	Feb Sales	Mar Sales	
2	Jane Smith	15,000	16,500	18,250	
3	Keith Forbes	15,000	22,000	18,500	
4	Wendy Turner	10,000	12,750	15,000	
5	Dave Sutherland	22,000	27,500	34,250	
6					

The data is copied to the new location and a link is created (using a formula) between the two sets of data. Any changes that are made to the original data will also be reflected in the linked data.

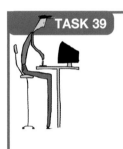

TASK 39

1 **Open the workbook called 'Budget Version 1'.**

2 **Delete the data on Sheet 2.**

3 **Copy and Paste Link the heading and items from Sheet 1 onto Sheet 2. (Resize the column appropriately).**

4 **On Sheet 1, change the item name from Bedding & Linen to Linen. Change the item name Furniture & Fittings to Fixtures. Notice how they also change on Sheet 2.**

5 **Save and close the workbook.**

 ## Linking Excel workbooks

Data that you want to work with may be saved in different workbooks. You can calculate data across the workbooks by linking them. There are two ways to link data: by writing a formula that refers to another workbook or by using Paste Link. (For information on how to write formulas and use functions, please refer to page 291.)

Creating a formula that refers to another workbook

The most efficient way to create a formula that refers to another workbook is to have both the 'source' workbook (i.e. the one that contains the original data) and the 'dependent' workbook (i.e. the one that will contain the link) open on the screen side-by-side.

Open both workbooks and then choose **Arrange** from the **Window** menu. The Arrange Windows dialog box opens.

Click on **Tiled** and then click on **OK**. The two workbooks will now appear on the screen side-by-side.

Click in the cell where you wish the result of the formula to appear. Write the formula in the normal way, clicking into the appropriate window and onto the appropriate cell. Excel will insert the appropriate workbook name, sheet name and cell reference as you use your mouse to click onto the cells.

In the this example, to calculate **Fee Due**, click on cell B2 in Consultant Fees.xls (on the right). Start the formula =

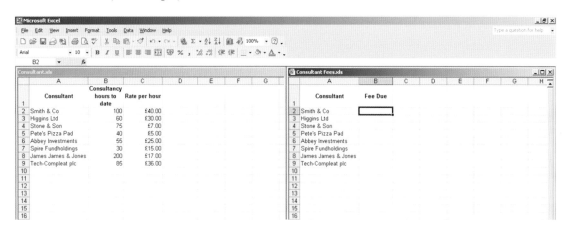

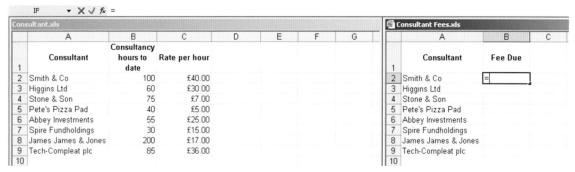

Then click onto cell B2 in the workbook on the left. The reference **[Consultant.xls]Consultants!$B$2** is inserted into the formula.

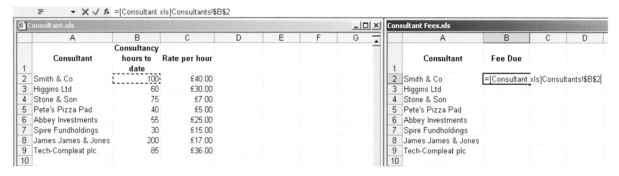

Now type * (multiply), then click onto cell C2 in the workbook on the left. The reference **[Consultant.xls]Consultants!$C$2** is inserted into the formula.

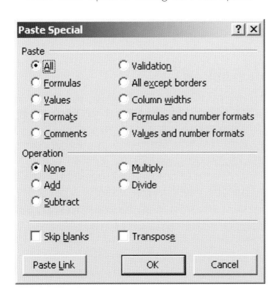

IF   ▾ X ✓ ƒ× =[Consultant.xls]Consultants!$B$2*[Consultant.xls]Consultants!$C$2

	A	B	C	D	E	F	G
1	Consultant	Consultancy hours to date	Rate per hour				
2	Smith & Co	100	£40.00				
3	Higgins Ltd	60	£30.00				
4	Stone & Son	75	£7.00				
5	Pete's Pizza Pad	40	£5.00				
6	Abbey Investments	55	£25.00				
7	Spire Fundholdings	30	£15.00				
8	James James & Jones	200	£17.00				
9	Tech-Compleat plc	85	£36.00				
10							

Consultant Fees.xls

	A	B	C	D	E	F	G
1	Consultant	Fee Due					
2	Smith & Co	=[Consultant.xls]Consultants!$B$2*[Consultant.xls]Consultants!$C$2					
3	Higgins Ltd						
4	Stone & Son						
5	Pete's Pizza Pad						
6	Abbey Investments						
7	Spire Fundholdings						
8	James James & Jones						
9	Tech-Compleat plc						
10							

The completed formula looks like this:

=[Consultant.xls]Consultants!$B$2*[Consultant.xls]Consultants!$C$2

When you click into the workbook on the left side, Excel inserts the name of the workbook, **Consultant.xls**. Excel also references the sheet, **Consultant**, and then the actual cell that you clicked onto. When writing formulas across workbooks, Excel makes the cell references absolute (for more information on absolute cell referencing, please refer to page 295). You need to remove the dollar signs from the formula before you can copy the formula down or across on the worksheet.

Using Paste Link

If you wish to use Paste Link across workbooks, it is a good idea to open both workbooks and then tile them on the screen so that they are side-by-side. (For more information on tiling windows, see pages 333–4)

Select the cells in the workbook that you wish to copy to a new location. Choose **Copy** from the **Edit** menu.

Alternatively, press the Copy button on the Standard toolbar.

Copy

You can also use [Control]+[C]

Move to the new location and choose **Paste Special** from the **Edit** menu.
The Paste Special dialog box will open.

Paste Special   ? X

Paste
- ● All
- ○ Formulas
- ○ Values
- ○ Formats
- ○ Comments
- ○ Validation
- ○ All except borders
- ○ Column widths
- ○ Formulas and number formats
- ○ Values and number formats

Operation
- ● None
- ○ Add
- ○ Subtract
- ○ Multiply
- ○ Divide

☐ Skip blanks   ☐ Transpose

[Paste Link]   [OK]   [Cancel]

Click on the **Paste Link** button in the bottom left of the Paste Special dialog box. The data is copied to the new location and a link is created (using a formula) between the two sets of data. Any changes that are made to the original data will also be reflected in the linked data.

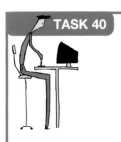

TASK 40

1 Open the workbook called 'VAT Calculation'. Ensure you are on Sheet 1.

2 Start a new workbook and tile both workbooks on the screen.

3 Copy and Paste Link the ITEM heading and items from the 'VAT Calculation' workbook.

4 Type a heading, **INCREASED PRICE**, in cell B1 of the new workbook.

5 Calculate the increased price – the current Nett Price + 5% – for White Wine.

6 Copy this formula to the other items. Your new workbook should look like this:

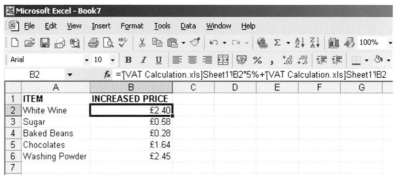

7 Save and close the original workbook – VAT Calculation.

8 Save the new workbook in your Tasks for ITQ folder with the filename 'Increased Price'. Close the workbook.

Sorting and filtering data

Excel can be used to store lists of information. An Excel worksheet has 65,536 rows, so you can create quite large lists. There are some database features in Excel which make it easier to analyse and extract the data in the list.

Sorting data in a list

If you are intending to sort data in a list on an Excel worksheet, there are a few rules you need to follow when creating the list. The column headings should be formatted differently to the detail in the list (this is something most people tend to do automatically, so that they look like headings). Excel can then recognise that this is the 'header row' and does not include it when sorting. Also, each column should contain the appropriate information as per its column heading and the list must be made up of consecutive rows. (If there is a blank row, Excel interprets this as the end of one list and anything after the blank row is treated as a separate list.)

	A	B	C	D	E	F	G
1	**Invoice**	**Date**	**Company Number**	**Company**	**Amount**	**Tax**	**TOTAL**
2	11560	22-Jul-96	101	Blue Sky Airlines	£3,299.00	£260.62	£3,559.62
3	11561	25-Jul-96	85	National Museum	£601.00	£47.48	£648.48
4	11562	30-Jul-96	101	Blue Sky Airlines	£7,823.00	£618.02	£8,441.02
5	11563	07-Aug-96	54	Northwind Traders	£112.00	£8.85	£120.85
6	11564	19-Aug-96	101	Blue Sky Airlines	£430.00	£33.97	£463.97
7	11568	21-Aug-96	12	Ferguson & Bardell	£245.00	£19.36	£264.36
8	11570	26-Aug-96	85	National Museum	£90.00	£7.11	£97.11
9	11573	02-Sep-96	54	Northwind Traders	£3,084.00	£243.64	£3,327.64
10	11574	03-Sep-96	12	Ferguson & Bardell	£312.00	£24.65	£336.65
11	11576	08-Sep-96	85	National Museum	£163.00	£12.88	£175.88
12	11580	12-Sep-96	101	Blue Sky Airlines	£2,650.00	£209.35	£2,859.35
13	11582	13-Sep-96	54	Northwind Traders	£411.00	£32.47	£443.47
14	11584	14-Sep-96	12	Ferguson & Bardell	£4,235.00	£334.57	£4,569.57
15	11586	16-Sep-96	85	National Museum	£122.00	£9.64	£131.64
16	11588	18-Sep-96	101	Blue Sky Airlines	£538.00	£42.50	£580.50
17							

Above is an example of how a list on an Excel worksheet should look. The column headings are formatted using bold and each column contains the appropriate information as per the column heading. There are no blank rows.

Using quick sort

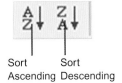

Sort Ascending   Sort Descending

There are two ways to sort data in a list. You can use the quick sort buttons on the Standard toolbar.

Click in the column on the worksheet that you wish to sort by.

	A	B	C	D	E	F	G
1	**Invoice**	**Date**	**Company Number**	**Company**	**Amount**	**Tax**	**TOTAL**
2	11560	22-Jul-96	101	Blue Sky Airlines	£3,299.00	£260.62	£3,559.62
3	11561	25-Jul-96	85	National Museum	£601.00	£47.48	£648.48
4	11562	30-Jul-96	101	Blue Sky Airlines	£7,823.00	£618.02	£8,441.02
5	11563	07-Aug-96	54	Northwind Traders	£112.00	£8.85	£120.85
6	11564	19-Aug-96	101	Blue Sky Airlines	£430.00	£33.97	£463.97
7	11568	21-Aug-96	12	Ferguson & Bardell	£245.00	£19.36	£264.36
8	11570	26-Aug-96	85	National Museum	£90.00	£7.11	£97.11
9	11573	02-Sep-96	54	Northwind Traders	£3,084.00	£243.64	£3,327.64
10	11574	03-Sep-96	12	Ferguson & Bardell	£312.00	£24.65	£336.65
11	11576	08-Sep-96	85	National Museum	£163.00	£12.88	£175.88
12	11580	12-Sep-96	101	Blue Sky Airlines	£2,650.00	£209.35	£2,859.35
13	11582	13-Sep-96	54	Northwind Traders	£411.00	£32.47	£443.47
14	11584	14-Sep-96	12	Ferguson & Bardell	£4,235.00	£334.57	£4,569.57
15	11586	16-Sep-96	85	National Museum	£122.00	£9.64	£131.64
16	11588	18-Sep-96	101	Blue Sky Airlines	£538.00	£42.50	£580.50
17							

Click on the Sort Ascending or the Sort Descending button, depending whether you want to sort the list in Ascending or Descending order. The whole list will be sorted according to the data in the column you are sitting in.

	A	B	C	D	E	F	G
1	Invoice	Date	Company Number	Company	Amount	Tax	TOTAL
2	11560	22-Jul-96	101	Blue Sky Airlines	£3,299.00	£260.62	£3,559.62
3	11562	30-Jul-96	101	Blue Sky Airlines	£7,823.00	£618.02	£8,441.02
4	11564	19-Aug-96	101	Blue Sky Airlines	£430.00	£33.97	£463.97
5	11580	12-Sep-96	101	Blue Sky Airlines	£2,650.00	£209.35	£2,859.35
6	11588	18-Sep-96	101	Blue Sky Airlines	£538.00	£42.50	£580.50
7	11568	21-Aug-96	12	Ferguson & Bardell	£245.00	£19.36	£264.36
8	11574	03-Sep-96	12	Ferguson & Bardell	£312.00	£24.65	£336.65
9	11584	14-Sep-96	12	Ferguson & Bardell	£4,235.00	£334.57	£4,569.57
10	11561	25-Jul-96	85	National Museum	£601.00	£47.48	£648.48
11	11570	26-Aug-96	85	National Museum	£90.00	£7.11	£97.11
12	11576	08-Sep-96	85	National Museum	£163.00	£12.88	£175.88
13	11586	16-Sep-96	85	National Museum	£122.00	£9.64	£131.64
14	11563	07-Aug-96	54	Northwind Traders	£112.00	£8.85	£120.85
15	11573	02-Sep-96	54	Northwind Traders	£3,084.00	£243.64	£3,327.64
16	11582	13-Sep-96	54	Northwind Traders	£411.00	£32.47	£443.47
17							

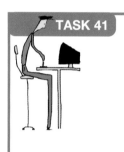

TASK 41

1 **Start a new workbook and type the following headings:**

   First Name   Last Name   Address 1   Address 2   Town/City   County

2 **Type 20 records of information under these headings.**

3 **Use Quick Sort to sort the list by the Last Name column in Ascending order.**

4 **Use Quick Sort to sort the list by the Town/City column in Descending order.**

5 **Save the workbook in your Tasks for ITQ folder with the filename 'Sorted List'.**

Using data sort

If you wish to sort by more than one column, e.g. sort a list by Last Name, then by First Name, choose **Sort** from the **Data** menu.

You do not need to select the list prior to choosing **Data**, **Sort** as Excel will select the list for you when you choose this option from the menu. Just click somewhere in the list.

The Sort dialog box opens.

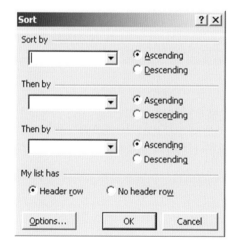

Choose the first column you want to sort by. Click on the drop-down arrow by the **Sort by** box to see the column headings in the list. Choose **Ascending** or **Descending**.

You can choose two levels of sub-sort (**Then by**), so that you can sort the list by three columns in all. Click on **OK**.

In this example the list has been sorted by Company, then by Amount and then by Invoice.

	A	B	C	D	E	F	G
1	Invoice	Date	Company Number	Company	Amount	Tax	TOTAL
2	11564	19-Aug-96	101	Blue Sky Airlines	£430.00	£33.97	£463.97
3	11588	18-Sep-96	101	Blue Sky Airlines	£538.00	£42.50	£580.50
4	11580	12-Sep-96	101	Blue Sky Airlines	£2,650.00	£209.35	£2,859.35
5	11560	22-Jul-96	101	Blue Sky Airlines	£3,299.00	£260.62	£3,559.62
6	11562	30-Jul-96	101	Blue Sky Airlines	£7,823.00	£618.02	£8,441.02
7	11568	21-Aug-96	12	Ferguson & Bardell	£245.00	£19.36	£264.36
8	11574	03-Sep-96	12	Ferguson & Bardell	£312.00	£24.65	£336.65
9	11584	14-Sep-96	12	Ferguson & Bardell	£4,235.00	£334.57	£4,569.57
10	11570	26-Aug-96	85	National Museum	£90.00	£7.11	£97.11
11	11586	16-Sep-96	85	National Museum	£122.00	£9.64	£131.64
12	11576	08-Sep-96	85	National Museum	£163.00	£12.88	£175.88
13	11561	25-Jul-96	85	National Museum	£601.00	£47.48	£648.48
14	11563	07-Aug-96	54	Northwind Traders	£112.00	£8.85	£120.85
15	11582	13-Sep-96	54	Northwind Traders	£411.00	£32.47	£443.47
16	11573	02-Sep-96	54	Northwind Traders	£3,084.00	£243.64	£3,327.64
17							

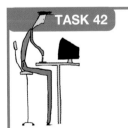 **TASK 42**

1 **Use Data Sort to sort your list by Last Name, then by First Name, then by Town/City.**

2 **Save the changes you have made.**

Sort options

If you do not want to sort by the default A–Z or Z–A sort order (e.g. if you want to sort by month), you can change the 'first key sort order'. Click on the **Options** button in the **Sort** dialog box.

The Sort Options dialog box opens, as in Figure 209.268.

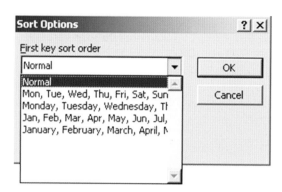

To choose a different **First key sort order**, click on the drop-down arrow and choose from the list.

Click on **OK** and then **OK** again to carry out the sort.

Filtering data in a list

Because of the size of an Excel worksheet, a list could potentially be very long. Finding information in the list could then prove laborious. However, a feature called AutoFilter makes it very easy to pick records from the list based on criteria.

Click somewhere on the list on the worksheet and choose **Filter** from the **Data** menu. Click on **AutoFilter** in the sub-menu.

Filter arrows appear at the top of each column.

	A	B	C	D	E	F	G
1	Invoice	Date	Company Number	Company	Amount	Tax	TOTAL

To pick records from the list based on their column entry, click on the drop-down arrow on the appropriate column and pick the records that meet your criteria. For example, to filter the list so that you only see companies with the number 54, click on the drop-down arrow in the Company Number column heading and choose **54** from the list.

	A	B	C	D	E	F	G
1	Invoice	Date	Company Number	Company	Amount	Tax	TOTAL
2	11560	22-Jul-9	(All)	Blue Sky Airlines	£3,299.00	£260.62	£3,559.62
3	11561	25-Jul-9	(Top 10...) (Custom...)	National Museum	£601.00	£47.48	£648.48
4	11562	30-Jul-9	12	Blue Sky Airlines	£7,823.00	£618.02	£8,441.02
5	11563	07-Aug-9	54	Northwind Traders	£112.00	£8.85	£120.85
6	11564	19-Aug-9	85	Blue Sky Airlines	£430.00	£33.97	£463.97
7	11568	21-Aug-96	101 12	Ferguson & Bardell	£245.00	£19.36	£264.36
8	11570	26-Aug-96	85	National Museum	£90.00	£7.11	£97.11

The list will be filtered and only records with company number 54 will be shown.

	A	B	C	D	E	F	G
1	Invoice	Date	Company Number	Company	Amount	Tax	TOTAL
5	11563	07-Aug-96	54	Northwind Traders	£112.00	£8.85	£120.85
9	11573	02-Sep-96	54	Northwind Traders	£3,084.00	£243.64	£3,327.64
13	11582	13-Sep-96	54	Northwind Traders	£411.00	£32.47	£443.47

The record numbers are shown in blue (to indicate they are filtered) and the drop-down arrow for the column that you have filtered also goes blue. The status bar at the bottom of the screen indicates the number of records that have been found matching the criteria.

To remove the filter, click on the drop-down arrow again and choose **All** from the list.

You can add filter on top of filter. For example, having filtered the list to show only company number 54, you can then filter using another column heading to narrow down the selection further.

If you have filtered the data in the list using lots of columns, it is quicker to remove the filter by using the Filter menu. Choose **Data**, **Filter** and then click on **Show All**.

TASK 43

1 **Switch on AutoFilter for this list.**

2 **Filter the list by the Town/City column. Pick one of your towns. Choose All from this list to view the whole list again.**

3 **Filter the list by the County column. Pick one of your counties. Choose All from this list to view all the list again.**

Using custom AutoFilter

Sometimes you might want to filter the list based on criteria other than what appears in the column list. Click on the drop-down arrow for the column you want to filter by and choose **Custom** from the list. The Custom AutoFilter dialog box opens.

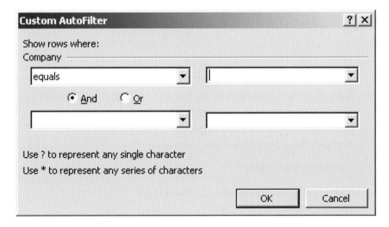

Choose the criteria you require by clicking on the drop-down arrows and picking from the lists or by typing in the criteria.

For example, to see Blue Sky Airlines and Ferguson & Bardell in the list above, the Custom AutoFilter dialog box would look like this:

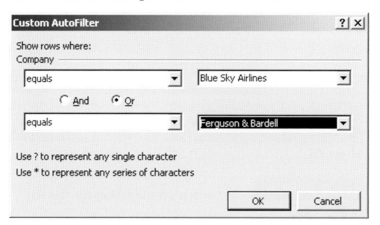

In this case, the search operator is **Or** (to see rows where the company is either Blue Sky Airlines or Ferguson & Bardell). If the search operator was left as **And**, no records would be returned as there are no rows that contain both companies.

Click on **OK** to carry out the Custom AutoFilter.

In this case the equals operator has been used. However, the list also contains other logical operators.

You can also add filter on top of filter using the Custom AutoFilter. For example, having filtered the list to show only the companies Blue Sky Airlines and Ferguson & Bardell, you could then carry out another custom filter using another column heading to narrow down the selection further.

The AutoFilter arrows do not print, they just appear on the screen. If you are working on a list where you use the AutoFilter regularly, you can leave the AutoFilter arrows switched on all the time.

However, if you do want to remove the AutoFilter arrows and reset the list so all records are displayed, choose **Data**, **Filter** and click on **AutoFilter** again to switch off the arrows.

TASK 44

1 **Use Custom AutoFilter to view records for two of your towns. The Custom AutoFilter dialog box should be completed as follows:–**

2 **Remove this filter.**

3 **Use Custom AutoFilter to view only records with a Last Name starting with L through to Z. The Custom AutoFilter dialog box should be completed as follows:–**

4 **Remove this filter.**

5 **Close the workbook without saving any changes.**

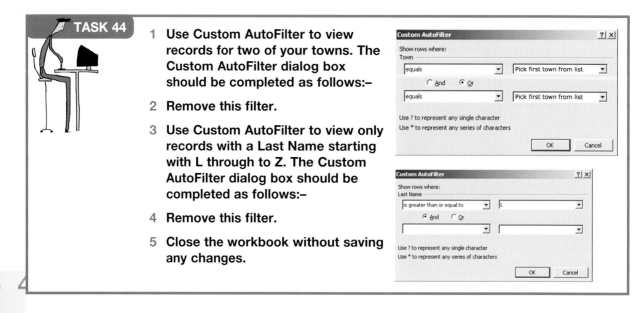

Automatic subtotals

This feature enables you to easily break a list into sections and see information, such as subtotals, at the end of each section. Once you have extracted the information you require from the list, it is then very easy to reset the list back to its 'list' state ready for new records to be added.

Firstly, sort the list into the chunks of data that you want to subtotal. (In this example, the list has been sorted by Company, then by Amount.)

	A	B	C	D	E	F	G
1	Invoice	Date	Company Number	Company	Amount	Tax	TOTAL
2	11564	19-Aug-96	101	Blue Sky Airlines	£430.00	£33.97	£463.97
3	11588	18-Sep-96	101	Blue Sky Airlines	£538.00	£42.50	£580.50
4	11580	12-Sep-96	101	Blue Sky Airlines	£2,650.00	£209.35	£2,859.35
5	11560	22-Jul-96	101	Blue Sky Airlines	£3,299.00	£260.62	£3,559.62
6	11562	30-Jul-96	101	Blue Sky Airlines	£7,823.00	£618.02	£8,441.02
7	11568	21-Aug-96	12	Ferguson & Bardell	£245.00	£19.36	£264.36
8	11574	03-Sep-96	12	Ferguson & Bardell	£312.00	£24.65	£336.65
9	11584	14-Sep-96	12	Ferguson & Bardell	£4,235.00	£334.57	£4,569.57
10	11570	26-Aug-96	85	National Museum	£90.00	£7.11	£97.11
11	11586	16-Sep-96	85	National Museum	£122.00	£9.64	£131.64
12	11576	08-Sep-96	85	National Museum	£163.00	£12.88	£175.88
13	11561	25-Jul-96	85	National Museum	£601.00	£47.48	£648.48
14	11563	07-Aug-96	54	Northwind Traders	£112.00	£8.85	£120.85
15	11582	13-Sep-96	54	Northwind Traders	£411.00	£32.47	£443.47
16	11573	02-Sep-96	54	Northwind Traders	£3,084.00	£243.64	£3,327.64
17							

Choose **Subtotals** from the **Data** menu.

The Subtotal dialog box opens.

Choose where you want the subtotals to appear by choosing from the drop-down list in the **At each change in:** box. In this example, the Company column heading is chosen from the drop-down menu.

Choose which function you want to use from the drop-down list in the **Use function:** box – Sum, Count, Average, Min, Max or Product.

Tick the boxes to indicate where you want to see the subtotals on the worksheet. You can only put subtotals at the bottom of figure columns.

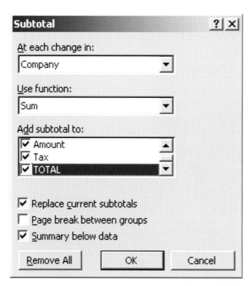

Click on **OK**.

Rows are inserted into your list, at the end of each section, and the appropriate function has been used.

1 2 3		A	B	C	D	E	F	G
	1	Invoice	Date	Company Number	Company	Amount	Tax	TOTAL
	2	11560	22-Jul-96	101	Blue Sky Airlines	£3,299.00	£260.62	£3,559.62
	3	11562	30-Jul-96	101	Blue Sky Airlines	£7,823.00	£618.02	£8,441.02
	4	11564	19-Aug-96	101	Blue Sky Airlines	£430.00	£33.97	£463.97
	5	11580	12-Sep-96	101	Blue Sky Airlines	£2,650.00	£209.35	£2,859.35
	6	11588	18-Sep-96	101	Blue Sky Airlines	£538.00	£42.50	£580.50
	7				**Blue Sky Airlines Total**	**£14,740.00**	**£1,164.46**	**£15,904.46**
	8	11568	21-Aug-96	12	Ferguson & Bardell	£245.00	£19.36	£264.36
	9	11574	03-Sep-96	12	Ferguson & Bardell	£312.00	£24.65	£336.65
	10	11584	14-Sep-96	12	Ferguson & Bardell	£4,235.00	£334.57	£4,569.57
	11				**Ferguson & Bardell Total**	**£4,792.00**	**£378.58**	**£5,170.58**
	12	11561	25-Jul-96	85	National Museum	£601.00	£47.48	£648.48
	13	11570	26-Aug-96	85	National Museum	£90.00	£7.11	£97.11
	14	11576	08-Sep-96	85	National Museum	£163.00	£12.88	£175.88
	15	11586	16-Sep-96	85	National Museum	£122.00	£9.64	£131.64
	16				**National Museum Total**	**£976.00**	**£77.11**	**£1,053.11**
	17	11563	07-Aug-96	54	Northwind Traders	£112.00	£8.85	£120.85
	18	11573	02-Sep-96	54	Northwind Traders	£3,084.00	£243.64	£3,327.64
	19	11582	13-Sep-96	54	Northwind Traders	£411.00	£32.47	£443.47
	20				**Northwind Traders Total**	**£3,607.00**	**£284.96**	**£3,891.96**
	21				**Grand Total**	**£24,115.00**	**£1,905.11**	**£26,020.11**
	22							

An outline appears at the left side of the screen. A Grand Total appears at the bottom of the list.

The numbered buttons at the top of the outline indicate how many levels there are in the list. (In the above example, there are three levels in the list – by clicking on **1**, the list would be collapsed so that you just see the Grand Total. By clicking on **2**, you would see the Grand Total and the Subtotals and by clicking on **3**, you would see the detail in between the sub-totals.

You can also use the + and − buttons at the side of the outline to collapse and expand the list. A − button indicates that the list can be collapsed, a + button indicates that the list can be 'expanded'.

Adding further information to a list

You can use the Subtotals feature again, to do a different calculation on the same data or to add subtotals to a different set of data.

When you have chosen where to put the subtotals, what function to use and where you want to see the subtotals on the worksheet, make sure you uncheck the **Replace current subtotals** box. Click on **OK**.

If you wish to put the subtotals at the top of the group of data that they refer to, uncheck the **Summary below data** box in the Subtotal dialog box.

If you wish to have a page break between each section in the list (so that they print onto separate pages), check the **Page break between groups** box in the Subtotal dialog box.

TASK 45

1 **Start a new workbook and type the following data:**

LAST NAME	FIRST NAME	LOCATION	SALES
Youndle	Mike	London	£33,567
Pilling	Susan	Edinburgh	£36,600
Smith	Vicky	London	£25,430
Masterson	Judith	London	£38,430
Dickens	Neil	Edinburgh	£44,320
Taylor	Sarah	Slough	£35,000
Cartwright	Chris	Slough	£45,051
Duckworth	Donald	London	£37,950
Jamieson	Alex	Edinburgh	£39,230
Batty	Norah	Slough	£38,540

2 **Sort the list by Location.**

3 **Insert Subtotals at the end of each location to show the Total sales (Sum).**

4 **Also insert Subtotals at the end of each location to show the Average sales. Your worksheet should look like this:**

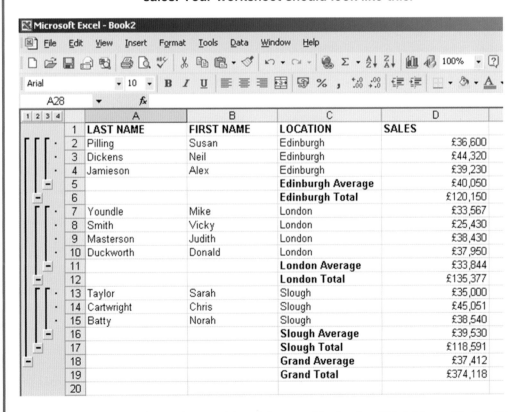

5 **Save the workbook in your Tasks for ITQ folder with the filename 'Subtotalled List'. Close the workbook.**

Presenting spreadsheet data

If you need to present complex data, it is sometimes more effective to present the data in a graph (chart) format. Below is a list of the different graph (chart) types available and how they present the data:

Standard type	Sub-type	How it presents the data
Column	Clustered Column, 3-D Clustered Column	Compares values across categories
	Stacked Column, 3-D Stacked Column	Compares the contribution of each value to a total across categories
	100% Stacked Column, 3-D 100% Stacked Column	Compares the percentage each value contributes to a total across categories
	3-D Column	Compares values across categories and across series
Bar	Clustered Bar, 3-D Clustered Bar	Compares values across categories
	Stacked Bar, 3-D Stacked Bar	Compares the contribution of each value to a total across categories
	100% Stacked Bar, 3-D 100% Stacked Bar	Compares the percentage each value contributes to a total across categories
Line	Line, Line with markers	Displays trend over time or categories
	Stacked Line, Stacked Line with markers	Displays the trend of the contribution of each value over time or categories
	100% Stacked Line, 100% Stacked Line with markers	Displays the trend of the percentage each value contributes over time or categories
	3-D Line	Line with a 3-D visual effect
Pie	Pie, 3-D Pie	Displays the contribution of each value to a total
	Pie of Pie	Pie with user-defined values extracted and combined into a second pie
	Exploded Pie, 3-D Exploded Pie	Displays the contribution of each value to a total while emphasising individual values
	Bar of Pie	Pie with user-defined values extracted and combined into a stacked bar
XY (Scatter)	Scatter, Scatter with data points connected, Scatter without markers	Compares pairs of values

Standard type	Sub-type	How it presents the data
Area	Area, 3-D Area	Displays the trend of values over time or categories
	Stacked Area, 3-D Stacked Area	Displays the trend of the contribution of each value over time or categories
	100% Stacked Area, 3-D 100% Stacked Area	Displays the trend of the percentage each value contributes over time or categories
Doughnut	Doughnut	Like a pie chart, but can contain multiple series
	Exploded Doughnut	Like an exploded pie chart, but can contain multiple series
Radar	Radar, Radar with markers	Displays changes in values relative to a centre point
	Filled Radar	Radar with the area covered by a data series filled with a colour
Surface	3-D Surface	Shows trends in values across two dimensions in a continuous curve
	Wireframe 3-D Surface	3-D surface chart without colour
	Contour	Surface chart viewed from above. Colours represent ranges of values
	Wireframe Contour	Contour chart without colour
Bubble	Bubble, 3-D Bubble	Compares sets of three values. Like a scatter chart with the third value displayed as the size of the bubble marker
Stock	High-Low-Close	Requires three series of values in this order
	Open-High-Low-Close	Requires four series of values in this order
	Volume-High-Low-Close	Requires four series of values in this order
	Volume-Open-High-Low-Close	Requires five series of values in this order
Cylinder/Cone/ Pyramid	Column, Bar with a cylindrical shape, conical shape, pyramid shape	Compares values across categories
	Stacked column, bar with a cylindrical shape, conical shape, pyramid shape	Compares the contribution of each value to a total across categories
	100% stacked column, bar with a cylindrical shape, conical shape, pyramid shape	Compares the percentage each value contributes to a total across categories
	3-D Column with a cylindrical shape, conical shape, pyramid shape	Compares values across categories and across series

For information on how to create graphs (charts), please see page 317.

Improving efficiency

For information on how you can improve efficiency by using buttons and shortcut keys, please refer to Unit 208 – Word-processing software.

 # Inserting pictures and other information into Excel

For information on inserting pictures and data from another application, please refer to Unit 208 – Word-processing software.

 # Suggests tasks for evidence

All evidence for this unit must be produced in the workplace. The suggested tasks below provide guidance on the type of work that you can produce as evidence for this unit. You may come across one or more of these scenarios in your workplace. By following the guidelines below, you will have produced a piece of evidence for this unit.

To ensure that your work can be used as evidence towards your ITQ, take screenshots at every stage to show the changes you are making to the document. The finished documents should also be provided.

Suggested Task 1

You have been asked to set up a list of contact information in Excel. The list should include name, address, e-mail address, telephone and web address. Consider the following and then produce the list:

- What column headings should be included? Should the name and address information be broken into separate cells?
- How should the list be formatted?
- Should the list be sorted?
- Should there be a header and/or footer on the printed page?

Include your company logo at the top of the list. Set it up and print.

Suggested Task 2

Create a spreadsheet that can make use of absolute cell references (e.g. to carry out VAT calculations). Format the worksheet and print to show the figures. View the formulas and print the worksheet again to show the formulas.

Suggested Task 3

Write a short report listing the different error messages that can appear when working with formulas in Excel. Write a short description of what each error message means.

Suggested Task 4

Create a spreadsheet that includes these formulas: Sum, Average, Min, Max, Count and Round.

Create two print-outs, one to show the results of the formulas and the other to show the formulas themselves. (You can switch this on in **Tools**, **Options**.)

Suggested Task 5

Open an existing workbook and split the data in the workbook across two or more sheets. Write formulas and use Paste Link to link the data together. Create appropriate screenshots and print-outs to show the linking.

Suggested Task 6

Open a spreadsheet that contains a list of information. Print the full list. Use AutoFilter to filter this list. Format and print just the filtered list.

Suggested Task 7

Open an existing workbook and create a chart from some of the worksheet data. Print the default chart. Change the chart type and format appropriately. Print the chart on its own and with the worksheet data.

Database software

Unit value = 20

Overview

You are likely to be in a role which involves modifying simple (e.g. single table, non-relational) databases and creating queries using multiple selection criteria and reports (e.g. about sales activities, order details or project management).

The database software outlined in this unit is Microsoft® Access. Microsoft® Access is part of the Microsoft® Office suite of applications. It offers a comprehensive set of tools for designing, managing and using databases. It is used in offices for storing large amounts of information. Once the information has been input, a database can be queried to extract data and present it efficiently and professionally using reports. Databases are an effective management tool to ensure that the kind of data that is required is stored and used in whatever format is quick and easy.

Competent people can use database software to enter data, retrieve a range of information and produce formatted reports. They can create and modify database fields and maintain data integrity. They will understand the principles of database design and structure.

 ## Required skills and techniques for Level 2

Entering data	Creating fields for entering data with the required field characteristics, such as name, type, size and format.
Modifying databases	Modifying field characteristics within a simple (e.g. single-table, non-relational) database while maintaining the integrity of existing data, such as name, type and size.
Formatting data	Using appropriate tools and techniques to format data that is text and numbers. Formatting reports from simple (e.g. single-table, non-relational) databases using appropriate tools and techniques for page layout, such as page size, page orientation, page numbering, headers and footers and margins.
Checking data	Using automated facilities, such as spell checking, for checking data and reports and sorting data. Checking reports are formatted and laid out appropriately.
Database queries	Creating and using multiple criteria queries to extract data.
Database reports	Planning and producing reports from single (e.g. single-table, non-relational) databases.
Improving efficiency	Setting up shortcuts.

 ## Requirements of this unit

You will need to carry out at least *two* comprehensive tasks to demonstrate your competence in entering data into a database, modifying a table design, formatting data and creating queries and reports. You will not be required to actually design a database, but you need to have knowledge of how they are designed and how they work. You need to demonstrate your understanding of the differences between databases and spreadsheets.

In your workplace, you may be asked to input some data into a database (possibly modifying field characteristics in the process), create queries to extract data from the database and present the data in a report.

 ## Tasks in this unit

The tasks that appear throughout this unit are designed to help you practise using the feature that has just been discussed. However, if you wish, you can provide these as extra pieces of evidence in addition to the two main pieces that are required by the unit.

The tasks at the end of the unit are suggested ways in which you could provide the main evidence for this unit.

 ## What will I achieve?

By accomplishing a Level 2 in this unit, you will also have achieved Level 1 in most cases. Below is a table to show what levels you will have achieved.

Required skill	Level 1	Level 2	Level 3
Entering data	●————————●		
Modifying databases	N/A	●	
Formatting data	N/A	●	
Checking data	●————————●		
Database queries	●————————●		
Database reports	●————————●		
Improving efficiency	N/A	●	

 ## What is a database?

If you need to store information about customers, suppliers, products, etc., and want to be able to extract any of the stored information, in different ways and formats, you need to store the information in a database. A database is like a multi-layered list. Each record in the list can be stored in such a way that individual parts of that record can be extracted without having to pull off the whole record.

Most computerised databases are 'relational'. This means that you create a number of tables containing different bits of information. These tables are then related to each other. This is more efficient than creating one huge table containing all the information that needs to be stored in the database.

 ## Database design

Microsoft Access is a database design tool. It provides you with all the tools required to design a database to suit what data you need to store and what information you need to extract from the database.

The design stage of a database is very important. Database designers will take a lot of time discussing the requirements of the database and what information it needs to provide prior to sitting down at the computer and starting to actually design it. It is much better to get it right at the outset rather than trying to amend a database that already contains hundreds of records. By establishing what needs to come out of the database, this will indicate what needs to be put into the database and the framework of the database.

The question of 'what do we want from the database' must be borne in mind during the whole design and creation process.

Access databases

An Access database consists of four basic elements:

Tables create the basic framework of the database and are where the data resides. You create fields in a table and properties can be assigned to these fields to control what data is allowed to be input.

Forms are a 'user-friendly' way of inputting data into a database. A data inputter would enter information into a form rather than directly into the table. However, the form is linked to the table so that the information actually 'lives' in the table. The form is a user interface between the data inputter and the database and is easier to navigate and use.

Queries If you wish to extract information from the database, you create a query. You can choose the fields you wish to extract information from and also set conditions that must be met for the information to be extracted. For example, the last name and first name of all people who are aged 21 and over.

Reports Although tables, forms and queries can all be printed, reports enable you to present your data in a professionally formatted way. You can base a report on a complete table or on a query you have created. Reports can be produced on portrait or landscape paper and the text in the report can be formatted to suit your requirements.

Opening Access

Microsoft Access

Very often there will be a shortcut on the desktop directly to the actual database that you want to use. If there isn't, you need to launch Access first and then open the database you want to work in.

Access can be launched by **double-clicking** on the Access **shortcut** on the desktop (if there is one).

Alternatively, click on **Start**, **Programs** and then choose **Microsoft Access** from the menu. (If you have Windows® XP, it is **Start, All Programs, Microsoft Access**).

Opening an existing database

Choose **Open** from the **File** menu.

Open

Alternatively, click on the **Open** button on the Standard toolbar.

You can also use [Control]+[O]

The Open dialog box opens.

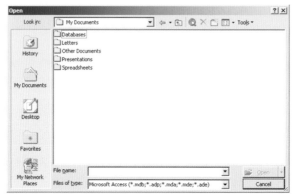

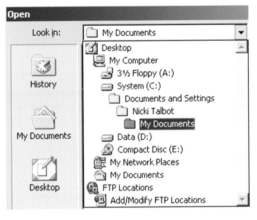

To change to a different drive, click on the drop-down arrow at the end of the **Look in:** box to open a list of locations. Choose the drive that you wish to use from the list.

Once you have chosen the appropriate drive from the **Look in:** list, the main area of the Open dialog box will display the folders that are already on that drive. To open a folder, double-click on the appropriate folder name.

Use the **Back** button or **Up One Level** button to move up out of a folder.

Locate the database you wish to open, click on it and then click on the **Open** button at the bottom right of the dialog box. (Alternatively, you can double-click on the file.)

TASK 1

If you have an existing Access database that you can use, open it.

Saving a database

When you create an Access database, you are asked to give the database a name. A database contains various elements: Tables, Forms, Queries and Reports (see page 352). Each element in the database is created and saved rather like saving a Word document or an Excel spreadsheet.

Click on the **File** menu and choose **Save**.

Alternatively, click on the **Save** button on the Standard toolbar.

You can also use ⌷Control⌷ + ⌷S⌷

If the table, form, query or report has not been saved before the Save As dialog box will appear.

Type a name in the box and click on OK.

Save

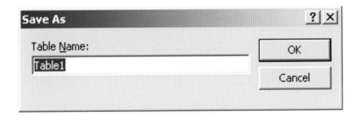

Because each element in the database is saved as it is created, you do not need to save the whole database when you make changes. You can simply close the database window when you are finished using it.

Closing a database

When you have finished working with the database, make sure any items in the database (i.e. tables, forms, queries or reports) have been closed.

Choose **Close** from the **File** menu.

Alternatively, you can click on the Close Window button at the top right of the screen.

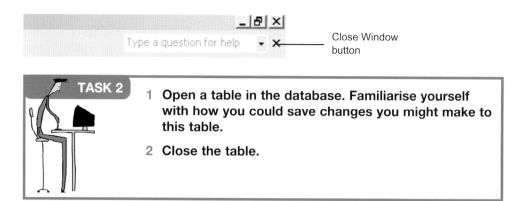

Close Window button

TASK 2

1 **Open a table in the database. Familiarise yourself with how you could save changes you might make to this table.**

2 **Close the table.**

Working with tables

To open an existing table in a database, click on the **Tables** link on the left side of the Database window.

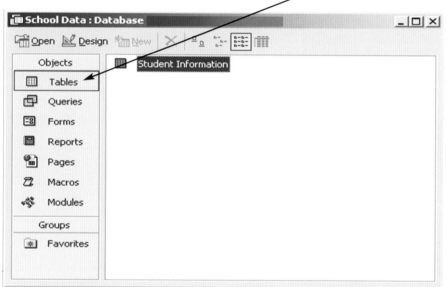

The tables in the database will be listed. (In the example above there is just one table, Student Information.) Select the table you wish to open and click on **Open** on the toolbar at the top of the window.

Alternatively, you can double-click on the table you wish to open.

The table opens into **Datasheet** view (it looks rather like an Excel spreadsheet). This view can be used to enter data into the table.

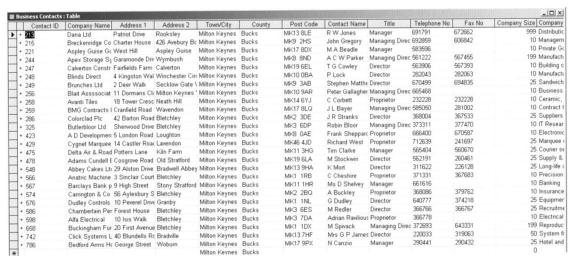

Contact ID	Company Name	Address 1	Address 2	Town/City	County	Post Code	Contact Name	Title	Telephone No	Fax No	Company Size	Company
213	Dana Ltd	Patriot Drive	Rooksley	Milton Keynes	Bucks	MK13 8LE	R W Jones	Manager	691791	672662	999	Distributic
215	Breckenridge Co	Charter House	426 Avebury Bc	Milton Keynes	Bucks	MK9 2HS	John Gregory	Managing Direc	692859	606842	10	Managem
221	Aspley Guise Gc	West Hill	Aspley Guise	Milton Keynes	Bucks	MK17 8DX	M A Beadle	Manager	583596		10	Private Gc
244	Apex Storage Sy	Garamonde Dri	Wymbush	Milton Keynes	Bucks	MK8 8ND	A C W Parker	Managing Direc	561222	567455	199	Manufactu
247	Calverton Constr	Fairfields Farm	Calverton	Milton Keynes	Bucks	MK19 6EL	T G Cowley	Director	563906	567393	10	Building c
248	Blinds Direct	4 Kingston Wal	Winchester Circ	Milton Keynes	Bucks	MK10 0BA	P Lock	Director	282043	282063	10	Manufactu
249	Brunches Ltd	2 Deer Walk	Secklow Gate \	Milton Keynes	Bucks	MK9 3AB	Stephen Matthe	Director	670499	694835	25	Sandwich
256	Blair Asssociat	11 Dormans Clc	Milton Keynes '	Milton Keynes	Bucks	MK10 9AR	Peter Gallagher	Managing Direc	665468		10	Business
258	Avanti Tiles	18 Tower Cresc	Neath Hill	Milton Keynes	Bucks	MK14 6YJ	C Corbett	Proprietor	232228	232228	10	Ceramic,
259	BMG Contracts I	Cranfield Road	Wavendon	Milton Keynes	Bucks	MK17 8LQ	J L Bayer	Managing Direc	585050	281002	10	Contract I
286	Colorclad Plc	42 Barton Road	Bletchley	Milton Keynes	Bucks	MK2 3DE	J R Stranks	Director	368004	367533	25	Suppliers
325	Butlerbloor Ltd	Sherwood Drive	Bletchley	Milton Keynes	Bucks	MK3 6DP	Robin Bloor	Managing Direc	373311	377470	10	IT Resear
423	A D Developmen	5 London Road	Loughton	Milton Keynes	Bucks	MK8 0AE	Frank Sheppard	Proprietor	666400	670587	10	Electronic
429	Cygnet Marquee	14 Castler Roac	Lavendon	Milton Keynes	Bucks	MK46 4JD	Richard West	Proprietor	712639	241697	25	Marquee c
475	Delta Air & Road	Potters Lane	Kiln Farm	Milton Keynes	Bucks	MK11 3HG	Tim Clarke	Manager	565404	560670	25	Courier se
478	Adams Cundell C	Cosgrove Road	Old Stratford	Milton Keynes	Bucks	MK19 6LA	M Stockwin	Director	562191	260461	25	Supply &
548	Abbey Cakes Ltc	29 Alston Drive	Bradwell Abbey	Milton Keynes	Bucks	MK13 9HA	K Mort	Director	311622	226128	25	Long-life c
566	Anatric Machine	3 Sinclair Court	Bletchley	Milton Keynes	Bucks	MK1 1RB	C Cheshire	Proprietor	371331	367683	10	Precision
567	Barclays Bank p	9 High Street	Stony Stratford	Milton Keynes	Bucks	MK11 1HR	Ms D Shelvey	Manager	661616		10	Banking
574	Carrington & Co	56 Aylesbury S	Bletchley	Milton Keynes	Bucks	MK2 2BQ	A Buckley	Proprietor	368086	379762	10	Insurance
576	Dudley Controls	10 Peverel Drive	Granby	Milton Keynes	Bucks	MK1 1NL	G Dudley	Director	640777	374218	25	Equipmen
586	Chamberlain Per	Forest House	Bletchley	Milton Keynes	Bucks	MK3 6ES	M Redler	Director	366766	366767	25	Recruitme
598	Alfa Electrical	10 Isis Walk	Bletchley	Milton Keynes	Bucks	MK3 7DA	Adrian Ravilious	Proprietor	366778		10	Electrical
658	Buckingham Fur	20 First Avenue	Bletchley	Milton Keynes	Bucks	MK1 1DX	M Spivack	Managing Direc	372693	643331	199	Reproduc
742	Click Systems L	40 Blundells Rc	Bradville	Milton Keynes	Bucks	MK13 7HF	Mrs G P James	Director	220033	319063	50	System fr
786	Bedford Arms Hc	George Street	Woburn	Milton Keynes	Bucks	MK17 9PX	N Canzio	Manager	290441	290432	25	Hotel and
				Milton Keynes	Bucks						0	

Alternatively, you may wish to open a table in **Design** view. This view is used to change the design of the table, to create or modify fields and their properties. To open a table in Design view, select the table in the list and click on **Design** on the toolbar at the top of the window.

The table opens into **Design** view.

If you have already opened a table into Datasheet view and you wish to switch to Design view, choose **Design View** from the **View** menu.

Alternatively, click the **View** button on the Standard toolbar.

The table switches to Design View. You can use the **View** menu or the **View** button to switch back to Datasheet view again.

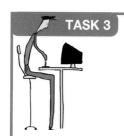

TASK 3

1 **Open a table in the database and practise switching between Design View and Datasheet View.**

2 **Close the table and then close the database.**

Design of tables

Tables form the basic framework of a database. The data in a database resides in tables in the database. These tables have field names so that the data inputter knows what to put in each field in the table. The database designer can also set field types and field properties to control what can be input into a field.

The first step in setting up a database is to design the tables. To create a new table, click on the **Tables** link on the left side of the Database window. Click on the **New** button on the toolbar at the top of the window.

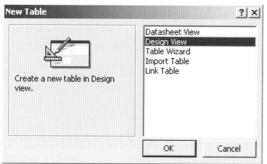

The New Table dialog box opens.

Choose Design View from the list and click on **OK**. A blank table design window opens.

There are two sections to the Design View window:

■ The top section of the window lists the **Field Names**, **Data Types** and a **Description** of the field.

■ The bottom section of the window contains the **Field Properties**.

Field names

The field names become the column headings when you switch to datasheet view. This makes it easier for a data inputter to know what to type into a field. You also use these field names when creating queries and reports.

Field names can be up to 64 characters long and can include any combination of letters, numbers, spaces and special characters. The only characters you cannot use are full stop (.), exclamation mark (!), speech marks (") and square brackets ([ ]).

A field name can only be used once in a table, i.e. you cannot have two fields with the same name.

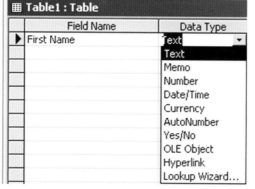

Data types

There are a range of data types you can pick from to determine the type of data that will be allowed in a field.

Once you have named a field, move into the next column (headed **Data Type**) and click on the drop-down arrow to open the list of available data types.

■ **Text** – use this data type for text or a combination of text and numbers. You can also use it for numbers that do not require calculations, such as phone numbers or post codes. Fields with this data type can have up to 255 characters.

- **Memo** – use this data type for longer amounts of text, up to 65,536 characters. This data type is useful for a comments or notes field.
- **Number** – use this data type for data which is to be included in mathematical calculations. (Except for money fields, which should use the Currency data type.)
- **Date/Time** – use this data type for dates and times.
- **Currency** – use this data type for currency values and to prevent rounding off during calculations.
- **AutoNumber** – use this data type if you want Access to generate a unique sequential number automatically when a new record is added.
- **Yes/No** – use for data that can be only one of two possible values, Yes/No, True/False, etc.
- **OLE Object** – use for inserting OLE objects, such as a Microsoft® Word document or Microsoft® Excel spreadsheet. Also pictures and sounds that were created in other programs.
- **Hyperlink** – use this data type if you wish to insert a hyperlink, such as a web address.
- **Lookup Wizard** – this data type launches a wizard which enables you to choose a value from a list or another table in the database.

Field descriptions

The next column in the Table Design window is **Description**. A description of the field is optional. If you do type a description in this box, the description will appear in the Status Bar when the user clicks into the field in Datasheet view. Sometimes the field names on their own do not give enough information to the data inputter as to what should be input into the field. You can add a description to give the user more information about the field.

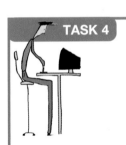

TASK 4

1 **Create a new blank database and call it Student Information. (Create it in your Tasks for ITQ folder.)**

2 **Create a new table. (Open it in Design View.)**

3 **Set up the following Field Names and Data Types:**

Field Name	Data Type
Student Code	Number
Last Name	Text
First Name	Text
House	Text
Teacher	Text
Enrolment Date	Date/Time
Comments	Text
Boarder?	Yes/No

4 **Type the following Descriptions:**

Student Code	Type the three digit number that appears on the student's enrolment form.
Enrolment Date	Please type in the date stamped on the application form.
Comments	Please add any comments about the character/personality of the child.

Your design view should look like this:

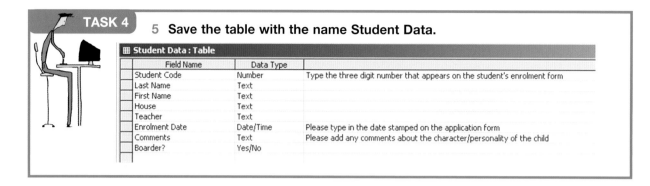

TASK 4

5 **Save the table with the name Student Data.**

Student Data : Table

Field Name	Data Type	
Student Code	Number	Type the three digit number that appears on the student's enrolment form
Last Name	Text	
First Name	Text	
House	Text	
Teacher	Text	
Enrolment Date	Date/Time	Please type in the date stamped on the application form
Comments	Text	Please add any comments about the character/personality of the child
Boarder?	Yes/No	

Field properties

The bottom section of the Table Design window contains the **Field Properties** for a selected field. Click on the field in the top section of the window to see the properties for that field.

Different Field Properties are available depending on the Data Type chosen in the top section of the Table Design window.

General	Lookup	
Field Size	50
Format	
Input Mask	
Caption	
Default Value	
Validation Rule	
Validation Text	
Required	No
Allow Zero Length	Yes
Indexed	No
Unicode Compression	Yes
IME Mode	No Control
IME Sentence Mode	None

The example above shows Field Properties for the Text Data Type.

Field Properties that you might want to set are:

■ **Field Size** – the maximum number of characters that will be allowed in the field (up to 255).
■ **Format** – the format of the data that is input. For a Text data type, you can type > to force all characters to uppercase or < to force all characters to lowercase.
■ **Input Mask** – a control over how data is entered into a field. For example, you could specify an input mask that would ensure that a set number of digits is entered for a phone number and that only numbers can be entered. The data inputter simply fills in the blanks. An input mask provides a lot more control over what is allowed in a field, thus providing more control over what information the database contains. This is fundamental to good database design as it ensures that you extract the data you want from the database.
■ **Caption** – if you want the column heading in datasheet view to be something other than the field name, type the caption in here.
■ **Default Value** – if a field should always contain a certain value, unless the user changes it, you can specify that value here. For example, if the Town for most of the records is going to be Milton Keynes, you can specify that as the default value. This will save the data inputter typing it each time. However, they can type a different town if required.

■ **Validation Rule** – a 'rule' that the field must conform to. For example, >9 will ensure that a number greater than 9 must be input into the field. Setting a validation rule means that the field cannot be left empty. If the field can be left empty, you must specify 'Or is Null' as part of the validation rule.

■ **Validation Text** – if you are setting a validation rule you can specify a message that should appear if the data inputter 'breaks' the rule. For example, the message might read 'Please enter an amount greater than 9'.

■ **Required** – setting this to Yes means that there must be an entry in this field and it cannot be left blank.

Field properties for a Date/Time field

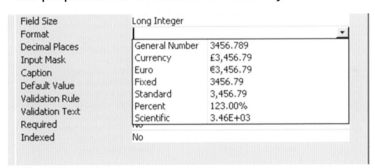

Format	Long Date	
Input Mask	General Date	19/06/1994 17:34:23
Caption	Long Date	19 June 1994
Default Value	Medium Date	19-Jun-94
Validation Rule	Short Date	19/06/1994
Validation Text	Long Time	17:34:23
Required	Medium Time	05:34 PM
Indexed	Short Time	17:34
IME Mode	No Control	
IME Sentence Mode	None	

You can specify the date format by clicking on the drop-down arrow in the **Format** field property and choosing the date format you require.

Field properties for a Number or Currency field

Field Size	Long Integer	
Format		
Decimal Places	General Number	3456.789
Input Mask	Currency	£3,456.79
Caption	Euro	€3,456.79
Default Value	Fixed	3456.79
Validation Rule	Standard	3,456.79
Validation Text	Percent	123.00%
Required	Scientific	3.46E+03
Indexed	No	

You can specify the number format by clicking on the drop-down arrow in the **Format** field property and choosing the number format you require.

Setting field properties

You need to be careful when changing the properties of fields that already contain data.

For example, if you change the field size so that existing data does not fit, you will receive the message below.

Microsoft Access ✕

⚠ **Some data may be lost.**

The setting for the FieldSize property of one or more fields has been changed to a shorter size. If data is lost, validation rules may be violated as a result.
Do you want to continue anyway?

[Yes]   [No]

Changing field properties of fields that already contain data may result in lost data. Lost data may result in validation rules being violated. (For more information on validation rules, see page 359.)

TASK 5

1 Set field properties as below:

Student Code	Long Integer	Decimal Places = 0	Required = Yes
Last Name	Field Size = 30	Required = Yes	
First Name	Field Size = 20		
House	Field Size = 10		
Teacher	Field Size = 20		
Enrolment Date	Format = Long Date		

2 Change the Data Type of the Comments field to Memo.

3 Save the changes you have made to the table.

Entering data into a table

To open a table that has already been designed, see page 354. Alternatively, if you are in Design View, you can use the **View** menu or click on the **View** button to switch to Datasheet View.

Student Information : Table

	Student Code	Last Name	First Name	House	Teacher	Enrolment Date	Comments	Boarder
▶	**111** Gerrard	Malcom	Yellow	Clarke	02 September 2001	Team worker	N
	172 Johnson	Nichola	Green	Webb	14 May 2000	Team worker	Y
	199 Hill	Andrew	Blue	Webb	05 September 1999	Shy	N
	200 Bowyers	Sarah	Green	Lidington	12 October 1998	Problem solver	Y
	203 Smith	Sue	Red	Hazel	03 November 2001	Team worker	N
	222 Baker	Ann	Yellow	Lidington	03 February 2002	Outgoing	Y
	256 Linekar	Simon	Red	Webb	19 January 1999	Outgoing	Y
	264 Spencer	Jon	Yellow	Lidington	23 June 2000	Shy	Y
	270 Mayfield	Chris	Blue	Webb	24 May 2001	Team worker	N
	288 Bowers	Ian	Yellow	Webb	18 January 1997	Team worker	N
	301 Smith	Caitlin	Blue	Hazel	03 February 1996	Team worker	N
	329 Wong	Emily	Blue	Hazel	23 May 1997	Outgoing	N
	333 Watkins	Gregory	Green	Clarke	07 September 2000	Shy	Y
	362 Lewis	Lennox	Blue	Hazel	17 September 2001	Problem solver	N
	365 Dale	Daniel	Green	Lidington	02 March 1996	Outgoing	Y
	377 Smith	Sam	Red	Clarke	15 March 2000	Outgoing	Y

The Field Names become the column headings in Datasheet view. The data is input into **fields** and each row in the table is called a **record**.

Working with fields and records

To edit a record in the table, click in the field you wish to edit and make your amendments. As soon as you click outside the field, the amendment is saved.

To add a new record to the table, click in the empty row at the bottom of the table (indicated by the *) and type data into the fields. Press Return on the keyboard to enter that record and move to the next new record.

To delete a record from the table, select the record by clicking on the grey tile to the left of the row.

	Student Code	Last Name	First Name	House	Teacher	Enrolment Date	Comments	Boarder
	111 Gerrard	Malcom	Yellow	Clarke	02 September 2001	Team worker	N
▶	172 Johnson	Nichola	Green	Webb	14 May 2000	Team worker	Y
	199 Hill	Andrew	Blue	Webb	05 September 1999	Shy	N

TASK 6

1 Switch to Datasheet view and enter the following data into the table:

Student Code	Last Name	First Name	House	Teacher	Enrolment Date	Comments	Boarder?
152	Jackson	Nicole	Sky	Walters	14 May 2000	Team worker	Y
161	Gregory	Matthew	Earth	Carter	02 Sept 2001	Team worker	N
173	Hall	Alistair	Fire	Walters	05 Sept 1999	Shy	N
210	Smythe	Shelley	Water	Hopkins	3 Nov 2001	Team worker	N
227	Boston	Annabel	Earth	Best	3 Feb 2002	Outgoing	Y
249	Bowman	Isobel	Earth	Walters	18 Jan 1997	Outgoing	N
251	Bowland	Susan	Sky	Best	12 Oct 1998	Problem solver	Y
266	Lineham	Stephen	Water	Walters	19 Jan 1999	Outgoing	Y
277	Mayhew	Carl	Fire	Walters	24 May 2001	Team worker	N
284	Spalding	Jonathan	Earth	Best	23 June 2000	Shy	Y
340	Spencer	Cathy	Fire	Hopkins	3 Feb 1996	Team worker	N
342	Wang	Eleanor	Fire	Hopkins	23 May 1997	Outgoing	N
348	Walters	Betty	Fire	Walters	27 June 2000	Shy	N
359	Llewellyn	Lucy	Fire	Hopkins	17 Sept 2001	Problem solver	N
366	Wilson	Janet	Water	Carter	6 Sept 2001	Team worker	Y
372	Davidson	David	Sky	Best	2 March 1996	Outgoing	Y
374	Bates	Toby	Sky	Best	10 Oct 2001	Team worker	Y
380	Sampson	Caitlin	Water	Carter	15 March 2000	Outgoing	Y
395	Watson	Gareth	Sky	Carter	7 Sept 2000	Shy	Y
396	Dawson	Julie	Sky	Hopkins	12 Feb 1996	Outgoing	N
424	Dennis	Daniel	Water	Walters	30 Nov 2000	Problem solver	Y
478	Johnson	Frederick	Earth	Hopkins	18 April 1997	Problem solver	Y
479	Coles	Claire	Sky	Best	7 April 1998	Outgoing	Y
484	Cuthberts	Tanya	Fire	Carter	2 Sept 2000	Team worker	N
488	Goodson	Michael	Fire	Walters	3 Sept 2001	Team worker	Y
522	Hillard	Barbara	Earth	Walters	8 Sept 2000	Outgoing	Y
553	Dilbert	Francis	Fire	Hopkins	2 Sept 2000	Outgoing	N
579	Spellman	Gail	Fire	Hopkins	12 Dec 2000	Team worker	N
633	Murray	Julia	Fire	Carter	4 May 2000	Shy	N
639	Hill	Gregory	Water	Hopkins	18 Oct 2001	Problem solver	N
657	Carter	Nigel	Sky	Best	25 March 2002	Outgoing	Y
674	Barton	Natasha	Fire	Walters	8 May 2002	Team worker	N
721	Day	Linda	Fire	Carter	23 Feb 1999	Problem solver	N
778	Freeman	Henry	Water	Walters	15 Sept 2001	Team worker	Y
825	Milner	Diane	Sky	Carter	29 March 1999	Problem solver	N
868	Engles	Elise	Fire	Carter	10 Oct 1998	Outgoing	N

2 Close the table.

Choose **Delete Record** from the **Edit** menu.
Alternatively, click on the **Delete Record** button on the Standard toolbar.

Delete
Record

This message appears:

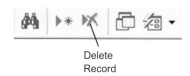

Click on **Yes** to delete the record.

 # Formatting a table

In Datasheet view you can use the **Format** menu to format the table.

Formatting the data

Any formatting changes you make apply to all the data in the table. You cannot select individual text in the table and format it.
Choose **Font** from the **Format** menu. The Font dialog box opens.

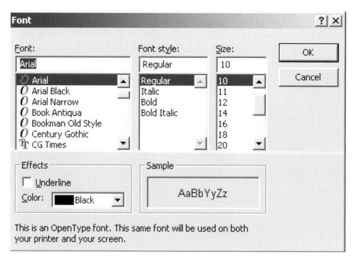

You can change the **Font**, **Font style** and **Size**. You can add **Underline** and change the font **Colour**.
Click on **OK** to make the changes to the table.

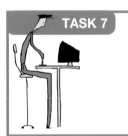

TASK 7

1 **Open the Student Data table.**

2 **Change the font of the data in the table to Arial 11pt, Blue.**

Formatting the datasheet

Any formatting changes you make apply to the whole table. You cannot make changes to just part of the table.

Choose **Datasheet** from the **Format** menu. The Datasheet Formatting dialog box opens.

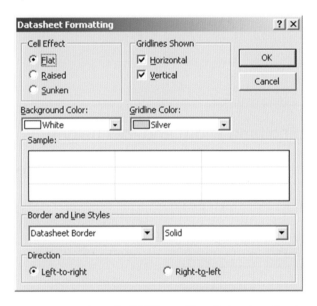

You can apply a **Cell Effect**, Flat, Raised or Sunken, to the fields.

You can choose which **Gridlines** should show in the table, Horizontal and/or Vertical.

You can choose a background colour for the fields from the **Background Color** drop-down list and a gridline colour for the lines around the fields from the **Gridline Color** drop-down list.

You can also choose line styles for the various borders and lines in the table.

Choose the border or line for which you wish to set the style from the drop-down list: Datasheet Border, Horizontal Gridline, Vertical Gridline or Column Header Underline.

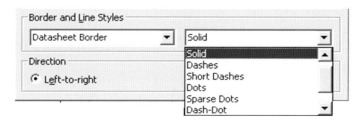

Then choose a line style from the drop-down list.

In Access 2002, you can also choose how data is input – **Left-to-right** or **Right-to-left**.

Click on **OK** to make the changes to the table.

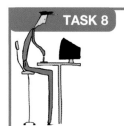

TASK 8

1 **Change the background colour of the cells to Silver.**

2 **Change the gridline colour to Blue.**

Changing column width and row height

You can change the row height of all the rows in a table. You cannot change the row height of individual rows in the table. Choose **Row Height** from the **Format** menu. The Row Height dialog box opens.

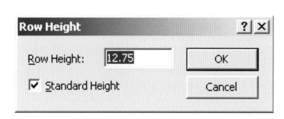

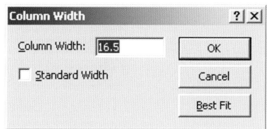

Specify the **Row Height** you require and click on **OK**.

You can change the width of individual columns in the table. Click in the column and choose **Column Width** from the **Format** menu. The Column Width dialog box opens.

Specify the **Column Width** you require and click on **OK**. Alternatively, click on **Best Fit** and Access will adjust the column width to fit the widest entry.

TASK 9

1 **Change the height of all the rows in the table to 20.**

2 **Change the width of all the columns in the table to Best Fit.**

Sorting records in a table

Open the appropriate table in Datasheet view.
Click in the column that you want to sort by and choose **Sort** from the **Records** menu.

Choose whether you wish to sort the column in **Ascending** or **Descending** order.
Alternatively, click the Sort buttons on the Standard toolbar.

Sort Ascending will sort the column in alphabetical order A–Z or in numerical order lowest to highest.
Sort Descending will sort the column in alphabetical order Z–A or in numerical order highest to lowest.

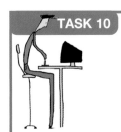

TASK 10

1 **Sort the table by the Last Name column (ascending).**

2 **Close the table.**

Finding data in the database

If you wish to simply locate records in a database, you can use the Find feature in the appropriate table.
Open the appropriate table in Datasheet view. Choose **Find** from the **Edit** menu. Alternatively, click on the Find button on the Standard toolbar.

Find

You can also use ⌃ Control + F
The Find and Replace dialog box opens.

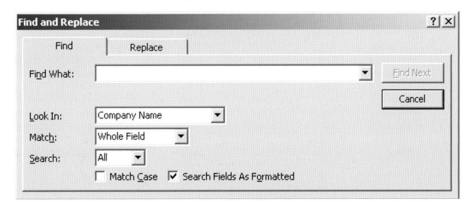

Type the word you wish to find in the **Find What** box. Choose which field to look in from the **Look In** drop-down list. Click on **Find Next** to start the search.
Access stops at the first match it finds. If this is not the record you require, click on **Find Next**. If it is the record you require, click on **Cancel** to close the Find dialog box.
Other features in the Find dialog box are:

- **Match** – in which you can choose to match the **Whole Field**, **Any Part of Field** or the **Start of Field**.
- **Search** – in which you can choose whether you want to search **All** the table, or just **Up** or **Down** from where you are currently sitting in the table.

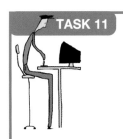

TASK 11

1 **Open the Student Data table.**

2 **Use the Find feature to find the following records in the table:**

Student Code	522
Last Name	Smythe
First Name	Caitlin
Enrolment Date	2 September 2001

Filtering records in a table

Find is useful to find one record at a time that matches your criteria. However, if you want to see a list of records that match your criteria, you can use a filter.

Open the appropriate table in Datasheet view. Choose **Filter** from the **Records** menu and choose **Filter By Form** from the sub-menu.

Filter By Form

Alternatively, click on the Filter By Form button on the Standard toolbar.

A blank table record appears with the words 'Filter by Form' in the Title bar.

Student Information: Filter by Form

Student Code	Last Name	First Name	House	Teacher	Enrolment Date	Comments	Boarder

Enter the criteria that you require for the filter in the appropriate fields. (For example, if you want to see only students who have Mr Clarke as their teacher, type Clarke in the Teacher field.)

Choose **Apply Filter/Sort** from the **Filter** menu.

Apply Filter

Alternatively, click on the **Apply Filter** button on the Standard toolbar.

Student Information : Table

Student Code	Last Name	First Name	House	Teacher	Enrolment Date	Comments	Boarder
333 Watkins	Gregory	Green	Clarke	07 September 2000	Shy	Y
627 Watson	Jane	Blue	Clarke	04 May 2000	Shy	N
377 Smith	Sam	Red	Clarke	15 March 2000	Outgoing	Y
392 Watson	John	Red	Clarke	06 September 2001	Team worker	Y
888 Barker	Diane	Green	Clarke	29 March 1999	Problem solver	N
666 Cartland	Fred	Green	Clarke	08 May 2002	Team worker	N
481 Cromwell	Tracey	Blue	Clarke	02 September 2000	Team worker	N
819 Jones	Ian	Green	Clarke	04 May 1997	Outgoing	N
111 Gerrard	Malcom	Yellow	Clarke	02 September 2001	Team worker	N
873 Day	Lynne	Blue	Clarke	15 September 2001	Team worker	Y

The list is filtered according to the criteria and only the records that match the criteria are listed.

Record: ◄◄ ◄ 1 ► ►► ►* of 10 (Filtered)

The number of records that have been returned appears in the bar at the bottom of the screen. (It also specifies that this is a filtered set of records.)

Remove Filter

To remove the filter and show all the records again, choose **Remove Filter/Sort** from the **Records** menu.

Alternatively, click on the Remove Filter button on the Standard toolbar.

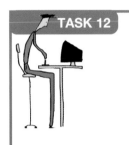

TASK 12

1 **Filter the records in the table where the House field = Earth. Remove the filter.**

2 **Filter the records in the table where the Teacher field = Carter. Remove the filter.**

3 **Filter the records in the table where the Comments field = Team worker. Remove the filter.**

4 **Filter the records in the table where the Boarder? field = Y. Remove the filter.**

Extracting data from the database

If you wish to extract information from a database and save the data as a subset of the database, you can create a 'query'. Queries can extract information from different tables in the database and you can set criteria for the query so that only records that match your criteria are extracted.

Creating a query

Click on the **Queries** link on the left side of the Database window.

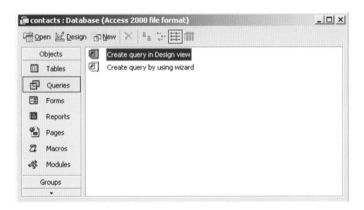

Double-click on **Create query in Design view** or click on the **Design** button on the toolbar at the top of the window.

The Query Design window opens and the Show Table dialog appears, as below:

Choose the tables from which you wish to extract information. Click on the Table in the list and click on **Add**. Repeat for each table you wish to add to the Query Design window.

When you have added all the tables you wish to use, click on **Close** to close the Show Table dialog box.

The tables you have added to the Query Design Window show in the top section of the window. The bottom section of the window contains a grid where you will build the query.

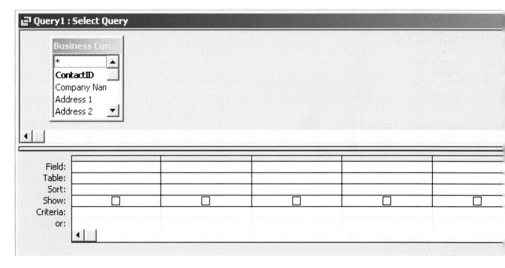

The table shows as a list of the fields. If this list is not wide enough, you can resize it by moving the mouse over the right edge of the list box and clicking and dragging the resizing handle.

TASK 13

Start a new query and add the Student Data table to the Query Design Grid.

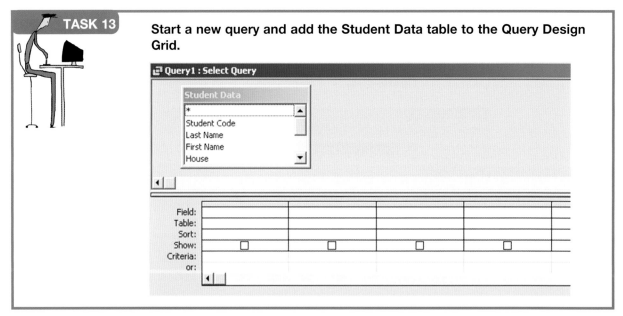

Adding fields to the query design grid

To build the query, you put the fields you want in the design grid at the bottom. You can click and drag the fields from the Table list at the top into the design grid at the bottom, or double-click on the field in the Table list and it will be added to the next column of the design grid.

For example, to create a query to show Company Name, Town/City, Contact Name, Title, Telephone Number, Company Size and Company Type, the query design grid would look like this:

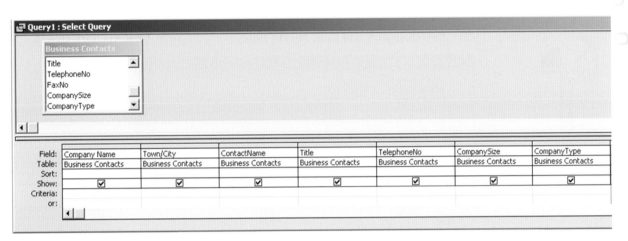

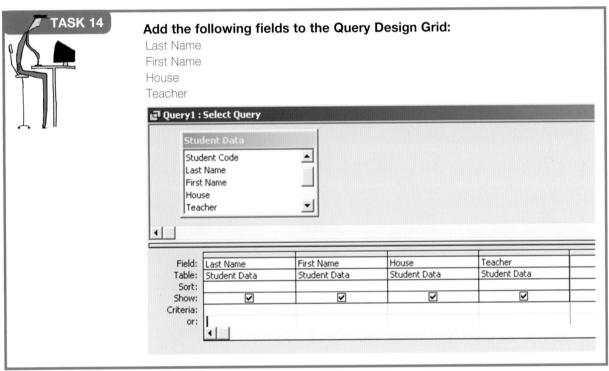

TASK 14

Add the following fields to the Query Design Grid:
Last Name
First Name
House
Teacher

Sorting fields in a query

If you wish to sort by any of the fields that you have brought down into the query design grid, click in the Sort row of the field you wish to sort, click on the drop-down arrow and choose **Ascending** or **Descending**.

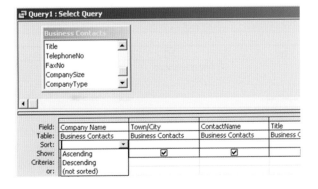

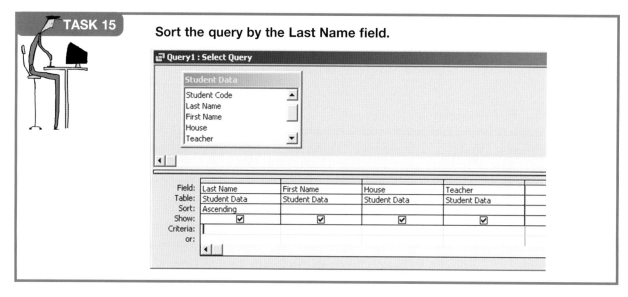

TASK 15

Sort the query by the Last Name field.

Showing or hiding data in a query

Sometimes you need to include a field in the query design but you do not want the data to be shown in the resulting query. For example, to return a list of companies in Milton Keynes, the Town/City field would need to be included in the query design with Milton Keynes as the criterion for this field. However, it would not be necessary for Milton Keynes to be listed against all the companies in the resulting query, as the query would probably be called 'Companies in Milton Keynes'.

If you do not want to show the data in the resulting query, deselect the box for the field that you do not wish to show.

Field:	Company Name	Town/City	ContactName	Title
Table:	Business Contacts	Business Contacts	Business Contacts	Business Contacts
Sort:				
Show:	☑	☐	☑	☑
Criteria:				
or:				

Setting criteria for queries

In the Criteria row of the query design grid, you can set criteria for the fields you are including in your query. For example, to return a list of companies in Milton Keynes, the criteria field on the Town/City field should be set. If you wish only records which match the criteria to be extracted, type the word which the records should match in the appropriate field of the query design grid. You must make sure that the word you type will exactly match the field it is set on.

Field:	Company Name	Town/City	ContactName	Title
Table:	Business Contacts	Business Contacts	Business Contacts	Business Contacts
Sort:				
Show:	☑	☑	☑	☑
Criteria:		"Milton Keynes"		
or:				

Using And criteria

You can set more than one criterion for extracting data (known as multiple criteria). For example, to extract records where the Last Name field is Smith <u>and</u> the town is Manchester, both criteria would be entered on the **same row** of the appropriate fields in the query design grid. Criteria that are on the same row act as 'and' criteria. This means that the record must match both criteria to be extracted.

In the example below only records that have the Town/City of Milton Keynes and the Title of Managing Director should be returned.

Field:	Company Name	Town/City	ContactName	Title
Table:	Business Contacts	Business Contacts	Business Contacts	Business Contacts
Sort:				
Show:	☑	☑	☑	☑
Criteria:		"Milton Keynes"		"Managing Director"
or:				

Using Or criteria

To extract records where the Last Name field is Smith or the town is Manchester, you enter the two criteria in two separate rows in the query design grid. Criteria that are on different rows act as 'or' criteria. This means that the records must match either criterion to be extracted.

In the example below records that have the Town/City of Milton Keynes or the Title of Managing Director should be returned.

Field:	Company Name	Town/City	ContactName	Title
Table:	Business Contacts	Business Contacts	Business Contacts	Business Contacts
Sort:				
Show:	☑	☑	☑	☑
Criteria:		"Milton Keynes"		
or:				"Managing Director"

In this case, more records will be returned than for the 'and' query as all records that have Milton Keynes as the Town/City, regardless of Title, and all records that have Managing Director as the Title, regardless of Town/City, will be returned.

You can mix **And** and **Or** criteria by placing the criteria on appropriate lines in the design grid.

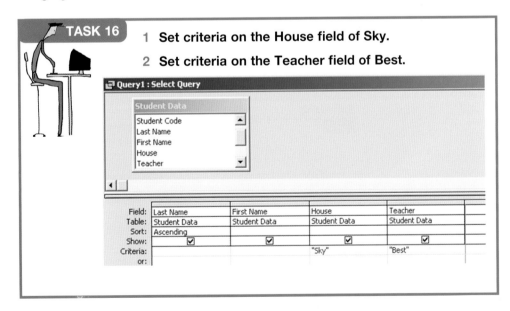

TASK 16

1 **Set criteria on the House field of Sky.**

2 **Set criteria on the Teacher field of Best.**

Running a query

Once you have set up the fields you require in the query and have specified Sort, Show and any Criteria, you are ready to run the Query.

Choose **Run** from the **Query** menu

Alternatively, click on the Run button on the Standard toolbar.

The records which match all the criteria are returned in datasheet view. (Inthis example only two records match all the criteria, i.e. Town/City = Milton Keynes, Title = Director and Company Size = 10).

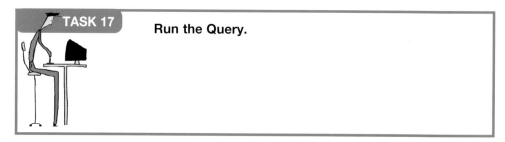

Company Name	Town/City	Contact Name	Title	Telephone No	Company Size	Company Type
Calvert Construction Ltd	Milton Keynes	T Cox	Director	563906	10	Building contractors
Blinds Direct	Milton Keynes	R Latimer	Director	282043	10	Manufacturer of blinds, curtains and interiors

Record: I◄ ◄ | 1 | ► ►I ►✱ of 2

If you wish to switch back to Design View, choose **Design View** from the **View** menu or click on the Design View button on the Standard toolbar.

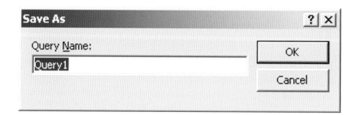

TASK 17 **Run the Query.**

Saving a query

Save

Once you have run the query and are satisfied with the results that have been returned, you can save the query.

Choose **Save** from the **File** menu

Alternatively, click on the Save button on the Standard toolbar.

You can also use [Control]+[S]

The Save As dialog box opens.

Save As	? ✕
Query **N**ame:	OK
Query1	Cancel

Type a name for the query in the **Query Name** box and click on **OK**.

A query is 'dynamic'. This means that each time you run the query, any new records that have been added to the database which meet the criteria of the query are also included in the results.

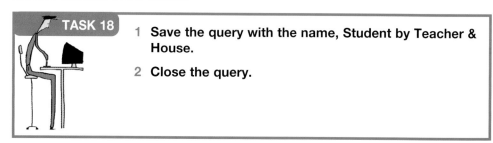

TASK 18

1 **Save the query with the name, Student by Teacher & House.**

2 **Close the query.**

Setting multiple criteria

In the example below, criteria have been set for the Town/City (Milton Keynes), the Title of the contact (Director) and the Company Size (10). Access adds speech marks around text criteria to indicate a text string.

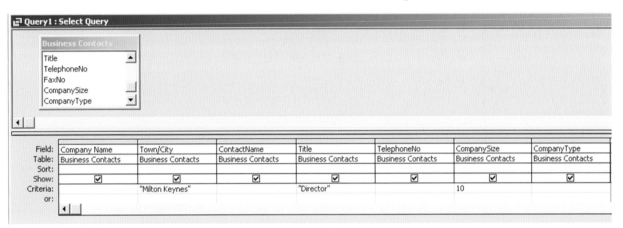

Because the criteria have been set on the same row in the query design grid, they are **And** criteria. This means that the records must match all criteria to be returned.

Other criteria

This is a list of other criteria that you can use in the query design grid:

- **Not** – if you type Not Smith in the Last Name field, only records that do not have Smith in the Last Name field will be extracted.
- **Null** – if you wish to find records that don't contain any value in the field, you can type 'Is Null' in the criteria line.
- **Current Date** – if you wish to find fields that have the current date, type 'Date()' in the appropriate field in the query design grid.
- **Date** – if the criteria is in a date field, type the date you wish to find. The date must be in the same format as it appears in the database. If you wish to find a date range for a field, type Between [first date] and [second date]. For example, Between 1/1/00 and 30/6/02 will find all records from 1 January 2000 to 30 June 2002. Access automatically places hashes around any dates set as criteria.
- **Number** – if the criteria is in a number field, type the number you wish to find. If you wish to find numbers greater than or less than a certain number, use > (greater than) or < (less than). You can also use >= (greater than and equal to) and <= (less than or equal to) if you also wish to include the number you specify in the query.

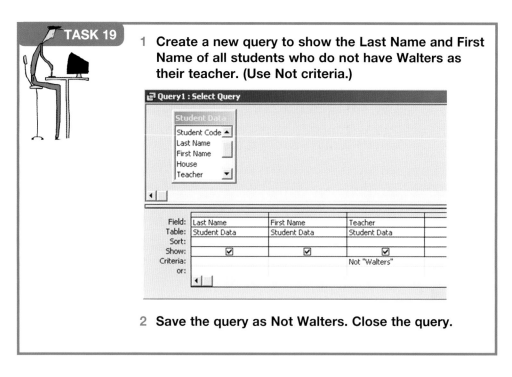

TASK 19

1 **Create a new query to show the Last Name and First Name of all students who do not have Walters as their teacher. (Use Not criteria.)**

2 **Save the query as Not Walters. Close the query.**

Using wildcards in criteria

You can use wildcards when setting criteria. For example, typing C* in the Company Name criterion field would return all companies starting with the letter C. You can also use the wildcard ? to match one character, e.g. b?ll would find ball, bell, bill, etc.

Below is a list of common wildcard characters that you can use when setting criteria for queries:

* matches any number of characters. It can be used as the first or last character in criteria, e.g. **wh*** finds what, white and why.
? matches any single alphabetic character, e.g. **b?ll** finds ball, bell and bill.
[ ] matches any single character within the brackets, e.g. **b[ae]ll** finds ball and bell but not bill.
! matches any character not in the brackets, e.g. **b[!ae]ll** finds bill and bull but not ball or bell.
- specifies a range of characters to match, e.g. **b[a-c]d** finds bad, bbd and bcd.
matches any single numeric character, e.g. **1#3** finds 103, 113 and 123.

You can mix logical operators and wildcards when setting criteria. For example, >D* would return all records beginning with D through to Z.

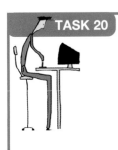

TASK 20

1 **Create a new query to show the Last Name and First Name of all students whose last name begins with B. (Use the * wildcard.)**

2 **Save the query as Last Name = B. Close the query.**

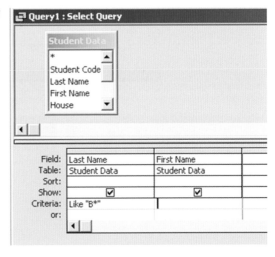

Database reports

If you are using a database that has already been designed, there may already be some reports set up in the database. You would usually just need to click on a button or choose an option in a menu to generate the report.

In the figure below, the database has a form, Update Contacts, and two reports, Monthly Stats Report and Current Contacts Reports. To run these reports, the user would simply click on the appropriate button. The report is produced and shown in Print Preview.

A good database would generally have this type of form (known as a Switchboard) as the front screen. The users of the database don't need to see the database structure, i.e. the tables, forms, queries and reports. They simply click on buttons to get to the different parts of the database that they need access to and to run reports.

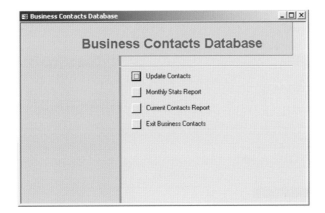

Creating a report

While you can print table and query datasheets, if you wish to present the data you have extracted from the database in a more professional manner, you can create a report.

If the reports have not already been created, you might need to produce them yourself. A report can be based on a table, or on a query that you have created and saved.

Click on the **Reports** link on the left side of the Database window.

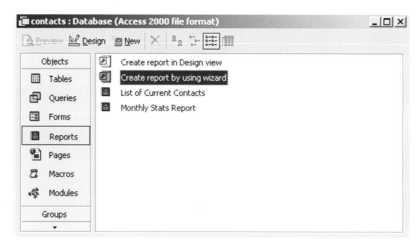

You can create the report by going to Design View or by using the Report Wizard. In the case of reports, it is more efficient to use the Wizard to get started and then you can use Design View to continue working with the report.

Double-click on **Create report by using wizard**. This launches the Report Wizard.

Step 1 of the Wizard asks you to choose which Table or Query to base the report on and the fields that you require on the report. Click on the drop-down arrow in the **Tables/Queries** box and choose the Table or Query that you are basing the report on.

When you have chosen the appropriate Table or Query, the list of **Available Fields** will change to show you the fields in that Table or Query. To use a field, click on it in the list on the left and click on the button to put the field name in the list of **Selected Fields** on the right. Select all the fields you require in the report in this way. (To put all the fields from the **Available Fields** list into the **Selected Fields** list, click on the button.)

Click on **Next**.

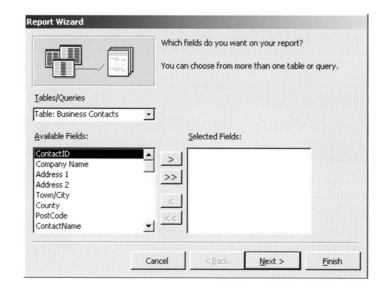

Step 2 of the Wizard asks if you want to add any grouping levels to the report. For example, the report may have been grouped by Company Name. The Company Name becomes a 'subheading' and the detail for that company will be shown underneath the heading.

Click on **Next**.

Step 3 of the Wizard asks if you want to sort by any of the fields in the report. If the report is based on a query, you may have already set sorting options on the fields in the query. These will be reflected in the report.

You can sort by up to four fields in Ascending or Descending order.

Click on **Next**.

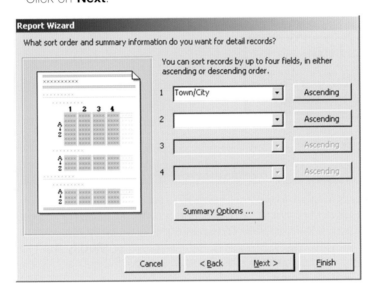

Step 4 of the Wizard asks you to choose a **Layout** for the report. You can also choose the page **Orientation** you require. When you select a Layout, you can see a preview of that layout in the box on the left.

You can also choose to **Adjust the field width so all fields fit on a page**.

Click on **Next**.

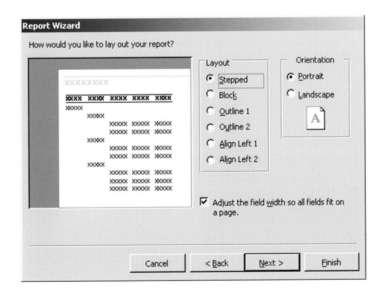

Step 5 of the Wizard asks you to choose a style for your report. You can choose from a range of built-in styles. When you select a Style, you can see a preview of that style in the box on the left. Choose a style by clicking on it in the list.

Click on **Next**.

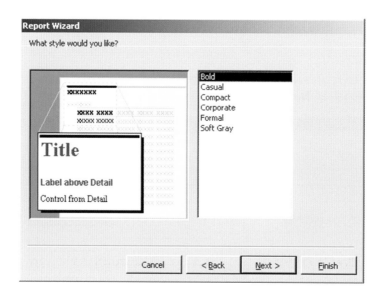

The final step of the Wizard asks you to type a title for the report (this also becomes the filename). You can choose whether you wish to **Preview the report**, which will open the report in Print Preview, or **Modify the report's design**, which will open the report in Design View.

Click on **Finish**.

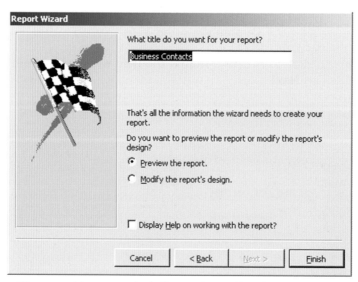

The report is generated. If you chose **Preview the report** then the report opens in Print Preview.

Business Contacts

Company Name	Address 1	Address 2	Town/City	Post Code	Contact Nam	Title	Telephone	Fax No
A D Developments								
	5 London Road	Loughton	Milton Keynes	MK8 0AE	Frank Sheppard	Proprietor	666400	670587
Abbey Cakes Ltd								
	29 Alston Drive	Bradwell Abbey	Milton Keynes	MK13 9HA	K Mott	Director	311622	226128
Adams Cundell Engineers								
	Cosgrove Road	Old Stratford	Milton Keynes	MK19 6LA	M Stockwin	Director	562191	260461
Alfa Electrical								
	10 Iris Walk	Bletchley	Milton Keynes	MK3 7DA	Adrian Ravilious	Proprietor	366778	
Anatric Machine Tools								
	3 Sinclair Court	Bletchley	Milton Keynes	MK1 1RB	C Cheshire	Proprietor	371331	367683
Apex Storage Systems Lt								
	Garamonde Drive	Wymbush	Milton Keynes	MK8 8ND	A C W Parker	Managing Direct	561222	567455
Aspley Guise Golf Club								
	West Hill	Aspley Guise	Milton Keynes	MK17 8DX	M A Beadle	Manager	583596	
Avanti Tiles								
	18 Tower Crescent	Neath Hill	Milton Keynes	MK14 6YJ	C Corbett	Proprietor	232228	232228
Barclays Bank plc								
	9 High Street	Stony Stratford	Milton Keynes	MK11 1HR	Mr D Shelvey	Manager	661616	
Bedford Arms Hotel								
	George Street	Woburn	Milton Keynes	MK17 9PX	N Caccio	Manager	290441	290432

14 July 2004   Page 1 of 3

TASK 21

1. **Create a report using the Report Wizard. Base the report on the Student by Teacher & House query.**

2. **Include all the fields from the query on the report.**

3. **There will be no grouping on the report, but sort by the Last Name field.**

4. **Choose the Columnar layout and Portrait orientation.**

5. **Choose Bold as the Style.**

6. **Give the report the title of 'Student List' and choose to Preview the report.**

Changing the design of a report

If you wish to work with the design of the report, choose **Design View** from the **View** menu or click on the Design View button on the Standard toolbar.

A report has various sections. These sections will vary according to the layout you chose in the Wizard. The report on page 380 has the following sections:

■ **Report Header** – contains the heading for the report and appears once at the top of the first page of the report.

■ **Page Header** – contains the column headings from the table or query and appears at the top of every page of the report.

■ **Company Name Header** – contains the Company Name, because this grouping level was chosen in the Wizard. The Company Name is now like a sub-heading and the detail for that company name appears underneath.

■ **Detail** – contains the detail for each company.

■ **Page Footer** – contains some pre-defined expressions. =**Now()** returns the current date. (This is useful when you print the report.) = **'Page' &[Page] & 'of' & [Pages]** returns the current page number and the total number of pages in the report. You can delete these objects if you do not want them to appear in the report. Information in this section of the report appears at the bottom of every page of the report.

■ **Report Footer** – contains nothing in this case, but information in this section of the report will appear once at the bottom of the last page in the report.

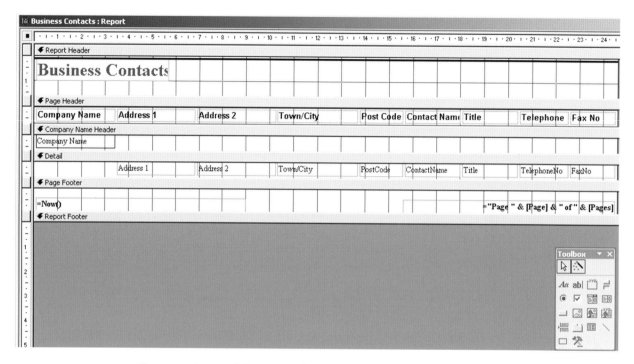

To expand any of these sections, move the mouse over the bottom grey border of the section you wish to work with. The mouse pointer changes to a resizing handle. Click and drag down to resize that section.

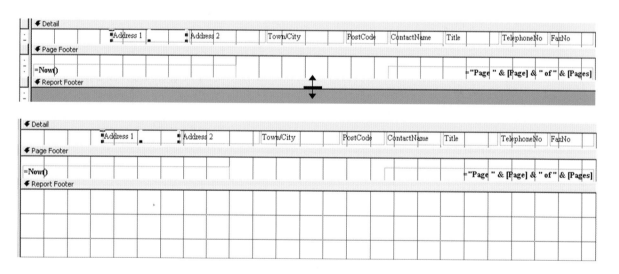

Moving items on the report

To move an item on the report, click on the text box to select it. (The mouse pointer changes to a hand.) Hold down the mouse button and drag the object to its new location.

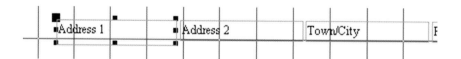

Resizing items on the report

To resize an item on the report, click on the text box to select it. It now has black handles around it. Move the mouse over one of the black handles. The mouse pointer changes to a double-headed arrow. Click and drag the double-headed arrow to enlarge or reduce the size of the item.

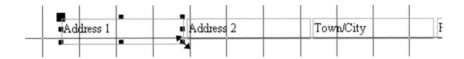

Other options for items on the report

To align more than one item, select all the items that you wish to align. (To select multiple items, hold down Shift on the keyboard as you click on each item.)

Choose **Align** from the **Format** menu and choose the alignment you require: **Left**, **Right**, **Top**, **Bottom**, **To Grid**.

In this example the three selected items have been aligned by their Tops.

To size multiple items, select all the items and choose **Size** from the **Format** menu. Choose the Sizing option you require: **To Fit**, **To Grid**, **To Tallest**, **To Shortest**, **To Widest**, **To Narrowest**.

In this example the three selected items have been sized to the Tallest.

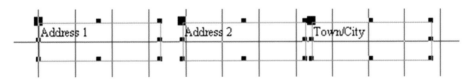

To change the spacing of multiple objects, select all of the objects and choose **Horizontal Spacing** or **Vertical Spacing** from the **Format** menu. Choose the Spacing option you require: **Make Equal**, **Increase**, **Decrease**.

In this example the space between the three selected items has been made equal.

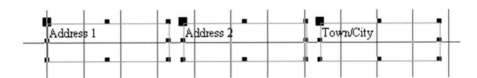

TASK 22

1 Switch to Design View.

2 Move the First Name, Last Name, House and Teacher controls away from their labels.

3 Resize the First Name, Last Name, House and Teacher labels and controls as appropriate. (You can switch back to Preview to view your changes and then switch back to Design view to continue making changes.)

4 Make sure the First Name, Last Name, House and Teacher labels are aligned on their left sides.

5 Make sure the First Name, Last Name, House and Teacher controls are aligned on their left sides.

6 Save the changes you have made to the report design.

Formatting a report

To format an item in the report, select the item by clicking on it.

You can use the buttons on the Formatting toolbar to format the selected item.

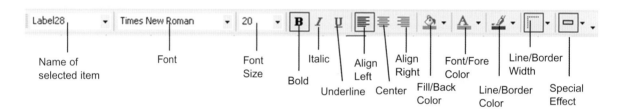

TASK 23

1 Select the First Name, Last Name, House and Teacher labels.

2 Experiment with the buttons on the Formatting toolbar to change the font, size and colour.

3 Experiment with the buttons on the Formatting toolbar to change the box colour, border, width and other special effects.

4 Save the changes you have made to the report design.

Adding page numbers to a report

The Page Footer area contains two expressions by default:

=**Now()** inserts the current date

=**'Page' & [Page] 'of' & [Pages]** inserts the current page number and the total number of pages

You can remove these expressions if you do not want them. Click on the item and press **Delete** on the keyboard.

To insert page numbers, choose **Page Numbers** from the **Insert** menu.

The Page Number dialog box opens.

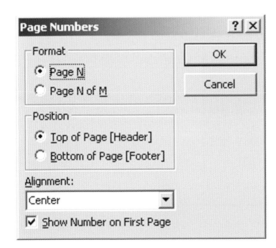

Choose whether you wish to display just the current page number, **Page N**, or the current page number and the total number of pages in the report, **Page N of M**.

Choose where you want the page number, at the **Top of Page [Header]** or at the **Bottom of Page [Footer]**.

Choose the **Alignment** of the page number from the drop-down list: **Left**, **Center** or **Right**. (You can also choose **Inside** and **Outside** for a multi-page report.)

Choose whether you want the page number to display on the first page of the report.

Click on **OK** to apply the changes.

TASK 24

1 **Remove any items in the Page Footer area of the report.**

2 **Insert the Page Number in the centre of the report in the Page Footer area. Make the page number Arial 9 pt.**

3 **Save the changes you have made to the report design.**

Adding page headers and footers to a report

Dependent upon which type of report you have created, the Page Header and Page Footer section may already show in the report design view.

✦ Page Header								
Company Name	Address 1	Address 2	Town/City	Post Code	Contact Name	Title		Telep

✦ Page Footer								
=Now()						="Page " & [Page] & " of " & [Pages]		

If the Page Header and/or Page Footer section is not showing in the design view, choose **Page Header/Footer** from the **View** menu.

For more information about the different sections of a Report, see page 379.

If you wish to type additional text in the page header or page footer area, you need to draw a label. Click on the **Label** button in the **Toolbox**. (If the Toolbox is not switched on, choose **Toolbox** from the **View** menu.)

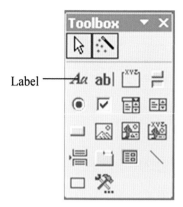

Label

The mouse pointer changes to a crosshair with an **A** attached to it.

Click and drag in the page header or footer area of the report to draw the label.

A

When you release the mouse button, the cursor will appear inside the label. Type the text you require. You can use the buttons on the Formatting toolbar to format the label.

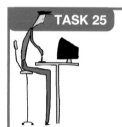

TASK 25

1 **Create a label on the right side of the page footer area and type your name in the label.**

2 **Save the changes you have made to the report design.**

Page Setup

Before you print your report, you can use the Page Setup dialog box to specify page orientation and margins.

Choose **Page Setup** from the **File** menu.

The Page Setup dialog box opens.

This dialog box has three tabs: **Margins, Page** and **Columns**.

On the **Margins** tab you can specify the margins for the page.

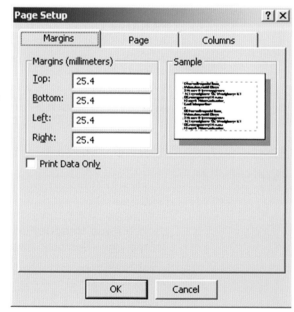

On the Page tab you can specify the page orientation, Portrait or Landscape. You can specify the Paper Size (usually A4) and the Printer to use.

Click on **OK** to make the changes to the page setup.

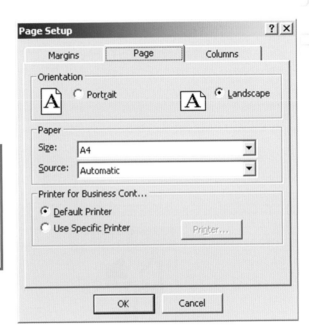

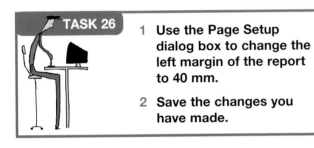

TASK 26

1 **Use the Page Setup dialog box to change the left margin of the report to 40 mm.**

2 **Save the changes you have made.**

Printing the report

Once you have finished working in Design View, you can switch back to Print Preview. Choose **Print Preview** from the **View** menu.

 Alternatively, click on the Print Preview button on the Standard toolbar.

The toolbar in the Print Preview window allows you to view your report prior to printing.

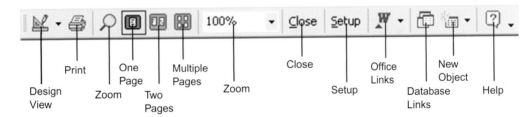

- **Design View** – switch back to Design View.
- **Print** – print the report.
- **Zoom** – zoom between 100% and Fit to window.
- **One Page** – view one page of the report.
- **Two Pages** – view two pages of the report.
- **Multiple Pages** – view multiple pages of the report (up to six).
- **Zoom** – click on the drop-down arrow to choose the zoom percentage.
- **Close** – close the Print Preview window and return to the previous screen.
- **Setup** – open the Page Setup dialog box. (This button is not on the toolbar in Access 2000. Access the Page Setup dialog box from the File menu in Print Preview.)
- **Office Links** – click on the drop-down arrow to choose to export the data in the report to Word or Excel.
- **Database Window** – brings the database container on top.
- **New Object** – click on the drop-down arrow to choose what object you wish to create.
- **Help** – launch Access help.

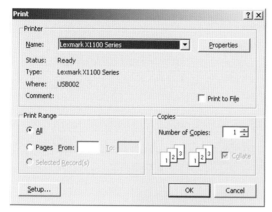

You can print the report straight from the Print Preview window by clicking on the Print button.

If you wish to open the Print dialog box, choose **Print** from the **File** menu.

Choose which printer you want to print to from the **Name** drop-down list.

Choose whether you wish to print **All** of the report or just a page range.

Choose the **Number of Copies** you want to print.

Click on **OK.**

TASK 27   **Print two copies of the report.**

 ## Issues relating to data accuracy

While the spell check facility will find words that are not in the dictionary, it will not find words that are wrong, but are spelt correctly. It is important that the data inputter checks the data they have input for accuracy. A database is only as good as the data it contains and it is the responsibility of anyone who enters data into the database to ensure that the data is accurate.

While setting Data Types and Field Properties for table fields can control data input to some extent, it cannot legislate for careless inputting. If the data in the database is not accurate, records will be missed when searches and queries are carried out.

It is also important that the layout of reports is checked manually. Print Preview provides a useful way of seeing how the report will look when printed.

Open the table or report for which you wish to check the spelling. Choose **Spelling** from the **Tools** menu.

The spell check is launched and stops at the first word that it does not recognise. The Spelling dialog box opens.

Spell checking works in Access in exactly the same way as in Word. (For more information on spell checking and other hints and tips for proofing, see Proofreading Tools in Unit 208 – Word-processing software.)

 ## Improving efficiency

For information on how you can improve efficiency by using buttons and shortcut keys, please refer to Unit 208 – Word-processing software.

Suggested tasks for evidence

All evidence for this unit must be produced in the workplace. The suggested tasks below provide guidance on the type of work that you can produce as evidence for this unit. You may come across one or more of these scenarios in your workplace.

By following the guidelines below, you will have produced a piece of evidence for this unit.

To ensure that your work can be used as evidence towards your ITQ, take screenshots at every stage to show the changes you are making to the database. Appropriate print-outs of tables, queries and reports should also be provided.

Suggested Task 1

You have been asked to set up a database to store some work-related information. Consider the following and then plan and design the database:

- What information needs to be input into the database and what data needs to be extracted?
- What tables and reports should the database contain?
- What fields should each table contain? Consider data types and field properties. Why is it important to set data types and field properties?

Create the tables using appropriate data types and field properties. Create any queries that are required to extract the data and then create reports based on these queries.

Take screenshots and print-outs to show the various stages of design and the finished tables, queries and reports.

Suggested Task 2

Produce a report in Word to discuss the differences between databases and spreadsheets. Include when a spreadsheet would be sufficient to store information and when it might be better to use a database.

unit
211

Website software

Overview

You are likely to be in a role which involves producing multi-page websites (e.g. a website about your organisation, what it does and the products or services offered).

The website software outlined in this chapter is Microsoft® FrontPage®. Microsoft® FrontPage® is part of the Microsoft® Office suite of applications. It offers a comprehensive set of tools for creating and publishing sophisticated websites. It includes templates, layout and graphics tools and the ability to generate Hypertext Markup Language (HTML) code quickly and easily.

Competent people can use website software to produce multi-page websites that combine different types of information. They can plan, format and layout Web pages and use text and images to communicate effectively. They have the knowledge to upload the website to a server and maintain it.

 ## Required skills and techniques for Level 2

Handling files	Using appropriate techniques to handle, organise and save files.
Combining information	Linking information within the same type of software. Adding information from one type of software to information produced using different software, such as a spreadsheet graph to a word-processing document; text to an image file; a picture to a presentation slide; or simple information from a database onto a website.
Planning and producing	Planning and producing simple, multi-page websites and interactive websites: ■ choosing content and features to include ■ planning layout and how the features will be used ■ using appropriate tools and techniques such as bookmarks, hyperlinks and altering simple code.
Editing, formatting and laying out content	Using a wide range of editing and formatting tools to produce content: ■ character, line, paragraph and page formatting ■ resize, align, rotate, flip and arrange images ■ using tables and frames to layout pages.
Checking text	Using proofreading techniques and checking layout.
Checking images	Ensuring images are appropriate – filters, resolution, etc.
Uploading	Using a file exchange programme to upload and publish the website.

 ## Requirements of this unit

You will need to demonstrate skills in the *entire process* of producing a multi-page website. You will need to carry out at least *two* comprehensive tasks to demonstrate that you can produce a fully functioning multi-page website from plan/design stage through to uploading the finished product. You need to provide all notes, sketches, layouts, etc., that you produce, so that the process can be seen at every stage of the development.

You need to demonstrate the ability to produce a website with text and images according to any guidelines given and possibly also create an alternative version of the website, to demonstrate different formats, features, colours and fonts.

Tasks in this unit

The tasks that appear throughout this unit are designed to take you step-by-step through the feature being discussed. It is recommended that you use the tasks completed as evidence in addition to the two main pieces that are required by the unit.

The tasks at the end of the unit are suggested ways in which you could provide the main evidence for this unit.

What will I achieve?

By accomplishing a Level 2 in this unit, you will also have achieved Level 1 in all cases. Below is a table to show what levels you will have achieved.

Required skill	Level 1	Level 2	Level 3
Handling files	●————●		
Combining information	●————●		
Planning and producing	●————●		
Editing, formatting and laying out content	●————●		
Checking text	●————●		
Checking images	●————●		
Uploading	●————●		

What is a website?

A website is a group of related pages that is hosted by an HTTP server on the World Wide Web. The pages in a website generally cover one or more topics and are connected by **hyperlinks**. Most websites have a **home page** as their starting point.

■ The **home page** is the main page of the Website. It usually contains hyperlinks to other pages in the site. It may also contain hyperlinks to other Websites.
■ A **hyperlink** is coloured and underlined text or a graphic that you click on to go to another Web page or another website.

Using FrontPage® to build a website

The templates in FrontPage® enable you to create a website quickly by generating pre-designed pages which already include formatting and design elements. You can create your website online or create it on your own computer and then publish it to the Web server after. Once you have published your website, you can keep it up-to-date easily and quickly by adding or updating pages and importing files.

You can enhance the visual impact of your site by using themes. Themes contain consistent, related visual elements, which give your Website a professional appearance. You can also use drawing objects, graphics and clipart.

In FrontPage® 2002 you can use Link bars, which contain a set of hyperlinks, to make navigating around your website easy for the visitor. You can create search forms so visitors can search your website for specific words or phrases.

 ## Planning a website

It is a good idea to spend some time planning your website, before you actually start creating it in FrontPage®.

Ask yourself why you want a website in the first place. What are you hoping to achieve with the site? Write down your goals so that you can keep referring to them during the design process.

Once you have focused on your goals, you need to think about the structure of the site. When you create a new website using a FrontPage® template, you will be offered a folder structure to use. You can, of course, create new folders within this structure. It is a good idea to keep all the pages related to the website in one location (i.e. a folder or set of folders).

Break your site into different sections and create a sub-folder within the main site folder for each different section. Put all pages relating to a section in the relevant folder. This will make your site easier to maintain and navigate.

Decide where you wish to store images and sounds. It is common to create a folder called 'Images' and then store all the images for a Website in that folder.

It is a good idea to create your website 'offline'. This allows you to create and edit pages and test changes before you upload the files to a Web server.

Next you need to design the 'look' of your site. Plan the design and layout before you begin working in FrontPage®. It is useful to create a 'blueprint' on a sheet of paper to give you an overview of how you want the site to look.

Be consistent in the layout of pages in the site. This gives a professional and related look to the pages in your site. For example, the navigation for the site should be in the same place on each page so that the user can click through the pages in your site without getting confused.

Next you need to think about how visitors will navigate around the site. How will they get from one area to another? Navigation should be consistent throughout the site. Visitors should know where they are in the site at any time and be able to return to the home page easily.

You might want to make use of search features and indexes to help visitors find information on the site. You may also want to consider feedback features so that visitors can contact the people related to the website or in the organisation.

Next you need to gather together all the files you will need for your site, including images, sounds, text, etc. (These are sometimes known as 'assets'.) It is a good idea to get all your files together and store them in appropriate folders in your Web project, so that you can get to them easily when needed for your design.

 ## Launching FrontPage®

FrontPage® can be launched by **double-clicking** on the FrontPage **shortcut** on the desktop (if there is one).

Alternatively, click on **Start**, **Programs** and then choose **Microsoft FrontPage** from the menu. (If you have Windows® XP, it is **Start, All Programs, Microsoft FrontPage**.)

The FrontPage® screen

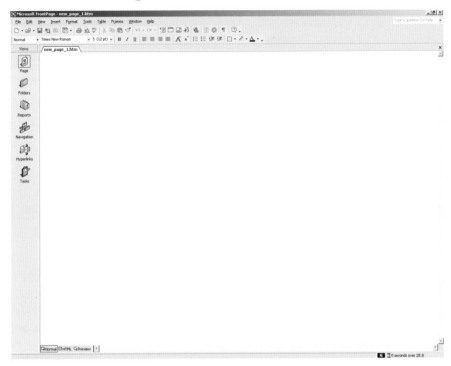

The **Title Bar** across the top of the screen informs you that you are in Microsoft FrontPage and the name of the current file you are working in.

The **Menu Bar** contains menus: **File, Edit, View, Insert, Format, Tools, Table, Frames, Window, Help**. To open a drop-down menu, click on the menu word on the Menu Bar.

Under the Menu Bar are **Toolbars**. These contain buttons which you can use for the more popular features, instead of using the menus.

Down the left side of the screen is the **Views Bar**.

Down the right side of the screen is the vertical scroll bar.

The main part of the screen is taken up by the editing window.

Along the bottom of the editing window is the horizontal scroll bar. At the left end of the horizontal scroll bar are three tabs. Normal is the window you will usually work in. HTML allows you to see the code that is created as you enter information and add elements to your Web page. Preview allows you to see what the Web page will look like when viewed with a browser.

Along the bottom of the screen is the Status Bar. This bar displays information and messages depending on what you have selected.

FrontPage® views

Down the left side of the screen is the Views Bar. When working in FrontPage®, you can use six different views:

- **Page** view – most of the work you do in FrontPage® will be undertaken in this view. You can see all the text, graphics, tables, etc., that you are putting on your web page in a 'WYSIWYG' environment. (WYSIWYG – What You See Is What You Get).
- **Folders** view – the Folders view opens a Windows Explorer-style list of the files and folders that make up the current Web project. You can open, move, rename

Views

Page

Folders

Reports

Navigation

Hyperlinks

Tasks

and delete files in this view. You can also see the title, size and modification date of each page in the Web.

■ **Reports** view – the Reports view shows a list of reports that tell you more about your Web project. It lists the report name, how many items are contained in that report, the size of the files in the report and a description of the contents of the report.

■ **Navigation** view – the Navigation view shows you a Web project's navigational structure. Each icon in the Navigation view represents a page in the Web project.

■ **Hyperlinks** view – the Hyperlinks view displays the relationship between a page and all the Web addresses to which it links, whether they are part of the same Web project or elsewhere on the World Wide Web.

■ **Tasks** view – the Tasks view can be used to create and manage a 'to-do' list of the tasks associated with your Web project. The Tasks view provides a built-in 'project manager' so that you can keep track of progress or collaborate with others.

 # Working with websites

Creating a new website from a template

To start creating your new website from a FrontPage® template, choose **New** from the **File** menu and then choose **Page or Web . . .** from the sub-menu.

The New Page or Web task pane opens down the right side of the screen. Under **New from template**, click on **Website Templates** . . .

The Website Templates dialog box opens.

Click the template you wish to use.

Under **Specify the location of the new web:** type the full path of where you want the new website to be stored on your computer, while you are creating it. (Alternatively, you can click on **Browse** . . . to navigate to the location where you wish to store the site.)

Click on **OK**.

A new website is created in the location (this is usually within My Documents in a folder called My Webs). The new website has the name myweb.

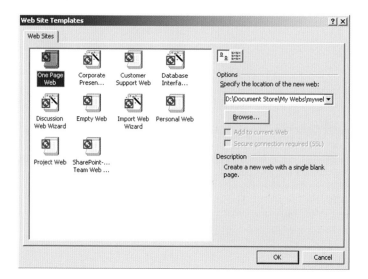

TASK 1   Start a new website using one of the FrontPage®
templates.

Closing a website

Once you have saved the Web pages you have been working on, if you wish to
remove the website project from the screen, you need to close it.

Choose **Close Web** from the **File** menu.

TASK 2   Close the website that is on the screen.

Opening an existing website

You may wish to open a website project that you have already starting working on
and previously saved.

Choose **Open Web** from the **File** menu.

The Open Web dialog box opens.

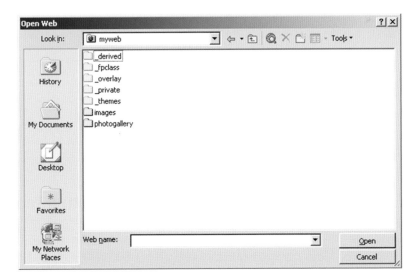

To move into a different folder, double-click on the appropriate folder name.

Use the **Back** or **Up One Level** buttons to move up out of a folder.

Locate the website project you wish to open, click on it and then click on the
Open button at the bottom right of the dialog box. (Alternatively, you can double-
click on the file.)

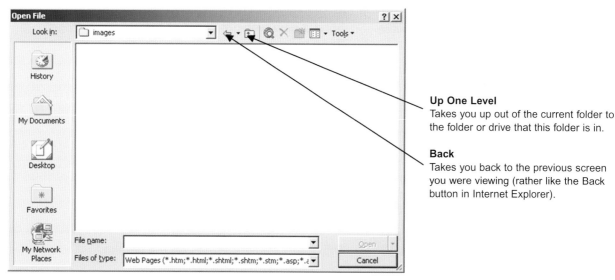

Up One Level
Takes you up out of the current folder to the folder or drive that this folder is in.

Back
Takes you back to the previous screen you were viewing (rather like the Back button in Internet Explorer).

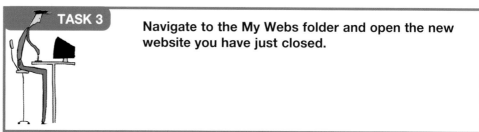

TASK 3

Navigate to the My Webs folder and open the new website you have just closed.

Working with Web pages

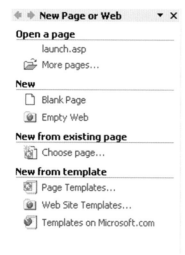

A website is usually made up of a number of pages. Web pages are written in HyperText Markup Language (HTML). FrontPage® provides a range of page templates that you can use to quickly create pages with a variety of layouts.

Alternatively, you can create blank pages and add your own elements, such as text, graphics, page banners, hyperlinks, etc. You can use frames, tables or absolute positioning to place the text and graphics on the page.

You can set the background colour for a page or use a graphic as the background to a page.

Creating a new Web page from a template

Choose **New** from the **File** menu and then choose **Page or Web . . .** from the sub-menu.

The New Page or Web task pane opens down the right side of the screen. Under **New from template**, click on **Page Templates** . . .

The Page Templates dialog box opens.

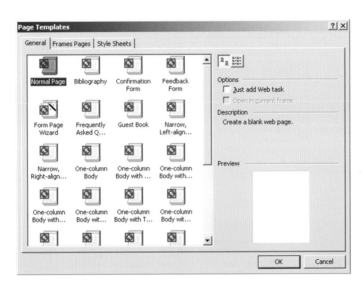

Select the template you wish to use for the new page and click on **OK**.

Creating a new blank Web page

New

If you wish to create a new blank page, choose **New** from the **File** menu and click on **Page or Web** . . . in the sub-menu. In the New Page or Web task pane, click on **Blank Page**.

Alternatively, click the **New** button on the Standard toolbar.

You can also press $\boxed{\text{Control}}$+$\boxed{\text{N}}$

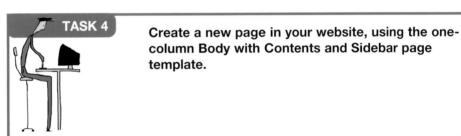

TASK 4

Create a new page in your website, using the one-column Body with Contents and Sidebar page template.

Saving a Web page

Save

Once you have set up the Web page, you can choose where in the project you wish to save it.

Click on the **File** menu and choose **Save**.

Alternatively, click on the **Save** button on the Standard toolbar.

You can also use $\boxed{\text{Control}}$+$\boxed{\text{S}}$

The Save As dialog box opens.

When you create a new website from a template, a folder is created called **myweb**. When you click on Save, you are automatically taken into the **myweb** folder. In this folder there are already a number of sub-folders.

You have to do two things in this dialog box: decide where in the website you want to store the page – at the top level or in one of the sub-folders – and what you want to call the page (File name and Page title).

Double-click on a folder to move into it. Use the **Back** or **Up One Level** buttons to move up out of a folder.

Navigate to the folder that you wish to store the page in.

Type a file name for the page in the File name box. If you wish to change the Page title, click on the **Change title** . . . button.

Type a title for the page. (This will appear in the Title Bar of the browser window.) Click on **OK**.

Once you have moved into the appropriate folder and given the page a file name, click on the **Save** button at the bottom right of the dialog box. Once you have saved the page, the file name of the page appears in the Folder List of your website and on the tab at the top of the page.

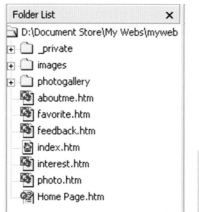

All FrontPage® Web pages are given the file extension .htm. This will help you recognise which of your files are Web pages when you are viewing files in folders.

If you have previously saved the page and then made some changes to it, choosing Save will overwrite the previous version of the page with the newly updated version. (It still has the same name and is stored in the folder that you initially put it in.)

TASK 5

1 Click on the placeholder 'Your Heading Goes Here' and type the heading 'What I do'.

2 Save the Web page in your website with the filename 'what I do.htm'. (Save it at the top level, under myweb.) Also change the Page Title to 'What I Do'.

3 If prompted to save Embedded Files, click on OK. This means any pictures are also saved in your website.

4 Close the Web page (File, Close).

Opening an existing Web page

You may wish to open a Web page file that you have already starting working on and previously saved.

Choose **Open** from the **File** menu.

Alternatively, click on the **Open** button on the Standard toolbar.

You can also use [Control] + [O]

The Open dialog box opens.

Open

Click on the Web page you wish to open and click on the **Open** button at the bottom right of the dialog box. (Alternatively, double-click on the file you wish to open.)

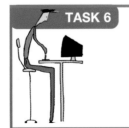

TASK 6

1 Open the What I Do Web page that you previously closed.

2 Change the heading on the page to 'My Friends'.

Using Save As

If you have opened an existing Web page and made changes to it, but you do not wish to overwrite the original file, you can use Save As. You can then give the new version of the Web page a different name or store it in a different folder.

Choose **Save As** from the **File** menu and follow the same steps as for saving a workbook.

TASK 7

Use Save As and save the page as 'my friends.htm'. Also change the Page Title to My Friends.

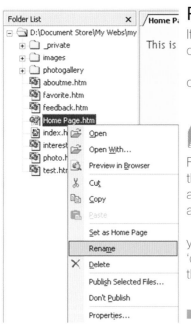

Renaming a Web page

If you change your mind about what you would like the Web page to be called after you have saved it, you can rename it.

Right-click on the page you wish to rename in the Folder List and choose **Rename** from the sub-menu.

Type the new name for the page and press **Return** on the keyboard.

Working with themes

FrontPage® provides 'themes' that you can apply to your websites. A theme is a set of design elements and colour schemes that you can apply to Web pages, to give them a professional look. Using a theme is a very quick and easy way to apply consistent formatting to your pages.

You can apply a theme to individual pages or to an entire website. If you apply a theme to all the pages in a website, it will become the 'default' theme for the site. When you create a new page, the default theme will automatically be applied.

A theme affects three main elements of a page's appearance:

■ **Colours** – a theme applies a colour to body text, headings, hyperlinks, banners, link bar labels, table borders and the page background.
■ **Graphics** – a theme can apply a background picture. It also affects the look of a page banner and any bullets, navigation buttons and horizontal lines on the page.
■ **Styles** – a theme contains fonts, font styles and font sizes.

Customising a theme

You can customise an existing FrontPage® theme to create your own theme. You can change the colours and/or graphics of a theme.

Applying a theme

To apply a theme to the current page, open the page to which you wish to apply the theme. Ensure you are in Page view.

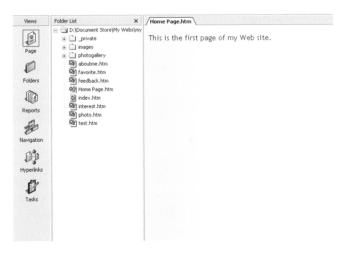

Choose **Theme** from the **Format** menu.
The Themes dialog box opens.

Click on the theme you wish to apply in the list on the left. Click on **OK**.

To apply a theme to more than one page, ensure you are in Folder view and select the pages to which you wish to apply the theme. To select more than one page, hold down **Ctrl** as you click on the pages you wish to select.

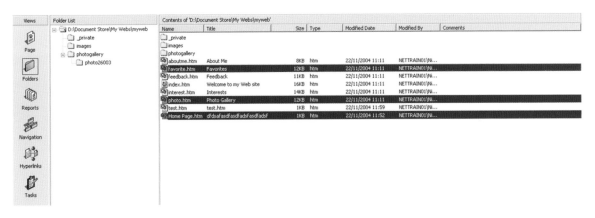

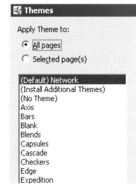

Choose **Theme** from the **Format** menu. Click on **Selected page(s)** at the top of the list of themes on the left side of the dialog box.

Select the theme you want to apply.

To apply a theme to the entire website, choose **Theme** from the **Format** menu.

Click on **All pages** at the top of the list of themes on the left side of the dialog box.

Select the theme you want to apply.

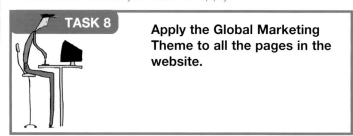

TASK 8

Apply the Global Marketing Theme to all the pages in the website.

Setting other theme options

In the Themes dialog box, you can select other options to set the appearance of the theme:

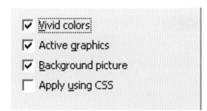

- **Vivid colors** – to use a bright colour, select the Vivid colors check box. To use the normal colour set, clear this box.
- **Active graphics** – to use a more elaborate set of banners, buttons, bullets and other graphical elements, select the Active graphics check box. To use the normal graphic set, clear this box.
- **Background picture** – this box is selected by default. If you do not want to use a background picture for your theme, clear this box.

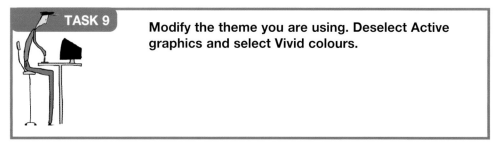

TASK 9

Modify the theme you are using. Deselect Active graphics and select Vivid colours.

Changing the colour scheme of a theme

Choose **Theme** from the **Format** menu. Click on the theme in the list for which you wish to change the colours. Click on the **Modify** button and click on **Colors ...**

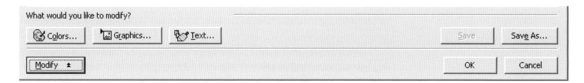

The Modify Theme dialog box opens.

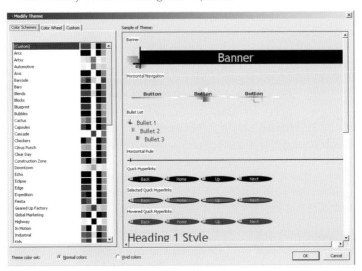

Choose whether you wish to change the colours in the **Normal** or **Vivid colors** set.

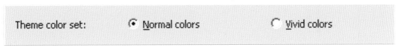

To use a preset colour scheme, click on the **Color Schemes** tab. Select the colour scheme you want to use and click on **OK**.

To create a new colour scheme, click on the Color Wheel tab.

Create the custom colour scheme you want to use and then click on **OK**.

Click on **Save As ...** to save the modified theme. You must give the modified theme a new name to create a new theme. You cannot overwrite a preset theme.

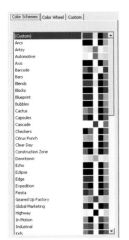

TASK 10

1 Change the colour scheme of the Global Marketing theme. Use the Industrial preset colour scheme.

2 As you cannot overwrite the existing Global Marketing theme, you will be prompted to save the theme with a new name. Call it My Global Marketing.

Removing a theme

To remove a theme from the current page, open the page from which you wish to remove the theme. Ensure you are in Page view.

Choose **Theme** from the **Format** menu. In the Themes dialog box, click on **No Theme** in the list of themes. Click on **OK**.

To remove a theme from more than one page, ensure you are in Folder view and select the pages from which you wish to remove the theme. To select more than one page, hold down **Ctrl** as you click on the pages you wish to select.

Choose **Theme** from the **Format** menu. In the Themes dialog box, make sure **Selected page(s)** is selected and click on **No Theme** in the list of themes. Click on **OK**.

To remove a theme from an entire website, choose **Theme** from the **Format** menu. In the Themes dialog box, make sure **All pages** is selected and click on **No Theme** in the list of themes. Click on **OK**.

TASK 11

Remove the My Global Marketing theme from all pages in the website.

Working with text

You can type text on a Web page just like you would type text in a Word document. You will notice the cursor flashing when you create a new page. Simply start typing.

Formatting text

You can format text on a Web page just like you format text in a Word document. Select the text you want to format and choose **Font** from the **Format** menu.

You can choose a font from the **Font** list. You can choose a **Font style** and a **Size**. You can change the font colour. Click on the drop-down arrow in the **Color** box and choose the colour you want from the palette. You can add other text effects by checking the appropriate boxes.

The Preview at the bottom of the dialog box allows you to see what effect the changes you are making are having on your selected text.

Click on **OK** to apply the changes and close the dialog box. Alternatively, you can format the selected text by using the buttons on the **Formatting** toolbar.

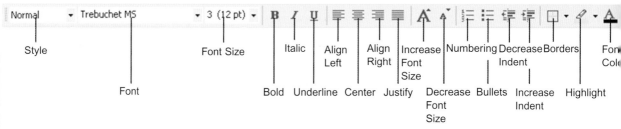

- **Style** – click on the drop-down arrow to choose from a list of styles that you can apply to text.

- **Font** – click on the drop-down arrow to choose from a list of fonts that you can apply to the selected text.

- **Font Size** – click on the drop-down arrow to choose from a list of font sizes that you can apply to the selected text.

- **Bold** – click on the button to apply **bold** formatting to the selected text. (Click on the button again to release it and remove the bold formatting.)

- **Italic** – click on the button to apply *italic* formatting to the selected text. (Click on the button again to release it and remove the italic formatting.)

- **Underline** – click on the button to apply <u>underline</u> formatting to the selected text. (Click on the button again to release it and remove the underline formatting.)

- **Align Left** – aligns the selected text to the left side of the page.

- **Center** – centres the selected text on the page.

- **Align Right** – aligns the selected text to the right side of the page.

- **Justify** – justifies the selected text so that it lines up at the left and right sides of the page.

- **Increase Font Size** – clicking on this button will increase the font size of the selected text in stages.

- **Decrease Font Size** – clicking on this button will decrease the font size of the selected text in stages.

- **Numbering** – applies numbering to the selected text.

- **Bullets** – applies bullets to the selected text.

- **Decrease Indent** – decreases the indent (moves the text back to the left once you have applied an indent).

- **Increase Indent** – moves the text to the right away from the left side of the page.

- **Borders** – applies a border to selected text. Click on the drop-down arrow to open a palette of different borders that you can apply.

- **Highlight** – applies highlighting to selected text. Click on the drop-down arrow to open a palette of different highlight colours that you can use.

- **Font Color** – applies a font colour to selected text. Click on the drop-down arrow to open a palette of different font colours that you can use.

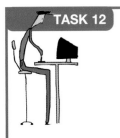

TASK 12

1 **Move to the About Me page. Make sure the Folder List is switched on (View menu) so you can see all the pages in the website.**

2 **Replace the text 'Welcome to my Website!' with 'Welcome to my World!'.**

3 **Change the Font to Verdana and the size to 16 pt. Add Bold and Italic. Centre the heading. Change the font colour to Maroon.**

4 **Save the changes you have made to the page.**

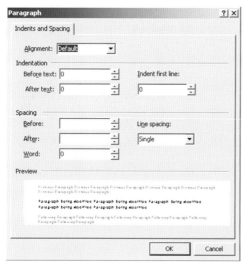

Formatting paragraphs

You can indent paragraphs of text and change the spacing of the lines in the paragraph. If you wish to format one paragraph, put the cursor in that paragraph. If you wish to format more than one paragraph, select the paragraphs that you wish to format.

Choose **Paragraph** from the **Format** menu.

The Paragraph dialog box opens.

You can change the **Alignment** of the text in the selected paragraphs. (You can also use the buttons on the Formatting toolbar to do this.)

You can apply **Indentation** before and after text. You can also choose to **Indent first line** of a paragraph.

You can apply **Spacing Before** or **After** lines in a paragraph. You can also change the **Line spacing** of lines in a paragraph.

Click on **OK** to apply the changes you have made.

 **TASK 13**

1 **On the About Me page, type three paragraphs of text about yourself.**

2 **Change the font to Verdana, 10 pt.**

3 **Fully justify the paragraphs and change the line spacing to 1.5.**

4 **Save the changes you have made to the page.**

Creating bulleted and numbered lists

You can create bulleted or numbered lists on your Web page. You can switch on the bullets or numbers before you start typing, or you can select existing text and apply bullets and numbers to it.

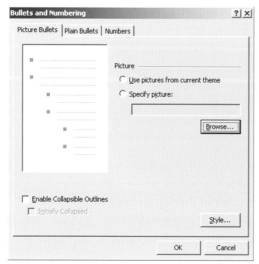

Applying bullets to existing text

Select the text to which you wish to apply bullets. Choose **Bullets and Numbering** from the **Format** menu.

The Bullets and Numbering dialog box opens.

To use picture bullets, click on the **Picture Bullets** tab. Choose **Use pictures from current theme** or **Specify picture** and then click on the **Browse ...** to locate the picture you want to use as the bullet. Click on **OK** to apply the bullets to the selected text.

To use plain bullets, click on the **Plain Bullets** tab.

Click on the bullet style you wish to use and click on **OK**.

If you are using a Theme, the Plain Bullets tab is unavailable.

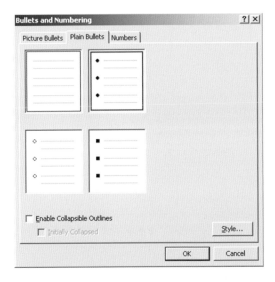

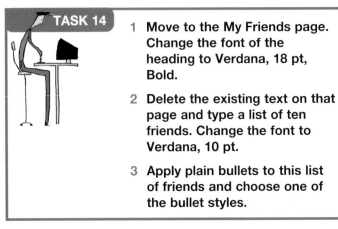

TASK 14

1 Move to the My Friends page. Change the font of the heading to Verdana, 18 pt, Bold.

2 Delete the existing text on that page and type a list of ten friends. Change the font to Verdana, 10 pt.

3 Apply plain bullets to this list of friends and choose one of the bullet styles.

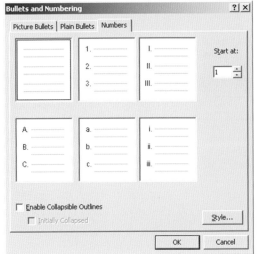

Applying numbering to existing text

Select the text that you wish to apply numbering to. Choose **Bullets and Numbering** from the **Format** menu.

The Bullets and Numbering dialog box opens.

Click on the **Numbers** tab. Choose the Number scheme you wish to use and click on **OK**.

TASK 15

1 Change the bullets in the list of friends to numbers.

2 Use one of the number styles.

3 Now change the numbers to picture bullets. Use a picture you have stored on your computer.

4 Save the changes you have made to the page.

Cut, copy and paste

You can move text on a Web page, or from one Web page to another, just as you would move text in a Word document.

For more information on moving and copying text using cut, copy and paste, see Unit 208 – Word-processing software.

Find and Replace

The Find and Replace feature in FrontPage® works just as it does in Word. You can search for text on a Web page and replace it with other text. For more information on using the Find and Replace feature, see Unit 208 – Word-processing software.

 ## Working with images

You can use graphics on a Web page, not just for decorative purposes, but as navigational buttons. You can use a graphic as the background to a Web page or you can create a graphical banner or a link bar containing graphic navigation buttons. You might want to put a company logo on the Web page or use graphical bullets.

Types of graphic

The most popular type of graphic used on Web pages are GIFs and JPEGs.

Graphics in GIF format can contain up to 256 colours. You can also select one colour to be transparent. Graphics in JPEG format are commonly used for photo-realistic images containing millions of colours. The JPEG format is useful because you can control the size of the file by changing the graphic quality.

Other file formats, such as BMP, TIFF, WMF or EPS can also be used on Web pages. For more information on different graphic file formats, see Unit 208 – Word processing software.

You can also add animated GIFs and videos to Web pages. You can find and download animated GIFs from the Web. You can use videos that can be played by the Windows® Media Player (files in the AVI format).

Adding a graphic to a Web page

Adding an image from a file

In Page view, place the cursor where you want to insert the graphic. Choose **Picture** from the **Insert** menu and choose **From File** from the sub-menu.

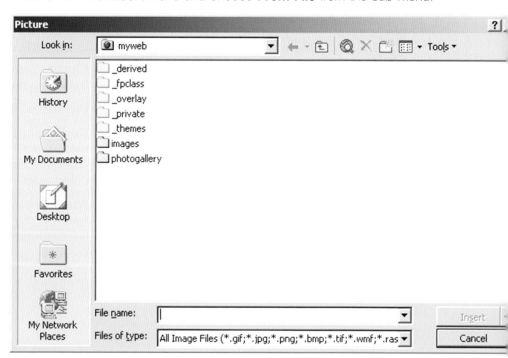

Locate the graphic file you wish to use, select it in the list and click on **Insert**.

When you save the page that contains the graphic, FrontPage® will prompt you to save the graphic to your website. Graphics with less than 256 colours are automatically converted to GIF format. All other graphics are converted to JPEG format.

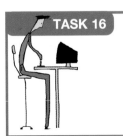

TASK 16

Move to the About Me page and insert a picture (photograph) that you have stored on your computer at the bottom of the paragraphs of text.

Adding an image from the Microsoft® Clip Gallery

In Page view, place the cursor where you want to insert the graphic. Choose **Picture** from the **Insert** menu and choose **Clip Art** from the sub-menu.

The **Insert Clip Art** task pane appears down the right side of the screen. You can search for an appropriate clip art by typing keywords in the **Search text** box. Click on **Search** and clips that contain your keywords will be shown in the task pane.

If the keyword 'symbols' is typed into the **Search text** box, it returns the images on the left. Click on a clip to insert it into your document.

Alternatively, you can click on the **Clip Organizer** link at the bottom of the task pane.

Modify

See also

Clip Organizer...

Clips Online

The Microsoft Clip Organizer dialog box opens.

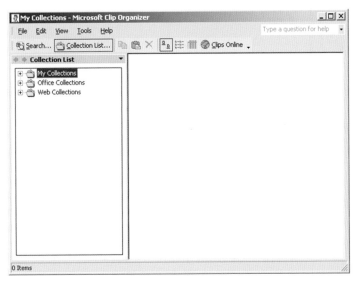

To view the categories of clips that are available in each folder, click on the + icon beside the folder you wish to view. For example, to view the categories in the Office Collections folder, click on the + icon to the left of the folder name.

To view the clips in a category, click on the category name in the list on the left. The clips in that category will show on the right side of the screen. (If there is a + icon beside a category name, that indicates that there are more sub-categories under the main category. Click on the + icon to see the sub-categories. Click on the category to view the clips in it.)

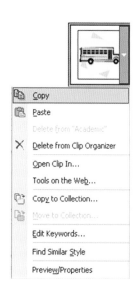

To insert a clip from the Clip Organizer, point to the clip that you wish to insert and click on the drop-down arrow that appears.

Choose **Copy** from the shortcut menu

Click in your document and press the **Paste** button on the Standard toolbar, choose **Paste** from the **Edit** menu, use [Control]+[V] or right-click and choose **Paste** from the shortcut menu.

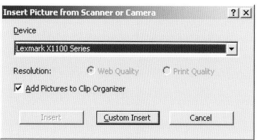

TASK 17

Move to the My Friends page and insert a picture from the Clip Gallery at the bottom of the list of friends.

Adding an image from a scanner or digital camera

In Page view, place the cursor where you want to insert the graphic. Choose **Picture** from the **Insert** menu and choose **From Scanner or Camera** from the sub-menu. Select the **Device** from where you are adding the graphic from the drop-down list.

Depending what type of device you have chosen, choose the **Resolution**. If you want to be able to access the picture easily again, check the **Add Pictures to Clip Organizer** box.

Click on **Insert** or **Custom Insert** and follow the instructions for your specific device.

Using the Pictures tool bar

If you want to work with the graphics you have placed onto the Web page, you will find it useful to use the Pictures toolbar. To switch on the Pictures toolbar, choose **Toolbars** from the **View** menu and click on **Pictures**.

Resizing a graphic

Click on the graphic you wish to resize. The graphic now has black squares around it. (These are selection handles.) Move the mouse over one of the black squares and the mouse pointer changes to a double-headed arrow. Click and drag to resize the graphic.

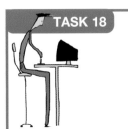

TASK 18

1 **Select the graphic you have inserted onto the About Me page and make it smaller.**

2 **Select the graphic you have inserted onto the My Friends page and make it smaller.**

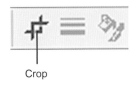

Crop

Cropping a graphic

Select the graphic that you wish to crop and click on the Crop button on the Pictures toolbar.

A cropping box appears on the graphic. (It looks like a box with a dashed border.) When you move the mouse over any of the squares around the edge of the cropping box, the mouse pointer changes to a double-headed arrow. Click and drag with the mouse to resize the cropping box so you can see the part of the picture you want to keep. Click on the Crop button on the toolbar again to remove the area outside of the cropping box.

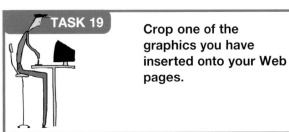

TASK 19

Crop one of the graphics you have inserted onto your Web pages.

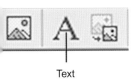

Text

Adding text to a graphic

Select the graphic to which you wish to add text. Click on the Text button on the Pictures toolbar.

If the graphic is a JPEG, you will receive a message informing you that the picture will need to be converted to a GIF. When the file is converted to a GIF, the number of colours in the graphic might be reduced and the file might become larger.

Type the text into the box that appears on the graphic. You can format the text in the box just as you would text on the Web page.

To move the text box on the graphic, click inside the box and drag it to a new location.

To resize the text box, click onto a resizing handle and drag to make the text box larger or smaller.

TASK 20

1 **Go to the My Friends page and type some text on the graphic you have inserted.**

2 **Format the text you have just typed and move and resize the text box.**

Changing the brightness and contrast of a graphic

Select the graphic that you wish to change. If you want to change the contrast of the graphic, click on More Contrast or Less Contrast on the Pictures toolbar. If you want to adjust the brightness of the graphic, click on More Brightness or Less Brightness on the Pictures toolbar.

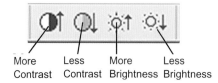

More Contrast   Less Contrast   More Brightness   Less Brightness

1 **Move to the About Me page and select the photograph you have inserted.**

2 **Adjust the brightness and contrast of the photograph.**

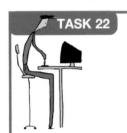

Applying a grayscale or washed out effect to a graphic

Select the graphic that you wish to change. Click on the Color button on the Pictures toolbar.

Choose Grayscale or Wash Out from the drop-down menu.

TASK 22

1 **Go to the My Friends page and select the graphic you have inserted.**

2 **Apply the Wash Out effect to the graphic.**

Rotating and flipping a graphic

Select the graphic that you wish to rotate or flip. Click the appropriate button on the Pictures toolbar.

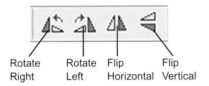

| Rotate | Rotate | Flip | Flip |
| Right | Left | Horizontal | Vertical |

- **Rotate Right** – rotates the selected graphic right through a 45° angle.
- **Rotate Left** – rotates the selected graphic left through a 45° angle.
- **Flip Horizontal** – flips the selected graphic through a horizontal axis (to produce a mirror image).
- **Flip Vertical** – flips the selected graphic through a vertical axis (to produce a mirror image).

TASK 23

1 **Move to the About Me page and rotate the photograph so that it is on its side.**

2 **Move to the My Friends page and flip the graphic so that it is facing the other way.**

 ## Page formatting

Using a graphic as a page background

Choose **Background** from the **Format** menu.

The Page Properties dialog box opens.

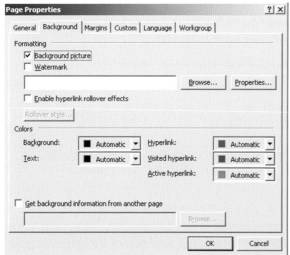

Click on the **Background** tab and check the **Background picture** box. Click on the **Browse ...** button to locate the picture you wish to use as the background of the page.

Locate the file, click on it and click on **Open**.

If you want the picture to be a watermark on the background of the page, check the **Watermark** box in the Page Properties dialog box.

TASK 24

1 Move to the What I do page and delete the existing text on the page.

2 Insert a graphic as the page background. Make the graphic a watermark.

3 Save the changes you have made to the page.

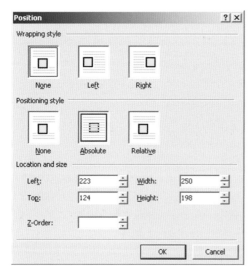

Positioning elements on the page

Select the element on the page to which you wish to apply absolute positioning. Choose **Position** from the **Format** menu. The Position dialog box opens.

Choose the **Wrapping style** and **Positioning** style you require for the selected element.

You can move and resize a page element using the mouse or you can specify measurements under **Location and size** in the Position dialog box.

Click on **OK** to apply your changes.

TASK 25

1 Move to the About Me page and move the picture so that it is on top of the text on the page.

2 Change the text wrapping so that it wraps around the right side of the picture.

 ## Working with tables

A table can be used on a Web page to present information. Just like a Word table, the table is made up of rows and columns of cells into which you can insert text and graphics.

You can use a table to present information in a grid-like format, such as a timetable. You can also use tables to assist you in laying out the text and graphics on a Web page.

Insert a table on a page

Place the cursor where you want to insert the table. Choose **Insert** from the **Table** menu and click on **Table** in the sub-menu.

The Insert Table dialog box opens.

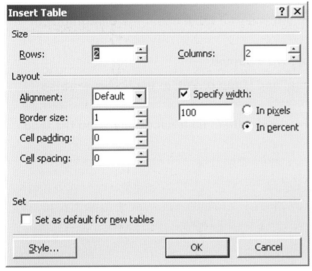

Specify the number of rows you require in the **Rows** box. Specify the number of columns you require in the **Columns** box. You can choose the position of the table on the page in the **Alignment** box. You can specify the width you want for the table border in the **Border size** box. (If you do not want a border, type 0.) You can also specify the **Cell padding** (the space between the cell border and its contents) and the **Cell spacing** (the space between cells). You can specify the width of the table in pixels or as a percentage of the screen width.

You can create a simple table by specifying only the number of rows and columns you require. Default properties are used for the table.

Alternatively, you can click on the Insert Table button on the Standard toolbar and drag with the mouse to highlight the number of rows and columns you require.

2 by 3 Table

A table will be inserted with the number of rows and columns you have specified. The other table properties will be set to default values.

Drawing a table on a page

Choose **Draw Table** from the **Table** menu.

The Tables toolbar appears with the first button selected. The mouse has changed to a 'pencil' icon.

Draw the outside border of the table by clicking and dragging with the mouse, as if you had a pencil in your hand. To make cells, draw vertical and horizontal lines within the table.

If you draw a line and then decide you don't want it, click on the Eraser button on the Tables toolbar. The mouse pointer changes to an 'eraser' icon. Drag over the line with the mouse to erase the line.

Once you have finished drawing the table, click on the Draw Table button on the Tables toolbar to switch off the 'pencil' icon.

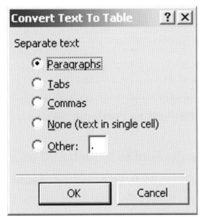

Converting existing text to a table

Select the text that you want to convert into a table. You need to separate the text using commas or tabs before converting it to a table.

Choose **Convert** from the **Table** menu and click on **Text To Table** in the sub-menu.

The Convert Text To Table dialog box opens.

Specify the character that is currently being used to separate the text. If you choose None, a one-cell table will be created with all the text in that one cell. Click on **OK**.

TASK 26

1 Move to the About Me page and insert a table under the paragraphs of text.

2 Make the table four rows by two columns.

3 Type the headings 'Pet Name' and 'Type of Pet' in the first row of the table.

4 Type the names of three pets (make them up if necessary!) and the type of pet they are.

Selecting parts of a table

To select the entire table, click anywhere in the table you wish to select. Choose **Select** from the **Table** menu and then choose **Table** from the sub-menu.

To select a cell in the table, click in the cell you wish to select. Choose **Select** from the **Table** menu and then choose **Cell** from the sub-menu. To select multiple cells, follow the procedure above to select the first cell, hold down **CTRL** and click to select each additional cell.

To select a row in the table, click in the row you wish to select. Choose **Select** from the **Table** menu and then choose **Row** from the sub-menu.

Alternatively, you can move the mouse to the left end of the row you wish to select. The mouse pointer changes to a black arrow pointing towards the row. Click to select the row.

To select more than one row, click and drag up or down with the black arrow.

To select a column in the table, click in the column you wish to select. Choose **Select** from the **Table** menu and then choose **Column** from the sub-menu.

Alternatively, you can move the mouse to the top of the column you wish to select. The mouse pointer changes to a black arrow pointing towards the column. Click to select the column.

To select more than one column, click and drag right or left with the black arrow.

TASK 27

1 Select the first row of the table and change the Font to Verdana, 10 pt, Bold.

2 Select the other rows in the table and change the Font to Verdana, 10 pt.

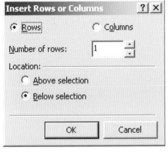

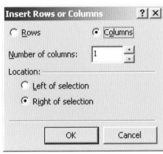

Inserting rows and columns

To insert a cell into the table, place the cursor in the cell to the right of where you want to insert a cell. Choose **Insert** from the **Table** menu and click on **Cell** in the sub-menu.

To insert a row into the table, place the cursor where you wish to insert the row. Choose **Insert** from the **Table** menu and click on **Rows or Columns** in the sub-menu.

Select **Rows** and type the **Number of rows** you wish to insert. Under **Location** specify where you want to insert them – **Above selection** or **Below selection**. Click on **OK**.

To insert a column into the table, place the cursor where you wish to insert the column. Choose **Insert** from the **Table** menu and click on **Rows or Columns** in the sub-menu.

Select **Columns** and type the **Number of columns** you wish to insert. Under **Location** specify where you want to insert them – **Left of selection** or **Right of selection**. Click on **OK**.

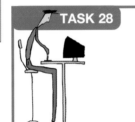

TASK 28

1 **Insert a row above the last row of the table and type the details for another pet.**

2 **Insert a column after the last column and type the heading 'Age of Pet'. Type the ages of the pets.**

Deleting rows and columns

To delete a cell in the table, select the cell in the table that you wish to delete. Right-click and choose **Delete Cells** from the shortcut menu.

To delete a row or column in the table, select the row or column that you wish to delete. Right-click and choose **Delete Cells** from the shortcut menu.

To delete the entire table, select the table that you wish to delete. Right-click and choose **Delete Cells** from the shortcut menu.

Making columns and/or rows the same size

Select the columns or rows that you want to make the same size.

Right-click and choose **Distribute Rows Evenly** or **Distribute Columns Evenly** from the shortcut menu.

TASK 29

Make the columns in the table the same size.

Resizing parts of a table

To resize a table, right-click on the Table and choose **Table Properties** from the shortcut menu. For more information on Table Properties, see page 417.

To resize a cell, row or column, select the cell, row or column you wish to resize. Right-click and choose **Cell Properties** from the shortcut menu.

The Cell Properties dialog box opens.

Cell Properties

Layout

Horizontal alignment:	Default	☑ Specify width:
Vertical alignment:	Default	25 ○ In pixels ● In percent
Rows spanned:	1	☑ Specify height:
Columns spanned:	1	22 ● In pixels ○ In percent

☐ Header cell
☐ No wrap

Borders

Color: [dropdown]   Light border: ■ Automatic
                     Dark border: ■ Automatic

Background

Color: ■ Automatic
☐ Use background picture

[Browse...] [Properties...]

[Style...]   [OK] [Cancel] [Apply]

Specify the width or height in pixels or as a percentage of the screen size.

Other cell properties

You can change the **Horizontal alignment** and **Vertical alignment** of the contents of selected cells. Choose the alignment you require from the drop-down lists. (Left, Right, Center or Justify for Horizontal and Top, Middle, Baseline or Bottom for Vertical.)

You can adjust the width of columns or the height of rows by specifying how many columns or rows they should span. In the **Layout** section of the Cell Properties dialog box, specify the number of rows or columns you want the selected rows or columns in the table to span in the **Rows spanned** or **Columns spanned** box.

To emphasise cells in the table, you can make them header cells. Select the cells in the table to which you wish to apply this formatting and check the **Header cell** box in the Cell Properties dialog box.

To prevent text wrapping in its cell, check the **No wrap** box in the **Layout** section of the Cell Properties dialog box.

To apply borders to cells, select the cell or cells to which you wish to apply the border. Right-click and choose **Cell Properties** from the shortcut menu.

To set a one-colour border, in the **Borders** section, choose a **Color** from the drop-down palette.

To set a two-colour border, in the **Borders** section, choose a **Light border** colour from the drop-down palette and a **Dark border** colour from the drop-down palette.

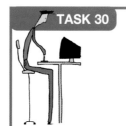

TASK 30

1 **Centre the text in the cells.**

2 **Put a border around the cells.**

3 **Apply a background colour to the cells.**

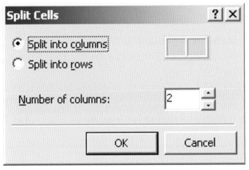

Splitting and merging table cells

To split a cell into more than one row or column, right-click on the cell you want to split and choose **Split Cells** from the shortcut menu.

Choose whether you wish to split the cell into columns or rows. Specify the number of columns or rows you want to split the cell into. Click on **OK**.

To merge more than one cell to make a larger cell, select the cells that you wish to merge. Right-click and choose **Merge Cells** from the shortcut menu. The selected cells are merged into one cell.

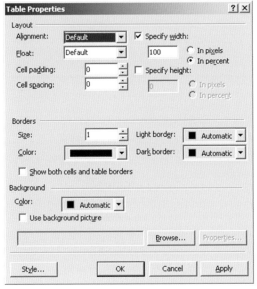

Table properties

Right-click on the table and choose **Properties** from the shortcut menu.

The Table Properties dialog box opens.

Layout

- You can choose the **Alignment** of the table on the page – **Left**, **Right** or **Center**.
- You can choose how text should flow around the table from the **Float** drop-down list – **Left** or **Right**. If you don't want text to flow around the table, choose **Default**.
- To change the space between a cell border and its contents, type a number in the **Cell padding** box.
- To change the space between the table cells, type a number in the **Cell spacing** box.
- To specify the width of the table, in pixels or as a percentage of the screen width, check the **Specify width** box and type a number in the box. (Select **In pixels** or **In percent**.)
- To specify the height of the table, in pixels or as a percentage of the screen depth, check the **Specify height** box and type a number in the box. (Select **In pixels** or **In percent**.)

Note: If a table is sized in pixels, its size will remain the same, regardless of the size of the page. If a table is sized as a percentage of the browser window, its size changes depending on the size of the window. If height or width is not specified, the table is sized according to its contents.

Borders

In the Borders section of the Table Properties dialog box, you can specify the **Size** width of the table border in pixels. If you do not want a border, type 0 in this box.

To set a one-colour border for the table, select a colour from the **Color** drop-down palette.

To set a two-colour border for the table, select a colour from the **Light border** drop-down palette and a colour from the **Dark border** drop-down palette.

If you wish the colours to apply to cell borders as well as the table border, check the **Show both cells and table borders** box.

Background

In the Background section of the Table Properties dialog box, you can specify a background colour for the table. Choose a colour from the **Color** drop-down palette.

Color: ■ Automatic ▼
☑ Use background picture
[   ] Browse... Properties...

Alternatively, you can use a picture for the background of the table.

Check the **Use background picture** box in the Table Properties dialog box and click on the **Browse...** button to locate the picture you wish to use.

Locate the picture you wish to use, click on it and click on **Open**.

Click on **OK** to apply changes you have made in the Table Properties dialog box.

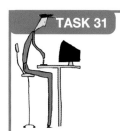

TASK 31

Put a border around the edge of the table.

Working with frames

Frames are another way of laying out content for when it is viewed in a browser window. A frames page divides the browser window into different areas, each of which can show a different page.

The frames page itself does not contain anything – it is just a container that specifies which pages show. For example, if you click a hyperlink in one frame, the page pointed to by that hyperlink can open in another frame (known as the target frame).

Frames are often used for catalogues or lists of items. When you click on a hyperlink in one frame, the item itself shows on a page in another frame.

FrontPage® provides a range of frames page templates. By using these templates, the navigation between the frames is already set up. You simply set the initial page that you want shown in each frame.

You can split, resize and delete frames on a page. You can also control space between frames, margins inside frames, whether or not a frame can be resized in the browser and whether or not scroll bars will be available in the frame.

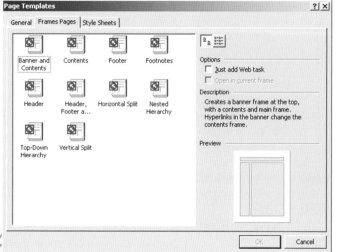

Creating a frames page

Choose **New** from the **File** menu and click on **Page or Web ...** in the sub-menu.

The New Page or Web task pane opens down the right side of the screen. Choose **Page Templates** under **New from template**. The Page Templates dialog box opens.

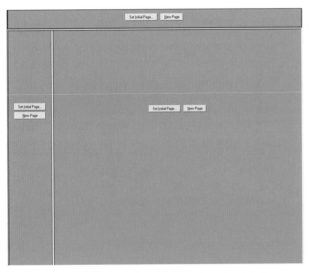

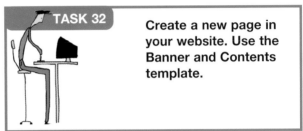

Click on the **Frames Pages** tab. Select the template you want to use and click on **OK**.

The example left shows the Banner and Contents frames page template.

TASK 32

Create a new page in your website. Use the Banner and Contents template.

Setting the initial page

Click on **Set Initial Page ...** in the frame whose initial page you want to set. The Insert Hyperlink dialog box opens.

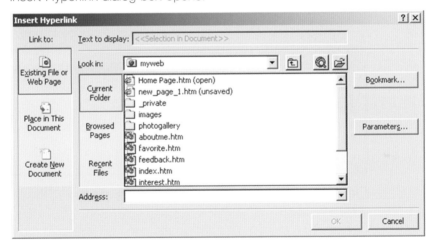

Select the page from the **Current Folder** that you wish to set as the initial page. (If the page you want to use is not in the Current Folder, navigate to the folder that it is stored in.) Click on **OK**.

TASK 33

Set the Initial Page for the Banner area (the top frame). Choose About Me as the page to display in that frame.

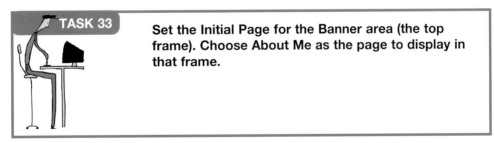

Saving a frames page

To save the frames page that holds the content, choose **Save As** from the **File** menu.

The Save As dialog box shows the layout of the frames page with a heavy blue border around the edge. This indicates that you are saving the frames page, not the individual pages within it.

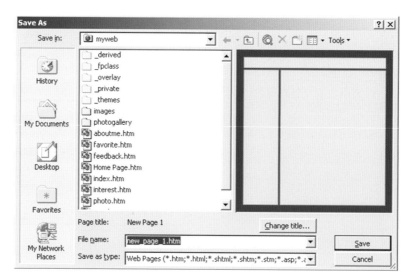

Type a name for the page in the **File name** box. If you want to change the page title, click on **Change title ...** and type the new page title. Navigate to where you want to store the frames page and click on **Save**.

When you click on Save, you will be prompted to save each of the pages shown in the frame.

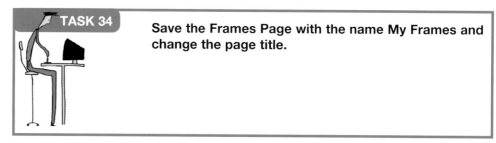

TASK 34

Save the Frames Page with the name My Frames and change the page title.

Deleting a frame from a frames page

When you delete a frame from a frames page, the page shown in that frame is deleted. The remaining frames on the page expand to fill the space.

Click in the frame you want to delete. Choose **Delete Frame** from the **Frames** menu.

If the frames page contains only one frame, you cannot delete it.

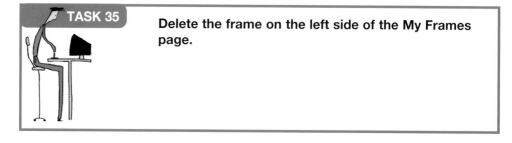

TASK 35

Delete the frame on the left side of the My Frames page.

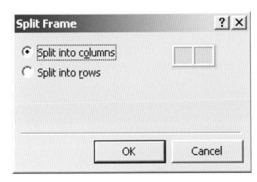

Splitting a frame

Drag any frame border while holding down **CTRL** or click in the frame you want to split and choose **Split Frame** from the **Frames** menu.

Choose whether you wish to split the frame into columns or rows and specify the number of columns or rows. Click on **OK**. (This will split the frame into evenly sized rows or columns.)

When you split a frame, the content stays in the original frame and a new frame is created.

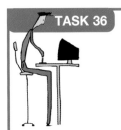

TASK 36

Split the large frame on the My Frames page into two columns.

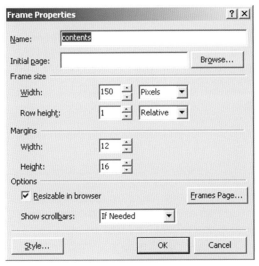

Resizing a frame

You can resize a frame by simply dragging its borders. Move the mouse over a frame border and it changes to a double-headed black arrow. Click and drag to resize the frame.

Alternatively, you can use Frame Properties to specify the measurement of the frame. Right-click in the frame you wish to resize and choose **Frame Properties** from the shortcut menu.

Under **Frame size**, specify the **Width** and **Row height** of the frame. (You can specify the sizes in pixels or as a percentage of the browser window. You can also size the frame relative to other frames in the same row or column.)

TASK 37

1 **Resize the frame on the left by dragging its right border to the right.**

2 **Resize the frame on the right using Frame Properties. Specify the width as 40.**

Setting other frame properties

In the **Options** section of the Frame Properties dialog box, click on the **Frames Page ...** button.

To display or hide the borders around a frame, check or uncheck the **Show Borders** box. Click on **OK**. When you switch on borders, they will appear around all the frames on the page.

Specify the amount of spacing (in pixels) in the **Frame spacing** box. Click on **OK**.

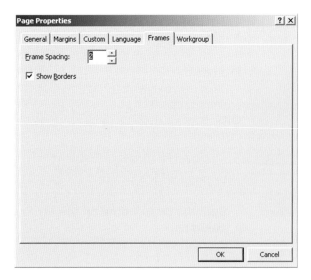

To create invisible frames, clear the **Show borders** check box and set the **Frame spacing** to 0.

To adjust the margins of a frame, click on the **Margins** tab and specify the **Width** and **Height**.

To show or hide scrollbars in a frame, go to the Options section of the Frame Properties dialog box and choose the scrollbars option you require (If Needed, Never or Always) from the **Show scrollbars** drop-down list.

Working with hyperlinks

Once you have created the individual pages in your website, you need a way that a visitor can navigate around the different pages. You create hyperlinks on the pages that can be clicked to go to another part of the page, another page or even another website.

You can create hyperlinks that navigate to an existing file on a network or to a Web page on an intranet or the Internet. You can create hyperlinks that navigate to a file or a Web page that you plan to create in the future. You can create a hyperlink that launches an e-mail editor, so the user can send an e-mail, or that starts a file download.

A hyperlink can be placed on text or a graphic. When the visitor points to a hyperlink, the mouse pointer becomes a hand with a finger pointing. This indicates that this item can be clicked on to hyperlink to somewhere else.

A Web browser will usually underline text hyperlinks and display them in a different colour (usually blue for an unused hyperlink).

If a hyperlink is placed on a picture, there are two options: the entire picture can be a hyperlink – the visitor can click on any part of the picture – or the picture can have 'hotspots'. The picture may have more than one hotspot and the visitor clicks on the appropriate hotspot to go to the destination linked to that hotspot.

Creating a hyperlink
Linking to an existing Web page or a file

Select the text or picture to which you wish to assign the hyperlink. Choose **Hyperlink** from the **Insert** menu.

Alternatively, click on the **Insert Hyperlink** button on the Standard toolbar.

You can also press `Control` + `K`

The Insert Hyperlink dialog box opens.

Insert Hyperlink

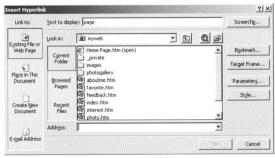

Click on **Existing File or Web Page** in the **Link to** list. Select the page or file you want to link to from the list. (If the page or file is in a different folder, navigate to that folder by clicking on the drop-down list by **Look in:**.) Click on **OK**.

Linking to a page that does not yet exist

Select the text or picture to which you wish to assign the hyperlink and select **Insert, Hyperlink**, click on the **Insert Hyperlink** button or press [Control]+[K].

Click on **Create New Document** in the **Link to** list in the Insert Hyperlink dialog box. Type the name of the new document and choose whether you want to **Edit the new document later** or **Edit the new document now**. Click on **OK**.

Linking to a page or file on the Web

Select the text or picture to which you wish to assign the hyperlink and open the Insert Hyperlink dialog box.

Click on **Existing File or Web Page** in the **Link to** list. Click on the **Browse the Web** button.

In the Web browser, navigate to the page to which you want to link and then press [Alt]+[Tab] on the keyboard to switch back to FrontPage®. The location of the page is displayed in the **Address** box in the Insert Hyperlink dialog box.

Click on **OK**.

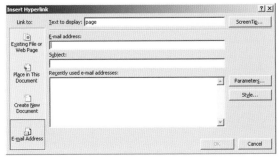

Linking to an e-mail address

Select the text or picture to which you wish to assign the hyperlink and open the Insert Hyperlink dialog box.

Click on **E-mail Address** in the **Link to** list. Type the address in the **E-mail address** box or select an address from the **Recently used e-mail addresses** list. Type the subject of the e-mail message in the **Subject** box. Click on **OK**.

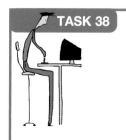

TASK 38

1 Move the About Me page in your website. Select a word on the page and create a hyperlink to jump to the What I do page.

2 Create a hyperlink on the graphic on that page to jump to the My Friends page.

3 Move to the My Friends page and create a hyperlink on that page that links to another website on the Web.

4 Click on the What I do page and create a hyperlink that opens an e-mail message window. The e-mail address should be info@aboutme.co.uk. The Subject line should be 'More information please'.

5 Save the changes.

Using bookmarks

You can create a bookmark on a page by selecting and marking specific text. You can then use the bookmark as the location for a hyperlink. Rather than a visitor being taken to the top of a page when they click on a hyperlink, they can be taken to a specific place on the page (marked by the bookmark).

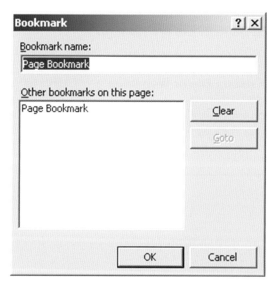

Creating a bookmark

Place the cursor where you want to create the bookmark (or select the text that you want to assign to the bookmark). Choose **Bookmark** from the **Insert** menu. The Bookmark dialog box opens.

Type a name for the bookmark and click on **OK**. (If you selected text to bookmark, the text is displayed with a dashed underline.)

Creating a hyperlink to a bookmark

Select the text or picture to which you wish to assign the hyperlink and open the Insert Hyperlink dialog box.

Click on **Place in This Document** in the **Link to** list. All the bookmarks are listed. Click on the bookmark you want to use and then click on **OK**.

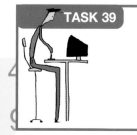

TASK 39

1 Move to the About Me page in your website.

2 Create a bookmark on a word in the last paragraph on that page.

3 Create a hyperlink from the My Friends page that takes you to the bookmarked text.

6

7

Setting colours for hyperlinks

You can specify the colours that a Web browser will use to display hyperlinks. You can set three colours for a hyperlink:

■ Hyperlink – a colour for a hyperlink that has not been followed (i.e. is not in the temporary Internet files folder).
■ Active hyperlink – a colour for a hyperlink that is currently selected (i.e. the cursor is over it).
■ Visited hyperlink – a colour for a hyperlink that has been followed (i.e. is in the temporary Internet files folder).

Right-click on the page and choose **Page Properties** from the shortcut menu. The Page Properties dialog box opens.

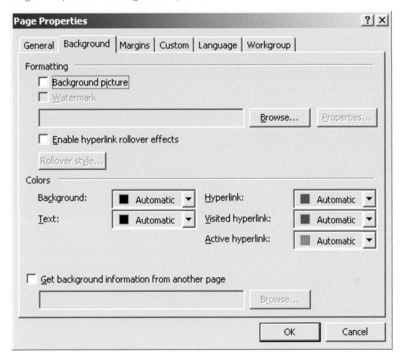

Click on the **Background** tab. Choose a colour from the drop-down palette for **Hyperlink**, **Visited hyperlink** and **Active hyperlink**. Click on **OK**.

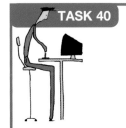

TASK 40

1 **Move to the About Me page in your website.**

2 **Change the colours for Hyperlinks, Visited hyperlinks and Active hyperlinks.**

Removing a hyperlink

To delete the hyperlink and the hyperlink text, select the hyperlink you wish to remove and press **Delete** on the keyboard.

To delete the hyperlink but leave the hyperlink text, select the hyperlink and choose **Hyperlink** from the **Insert** menu or click on the Insert Hyperlink button on the Standard toolbar.

Click on **Remove Link** in the Edit Hyperlink dialog box. Click on **OK**.

TASK 41

Move to the What I Do page and remove the hyperlink to the e-mail.

Managing hyperlinks

If you rename a page in your website, FrontPage® will automatically check to see whether there are any hyperlinks to that file. If there are, they are automatically updated with the new file name.

If you move a file in the website (for example, into a different folder), FrontPage® will automatically check to see whether there are any hyperlinks to the file and automatically update them to the new file location.

Before you publish a website, you should test all the hyperlinks. Broken hyperlinks should be repaired. A broken hyperlink is one that has an invalid destination. When a visitor clicks on a broken hyperlink, an error message will be displayed. A hyperlink could be broken because the Web address (URL) has simply been mistyped or because it points to a page that you have since deleted from your website.

Viewing internal hyperlinks

Make sure the Folder List is switched on. (Choose **Folder List** from the **View** menu.) Choose **Hyperlinks** from the **View** menu. Click on the page in the Folder List for which you wish to view the hyperlinks.

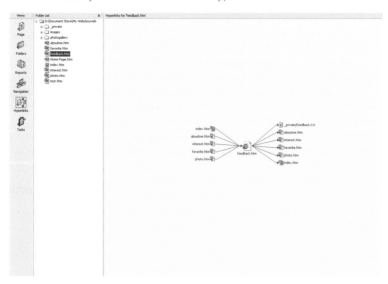

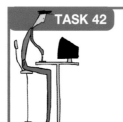

TASK 42

View all the hyperlinks in your website.

Verifying external links

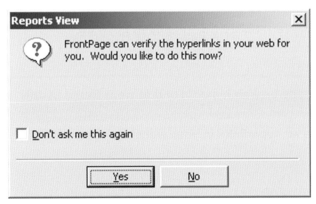

Reports View

? FrontPage can verify the hyperlinks in your web for you. Would you like to do this now?

☐ Don't ask me this again

[Yes]   [No]

You can run a report to verify that external links are valid. Switch to Hyperlinks view (View menu) and make sure you have saved all open pages. Choose **Reports** from the **View** menu, click on **Problems** and then click on **Broken Hyperlinks**.

When you run the report, you will receive the message on the left.

Click on **Yes**. All the external hyperlinks are listed and FrontPage® verifies each one in turn.

Broken Hyperlinks

Status ▼	Hyperlink ▼	In Page ▼	Page Title ▼	Modified By ▼
✓ OK	http://communities.msn.com/people	index.htm	Welcome to my Web site	NETTRAIN01\Nicki Talbot
✓ OK	http://moneycentral.msn.com/home...	interest.htm	Interests	NETTRAIN01\Nicki Talbot
✿ Broken	http://www.carpoint.com/	interest.htm	Interests	NETTRAIN01\Nicki Talbot
✓ OK	http://www.expedia.com	favorite.htm	Favorites	NETTRAIN01\Nicki Talbot
✓ OK	http://www.expedia.com	index.htm	Welcome to my Web site	NETTRAIN01\Nicki Talbot
✓ OK	http://www.expedia.com/	interest.htm	Interests	NETTRAIN01\Nicki Talbot
✿ Broken	http://www.msn.com	index.htm	Welcome to my Web site	NETTRAIN01\Nicki Talbot
✿ Broken	http://www.msn.com/	favorite.htm	Favorites	NETTRAIN01\Nicki Talbot
✓ OK	http://www.msnbc.com	favorite.htm	Favorites	NETTRAIN01\Nicki Talbot
✓ OK	http://www.msnbc.com	index.htm	Welcome to my Web site	NETTRAIN01\Nicki Talbot

The Status column shows whether a hyperlink is OK or Broken.

If you do not click on **Yes** at the prompt, you can check the status of a hyperlink manually. Right-click on the file for which you wish to check the hyperlinks and choose **Verify Hyperlink** from the shortcut menu.

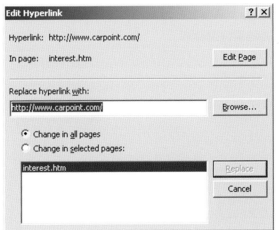

TASK 43   **Run the report to verify external links.**

Repairing broken hyperlinks

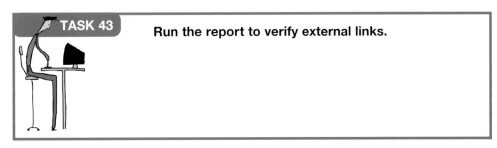

Edit Hyperlink   ? ✕

Hyperlink: http://www.carpoint.com/

In page: interest.htm   [Edit Page]

Replace hyperlink with:

[http://www.carpoint.com/]   [Browse...]

⊙ Change in all pages
○ Change in selected pages:

| interest.htm | [Replace]

                                          [Cancel]

Double-click a broken hyperlink in the list to open the Edit Hyperlink dialog box.

To display the page, click on **Edit Page** or type the correct URL of the page you want to link to in the **Replace hyperlink with** box. (Alternatively, click on **Browse ...** to navigate to the page.)

To repair this link on all pages in the current website, select **Change in all pages**. To repair this link on selected pages, select **Change in selected pages**. Click on **Replace**.

The hyperlink is no longer displayed as a broken hyperlink in the report.

Updating hyperlinks

To update all hyperlinks in your website, choose **Recalculate Hyperlinks** from the **Tools** menu.

TASK 44

1 **Repair any broken hyperlinks that were found by the report.**

2 **Update all hyperlinks in your website.**

Working with link bars

A link bar is a set of hyperlinks that you use to navigate around a website. You can display a link bar on every page in the website. You can use buttons or text hyperlinks on a link bar.

You can set up the navigation structure of your website and then let FrontPage® create the link bars for you. FrontPage® then maintains these link bars, if you add, delete or move a page.

There are three types of link bar:

- **Custom Link Bar** – you can add any pages in your website and external pages to a custom link bar. You can set up the link bar yourself and add and remove pages from it at any time.
- **Link Bar with Back and Next links** – FrontPage® interprets the navigation structure of your website and determines which pages to link when the Back button and the Next button are clicked. You can also include links to the website's home page, other pages within the site and external Web pages.
- **Link Bar based on the Navigation structure of the website** – to use this type of link bar you need to set up the navigation structure of the site. This determines which hyperlinks will appear on the link bar. FrontPage® will then set up each link bar according to the navigation structure.

Adding a custom link bar to a page

Place the cursor where you want the Link Bar to appear. Choose **Navigation** from the **Insert** menu.

The Insert Web Component wizard launches.

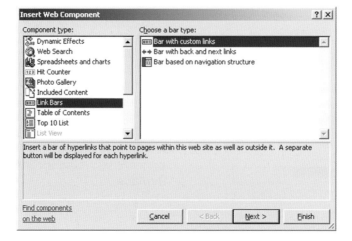

Choose Bar with custom links in the **Choose a bar type** list. Click on **Next**.

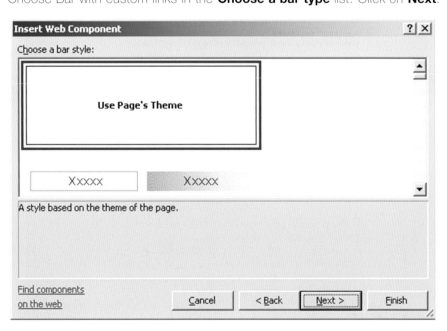

Select a bar style from the gallery. If your page uses a theme, click on **Use Page's Theme**. (For more information on themes, see page 398.) Click on **Next**.

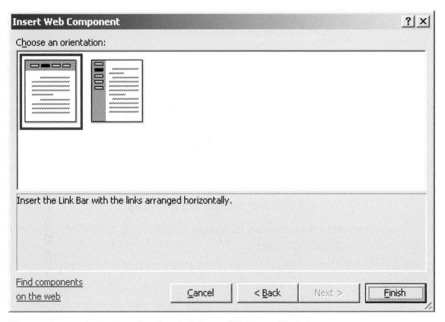

Choose an orientation for the link bar. Click on **Finish**.
In the Create New Link Bar dialog box, type a name for the link bar. Click on **OK**.

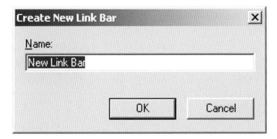

The Link Bar Properties dialog box now opens. To add links to the link bar, click on **Add link ...**

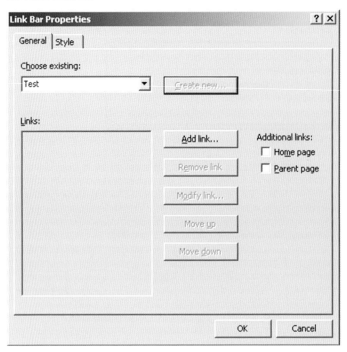

In the Add to Link Bar dialog box, click on **Existing File or Web Page** in the **Link to** list.

Select the page you want to link to. Type the text you want displayed on the link bar in the **Text to display** box. Click on **OK**.

Click on **Add link...** again and repeat this process for each link you want to add to the link bar.

TASK 45

1 **Move to the About Me page of your website.**

2 **Create a custom link bar. Choose a style from the gallery and choose for the links on the link bar to be arranged vertically.**

3 **Call the link bar 'About Me Link Bar'.**

4 **Add links to the Link Bar to take you to the My Friends page and the What I Do page.**

To add other types of link bar, follow the same process as for Adding a Custom Link Bar, but choose **Bar with back and next links** in the first step of the wizard.

Changing the style of a link bar

Select a link bar that contains text that you wish to format and choose **Font** from the **Format** menu. Choose the options you require in the Font dialog box and click on **OK**.

Double-click a link bar that contains text that you wish to format. The Link Bar Properties dialog box opens. Click on the **Style** tab. Select the style that you wish to use and click on **OK**.

Deleting a link bar

Click on the Link Bar that you wish to delete and press **Delete** on the keyboard.

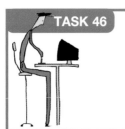

TASK 46

1 **Change the style of the link bar you have created.**

2 **Delete the link bar.**

 ## Working with hotspots

A hotspot is an area on a picture where there is a hyperlink. A graphic that contains more than one hotspot is called an image map. For example, you may have a picture of a product that contains a hotspot for each part of the product. The visitor can click on the different areas of the product to link to a page which explains that part of the product in more detail.

Creating a hotspot on a picture

Select the graphic on which you wish to create a hotspot. Click the appropriate Hotspot button on the Pictures toolbar. (To switch on the Pictures toolbar, choose **Toolbars** from the **View** menu and click on **Pictures**.)

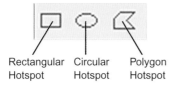

Rectangular   Circular   Polygon
Hotspot   Hotspot   Hotspot

On the graphic, click and drag to draw the rectangle, circle or polygon. When you release the mouse button, the Insert Hyperlink dialog box opens. Follow the steps from page 422.

TASK 47

1 **Move the About Me page in your website.**

2 **Create a circular hotspot on the picture on that page. Hyperlink to the My Friends page.**

Creating a text hotspot on a picture

Select the graphic and click the Text button on the Pictures toolbar. A text box will appear on the graphic. Type the text you require and double-click the edge of the text box to open the Insert Hyperlink dialog box. Follow the steps for inserting a hyperlink (see page 422).

Changing a hotspot

Click on a picture to display the hotspots that are on it.

■ To edit the destination of the hotspot, double-click it and change the destination in the **Address** box.
■ To move a hotspot, click and drag it to a new location on the picture.
■ To resize a hotspot, click and drag one of the selection handles.

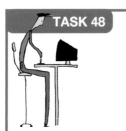

TASK 48

1 **Change the destination of the hotspot to the What I Do page.**

2 **Move and resize the hotspot on the picture.**

Deleting a hotspot

Click on the picture to display the hotspots that are on it. Click on the hotspot that you wish to delete and press **Delete** on the keyboard.

Working with HTML code

Websites are created using a language called HyperText Markup Language (HTML). HTML contains 'tags' that dictate how a Web browser should display the page elements such as text and graphics.

When you use FrontPage® to design your website, the HTML code is generated automatically for you as you add page elements in the Normal pane. You therefore don't need to know HTML code to create a website in FrontPage®. However, if you want to see the HTML code that is being generated as you add page elements, click on the **HTML** tab at the bottom of the screen.

This example shows how a Web page looks in Normal view (the view you use to add text and other elements to your page).

To view the HTML code that has been generated to create that page, click on the HTML link at the bottom of the page.

```
Home Page.htm*  aboutme.htm
<html>

<head>
<meta http-equiv="Content-Language" content="en-gb">
<meta name="GENERATOR" content="Microsoft FrontPage 5.0">
<meta name="ProgId" content="FrontPage.Editor.Document">
<meta http-equiv="Content-Type" content="text/html; charset=windows-1252">
<title>dfdsafasdfasdfadsfasdfadsf</title>
<meta name="Microsoft Theme" content="none">
</head>

<body>

<p>This is the first <a name="Page Bookmark" href="#Page Bookmark">page</a> of my Web site.</p>

<p> </p>

<p>
<img border="0" src="../../Mum%20&%20Dad/Mum%20and%20Dad.bmp" width="187" height="141"></p>
|
</body>

</html>
```

Normal HTML Preview

This example shows the HTML code that has been generated for the same page.

As you build websites using FrontPage®, you can begin to learn HTML code by seeing the code that is generated for certain page elements. You can click on the HTML tab and can also type HTML code straight onto the page.

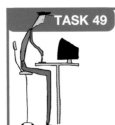

TASK 49

Look at the HTML code that has been generated from the work you have done on the various pages in Normal view.

 # Checking the website

It is important to check each page in your website for spelling and layout. It is also important to check that your website is easy to use and navigate around. The best way to do this is to preview your site as it will look in a browser window and then practise navigating around it.

You may want to ask someone else to test out your website. They will not already know what pages are where and will be able to provide a more objective test of how easy it is to use.

Before you publish your website, you should check for broken hyperlinks (see page 427), check that the pages look the way you want them to look and preview the website in a Web browser.

Checking spelling on a Web page

Open the page that you wish to spell check. Choose **Spelling** from the **Tools** menu.

Alternatively, click on the Spelling button on the Standard toolbar. You can also use shortcut icon ⬚.

Spelling

The spell check is launched and stops at the first word that it does not recognise. The Spelling dialog box opens.

Spell checking works in FrontPage® in exactly the same way as in Word. (For more information on spell checking and other hints and tips for proofreading, see Proofreading Tools in Unit 208 – Word-processing software.)

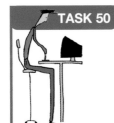

TASK 50

Spell check the pages in your website.

Previewing a Web page in a browser window

Open the page that you wish to preview. Choose **Preview in Browser** from the **File** menu.

Alternatively, click on the **Preview in Browser** button on the Standard toolbar.
Note: You must save a page before previewing it in the browser.
Your Web browser will launch and you will see the Web page exactly as it would

Preview in Browser

look to anyone viewing it on the Web. You can check the layout and visuals and also test the links.

TASK 51

1 **Preview your Web pages in the browser window. Check how the pages look when viewed in the browser window.**

2 **Check that all the hyperlinks work.**

Uploading and publishing the website

A website is a group of files (pages) that are connected using hyperlinks. A website can be a single HTML page, but is more likely to comprise a number of pages that include text, graphics, hyperlinks and even forms or databases.

Publishing a website means copying all the files that make up the website to a specific location. Usually, you create your website in a location that cannot be viewed using a Web browser (for example, your own computer). When you are ready to let others view the website on the Internet or on your company intranet, you copy the files to a Web server.

You can also use the publishing feature in FrontPage® to make a copy or backup of your website. You can save this to your own computer or onto the network.

You can choose to publish all the files in your website, or just those that have been changed.

Publishing a website using HTTP

Choose **Publish Web** from the **File** menu. The Publish Destination dialog box opens.

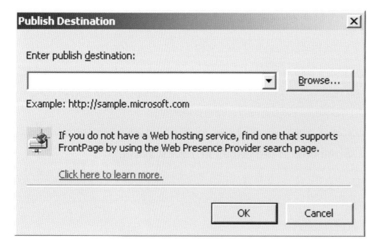

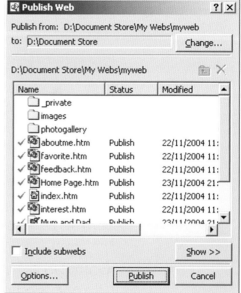

Type the location of the Web server or click on **Browse ...** and locate the publishing location. Click on **OK**.

In the Publish Web dialog box, select the pages that you wish to publish by clicking on the **Options ...** button. Click on the **Publish** tab and choose whether you wish to publish **Changed pages only** or **All pages**.

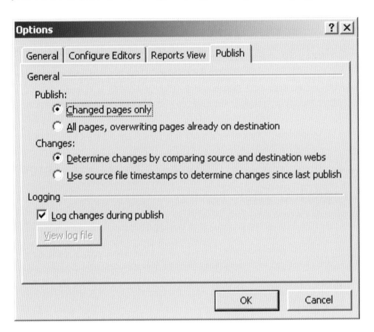

Click on **OK** and then click on **Publish**.

Your website is published to the Web server you have specified. To verify that your website has been successfully published, click the hyperlink that is displayed – your Web browser will open to the site you have just published.

Publishing a website using FTP

Follow the steps as for publishing a website using HTTP. Type the location of the FTP server in the Publish Destination dialog box. Click on OK and specify the pages you want to publish.

Your website is published to the FTP server you have specified.

Publishing a website to a PC or network location

Follow the steps as for publishing a website using HTTP. Type the path to the folder on your system or click on **Browse ...** to navigate to it in the Publish Destination dialog box. Click on OK and specify the pages you want to publish.

Your website is published to the location you have specified.

 ## Managing a website on a server

You should carry out regular management and maintenance of your website to ensure it is kept up-to-date and relevant.

Deleting files that have been published

When you publish your website, FrontPage® compares the files on your own computer with the files on the Web server. So, to delete a file from the server, first delete it from your own computer. When you publish the website again, you will be prompted to delete the same file from the Web server.

Changing the publishing location

Choose **Publish Web** from the **File** menu. In the Publish Web dialog box, click on

Change ... Type the new location of the Web server or FTP server, or click on **Browse ...** to navigate to it.

Click on **Publish** once you have made the changes.

 ## Suggested tasks for evidence

All evidence for this unit must be produced in the workplace. The suggested tasks below provide guidance on the type of work that you can produce as evidence for this unit. You may come across one or more of these scenarios in your workplace. By following the guidelines below, you will have produced a piece of evidence for this unit.

To ensure that your work can be used as evidence towards your ITQ, take screenshots at every stage to show the changes you are making to the website. Appropriate print-outs of pages and graphics should also be provided.

Suggested Task 1

You have been asked to create a small website for a project that is being run by your organisation. The website will be hosted on your company intranet and will be viewed by the people involved in the project. You need to find out exactly what is to be included in the website and draw up a plan. Consider the following:

■ Format and layout of the site – colours, fonts, graphics, themes, etc. Is there an organisational template that should be used?
■ What logos and other images are to be included?
■ Who is the intended audience?
■ How will visitors navigate around the site?

Create the pages for the website including themes, text and graphics. Add all the hyperlinks that are required to navigate around the website efficiently and easily. Save the website in stages as you produce the different pages and add page elements and hyperlinks.

Check the site for accuracy of content and also formatting and layout. Test the site yourself and get a colleague to use the site to check that it is easy to navigate.

Make any suggestions for improvements to the website and create an alternative version of the site.

Create notes to explain the different elements of the site and how it works.

Suggested Task 2

Create a short report providing tips for creating an effective website, taking into account what message needs to be conveyed and the intended visitors to the site.

Artwork and imaging software

Overview

You are likely to be in a role which involves creating and modifying artwork and images for printing or display on screen.

The software outlined in this unit is Adobe Photoshop®. Adobe Photoshop® is a powerful application which is used to manipulate images. Pictures can be changed by changing colours, sharpening images or moving or removing parts of a picture. It is a useful tool to work with digital photographs and scanned images.

A competent person can use this type of software effectively to produce artwork and images that communicate clearly and effectively. This includes creating and modifying artwork and images and understanding the image file formats that are appropriate for different media. It also includes a general working knowledge of the laws affecting the use of IT.

 ## Required skills and techniques for Level 2

Handling files	Using appropriate techniques to handle, organise and save files.
Creating drawings, artwork and images	Creating simple and more complex drawings and artwork: ■ choosing the right software to use ■ taking account of page size, colours and file size and format when creating images.
Inserting, manipulating and editing artwork and images	Using tools appropriately: ■ group and ungroup ■ filters to create special effects ■ editing existing templates.
Checking images	Checking images to ensure they are effective and fit for purpose: ■ checking colours and filters ■ checking image resolution is suitable for how it will be used.
Checking text	Checking text to ensure it is accurate, consistent and well laid out: ■ using appropriate proofreading techniques ■ checking line, paragraph and page breaks and that formatting techniques are used consistently and appropriately.

 ## Requirements of this unit

You will need to carry out at least *two* comprehensive tasks to demonstrate that you can produce different types of artwork and images for a wide variety of uses. You need to demonstrate knowledge of what file formats are suitable for different media, e.g. print and websites. You need to have a general working knowledge of the laws that affect the use of IT.

Tasks in this unit

The tasks that appear throughout this unit are designed to take you step-by-step through the feature being discussed. It is recommended that you use the tasks completed as evidence in addition to the two main pieces that are required by the unit.

The tasks at the end of the unit are suggested ways in which you could provide the main evidence for this unit.

What will I achieve?

By accomplishing a Level 2 in this unit, you will also have achieved Level 1 in all cases and a Level 3 in some cases. Below is a table to show what levels you will have achieved.

Required skill	Level 1	Level 2	Level 3
Handling files	●———————●		
Creating drawings, artwork and images	●———————●		
Inserting, manipulating and editing artwork	●———————●		
Checking images	●———————————●———————————●
Checking text	●———————————●———————————●

Launching Photoshop®

Adobe Photoshop® can be launched by double-clicking on the **Photoshop** shortcut on the desktop (if there is one).

Alternatively, click on **Start**, **Programs** and then choose **Adobe Photoshop** from the menu. (If you have Windows® XP, it is **Start, All Programs, Adobe Photoshop**.)

The Photoshop® Screen

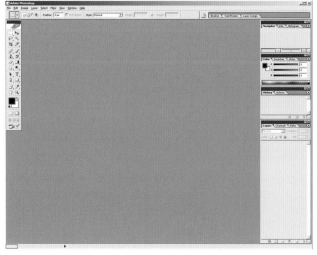

Adobe Photoshop® is not a Microsoft® product. However, all Windows®-based applications share common elements, regardless of who the software was created by.

The **Title Bar** across the top of the screen informs you that you are in Adobe Photoshop.

The **Menu Bar** contains menus: **File, Edit, Image, Layer, Select, Filter, View, Window, Help**. To open a drop-down menu, click on the word on the Menu Bar.

Under the Menu Bar is the **Options Bar**. This bar is context-sensitive and changes depending on what tool is currently selected.

At the right end of the Options Bar is the **Palette Well**. This helps you to organise and manage palettes. The palette well stores palettes that you use frequently. (It shows Brushes, Tool Presets and Layer Comps.)

Down the left side of the screen is the **Toolbox**. This contains the tools you use to create and edit images.

Down the right side of the screen are the **palettes**. (Navigator, Color, History and

Layers palettes.) You use palettes to monitor and modify images. By default, palettes are stacked in groups. You can move palette groups, rearrange palettes in a group and remove palettes from a group.

The main part of the screen is called the **active image area**.

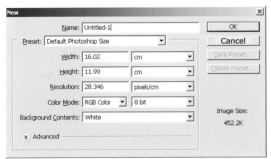 Working with files

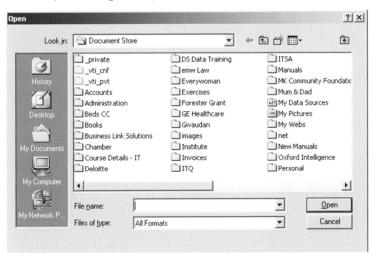

You can open and import images in most graphic file formats.

Creating a new file

Choose **New** from the **File** menu.

Alternatively, press [Control]+[N]

The New dialog box opens.

Type a name for the file in the **Name** box. Choose a preset size by clicking on the drop-down arrow by the **Preset** box. Click on **OK**.

Opening a file

Choose **Open** from the **File** menu.

Alternatively, press [Control]+[O]

The Open dialog box opens.

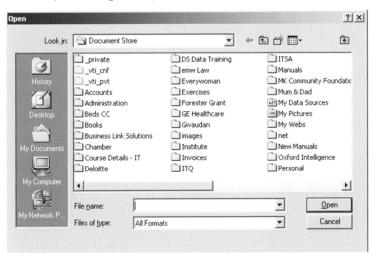

Navigate to where the file that you wish to open is stored. Select the file (or type the filename in the **File name** box) and click on **Open**. (For more information on navigating to folders, see Unit 208 – Word-processing software.)

Opening recently used files

You can quickly reopen a file you have used recently. Choose **Open Recent** from the **File** menu and choose the file you want to open from the sub-menu.

TASK 1

Open a jpeg or bmp file you have on your computer into Photoshop®.

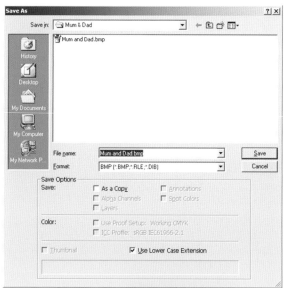

Saving a file

If you wish to save the changes you have made to the image, choose **Save** from the **File** menu.

Alternatively, press [Control]+[S]

The original file is overwritten with the new version of the file.

If you wish to save the changed image with a different file name (so that you also keep the original), choose **Save As** from the **File** menu.

Alternatively, press [Shift]+[Control]+[O]

The Save As dialog box opens.

Navigate to where you wish to save the amended file. (For more information on navigating to folders, see Unit 208 – Word-processing software.)

Type a name for the file in the **File name** box and click on **Save**.

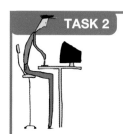

TASK 2

Use Save As to save the file you have opened with a different file name. Save it in your Tasks for ITQ folder.

Closing a file

Once you have saved the file, if you wish to remove it from the screen, you must close the file. Choose **Close** from the **File** menu.

Alternatively, press [Control]+[W]

Printing a file

To print the file with the current options, choose **Print** from the **File** menu.

Alternatively, press [Control]+[P]

The Print dialog box opens.

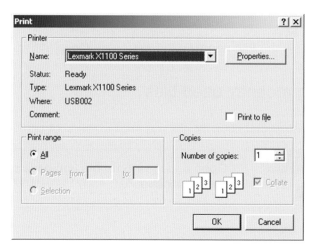

Select the printer you wish to use to print the file from the **Name** drop-down list.

Choose the **Number of copies** you want to print and click on **OK**.

Using Page Setup

You may wish to use Page Setup before you print. Choose **Page Setup** from the **File** menu.

Alternatively, press [Shift] + [Control] + [P]

The Page Setup dialog box opens.

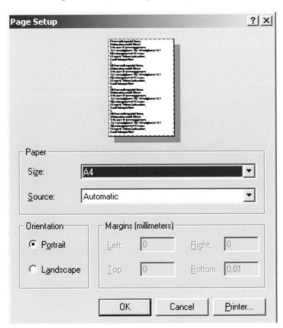

You can specify the **Paper Size** and **Orientation**. Click on **OK** to apply any changes.

Print with Preview

If you wish to adjust the printed output and use the Photoshop® colour management options, you can use Print with Preview.

Choose **Print with Preview** from the **File** menu. The Photoshop® Print dialog box opens.

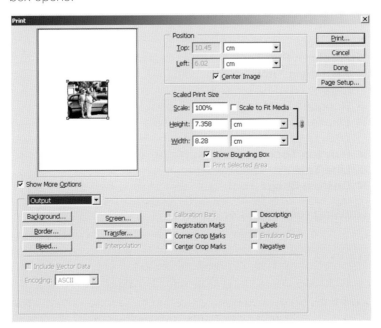

You can choose the position of the image on the printed page by specifying a measurement for **Top** and **Left** in the **Position** section.

You can scale the image by choosing a **Scale** percentage or by specifying the **Height** and **Width** in the **Scaled Print Size** section.

If your file is going to be commercially printed direct from Photoshop®, you can specify **Output** options.

You can use colour management options to ensure that the colours on the monitor are as close as they can be to the colours on the printer.

Click on **Print** to print the image. Click on **Done** to preserve the new settings and close the dialog box.

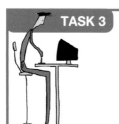

TASK 3

1 **Use Page Setup to set the printed page to Landscape.**

2 **Print one copy of the graphic file.**

Using the drawing tools

You can use the drawing tools in Photoshop® to create shapes and paths. Shapes will maintain crisp edges when resized, printed, saved in a PDF file or imported into another application. Paths are used to define an area of an image. The outline of a shape is a path. Paths can be made up of one or more straight or curved segments. Each segment is marked by anchor points (rather like pins holding wire in place). You can change the shape of a path by editing its anchor points.

Creating shapes

Select a shape tool from the **Options Bar**.

- ■ **Pen Tool** – creates straight or curved lines.
- ■ **Freeform Pen Tool** – creates freeform lines.
- ■ **Rectangle Tool** – draws rectangles. (Hold down SHIFT on the keyboard as you draw to create a square.)
- ■ **Rounded Rectangle Tool** –draws rectangles with rounded corners.
- ■ **Ellipse Tool** – draws ellipses (ovals). (Hold down SHIFT on the keyboard as you draw to create a circle.)
- ■ **Polygon Tool** – creates a polygon shape.
- ■ **Line Tool** – creates a line.
- ■ **Custom Shape Tool** – selects from a set of custom shapes.

Drawing rectangles or squares

Click on the **Rectangle** tool in the Options Bar and click and drag on the active image area to draw the rectangle. To draw a square, hold down SHIFT on the keyboard as you drag to draw the shape. If you wish to draw a rectangle with rounded corners, use the Rounded Rectangle tool. The shapes are filled with the default fill colour.

Drawing ellipses or circles

Click on the **Ellipse** tool in the Options Bar and click and drag on the active image area to draw the ellipse. To draw a circle, hold down SHIFT on the keyboard as you drag to draw the shape. The shapes are filled with the default fill colour.

Drawing lines

Click on the **Line** tool in the Options Bar and click and drag on the active image area to draw the line.

Drawing polygons

Click on the **Polygon** tool in the Options Bar and click and drag on the active image area to draw the polygon. The shape is filled with the default fill colour.

Drawing custom shapes

Click on the **Custom Shape** tool in the Options Bar and then click on the drop-down arrow by the Shape box to open a gallery of custom shapes.

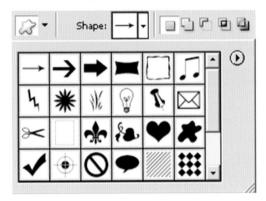

Click on the shape you wish to draw and then click and drag on the active image area to draw the shape.

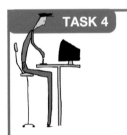 **TASK 4**

1 **Create a new file. Call the file 'Drawings' and choose A4 as the Preset size.**

2 **Draw a rectangle, a square, a circle, an ellipse, a rectangle with rounded corners, a polygon and a line.**

3 **Save the file in your Tasks for ITQ folder.**

Changing the colour of the shape or line

If you do not want the shape or line to be the default colour, you can choose a colour for it before you draw it. Once you have selected the shape you wish to draw, click on the Color picker button.

The Color Picker dialog box opens.

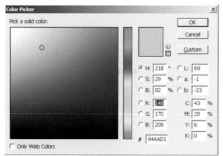

You can pick a colour for the shape by dragging the sliders on the bar to pick the main colour. You can then click in the solid colour area to select the exact colour you require. Click on **OK** to apply the colour.

Alternatively, you can change the colour of a shape you have already drawn. Use the selection tool to select the shape and then click on the **Color** button on the Options Bar.

TASK 5

Practise changing the colour of the shapes you have drawn.

Using a preset style for a shape

You can assign a preset style to a shape or a line before you draw it. Once you have selected the shape you wish to draw, click on the drop-down arrow by the Style button.

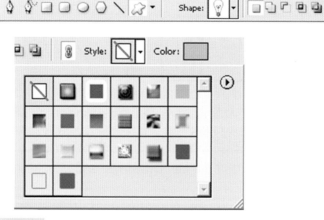

Choose a Style from the gallery. To switch to different galleries, click on the arrow button at the right side of the current gallery to open a menu listing other Style galleries.

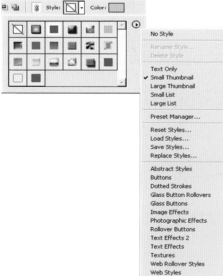

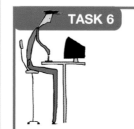

TASK 6

1 **Practise changing the style of the shapes you have drawn. Look at the different galleries available.**

2 **Save and close the file.**

Drawing multiple shapes

You can draw shapes on top of each other to create a 'picture'. There is a set of tools you can use to create different effects as you draw shapes on top of each other.

Select the shape you wish to draw and choose any colour or style you want to apply. Before you draw the shape, choose from the following options:

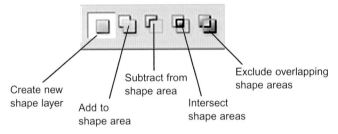

Create new
shape layer

Add to
shape area

Subtract from
shape area

Intersect
shape areas

Exclude overlapping
shape areas

- **Create new shape layer** – creates a new shape on a new layer, so it does not affect any shapes that are already drawn.

- **Add to shape area** – adds the new shape to the existing shape area.

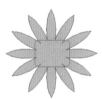

- **Subtract from shape area** – removes the new shape from the existing shape area.

- **Intersect shape areas** – combines the two shape areas.

- **Exclude overlapping shape areas** – excludes any overlap areas in the new consolidated shape.

TASK 7

1 **Create a new file. Call the file 'Picture' and choose A4 as the Preset size.**

2 **Draw multiple shapes using the shape tools to create a 'picture'.**

3 **Save the file in your Tasks for ITQ folder. Close the file.**

Working with drawn objects

You can change the colour of a shape once you have drawn it. You can also move, reshape and delete parts of a shape. You can align and distribute shapes and rotate, flip and skew them. You can resize shapes, crop shapes and use copy and paste to create duplicate shapes.

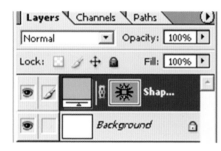

Changing the colour of a shape

Double-click the shape's thumbnail in the Layers palette and choose a different colour using the Color Picker.

You can also fill the shape with a pattern or gradient fill. Select the shape layer in the Layers palette. Choose **Change Layer Content** from the **Layer** menu and choose whether you want **Gradient** or **Pattern** from the sub-menu.

Using a gradient fill

In the Gradient Fill dialog box, choose a **Gradient** from the gallery and pick a **Style** (Linear, Radial, Angle, Reflected or Diamond). You can also specify the **Angle** and **Scale**. Click on **OK** to apply the changes.

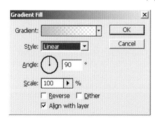 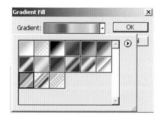

Click on the drop-down arrow to open the Gradient gallery. Click on the arrow to the right of the current gallery to open a menu listing other galleries.

Using a pattern fill

In the Pattern Fill dialog box, choose a pattern from the gallery. You can also specify the **Scale**. Click on **OK** to apply the changes.

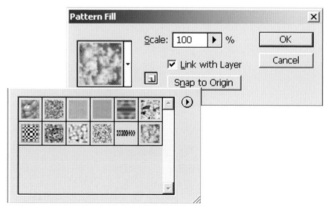

Click on the drop-down arrow to open the pattern gallery. Click on the arrow to the right of the current gallery to open a menu listing other galleries.

TASK 8

1 **Open the file called 'Drawings'.**

2 **Experiment with applying gradient and pattern fills to the shapes. (Look at the different galleries available.)**

3 **Save the changes you have made. Close the file.**

Moving a segment of the picture

When you have drawn various shapes to build a picture, you can move the individual shapes you have drawn.

Click on the Path Selection tool in the Toolbox. Click and drag the shape you wish to move.

Deleting a segment of the picture

Click on the Direct/Path Selection tool in the Toolbox and click on the shape you want to delete. Press **Delete** on the keyboard.

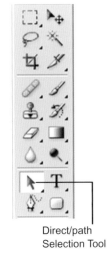

Direct/path
Selection Tool

TASK 9

1 **Open the file called 'Picture'.**

2 **Move the shapes in your picture**

3 **Delete one of the shapes in your picture.**

4 **Close the file without saving any changes.**

Aligning shapes

Use the Path Selection Tool to select the shapes you want to align. Hold down **Shift** on the keyboard as you click on each shape to select multiple shapes. Choose one of the alignment options from the Options Bar.

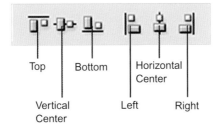

Top | Bottom | Horizontal Center

Vertical Center | Left | Right

Distributing shapes

Use the Path Selection Tool to select the shapes you want to distribute. There must be at least three shapes selected. Choose one of the distribution options from the Options Bar.

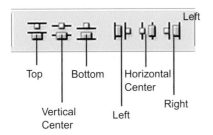

Left

Top | Bottom | Horizontal Center

Vertical Center | Left | Right

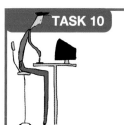

TASK 10

1 **Open the file called 'Drawings'.**

2 **Practise aligning the shapes using the different alignment options.**

3 **Practise distributing the shapes using the different distribution options.**

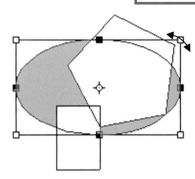

Rotating a shape

Use the Direct/Path Selection Tool to select the shape you want to rotate.

Choose **Transform** (or **Transform Path**) from the **Edit** menu and choose **Rotate** from the sub-menu. A selection box appears around the shape and the mouse pointer changes to a rotate handle.

Move the rotate handle over on the handles of the selection box and click and drag to rotate the shape.

Alternatively, you can choose **Rotate 180°**, **Rotate 90° CW** or **Rotate 90° CCW** from the Transform menu.

Flipping a shape

Use the Direct/Path Selection Tool to select the shape you want to flip.

Choose **Transform** (or **Transform Path**) from the **Edit** menu and choose **Flip Horizontal** or **Flip Vertical** from the sub-menu.

TASK 11

1 **Select the different shapes and experiment with the rotation options.**

2 **Select the different shapes and experiment with the flip options.**

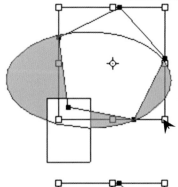

Skewing a shape

Use the Direct/Path Selection Tool to select the shape you want to skew.

Choose **Transform** (or **Transform Path**) from the **Edit** menu and choose **Skew** from the sub-menu. A selection box appears around the shape and the mouse pointer changes to a skew handle.

Point to one of the handles of the selection box with the skew handle and click and drag to skew the shape.

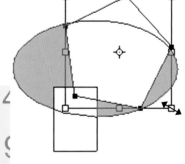

Scaling a shape

Use the Direct/Path Selection Tool to select the shape you want to scale.

Choose **Transform** (or **Transform Path**) from the **Edit** menu and choose **Scale** from the sub-menu. A selection box appears around the shape.

Point to one of the handles of the selection box and the mouse pointer changes to a double-headed arrow. Click and drag inwards or outwards to resize the shape.

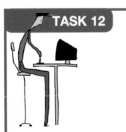

TASK 12

1   **Select the different shapes and experiment skewing them in different ways.**

2   **Select the different shapes and experiment with scaling them to different sizes.**

Cropping a shape

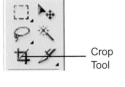

Crop Tool

Use the Direct/Path Selection Tool to select the shape you want to crop.

Click on the Crop tool in the toolbox.

The mouse pointer changes to a crop handle. Click and drag over the part of the image that you want to keep. A moving border appears around the area you have just created. Click on the Crop tool again.

Click on **Crop** to finish the process.

TASK 13

Practise using the crop tool on the different shapes.

Using copy and paste

If you want to create a duplicate of a shape you have already created, you can use the copy and paste commands.

Use the Direct/Path Selection Tool to select the shape you want to copy. Choose **Copy** from the **Edit** menu. Click outside the shape to deselect it and choose **Paste** from the **Edit** menu. The shape is copied on top of the original shape. You can click and drag to move it to a new location.

TASK 14

1   **Use Copy and Paste to create duplicates of the shapes. Move them to a different location on the page.**

2   **Close the file without saving any changes.**

Working with text

You can create horizontal or vertical text anywhere on an image. There are two types of text you can enter – point type and paragraph type. Point type is used for entering a single word or a line of characters. Paragraph type is used for entering and formatting type as one or more paragraphs.

Creating point type

When you enter point type, the length of a line of text will grow or shrink as you edit it. It does not wrap to the next line.

Select the Type tool in the toolbox.

Type Tool

Click on the active work area where you want to type. The cursor appears. Type the text you require. Press [Control]+[Return] when you have finished.

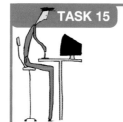

TASK 15

1 **Create a new file. Call the file 'Text' and choose A4 as the Preset size.**

2 **Type your name using Point Type.**

3 **Save the file in your 'Tasks for ITQ' folder.**

Creating paragraph type

When you enter paragraph type, the lines of type will wrap to fit the dimensions of the text box. If you resize the text box, the type will reflow within the adjusted box. Select the Type tool in the toolbox.

Click and drag on the active work area to create a text box. When you release the mouse button, the cursor appears in the text box. Type the text you require. Press [Control]+[Return] when you have finished.

Type Tool

TASK 16

Type a paragraph of text under your name using paragraph type.

Formatting text

You can use the other buttons on the Options Bar to format text you have typed. Select the text you want to format and then use the appropriate button on the Options Bar.

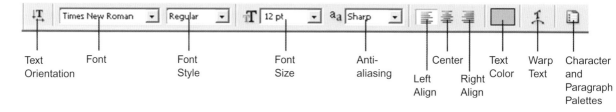

Text Orientation	Font	Font Style	Font Size	Anti-aliasing	Left Align / Center / Right Align	Text Color	Warp Text	Character and Paragraph Palettes

- **Text Orientation** – changes the orientation of the selected text (toggles between horizontal and vertical).
- **Font** – enables you to choose a Font from the list.
- **Font Style** – enables you to choose a Font Style from the list.
- **Font Size** – enables you to choose a Font Size from the list.
- **Anti-aliasing** – enables you to choose an anti-aliasing option from the list to smooth the edges of typed text.
- **Left Align** – aligns the selected text to the left side.
- **Center** – aligns the selected text to the centre.
- **Right Align** – aligns the selected text to the right side.
- **Text Color** – opens the Color Picker. Select a new colour by dragging the

sliders and clicking on the colour palette. Click on **OK** to apply the new colour to the selected text.

- **Warp Text** – opens the Warp Text dialog box. Choose a warp **Style** from the drop-down list. Click on **OK** to apply the changes to the selected text.

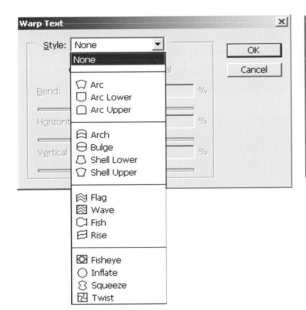

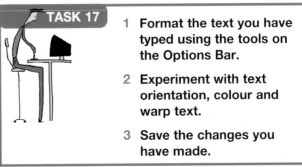

TASK 17

1. **Format the text you have typed using the tools on the Options Bar.**

2. **Experiment with text orientation, colour and warp text.**

3. **Save the changes you have made.**

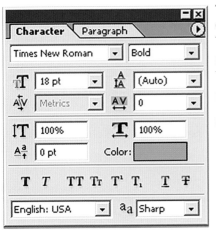

The Character and Paragraph Palettes button switches on the Character and Paragraph Palettes (which are grouped together). These palettes offer more options for working with character and paragraph text. You can also use this button to toggle between the two palettes.

Extra options on the Character palette are:

- **Leading** – adjusts the space between lines of type. It is measured from the baseline of one line of type to the baseline of the next line of type. (The baseline is an invisible line on which type lies.) Choose an amount from the drop-down list.
- **Kerning** – adjusts the space between characters. Positive kerning moves characters apart and negative kerning moves characters closer together. Alternatively, you can switch on automatic kerning – Metrics or Optical. Place the cursor between the characters you wish to kern and choose an option from the drop-down list.
- **Tracking** – creates an equal amount of space across a range of letters. Positive tracking moves characters apart and negative tracking moves characters closer together. Select the characters that you wish to set tracking for and choose an amount from the drop-down list.
- **Vertically/Horizontally Scale** – enables you to scale the type vertically and horizontally. Select the text and enter a percentage in the Vertical scale or Horizontal scale box.
- **Baseline shift** – controls the distance that type appears from its baseline. Select the text and enter the amount you wish to move the text away from its baseline. A positive value moves horizontal type above and vertical type to the right of the baseline. A negative value moves horizontal type below and vertical type to the left of the baseline.
- **Faux Bold/Faux Italic** – applies a 'fake' bold or italic using these buttons if the

font you have chosen does not include a Bold or Italic option. Select the text and click the appropriate button.

- **All Caps/Small Caps** – applies All Caps or Small Caps to the selected text.
- **Superscript/Subscript** – applies superscript or subscript to the selected text.
- **Underline** – applies underline to the selected text.
- **Strikethrough** – applies strikethrough to the selected text.

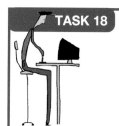

Extra options on the Paragraph palette are:

- **Justify last left** – justifies all lines except the last, which is left-aligned. Select the paragraphs you want to justify and click this option.
- **Justify last centered** – justifies all lines except the last, which is centre-aligned. Select the paragraphs you want to justify and click this option.
- **Justify last right** – justifies all lines except the last, which is right-aligned. Select the paragraphs you want to justify and click this option.
- **Justify all** – justifies all lines, including the last. Select the paragraphs you want to justify and click this option.
- **Indent left margin** – indents the text from the left edge of the paragraph by the amount you specify.
- **Indent right margin** – indents the text from the right edge of the paragraph by the amount you specify.
- **Indent first line** – indents the first line of text in the paragraph by the amount you specify.
- **Space before paragraph/Space after paragraph** – increases the space before and after paragraphs. Select the paragraphs you want to adjust and type a value in the appropriate box.

TASK 18

1 **Experiment with the different options in the Character and Paragraph palettes.**

2 **Save the changes you have made and close the file.**

Working with images

Types of image
Bitmap images

Bitmap images are made up of dots, known as pixels. They contain a fixed number of pixels and each pixel has a specific location and colour. Bitmap format is the most common electronic format for photographs – because of the pixels, they can represent subtle grades of shades and colour. However, because of the fixed number of pixels, they can lose detail when made larger on screen and can look jagged if printed at too low a resolution.

Vector images

Vector images are made up of mathematically defined lines and curves, called vectors. This means that you can work with a line (move it, resize it or change its colour) without losing the quality of the graphic. Vector graphics can be resized and printed at any resolution without losing detail or clarity.

File formats supported in Photoshop®

You can open images of various file formats into Photoshop®, including:

- **BMP** – Bitmap is a standard Windows®-based image format.
- **GIF** – Graphics Interchange Format is the format commonly used to display images in HTML documents on the Web. GIF is a compressed format designed to minimise file size.
- **JPEG** – Joint Photographic Experts Group format is commonly used to display photographs in HTML documents on the Web. JPEG compresses file size by selectively discarding data.
- **PDF** – Portable Document Format can be used in lots of applications. PDF files accurately display and preserve fonts, page layouts and both vector and bitmap graphics.
- **TIFF** – Tagged-Image File Format is used to exchange files between different applications. TIFF is a bitmap image format which is supported by almost all paint, image-editing and page-layout applications. Most desktop scanners can produce TIFF images.
- **EPS** – Encapsulated PostScript format can contain both vector and bitmap graphics and is supported by virtually all graphic, illustration and page-layout programs.
- **PSD** – Photoshop® format is the default format used by Photoshop® and is the only format that supports all Photoshop® features.
- **PSB** – Large Document Format supports documents up to 300,000 pixels.
- **PNG** – Portable Network Graphics format is used for lossless compression and for the display of images on the Web. However, not all Web browsers support PNG images.

For information on opening files, see page 439).

Scanned images and images from a digital camera

You can import scanned images directly into Photoshop® (see your scanner instructions). Alternatively, you can save the file in any of the above file formats and then open it into Photoshop®.

You can import images directly from a digital camera (see your camera instructions). Alternatively, you can save the file in any of the above file formats and then open it into Photoshop®.

TASK 19

Open the JPEG or BMP file you saved in your Tasks for ITQ folder.

Resizing an image

Choose **Image Size** from the **Image** menu.

The Image Size dialog box opens.

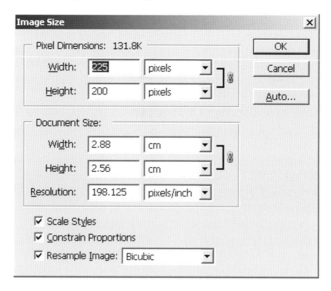

Type a value in the **Width** and **Height** box and click on **OK**.

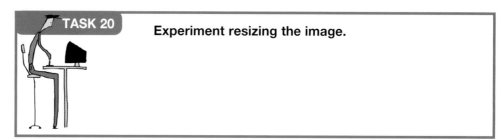

TASK 20

Experiment resizing the image.

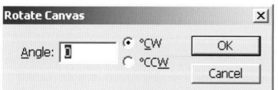

Rotating and flipping the image canvas

Choose **Rotate Canvas** from the **Image** menu and choose an option from the sub-menu.

Arbitrary enables you to specify an angle to rotate the image canvas.

Type a value in the **Angle** box and choose **CW** (clockwise) or **CCW** (counter-clockwise). Click on **OK**.

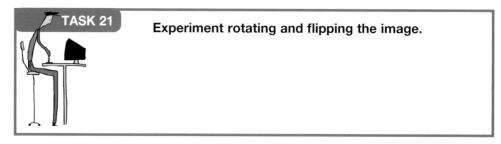

TASK 21

Experiment rotating and flipping the image.

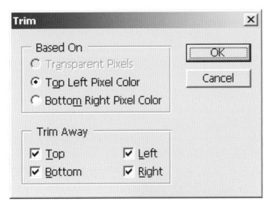

Cropping the image

Select the Crop tool in the toolbox.

The mouse pointer changes to the crop handle.

Click and drag over the part of the image that you want to keep. That part of the image is highlighted by a moving dashed border.

Crop tool

Press **Enter** on the keyboard. The picture is cropped.

Trimming the image

Choose **Trim** from the **Image** menu. The Trim dialog box opens.

Choose on what the trim should be based. **Transparent Pixels** will trim away transparency at the edges of the image. **Top Left Pixel Color** will remove an area the colour of the upper left pixel. **Bottom Right Pixel Color** will remove an area the colour of the bottom right pixel.

Select the areas of the image you want to trim away: **Top**, **Bottom**, **Left**, or **Right**. Click on **OK**.

Trim ☒

Based On
- ○ Transparent Pixels
- ● Top Left Pixel Color
- ○ Bottom Right Pixel Color

OK
Cancel

Trim Away
- ☑ Top   ☑ Left
- ☑ Bottom ☑ Right

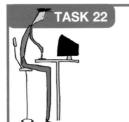

TASK 22   **Experiment cropping and trimming the image.**

Sharpening the image

Sharpening an image will enhance the definition around the edges of the image. However, sharpening can only go so far – it will not correct the problems of a severely blurred image.

Choose **Sharpen** from the **Filter** menu and then choose a Sharpen option from the sub-menu.

- ■ **Sharpen** – focuses the image and improves its clarity.
- ■ **Sharpen Edges** – finds the areas in the image where significant colour changes occur and sharpens them.

- **Sharpen More** – applies a stronger sharpening than Sharpen.
- **Unsharp Mask** – opens the Unsharp Mask dialog box.

Choose **Unsharp Mask ...** from the Sharpen sub-menu. The Unsharp Mask dialog box opens.

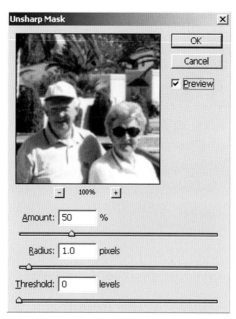

Drag the **Amount**, **Radius** and **Threshold** sliders to adjust the image. (It is a good idea to move the dialog box so that you can see how the change affects the image.) Click on **OK** to apply any changes.

Amount affects the contrast of the edge. The higher the amount, the more contrast there is at the edges of pixels. (For a high-resolution printed image, you will probably want an amount between 150% and 200%.)

Radius specifies the width of the edge created by sharpening. Be careful not to set this too high, otherwise the edges will have a 'halo' effect.

Threshold specifies the difference needed between shades before the filter sharpens the edge between them. A threshold of 0 will sharpen all the pixels in the image. A high threshold value only sharpens the edges between significantly different shades.

Adjusting the brightness and contrast of the image

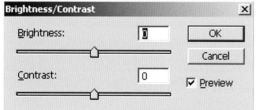

Choose **Adjustments** from the **Image** menu and click on **Brightness/Contrast** in the sub-menu.

The Brightness/Contrast dialog box opens.

Drag the appropriate slider to adjust the **Brightness** and/or **Contrast** of the image. (You will see the changes on the image as you drag the sliders.) Click on **OK** to apply any changes.

Adjusting the hue and saturation of the image

Choose **Adjustments** from the **Image** menu and click on **Hue/Saturation** in the sub-menu.

The Hue/Saturation dialog box opens.

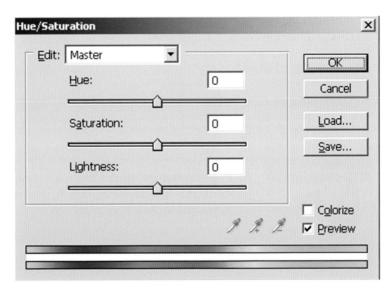

Click on the drop-down arrow by the **Edit** box and choose which colours in the image you want to edit.

Drag the **Hue**, **Saturation** and **Lightness** sliders to adjust those colours in the image. You will be able to see the changes on the image as you drag the sliders.

Choose each colour from the **Edit** drop-down list and adjust the sliders until you are happy with the image.

Click on **OK** to apply changes.

Desaturating the image

The Desaturate command converts a colour image to a grayscale image. (This command has the same effect as setting Saturation to 100 in the Hue/Saturation dialog box.)

To desaturate the image, choose **Adjustments** from the **Image** menu and click on **Desaturate**.

Adjusting shadows and highlights in the image

This tool is useful where the original image has shadowed areas, due to strong backlighting.

Choose **Adjustments** from the **Image** menu and click on **Shadow/Highlight** in the sub-menu.

The Shadow/Highlight dialog box opens.

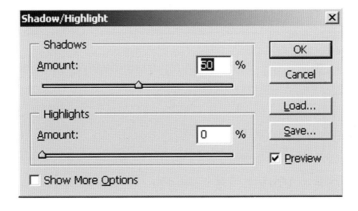

Drag the **Shadows** and **Highlights** sliders to adjust the shadows and highlights in the image. You will be able to see the changes on the image as you drag the sliders.

The **Shadows** slider adjusts the amount of shadow lightening to apply. The larger the percentage, the greater the lightening of the shadows.

The **Highlights** slider adjusts the amount of highlight darkening to apply. The larger the percentage, the greater the darkening of highlights.

Click on **OK** to apply changes.

TASK 23

Experiment using the sharpen, brightness and contrast, hue and saturation, and shadow and highlight tools on your image.

Inverting the colours of the image

The Invert command inverts the colours in the image (so it looks like a negative of the photograph).

To invert the colours of the image, choose **Adjustments** from the **Image** menu and click on **Invert**.

Equalising the colours of the image

The Equalize command balances the brightness values in an image so that they are more evenly distributed across the image. You can use this to balance a dark image to produce a lighter image.

To equalise the colours of the image, choose **Adjustments** from the **Image** menu and click on **Equalize**.

Posterizing the colours of the image

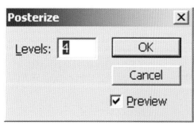

The Posterize command is useful for creating a special effect on a coloured image.

Choose **Adjustments** from the **Image** menu and click on **Posterize** in the sub-menu.

The Posterize dialog box opens.

Choose the number of tonal levels you want and click on **OK**. As you specify the number of levels, you will be able to see how your changes affect the image.

TASK 24

Experiment using the invert, equalize and posterize tools on your image.

Using the Variations Gallery

The Variations Gallery enables you to pick a variation on your original image. The variations have colour balance, contrast and saturation adjusted. You can pick a variation rather than adjusting these elements manually on your image.

Choose **Adjustments** from the **Image** menu and click on **Variations** in the sub-menu. The Variations gallery opens, as in the figure below.

The first two images in the gallery show the **Original** picture and the **Current Pick** (the option you have selected).

Click on the appropriate picture to apply that saturation: **More Green**, **More Yellow**, **More Cyan**, **More Red**, **More Blue**, **More Magenta**.

Click on the appropriate picture to apply that brightness: **Lighter**, **Darker**.

Click on **OK** to apply your changes to the image.

TASK 25

1 Use the Variations Gallery to make changes to your image.

2 Save any changes you have made and close the file.

Working with special effects and filters

You can use filters to apply special effects to an image. You can apply more than one filter to the image to create a cumulative effect. Photoshop has many filters – 14 different groups, each of which contains a range of filters:

- ■ Artistic filters
- ■ Blur filters
- ■ Brush stroke filters
- ■ Distort filters
- ■ Noise filters
- ■ Pixelate filters
- ■ Render filters
- ■ Sharpen filters
- ■ Sketch filters
- ■ Stylize filters
- ■ Texture filters
- ■ Video filters
- ■ Digimarc filters
- ■ Other filters

Applying a filter manually

Choose a filter from the **Filter** menu and then choose an option from the sub-menu.

Applying a filter using the Filter Gallery

Choose **Filter Gallery** from the **Filter** menu. The Filter Gallery opens.

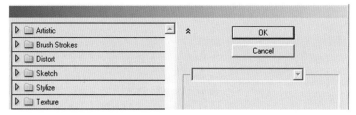

Choose a filter group by clicking on the arrow beside the appropriate folder.

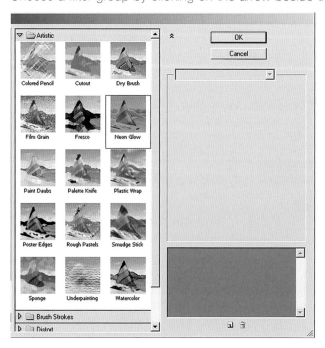

Click on a filter to see how it affects your image. You can click on different filters and see immediately how each filter will affect your image. You can also adjust options for each filter you choose. (The options vary according to the filter chosen.) Click on **OK** to apply any changes.

TASK 26

1 **Open the JPEG/BMP file again.**

2 **Experiment applying different filters manually and using the Filter Gallery.**

3 **Save any changes you have made.**

 ## Using suitable file formats for different media

Saving files with different formats

When you use the Save command (File menu), the image will be saved in its original format. By using Save As (File menu), you can change the file format, so that it is suitable for whatever media you want to use it in. (For more information on different file formats, see page 452.)

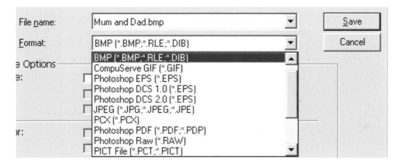

Saving files for the web

When you are going to use an image on the Web, you need to balance image quality with file size and download time. There is a Save command in Photoshop® that allows you to specify options for saving an image file that will be used on the Web. You can preview different settings for your image file – each preview lets you know what the file size will be and the approximate download time.

Choose **Save for Web** from the **File** menu. The Save for Web dialog box opens.

There are four tabs at the top of the dialog box: **Original**, **Optimized**, **2-Up** and **4-Up**. Click on the appropriate tab for the view you want. (2-Up and 4-Up are the recommended views, as they let you see how your presets will look on the image.)

Choose a **Preset** from the drop-down list. You will be able to see how this Preset affects the quality of your image and, at the bottom of the screen, it will tell you the size of the file in this format and the estimated download time. You can choose different Presets from the list until you are happy with the balance of image quality, file size and download time. When you are happy with the settings, click on **Save**.

TASK 27 — Use the Save for Web dialog box to optimise your image file for use on the Web.

Creating images for printing

It is impossible for a standard desktop printer to reproduce an image with all the colours that can be displayed on a computer monitor. However, there are certain steps you can take to achieve predictable results when printing images to a desktop printer.

You can use the Proof Colors feature in Photoshop® to preview what the image will look like when printed to your desktop printer.

For accurate colour reproduction between the screen and the printed page, you should use the colour management tools in Photoshop®.

For information on the Photoshop® colour management tools, see page 458.

Suggested tasks for evidence

All evidence for this unit must be produced in the workplace. The suggested tasks below provide guidance on the type of work that you can produce as evidence for this unit. You may come across one or more of these scenarios in your workplace. By following the guidelines below, you will have produced a piece of evidence for this unit.

To ensure that your work can be used as evidence towards your ITQ, take screenshots at every stage to show the changes you are making to image files. Appropriate print-outs of the images at various stages of change should also be provided.

Suggested Task 1

You have been asked to supply the photographs and graphics for your website. Collect together a range of graphics and photographs and use Photoshop® to create interesting effects, using filters, text on picture, etc.

Save them in a format for optimum Web viewing.

Suggested Task 2

Your organisation is creating a brochure to display the products that they sell. While the brochure is going to be produced by an external printing agency, you need to prepare the photographs for use in the brochure.

Collect together a range of photographs and use Photoshop® to create interesting effects, using filters, text on picture, etc.

Save them in a format appropriate for optimal printing.

Presentation software

Overview

You are likely to be in a role which involves producing more complex presentations (e.g. slide shows with animation).

The presentation software outlined in this unit is Microsoft® PowerPoint®. Microsoft® PowerPoint® is part of the Microsoft® Office suite of applications. It offers a set of comprehensive tools for producing on-screen slide shows: graphics, text, animation, sound, etc. It also offers a large range of desktop publishing tools that enable the user to produce newsletters, flyers, leaflets and other graphical material. It is used in offices to present information to clients and staff in a graphical way – either by OHP or on-screen slide show.

Competent people can use presentation software to produce complex presentations to communicate effectively with an audience. They will be able to handle files, edit and check presentations, format slides and present slides in slide show.

 ## Required skills and techniques for Level 2

Handling files	Using appropriate techniques to handle, organise and save files.
Combining information	Linking information within the same type of software. Adding information from one type of software to information produced using different software, such as a spreadsheet graph to a word processing document; text to an image file; a picture to a presentation slide; or simple information from a database onto a website.
Editing presentations	Using a wide range of editing techniques appropriately for more complex presentations, such as: ■ inserting objects and other resources ■ resizing images ■ changing the position or orientation of other objects.
Checking presentations	Using proofreading techniques to check that text and images look professional. Checking text formatting techniques are used appropriately. Checking images and other objects are positioned and edited appropriately.
Formatting slides	Formatting complex presentations using appropriate tools and techniques, such as changing colour schemes for slides or using an organisational house style.
Producing presentations	Choosing an appropriate method and presentation style to suit audience needs. Choosing, using and adjusting templates for presentations.
Presenting slides	Saving a presentation as a slide show. Printing speaker notes.

Requirements of this unit

You will need to carry out at least *two* comprehensive tasks to demonstrate that you can produce fairly complex presentations. You need to demonstrate the ability to produce slides with text and images according to the guidelines given, save copies of the presentation as you build it and also create an alternative presentation for consideration. You will also need to order the slides appropriately, check the presentation for accuracy, animate slides where appropriate and add transitions and timings. Finally, you must produce speaker notes to accompany the presentation.

In an office situation you may be given some text and images and some instructions as to the general format of the presentation – colours, fonts, etc., and the standard elements, such as company logo and background. You would need to understand what is required of the finished product and the intended audience. You would need to discuss the details of the presentation with the person who will deliver it.

Tasks in this unit

The tasks that appear throughout this unit are designed to take you step-by-step through the feature being discussed. It is recommended that you use the tasks completed as evidence in addition to the two main pieces that are required by the unit.

The tasks at the end of the unit are suggested ways in which you could provide the main evidence for this unit.

What will I achieve?

By accomplishing a Level 2 in this unit, you will also have achieved Level 1 in most cases. Below is a table to show what levels you will have achieved.

Required skill	Level 1	Level 2	Level 3
Handling files	●	●	
Combining information	●	●	
Editing presentations	●	●	
Checking presentations	●	●	
Formatting slides	●	●	
Producing presentations	N/A	●	
Presenting slides	●	●	

Launching PowerPoint®

PowerPoint® can be launched by double-clicking on the **PowerPoint®** shortcut on the desktop (if there is one).

Alternatively, click on **Start**, **Programs** and then choose **Microsoft PowerPoint®** from the menu. (If you have Windows® XP, it is **Start, All Programs, Microsoft PowerPoint®**.)

What type of presentation?

While PowerPoint® is a tool which enables you to create on-screen slide shows, you can also create a presentation that you are going to deliver by using OHP transparencies or simply by giving out handouts.

If you are creating a presentation for OHP transparencies (or for handouts) you should choose a lighter colour scheme for your slides. It is not a good idea to try and print a dark background onto a transparency!

If this is the type of presentation that you are creating, you only need to create the individual slides. Check the colours on each slide are appropriate prior to printing. If necessary you can change the colour scheme or design template – see pages 493–6.

 # Design templates

A design template is like a 'blueprint' for a presentation. It determines the colour scheme of the presentation and what fonts, size and colour are used. In the case of a corporate template, it may also include a corporate logo and other corporate elements. If everyone uses the same corporate template then all presentations have the same look and feel to them, which maintains the corporate image.

A well-designed template will have a number of different colour schemes to suit different media (or you can have different design templates for different media).

For example, on-screen slide shows often look best with a dark background. However, for slides that are going to be printed, a lighter coloured background is preferable. If a design template has been created properly, it is simply a case of changing the colour scheme or choosing a different design template for printing.

Of course, there may be times when you need to print in black and white and there should also be a colour scheme that accommodates this. If there isn't a black and white colour scheme or template, you can print a coloured scheme to a black and white printer, but you need to check how the printer will interpret the different colours and if they are appropriate for printing.

A well-designed template makes it easier for the person creating the presentation. They don't have to worry about layout and colours, etc., as these are already set up. They can just concentrate on the content of the presentation.

 # Creating a new presentation

Creating a default presentation

What you see when you first launch PowerPoint® depends on which version you are using.

PowerPoint® 2002

A new presentation automatically opens. This presentation is based on the default template. This template has a plain white background and uses a default font. (Default means the setting that will be used unless the user changes it.)

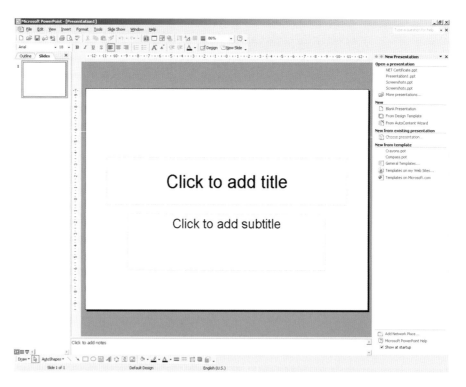

New

To begin creating your presentation, click on a placeholder ('Click to add . . .') and start typing.

If you want to create a new presentation at any time (based on the default template), click the New Document button on the Standard toolbar.

Alternatively, use `Control` + `N`

PowerPoint® 2000

The PowerPoint® dialog box opens.

To start a presentation based on the default template (a plain white background), choose **Blank presentation**. Click on **OK**.

Rather than creating your presentation on a blank white background, you can choose from a range of design templates which provide a background colour and theme, a colour scheme and fonts.

Creating a new presentation using a design template
PowerPoint® 2002

When you launch PowerPoint® 2002 the New Presentation task pane will appear down the right side of the screen.

Click on **General Templates ...** under the **New from template** section to open the Templates dialog box.

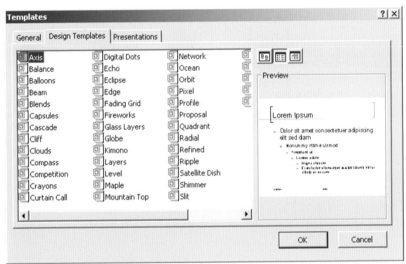

Click on a template to **Preview** it. Double-click on a template to select it, or click on it and click on **OK.**

PowerPoint® 2000

To access the Design Templates, choose **New** from the **File** menu.
The New Presentation dialog box opens. Click on the **Design Templates** tab.

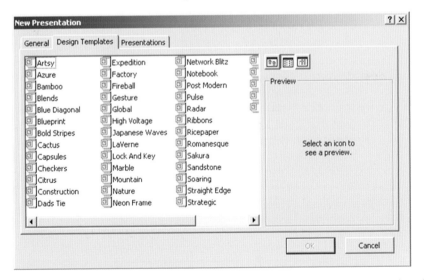

Click on a template to **Preview** it. Double-click on a template to select it, or click on it and click on **OK.**

TASK 1

Start a new presentation and choose a design template for it. Start with the Title AutoLayout.

Saving a presentation

The first time you save a presentation, you will be prompted to give the file a name and to choose the folder into which you wish to save it.

Click on the **File** menu and choose **Save**.

Alternatively, click on the **Save** button on the Standard toolbar.

Alternatively, use <kbd>Control</kbd>+<kbd>S</kbd>

The **Save As** dialog box opens.

Save

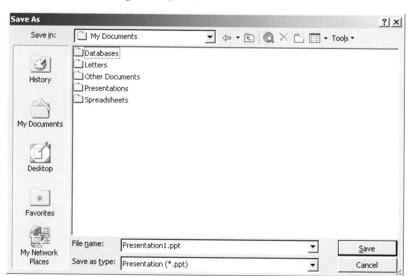

You have to do two things in this dialog box: decide where you want to store the presentation (in a folder) and what you want to call the presentation (file).

(For more information on storing files, see Choosing where to store the file in Unit 208 Word-processing software, page 156.)

Once you have chosen the appropriate drive and folder, you need to give your presentation a name. Type a name for the presentation in the **File name** box and ensure that it will be saved as a presentation (**Save as type** should be set to **Presentation (*.ppt)**).

Your filename can be up to 250 characters long – use an obvious name for your file so that you remember what you called it in the future!

You do not need to type the .ppt filename extension as this will be added automatically. (The filename extension will only be visible if you have set it to show in Windows Explorer.)

Once you have chosen the appropriate folder and given the file a name, click on the **Save** button at the bottom right of the dialog box.

Once you have saved the presentation, the name of the file will appear in the Title Bar across the top of the screen.

Microsoft PowerPoint - [My Presentation.ppt]

All PowerPoint® presentations have the file extension .ppt. This will help you recognise which of your files are PowerPoint® presentations when you are viewing files in folders.

The PowerPoint® icon also appears to the left of the file in the Open or Save dialog box.

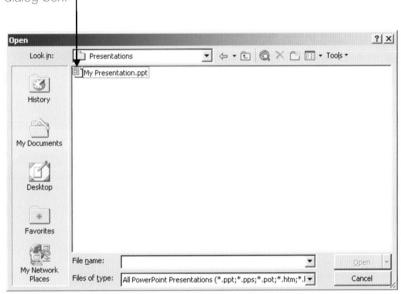

If you have previously saved the presentation, choosing Save will overwrite the previous version of the presentation with the newly updated version. (It still has the same name and is stored in the folder that you initially put it in.)

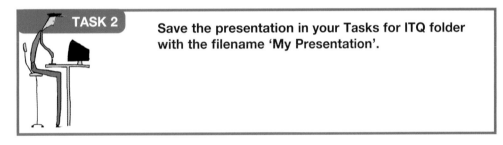

TASK 2

Save the presentation in your Tasks for ITQ folder with the filename 'My Presentation'.

 ## Closing the presentation

Once you have saved the file, if you wish to remove the presentation from the screen, you need to close it.

Choose **Close** from the **File** menu.

Alternatively, you can click on the Close Window button at the top right of the screen.

Close Window button

If you haven't previously saved the presentation or you have made more changes since you last saved the presentation, this message will appear on the screen.

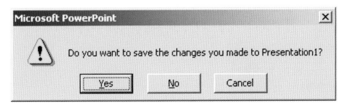

Click on **Yes** to save any further changes you have made and close the file. If you do not wish to save any further changes you have made, click on **No**. Clicking on **Cancel** will remove the dialog box from the screen without closing the file. If you wish to close the presentation, you will need to choose **File**, **Close** again.

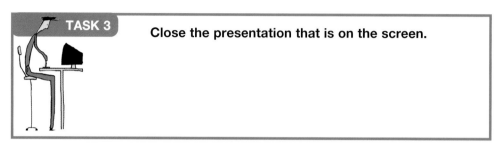

TASK 3

Close the presentation that is on the screen.

Opening an existing presentation

You may wish to open a presentation that you have already starting working on and previously saved.

Choose **Open** from the **File** menu.

Alternatively, click on the Open button on the Standard toolbar.

Alternatively, use $\boxed{\text{Control}}+\boxed{\text{O}}$

The Open dialog box opens.

Open

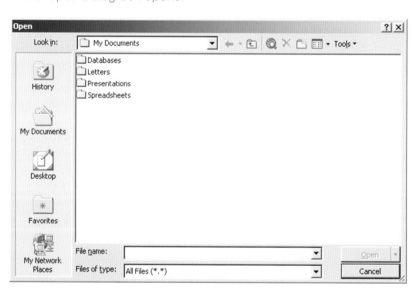

To change to a different drive, click on the drop-down arrow at the end of the **Look in:** box to open a list of locations. Choose the drive that you wish to view from the list.

Once you have chosen the appropriate drive from the Look in: list, the main area of the Open dialog box will display the folders that are on that drive. To open a folder, double-click on the appropriate folder name.

Use the **Back** or **Up One Level** buttons to move up out of a folder.

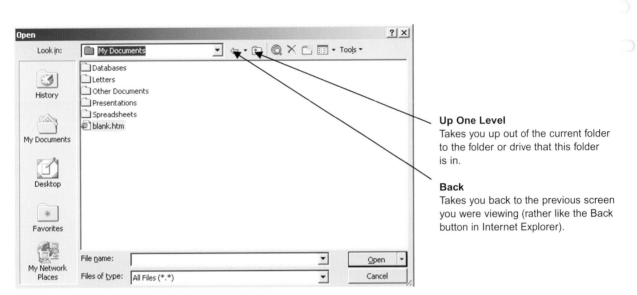

Locate the presentation you wish to open, click on it and then click on the **Open** button at the bottom right of the dialog box. (Alternatively, you can double-click on the file.)

Using Save As

If you have opened an existing presentation and made changes to it but you do not wish to overwrite the original presentation, you can use **Save As**. You can then give the new version of the presentation a different name or store it in a different folder.

Choose **Save As** from the **File** menu and follow the same steps as for saving a presentation.

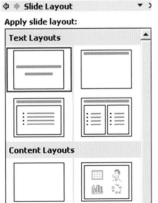

TASK 4

1 **Navigate to the Tasks for ITQ folder and open the presentation called 'My Presentation' again.**

2 **Change the design template that you are using.**

3 **Save the presentation in your Tasks for ITQ folder with the filename 'My Presentation' Version 2.**

Creating slides in a presentation

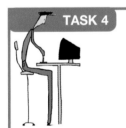

Once you have chosen the design template that you are going to use for your presentation, you can then start creating the slides for the presentation.

The first slide in PowerPoint® 2002

You will automatically be offered the Title Slide as the first slide in your presentation. Simply click on the text placeholders (the boxes which say 'Click to add . . .') and type the text that you wish to appear on the title slide. You have two placeholders – for a title and a subtitle.

If you wish to pick a slide layout other than Title Slide, click on a different slide layout on the Task Pane on the right side of the screen.

If the Slide Layout Task Pane is not showing down the right side of the screen, choose **Slide Layout** from the **Format** menu to open the appropriate Task Pane. Click on the slide layout you wish to use. When you

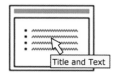

point to a slide layout on the Task Pane, a tooltip shows you what the slide layout is called.

The first slide in PowerPoint© 2000

Once you have chosen the design template you wish to use for the presentation, you will be offered the Slide Layout dialog box. Click on the slide layout you wish to use for the first slide in the presentation (e.g. Title Slide) and click on OK. Now click on the 'Click to add . . .' placeholders and type the text that you wish to appear on this slide. You have two placeholders – for a title and a subtitle.

To change the layout, choose **Slide Layout** from the **Format** menu to open the Slide Layout dialog box.

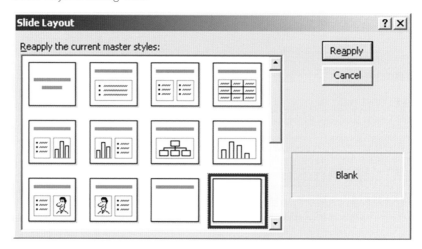

Click on the slide layout you wish to use and click on **OK**.

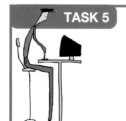

TASK 5

1 **Ensure you have chosen the Title Slide layout. Type the following text on the Title Slide:**

   Starlight Fashions

   Annual Report 2004

2 **Save the presentation.**

Inserting new slides into the presentation

A PowerPoint® presentation is made up of a number of individual slides containing text, pictures and other objects that are shown one after the other in a presentation format. Once you have created the first slide in the presentation, you will then want to create the next slide.

To insert a new slide into the presentation, choose **New Slide** from the **Insert** menu.

Alternatively, click on the **New Slide** button (on the Formatting toolbar in PowerPoint® 2002 and on the Standard toolbar in PowerPoint® 2000).

Alternatively, you can press [Control]+[M]

PowerPoint® 2002

A new slide with the Title and Text layout is inserted after the current slide. The Slide Layout task pane also appears down the right side of the screen. If you require a different layout, click on the slide layout you want on the task pane.

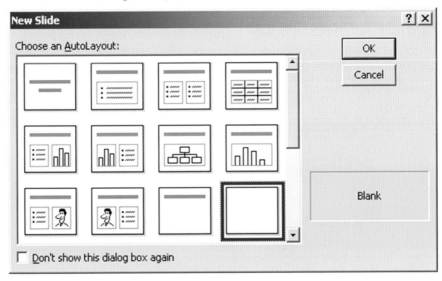

PowerPoint® 2000

The New Slide dialog box opens.

Select the slide layout you require by clicking on it and then click on **OK**. A new slide with your chosen layout is inserted after the current slide.

Inserting a duplicate slide

Sometimes you might want to insert another slide which is similar in content to the existing slide. For example, if you want to continue a bulleted list, it may be more efficient to insert a duplicate slide and then amend the text for the new slide.

Choose **Duplicate Slide** from the **Insert** menu.

A new slide, identical to the current slide, is inserted after the current slide.

TASK 6

1 Insert a new slide into the presentation. It should use the Title and Text layout in PowerPoint® 2002 and the Bulleted List layout in PowerPoint® 2000.

2 Type the heading:

   Starlight Fashions performed well ...

3 Type the following text in the bulleted list area of the slide:
   - Operating profits once again reached record levels
   - Our cost:income ratio improved for the second year, by 4%
   - Asset quality has improved

4 Insert a duplicate slide and change the bullet text.
   - Targets in all areas were reached
   - Wholesale – up 5%
   - Retail – up 10%
   - Mail Order – up 10%
   - Staff turnover is the lowest for 5 years

5 Save the presentation.

Formatting text on a slide

Formatting text

Before you can make changes to existing text, you need to select the text that you wish to change. To select text, point to the start of the text with the mouse, click and hold the left mouse button down and drag the mouse over the text you wish to select. The text is 'highlighted'.

Once you have selected the text, you can format it using the Formatting toolbar.

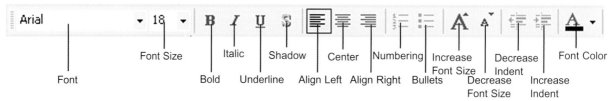

- **Font** – enables you to open a list of available fonts and change the font of the selected text.
- **Font Size** – enables you to open a list of font sizes (the bigger the number, the larger the text) and change the font size of the selected text.
- **Bold** – applies bold formatting to the selected text.
- **Italic** – applies italic formatting to the selected text.
- **Underline** – applies underline formatting to the selected text.
- **Shadow** – apply shadow formatting to the selected text.
- **Align Left** – aligns the selected text to the left.
- **Centre** – centres the selected text.
- **Align Right** – aligns the selected text to the right.
- **Numbering** – applies list numbering to the selected text.
- **Bullets** – applies bullets to the selected text.
- **Increase Font Size** – increases the font size of the selected text.
- **Decrease Font Size** – decreases the font size of the selected text.
- **Decrease Indent** – decreases the indentation of the selected text. (This button is called Promote in PowerPoint® 2000.)
- **Increase Indent** – increases the indentation of the selected text. (This button is called Demote in PowerPoint® 2000.)
- **Font Color** – enables you to open a colour palette and change the colour of selected text. (This button is not on the Formatting toolbar in PowerPoint® 2000 but on the Drawing toolbar.)

Alternatively, you can use the Font dialog box to format text you have typed on the slide. Select the text and choose **Font** from the **Format** menu.

The Font dialog box opens.

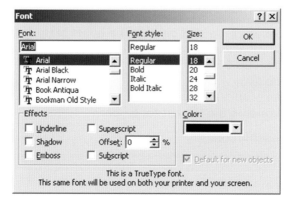

You can change the **Font**, **Font style** and **Size.** You can also add effects such as **Underline, Shadow, Emboss, Superscript and Subscript.** You can change the font **Color**. Click on **OK** to apply the changes to the selected text.

Changing text alignment

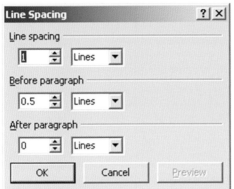

The three most common alignments (Left, Center and Right) have been assigned to buttons on the Formatting toolbar.

However, you can also use the menus to choose alignment. Select the text whose alignment you wish to change. Choose **Alignment** from the **Format** menu and choose the alignment you require: **Align Left, Center, Align Right** or **Justify.**

Alternatively, you can use the following shortcut key combinations:

- Align Left   `Control` + `L`
- Center   `Control` + `E`
- Align Right   `Control` + `R`

Changing line spacing

Select the text whose line spacing you wish to change. Choose **Line Spacing** from the **Format** menu.

The Line Spacing dialog box opens.

You can change the **Line spacing** of the selected text. You can also choose if you want space **Before paragraph** or **After paragraph**. Click on **OK** to apply the changes.

TASK 7

1   **Move to the Title Slide of the presentation. Select the main title – Starlight Fashions Ltd – and change the font to Verdana, 48 pt and Bold. Change the colour of the main title.**

2   **Select the subtitle – Annual Report 2004 – and change the font to Verdana, 32 pt. Change the colour of the subtitle and add text shadow.**

3   **Move to the first bullet slide and select the main heading – Starlight Fashions performed well ... Change the font to Verdana, 36 pt. Make the same change to the heading on the second bullet slide.**

4   **Select the bulleted text on each bullet slide and change the spacing to 0.6 before each paragraph.**

5   **Save the changes you have made.**

Working with bullets and numbering

If you wish to create a bulleted or numbered list on a slide, you can choose an appropriate slide layout. There is a range of slide layouts which include a placeholder for a bulleted list – Title and Text, Title and 2-Column Text, Title, Text and Content, etc. For more information on choosing a slide layout, see pages 471–3.

This example shows the Title and Text slide layout.

When you choose a slide which includes a bulleted text area, the bullets you are offered depend on the template that is being used. Click on the 'Click to add text' placeholder and type the text for the first bullet. When you press Return, the next bullet appears in the list. Type the text for the next bullet and so on.

Changing the bullet character

You can change the bullet character that you are offered by the template. In order to change the bullets, you need to select the text of each bullet (you cannot select the bullet character itself).

Choose **Bullets and Numbering** from the **Format** menu. The Bullets and Numbering dialog box opens.

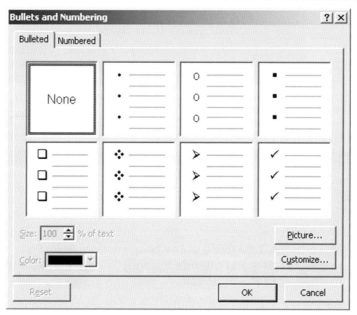

Select the bullet scheme that you wish to use from those offered, or click on **Customize ...** to open the Symbol dialog box (in PowerPoint® 2000 this button is called **Character ...**).

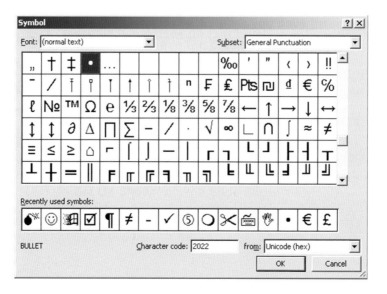

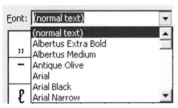

Choose the Font set from which you wish to view symbols by clicking on the drop-down arrow by the **Font** text box.

Choose the symbol you wish to use by clicking on it and clicking on **OK**.

You can also choose the colour that you wish the bullet symbol to be and the size of the bullet symbol in relation to the size of the text.

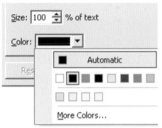

TASK 8

1 Select the bulleted text on the first bullet slide and change the bullet character to Wingdings 216. Change the colour of the bullet.

2 Repeat this process on the second bulleted slide.

3 Save the changes you have made.

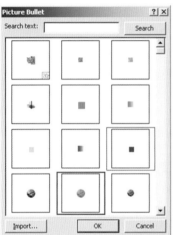

Using picture bullets

Rather than using a symbol as the bullet character, you can choose from a range of picture bullets.

Choose **Bullets and Numbering** from the **Format** menu to open the Bullets and Numbering dialog box. Click on the **Picture ...** button at the bottom of the dialog box to open the Picture Bullet dialog box.

Click on the picture bullet you wish to use from the gallery and click on **OK**.

You cannot change the colour or size of a picture bullet.

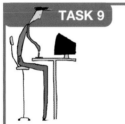

TASK 9

1 Select the bulleted text on the first bullet slide and change the bullets to a picture bullet.

2 Repeat this process on the second bulleted slide.

3 Save the changes you have made.

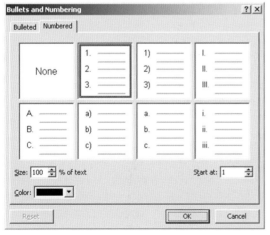

Changing to a numbered list

If you wish to have a numbered list instead of a bulleted list, select the text in the bulleted list and choose **Bullets and Numbering** from the **Format** menu to open the Bullets and Numbering dialog box. Click on the Numbered tab.

Select the numbering scheme that you wish to use from those offered. You can also choose the colour for the number and the size of the number in relation to the size of the text. Click on **OK**.

TASK 10

1 Select the bulleted text on the first bullet slide and change the bullets to numbers.

2 Change them back to the picture bullet you had before.

3 Save the changes you have made.

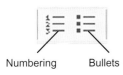

Numbering   Bullets

Creating a bullet or number text area

You can also create a bulleted or numbered list on a slide that doesn't already have a bullet text area.

You will need to create a text box first (see page 479). Once you have drawn the text box, you can switch on the default bullet or numbering scheme by clicking on the appropriate button on the Formatting toolbar.

Alternatively, to select the bullets or numbering you wish to use, choose **Bullets and Numbering** from the **Format** menu. Continue as for changing the bullet character or number (see pages 476–7).

Increasing the space between a bullet/number and the text

Select the bulleted text that you wish to adjust. (Remember, you cannot select the bullets/numbers themselves.) Make sure you have the Ruler switched on. (Choose **Ruler** from the **View** menu.)

When you are in a bulleted or numbered text box, an indent marker appears on the ruler. The top triangle of the indent marker represents the bullet or number and the bottom triangle of the indent marker represents the text. By dragging the bottom triangle away from the top triangle, you increase the space between the bullet/number and the text.

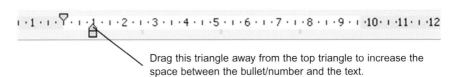

Drag this triangle away from the top triangle to increase the space between the bullet/number and the text.

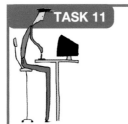

TASK 11

1 **Select the bulleted text on the first bullet slide and move the text away from the bullet.**

2 **Repeat this process on the second bullet slide.**

3 **Save the changes you have made.**

Creating a multi-level list

If you have sub-items you wish to include in your list, you can create a multi-level bulleted or numbered list.

Start your bulleted or numbered list by choosing an appropriate slide layout or switching on bullets or numbering in a text box. Type the text for your bulleted or numbered list, pressing Return at the end of each line. On the line where you wish to type a sub-item, you need to indent or 'demote' the bullet or number down to the next level.

In PowerPoint® 2002, click on the Increase Indent button on the Formatting toolbar.

In PowerPoint® 2000, click on the Demote button on the Formatting toolbar.

A sub-bullet or number is inserted, indented further to the right. Type the text for the sub-item. When you press Return this time, you will be offered another bullet or number on this new level. To go back to the top level, you need to decrease the indent or 'promote' the bullet or number.

In PowerPoint® 2002, click on the Decrease Indent button on the Formatting toolbar.

In PowerPoint® 2000, click on the Promote button on the Formatting toolbar.

You can indent or demote text up to four times. When you create a multi-level list, there will be a set of indent markers on the ruler for each level in the list. The top triangle of each set represents the bullet or number and the bottom triangle in the set represents the text.

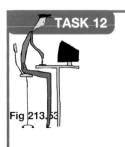

TASK 12

Fig 213.53

1 **Move to the second bullet slide and put the cursor in front of the text Wholesale ... Demote this to a second level bullet. Also demote Retail ... and Mail Order ...**

2 **Move the demoted text away from the bullet. The bullets should look like this:**

3 **Save the changes you have made.**

Starlight Fashions performed well...

⬇ Targets in all areas were reached
   ⬇ Wholesale – up 5%
   ⬇ Retail – up 10%
   ⬇ Mail Order – up 10%
⬇ Staff turnover is the lowest for 5 years

Adding more text to a slide

If you wish to add more text to the slide than you have text placeholders for, you can draw a text box and then type text into that box.

Choose **Text Box** from the **Insert** menu.

Alternatively, you can click on the Text Box button on the Drawing toolbar at the bottom of the PowerPoint® screen.

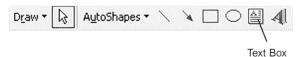

Text Box

The mouse pointer changes to a 'crosshair'. Move onto the slide, click and hold down the left mouse button and drag with the mouse to draw a box.

When you release the mouse button the cursor will appear in the box so that you can type text.

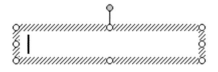

The size of a text box depends on the amount of text inside it. As you type text, it will wrap inside the box and the box will get larger as required. If you press Return, the box will also increase in size.

Once you have finished typing the text in the box, if you wish to move the text box on the screen, point to the edge of the box. Click and hold the left mouse button and drag the box to a new location.

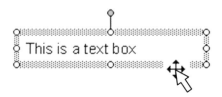

You can format the text inside the text box by using the Formatting toolbar or the Format Font dialog box (see page 474 for more information on formatting text).

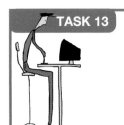

TASK 13

1 **Move to the Title Slide and draw a text box in the bottom right corner of the slide.**

2 **Type your own name in the text box. Select the text and choose an appropriate font and size.**

3 **Save the changes you have made to the presentation.**

The Drawing toolbar

As well as drawing text boxes on a slide to type text, there is a range of other objects you can insert using the Drawing toolbar.

When you launch PowerPoint® there are three toolbars that switch on automatically: the Standard and Formatting toolbars, which appear across the top of the screen, and the Drawing toolbar, which appears under the PowerPoint® slide area.

Drawing lines and arrows

If you wish to draw a line on the slide, click on the Line tool on the Drawing toolbar.

Line

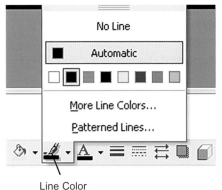

Line Color

The mouse pointer changes to a crosshair. Click and drag on the slide to draw the line.

To move the line, point to the line itself with the mouse. A four-headed arrow appears attached to the mouse pointer. Click and drag the line to the new location.

To resize the line, move the mouse over one of the handles at the end of the line (white circles in PowerPoint® 2002 and white squares in PowerPoint 2000) – the mouse pointer changes to a double-headed black arrow. Click and drag to resize the line.

To change the colour of the line you have drawn, click on it to select it.

Click on the Line Color button on the Drawing toolbar and choose a colour from the palette. If you do not like the colours in the palette, click on **More Line Colors ...** to open the Colors dialog box and choose any colour. Click on **OK**.

To change the style of the line (thickness or number), click on the Line Style button on the Drawing toolbar and choose a line style from the pop-up menu.

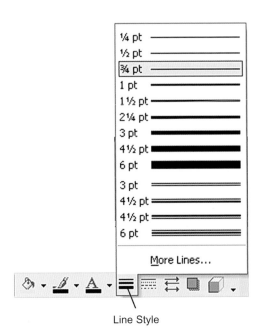

Line Style

If you wish to draw a line with an arrowhead on the slide, click on the Arrow tool on the drawing toolbar.

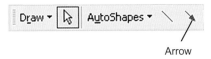

Arrow

The mouse pointer changes to a crosshair. Click and drag on the slide to draw the line. Drag towards what you want to point at – the arrowhead appears at the end of the line. To draw a straight line, hold down the Shift key on the keyboard as you click and drag with the mouse to draw the line.

You can move and resize an arrow in the same way you move and resize a line.

You can change the colour or style of the arrow line in the same way as for an ordinary line.

To change the arrowhead, click on the arrow line to select it. Click on the **Arrow Style** button on the Drawing toolbar and choose an arrow style from the pop-up menu.

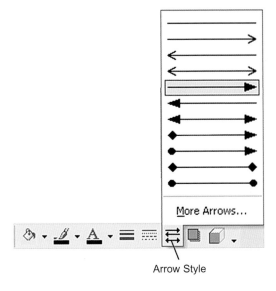

Arrow Style

Drawing shapes

If you wish to draw a rectangle on the slide, click on the Rectangle tool on the Drawing toolbar.

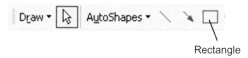

Rectangle

The mouse pointer changes to a crosshair. Click and drag on the slide to draw the rectangle. A rectangle is a filled object. It will be filled with the 'default' fill colour.

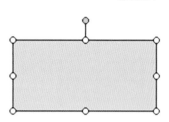

To draw a square, hold down the Shift key on the keyboard as you click and drag the mouse to draw the shape.

You can move the rectangle on the slide in the same way you move a line or arrow.

To resize the rectangle, click on it to select it. It will now have 'handles' around the edges.

Move the mouse over one of the handles (white circles in PowerPoint® 2002 and white squares in PowerPoint® 2000) – the mouse pointer changes to a double-headed black arrow. Click and drag to resize the rectangle. (To keep the dimensions of the rectangle, click and drag a corner handle.)

To change the colour of the line around the edge of the rectangle or square, click on the shape to select it and click on the Line Color button on the Drawing toolbar. Choose a colour from the palette.

To change the style of the line around the edge of the rectangle or square, click on the shape to select it and click on the Line Style button on the Drawing toolbar. Choose a line style from the pop-up menu.

To change the fill colour of the rectangle or square, click on the shape to select it. Click on the Fill Colour button on the Drawing toolbar and choose a colour from the palette. If you do not like the colours in the palette, click on **More Fill Colors ...** to open the Colours dialog box and choose any colour. Click on **OK**.

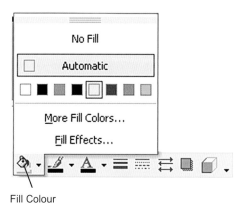

Fill Colour

If you wish to draw an oval on the slide, click on the Oval tool on the Drawing toolbar.

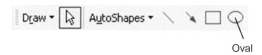

Oval

The mouse pointer changes to a crosshair. Click and drag on the slide to draw the oval. An oval is a filled object. It will be filled with the 'default' fill colour.

To draw a circle, hold down the Shift key on the keyboard as you click and drag with the mouse to draw the shape.

You can move the oval on the slide in the same way you move a line, arrow or other shape. You can resize the oval in the same way you resize a rectangle.

You can change the colour and style of the line around the edge of the oval or circle in the same way as for a rectangle or square.

You can change the fill colour of the oval or circle in the same way as for a rectangle or square.

Applying a shadow to a shape

Click on the shape to select it. Click on the Shadow Style button on the Drawing toolbar and choose a shadow from the palette.

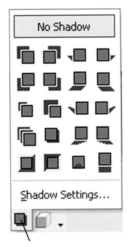

Shadow Style

Applying a 3-D effect to a shape

Click on the shape to select it. Click on the 3-D Style button on the Drawing toolbar and choose a 3-D effect from the palette.

3-D Style

Drawing other shapes

As well as rectangles, squares, ovals and circles, there is a whole range of AutoShapes you can draw. Click on the **AutoShapes** button on the Drawing toolbar to open a pop-up menu.

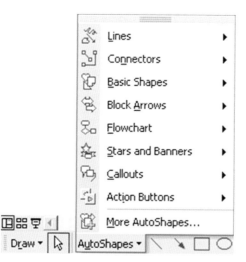

Click on a category in the pop-up menu to open a palette of shapes in that category.

Click on the shape you require. The mouse pointer changes to a crosshair. Click and drag on the slide to draw the shape.

You can format the line, fill and effects of AutoShapes just as you can lines and basic shapes.

Selecting multiple objects on a slide

To select individual objects on a slide, simply click on the object you wish to select.

However, there may be times when you wish to select more than one object on the slide. There are two ways you can select multiple objects:

- Click on the first object you wish to select. Hold down the Shift key on the keyboard and click on the next object you wish to select. Continue to hold the Shift key down and click on each object that you wish to select.
- Click and hold the left mouse button and drag to draw a selection area around all the objects you wish to select. When you release the mouse button, all the objects that are within the area are selected. The objects that you wish to select must be completely inside the selection area.

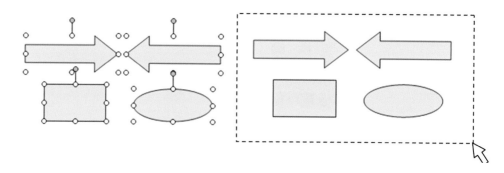

TASK 14

1 Insert a new slide in the presentation (after the second bullet slide) and choose the Blank AutoLayout.

2 Create the following diagram on the slide using the drawing tools:

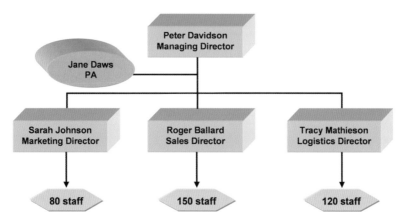

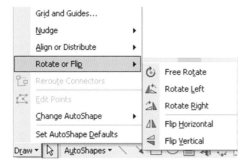

3 Use AutoShapes, Shadow Effects and 3-D Effects.

4 Use different colours and fill effects.

5 Save the changes to the presentation. Close the presentation.

The Draw menu

The **Draw** menu contains more commands for working with your drawn objects.
Select the object you wish to work with by clicking on it and then click on the **Draw** button on the Drawing toolbar to open the Draw menu.

Rotating or flipping a drawn object

Select the object you wish to rotate or flip and choose **Rotate or Flip** from the **Draw** menu.

Grid and Guides...
Nudge ▶
Align or Distribute ▶
Rotate or Flip ▶

⟳	Free Rotate
	Rotate Left
	Rotate Right
	Flip Horizontal
	Flip Vertical

Reroute Connectors
Edit Points
Change AutoShape ▶
Set AutoShape Defaults

Draw ▾ | AutoShapes ▾

Choose the option you require from the sub-menu:

■ **Free Rotate** – the white handles around the selected object become green circles. Move the mouse pointer over one of the green circles. The mouse pointer changes to a black circular arrow. Drag the object around to rotate it.

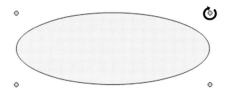

■ **Rotate Left/Rotate Right** – the selected object is rotated through a 45° angle left or right.

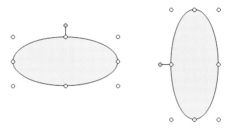

■ **Flip Horizontal/Flip Vertical** – the selected object will be flipped through a horizontal or vertical axis (to get a mirror image).

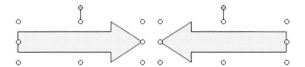

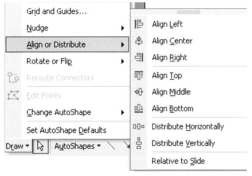

Aligning and distributing objects

Select the objects you wish to align or distribute and choose **Align or Distribute** from the **Draw** menu. (For information on how to select multiple objects, see page 484.)

Choose the option you require from the sub-menu:

■ **Align Left/Center/Right** – the selected objects are aligned by their left sides, their centres or their right sides.

■ **Align Top/Middle/Bottom** – the selected objects are aligned by their tops, middles or bottoms.

■ **Distribute Horizontally/Distribute Vertically** – the selected objects are distributed across the page (horizontally) or down the page (vertically).

The objects in this example are aligned by their left sides.

The objects in this example are aligned by their tops.

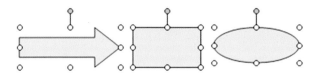

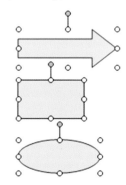

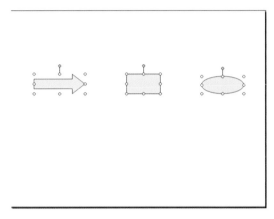

The objects in the example above are distributed horizontally across the slide.

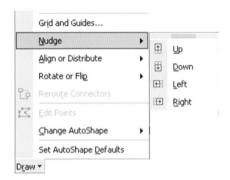

Nudging objects on the slide

Using Nudge enables you to move objects a small amount. (It can be difficult to move objects a small amount using the mouse.)

Select the object or objects that you wish to nudge and choose **Nudge** from the **Draw** menu.

Choose the direction you wish to nudge the objects.

Alternatively, you can use the arrow keys on the keyboard to nudge objects on the slide. Select the object or objects that you wish to nudge and press the appropriate arrow key to indicate the direction you wish to move the object.

Working with grids and guides

Displaying grids and guides enables you to place objects on the slide with more accuracy. Choose **Grid and Guides** from the **Draw** menu (this is only available in PowerPoint® 2002). The Grid and Guides dialog box opens.

The grid consists of dots which cover the slide. By default, you do not see these dots, although you can switch them on by choosing **Display grid on screen**. You can choose **Snap objects to grid** to have objects on the slide align to the nearest dot intersection on the grid.

You can choose **Snap objects to other objects** to have an object align to another object as you move objects on the slide.

Under **Grid settings** you can change the density of the dots in the grid by choosing how far apart they should be (spacing).

Under **Guide settings** you can display the drawing guides on screen.

In PowerPoint® 2000, there is no Grid and Guides dialog box. Choose Snap from the Draw menu to switch off Snap To Grid.

Changing the order of objects on a slide

The Order option in the Draw menu enables you to change the layering order of objects that overlap on the slide. For example, if you have drawn a text box on the slide and then decide to have that text box in an oval, because the oval was drawn second, it sits on top of the text box. The order option in the Draw menu enables you to bring the text box to the front of the oval.

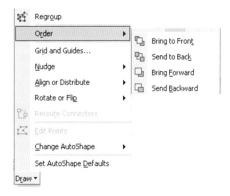

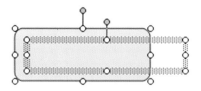

Select the object that you wish to change the order for and choose **Order** from the **Draw** menu.

Choose the option you require from the sub-menu.

■ **Bring to Front/Send to Back** – the selected object will be brought to the front of the other objects or sent to the back of the objects.

■ **Bring Forward/Send Backward** – the selected object will be brought forward one layer or sent backward one layer. (For example, if you have three objects on top of each other, you can move the selected object back or forward just one layer.)

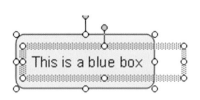

In the example above the text box is behind the blue shape.

In the example on the left the blue shape has been sent to the back so that the text in the text box is visible.

Grouping objects on a slide

You can group individual objects together on the slide so that they are treated as one object. For example, if you have drawn a number of objects to create a diagram, you can group these objects together so that PowerPoint® treats them as one object. They can then be moved and resized as one object.

Select the objects on the slide that you wish to group and choose **Group** from the **Draw** menu. There will now only be one set of selection handles around the whole group.

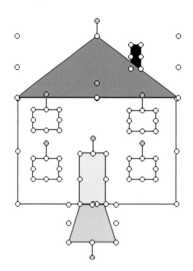

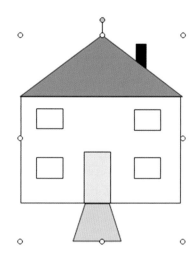

This example shows a group of objects before and after they have been grouped. After grouping, PowerPoint® treats the object as a 'house' rather than some rectangles, squares and triangles.

If you wish to ungroup the objects again, in order that you can work with the individual shapes, click on the grouped object to select it and choose **Ungroup** from the **Draw** menu.

TASK 15

1 **Start a new blank presentation and use the drawing toolbar to draw shapes on the slide.**

2 **Practise using the drawing tools to work with colours, shadow effects and 3-D effects.**

3 **Use the Draw menu to work with rotation, alignment, grouping, etc.**

4 **Save the presentation in your 'Tasks for ITQ' folder with the filename 'Drawing'. Close the presentation.**

Inserting pictures into a presentation

For more information on inserting pictures, see Inserting pictures into a document in Unit 208, Word Processing Software, page 192.

Positioning a picture on a slide

To move a picture on a slide, click on the picture with the mouse to select it. (The selection handles in PowerPoint® 2002 are white circles, the selection handles in PowerPoint® 2000 are white squares.) When the mouse pointer is on the picture, a four-headed arrow is attached

Click and hold the left mouse button and drag the picture to its new location. As you drag the picture, a dashed border appears.

When you release the mouse button the picture is moved to the new location.

Resizing a picture on a slide

To resize a picture, click on it to select it. Move the mouse over one of the selection handles (white circles or squares). The mouse pointer changes to a double-headed black arrow.

Click and drag this arrow inwards or outwards, depending whether you wish to make the picture smaller or larger. Resizing using the handles on the left or right of the picture will make the picture narrower or wider. Resizing using the handles on the top or bottom of the picture will make the picture shallower or deeper. Resizing using the handles in the corners of the picture will resize horizontally and vertically at the same time.

Rotating a picture on a slide

To rotate a picture, click on it to select it.

PowerPoint® 2002

Move the mouse over the green circle at the top of the picture. The mouse pointer changes to a circular black arrow.

Click and drag this arrow to the right or left. The picture rotates in the direction you are dragging.

As you drag the handle, a dashed border appears. When you release the mouse button, the picture is rotated.

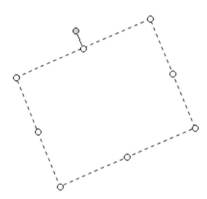

PowerPoint® 2000

Click on the **Free Rotate** tool on the Drawing toolbar. The mouse pointer changes to a circular black arrow and the handles around the picture are now green circles. Move the mouse over one of the green circles.

Click and drag this arrow to the right or left. The picture rotates in the direction you are dragging.

As you drag the handle, a dashed border appears. When you release the mouse button, the picture is rotated.

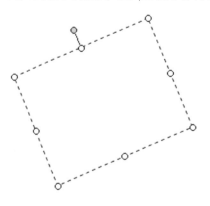

TASK 16

1　Open the presentation called 'My Presentation Version 2' and move to the Title Slide.

2　Insert a picture from the clipart gallery and position it under the title and subtitle on the slide. (If necessary, move the title and subtitle on the slide to accommodate the picture.)

3　Resize the picture to an appropriate size.

4　Insert a new slide as the last slide in your presentation. Insert an appropriate picture and practise resizing, moving and rotating the picture.

5　Save the changes you have made.

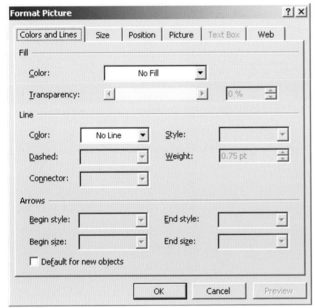

Formatting a picture

Double-click on the picture to open the Format Picture dialog box.

This dialog box has tabs across the top: **Colors and Lines**, **Size**, **Position**, **Picture**, **Text Box** and **Web**.

The **Colors and Lines** tab enables you to put the picture in a 'box' by choosing a **Line** colour and style for around the edge of the picture and a **Fill** colour inside the box.

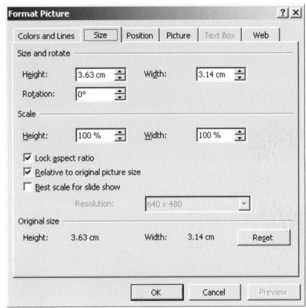

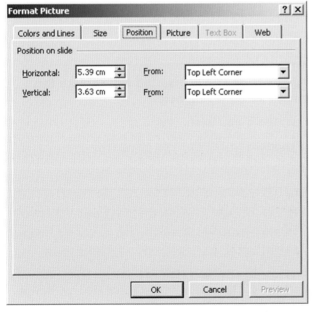

The **Size** tab enables you to specify a height and width for your picture (rather than resizing using the handles). You can also specify a rotation angle (rather than rotating using the handle).

You can also **Scale** the picture as a percentage of its original size (100%). Ensure the **Relative to original picture size** box is ticked.

If the **Lock aspect ratio** box is ticked, the height and width will change in relation to each other, i.e. when you specify the height measurement, the width measurement will change automatically so the picture still has the same dimensions.

You can choose **Best scale for slide show** to adjust the picture to the best size for a slide show. (You also need to specify the resolution of your monitor in the **Resolution** box.)

The **Position** tab enables you to choose the position of the picture on the slide. You can specify the **Horizontal** and **Vertical** distance from the **Top Left Corner** or **Center**.

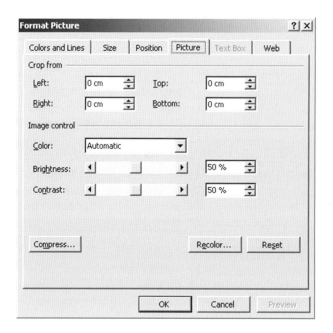

The **Picture** tab enables you to **Crop** the picture (remove unwanted material from the edge). Choose which side of the picture you wish to crop and by how much.

You can also work with the **Image control** settings on the **Picture** tab. Click on the drop-down arrow by **Color** and choose Automatic, Grayscale, Black and White or Washout.

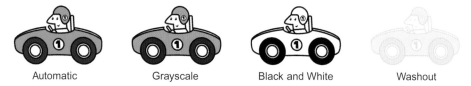

| Automatic | Grayscale | Black and White | Washout |

To adjust the **Brightness** and **Contrast** of the picture, either drag the slider to the left or right or choose a percentage in the box.

TASK 17

1 **Double-click on one of the pictures you have inserted and explore the options available in the Format Picture dialog box.**

2 **Apply any changes to your picture if you wish.**

3 **Save any changes you have made.**

Formatting slides

Changing the background colour of slides

You can change the background colour of one slide or all the slides in the presentation. Choose **Background** from the **Format** menu.
The Background dialog box opens.

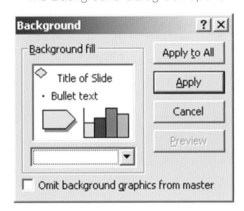

To change the background colour, click on the drop-down arrow and choose a colour from the palette.

If you don't like any of the colours offered in the palette, click on **More Colors** to open the Colors dialog box.

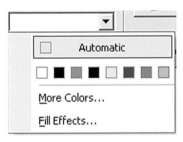

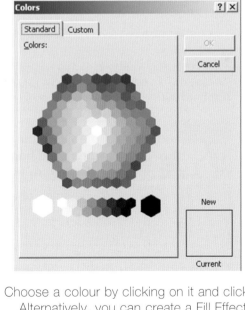

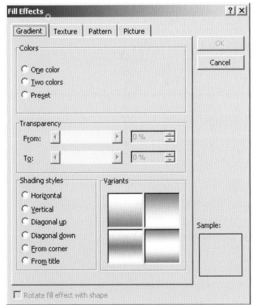

Choose a colour by clicking on it and click on **OK.**

Alternatively, you can create a Fill Effect for the slide background. Click on the drop-down arrow in the Background dialog box and click on **Fill Effects**. The Fill Effects dialog box opens.

You can create **Gradient** fill effects, **Texture** fill effects, **Pattern** fill effects or insert a **Picture** as the background of the slide.

With a **Gradient** fill, you can choose either **One color** or **Two colors** and then choose the colours you wish to use. Alternatively, choose **Preset** and then choose from a list of preset gradient fills. Choose one of the **Shading styles**: horizontal, vertical, diagonal, etc., and then choose the **Variant** that you wish to use by clicking on it.

When you have created the effect you require, click on **OK.**

With a **Texture** fill, you can choose the texture effect you wish to use by clicking on it and then clicking on **OK**.

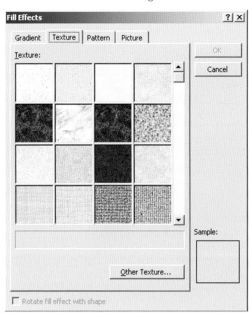
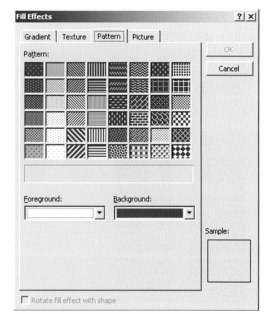

For a **Pattern** fill effect, choose the pattern you wish to use by clicking on it and then choose the Foreground and Background colour for the pattern. Click on **OK**.

For a **Picture** fill, click on **Select Picture ...** and browse for the picture you wish to use. Click on the Picture and click on **Insert**. Click on **OK**.

To apply the changes to the current slide, click on **Apply** in the Background dialog box. To apply the changes to all the slides in the presentation, click on **Apply to All** in the Background dialog box.

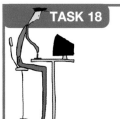

TASK 18

1 **Move to the last slide in your presentation. Change the slide background for just this slide. You can use a fill colour, fill effects or a picture.**

2 **Save the changes you have made.**

Changing the slide colour scheme

Most design templates have a range of different colour schemes you can choose from.

PowerPoint® 2002

Choose **Slide Design** from the **Format** menu. The Slide Design task pane appears on the right side of the screen.

Click on the **Color Schemes** link at the top of the Slide Design task pane.

The colour schemes that are available for that template now appear in the task pane on the right side of the screen. To apply a different colour scheme, click on it in the task pane.

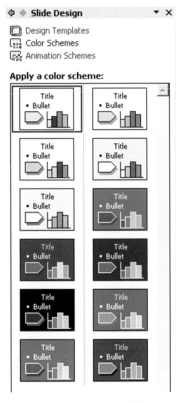

You can experiment with colour schemes by clicking on different ones to see how they look on your presentation.

PowerPoint® 2000

Choose **Slide Color Scheme** from the **Format** menu.

The Color Scheme dialog box opens. This shows the colour schemes that are available for the current template.

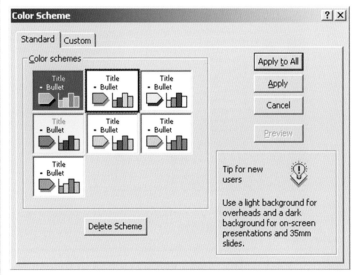

Choose a colour scheme and click on **Apply** to apply it to just the current slide or **Apply to All** to apply it to all the slides in the presentation.

Changing the design template

It may be that, as you are creating your presentation, you change your mind about the template you wish to use or you have to apply a different organisational template.

PowerPoint® 2002

Choose **Slide Design** from the **Format** menu. The Slide Design task pane appears on the right side of the screen.

Click on the **Design Templates** link at the top of the Slide Design task pane.

The design templates are now listed in the task pane on the right side of the screen. Click on a design template to apply it to your presentation.

You can experiment with design templates by clicking on different ones to see how they look on your presentation.

PowerPoint® 2000

Choose **Apply Design Template** from the **Format** menu.

The Apply Design Template dialog box opens. This lists the design templates that are available.

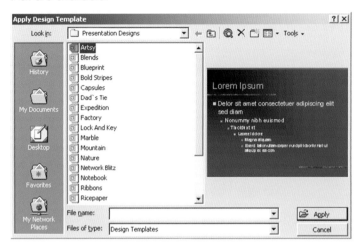

Choose a design template (you will see a preview when you click on a design template in the list) and click on **Apply**.

TASK 19

1 **Look at the colour schemes that are available for the design template you are using.**

2 **Practise applying different colour schemes and see how they change the look of your presentation. Apply the original colour scheme again.**

3 **Look at the design templates that are available. Apply some different design templates to your presentation and notice how the colours and layout of your presentation are updated for the new design template that has been applied. Apply your original design template again.**

4 **Save the changes you have made.**

Viewing and re-ordering slides

The default view when working with the individual slides in the presentation is called **Normal** view. This view enables you to see one slide at a time.

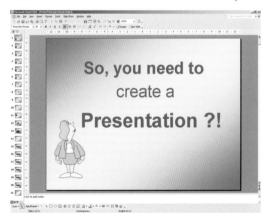

However, if you wish to see an overview of the whole presentation, you can switch to **Slide Sorter** view. Choose **Slide Sorter** from the **View** menu.

This view enables you to see a miniature of each of the slides in your presentation.

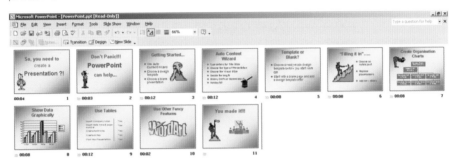

It is very easy, in Slide Sorter view, to rearrange the slides in your presentation. To move a slide, point to it with the mouse, click and hold the left mouse button and drag the slide to its new location. (A vertical line will appear to help you see where the slide will be inserted when you release the mouse button.)

To switch back to Slide view for a slide, double-click on the slide in Slide Sorter view.

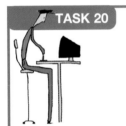

TASK 20

1 **Switch to Slide Sorter view and move the slide containing the organisation diagram so that it is before the two bulleted slides.**

2 **Save the changes you have made.**

Producing a slide show

The first stage of producing a presentation is to produce the individual slides that you wish to include in the presentation. If you wish to deliver this presentation as a slide show (i.e. on a computer, with one slide moving onto the next slide), there are two other stages you need to work through.

You may wish to add 'animation' to your slides. You can decide how each object on a slide is going to arrive, and in what order they will arrive.

Once you have added animation to the individual slides, you should then add 'transitions'. A transition is how one slide moves into the next slide. Rather than the next slide just appearing in the slide show, you can choose from a range of effects to apply as each new slide appears.

Adding animation to slides

In PowerPoint® 2000, you can choose how objects arrive on the slide. In PowerPoint® 2002 you can also animate objects while they are on the slide and choose how they leave the slide. Don't over-do animation. A presentation with a small amount of animation is far more professional than one that has every object on every slide animated!

Animation in PowerPoint® 2002

Move to the slide in the presentation to which you wish to add animation. (You can use the vertical scroll bar on the right side of the screen, or click on the Previous Slide or Next Slide buttons at the bottom of the vertical scroll bar.)

Choose **Custom Animation** from the **Slide Show** menu.
The Custom Animation task pane appears down the right side of the screen.

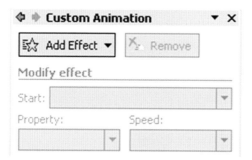

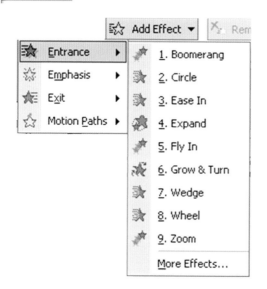

Select the object on the slide that you wish to animate.

Choose when you want to add an effect from the **Add Effect** drop-down list: on **Entrance**, for **Emphasis** (whilst on the slide) or on **Exit**.

Choose an effect from the sub-menu or, to see more effects, click on **More Effects ...** to open the Add Effect dialog box.

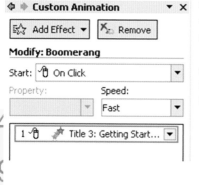

Choose an Effect by clicking on it. If you wish to preview the effect when you click on it, check the **Preview Effect** box. To use an Effect, click on **OK**.

The number 1 appears next to the object to which you have just added animation. This indicates that this is the first object on the slide that will be animated. The effect you have chosen appears in the Custom Animation task pane.

Choose an option from the **Start** drop-down list to choose when to start the effect: **On Click** (on mouse click), **With Previous** (at the same time as the previous effect), **After Previous** (after the previous effect).

Choose a **Speed** from the drop-down list: **Very Fast**, **Fast**, **Medium**, **Slow** or **Very Slow**.

To choose other options for the animation effect you have chosen, click on the drop-down arrow to the right of the animation listed in the task pane and choose **Effect Options**.

This dialog box will vary according to the animation you have chosen and the type of object selected.

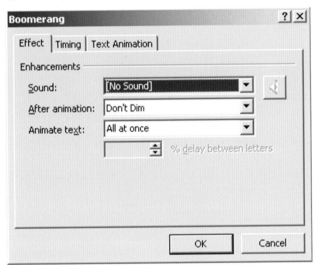

This example has three tabs: **Effect, Timing** and **Text Animation**.

On the Effects tab, you can alter:

■ **Sound** – you can choose to have a sound playing as the object is animated. Pick a sound from the drop-down list or click on **Other Sound ...** at the bottom of the list to browse for other sound files.

■ **After animation** – you can choose what the object should do after it has been animated. Pick an option from the drop-down list (**Colors, Don't Dim, Hide After Animation** or **Hide on Next Mouse Click**).

■ **Animate text** – you can choose how text should be animated. Pick an option from the drop-down list (**All at once, By word** or **By letter**).

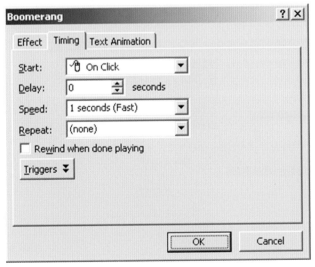

On the Timing tab, you can alter:

■ **Start** – you can choose how the object should start to be animated. Pick an option from the drop-down list (**On Click**, **With Previous** or **After Previous**).

■ **Delay** – you can choose if there should be a delay before the animation starts. Choose the number of seconds delay you require.

■ **Speed** – you can choose the speed of the animation. Pick an option from the drop-down list (**5**, **3**, **2**, **1** or **0.5**).

■ **Repeat** – you can choose to have the animation repeating. Pick an option from the drop-down list (**2**, **3**, **4**, **5**, **10**, **Until Next Click** or **Until End of Slide**).

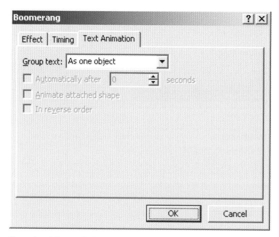

On the Text Animation tab, you can choose how the text should be grouped as it is animated. Pick an option from the drop-down list (**As one object**, **All paragraphs at once** or **By 1st level paragraphs**).

Click on **OK** once you have chosen your options.

To remove the animation from the object, click on the drop-down arrow of the animation in the task pane and click on **Remove**.

In order to discover what looks good and what doesn't look good, you will need to experiment with the animation of objects on slides.

Animation in PowerPoint® 2000

Move to the slide in the presentation to which you wish to add animation. (You can use the vertical scroll bar on the right side of the screen, or click on the Previous Slide or Next Slide buttons at the bottom of the vertical scroll bar.)

Choose **Custom Animation** from the **Slide Show** menu.

The Custom Animation dialog box opens.

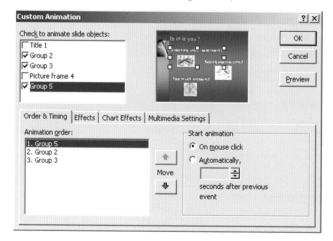

Tick the box next to the object on the slide that you wish to animate in the **Check to animate slide objects** list. The Preview window enables you to check which object you have selected. The object you have ticked will now appear in the **Animation order** list on the **Order & Timing** tab in the bottom section of the dialog box.

Choose how you wish to **Start animation**: **On mouse click** or **Automatically** (choose how many seconds after the previous event.

If you wish to control the speed of the presentation yourself, e.g. if there may be discussion about each slide and you don't know how long it will take, choose **On mouse click**. If the slide show is to run with no interruptions (for example, at a trade show) then choose **Automatically** and set timings.

Now click on the **Effects** tab.

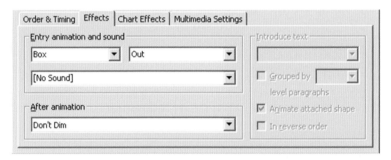

Choose an **Entry animation** from the drop-down list. Depending which animation you choose, you may be able to choose other options from a second drop-down list to the right.

Choose a **Sound** (if required) from the **Sound** drop-down list. (Be careful when using sound – lots of small sounds on slides can become very distracting and annoying, especially if you are creating a presentation where someone will be speaking about each slide.)

You can also choose what should happen to the object **After animation**. Choose an option from the drop-down list (**Don't Dim**, **Hide After Animation** or **Hide on Next Mouse Click**).

In order to discover what looks good and what doesn't look good, you will need to experiment with the animation of objects on slides.

Repeat this process for each object on the slide that you wish to animate (switching between the **Order & Timing** tab and the **Effects** tab).

If you wish to Preview how the animations will look on the slide, click on the Preview button in the top section of the Custom Animation dialog box.

You apply animation to text objects in the same way as other objects. There is another section of the Custom Animation dialog box that specifically allows you to work with text animation. Click on the **Effects** tab.

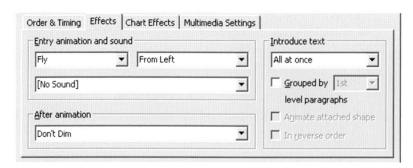

You can choose how the text should be introduced onto the slide in the **Introduce text** section of the dialog box. Choose an option from the drop-down list: **All at once**, **By Word** or **By Letter**. You can also introduce the text grouped in paragraphs. Tick the **Grouped by** box and choose the grouping level.

Animating charts
PowerPoint® 2002

If you have selected a chart object on the slide to animate, the Effect Options for the chart will also include a **Chart Animation** tab.

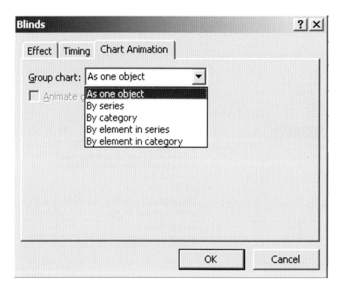

Depending on the type of chart you have created and the animation you are using for the chart object, you can choose to introduce the chart elements **As one object**, **By series**, **By category**, **By element in series** or **By element in category**.

PowerPoint® 2000

If you have selected a chart object on the slide to animate, once you have chosen options on the **Order & Timing** tab, click on the **Chart Effects** tab.

You can choose how to **Introduce chart elements** from the drop-down list: **All at once**, **by Series**, **by Category**, **by Element in Series**, **by Element in Category**.

You can also choose an **Entry animation and sound**. Click on **OK** once you have set all the animation you require for that slide.

Repeat this process for each slide in the presentation.

Custom Animation   ? X

Check to animate slide objects:
☐ Title 1   Click to add title
☐ Chart 2   □   □
                                                          OK

                                                        Cancel

                                                        Preview

Order & Timing | Effects | Chart Effects | Multimedia Settings

┌Introduce chart elements─────┐ ┌Entry animation and sound──────┐
│ All at once   ▼ │ │ No Effect   ▼ │   ▼ │
│   │ │   │
│ ☐ Animate grid and legend │ │ [No Sound]   ▼ │
└────────────────────────────┘ │   │
                                 │ ┌After animation──────────────┐
                                 │ │ Don't Dim   ▼ │
                                 │ └──────────────────────────────┘

TASK 21

1 **Move to the Title Slide in the presentation. Select the Title and add an entry animation. Select the subtitle and add an entry animation. Finally, select the picture and add an entry animation.**

2 **Move to the first of the bullet slides. Select the bulleted list and add an entry animation. Have the bullets coming in one at a time. Choose an appropriate colour so each bullet appears to dim when the next bullet comes in.**

3 **Move to the next bullet slide. Select the bulleted list and add an entry animation. Have the main bullets and the sub-bullets coming in one at a time. (You will need to introduce the text by 2nd level paragraphs.) Choose an appropriate colour so each bullet appears to dim when the next bullet comes in.**

4 **Save the changes you have made to the presentation.**

Adding slide transitions

Once you have added any animation you require to the individual slides, you now need to decide how each slide will move into the next slide. In PowerPoint® this is called a 'transition'.

While it is not necessary to apply animation to every object on every slide, it does look more professional if you use transitions to move from one slide to the next in a slide show.

PowerPoint® 2002

Move to the first slide in the presentation. (You can use the vertical scroll bar on the right side of the screen, or click on the Previous Slide or Next Slide buttons at the bottom of the vertical scroll bar.)

Choose **Slide Transition** from the **Slide Show** menu.

The Slide Transition task pane appears down the right side of the screen.

Choose a slide transition from the list. Choose the **Speed** of the transition from the drop-down list and choose a **Sound** if required. The sound will start to play as the slide arrives on the screen.

Choose whether you wish to advance the slide **On mouse click** or **Automatically** (you can tick both boxes and choose each time you are going to run the presentation).

The transition is now applied to the current slide. Move to the next slide and choose settings for that slide. If you wish to apply the same settings to all slides in the presentation, click the **Apply to All Slides** button.

PowerPoint® 2000

Move to the first slide in the presentation. (You can use the vertical scroll bar on the right side of the screen, or click on the Previous Slide or Next Slide buttons at the bottom of the vertical scroll bar.)

Choose **Slide Transition** from the **Slide Show** menu.

The Slide Transition dialog box opens.

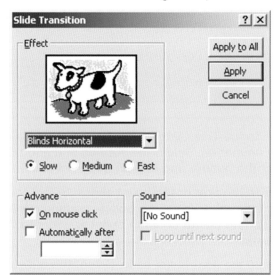

Choose a transition effect from the drop-down list.

Choose the speed of the transition: **Slow, Medium** or **Fast**.

Choose how you want the slide to **Advance** to the next slide: **On mouse click** or **Automatically after** a specified number of seconds.

Choose a **Sound** if you require. (The sound will start to play as the slide arrives on the screen.)

Click on **Apply to All** to apply the same settings to every slide in the presentation, or click on **Apply** to apply the settings to just the current slide in the presentation.

In order to discover what looks good and what doesn't look good, you will need to experiment with the slide transitions.

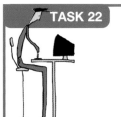

TASK 22

1 **Add a different slide transition to each of the slides in your presentation.**

2 **Save the changes you have made.**

Adding timings to a slide show

If you want a slide show to run through automatically, without having to click the mouse, you can add timings to the slide show. There are two ways to add timings: by setting the time when you add the transitions and by using the Rehearse Timings feature.

To add slide timings manually to each slide, specify how long you want the slide to remain on the screen under the **Advance** section in the Slide Transition dialog box. (For more information on adding transitions, see pages 503–4.)

Alternatively, open the slide show for which you wish to set timings and choose **Rehearse Timings** from the **Slide Show** menu.

The slide show will be launched and a timer appears in the top left corner of the screen.

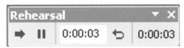

Click on the slide when you are ready to move on. The length of time that the slide was on the screen is stored by the timer. Continue working through the slide show, clicking when you are ready to move on.

When the slide show has finished running through, the message appears.

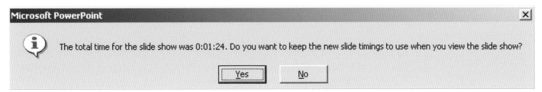

If you wish to use the new slide timings, click on **Yes**. If you wish to discard the timings, click on **No**.

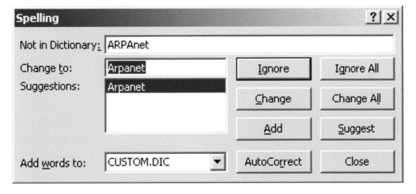

TASK 23

1 **Use the Rehearse Timings feature to add timings to your slide show.**

2 **Save the timings and save the presentation.**

Checking the presentation for spelling

Choose **Spelling** from the **Tools** menu.

Alternatively, click on the Spelling button on the Standard toolbar.

Spelling

You can also use ⟦F7⟧

The spelling checker is launched and stops at the first word that it does not recognise. The Spelling dialog box opens.

Spell checking works in PowerPoint® in exactly the same way as in Word. (For more information on spell checking and other hints and tips for proofreading, see Proofreading tools in Unit 208 – Word-processing software.)

TASK 24

1 **Spell check the presentation.**

2 **Save any changes you make.**

 # File properties

If you wish to keep tabs on how many slides, paragraphs, words, etc., there are in the presentation, you can look at the Properties for the presentation.

Choose **Properties** from the **File** menu.

The Properties dialog box has several tabs: **General**, **Summary**, **Statistics**, **Contents** and **Custom.** Click on the **Statistics** tab to see information about the contents of the presentation.

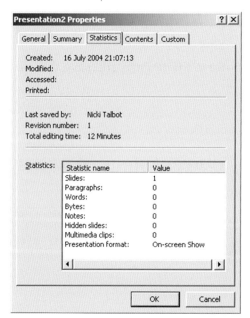

Click on **OK** once you have finished with this dialog box.

 # Tips for presentation design

Design basics

Below are some tips for slide design:

■ Use hierarchy in the slide design – decide what you want the audience to see first. Rank the elements on your slide in order of importance. Use contrast to give different emphasis to different elements of the slide. This can be achieved by grouping and spacing elements, working with type size, style and colour.

■ Keep it simple – too many elements or too big, too bold or too colourful is too much! Space on the slide is good.

- Group related items – bullet points, lists, names, etc., and isolate them from other elements on the slide.
- Use fonts carefully – do not use more than three fonts and sizes per presentation. Take font sizes up four points larger than you think. Don't go smaller than 18 point size – the people in the back row need to be able to see the text! Vary the font style – bold, italics, underline, small caps – to add emphasis and lead the audience. Make sure the text contrasts with the background.
- Use colour carefully – colours need to be bold and contrast well with the background and each other. Create a colour palette for the whole presentation and stick to those colours. Think about what message the colours are trying to convey. Create relationships with colours. Remember, colours are never viewed in isolation – they are judged in their environment and influenced by neighbouring colours.
- Establish a focal point on each slide – make it clear which is the most important part of the slide.
- Consider the medium – dark backgrounds are good for on-screen presentations; light colours are too bright and can make the audience uncomfortable. Use medium colours when you want a softer impact. Photographs and textures are more professional as backgrounds than solid colours.
- Be consistent with design throughout the presentation – consistency maintains clarity. Keep the headlines in the same place on each slide, use the same typeface and sizes, colours and lines.

Checking the effect of the presentation

Below are some things to bear in mind when creating a presentation:

- Don't overcrowd slides – audiences 'switch off' and the main points are obscured.
- Don't overuse effects – you want your audience to focus on the content of the presentation and you, not what is happening on the slides! Use sound, video and animation sparingly.
- Don't reproduce handouts – use slides to illustrate what you are saying, not to replace you. Don't cram them with information that belongs in the handout. Limit your points to 3–5 per slide.
- Avoid subheadings – break major points into separate slides.
- Be consistent – use the same backgrounds and styles throughout the presentation. Use the same animation effect for similar objects, e.g. bullets in a list.
- Use headlines – these add energy and power to your presentation.
- Find your own style – use what you are comfortable with. Don't use a PowerPoint® element unless you can do it well and are comfortable with it.
- Think like the audience – picture what your audience will see and hear. Spend more time on content than design. Use large fonts for easy readability. Break points onto separate slides.
- Never forget the conclusion slide – this should contain 3–5 summary points or action steps. This may be your 'call to action' – make sure it is uncluttered, simple and bold. What do you want the audience to do now? Leave the audience with a strong impression.
- Graphic art adds emotional impact – Photographs are effective, but avoid cartoons. Fifty per cent of the slides should have a graphic element.

Preparing to deliver the slide show

Before you are ready to deliver the presentation, there are a few 'finishing touches' that you need to think about.

Speaker notes

For each slide in the presentation, you can create speaker notes. These have a number of uses – they can be used by the presenter as a prompt as to what they need to say for each slide or they can be given out to the audience as handouts.

You can create speaker notes on the normal screen. There is an area for notes at the bottom of the screen under the Slide area. (The placeholder says **Click to add notes**.) This area can be enlarged if you wish to have more space for typing notes. Move the mouse over the horizontal grey bar that separates the notes area from the slide area. The mouse pointer changes to a double-headed black arrow. Click and drag up to enlarge the notes area.

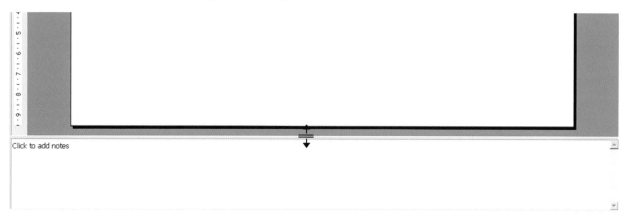

Alternatively, you can switch to Notes Page view to create your notes for each slide.

Choose **Notes Pages** from the **View** menu.

In Notes Page view the page is shown A4 Portrait. The slide is at the top of the page and there is an area under the slide for notes.

Click on the **Click to add text** placeholder and type the notes.

TASK 25

1 **Create a notes page for the two bulleted slides in the presentation.**

2 **Save the changes to the presentation.**

Setting up the show

Before running the slide show, you can set options in the Set Up Show dialog box to control how the show will run.

Choose **Set Up Show** from the **Slide Show** menu.

The Set Up Show dialog box opens.

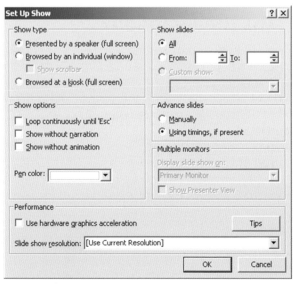

PowerPoint® 2002

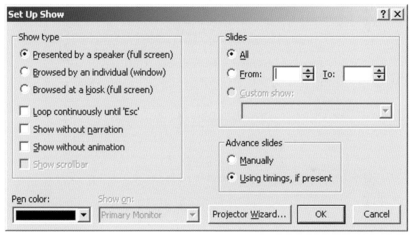

PowerPoint® 2000

Under **Show options** (**Show type** in PowerPoint® 2000), you can choose to have the slide show **Loop continuously until 'Esc'**. This is useful if you are running the slide show at an exhibition where you want it to be continuous. After the last slide has been shown, the slide show will start again. It will continue cycling around until the Esc key is pressed on the keyboard.

Under **Show slides** (**Slides** in PowerPoint 2000) you can choose whether you wish to show **All** the slides in the presentation or a range of slides **From** (slide number) **To** (slide number).

Under **Advance slides**, you can choose whether you wish to show the slide show **Manually** (i.e. using mouse click) or **Using timings, if present**.

Click on **OK** to apply the changes to your presentation.

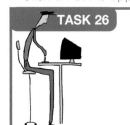

TASK 26	
1	Use the Set Up Show dialog box to advance slides using timings, if present.
2	Also make the slide show loop continuously until Esc.
3	Save the changes you have made.

Printing the presentation

Finally, you need to think about whether you wish the audience to take away a printed form of the slide show. You have various choices when it comes to printing.

If you press the Print button on the Standard toolbar, your slides will print one slide per page, A4 landscape. This is the default setting. However, you can also choose to print handouts and speaker notes. To do this, you need to choose **Print** from the **File** menu.

Alternatively, you can press ⌃Control + P

The Print dialog box opens, as below.

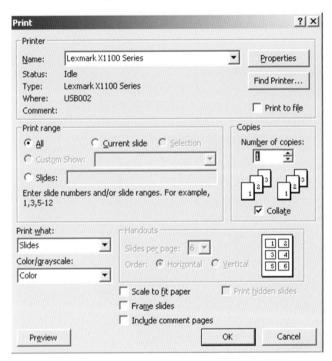

Choose the printer to which you wish to print from the **Name** drop-down list.

Choose whether you wish to print **All** the slides, just the **Current slide** or a slide range. In the **Slides** box type the numbers of the slides you wish to print.

Choose the **Number of copies** you require.

Choose what you want to print from the **Print what** drop-down list.

Slides is the default setting. PowerPoint® prints one slide per page, A4 landscape.

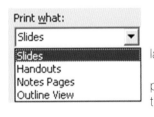

If you choose **Handouts** from the list, you can choose how many slides per page you wish to print – **1**, **2**, **3**, **4**, **6** or **9**. You can also choose the ordering of the slides on the handout, **Horizontal** or **Vertical**.

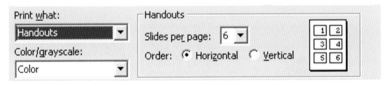

Notes Pages print one slide per page, A4 portrait, with the notes underneath.

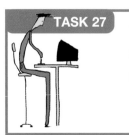

TASK 27

1 **Print each slide in the presentation.**

2 **Print the two notes pages in the presentation.**

3 **Print the five slides in the presentation as a handout on one A4 page.**

 ## Running the slide show

It is important that you test run the slide show a number of times to check the content, animation, transitions, etc. It is a good idea to get someone else to view the presentation also. If you have been working on it for some time, it is hard to take an objective view of it. Of course, the person who is going to present the slide show should also see it and practise running it.

There are various ways to run the slide show: choose **View Show** from the **Slide Show** menu, choose **Slide Show** from the **View** menu or press ⌨. (In PowerPoint® 2002, you can also click on the Slide Show button at the bottom of the Custom Animation and Slide Transition task panes.)

If you wish to stop the slide show while it is running, press Esc on the keyboard.

Saving a presentation as a slide show

Once you have finished creating your presentation and there will be no more changes made to it, you can save the presentation as a slide show.

This looks much more professional when presenting to an audience – rather than having to start up PowerPoint®, open the file and then run the slide show, you simply open the slide show file and it launches straight into the slide show.

Choose **Save As** from the **File** menu to open the Save As dialog box.

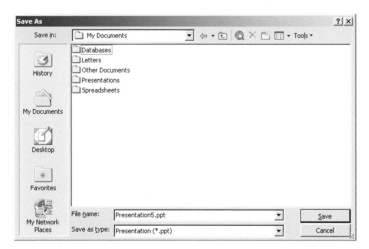

Type a name for the slide show in the **File name** box.

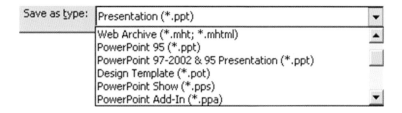

Click on the drop-down arrow in the **Save as type** box and choose PowerPoint® Show (*.pps) from the list.

Click on **Save**. You will now have two files – the presentation (.ppt) and the slide show (.pps).

TASK 28

1 **Run the slide show and check timings, animation, transitions, etc. Make any necessary adjustments.**

2 **Save the presentation as a slide show.**

Suggested tasks for evidence

All evidence for this unit must be produced in the workplace. The suggested tasks below provide guidance on the type of work that you can produce as evidence for this unit. You may come across one or more of these scenarios in your workplace. By following the guidelines below, you will have produced a piece of evidence for this unit.

To ensure that your work can be used as evidence towards your ITQ, take screenshots at every stage to show the changes you are making to the presentation. Appropriate print-outs of slides, speaker notes and handouts should also be provided.

Suggested Task 1

You have been asked to create a presentation for your colleague to deliver at a conference. Gather information and notes about the content of the presentation. Consider the following:

■ General format of presentation – colours, fonts, etc. Is there an organisational template that should be used?
■ Are there logos and other images to be included?
■ Who is the intended audience?
■ Is it going to be delivered as a slide show or as OHP transparencies?

Create the slides for the presentation including all text and images that have been provided. Add animation and transitions where and if appropriate. Save the presentation in stages as you produce the slides.

Liaise with the person who is going to deliver the presentation to ensure that the content is accurate and appropriate and that the layout is suitable and consistent.

Make any suggestions for improvements to the presentation and create an alternative version of the presentation.

Create speaker notes for the presenter and save the presentation as a slide show.

Suggested Task 2

Create a short report providing tips for delivering an effective presentation, taking into account what message needs to be conveyed and the intended audience.

Specialist or bespoke software

Unit value = 20

Overview

You are likely to be in a role which involves using a specialist or bespoke software application to carry out tasks specific to your organisation. You will understand the capabilities of the software and the types of tasks for which it is suitable.

It is clearly not possible to outline all the specialist or bespoke software applications that are used in organisations. You will obviously know if you use a specialist/bespoke piece of software, but before undertaking this unit, you need to be sure that you understand enough about the software, how it works and what it can do.

This unit provides three case studies discussing three very different specialist applications. While the specialist software you use may not be the same as those covered in the case studies, it will give you some pointers as to what you would need to provide as evidence of your knowledge of your specialist software.

 ## Required skills and techniques for Level 2

Handling files	Using appropriate techniques to handle, organise and save files.
Combining information	Linking information within the same type of software. Adding information from one type of software to information produced using different software, such as a spreadsheet graph to a word processing document; text to an image file; a picture to a presentation slide; or simple information from a database onto a website.
Entering, editing and processing information	Carrying out more complex tasks using appropriate tools and techniques for entering, editing and processing information.
Checking information	Using appropriate techniques to check more complex information.

 ## Requirements of this unit

You will need to carry out at least *two* comprehensive tasks to demonstrate your competence in using the piece of software. You need to demonstrate the ability to use the software efficiently – handling and organising files, linking information, entering, editing and processing data in the software application, and checking the data. You must also understand what the software application is for and how it delivers what is required of it.

 ## What will I achieve?

By accomplishing a Level 2 in this unit, you will also have achieved Level 1 in all cases and Level 3 in one case. Below is a table to show what levels you will have achieved.

Required skill	Level 1	Level 2	Level 3
Handling files	●————————●		
Combining information	●————————●		
Entering, editing and processing information	●————————●		
Checking information	●————————●————————●		

Case study 1 – Using a CRM system

Katie is the Administrator for a busy sales team in BusArt Ltd, a company offering specialist business advice to small- and medium-sized businesses. She manages the Customer Relationship Management (CRM) system for the team – inputting new records and logging all activity that the sales team have with their various clients.
   She carries out the following tasks in the system:

- If one of the sales team is going to visit a client, she will pull up that client record to see the history that is already logged against that client. This gives the sales person an overview of what dealings BusArt Ltd have previously had with the client.
- If one of the sales team has a new lead, Katie creates a new record in the system to store the contact information and company information for that lead.
- If Katie has received a phone call from a client, she will log that activity against the appropriate client record in the system.
- If Katie has supplied some information to a client or potential client, she will log that activity against the appropriate client record in the system. In the case of a potential client, she will create the client record first.
- Katie manages the diaries of the sales team. She logs all pending activity that the sales team need to carry out on the appropriate sales person's activity list. This can include telephone calls, meetings and other things to do.
- She sends e-mails from the system to clients and creates letters from the system to clients.
- She is very familiar with navigating around the system and knows how to set up different screens to suit her own requirements. She can use all the features of the system that are relevant to her work and also knows how to interrogate the database to extract reports for different purposes.

Case study 2 – Using a stock control system

Tony is the Warehouse Manager for a large toy manufacturer. He uses the stock control system on a daily basis to manage the stock levels in the warehouse:

- He locates stock records in the system to check the details of the stock and its location in the warehouse.
- He creates new stock records when new items are added to the stock.
- He generates stock orders from the system when stock levels need replenishing. He then logs the new stock onto the system when it arrives in the warehouse.
- He generates sales orders when stock is sold to customers. He then logs the stock out of the system when it is delivered to the customer.
- He is able to interrogate the system and produce reports showing different stock information.

■ He is very familiar with navigating around the system and knows how to set up different screens to suit his own requirements. He can use all the features of the system that are relevant to his work.

 ## Case study 3: Using a team collaboration tool

Ottingers Inc is an international organisation that has offices in countries all around the world. Their staff need to collaborate regularly on projects, but the project team is usually based in different locations around the world. They make use of a team collaboration tool that is hosted on the Web to share information, files and resources.

■ The users of this tool can create secure work spaces for the project team to access.
■ They can create different types of folder in the workspace, to hold different types of information. They can create different types of pages within the folders to share information and they can upload files to the workspace for others to work on and download.
■ They can use the task and team calendars to communicate and collaborate.
■ They can manage the workspace, cleaning up and removing folders in order to keep everything up-to-date and relevant.
■ They know how to use all the features of this application and are able to use it to maximise productivity within the project team.

 ## Evidence

All evidence for this unit must be produced in the workplace. The case studies provide guidance on the type of work that you can produce as evidence for this unit.

To ensure that your work can be used as evidence towards your ITQ, take screenshots and print-outs at every stage to show the changes you are making to the system. You will also need to explain what you have done and why you have done it, in order to show that you understand what the system is for and how it works.

Evaluate the impact of IT

Unit value = 15

Overview

This unit assesses your ability to evaluate the impact of using IT in a variety of situations, such as home, work, school or other environments.

This unit covers the use of IT in general – how it is used to help people in their work and to help businesses become more efficient and profitable. It is also about how IT is changing our lives – the use of on-line services such as banking, shopping and communication. You need to demonstrate your understanding of the difficulties some people have in accessing IT. You should have a general awareness of safety and security when using IT. Finally, you should be aware of what is available to you to improve your IT skills – from formal training sessions to self-help tools and tips on the Web.

 ## Required skills and techniques for Level 2

Analysing and evaluating	Analysing and evaluating the benefits and drawbacks of using IT in different settings:
	■ gathering information to help make judgements
	■ analysing information about how IT is used
	■ evaluating the benefits and drawbacks of using IT
	■ commenting on the impact of IT use.
Learning	Learning IT skills with help and advice from others:
	■ identifying own learning needs in using IT, with help from other people
	■ finding sources of information about opportunities for learning IT skills
	■ using appropriate sources of information to find out about developments in using IT
	■ getting advice about the most suitable ways of learning.

 ## Requirements of this unit

You will need to produce at least *two* comprehensive and different pieces of work, demonstrating skills, techniques and knowledge in using IT in general and how that use impacts on you, others, your organisation and people's lives.

Tasks in this unit

The tasks at the end of this unit are suggested ways in which you could provide the main evidence for this unit.

 ## What will I achieve?

By accomplishing a Level 2 in this unit, you will also have achieved Level 1 in all cases. Below is a table to show what levels you will have achieved.

Required skill	Level 1	Level 2	Level 3
Analysing and evaluating	●———————●	
Learning	●———————●	

How computers are changing how people work and live

Our day-to-day lives have changed dramatically over the last 20 years by the arrival of the personal computer. Many people spend hours each day in front of a screen, typing. We now have access to vast stores of information. The number of people we communicate with has increased dramatically and the way we communicate with them has changed too.

IT in commerce

You only have to walk into any office today to see the impact that computers have had on the way we work. Computers have revolutionised the way we receive, process, store and despatch information. Software programs mean that users can carry out complex tasks with relative ease. Fax, e-mail and the Internet have completely changed the way businesses communicate. Practically every business today is driven by technology: they can accomplish more with greater levels of productivity, better performance and improvements in accuracy and efficiency. They can now communicate with anyone, anywhere in the world, at any time.

Products can now be ordered 'on-line' over the Internet, money can be transferred electronically and *e-commerce* is changing the way businesses advertise, order and sell products.

Computerised stock control has enabled businesses to reduce costs. They can manage their stock levels more accurately and efficiently and are able to stock more products than before. Computers in shops can be linked to warehouses and the process of sending new stock from the warehouse to the shop is completely automated.

Banking

Banking as we know it today is one industry that could not function without computers. Most payments – salaries, mortgage, monthly bills, etc. – are paid electronically. Credit and debit cards are now used in shops as frequently as cash. If a person does want cash, they can visit an Automated Teller Machine (ATM). The ATM is linked to the bank's computer system so that it can provide information about the user's account. Home banking is becoming more popular, as it enables people to check their accounts and carry out transactions at home at any time of the day or night.

The use of credit cards means that more and more shopping can be carried out without leaving home, not only using a computer and the Internet, but cable and digital TV shopping channels.

IT in manufacturing

Many manufacturing industries now use Computer-Aided Design (CAD) and Computer-Aided Manufacturing (CAM) systems. Using computerised systems results in higher and more consistent quality and, as a computer can probably produce something much quicker than a human, this also leads to increased productivity.

Computerised systems can cut down on wastage, as they optimise the use of raw materials. More automation leads to shorter working hours for staff. However, it usually also leads to fewer staff being required.

Computers have also created jobs – in hardware sales, repair and maintenance, technical support, training and consultancy.

New products are now being manufactured because of computers, for example, CDs, videos and microwaves.

IT and medicine

Information about patients is stored by hospitals and surgeries. Pharmacists can also keep records about patients and their prescriptions.

IT also helps in the diagnosis and monitoring of patients' illnesses. Computers are used in most aspects of hospital life – ultrasound scanners, X-rays, heart monitors, etc.

IT is also used in the operating room – robotic arms can be used to move cameras and instruments inside a patient. The surgeon controls the movement of these 'arms' from a console, where he can see the images that are being fed back from the camera.

IT and education

Computers are now commonplace in schools and colleges. Software packages can be used to complement and enhance the learning process. Better communications have provided new opportunities for distance learning and video-conferencing can be used for lectures – both of which are useful for remote and under-populated areas of the world. The Internet is now a major research tool in schools and colleges.

Computer-Based Training (CBT) is used in many industries, for example, flight simulators in the airline industry.

Most schools and colleges enter students for exams electronically and some schools are now using electronic registration. Students who apply to UCAS for university places are likely to do this electronically.

IT in the home

Computers are used in the home to control many functions, such as heating, ventilation, hot water and security.

We use computer communications to access the Internet where we can shop online, carry out research, check our bank accounts and chat with friends. The use of e-mail to communicate with friends and family around the world is now commonplace. Home computers and games consoles offer new forms of entertainment.

Changing work patterns

Some jobs have changed radically because of computers; some have disappeared completely. Other jobs have been affected little by the IT revolution.

One of the major changes as a result of IT is the shift to working from home (or another place away from the office). Because of the advancements in technology and communications, workers are now able to access their organisation's computer systems from anywhere in the world. Most people will work from home for part of the time but go into the office for the other part. 'Hot-desking' has become commonplace. This is where, instead of having a workstation for every employee, those who only come into the office on some days each week use 'hot desks' where they share resources. This saves the cost of office space for a business.

'Mobile working' means that companies can use labour resources from anywhere in the world. Businesses are able to get the best person for the job, regardless of their geographical location, if they are able to work remotely.

Remote working offers many advantages to workers – flexible hours, no wasting time in rush-hour traffic, choice of where to live, etc. However, it does have some drawbacks – the lack of social interaction is a major disadvantage cited by remote workers. Most people form friendships at work and remote working removes this social aspect to working life. Some people find it hard to get down to work by themselves, others find it hard to work as part of a team when they never actually see the other members of the team. Also, if you work from home, the lines between work and private life can become blurred and work can take up more and more of your time, affecting your quality of life.

 # Benefits of storing and organising information using IT

The value of information

Today, information is a commodity like oil or gold. It can be very valuable. Its value depends on what the information is, how accurate it is and what you intend to do with it.

A successful business needs information to make the right decisions. For example, it needs sales figures so managers know how they are doing; it needs financial information to plan ahead; it needs information about competitors, so it can remain competitive; and it needs data about current and potential customers.

Some information is publicly available and is free. Other information, a business has to purchase. Usually, the more information that is required and the more detailed the information, the more it will cost to obtain. The business can collect other information itself, such as sales figures and customer information.

Of course, the information that is stored must be kept up-to-date. Out of date information is not very useful for a business to use to plan ahead. Keeping information up-to-date also has a cost implication.

How valuable information is is sometimes not realised until it is lost. If a business lost all the information about their current and potential customers, imagine how much that would affect their operations – they would not be able to communicate with current customers and would probably lose them and they wouldn't be able to communicate with potential customers, so would get no new customers! It wouldn't take long for the business to cease to exist!

A company that experiences a computer breakdown that lasts more than ten days will never fully recover financially.

Managing the information

As the information that a business stores is valuable, it needs to be kept securely and access to it controlled. Most computer systems will have different levels of access, depending what the user of that computer system needs to do in the system.

For more information on IT security, please refer to Unit 205 – IT Security for Users.

Why use computers to store information?

- **They are fast** – computers can process data very quickly, so are able to manage large amounts of data.
- **They can store large amounts of data** – and it doesn't take up huge amounts of physical space. Storage can be on hard disks or on portable storage media. Portable storage media is small and easy to manage. One CD can hold a large amount of data.
- **They are very accurate** – they are more efficient at performing repetitive tasks efficiently because they don't become bored or tired as humans do. If a computer program is set up to do a task, it will do that task in exactly the same way every time.
- **They can search quickly** – files can be located based on any criteria.

Searching through thousands of records manually would be a very time-consuming and labour-intensive exercise. A computer can do it in minutes.

- **They cut costs** – because they are able to process and search through data so quickly, it saves hundreds of man-hours and therefore saves money. They are able to perform a task millions of times just as easily as performing that task ten times.
- **They are automatic** – they can work 24 hours a day, 7 days a week and need little human supervision. Computers can be programmed to perform tasks without an operator being present.
- **They can manipulate and combine data** – data from different sources can be manipulated and combined to provide useful output.
- **They can link to other computer systems** – in fact they can link not only to other computer systems, but also to other electronic devices anywhere in the world. The Internet is the biggest example of computers linking to other computers.

There are many tasks that are carried out today that would not have been possible without computers.

Limitations of computers

Computers are only as good as the hardware that is currently available and there are always some tasks that computers are not quick enough or powerful enough to do . . . yet. Faster processors are being developed all the time – the pace of development in computers is phenomenal.

Hardware failure does occur and the results of this can be severe. Also, sometimes software can have 'bugs' in it which have an impact on how well the computer system works.

Computers can only process the data that is entered into the system. Very often, this data entry is carried out manually, so if incorrect data is input, then incorrect data will be output. It is important that appropriate procedures are in place to ensure that data entry is accurate, otherwise the data that the computer system outputs will be not be reliable.

A computer is a dumb tool and can only do what it has been programmed to do. Poorly designed computer programs will not yield the results that are required. If the programming is wrong, the output will be wrong.

It can take a long time to develop a new computer system – sometimes the system is out-of-date before it has even been used!

Computers cannot understand spoken or handwritten language very easily. This is still an area that humans are better at!

The speed of data transfer can be an issue when trying to transfer large amounts of data. Developments in this area are also occurring at a phenomenal rate, for example, broadband is now becoming commonplace, both in offices and at home. (For more information on broadband, see Unit 206 – The Internet and intranets.)

Difficulties people experience in accessing IT

There are two broad areas where people experience difficulties in accessing IT. Some people have physical disabilities that affect how they can use computers – these can be largely overcome by hardware and software. The second area is not so easy to quantify or deal with – the fact that the IT revolution has created a divided society and that many people in our society do not have access to IT and are therefore now 'missing out' on the information revolution.

Physical disabilities

There are many physical disabilities that can affect someone's use of computers, including:

- Communication problems
- Blindness or visual impairment
- Deafness
- Learning disabilities

There is hardware and software available which can overcome many of these problems, such as speech recognition software and screen readers for the blind and visually impaired. There is also a range of mouse and keyboard alternatives for people with these types of physical disability.

Speech recognition software

Essentially, speech recognition systems can convert voice into text. This type of software has been in development for a number of years and there were problems with the early software understanding accents and dialects and being able to turn voice into intelligible text.

The latest speech recognition software captures the voice in a digital format. The speech-recognition engine then performs the voice-to-text conversion.

Speech recognition systems can be used as assistive writing tools for people with learning disabilities such as dyslexia (a language-based disability) and dysgraphia (a writing disability).

Screen readers

A screen reader reads aloud information displayed on a computer screen. It can read aloud text in a document and other information within dialog boxes and error messages. They also read aloud menu selections, graphic icons and information from Web sites.

Mouse and keyboard alternatives

There are various products on the market that can be used instead of the conventional mouse or keyboard.

There are systems that can move the mouse pointer and cursor on the screen according to a person's eye movements, foot movements or head movements. There are also joysticks, trackballs, touch pads and touch screens, which can be used instead of a conventional mouse.

Other keyboard products include expanded keyboards with large keys, ergonomic keyboards which reduce fatigue and discomfort for some people, miniature keyboards and keyboards designed for use by one hand.

A very useful website for information about products that are available to assist people with various disabilities is www.abilityhub.com.

The 'Digital Divide'

The IT revolution has brought with it a society of 'haves' and 'have nots' as far as access to computers and the Internet are concerned. There are divides between different schools and school areas, between the old and young, between parents and children, between male and female, between the rich and the poor and between towns and the countryside.

Large parts of our society are getting left behind in the IT revolution. Those without money or access to institutions have no access to computers or the Internet. There are various government initiatives afoot to try to redress this balance.

Barriers to access include:

■ **Cost** – the cost of purchasing/renting a PC initially and then the ongoing cost of Internet access.
■ **Lack of public access** – throughout the country, there are not many places where you can gain free Internet access.
■ **Location** – those living in rural areas very often do not have the same level of access to computers as those who live in urban areas.
■ **Education** – research shows that better-educated adults are more likely to use computers and the Internet regularly.
■ **Age** – people over 60 years old are less likely to be regular computer users, unless they are still working.
■ **Ethnicity** – there are still marked differences in the numbers of people using computers regularly across different ethnic groups.

Developments in IT hardware and software

Technology continues to develop at a high speed. Wireless ways of working over both short and long distances will become the norm, Broadband will boom and the development of faster and more efficient processors will continue to transform what businesses are capable of achieving. Further advances in IT will bring new ways of working, create new revenue opportunities and provide better ways to achieve even higher levels of customer satisfaction. Of course, keeping abreast of the developments in IT is a bit like trying to keep up with a speeding train!

Below is a list of websites that you can visit regularly to keep up-to-date with new technology that is affecting businesses.

■ www.bcentral.co.uk   A Microsoft® website which offers lots of information and advice on technology in business. The site also contains links to many other sites.
■ www.businessbureau-uk.co.uk   This site contains many links to articles relevant to businesses, many of which are IT related.
■ www.dti.gov.uk/bestpractice   This site offers free information and resources about building best practice into a business. There is a whole section on IT and communications.

Improving IT skills

There are many ways that you can improve your IT skills. In fact, developing your IT skills is a process which is taking place informally every day that you use your computer. How many times have you stumbled across a feature that you didn't know about, or clicked on a button by mistake and discovered something new about the software?

IT is a continuous learning curve, even for those who appear to know a lot more than you do!

Informal learning

As mentioned above, informal learning takes place in the workplace on an ongoing basis. Either you stumble on something yourself or a colleague shows you something you were not aware of before. If you are interested in the area of IT generally, you will actively seek out new and more efficient ways to use your computer and be continually improving your skills and building your knowledge.

The Internet has facilitated informal learning – users can now seek out information and resources for themselves, control the pace and direction of their learning and consult with others. There are hundreds of sites on the Web offering access to different types of IT training – from formal classroom-based training to e-learning. There are also many sites offering tips and tricks to improve skills using a specific piece of software.

Traditional tutor-led training

This form of learning is good when you have a specific software application or process that you need to learn about in order to do your job more efficiently. There are many types of tutor-led training available, from night classes at a local college or Adult Education Centre, to business-focused day courses which you can attend at a separate training centre, or in your own workplace.

Advantages of tutor-led training include:

- Training is focused on exactly what you need to learn. A good trainer will tailor the training content to suit the participants on the course and make it relevant.
- You are motivated by the tutor and the structure and framework for the learning to take place is already set up for you.
- You can ask questions directly of the tutor and (hopefully) get answers. If you are attending a public training course, you can also interact with the other members of the group and learn from their experiences.
- You are taken out of your normal work environment and everyday demands, which means you can concentrate fully on the learning.
- Group settings are ideal places for people to solve problems, discover new knowledge and practise new skills.
- The training involves the 'human touch'.

The disadvantages of tutor-led training are that you need to allocate a block of time to attend the training. If you work in a busy office, taking a day or two out to attend training can be an issue. Also, you cannot always learn at your own pace. A training course will often involve a group of people with differing levels of ability and experiences. The training has to be paced according to the general needs of the group and you may find you are quicker or slower to pick up new information and skills than others in the group.

Computer-based training

Computer-based training (CBT) is a very powerful alternative to more traditional classroom-based training. It can be delivered via the Internet, a company intranet or on CD.

The costs of developing or purchasing computer-based training solutions can be higher than instructor-led training, but the costs of delivering this type of training are much lower. Therefore, CBT is a cost-effective method of delivering training if there are a large number of people who need to learn the same thing and particularly if the people who need the training are in different locations around the country, or world.

Advantages of CBT training include:

- No costs involved in people having to travel to a training location and the loss of man-hours involved in classroom-based training.
- CBT can reduce the time required to learn new skills. Studies show that computer-based training can reduce training time by as much as 48%.
- CBT can be taken just when it is needed, so the learner can put their new skills into practice straight away. This results in better reinforcement of what has been learnt and greatly increases long-term retention.
- Learners can work through the material at their own pace and can review the same material as many times as they like. It is a more personal learning experience.

- CBT is convenient – courses can be taken as and when time permits. The training is available to the user 24 hours a day, seven days a week. Training can be scheduled around the users' own time constraints.
- The delivery is consistent. The material used in a training session and the method of delivery is exactly the same for each user.

A major disadvantage of computer-based training is that the person undertaking the training must be self-motivated and prepared to focus on the learning at hand. Many CBT style courses are undertaken by learners at their desks, where it may be hard to concentrate fully on the learning due to interruptions from day-to-day work matters. Another disadvantage of CBT training is the loss of interaction with a tutor and other participants in a training course. New knowledge can often be acquired by hearing about the experiences of others.

E-learning

Whilst e-learning is a term that is used to describe learning over the Internet, it is actually the broad term for all types of electronic learning, including Web-based learning, computer-based learning and virtual classrooms. Content can be delivered via the Internet, a company intranet/extranet, video, TV or CD.
The advantages of e-learning (as well as those already outlined for CBT) include:

- Easy delivery of training to multiple users.
- Opportunities for group training (virtual classrooms).
- Content can be kept up-to-date and relevant easily.

However, a major barrier to the development of learning over the Web is the bandwidth issue. Web-based learning courses usually include sound, graphics and animation. It is not practical to try and access this type of content if you are using a standard dial-up connection.

Useful resources

There are many websites extolling the virtues of the different methods of training delivery. Below are listed some sites that you may find useful if you want to do more research into the different training options available or want to find out more about e-learning.

- www.e-learningcentre.co.uk – The e-Learning Centre is an independent consultancy to help organisations and individuals understand e-learning and provide practical advice on how to build effective e-learning solutions. The site also contains lots of links to e-learning resources.
- www.bcs.org – The website of the British Computer Society.
- www.learningcircuits.org – This site contains articles to inform and educate about e-learning and how to use the technology efficiently and effectively for learning. There are discussions, demos, resources and weekly articles.
- www.clearning.com/ITCStudy.pdf – This is an interesting document containing a case study comparing traditional classroom-based training with delivering the same training using CBT.

If you are interested in undertaking IT training on a personal basis, a good starting point is a local college or Adult Education Centre. There are many IT-related courses being offered using the different methods of training delivery.

 ## Laws and guidelines covering IT

For information on the laws and guidelines covering IT use, please refer to Unit 205 – IT security for users and Unit 207 – E-mail.

Security risks

For information on security when using IT, please refer to Unit 203 – IT troubleshooting for users, Unit 204 – IT maintenance for users and Unit 205 – IT security for users.

Health and safety issues

For information on health and safety, please refer to Unit 202 – Operate a computer and Unit 204 – IT maintenance for users.

Other information

This unit should be used in conjunction with the more specific units covering the Internet, operating a computer and IT security.

■ Unit 202 – Operate a computer
■ Unit 205 – IT security for users
■ Unit 206 – The Internet and intranets

Suggested tasks for evidence

Below are some suggestions for the type of task you can undertake in the workplace which would serve as evidence for this unit.

Suggested Task 1

Write a list of the tasks you undertake in your job role and specify whether they involve a computer or not. Discuss how the tasks might be performed better if they were done (or not done!) on a computer.

Suggested Task 2

Keep a log whenever you struggle to do something on your computer because of a lack of knowledge. Make use of the Internet, books and other resources to fill that gap in your knowledge. Make a note of when you acquired a new skill or gained some new knowledge and how you did it.

Suggested Task 3

As you are using the Internet, build a list of sites that you visit that provide useful information about any aspect of IT.

Suggested Task 4

Your organisation is going to undertake IT training to improve the general computer skills of everyone. Carry out research and write a report on the various methods of training available and why certain methods might be better suited to your organisation than others.

Suggested Task 5

Pick a process in your work that involves storing data about something. Write a report comparing storing this data electronically versus storing it manually using a paper-based system.

unit **216**

General uses of IT

This unit assesses your ability to make general use of IT systems, using IT to find information, using IT software and understanding the purposes of IT.

This is a 'stand-alone' unit and is designed for use by people whose primary role is not the use of IT, but who need to use IT as part of their job. The unit covers a broad range of IT use at a basic level.

 ## Required skills and techniques for Level 2

Handling files	Using appropriate techniques to handle, organise and save files.
Editing, formatting and checking information	Using appropriate editing and formatting tools and techniques: ■ characters, lines, paragraphs and pages (word processing) ■ enter data into existing forms (databases) ■ clear cells, add and change rows and columns (spreadsheets) ■ insert and change text and Clip Art (presentations and Web pages) ■ draw basic shapes; resize, align, rotate, flip and arrange images (art and design). Using proofreading techniques to check that documents look professional.
Searching	Searching for information on the Internet and an intranet: ■ choose a search engine that is appropriate for the information that is needed ■ carry out searches efficiently, such as by using meta search engines, wildcards, AND or NOT (Boolean notation).

 ## Requirements of this unit

You will need to carry out at least *two* comprehensive tasks to demonstrate your skills and techniques in the above areas. You will need to demonstrate your understanding of the purposes of IT software and how to judge what is appropriate for specific tasks. You need to demonstrate knowledge of how to produce information that communicates effectively and accurately taking into account time, content, meaning and the needs of the audience. Finally, you should be aware of health and safety issues when using IT.

 ## About this unit

Because all of the areas covered in this unit have already been discussed in this book, this unit contains 'signposts' to point you to the parts of the book that will aid your knowledge and understanding in a particular area.

Skill requirements

Handling files

Software being used	Applicable Unit
Word-processor	Unit 208 – Word-processing software
Spreadsheet	Unit 209 – Spreadsheet software
E-mail	Unit 207 – E-mail
Presentation	Unit 213 – Presentation software
Database	Unit 210 – Database software
Website	Unit 211 – Website software
Artwork and images	Unit 212 – Artwork and imaging software

Editing, formatting and checking information

Software being used	Applicable Unit
Word-processor	Unit 208 – Word-processing software
Databases	Unit 210 – Database software
Spreadsheets	Unit 209 – Spreadsheet software
Presentations and Web pages	Unit 213 – Presentation software Unit 211 – Website software
Art and design	Unit 212 – Artwork and imaging software

Searching

Software being used	Applicable Unit
Internet and intranet/Search engines	Unit 206 – The Internet and intranets

Purposes

Skill to evidence	Applicable Unit
Purposes for IT	Unit 215 – Evaluate the impact of IT
Choosing appropriate IT software	Unit 202 – Operate a computer

Produce information

Software being used	Applicable Unit
Word-processor	Unit 208 – Word-processing software
Databases	Unit 210 – Database software
Spreadsheets	Unit 209 – Spreadsheet software
Presentations and Web pages	Unit 213 – Presentation software Unit 211 – Website software
Art and design	Unit 212 – Artwork and imaging software

Health and safety issues

Skill to evidence	Applicable Unit
Health and safety issues when using IT	Unit 202 – Operate a computer Unit 204 – IT maintenance for users

Use IT systems

This unit assesses your ability to set up and use hardware day-to-day and protect hardware, software and the data within an IT system.

This is a 'stand-alone' unit and is designed for use by people whose primary role is not the use of IT but who need to use IT as part of their job. The unit covers setting up and managing IT hardware and software.

 ## Required skills and techniques for Level 2

Setting up	Setting up computer hardware and storage media:
	■ connecting up a computer with other hardware and storage media safely
	■ linking a computer to other hardware safely.
Accessing	Accessing files, networks and network software on a local area network (LAN) or a wide area network (WAN).
Protecting	Protecting hardware, software and data:
	■ setting password levels on software and data
	■ making backups of operating system data, where necessary
	■ downloading software patches to fix any security flaws
	■ taking appropriate action to keep risks to a minimum, when downloading software
	■ taking action to avoid risks from receiving and opening attachments from e-mails.

 ## Requirements of this unit

You will need to carry out at least *two* comprehensive tasks to demonstrate your skills and techniques in the above areas. You will need to demonstrate knowledge of the different types of computer hardware and how to use them. You will need to have a knowledge of the causes of errors and problems and how to sort them out and be aware of health and safety issues when using IT.

 ## About this unit

Because all of the areas covered in this unit have already been discussed in this book, this unit contains 'signposts' to point you to the parts of the book that will aid your knowledge and understanding in a particular area.

 ## Skill requirements

Setting up

Skill to evidence	Applicable Unit
Connecting a computer with other hardware and storage media	Unit 202 – Operate a computer
Linking a computer to other hardware safely	Unit 202 – Operate a computer

Accessing

Skill to evidence	Applicable Unit
Accessing files on a LAN or a WAN	Unit 202 – Operate a computer Unit 206 – Internet and intranets

Protecting

Skill to evidence	Applicable Unit
Setting password levels on software and data	Unit 205 – IT security for users
Making backups	Unit 204 – IT maintenance for users Unit 205 – IT security for users
Downloading software patches	Unit 203 – IT troubleshooting for users Unit 205 – IT security for users
Keeping risks to a minimum when downloading software	Unit 203 – IT troubleshooting for users Unit 205 – IT security for users
Avoiding risks when opening attachments	Unit 205 – IT security for users Unit 207 – E-mail

Types of computer hardware

Skill to evidence	Applicable Unit
What most types of computer hardware are	Unit 202 – Operate a computer
What storage media are available	Unit 202 – Operate a computer
How to use hardware and storage media	Unit 202 – Operate a computer

Errors

Skill to evidence	Applicable Unit
Correction of errors – hardware and storage media	Unit 203 – IT troubleshooting for users
Correction of errors – software	Unit 203 – IT troubleshooting for users
Correction of errors – combination of hardware and software	Unit 203 – IT troubleshooting for users
Correction of errors – data	Unit 203 – IT troubleshooting for users
Viruses	Unit 203 – IT troubleshooting for users Unit 205 – IT security for users Unit 207 – E-mail

Health and safety issues

Skill to evidence	Applicable Unit
Keep risks to people to a minimum	Unit 202 – Operate a computer Unit 204 – IT maintenance for users
Keep risks to hardware to a minimum	Unit 202 – Operate a computer Unit 204 – IT maintenance for users

Use IT to exchange information

This unit assesses your ability to send and receive messages and access and retrieve information from the Internet, intranets and the Web.

This is a 'stand-alone' unit and is designed for use by people whose primary role is not the use of IT but who need to use IT as part of their job. The unit covers using a computer for e-mail and Internet purposes.

 ## Required skills and techniques for Level 2

Sending and receiving	Sending and receiving e-mails using the facilities provided by the software: ■ using more advanced facilities, such as adding a signature or setting priority of messages ■ sending messages to groups of people using groups set up in an address book ■ sending and receiving instant messages with and without attachments ■ compressing messages on sending and decompressing messages that have been received ■ archiving e-mails where necessary, such as by using folders and sub-folders.
Searching	Searching for information on the Internet or an intranet: ■ choosing a search engine that is appropriate for the information that is needed ■ carrying out searches efficiently, such as by using meta search engines, wild cards, AND or NOT (Boolean notation).

 ## Requirements of this unit

You will need to carry out at least *two* comprehensive tasks to demonstrate your skills and techniques in the above areas. You will need to demonstrate knowledge of the different facilities that are provided by e-mail software, have an understanding of problems that can arise when exchanging information and be aware of the laws and guidelines applicable to using IT.

 ## About this unit

Because all of the areas covered in this unit have already been discussed in this book, this unit contains 'signposts' to point you to the parts of the book that will aid your knowledge and understanding in a particular area.

Skill requirements

Sending and receiving

Skill to evidence	Applicable Unit
Using signature and setting priority of messages	Unit 207 – E-mail
Sending messages to groups of people	Unit 207 – E-mail
Sending and receiving instant messages	Unit 207 – E-mail
Compressing/decompressing	Unit 207 – E-mail
Archiving e-mails	Unit 207 – E-mail

Searching

Software being used	Applicable Unit
Internet and intranet/search engines	Unit 206 – The Internet and intranets

E-mail facilities

Skill to evidence	Applicable Unit
Sending e-mails to groups	Unit 207 – E-mail
Archiving and compressing e-mails	Unit 207 – E-mail
Other resources provided by e-mail software	Unit 207 – E-mail

Problems with exchanging information

Skill to evidence	Applicable Unit
What to do with spam and chain e-mails	Unit 205 – IT security for users Unit 207 – E-mail
Difficulties with sending large e-mails	Unit 207 – E-mail
Limits to number and size of e-mails	Unit 207 – E-mail
Avoiding viruses	Unit 203 – IT troubleshooting for users Unit 205 – IT security for users Unit 207 – E-mail

Laws and guidelines

Skill to evidence	Applicable Unit
Laws and guidelines that affect use of IT	Unit 205 – IT security for users Unit 207 – E-mail

Use IT software

This unit assesses your ability to select and use a suitable software application to produce information for different tasks and users.

This is a 'stand-alone' unit and is designed for use by people whose primary role is not the use of IT but who need to use IT as part of their job. The unit covers general IT software use.

 ## Required skills and techniques for Level 2

Handling files	Using appropriate techniques to handle, organise and save files.
Combining information	Ways of combining information of various types: ■ linking information within the same type of software ■ adding information from one type of software to information produced using different software.

 ## Requirements of this unit

You will need to carry out at least *two* comprehensive tasks to demonstrate your skills and techniques in the above areas. You will need to demonstrate your understanding of the purposes of IT software and how to judge what is appropriate for specific tasks. You need to demonstrate knowledge of how to produce information that communicates effectively and accurately taking into account time, content, meaning and the needs of the audience.

About this unit

Because all of the areas covered in this unit have already been discussed in this book, this unit contains 'signposts' to point you to the parts of the book that will aid your knowledge and understanding in a particular area.

 ## Skill requirements

Handling files

Software being used	Applicable Unit
Word-processor	Unit 208 – Word-processing software
Spreadsheet	Unit 209 – Spreadsheet software
E-mail	Unit 207 – E-mail
Presentation	Unit 213 – Presentation software
Database	Unit 210 – Database software
Website	Unit 211 – Website software
Artwork and images	Unit 212 – Artwork and imaging software

Combining information

Software being used	Applicable Unit
Word-processor	Unit 208 – Word-processing software
Spreadsheet	Unit 209 – Spreadsheet software
Presentation	Unit 213 – Presentation software
Database	Unit 210 – Database software
Website	Unit 211 – Website software

Purposes

Skill to evidence	Applicable Unit
Purposes for IT	Unit 215 – Evaluate the impact of IT
Choosing appropriate IT software	Unit 202 – Operate a computer

Produce information

Software being used	Applicable Unit
Word-processor	Unit 208 – Word-processing software
Databases	Unit 210 – Database software
Spreadsheets	Unit 209 – Spreadsheet software
Presentations and Web pages	Unit 213 – Presentation software Unit 211 – Website software
Art and design	Unit 212 – Artwork and imaging software

Purposes for using IT

This unit assesses your ability to make selective use of IT and evaluate its use in a variety of situations, such as home, work, school and other environments.

This is a 'stand-alone' unit and is designed for use by people whose primary role is not the use of IT but who need to use IT as part of their job. The unit covers the broader aspects and implications of IT use.

 ## Required skills and techniques for Level 2

Explaining (use of IT)	Explaining decisions and actions about using IT: which software tools and techniques were chosen and how effectively they were used for particular tasks and uses.
Organising	Organising information appropriately for the task: using a variety of IT software tools and techniques to structure information to suit more complex tasks and audience needs, such as using large print for partially sighted readers.
Reviewing	Reviewing the effectiveness and appropriateness of own use of IT: ■ evaluating own strengths and weaknesses in using IT ■ take account of feedback from other people about own use of IT.

 ## Requirements of this unit

You will need to carry out at least *two* comprehensive tasks to demonstrate your skills and techniques in the above areas. You will need to demonstrate your understanding of the purposes of using IT and how to judge what is appropriate for specific tasks. You need to demonstrate knowledge of how to improve people's access to finding information and using IT. Finally, you should be aware of the laws and guidelines affecting people's use of IT.

 ## About this chapter

Because all of the areas covered in this unit have already been discussed in this book, this unit contains 'signposts' to point you to the parts of the book that will aid your knowledge and understanding in a particular area.

 ## Skill requirements

Analysing and evaluating

Skill to evidence	Applicable Unit
Gathering information to help make judgements	Unit 206 – The Internet and intranets
Analysing information about how IT is used	Unit 206 – The Internet and intranets Unit 215 – Evaluate the impact of IT
Evaluating the benefits and drawbacks of using IT	Unit 215 – Evaluate the impact of IT
Commenting on the impact of IT use	Unit 215 – Evaluate the impact of IT

Learning

Skill to evidence	Applicable Unit
Identifying own learning needs in using IT, with help from other people	Unit 215 – Evaluate the impact of IT
Finding sources of information about opportunities for learning IT skills	Unit 206 – The Internet and intranets Unit 215 – Evaluate the impact of IT
Using appropriate sources of information to find out about developments in using IT	Unit 206 – The Internet and intranets Unit 215 – Evaluate the impact of IT
Getting advice about the most suitable ways of learning	Unit 215 – Evaluate the impact of IT

Individuals and organisations

Skill to evidence	Applicable Unit
How what people do is changing because of using IT	Unit 215 – Evaluate the impact of IT
What benefits there may be in gathering and organising business information using IT	Unit 215 – Evaluate the impact of IT
How using online services is changing people's access to information	Unit 215 – Evaluate the impact of IT
Where and how to find information about changes and developments to IT hardware and software	Unit 206 – The Internet and intranets Unit 215 – Evaluate the impact of IT

Improve access

Skill to evidence	Applicable Unit
Difficulties that some people have in using IT	Unit 215 – Evaluate the impact of IT
Difficulties that some people have in accessing documents that have been produced using IT	Unit 215 – Evaluate the impact of IT
Where to get advice about software or equipment that can help people use IT	Unit 206 – The Internet and intranets Unit 215 – Evaluate the impact of IT

Health and safety issues

Skill to evidence	Applicable Unit
Ways to keep risks to people to a minimum	Unit 202 – Operate a computer Unit 204 – IT maintenance for users
Ways to keep risks to hardware to a minimum	Unit 202 – Operate a computer Unit 204 – IT maintenance for users

Security risks

Skill to evidence	Applicable Unit
Risks of downloading software from the Internet	Unit 203 – IT troubleshooting for users Unit 205 – IT security for users

Improving learning

Skill to evidence	Applicable Unit
The benefits and drawbacks of Web-based learning or e-learning compared with other methods of learning	Unit 215 – Evaluate the impact of IT

CITY OF WOLVERHAMPTON COLLEGE

Index